Total SNMP:

Exploring the Simple Network Management Protocol

Second Edition

Sean Harnedy

**To join a Prentice Hall PTR Internet mailing list, point to
http://www.prehnhall.com/register**

**Prentice Hall PTR
Upper Saddle River, NJ 07458
http://www.prenhall.com**

Library of Congress Cataloging-in-Publication Data

Harnedy, Sean J., 1955-
   Total SNMP : exploring the Simple Network Management Protocol /
Sean J. Harnedy. — 2nd ed.
     p. cm.
   Includes bibliographical references and index.
   ISBN 0-13-646994-9
   1. Simple Network Management protocol (Computer network protocol)
I. Title.
TK5105.55.H37 1997   97-14616
005.7'1—dc21   CIP

Editorial/production supervision: *Mary Sudul*
Cover design: *Bruce Kenselaor*
Cover design director: *Jayne Conte*
Manufacturing manager: *Alexis R. Heydt*
Marketing manager: *Steve Solomon*
Acquisitions editor: *Michael E. Meehan*
Editorial assistant: *Barbara Alfieri*
ISBN 0-13-646994-9

©1998 Prentice Hall PTR
Prentice-Hall, Inc.
A Simon & Schuster Company
Upper Saddle River, New Jersey 07458

The publisher offers discounts on this book when ordered
    in bulk quantities. For more information, contact:

Corporate Sales Department
    PTR Prentice Hall
    One Lake Street
    Upper Saddle River, NJ 07458

Phone: 800-382-3419
    Fax: 201-236-7141
E-mail (Internet): corpsales@prenhall.com

Product names mentioned herein are the trademarks or registered trademarks of their respective owners.

Printed in the United States of America

    10 9 8 7 6 5 4 3 2

Prentice-Hall International (UK) Limited, *London*
    Prentice-Hall of Australia Pty. Limited, *Sydney*
    Prentice-Hall Canada Inc., *Toronto*
    Prentice-Hall Hispanoamericana, S.A., *Mexico*
    Prentice-Hall of India Private Limited, *New Delhi*
    Prentice-Hall of Japan, Inc., *Tokyo*
    Simon & Schuster Asia Pte. Ltd., *Singapore*
    Editora Prentice-Hall do Brasil, Ltda., *Rio de Janeiro*

Contents

2   The "Theory" of SNMP   39

7   The Management Information Base for SNMP Version 1   195

Preface to the Second Edition

It is proof of high culture to say the greatest matters in the simplest way.
—Ralph Waldo Emerson[1]

When you think about it, a Simple Network Management Protocol (SNMP) sounds like an oxymoron. After all, what's so simple about managing a network?[2]

INTRODUCTION

SNMP is the acronym for the Simple Network Management Protocol. In a strict sense, SNMP refers to a protocol—a set of rules for transferring data—used to manage networks. In a more general sense, SNMP refers to the network management framework that uses this protocol: the Internet-standard Network Management Framework.

As I write the second edition of this book, SNMP has celebrated its eighth birthday. Although these eight solid years of implementation have shown

SNMP Version 1 to be a resounding success, the progression to Version 2 has been a long and somewhat bumpy road.

SNMPv2 has been moved along to draft status but is still lacking the much-sought-after security features and their accompanying administrative framework. The current flavor of SNMPv2—often referred to as "community-based SNMPv2" or SNMPv2c—uses the Version 1 message format with the new Version 2 protocol enhancements. Work is proceeding in the security arena and hope is high that these features will soon be added to the framework. A Working Group has been started on the next generation of SNMP that will be called SNMPv3.

Network Management with SNMP has matured in many supporting areas in the three years since the first edition of this book. Script languages and much more widespread use of object-oriented methodologies have increased the rate of deployment of network management applications. The World Wide Web browsers are also promising to provide innovative techniques for realizing Web-Based network management. New and exciting computer technologies are emerging and the prospects for Network Management 2000 are taking shape.

SNMP is a powerful and flexible solution that has aided network managers and administrators in making their unenviable task of controlling the ever-growing number of components of their internetwork more manageable. It has provided the means for hardware and software vendors to make their network devices controllable from centralized and integrated management platforms. Many new and exciting network management applications are constantly being released, further refining this necessary functionality. The SNMPv2 enhancements make the protocol more efficient, and at the same time still keep it relatively easy and cheap to implement. SNMPv3 will bring security and other features still being defined.

INFORMATION ON-LINE

In the nearly nine years that SNMP has been around, many new sources of information have been available on the subject, much of it free and on-line. Gone are the days when you were told to RTFRFC—"Read The RFCs"—when you needed SNMP information. The biggest problem now is dealing with what to read: culling the information from the data.

SNMP FAQ

An amazing store of Frequently Asked Questions exist at MIT on a number of computer topics. The SNMP ones are:

```
ftp://rtfm.mit.edu/pub/usenet/news.answers/snmp-faq/part1
ftp://rtfm.mit.edu/pub/usenet/news.answers/snmp-faq/part2
```

SNMP WEB SITES

Several excellent and very comprehensive Web sites are up that deal with SNMP and network management. Lots of links.

```
http://netman.cit.buffalo.edu/index.html
http://snmp.cs.utwente.nl
http://www.onramp.net/~cwk/net-manage.cgi
```

SNMP MAILING LISTS

A mailing list exists for SNMP Version 1, Version 2, and now Version 3.

```
For Version 1: snmp-request@psi.com
For Version 2: snmpv2-request@tis.com
For Version 3: snmpv3-request@tis.com
```

The body of the mail message should contain `subscribe <your e-mail address>`. No subject is required.

SNMP NEWS GROUPS

Also, three news groups deal with SNMP and network management.

```
comp.protocols.snmp
info.snmp
comp.dcom.net-management
```

AUDIENCE

This book is intended for anyone interested in the use of SNMP as a network management solution. SNMP is a fine example of a well-thought-out and easily implementable network management framework paradigm; it provides the specification for the manager, the agent, and a definition of the method for the two to communicate the necessary management information.

I have made several assumptions in this book that I should state up front.

The current networking world can be thought of as comprising three realms (David Crocker, quoted in[3]):

◆ The Internet and its TCP/IP-UNIX-dominated environment

◆ The "Big Net" of the mainframe- and telecommunications-oriented Wide Area Networks (WANs)

◆ The Local Area Networks (LANs) of PCs, Network Operating Systems (NOSs), and servers

Because the original SNMP charter was for the management of the Internet and TCP/IP, users of the first realm will naturally be interested in this book. The explosion of intranetworking keeps attention on the use of SNMP for managing these types of devices and connections.

Surprisingly, the direction of networking and network management is evolving at such a pace and in such a direction that the SNMP umbrella is beginning to affect (and even replace) the "Big Net" and LAN management frameworks also. The proprietary network management schemes of the "Big Net" are being made to interoperate with the open frameworks of SNMP. The management of LANs and PCs via SNMP is an especially hot topic.

The discussion of networks occurs in a general sense with the key term being internetworking—a network of networks. The management of such a diverse mix of hardware and software components from different vendors is crucial to maintain their interoperability in this environment.

This book is intended also for people who are seeking a comprehensive introduction to SNMP. I introduce and describe in detail the theory and practice of this protocol. Hopefully, I point you in the right direction for obtaining a deeper level of understanding where SNMP requires it.

I hope that management information systems managers, network supervisors, and administrators find this book helpful. For those individuals involved in technical support and management, I offer valuable information about the SNMP network management framework. Operations managers and field engineers will also find this book informative.

SNMP will become increasingly important in the PC and LAN arenas. LAN administrators and analysts will find this information increasingly relevant as their domains come under SNMP management.

In general terms, technology planners, system integrators, network consultants, and resellers will find this material worthwhile.

I have tried to make the "practice" section technical enough so that network and systems analysts and programmers can derive some useful information from this undertaking.

HOW THIS BOOK IS ORGANIZED

The book is organized into two major sections. The first section is an introduction to the theory of SNMP and contains Chapters 1 through 8. Section II is an introduction to the practice of SNMP and contains Chapters 9 through 16.

Chapter 1, Introduction to Network Management, introduces the overall topic of network management by discussing current trends in the field. It also presents the architecture and other important models for internetworking. It then introduces the functional requirements of network management along with an overview of SNMP.

Chapter 2, The "Theory" of SNMP, covers the analysis of SNMP and its major components. It offers a brief history of its development and a chronology of its major events. It also gives information about the Internet Architecture Board and Request for Comments. The chapter introduces the three major components of SNMP—the Structure of Management Information, the protocol, and the Management Information Base. The chapter presents and explains the SNMP Reference Model.

Chapter 3, The Structure of Management Information for Version 1, goes into detail about the SNMP guidelines for SMIv1. It explains Abstract Syntax Notation One, the Basic Encoding Rules, and the Management Information Base Object templates and macros that are used.

Chapter 4, The Structure of Management Information for Version 2, discusses the changes made to the original SMI to create SMIv2.

Chapter 5, The SNMP Protocol for Version 1, explains the protocol and the SNMP messages that are used to exchange information between the Network Management Stations and the managed agents. The chapter also explains protocol issues such as authentication and authorization.

Chapter 6, The SNMP Protocol for Version 2, explains the protocol enhancements and the new PDUs added for the second version of the protocol.

Chapter 7, The Management Information Base for Version 1, presents the objects that are the heart of SNMP. It introduces the standard MIB-II objects, as well as the additional objects defined for experimental purposes and by the many vendors and researchers working to create SNMP object definitions.

Chapter 8, The Management Information Base for Version 2, presents the MIBs that now use the Version 2 SMI. It includes the new standard MIB that should be used with SNMPv2.

Chapter 9, The "Practice" of SNMP for Version 1, revisits the SNMP Reference Model and then explains the implementations of SNMP and a generic protocol "engine" and library. Then the chapter applies these details to the agent and Network Management System. CASE diagrams and pseudocode for an agent implementation are also included to provide more detail.

Chapter 10, The "Practice" of SNMP Version 2, presents a network management application for Fault Management using object-oriented analysis and design.

Chapter 11, SNMP Development and Support Tools, discusses the various tools needed for SNMP development and implementation. It also discusses the MIB compiler in some detail.

Chapter 12, The Network Management Station, explains the Network Manager Station, its functionality, and the various components that comprise it.

Chapter 13, The Agent, explains the agent, the agent's functionality, and its various pieces. The chapter discusses a diagram of the proxy agent.

Chapter 14, Other Implementation Issues, revisits the functional attributes of the SNMP management framework. It also includes sections on Remote Network Monitoring (RMON), SNMP security, and the implementation of SNMP on other stacks.

Chapter 15, Current SNMP Implementations, compares the Network Manager offerings from the major network management vendors, agent offerings, and other SNMP related products.

Chapter 16, Recent Directions and Developments, discusses the recent enhancements to SNMP. Important topics include the development of standard Application Program Interfaces (API) such as WinSNMP and SNMP++, Desktop Management Task Force (DMTF), Agent Extensions, World Wide Web-Based management, use of distributed objects, the role of expert systems technology, and others.

Appendix A contains the chronology for SNMP Version 1. Appendix B includes the full listing of the MIB-II Standard Specification (RFC 1213) and Appendix C lists the SNMP protocol specification (RFC 1157). RFCs that deal with network management and associated issues are listed in Appendix D. The book also includes an Annotated Bibliography, a list of Acronyms, and a Glossary.

CONVENTIONS USED IN THIS BOOK

Listed below are the conventions for the various fonts used in this text.

`Constant Width`	is used for source code examples, and for quotations from source code within the text, including variable and function names. This font is also used for output printed by a computer and for the contents of files.
`Constant Bold`	is used for commands typed word-for-word by the user.
Italic	is used for command names, directory names, and filenames. It is also used for words that I define.
Bold	is used for command options. In addition, it is used for vectors in the mathematical sense.

ACKNOWLEDGMENTS

Again, I have to thank my family for their love, cooperation, help, and support—necessarily in that order! Without the assistance of my wife, Andrea, and our three boys, Ryan, Sean, and Andrew, this book would just not have been possible. I would also like to again thank Andrew and Gloria Laspino for the many kind favors they have done for me over the years. Their support is always appreciated. I would also like to thank my father and mother, John and Charlotte Harnedy.

Thanks to all my new friends and everyone I work with at the Racal Data Group in Sunrise, Florida. I have learned many new and exciting technologies since I started working in the Security Products Group under Geoffrey Stevenson. Also special thanks to Ronald Monzillo.

I would like to thank everyone whom I've met in my dealings with SNMP and internetworking over the World Wide Web. So many helpful, friendly and intelligent people are in the Internet community that I could not hope to thank everyone individually.

Finally, I would like to thank Mike Meehan, Mary Sudul, Christa Carroll, and everyone at Prentice Hall PTR who helped see this project through to completion.

Sean J. Harnedy
April, 1997
Boca Raton, Florida

REFERENCES FOR PREFACE

[1] Tripp, Rhonda Thomas (compiler). *The International Thesaurus of Quotations.* New York, NY: Thomas Y. Crowell Company. 1970.

[2] Mclachlan, Gordon. "Redefining Simple." *HP Professional* (June): 27. 1992.

[3] Burton, Craig. "NMS—Is Novell Working in a Vacuum?" *Network Computing* (September): 55. 1992.

CHAPTER 1

Introduction to Network Management

The aspects of things that are most important for us are hidden because of their simplicity and familiarity.

— *Ludwig Wittgenstein*[1]

Order and simplification are the first steps toward the mastery of a subject—the actual enemy is the unknown.

—*Thomas Mann*[2]

Networks exist to distribute information. This information needs to be communicated in an efficient, effective, and reliable manner. Network management is important because it allows this useful (net)work to properly commence and continue. It monitors the network activity, it controls the operations of the devices, and it can be responsible for any number of other related tasks. This book is about SNMP, the Simple Network Management Protocol. It has become the most popular network management solution in use today.

The curse of living in interesting times can seem especially onerous for anyone dealing with networking. The sheer number and complexity of the devices that constitute people's enterprises and how they communicate are making the task of managing the devices more and more intractable. Setting up an enterprise network and then modifying and controlling it have become a true Sisyphean ordeal. With even the slightest exposure to working with today's networks, one can say with Socratic clarity that: **The unmanaged network is not worth implementing**. Network management must be viewed as an essential part of any network.

For a number of reasons, the network "wagon" has long been in front of the management "horse." As network management "pushes" to monitor and control today's networks, networking technology emerges undeterred into developing more complex, faster, and more widely dispersed devices and related applications.

Although the observation that network management needs to be an essential part of today's networks may seem obvious, a number of factors at play leave most of the current networks in an "undermanaged" state.

NETWORK "UNDER"-MANAGEMENT

The following factors are prime examples of why many of today's networks are undermanaged:

- ◆ Today's network is often a heterogeneous collection of multi-vendor hardware and software that must be configured to operate together. Each vendor usually offers its own network management tools and features that must be reconciled.

- ◆ The network can be configured with various "generations" of networking technologies. The newest technology frequently must coexist with legacy systems that are already in place.

- ◆ The push towards distributed processing and the prominence of the client/server model has changed the network management model that needs to be applied to this new infrastructure. The mainframe-based management models are often no longer appropriate.

- ◆ Current networks are now often enterprise internetworks and intranetworks that have greatly increased in size, complexity, and scale.

Accompanying advances in networking management must be realized to manage these networks.

◆ Network management is a cost factor. In an effort to contain costs, companies try to do network planning, support, troubleshooting, debugging, operation, administration, and management automatically with fewer, and often less experienced, people.

◆ Security is a major concern in most networks. With nearly everyone connected to the Internet and to networks in other management domains, access and privileges need to be scrutinized. Vital data needs to be protected, authenticated, and often encrypted.

◆ Additional activities related to network management, such as network capacity planning and design, policy management, systems management, service management, and other activities, are not done properly or done with ad hoc and proprietary tools.

A viable network management framework must address and resolve these issues within the limits of functionality and cost. The framework must be able to evolve to handle the current and future issues that will arise with networking management. Accordingly, any network management framework is a compromise between the functionality that it provides versus the associated costs with fielding it in one's enterprise.

Management framework functionality is quite a discussed and studied topic. In Section 1.4 *Network Management Functional Requirements* I discuss the five major functional requirements for management that are always considered: Fault, Configuration, Accounting, Performance, and Security. In addition, I introduce other areas of network management functionality that do not fall handily under these general categories.

The cost of network management refers not only to the actual purchase price of the components, but in a broader sense to the human and computer resources required to field, administer, upgrade, and utilize the system.

Figure 1-1 shows that the ideal network management system offers the most comprehensive functionality at a very low cost.

But, as you can imagine, the ideal network management system is only for the perfect world. "The optimist proclaims that we live in the best of all possible worlds; the pessimist fears that this is true."[3] What you need then is a network management framework that can offer an effective compromise. At a minimum, it must address the reasons why so many of today's networks are undermanaged.

3

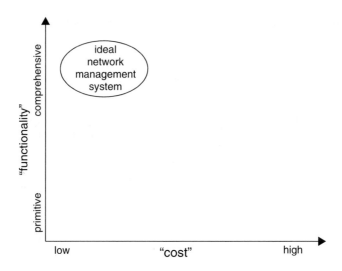

Figure 1-1. Network Management: Functionality vs. Cost

Perhaps you can create a network management "Wish List." Would it be something like the following?

A CURRENT NETWORK MANAGEMENT "WISH LIST"

◆ The network management framework must be open and standards-based so that it can work with many different types of equipment from different vendors. A great advantage is when the framework is easy to implement and operate.

◆ It must scale for new and existing hardware and software technologies while still accommodating the legacy systems.

◆ It must work with the new network paradigms that are being implemented.

◆ The framework must balance networking cost considerations with the performance, flexibility, availability, and control that are required for network operation.

◆ As needed, this framework must adequately deal with security issues.

◆ The framework must accommodate new networking technologies. LANs are being switched and virtualized. Their speeds are increasing in degrees of magnitude. WAN services such as Frame Relay, SMDS, and ATM are becoming widely implemented. Other new technologies, such as wireless, must also be considered.

♦ The framework must incorporate new computer technologies: new processors and platforms, new software advances, the World Wide Web and Web-based management, distributed data stores and objects, knowledge engineering and expert systems, parallel processing, and so on.

♦ The network management umbrella needs to include peripheral activities such as systems management, service management, network and capacity planning, policy enforcement, and others.

In network management today a disparity exists between your wish list and what is implemented for today's networks. Several reasons explain why this gap between what is needed and what is currently in place exists.

The major topic of this book, the Simple Network Management Protocol (SNMP), is a network management framework that offers itself as a solution. It is the most widely-used framework in place today. SNMP partially fills many of your wishes, and where it succeeds and fails as a framework is one of the main directions of this book.

Another reason a distance exists between the achieved and the achievable is a phenomenon I call "network management acceleration."

1.1. NETWORK MANAGEMENT ACCELERATION

In physics, acceleration is the rate of change in the speed and/or the direction of an object with respect to time. You accelerate when you change your pace; you accelerate when you change your direction. In the field of network management, the *what* is being managed and the *how* it is managed are constantly accelerating. We can take a snapshot of what network management is by asking the same question twice—with a slight shift in emphasis.

1.1.1. WHAT IS *NETWORK* MANAGEMENT?

A network is a collection of communicating computing resources. These resources are typically resident on network devices called nodes. These nodes run software for performing their requisite functions. Our network of interest is an important part of our enterprise. It is our collection of network devices. These enterprise resources need to be managed.

The area of network management is rapidly accelerating to include the management of other services heretofore not generally considered part of network management. These include:

◆ **system management:** the management of personnel computers and their components;

◆ **service management:** the wide area network service providers and their equipment management;

◆ **application management:** the management of user applications;

◆ **management of many other resources** (once considered out of the direct province of network management) including databases, storage devices, home electronic devices, electronic mail, and so forth.

The charter of what was formerly considered network management has been stretched "horizontally" to include these new types of management.

Network management is accelerating at an even quicker pace in the "vertical" direction. Where the SNMP framework was originally designed to manage network devices such as gateways, bridges, and routers that ran the TCP/IP protocol suite, it now manages just about any network device that has the processing ability to support an agent (or be proxied). This runs the gamut from personal digital assistants all the way up to the mainframe computer. Network management needs to run over the current networking protocols, such as IPX from Novell, the OSI stacks, AppleTalk from Apple, and others.

1.1.2. WHAT IS NETWORK *MANAGEMENT*?

Just as what is being managed is expanding in many new directions, the definition of management itself is also enlarging. The first-generation network management frameworks were largely in charge of monitoring vital network devices and a core set of operating statistics. The use of network management commands to control the devices was very limited, mainly due to the lack of security and the general limitations of how controls were implemented and administered. The user's view was often a minimal command line interface.

Today users interact with management consoles that use graphical user interfaces to present many different views of the network. Management tools and applications cull useful information from vast digital streams of management data. The results are stored in various databases for further analysis. Many new applications use advanced software techniques to make the information more clear and concise. The interpretation of the management information makes the analysis of network problems more straightforward for debugging and troubleshooting.

Much new functionality is also being added. The current generation frameworks are wrestling with the security issues of encryption and privacy, remote configuration, general framework administration, increased efficiencies in protocol operation, manager-to-manager communications, support of proxied devices, disparate platform technologies, and many, many other issues.

Figure 1-2 shows how network management has accelerated from its original, first-generation definition, to where it is today, to what it will hopefully encompass in the future.

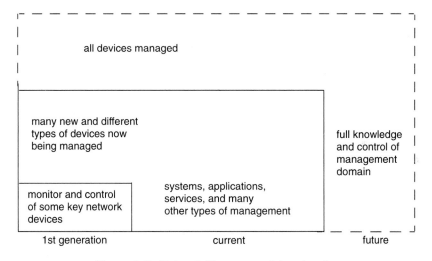

Figure 1-2. Network Management Acceleration

How then can this network acceleration be handled? Practical implementation and deployment experience, technology trends, academic research, and many other factors have directed the solution towards open, standards-based network management frameworks.

1.2. OPEN, STANDARDS-BASED NETWORK MANAGEMENT FRAMEWORKS

A network management framework that is open and based on standards has many benefits.

Open is definitely in. Open systems can be analyzed, tested, and expanded in ways that are not possible with closed, proprietary-based systems. A prime benefit of using open systems in the enterprise is that you can acquire the necessary hardware and software components from different vendors for the best solution. A high degree of probability exists that these multi-vendor computing systems so integrated and based on standards will successfully interoperate. Open systems possess an additional benefit in that properly engineered software can be ported with minimal changes. Competition in both cost and functionality results because the user is no longer locked into a particular vendor or product.

In order for these many computing systems from many different vendors in an enterprise to work together, they must be based on well-established and agreed-upon rules or standards. Two important open, standards-based network management frameworks are in use today: SNMP and the OSI-based Common Management Information Protocol (CMIP).

One reason SNMP is widely used is its evolution with the Internet. The standards that are of particular interest to the internetwork enterprise being discussed and managed by SNMP are the protocols in the TCP/IP protocol suite.

Although the acronym limits itself to the protocol—the set of rules for communicating between devices—it is more often used in the general sense of a network management framework and infrastructure. The framework includes:

◆ definition of the protocol operations

◆ administration

◆ security

◆ rules for how the management information is structured

◆ the list of managed variables

◆ several other closely related components

The other major standards-based network management framework of interest is the Open Systems Interconnection (OSI) network management framework. Note that this framework is also referred to by its defined services and protocol: The Common Management Information Service (CMIS) and the Common Management Information Protocol, respectively. Although a full discussion of CMIP is beyond the scope of this text, I introduce it later in this chapter in Section 1.6 *Introducing OSI Network Management: CMIP* for comparison and contrast with SNMP.

Before I delve into the particulars of these frameworks, I must establish general network management requirements. These requirements include a network management architecture and its environment. The functional requirements—fault, configuration, accounting, performance, and security management—must be presented and elaborated. Also, the network management requirements would not be complete without a discussion of network management terminology and models.

Two essential topics in understanding the definition of network management are:

♦ Network Management Architecture

♦ Network Management Functional Requirements

After one understands the ideal model and functional requirements of such a network management framework, the real-world solution offered up by a framework such as SNMP becomes much more understandable.

1.3. NETWORK MANAGEMENT ARCHITECTURE

A generalized network management architecture has three primary purposes:

1. To show the overall structure of the network management system

2. To show each individual component within the system

3. To show the relationships among these components

The architecture is represented by a model that depicts these purposes.

1.3.1. A NETWORK MANAGEMENT REFERENCE MODEL

Each communications network is a complex arrangement of computers, connections, systems software, and protocols. As these networks are connected to form an even more complex internetwork, the development of a network management system must be supported with techniques that allow the components to be modeled in a logical way and still maintain a framework for handling all of the actual physical complexities involved.

The first model presented, as shown in Figure 1-3, is the top-level view of a network management system for the manager/agent paradigm. It shows the overall structure of the system as well as the individual components and their relationship to each other.

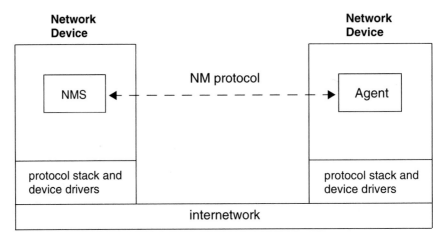

Figure 1-3. Network Management Architecture Model

This model depicts two network devices, a Network Management System (NMS), and a network management agent. The NMS and the agent communicate on the peer-to-peer level via a Network Management (NM) protocol. The model further depicts end-to-end communication over the internetwork between the two network devices, through a set of protocol stacks and device drivers for the application and internetworking communications.

This Network Management Architectural Model applies to SNMP, which uses the NMS/agent paradigm for NM protocol exchanges. The network devices using SNMP primarily use the TCP/IP protocol suite for applications services and internetworking protocols for end-to-end communications. The NMS and agent are both examples of application-level entities.

This model is a starting point for explaining network management in general, and SNMP in particular. By elaborating on each element in the model, I show in greater detail and complexity the network devices supporting both NMSs and agents in the SNMP environment.

1.3.2. INTERNETWORKING COMMUNICATIONS MODELS

For any network management system to be effective, it must be able to operate for the largest number of networks and systems. For a network to support communications on an internetwork, it must support common and interoperable protocols that allow for this communication.

The OSI Reference Model is used as the lowest common denominator for the basis of explaining how open systems communicate on the network and how networks can support communications with each other on the internetwork.

The model was standardized by the International Standards Organization (ISO) in 1978 and approved as a standard in 1983 (OSI guideline IS #7498[4]). It defines the communication between two end-systems in terms of seven layers. Each layer communicates with its corresponding peer-level layer via its protocol. A layer provides a well-defined set of services. Each layer n communicates and uses the services of the layer below it (n - 1) through its well-defined interface. Figure 1-4 shows the layers of the model:

7. Application:	provides user services
6. Presentation:	provides data transformation
5. Session:	provides application-to-application control
4. Transport:	provides reliable end-to-end communications
3. Network:	provides connections with the networks
2. Data Link:	provides for reliable data transfer over physical link
1. Physical:	provides reliable transmission of bits over the media

Figure 1-4. The ISO-OSI Seven Layer Reference Model

Much has been written about the model and how it can be implemented. A primary interest is to see how most communication protocol stacks and suites are matched to this model in terms of functionality, especially the TCP/IP protocol suite used with SNMP.

Before I examine the layers of the TCP/IP suite, let me subdivide the OSI model into two major layers: End-to-End Services (layers 1,2,3) and the Application Services (layers 5,6, and 7). Layer 4, the Transport Layer, helps facilitate the transition between the two services. This relationship appears in Figure 1-5.

Application	
Presentation	**APPLICATION SERVICES**
Session	
Transport Service	
Network	
Data Link	**END-TO-END SERVICES**
Physical	

Figure 1-5. Network Device Services Model

The lower layer, End-To-End Services, focuses on the data transmission among end-systems across the internetwork communications facility. The upper layer, Application Services, focuses on the user requirements and applications. The Transport Layer Service and its interface separate these two types of services. Their main purpose is to shield the application services from the details of the end-to-end services.

The various devices that are connected on an internetwork are characterized by the level of communication services that each can support. The OSI reference model provides a common ground for comparing these devices. When a connected device can communicate with the NMS by supporting the proper protocol, and it has an agent and the other necessary instrumentation code, it becomes a managed entity.

The types of managed entities are divided into two large categories:

◆ Managed Network Devices: devices that function to serve the network
◆ Managed Network Hosts: devices that serve the end-user

The Managed Network Devices operate at different levels of the OSI model. Figure 1-6 shows common network devices.

The most common network devices are:

◆ Repeaters
◆ Bridges
◆ Routers
◆ Gateways
◆ Other network devices

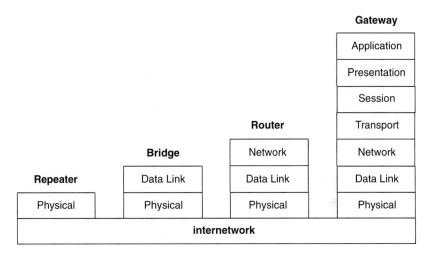

Figure 1-6. Network Devices

A repeater operates at the Physical layer by regenerating the media bit stream. This extends the length of a network by connecting segments of the same media type. A common scenario is adding a repeater to two Ethernet segments to create one logical LAN network. No software logic is involved—only electronic hardware.

A bridge operates at the Data Link layer to allow networks with different physical signaling, but with compatible Data Link addressing schemes, to communicate. A common example of where a bridge would be used is to allow users on an Ethernet LAN and a Token Ring LAN to communicate with each other. A bridge is media-dependent but protocol-independent.

A router operates up to the third layer, the Network Layer, and allows for the use of multiple communication paths through the network, based on knowledge of the source and destination addresses. Many routers operate on multiple protocols and can use any number of routing protocols. The most common routing protocols are SNMP-manageable. Routers are protocol-dependent but media-independent.

A gateway can include all seven of the OSI model layers and operates at the Application layer. (In 1970s terminology, gateway referred to what is known today as a router.) A gateway is a complex computing system that can be programmed to do any number of intricate protocol conversions and negotiations. Common types of gateways include OSI, DECnet, AppleTalk, SNA-to-TCP/IP, and others.

Also, many other network devices are based on various hardware and software configurations. These include hybrids such as brouters, routing bridges, and other devices such as hubs and multiplexors. Because these devices have such diverse communications capabilities, how they can support the communications protocols necessary for management becomes an issue.

The Managed Network Host serves the end-user. The end-user is one of the communicating end-systems that is performing the various functions desired by the users. The Internet term most often used is "host." "A host computer, or simply "host," is the ultimate consumer of communication services. A host generally executes application programs on behalf of user(s), employing network and/or Internet communication services in support of this function."[5]

Common classifications for hosts include mainframes, minicomputers, microcomputers, servers of various types (file, communications, print, database, and terminal), network printers, and so forth. Hosts typically implement application-level—or process-level in the TCP/IP model—communication services.

Several other devices do not handily fit in one of the two categories above, but can be managed, nonetheless. These include dedicated probe devices for monitoring various networks, uninterruptible power supplies (UPS), and many other unique and special-purpose devices. One of the first devices that was managed on a network by SNMP was a toaster. Another recent trade show had an SNMP-managed bathroom!

The TCP/IP protocol suite is the primary set of protocols used for internetworking communications. The TCP/IP protocol suite actually predates the OSI Reference Model and was originally developed from the ARPANET research and development effort from the late 1960s and early 1970s. By the early 1980s, all the computing systems wishing to communicate on the ARPANET internetwork were required to speak TCP/IP. Its use is still on the rise, and TCP/IP is a protocol that is allowing more and more devices to communicate on the internetwork.

Although any networking architecture must *include* services for communications, the TCP/IP suite has been designed *expressly* with reliable internetworking communications in mind. Four reasons for this fact are:[6]

◆ Network technology independence

◆ Universal interconnection

◆ End-to-End acknowledgments

◆ Application protocol standards

TCP/IP is based on the notion of sending packets called datagrams that help to make the protocol independent of any proprietary, single vendor's hardware or software platform. It allows any end-user or end-device to communicate to any other known end-user or end-device in a reliable manner; that is, acknowledgments can be sent, if so configured and desired. The fourth reason listed above, application protocol standards, is most important to SNMP. SNMP is an application-level protocol based on standardized specifications that allow end-user and network entities to manage and be managed. By being an open standard, SNMP is easily understood and capable of being extended in any number of anticipated—or unanticipated—directions.

The TCP/IP model, although providing the core functionality of the OSI seven-layer model, is represented in a more condensed fashion by using a four-layer model as shown in Figure 1-7.

4. **Process:**	provides application services for the end-user
3. **Host-to-Host:**	provides reliable end-to-end internetwork data exchange
2. **Internet:**	provides device-to-device internetwork data exchange
1. **Network Access:**	provides reliable host-to-network data exchange

Figure 1-7. The TCP/IP Four-Layer Reference Model

The Network Access Layer is the layer closest to the physical network. It accepts and delivers packets between the Internet Layer above it and the internetwork below. This layer has been developed for nearly every available network type, including local, metropolitan, and wide area networks.

The Internet Layer's prime component is the Internet Protocol (IP). By utilizing a global addressing scheme, this layer provides a delivery service that is independent of the network access layer below it. IP is a connectionless, datagram internetworking protocol that does not guarantee end-to-end delivery. Its features include the ability to specify type-of-service, Internet Layer addressing, fragmentation and reassembly, checksumming, and rudimentary security. The source reference for the current version of IP—IPv4—is the Internet Request for Comments (RFC) 791, *Internet Protocol* (I cover RFCs in depth in Chapter 2). Another important protocol included in the Internet Layer is the Internetwork Control Message Protocol (ICMP) for error and congestion reporting. The source reference for ICMP is RFC 792, *Internet Control Message Protocol*.

The Host-to-Host Layer offers the transport service necessary for allowing one host to communicate to another regardless of its place on the internetwork. This suite offers two transport protocols: the Transport Control Protocol (TCP) and the User Datagram Protocol (UDP). The source reference for TCP is RFC 793, *Transmission Control Protocol*, and for UDP, it is RFC 768, *User Datagram Protocol*. TCP is a reliable, connection-oriented service that provides end-to-end reliability, resequencing, error checking, and flow control. UDP is an unreliable, connectionless, datagram service that is the transport service of choice for SNMP.

The Process Layer is the application layer that provides services to the end-user and also a variety of common system functions. Common TCP/IP applications include the Telnet terminal program, the FTP file transfer program, the Simple Mail Transfer Protocol (SMTP) electronic mail program, and many others. The SNMP process resides at this layer.

Each of the four layers are implemented with many cooperating protocols. Now, many dozens of protocols comprise the full TCP/IP protocol suite. Figure 1-8 shows several of the primary TCP/IP protocols and how they fit into the TCP/IP model. The protocols in the boldface are of particular interest for SNMP. The Address Resolution Protocol (ARP) and the Reverse Address Resolution Protocol (RARP) can handle network access layer and Internet layer address mappings.

process layer	**SNMP**	TELNET		FTP	Other Applications
host-to-host layer	**UDP**		TCP		
internet layer	**IP (w/ICMP)**	ARP		RARP	Gateway Protocols
net access layer	**LAN Protocols**	**WAN protocols**			**MAN protocols**

Figure 1-8. TCP/IP Protocols

To serve as the foundation for a discussion on communication protocol layers and servicing, Figure 1-9 compares the TCP/IP model with the OSI model.

Application	Process
Presentation	
Session	
Transport	Host-to-Host
Network	Internet
Data Link	Network Access
Physical	

Figure 1-9. OSI and TCP/IP Model Comparison

1.3.3. INTERNETWORKING REQUIREMENTS

You need to understand the requirements of internetworking before reading about the functional requirements of network management.

1. For internetworking to be possible, all the networks that comprise the internetwork or intranet must be connected in such a way as to allow for the effective communication between two end points.

2. You must be able to route and deliver data between processes running on different computers on the connected networks.

3. The internetwork should be able to handle the different types of underlying networks and provide service in a transparent manner. The various network devices offer solutions for achieving interoperability for the internetwork. Global services for accounting, directories, electronic mail, and so on must be supported.

Differences among the various networks can cause problems. Here I list differences that you should consider.

◆ Networks have different addressing schemes, particularly the size and format of the addresses.

◆ The maximum and minimum packet sizes supported vary. The fragmenting and reassembly process for packets traversing the internetwork is required to handle this variation.

◆ The protocols used in the lowest layers vary, making the network access process different.

◆ Different networks use different time-out values that present problems if acknowledgments are not received in a timely manner. Having higher time-out values for internetwork communications is always desirable because of the longer time required for the end-to-end trip. Note that in a connection-based service, premature time-outs, before an acknowledgment can be received, cause needless retransmission and waste bandwidth.

◆ Internetworks should have a global error-reporting and error-recovery scheme.

◆ Internetworks should have mechanisms to report status and performance information.

◆ Routing on the internetwork must be robust to handle the way traffic is routed within and among the various networks.

◆ Internetworks should have reliable user access and control facilities.

◆ Optimally, the internetwork should provide a global connection service that is not predicated on the specific connection services—whether they be connection-oriented, virtual circuit-type, or connectionless, datagram-type—within each network.

1.4. NETWORK MANAGEMENT FUNCTIONAL REQUIREMENTS

In general, the functional requirements for sound network management have been analyzed in great detail, particularly with regards to the OSI model. The result of this analysis has been the subdivision of the network management functional requirements into five major groupings.

These five areas are so commonly used in network management design and implementation today, that they are often referred to by the acronym FCAPS. See Figure 1-10.

F	Fault management
C	Configuration management
A	Accounting management
P	Performance management
S	Security management

Figure 1-10. FCAPS

When desirable features are defined for inclusion into network management systems, these features are usually mapped into one or more of the FCAPS management categories by network management designers. FCAPS is often seen as the highest-level set of commands in Network Management Station implementations. Network Management applications are also categorized as one or more of these types.

Figure 1-11 (taken from [7]) depicts the interrelationships between the FCAPS functional areas for CMIP. These also hold true for SNMP.

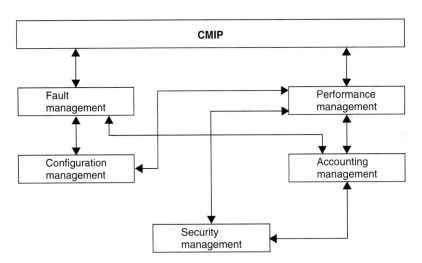

Figure 1-11. ISO Network Management Architecture

The relative priorities of the five areas have often been debated, but even the most rudimentary network management schemes must include fault and configuration management. Accounting, performance, and security management are often viewed as optional add-ons in some environments, but certainly necessary for a full-fledged network management implementation. The first specification of SNMP did, indeed, include fault and configuration management with a very rudimentary security management called trivial authentication. As befitting SNMP's aims for simplicity and extensibility, accounting, performance, and more rigid security management features are being added to the standard or made available through extension mechanisms.

Other ancillary network management topics do not handily fit into one of these five major categories. Such topics include:

◆ network rerouting capabilities

◆ report generation functions

◆ a central or distributed repository for various statistics and information

◆ non-attendant operation

◆ remote control features

◆ more integrated control with other features

◆ graphic user interfaces for the console and other network devices

◆ mainframe independence

◆ local user databases for various purposes

Discussing these other key areas is certainly important, but in the final analysis, these topics can ultimately be added to one or more of the FCAPS categories or viewed as implementation details.

FCAPS was developed for the OSI network management architecture. However, it also presents a clear model from which to view the capabilities and limitations of other network management frameworks such as SNMP. When I discuss SNMP practice in Section 14.3 *Revisiting FCAPS*, I reexamine FCAPS and see how these areas are applied to SNMP network management implementation details.

Looking in a little more detail at the specifics of each FCAPS category is beneficial. You can find a complete discussion of FCAPS in *Network Management: A Practical Perspective* (second edition) by Allan Leinwand and Karen Fang Conroy.[8]

1.4.1. FAULT MANAGEMENT

Fault Management (FM) detects, locates, and corrects problems in the network hardware and software. It determines, and usually records, that a fault has occurred, finds its location, and then attempts to mend the fault.

"Central to the definition of fault management is the fundamental concept of a 'fault.' Faults are to be distinguished from errors. A fault is an abnormal condition which requires management attention (or action) to repair. A fault is usually indicated by failure to operate correctly, or by excessive errors. Certain errors (e.g., CRC errors on communication lines), may occur occasionally and are not normally considered to be faults. Ordinarily, these errors are handled by an (n)-layer entity as part of (n)-layer operation."[9]

FM must be able to view the devices on the internetwork individually in order to determine that each is working properly. In close association with this awareness is the ability to isolate, correct, and repair any faults that may be detected. Faults are often catalogued for archiving and further analysis.

Implicit in the determination of whether a network device is operating properly is the knowledge of the "fault characteristics" of each device. Each device should have a predefined fault threshold. In conjunction with Configuration Management, these default thresholds should be changeable, either by having the NMS send set operations or by having these thresholds dynamically updated by the devices as they monitor the network operation.

The NMS should also implement fault filtering where faults can be prioritized to prevent the internetwork from being flooded by any fault notification. These priorities should also be configurable.

Routine preventive maintenance can also ensure properly functioning devices on the internetwork. Sophisticated Fault Management includes the proactive anticipation of failures. One way that this can be handled is by scheduling routine diagnostics to run on the devices. Depending on the capabilities of the device, these tests can range from simple loopbacks to rigorous diagnostic test suites.

1.4.2. CONFIGURATION MANAGEMENT

Configuration Management (CM) knows and controls the state of the internetwork. This includes knowing the devices and their interrelationships within the internetwork.

When discussing CM, a helpful abstraction is to characterize the devices within the internetwork as network objects that can be either end-host systems or network devices. These objects have characteristics, or attributes that are the properties that describe them. These properties are the list of management variables of interest that have values that can be set or examined.

CM comprises three major sub-areas:

♦ Initializing and maintaining the state of the internetwork

♦ Maintaining the status of each of the network objects

♦ Monitoring the relationship among the network objects

CM handles the starting up and shutting down of the internetwork. This includes the various issues involved in initialization and the warm and cold restarts that become necessary when the internetwork is operational.

The attributes of the managed object include such detailed information as the hardware and software inventory of the device, a name assigned to it as a convention, and its operational and administrative status. Various attribute values are configurable, thus allowing the NMS to affect the operational state of the network device.

In addition to knowing all about each device, the CM must also understand and monitor their relationships, often called the *network topology*. The primary need for network topology is to understand how the various network objects are interconnected. This is of paramount concern when Fault Management comes into play in determining and invoking alternative routing configurations and new traffic patterns.

The NMS typically represents the internetwork's configuration as a logical map depicting all of the network devices and a logical relationship that maps in some scale or perspective into the actual physical layout of the internet. Sophisticated GUI bitmaps present icons for the various network objects. The icons are often color-coded to represent the operational status of that device. The various connections also appear to show how the devices are interconnected. The use of graphics in CM presents a very useful top-level abstraction for network management.

Configuration Management works closely with Fault Management. As with all the network management areas, logging and authorization mechanisms are desirable, to verify and record any changes that are made and who makes them. Current directions in Configuration Management include the addition of provisioning the network devices with initial or updated software configurations, including operational software.

1.4.3. ACCOUNTING MANAGEMENT

Accounting Management (AM) gauges the usage of network resources by various end-users and applications. It calculates usage with various implementation-dependent algorithms based on connect time, length of connection, who the user is, and other parameters. This usage is typically logged into an accounting database. Accounting management provides a method for calculating the cost of running a particular network or segment. Accounting management also includes budgeting, verification, and billing.

This type of management is necessary when more than one group is using an internet or intranet. It is also useful in pointing out how resources are used and in what areas more networking resources may be required.

1.4.4. PERFORMANCE MANAGEMENT

Performance Management (PM) deals with the use of the network. Where Configuration Management is concerned with whether the internet was functioning properly, PM is concerned with how well it is working. PM allows network administrators to monitor such key network variables as throughput, response time, and general network availability, pointing out where and how performance can improve.

"At least conceptually, performance management of computer networks includes two broad functional categories-monitoring and tuning. Monitoring is the performance management function which tracks activities on the network. The tuning function enables performance management to make adjustments to improve network performance. Performance management enlists these mechanisms to provide an awareness of the degree to which the network is fulfilling the service expectations of the users and the degree to which the overall resources of the network are being used."[10]

PM has to deal with both the utilization and performance of each network object, as well as how they work together as a networking whole. The actual performance of the internet must approximate the expectations when the various PM metrics are calculated and analyzed.

23

1.4.5. SECURITY MANAGEMENT

Security Management (SM) is the regulation and administration of the access to the network resources and its important information. This includes verifying the access and privileges of network users to detect and record when an unauthorized user attempts an inappropriate action, either maliciously or unintentionally.

Many facets to SM are implementation-dependent, depending on the types of devices and the levels of security. Many of the communications security mechanisms—authentication, encryption, key management and recovery, certificate authorization, and others—are evolving and being incorporated into network management designs and implementations.

With the recent upsurge of interest in using the Internet for commercial purposes and using intranets for carrying mission-critical enterprise documents, the importance of security management has come to the forefront of network management agendas.

1.5. INTRODUCING SNMP

S	Simple
N	Network
M	Management
P	Protocol

The Simple Network Management Protocol provides a standardized network management framework for enabling the control and monitoring of an internetwork. The requirements for managing such a diverse range of network devices and hosts include a simple—yet extensible—set of standards that must be as robust and unobtrusive as possible. Consequently, SNMP is vendor-independent and relatively easy to implement.

SNMP was developed in 1988 as the short-term solution for the network management framework to be used in managing the devices connected to the Internet. The original plan was to supplant SNMP with the OSI network management standard CMIP after standards development and implementation experience proved this feasible.

This transition from SNMP to CMIP did not progress at the pace initially envisioned by the network management framework architects for a number of reasons. The CMIP implementations have been slow to be realized, and at the same time, SNMP has proliferated and gained a great deal of momentum and industry support. Very serious doubts exist now that this transition will ever occur.

SNMP's original charter of providing network management for Internet devices such as bridges, routers, and gateways is rapidly being expanded to include additional devices, other network environments, more protocols, and a variety of new features. Such a charter has allowed SNMP to be and evolve into a popular and effective network management scheme. The recommendation is that any device that wishes to connect to the Internet and use the Internet protocol suite have the capability to be managed by SNMP.

Of course, SNMP's widespread use has exposed it to the realities of what it is not and what it should or should not become.

1.5.1. WHAT SNMP IS

SNMP is the network management framework for internetwork devices that primarily contain the TCP/IP protocol suite. It has been adapted to run on other protocol stacks, but only if the TCP/IP stack is not available. It uses the manager/agent model, and its protocol operates at the application or "process" level of the TCP/IP model.

The first version of SNMP (SNMPv1) is very successful due to its balance of simplicity, flexibility, and extensibility. The second version of SNMP is now struggling through the IETF standards process. The additional requirements that are being added involve the introduction of complexity that makes consensus difficult to achieve. SNMPv2 is, at this writing, a draft standard based on the same community authentication scheme used in version 1. This version is represented by RFCs 1902-1908 that were released in January 1996.

SNMP is defined in a standardized way that encourages the framework's flexibility and extensibility. SNMPv1 is based on Internet standards that define its three major components: the Structure of Management Information (SMI), the Management Information Base (MIB), and the protocol itself, which is also referred to as SNMP (remember, the P stands for protocol). These standards are published as Request for Comments (RFC) and available for unlimited distribution. SNMP documentation is "free," and this fact has certainly engendered many commercial and reference manager and agent implementations.

The SMI is a standard notation for describing the management information. The MIB contains the variables of interest to be managed. By defining standard management objects and by providing the ability to define new MIB groups, SNMP has been extended to manage many new protocols and devices.

The generalized format of the MIB definition allows an MIB group to be defined for each new managed service. Vendors have a standard way to add their private managed objects. Additional efforts are underway to have SNMP work with other network management frameworks such as the IBM SNA world, various LAN schemes, and other popular proprietary network management schemes. By implementing a proxy agent, management information for devices that do not natively support SNMP and the TCP/IP protocol suite can also be managed.

SNMPv2 builds on the three major components that comprise the first version and contains updated versions of the SMI, MIB, and the protocol.

The SNMP network management model is centralized. Few active Network Management Stations and many passive agents converse in the protocol to exchange management information. One of the main reasons SNMPv1 is simple to implement and not resource-intensive is that the protocol contains only five request/response primitives:

◆ `get-request`
◆ `set-request`
◆ `get-next-request`
◆ `get-response`
◆ `trap`

The Network Management Stations can retrieve the variables of interest to its applications by sending `get-request` and `get-next-request` messages. The former is a specific read operation, and the latter provides a tree-traversal operator to determine which objects are supported by an agent. The NMS can modify an agent's variables by sending a `set-request` message.

The agent can reply to these three requests with the `get-response` primitive if no error occurs. Additionally, the `trap` primitive allows the agent to send an asynchronous alert to the NMS to signal certain predefined conditions.

Implementation experience and design improvements have caused SNMPv2 to refine the protocol by adding an improved NMS read operation, the `get-`

`bulk-request` message. It can be called to efficiently retrieve large amounts of data from a single request (such as the contents of a specific table). SNMPv2 has introduced manager-to-manager communication for status reporting by adding the `inform-request`. The `get-response` has been appropriately renamed to just `response`. The `trap` message has been modified to `snmpv2-trap` and it now has the same format as all of the protocol messages.

1.5.2. WHAT SNMP IS NOT

SNMP is not a panacea for the complete network management of the internetworked enterprise. Because SNMP evolved primarily from the Simple Gateway Management Protocol (SGMP), its original domain was to monitor and control specific internetwork devices such as routers. The original MIB (MIB-I) contained groups only for the general system description, the network interface, various addresses, the TCP protocols (IP, ICMP, TCP, and UDP), and the Exterior Gateway Protocol (EGP). The SMI was a small subset of ASN.1. SNMP has developed from this bottom-up evolution to become an enabling technology to manage many different devices in many different environments.

By definition simplicity implies limitation. Because SNMP was originally developed as a quickly implementable standard that was readily made available and required minimal system and network resources, several features and abilities that were originally unanticipated or not yet available became important. They need to be added to the SNMP standard and much of this progress is apparent when SNMPv1 is compared to SNMPv2. SNMP is purposely **not** a full-fledged object-oriented design. It uses a small set of ASN.1 and the BER encoding scheme to promote lean implementations.

Many of the perceived weaknesses of SNMP—such as having less functionality than CMIS/CMIP, rudimentary security, no manager-to-manager communications, little support for non-Internet protocols, poor bulk data transfer, scalability limits, and so forth—are hotly debated topics that are being addressed in the second and future versions of the standard.

1.5.3. SNMP VERSION 2

The second incarnation of SNMP is evolving to improve SNMPv1. The improvement includes adding security and a supporting administrative framework, improved protocol operations, fixing any SNMPv1 deficiencies, designing manager-to-manager communications, and remote SNMP-based configuration. The first proposal put on the standards track that appeared in April 1993 (RFCs 1441-1451) was an ambitious attempt to address all of these areas. Implementation experience, however, revealed problems.

The second attempt that was released in January 1996 (RFCs 1902-1908) is a much less comprehensive set of specifications that does not include security and remote configuration. Work still continues to improve this interim set of standards, as the security features and its administrative framework are seen as a required set of features for SNMP to continue its evolution and for people to foster its use.

Failure to produce an SNMPv2 standard with security in a timely way leaves the door open for alternatives. CMIP discussions continually resurface, and many vendors are experimenting with adding security features to the firmly entrenched SNMPv1 implementations. New network management paradigms based on WWW technologies are also at the door. Sun Microsystems has recently announced an SNMP-optional network management scheme based on the Java programming language.

CMIP has been around for as long as SNMP, but it has enjoyed very limited success. It claims a niche market for networks using the OSI protocol stacks and for several large telecommunications implementations.

1.6. INTRODUCING OSI NETWORK MANAGEMENT: CMIP

The OSI NM architecture (often referred to as the Common Management Information Protocol, or CMIP) also provides a network management framework for open systems that are running the OSI protocol suite. It is part of the much broader set of standards that has been developed for use in the OSI Reference Model. It is considered a fully elaborated set of standards that has been evolving for many years, although implementations have been slow to appear. Along with this evolution is the creation of an immense set of terminology and acronyms whose meanings and contexts must be understood. They are defined in over 30 network management standards documents produced by International Standards Organization.

The most important ISO Network Management Standards are:

◆ OSI Management Framework (IS 7498-4)

◆ Common Management Information Service (IS 9595)

◆ Common Management Information Protocol (IS 9596)

◆ Structure of Management Information (DIS 10165)

◆ System Management Overview (DIS 10040)

◆ System Management Functional Areas (DIS 10164)

The ISO Web page has many links to more information. It includes an introduction to ISO, its technical committees, its structure, a meeting calendar, worldwide member list, a catalog of its standards, publications and documents, information about ISO 9000, and even a "what's new" page. The ISO URL is http://www.iso.ch.

The OSI NM architecture is a complete object-oriented design. Along with this comes all of the object-oriented concepts including inheritance, containment, and associations among all of the management objects. Along with the design, the architecture comprises four major pieces that combine to provide this very comprehensive network management scheme. The architecture provides an Information Model, an Organization Model, A Communication Model, and a Functional Model to provide a rich set of services.

The Information Model includes a Structure of Management Information that is a superset of SNMP, a naming hierarchy, and the definition of managed objects (MO). Abstract Syntax Notation One (ASN.1) is used for the information exchange. The framework is organized in the same manner as SNMP, which is with the manager and agent paradigm. Both protocols operate at the application layer of the OSI reference model.

The Communication Model uses the OSI protocol suite but its architecture also includes Systems Management. It uses a connection-based service.

CMIP has a full set of operators. It has scoping and filtering rules for selectively viewing and prescreening the management information. *Scoping* can be applied to requests to view a selected subset of managed objects. *Filtering* is performed by applying boolean expressions against a request and only viewing the objects and their attributes that meet the truth criteria.

The Functional Model includes the specific management functional areas previously discussed: Fault, Configuration, Accounting, Performance, and Security Management.

The service definition for the network management is called Common Management Information Services (CMIS). CMIP defines how to implement the CMIS services by specifying the PDUs and the transfer syntax used in the protocol exchanges.

Three OSI application layer protocols (also called *service elements)* are necessary for implementation:

♦ Common Management Information Service Element (CMISE)

♦ Association Control Service Element (ACSE)

♦ Remote Operations Service Element (ROSE)

CMISE lets the user access the CMIS management services that in turn use CMIP for manager/agent communications. ACSE and ROSE are used by CMISE and are needed to control the application associations. ACSE handles the opening and closing of the manager and agent communications, and ROSE handles the requests and replies once the association has been established.

Figure 1-12 contains a table of the ten CMIS services.

The OSI NM framework was begun in the early 1980s and made into a standard about the same time as SNMP. Although its deployment has not enjoyed the same rapid success as SNMP for a variety of reasons, it is the predominant NM framework in most telecommunication providers and government agencies. Many people believe that the most important contribution of this framework is its use of object-oriented analysis and design.

The OSI NM framework is very elaborate, and you can very easily "accelerate" in many different directions when investigating and implementing it. Several good references are available (see the Bibliography at the end of this book) and the standards are a must-read to appreciate the complexity and scope of this architecture. Tools are slowly appearing that make working with the framework more straightforward.

Even for SNMP-only practitioners, understanding CMIP is important for several key reasons. You can benefit from examining all of the work that has gone into the concepts and modeling that has been used for nearly all of the general development of network management solutions. SNMP has been influenced by the OSI reference model, FCAPS, protocol operations, object-orien-

Service Name	Description
M-INITIALIZE	management association service used for establishment
M-TERMINATE	management association service used to break association
M-ABORT	management association service used for unconfirmed halting
M-EVENT-REPORT	management notification service that signals a pre-specified condition or event
M-GET	management operation service that retrieves (reads) the requested object attributes
M-CANCEL-GET	management operation service that allows the previous M-GET retrieval to be stopped
M-SET	management operation service that modifies (writes) the requested object attributes
M-ACTION	management operation service that allows a manager to specify that an operation be executed on the specified resource
M-CREATE	management operation service that allows the specified object instance to be created
M-DELETE	management operation service that allows the specified object instance to be destroyed

Figure 1-12. CMIS Services

tation, and many other key ideas. Many key CMIP concepts are realized in SNMP network management applications.

OSI NM has influenced other areas also. Two key examples are the integration of OSI network management into telecommunications and the development of consortiums such as the Network Management Forum to foster these types of network management frameworks.

1.6.1. TELECOMMUNICATIONS MANAGEMENT NETWORK (TMN)

The Telecommunications Management Network framework is a comprehensive set of specifications that deals with the managing and controlling of the network elements and resources in a telecommunications network. It provides standard interfaces so that management information can be accessed in a known and controllable manner.

31

In 1985, the International Telecommunications Union, Telecommunications Standardization Sector (ITU-T; previously the CCITT), began work on TMN—and it is now defined by the specifications found in the ITU-T document M.3000 series.[11] Figure 1-13 lists the ITU documents that represent the TMN Specifications.

TMN Recommendations	
M.3000	Overview of TMN Recommendations
M.3010	Principles for a Telecommunications Management Network
M.3020	TMN Interface Specification Methodology
M.3180	Catalog of TMN Management Information
M.3200	TMN Management Services: Overview
M.3300	TMN Management Capabilities Presented at the F Interface
M.3400	TMN Management Functions

Figure 1-13. TMN Specifications

TMN is object-oriented and primarily uses OSI constructs, such as MIBs and managed objects, CMIP managers and agents, and the OSI protocols for the management exchanges. TMN comes with its own set of terminology baggage that you need to understand before fully understanding the framework. For example, the functional areas of telecommunications networks are referred to as OAM&P: Operations, Administration, Maintenance, and Provisioning. This is similar to FCAPS. Another common TMN term encountered is the Q3 interface, which is the standardized interface that allows a manager and agent pair access to its MIB.

As the telecommunications and data worlds begin to collide in earnest, people working with internetworks will need to become familiar with many different frameworks. You can view much more information on the ITU from their home page at http://www.itu.ch.

1.6.2. NETWORK MANAGEMENT FORUM

A consortium of interested vendors, service providers, and government agencies named the Network Management Forum (NMF) have packaged a set of specifications dealing with the coexistence of many types of existing and emerging network management frameworks. They have dubbed this specification set OMNIPoint.[12]

The OMNIPoint approach attempts to be pervasive and include both telecommunications and data communications arenas. It allows for the use of many different types of protocol stacks and embraces both CMIP and SNMP. It is a very ambitious undertaking, and OMNIPoint-compliant products are being to appear. It comes with its own set of terminology and standardization formats. The NMF home page is at `http://www.nmf.org`.

1.7. COMPARING SNMP AND CMIP

SNMP and CMIP can be compared from many different vantage points. To the true network management zealot they exhibit a distinct difference in philosophies. To administrators and other pragmatists, the difference can be a commitment to what framework(s) are required for the platforms and resources to be managed. To object-oriented practitioners, CMIP is a complete object-oriented model with distributed, hierarchical objects, whereas SNMP is a flat, static model—"object-based" at best.

Facile comparisons include the connectionless, unreliable transport service of UDP versus the connection-oriented, reliable transport service used by the OSI protocol stack. People debate whether the added protocol operators of CMIP and such features as filtering and scoping can be truly emulated by the simpler SNMP constructs. Some even argue that the cost of obtaining the standards documents—the fairly hefty price tag of CMIP versus the virtually free price of SNMP—has affected the success and progress of these management frameworks.

If you revisit the functionality versus cost graph introduced earlier in the chapter (see Figure 1-1), you can now place SNMP and CMIP, as you see in Figure 1-14. The first thing you notice is the "SNMP/CMIP gap." How wide the gap is is a moot point but what is important is that CMIP is generally considered higher functionality at higher cost when compared to SNMP. The real

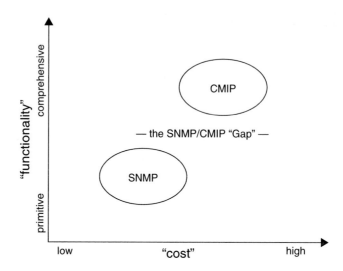

Figure 1-14. SNMP vs. CMIP: Functionality vs. Cost

question, then, is determining where your enterprise's network management needs lie.

ISO has created a super-flexible framework with high resource requirements. CMIP is resource-intensive in both the time required to implement it and the overhead required to run it on the managing and managed devices. CMIP definitely runs best in devices that have adequate resources. Its network management model has been criticized for lacking an adequate focus that can turn open standards into interoperable implementations. "As is the case with so many ISO standards, the OSI Network Management Framework (ISO/IEC 7498-4: 1989) describes a model that is incredibly general and can essentially mean almost anything to anyone."[13]

The Internet Architecture Board (IAB) has taken a near antithetical approach in espousing a simple, inexpensive, and easy to implement solution. The key tenet of SNMP is that it should have minimal impact on the system being managed. This is summarized succinctly in the Fundamental Axiom: "The impact of adding network management to a managed node must be minimal, reflecting a lowest common denominator."[14]

One general conclusion is fairly safe: if you're running a TCP/IP network, you reap overwhelming benefit from using SNMP; if you're using the OSI protocols, you should favor CMIP.

Network management zealots from both camps continue to argue that SNMP may be too simple and that CMIP is too complex. Can SNMP scale to an extremely large network? Will CMIP ever obtain the momentum to create a large user base? Are SNMP agents too "dumb"? Does SNMP require too much polling to be effective? Is CMIP too resource-intensive? And many others.

This debate continues, but the huge success of SNMPv1 is undeniable. If the next SNMP version cannot take up the network management baton with similar implementation success, as well as the desired security features, the CMIP standard may, perhaps, be discussed as an alternative open, standards-based NM framework solution.

Figure 1-15 (from [15]) presents a summary of the key features of SNMP Version 1 and CMIP.

Feature	SNMPv1	CMIP
Installed base	Huge	Small
Managed objects per managing station	Small	Large
Management model	Manager and agents	Manager and agents
View of managed objects	Simple variables arranged in MIB trees	Objects with inheritance defined in MIBs
Manager/agent interactions	Polling, infrequent traps	Event driven
Explicit manager to agent command invocations	No	Yes
Security	No	Yes
Manager-to-manager exchanges	No	Yes
Bulk transfers	No	Yes
Create/delete managed objects	No	Yes
Communication model	Datagram	Session-based
Standards body	Internet	ISO
Approximate memory requirements	40-200 KBytes	300-1000 KBytes

Figure 1-15. SNMP vs. CMIP: Feature Comparison

1.8. THE INTERNET

An introduction to network management for the 1990s would not be complete without a mention of the Internet. The Information Super Highway is on everyone's Top Ten List of the most overused buzz phrases, but its influence on anything having to do with communications and information-sharing—including network management frameworks such as SNMP—is undeniable.

The Internet has grown at an exponential rate from its ARPANET origin nearly three decades ago to the largest collection of communicating computers in the world. Millions of computers successfully intercommunicate because of the internetworking technology, including the TCP/IP protocol suite, that has been implemented.

A very positive side effect is the high availability and easy accessibility of valuable information such as the SNMP standards, internet drafts, RFCs, sample code, and reference implementations. Mailing lists and user groups allow people ready access to the most up-to-date information about topics such as network management and SNMP.

SNMP is growing with the Internet and is its primary tool for network management.

REFERENCES FOR CHAPTER 1

[1] Winoker, Jon, ed. *Zen to Go*. New York: Plume, Penguin Books. 1990.

[2] Bartlett, John. *Bartlett's Familiar Quotations, 16th edition*. Boston: Little, Brown, and Company. 1992.

[3] Rogers, James. *The Dictionary of Clichés*. New York: Ballantine Books. 1985.

[4] Information Processing Systems. Open Systems Interconnection. "Basic Reference Model." International Organization for Standardization. International Standard 7498. 1984.

[5] Braden, R. T., ed. *Requirements for Internet Hosts-Communications Layers, RFC 1122*. DDN Network Information Center: SRI International. 1989.

[6] Comer, Douglas E. *Principles, Protocols, and Architecture*. Vol. 1 of Internetworking with TCP/IP. Englewood Cliffs, NJ: Prentice Hall. 1991.

[7] Ball, Larry L. *Cost-Efficient Network Management*. New York: McGraw-Hill, Inc. 1992.

[8] Leinwand, Allan, and Karen Fang Conroy. *Network Management: A Practical Perspective*. Reading, MA: Addison-Wesley. 1996.

[9] Aronoff, R., M. Chernick, K. Hsing, K. Mills, and D. Stokesberry. *Management of Networks Based on Open Systems Interconnection (OSI) Standards: Functional Requirements and Analysis*. Gaithersburg, MD: National Institute of Standards and Technology. 1989.

[10] *Ibid*.

[11] CCITT, "Principles for a Telecommunications Management Network." M.3010. 1992.

[12] Network Management Forum. *Discovering OMNIPoint*. Upper Saddle River, NJ: Prentice Hall. 1993.

[13] Piscitello, David M., and A. Lyman Chapin. *Open Systems Networking: TCP/IP and OSI*. Reading, MA: Addison-Wesley. 1993.

[14] Rose, Marshall. *The Simple Book: An Introduction to Networking Management*. Upper Saddle River, NJ: Prentice Hall. 1996.

[15] Orfali, Robert, Dan Harkey, and Jeri Edwards. *Essential Client/Server Survival Guide*. New York: Van Nostrand Reinhold. 1994.

CHAPTER 2

The "Theory" of SNMP

Our life is frittered away by detail ... Simplify, simplify.

—*Henry David Thoreau*[1]

Everything should be as simple as possible, but not simpler.

—*Albert Einstein*[2]

The "theory" of SNMP is a general analysis of the pieces that make up this network management framework. This includes an overview of its history (the *why*), a chronology of its major developments (the *when* and the *who*), and the main components and their relationship to one another (the *what* and the *where*). This information is necessary before you can explore the implementation details of SNMP "practice" in Chapters 9 and 10. The "practice" of SNMP is the *how* and contains the details and specifics needed for implementation. Figure 2-1 encapsulates the five W's of SNMP.

SNMP is now the most common standardized network management framework being implemented today. SNMP is the application-level protocol offering network management service primarily via the Internet suite of protocols and its attached resources. It provides a basic framework for the administration

Simple Network Management Protocol	
Why?	A network management framework was needed for monitoring and controlling internetworks using primarily the TCP/IP protocol suite.
Who?	Jeffrey Case, Mark Fedor, Martin Schoffstall, and James Davin are considered the main SNMP designers and the writers of the SNMP Version 1 RFCs. Marshall Rose and Keith McCloghrie also made many contributions, wrote the SMI RFC, and edited the MIB-1 and MIB-2 RFCs. The four principles for Version 2 (often referred to as the "Gang of Four") are Jeffrey Case, Keith McCloghrie, Marshall Rose, and Steven Waldbusser.
When?	SNMP Version 1 implementations first appeared in 1988. The SNMPv2 proposed standards were originally published in April 1993, but greatly modified by the draft proposals presented in January 1996.
What?	SNMP is comprised of managers, agents, the management protocol, and the management information.
Where?	SNMP is an application layer process that primarily uses UDP/IP to communicate across the internetwork.

Figure 2-1. SNMP Overview

of authentication, authorization, access control, and privacy policies from which network management can be achieved.

SNMP uses the manager-agent model to monitor and control various manageable network devices on the internetwork. It is comprised of three elements:

◆ One or more network devices to be managed, each containing the agent. This managed network entity, or node, must have the capability of communicating across the internetwork.

◆ One or more managing network devices, each containing the network management station (NMS). This network manager must also have the ability to communicate across the internetwork.

◆ The protocol between the agents and the NMS used to exchange management information. This protocol is also referred to as SNMP.

SNMPv2 has added the refinement of the dual-role entity, which is a network device that contains both a manager and an agent. The agent can be managed by NMSs on other devices allowing for the configuration of a hierarchical scheme of managers. Work is continuing on inter-manager communications, but it is not, as of this writing, part of the official SNMP standards.

SNMP uses a fetch-and-store paradigm[3] to realize this network management between the NMS and the agents. Each agent, also called the SNMP server, manages a collection of meaningful and predefined data called the Management Information Base (MIB). An agent's MIB instantiation can be read by or written to by the NMS. The NMS is also called the client in SNMP parlance. Beware, however, that client-server terminology is not often used because the terms client and server have been widely overused. They have taken on a variety of differing and conflicting meanings in various computing contexts (see the third letter in Jeffrey Case's "Ask Dr. SNMP" column in *The Simple Times*[4]). In customary usage many clients are communicating with few servers; this model is the opposite of that found with SNMP.

The NMS is the active participant in the SNMP model. In the general case, users at the NMS platform execute network management applications that initiate requests to read and write to the nodes they wish to manage. The nodes contain agents that passively wait to service the requests. The agents translate the requests from the NMS, verify that the operation is permissible and possible, perform the operation, send the appropriate response, and then go back to "waiting."

One of the most important functions of the agent is to translate the generalized request for information by the NMS into equivalent operations on the local data structures. This function is accomplished by the agent's instrumentation procedures that map the SNMP commands to local operations. In order to execute in each node's environment, this mapping is different for each agent's implementation.

The agent is also capable of sending a trap message to the NMS. A trap is a message reporting an extraordinary, and predefined, event. The NMS is then responsible for further interaction with the agent to determine the nature of the problem and subsequent actions that can be taken.

To understand this common scenario more fully and to look deeper into the framework, look at the major standards that define SNMP. SNMP is comprised of three major standards:

The SMI contains the fundamental rules used to define SNMP. It delineates how the managed objects and the management information that is transferred between the NMS and its agents are defined. The SNMP protocol are the rules

The SNMP Standards
The Structure of Management Information (SMI)
The Network Management Protocol (SNMP)
The Management Information Base (MIB)

for how the network management information is exchanged. The MIB is the collection of managed objects.

As with all Internet protocols that are intended for standardization, the SNMP specifications are published as Request for Comments (RFC) and put on the standards track by the Internet Architecture Board (IAB). All three standards for SNMPv1 have reached the full standard status. The final version of the SMIv1 is RFC 1155. For the MIB-II, it is RFC 1213 and for the v1 protocol, it is RFC 1157. Note that RFC 1212, *Concise MIB Definitions*, clarifies and extends the format for defining MIB objects and is considered part of the SMI. The protocol, the SMI, and the MIB are also referred to as STD 15, STD 16, and STD 17, respectively.

The first SNMPv2 version (RFCs 1441-1452), which entered the standards track as a proposed standard, met with a great deal of resistance and many of the modifications that were submitted were rejected or slated for modification. The current revision of SNMPv2 (RFCs 1902-1908)—without much of the proposed functionality—has entered the next phase of standardization as a draft standard status. Version 2 is still evolving and until consensus can be reached on the administrative framework and security, full standard status will be delayed. When SNMPv2 finally reaches full standards status, SNMPv1 will be relegated to historical status.

2.1. A BRIEF HISTORY OF SNMP

Although no one would argue that the need for network management has been around for as long as networks have existed, the standardization process to create open frameworks such as SNMP did not gain critical momentum until the 1980s.

In less than a decade, SNMP has evolved from a simplistic monitoring program for routers into a very powerful network management framework. The complete details of SNMP history and related standards are presented in Appendix A.

2.1.1. SNMP VERSION 1

Early in 1988, the First Ad Hoc Network Management Review Group met to decide on the proper path for the specification of a network management protocol for the Internet. The group considered three major protocols:

♦ The High-Level Entity Management Systems (HEMS)

♦ The Simple Gateway Monitoring Protocol (SGMP)

♦ The OSI CMIP over TCP/IP (CMOT)

Since the SGMP protocol was already implemented to manage Internet routers and would only need minor modifications to make it more general purpose, it was chosen as the short-term solution for Internet management. The CMOT protocol was chosen as the long-term solution, although since 1988 its interoperability has been questioned and it has not been widely implemented. The HEMS system had considerable technical merit, but was not further considered in order to reach consensus.

SGMP was expanded and renamed to SNMP, and SNMP became the transitionary proposal to ease the eventual change to CMOT. The initial specifications for SNMP had already been completed by August 1988. They were collectively referred to as the "Internet-standard Network Management Framework." The three seminal specifications for the SMI, MIB, and protocol were published as RFCs 1065, 1066, and 1067, respectively. The specifications were approachable enough that several implementations appeared before the end of 1988.

In April 1989, the SNMP protocol status was promoted to "recommended" by the Internet Architecture Board. This was the blessing that devices should implement SNMP—effectively making it the *de facto* standard for the network management of internetworks that use the TCP/IP protocol suite. The Second Ad Hoc Network Management Review held in June 1989, reiterated that the dual track of SNMP and CMOT would be maintained with work on common managed object definitions and SMI for the two frameworks, but that implementation experience would help dictate the future and pace of the transition.

At the INTEROP trade show held in October 1989, more than 30 vendors demonstrated SNMP management in some fashion. By May 1990, the three major portions of SNMP were elevated to full standard protocol by the IAB. This step cleared the way for general vendor acceptance and widespread use and implementation. The SNMP/CMOT dual track proved intractable, and the SNMP framework became the *de jure* standard for network management.

The greatest emphasis in the early 1990s was the creation of enterprise MIBs to extend the set of managed objects in a standardized way. "MIB mania" ensued as nearly every vendor hopped on the SNMP bandwagon and created MIB objects for all of the variables that could possibly be managed in a particular device. Most of the legacy management variables were "mibified" to make their values available to SNMP. Concurrently, many network management applications were also developed to make use of these variables for turning all of this data into information about the health and well-being of the managed network.

With the first version complete and solidly in place, work recommenced improving the framework and starting the next iteration. People working with SNMP compiled quite a wish list of what features and modifications they would like to have incorporated into the SNMP framework. These suggestions included security, remote configuration, the extended management of new hardware devices and software components, and many others. These enhancements were to be done in keeping with the spirit of SNMP; it was to remain a framework that was simple to implement, and yet flexible enough to be extended to include the required network management functionality.

2.1.2. SECURE SNMP AND THE SIMPLE MANAGEMENT PROTOCOL

In early 1992, the IETF issued a call for proposals for the next version of SNMP. Three RFCs were issued in July 1992, by James Galvin, Keith McCloghrie, and James Davin, that described a new framework that included security. This framework was dubbed Secure SNMP and is detailed in RFCs 1351-1353.

- RFC 1351 *SNMP Administrative Model*

- RFC 1352 *SNMP Security Protocols*

- RFC 1353 *Definitions of Managed Objects for Administration of SNMP Parties*

Secure SNMP offered a security model that had both authentication and encryption to protect against such threats as interruption, interception, modification, and masquerade. Messages could be sent and received as non-secure, authenticated but not private, not authenticated but private, and both authenticated and private. In order to offer this new functionality, a new administrative framework was proposed. A cornerstone of this model was the notion of a party.

> *An SNMP **party** is a conceptual, virtual execution context whose operation is restricted (for security and other purposes) to an administratively defined subset of all possible operations of a particular SNMP entity.*

The party was the core element for this new administrative framework. The party structure was to replace the community name of Version 1 and contain the extra information needed for authentication and privacy. It defined the transports, the clocks, the keys, and access rights for the two communicating SNMP entities.

The Message Digest 5 (MD5) authentication algorithm was to check the message sender's identity by verifying a checksum that would be included in the message wrapper. MD5 is presented, along with its C source code reference implementation, in RFC 1321, *The MD5 Message Digest Algorithm*.

Encryption for message privacy was to be done using the Data Encryption Standard (DES) algorithm. DES is a symmetric encryption technique whereby the same key is used to both encrypt and decrypt the data. The algorithm involves a series of substitutions followed by a permutation on the message, using the particular configured secret key. (An excellent text on all phases of cryptography with full explanations of MD5, DES, and many other encryption algorithms is Bruce Schneier's Book, *Applied Cryptography*[5]).

The Secure SNMP RFCs offered many new improvements and innovative ideas. However, the fact that Secure SNMP was not backward compatible with Version 1—the message formats with the new authentication and security wrappers were completely different—made consensus impossible to reach.

The Simple Management Protocol (SMP) was an alternate proposal offered by Jeffrey Case, Keith McCloghrie, Marshall Rose, and Steven Waldbusser at approximately the same time (July 1992). They titled their framework "Simple Management Protocol" (SMP) to highlight the fact that the protocol would be network-independent. It also included the security features presented by the Secure SNMP proposal.

This new framework was developed as an extension to SNMP Version 1 to encompass the management of more network elements in a secure fashion. The design had also been simplified to allow for the management protocol to be network-independent. This new proposed protocol would be able to run on various transport levels in a standardized way. The proposal contained such new features as manager-to-manager communications, bulk table transfer, improved protocol error reporting, enhanced SMI, and other modifications to Version 1. It was also, however, not backward compatible with the first version.

Although several implementations of both frameworks were deployed to prove that they were implementable, Secure SNMP and SMP are of primary interest as the foundation for creating the proposed next version of SNMP. IETF Working Groups used both Secure SNMP and SMP later in 1992 for the upgrade effort of SNMP to move towards Version 2.

2.1.3. SNMP VERSION 2: TAKE 1

The new SNMPv2 addresses several key areas that were thought to be lacking or needed to be improved upon from the original version. It includes the Secure SNMP and SMP work and still maintains the spirit of the SNMP charter by attempting to minimize complexity at the agent and adding the new management functionality under the central control of the Network Management Station and its applications.

Five key SNMPv2 enhancements include:

◆ the security features deployed with "Secure SNMP"

◆ addition of the manager-to-manager facility to allow for hierarchical management

◆ capability of supporting a variety of transport services

◆ reduction of internetwork traffic by making the retrieval mechanism more efficient

◆ enhancements to the existing SNMPv1 protocol framework

Version 2 incorporated the security recommendations defined in RFCs 1351, 1352, and 1353. Two key differences exist, however. First, the use of the

Data Encryption Standard (DES) encoding is optional due to problems related to its restricted use outside of the U.S. (the U.S. government prohibits the exportation of encryption keys over 40 bits in length; DES requires a 56-bit key). Secondly, SNMPv2 would allow for the acceptance of packets that arrived at the NMS out of the order in which they were transmitted. The Version 2 architects felt that the additional processing that is required to handle packets arriving out of sequence would increase the robustness and response timing of the management. They felt that packets arriving out of order are more of a network performance problem than a security issue. "Secure SNMP requires packets to be delivered in order, since those that don't may be intercepted and copied by an unauthorized party. But most networks reorder packets in the course of regular data transmissions, especially during times of stress, precisely when network management is needed most."[6]

Like Secure SNMP and SMP, the implementation of these security features involved adding several new fields to the SNMPv1 message. These fields added to the message's "outer wrapper" and included information on the message's origin, integrity, replay protection, and privacy. It used the party concept introduced by Secure SNMP.

Manager-to-manager communications were to be another major improvement to SNMP. The original management architecture model of the manager-agent was now expanded to introduce a hierarchical ordering that is possible when managers are allowed to communicate with each other. This feature could greatly enhance enterprise manageability by scaling the management domain, as more and more agents are deployed. Strategically placed element managers could report the status of their agents that they are monitoring and controlling to a centralized NMS. In effect, these element managers, or mid-level managers, have dual roles of managing their network and its agents, and then acting as an agent for the top-level enterprise-wide NMS. Manager-to-manager communications were to be done with the new Inform-PDU type that was proposed. RFC 1451 defined the Manager-to-Manager MIB.

The newly proposed SNMPv2 also supported additional transport communication facilities in a standardized fashion. These included the use of the AppleTalk, IPX from Novell, and OSI CLNP stacks. UDP/IP was still endorsed as the transport service of choice for SNMP. For this reason, many devices took a dual approach and supported both their "native" transport and an additional UDP/IP stack for the management application. Proxy agents were also used for managing foreign network devices that did not have their own agents.

A new PDU was devised for bulk data transfer. The addition of the `Get-Bulk-PDU` could greatly increase the performance and efficiency of large data requests sent by the NMS. This new PDU is actually a refinement of the `Get-NextRequest-PDU`. It allowed for the retrieval of entire tables and the use of maximum message sizes without the need for issuing repeated read requests to the agent. Its use would reduce the management bandwidth overhead required for routers and other devices that maintain large amounts of tabular data.

Also, several welcome enhancements to the existing SNMPv1 protocol framework were discovered through implementation experience.

◆ A locking mechanism was to be implemented to assure that set requests were done properly when an agent was communicating with multiple NMSs. Each NMS could request the current lock count, and then send a set request with this value in one of the fields. The agents verified the value, incremented its counter, and then honored the request. Any requests with an invalid value in this field would not be executed by the agent; therefore, one request was done per lock value. This was called the `TestAndIncr` (test and increment) textual convention.

◆ The SMI was modified to include 64-bit counters (in addition to the 32-bit counters) to accommodate higher speed devices that cause these counters to wrap more quickly. Five new macros were also defined for object-types, object-groups, module compliance, agent capabilities, and traps. Several new data types and conventions were included for such items as the OSI addressing scheme, IPX addresses, and so forth.

◆ Error reporting was improved with an expanded set of error codes to more accurately explain why requests failed. This improvement provided more information to the NMS and its applications for handling error recovery.

◆ The agents could have accepted and processed partial requests for retrieving information. This was to make the monitoring function less bandwidth-intensive and recovery requests easier to formulate for the network management applications.

SNMP Version 2 was defined formally in a set of twelve consecutive RFCs that delineate these features and enhancements. All were issued in April 1993, and entered the standards track as proposed standards. If you are interested in the history and evolution of SNMP, they are all certainly worth a read.

Figure 2-2 lists the SNMP Version 2 RFCs. At over 400 pages of specification they are a little less "simple" than Version 1!

SNMP Version 2 (Proposed Standard) RFCs	
RFC	**Title**
1441	Introduction to Version 2 of the Internet-standard Network Management Framework
1442	Structure of Management Information for Version 2 of the Simple Network Management Protocol (SNMPv2)
1443	Textual Conventions for Version 2 of the Simple Network Management Protocol (SNMPv2)
1444	Conformance Statements for Version 2 of the Simple Network Management Protocol (SNMPv2)
1445	Administrative Model for Version 2 of the Simple Network Management Protocol (SNMPv2)
1446	Security Protocols for Version 2 of the Simple Network Management Protocol (SNMPv2)
1447	Party MIB for Version 2 of the Simple Network Management Protocol (SNMPv2)
1448	Protocol Operations for Version 2 of the Simple Network Management Protocol (SNMPv2)
1449	Transport Mappings for Version 2 of the Simple Network Management Protocol (SNMPv2)
1450	Management Information Base for Version 2 of the Simple Network Management Protocol (SNMPv2)
1451	Manager-to-Manager Management Information Base
1452	Coexistence between Version 1 and Version 2 of the Internet-standard Network Management Framework

Figure 2-2. SNMP Version 2 Draft RFCs

The transition to SNMPv2 was seen as a major issue, because a large number of SNMPv1 agents and managers had already been successfully implemented and deployed. For an indeterminate amount of time, the SNMP community would have to accommodate both versions. Two paths were proposed: bilingual implementations and proxy methods.

Bilingual agents and NMSs would support both versions. A bilingual NMS could talk SNMPv1 to Version 1 agents and SNMPv2 to Version 2 agents. These bilingual NMSs could also accept `Trap-PDUs` in either format. Bilingual agents would also be able to converse in both brands of the protocol.

The proxy method involves the use of additional software logic to transform and map the requests, responses, and traps between the two versions.

The upgrade to this new version of the SNMP management framework was advertised as more of a migration than a conversion. The upgrade required slight modifications to the existing SNMPv1 base. The MIBs were quickly updated across the versions, and the large investment in the current MIB base was to be retained. The Version 2 improvements actually made the MIB information more functional. A large percentage of the agent code was reusable, with changes needed to handle the security information in the SNMP message header, the SMI changes, new PDU types, additional error codes, and so forth. This situation is also true on the NMS side, with slight modifications needing to be done to handle the new functionality. Additional implementation facilities such as the interface and database handling would need to be updated.

2.1.4. SNMP VERSION 2: TAKE 2

After the 12 RFCs that comprised the SNMPv2 proposed standard were released in May 1993, the SNMPv2 Working Group was disbanded. This action is part of the normal IETF process and allows vendors and other interested parties to develop and field applications based on these new specifications.

The initial feedback was not positive. The general consensus was that the party-based administrative framework and security features were too complex and confusing to implement. Configuring the agents was very difficult. The security features prohibited the SNMP discovery feature that populated topology maps from discovering the agents. The general deployment and usage had become a daunting task; it was no longer simple.

The SNMPv2 Working Group was started up again in December 1994 to review the specifications and move the standard to the next level of acceptance (from proposed to draft). The administrative framework and security became the key points of discussion. After heated debates—and even the possibility of an interim SNMPv1.5 version—major changes clearly needed to be done before the SNMPv2 standard could be advanced.

2.1.5. SNMP VERSION 2: TAKE 3

The SNMP Working Group met many times in the first part of 1995, and the SNMPv2 mailing list volume rose dramatically. The SNMPv2 specifications were reworked. When consensus could not be reached on the administrative framework with security, the only compromise that could be reached was the use of the new protocol features (SNMPv2 PDUs) within the "traditional" Version 1 community-based message wrapper. The party-based framework was discarded completely and Version 2 was named: SNMPv2c-community-based SNMPv2. Figure 2-3 shows how the proposed RFCs (1441–1452) evolved into their draft RFCs successors (1901–1908).

"Proposed" SNMPv2 RFC and Title	Evolution to "Draft" SNMPv2
RFC 1441: *Introduction to Version 2 of the Internet-*standard Network Management Framework	modified to Experimental status and reissued as RFC 1901: *Introduction to Community-based SNMPv2*
RFC 1442: *Structure of Management Information for* Version 2 of the Simple Network Management Protocol (SNMPv2)	updated to Draft status and reissued as RFC 1902: *Structure of Management Information for Version 2 of the Simple Network Management Protocol (SNMPv2)*
RFC 1443: *Textual Conventions for Version 2 of the Simple* Network Management Protocol (SNMPv2)	updated to Draft Status and reissued as RFC 1903: *Textual Conventions for Version 2 of the Simple Network Management Protocol (SNMPv2)*
RFC 1444: *Conformance Statements for Version 2 of the* Simple Network Management Protocol (SNMPv2)	updated to Draft Status and reissued as RFC 1904: *Conformance Statements for Version 2 of the Simple Network Management Protocol (SNMPv2)*
RFC 1445: *Administrative Model for Version 2 of the Simple* Network Management Protocol (SNMPv2)	reclassified to Historical status in December 1995
RFC 1446: *Security Protocols for Version 2 of the Simple* Network Management Protocol (SNMPv2)	reclassified to Historical status in December 1995

Figure 2-3. SNMP Version 2 Proposed RFCs Evolution

"Proposed" SNMPv2 RFC and Title	Evolution to "Draft" SNMPv2
RFC 1447: *Party MIB for Version 2 of the Simple Network Management Protocol (SNMPv2)*	reclassified to Historical status in December 1995
RFC 1448: *Protocol Operations for Version 2 of the Simple Network Management Protocol (SNMPv2)*	updated to Draft Status and reissued as RFC 1905: *Protocol Operations for Version 2 of the Simple Network Management Protocol (SNMPv2)*
RFC 1449: *Transport Mappings for Version 2 of the Simple Network Management Protocol (SNMPv2)*	updated to Draft Status and reissued as RFC 1906: *Transport Mappings for Version 2 of the Simple Network Management Protocol (SNMPv2)*
RFC 1450: *Management Information Base for Version 2 of the Simple Network Management Protocol (SNMPv2)*	updated to Draft Status and reissued as RFC 1907: *Management Information Base for Version 2 of the Simple Network Management Protocol (SNMPv2)*
RFC 1451: *Manager-to-Manager Management Information Base*	reclassified to Historical status in December 1995
RFC 1452: *Coexistence between Version 1 and Version 2 of the Internet-standard Network Management Framework*	updated to Draft Status and reissued as RFC 1908: *Coexistence between Version 1 and Version 2 of the Internet-standard Network Management Framework*

Figure 2-3. SNMP Version 2 Proposed RFCs Evolution *(continued)*

The latest incarnation of SNMP uses the new SNMPv2 PDUs (as defined in RFC 1905) with their associated protocol operations such as Get-Bulk. It employs the new SMI and its MIB definitions. Note that this version of SNMPv2 is the current version in use as I'm writing this book. **Unless otherwise specifically stated, the SNMPv2 used in the remainder of the text refers to its draft standard as defined by RFCs 1902–1908.**

SNMPv2 uses the v1 administrative framework and the standard SNMPv1 message wrappers as they are defined in RFC 1157. The only difference in the wrapper is that the value of the version field is now set to 1 for Version 2 messages (the version field has a value of 0 for Version 1 messages). Several minor changes occurred between the draft standard and the proposed standard. These are detailed in Keith McCloghrie's column "The SNMP Framework" in

The Simple Times ([7, 8, 9]). RFC 1901 is classified as experimental, with the understanding that a new administrative framework and message wrapper need to be defined in order to realize the security and other features that will work with the current SNMPv2 PDUs.

2.1.6. SNMP VERSION 2: TAKE 4

While the current draft version of community-based SNMPv2 seeks to gain implementation momentum, much more consensus for security and the administration framework will be needed to move SNMPv2 along the standards track to a full standard.

Two major SNMPv2 efforts are ongoing. The original four authors of SNMPv2—the "Gang of Four"—has become two "Gang of Two's"—with additional posse members. Marshall Rose and Keith McCloghrie are now backing the User-based security model (USEC), and Jeffrey Case and Steven Waldbusser are espousing the SNMPv2* (or V2 star) proposal. The May 1996 issue of *Connexions* contains a detailed article on each these proposals.[10, 11]

2.1.6.1. *USEC*

USEC was presented as experimental RFCs in February 1996. RFC 1909, *An Administrative Infrastructure for SNMPv2*, and RFC 1910, *User-based Security Model for SNMPv2*, detail the administrative framework that would need to be added to include this flavor of security and other associated features into the next release of SNMP.

At this writing, the URL for the USEC home page is `http://www.sim-ple-times.org/pub/simple-times/usec`. This Web site contains an update status on the USEC effort, pointers to reference implementations in several languages, a FAQ section, and a short history on the project with comparisons to the competing proposal.

2.1.6.2. *SNMPv2 "Star"*

SNMPv2 "star" (or SNMPv2*) is another proposal for adding security and a new administrative framework. As of this writing the SNMPv2* proposals are only available in the draft format, but may be released as experimental RFCs.

The SNMPv2* home page is at `http://www.int.snmp.com/v2star.html`. At this Web site you find a project definition, current status, an open issues list, information on joining the mailing list, and other references to meetings and the project archive.

The second half of 1996 saw the initial deployment of community-based SNMPv2 agents and NMSs. Work continues in the security and administrative framework with usec and SNMPv2* debate/compromise and implementation experience. Consensus and "rough code" will hopefully drive the direction towards a full standard that will include these highly desirable features.

After bringing you up-to-date on SNMP's eight-year history—but before delving deeper into its details—a brief discussion of the Internet Standards Process would be helpful. In order to understand SNMP, you need to understand the standards track it evolves from, the Internet Architecture Board, and more information on exactly what RFCs are.

2.2. THE INTERNET STANDARDS PROCESS

SNMP in an Internet standard and, as such, its evolution is guided by the Internet Architecture Board (IAB).

2.2.1. INTERNET ARCHITECTURE BOARD

The Internet Architecture Board—renamed from the Internet Activities Board in 1992—is the controlling group over the development and general architecture of the Internet protocols, including SNMP. The IAB administers two subordinate groups, termed task forces, that vary on the timetable and the focus of their efforts. These two task forces are the Internet Research Task Force (IRTF) and the Internet Engineering Task Force (IETF). They are headed by the Internet Research Steering Group (IRSG) and the Internet Engineering Research Group (IERG), respectively. This relationship appears in Figure 2-4. The IRTF focuses on long-term research developments, whereas the IETF focuses on relatively short-term engineering projects.

The IETF is comprised of a large number of network operators, vendors, designers, and researchers who are interested in such things as Internet networking protocols and communication standards. It is an open organization and any interested individual can join. The IETF home page is `http://www.ietf.org`.

In order to work more efficiently, the IETF comprises a large number of Working Groups (WG) that are organized into different areas. Each has a very specific charter and generally meets three times a year. The IESG consists of the head of each area, called an Area Director, and the chairperson of the IETF. The Working Groups are dynamic and are comprised of technical contributors working towards developing specifications. These Working Groups are disbanded when their work is completed; the output is usually in the form of an RFC.

The Network Management Directorate currently has eight members and its IETF NM Area Director:

> Deirdre C. Kostick, NM Area Director
>
> Fred Baker
> Ted Brunner
> Jeff Case
> Keith McCloghrie
> Marshall Rose
> Bob Stewart
> Kaj Tesink
> Steve Waldbusser

The original SNMP Working Group was disbanded in November 1991. The SNMPv2 Working Group that produced the draft proposals of RFCs 1902-1908 was disbanded in the spring of 1995. Aside from the main SNMP standards work, many new groups are being formed and are working on a variety of related SNMP issues. For instance, Working Groups for each new MIB group are being developed.

A synopsis of network management Working Groups current for this writing appears in Figure 2-5.[12] Each Working Group has its own agenda and time table, and consequently new groups are continually being formed, as other groups are disbanded when their work is completed. A primary discussion vehicle for each Working Group is its mailing list. Anyone interested in the progress of the WG, obtaining an archive of its proceedings, "lurking" on current conversations and threads, or contributing ideas and comments can subscribe.

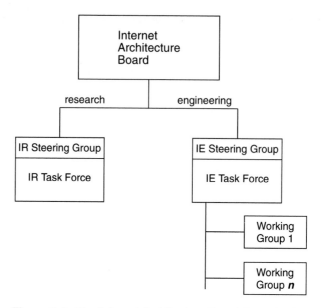

Figure 2-4. The Internet Architecture Board Organization

Working Groups Relating to SNMP and Network Management	
Working Group Name	**Mailing List Subscription Address**
100VG-AnyLAN MIB WG	`vgmib-request@hprnd.rose.hp.com`
Application MIB WG	`applmib-request@emi-summit.com`
AToM MIB WG	`atommib-request@thumper.bellcore.com`
BGP WG	`iwg-request@ans.net`
Bridge MIB WG	`bridge-mib-request@pa.dec.com`
Character MIB WG	`char-mib-request@decwrl.dec.com`
Data Link Switching MIB WG	`aiw-dlsw-mib@networking.raleigh.ibm.com`
DECnet Phase IV MIB WG	`phiv-mib-request@jove.pa.dec.com`
Distributed Management WG	`disman-request@nexen.com`
Entity MIB WG	`entmib-request@cisco.com`
FDDI MIB WG	`fddi-mib-request@cs.utk.edu`

Figure 2-5. Current IETF SNMP Working Groups

Working Group Name	Mailing List Subscription Address
Frame Relay Service MIB WG	`frftc-request@nsco.network.com`
Host Resources MIB WG	`hostmib-request@andrew.cmu.edu`
IEEE 802.3 Hub MIB WG	`hubmib-request@hprnd.rose.hp.com`
IDR WG	`bgp@ans.edu`
Interfaces MIB WG	`if-mib-request@dtl.labs.tek.com`
IP over AppleTalk WG	`apple-ip-request@cayman.com`
IPLPDN WG	`iplpdn-request@nri.reston.va.us`
IPv6 MIB WG	`ip6mib-request@research.ftp.com`
ISDN MIB WG	`isdn-mib-request@combinet.com`
IS-IS for IP Internets WG	`isis-request@merit.edu`
Mail and Directory Management WG	`ietf-madman-request@innosoft.com`
Modem Management WG	`modemmgt-request@telebit.com`
NOCtools WG	`noctools-request@merit.edu`
OSPF IGP WG	`ospf-request@gated.cornell.edu`
PPP Extensions WG	`ietf-ppp-request@merit.edu`
RIP WG	`ietf-rip-request@xylogics.com`
Remote Network Monitoring WG	`rmonmib-request@cisco.com`
Routing over Large Clouds WG	`rolc-request@nexen.com`
SNA DLC Services MIB WG	`snadlcmib-request@cisco.com`
SNA NAU Servces MIB WG	`snanaumib-request@cisco.com`
SNMP Agent Extensibility WG	`agentx-request@fv.com`
SNMPv2 WG	`snmpv2-request@tis.com`
TCP Client Identity Protocol WG	`ident-request@nri.reston.va.us`
DS1/DS3 MIB WG	`trunk-mib-request@cisco.com`
Uninterruptible Power Supply WG	`ups-mib-request@cs.utk.edu`
X.25 MIB WG	`x25mib-request@dg-rtp.dg.com`

Figure 2-5. Current IETF SNMP Working Groups *(continued)*

2.2.2. REQUEST FOR COMMENTS

A prime vehicle for disseminating information about the Internet and its standards is the Request for Comments (RFC) format.

The SNMP specifications in their various stages have been published as RFCs. In addition to formal specifications and standards such as SNMP and the protocols of the TCP/IP suite, many interesting documents are available: proposals, experiments, meeting notices, poems, biographies, glossaries, tutorials, lists of important numbers, and many miscellaneous documents containing additional technical information. The collection of RFCs is a wellspring of information, entertainment, and enlightenment.

It provides a powerful forum for refining standards and keeps them "open" by having them available for comment and criticism to a wide and diverse audience.

The RFCs are each assigned a unique incrementing number by the RFC office. "For over 20 years, Jon Postel, associate director of networking at Information Sciences Institute of the University of Southern California, has held his post of RFC editor. Postel and colleague Joyce Reynolds run the RFC office that handles the editing and distribution of new RFCs and guides the content of the informational documents."[13] The first RFC, RFC 1, was published in April 1969 by S. D. Crocker and was entitled *Host Software*. Now in 1997, the RFC numbering is over 2000.

The RFCs can be obtained through a variety of means from different sources. They are stored on-line and may be obtained at no charge over the Internet using electronic mail, anonymous FTP, or a Web browser. They are also available as hard copy for a small fee from SRI or in various other formats, such as CD. Figure 2-6 contains the latest mailing and Internet addresses and the current telephone and fax numbers that you can use for more information:

SRI INTERNATIONAL
Network Information Systems Center
333 Ravenswood Avenue
Room EJ291
Menlo Park, California 94025

Telephone: (415) 859-6387
            (415) 859-3695
Fax: (415) 859-6028

Internet Address   nisc@nisc.sri.com

Figure 2-6. RFC Information

Several sites worldwide allow anonymous FTP of RFCs. The first document to consult and retrieve is the RFC index (`rfc-index.txt`). Figure 2-7 contains four major sites that contain an up-to-date RFC repository.

Location	Name	IP Address
US East Coast	`ds.internic.net`	198.49.45.10
US West Coast	`venera.isi.edu`	128.9.0.32
Pacific Rim	`munnari.oz.au`	128.250.1.21
Europe	`nic.nordu.net`	192.36.148.17

Figure 2-7. RFC FTP Sites

In addition to RFCs a collection of Internet-draft documents represent working papers that are presented for discussion and input to RFCs. These documents should not be referenced, because they have no official status and can be deleted at any time. They typically carry a six-month expiration date. The Internet drafts are also available at the same site as the RFCs.

RFC 1310, *The Internet Standards Process*, describes the process of how specifications are proposed and progress to becoming standards. This evolution is depicted in Figure 2-8.[14]

A specification enters the standards track and can initially assume the status of proposed, experimental, or informational. The experimental and informational specifications either are not intended or do not fill the requirements to become full standards.

A proposed standard must be stable, meet with good reception, and be generally considered to be of value. After at least six months elapse (and two or more implementations are fielded), the proposed standard may be considered for draft status. The minimum time requirement from being elevated to a full standard is then reduced to four months. Many solid implementations should be operating to prove the specification's worthiness. After a time, the specification may be replaced by a newer version; in that case the former specification receives a historical status.

In addition to the standards status, an additional qualifier exists called the protocol status. This appears in Figure 2-9.

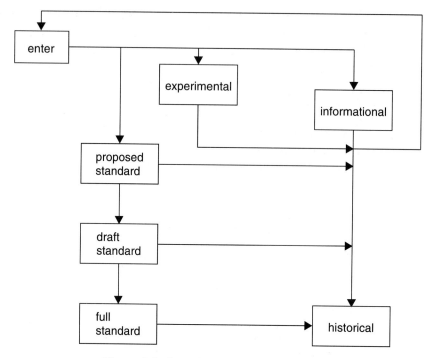

Figure 2-8. Specifications Standards Track

Internet Standards Protocol Status	
required	the protocol **must** be implemented on a system
recommended	the protocol **should** be implemented on a system
elective	the protocol **may** be implemented on a system
limited use	the protocol **may** be implemented under special circumstances
not recommended	the protocol **should not** be implemented on a system

Figure 2-9. Internet Standards Protocol Status

The three major standards that comprise SNMP Version 1—the SMI, the MIB, and the protocol—are all Full Standards with recommended protocol status. SNMP Version 2 is currently in the Draft Standard status with recommended protocol status.

Figure 2-10 shows a snapshot of the standards status of various SNMP MIB Modules and related standards.[15]

Full Standards
RFC 1643: Ether-Like Interface Type (SNMPv1)
Draft Standards
RFC 1493: Bridge MIB
RFC 1516: IEEE 802.3 Repeater MIB
RFC 1559: DECnet Phase IV MIB
RFC 1657: BGP Version 4 MIB
RFC 1658: Character Device MIB
RFC 1659: RS-232 Interface Type MIB
RFC 1660: Parallel Printer Interface Type MIB
RFC 1694: SMDS Interface Protocol (SIP) Interface Type MIB
RFC 1724: RIP Version 2 MIB
RFC 1742: AppleTalk MIB
RFC 1748: IEEE 802.5 Token Ring Interface Type MIB
RFC 1757: Remote Network Monitoring MIB
RFC 1850: OSPF Version 2 MIB
Proposed Standards
RFC 1285: FDDI Interface Type (SMT 6.2) MIB
RFC 1315: Frame Relay DTE Interface Type MIB
RFC 1381: X.25 LAPB MIB
RFC 1382: X.25 PLP MIB
RFC 1406: DS1/E1 Interface Type MIB
RFC 1407: DS3/E3 Interface Type MIB
RFC 1414: Identification MIB
RFC 1461: Multiprotocol Interconnect Over X.25 MIB
RFC 1471: PPP Link Control Protocol (LCP) MIB
RFC 1472: PPP Security Protocols MIB
RFC 1473: PPP IP Network Control Protocol MIB
RFC 1474: PPP Bridge Network Control Protocol MIB
RFC 1512: FDDI Interface Type (SMT 7.3) MIB
RFC 1513: Token Ring Extensions to RMON MIB
RFC 1514: Host Resources MIB
RFC 1515: IEEE 802.3 Medium Attachment Unit (MAU) MIB
RFC 1525: Source Routing Bridge MIB
RFC 1565: Network Services Monitoring MIB

Figure 2-10. SNMP MIB Modules Standards Summary

RFC 1566: Mail Monitoring MIB
RFC 1567: X.500 Directory Monitoring MIB
RFC 1595: SONET/SDH Interface Type MIB
RFC 1604: Frame Relay Service MIB
RFC 1611: DNS Server MIB
RFC 1612: DNS Resolver MIB
RFC 1628: Uninterruptible Power Supply MIB
RFC 1650: Ether-Like Interface Type (SNMPv2)
RFC 1666: SNA NAU MIB
RFC 1695: ATM MIB
RFC 1696: Modem MIB
RFC 1697: Relational Database Management System MIB
RFC 1747: SNA DLC MIB
RFC 1749: 802.5 Station Source Routing MIB
RFC 1759: Printer MIB
Experimental
RFC 1187: Bulk Table Retrieval with the SNMP
RFC 1224: Techniques for Managing Asynchronously Generated Alerts
RFC 1238: CLNS MIB
RFC 1592: SNMP Distributed Program Interface (SNMP-DPI)
RFC 1792: TCP/IPX Connection MIB Specification
Informational
RFC 1215: A Convention for Defining Traps for Use with the SNMP
RFC 1270: SNMP Communication Services
RFC 1303: A Convention for Describing SNMP-based agents
RFC 1321: MD5 Message-Digest Algorithm
RFC 1470: A Network Management Tool Catalog
RFC 1503: Automating Administration in SNMPv2 Managers
Historical
RFC 1156: Management Information Base (MIB-I)
RFC 1161: SNMP Over OSI
RFC 1227: SNMP MUX Protocol and MIB
RFC 1228: SNMP Distributed Program Interface (SNMP-DPI)
RFC 1229: Extensions to the Generic-Interface MIB
RFC 1230: IEEE 802.4 Token Bus Interface Type MIB
RFC 1231: IEEE 802.5 Token Ring Interface Type MIB

Figure 2-10. SNMP MIB Modules Standards Summary *(continued)*

RFC 1232: DS1 Interface Type MIB
RFC 1233: DS3 Interface Type MIB
RFC 1239: Reassignment of Experimental MIBs to Standard MIBs
RFC 1243: AppleTalk MIB
RFC 1252: OSPF Version 2 MIB
RFC 1253: OSPF Version 2 MIB
RFC 1269: BGP Version 3 MIB
RFC 1271: Remote LAN Monitoring MIB
RFC 1283: SNMP Over OSI
RFC 1284: Ether-Like Interface Type MIB
RFC 1286: Bridge MIB
RFC 1289: DECnet Phase IV MIB
RFC 1298: SNMP Over IPX
RFC 1304: SMDS Interface Protocol (SIP) Interface Type MIB
RFC 1316: Character Device MIB
RFC 1317: RS-232 Interface Type MIB
RFC 1318: Parallel Printer Interface Type MIB
RFC 1351: SNMP Administrative Model
RFC 1352: SNMP Security Protocols
RFC 1353: SNMP Party MIB
RFC 1368: IEEE 802.3 Repeater MIB
RFC 1389: RIPv2 MIB
RFC 1398: Ether-Like Interface Type MIB
RFC 1441: Introduction to SNMPv2
RFC 1442: SMI for SNMPv2
RFC 1443: Textual Conventions for SNMPv2
RFC 1445: Administrative Model for SNMPv2
RFC 1446: Security Protocols for SNMPv2
RFC 1447: Party MIB for SNMPv2
RFC 1448: Protocol Operations for SNMPv2
RFC 1449: Transport Mappings for SNMPv2
RFC 1450: MIB for SNMPv2
RFC 1451: Manager-to-Manager MIB
RFC 1452: Coexistence between SNMPv1 and SNMPv2
RFC 1596: Frame Relay Service MIB
RFC 1623: Ether-Like Interface Type MIB
RFC 1665: SNA NAU MIB

Figure 2-10. SNMP MIB Modules Standards Summary *(continued)*

2.3. THE THREE MAJOR SNMP COMPONENTS

Now that the background of SNMP's evolution and the environment in which it develops have been explained, look more closely at the three major components that make up SNMP—the SMI, MIB, and protocol for Version 1. Specific modifications for Version 2 are discussed in their appropriate chapter: SMIv2 in Chapter 4, the protocol in Chapter 6, and the MIB in Chapter 8. Generally, since the Version 2 changes are enhancements that build on the first version, learning Version 1 first is important. If you are not running Version 2 yet, this is all you need to know for now!

2.3.1. STRUCTURE OF MANAGEMENT INFORMATION

The Structure of Management Information lays the foundation for how the objects in the MIB are defined and encoded for transfer over the protocol. It was first defined in August 1988, and later reached Full Standard status with RFC 1155. Enhancements to how the objects are defined through a more concise macro format and a formalization of the trap mechanism format were introduced in 1991 with RFC 1212 and RFC 1215, respectively (note that RFC 1215 has informational status and is not, therefore, an official part of the SMI). Figure 2-11 shows an overview of the development of the SMI.

The Structure of Management Information		
History	**Date**	**RFC Number**
SMI is first defined	August 1988	1065
SMI is modified	May 1990	1155
Concise MIB format defined	March 1991	1212
Trap Definitions	March 1991	1215

Figure 2-11. SMI Summary

The SMI is the description of the common structures and generic types, along with the identification scheme, that are to be used in the implementation. The SMI is often likened to the schema of a database. Just as a schema describes the format and the layout of the objects in the database, the SMI describes the objects in the MIB. The key tenet of the SMI is that the formal definitions of the managed objects will be described using Abstract Syntax Notation One (ASN.1).

The collection of managed objects, which are explicitly defined for each implementation as its particular MIB, are called object types in the formal parlance of the SMI.

These object types have three basic attributes that describe them and allow them to be properly used in the SNMP implementation. These three attributes can be viewed as facets of the object type that are necessary in the various phases of the implementation. The three definable aspects of an SNMP object type are:

- its name
- its syntax
- its encoding

2.3.1.1. Object Type Name

The Object Type Name is a unique representation used as a means for identifying an object. It is also known as the object identifier. It is represented as a sequence of integers that traverse a global tree that contains all of the known objects in SNMP.

All of these known objects are defined in a hierarchy. The point of this hierarchy is to allocate the authority to assign names to many different interested organizations. Therefore, although any number of these groups may be assigning SNMP object names, this numbering scheme convention assures that all of the names created are unique and absolute because everyone knows the global scheme while being allocated its own individual branch.

Each level of the SNMP naming hierarchy is assigned a label. A period is used to separate each sub-level. Any name in the hierarchy is represented as a sequence of labels separated by periods. The label of the higher level always appears on the left; that is, as the name is decoded from left to right, we are traversing down the naming tree.

Names for objects in tables are even longer than names for simple variables because they contain additional labels that encode such information as the index of the table entry and the field desired in that entry.

Because all of these object identifiers are represented numerically, this organization lends itself naturally to lexicographic ordering. This is a very desirable feature in that it allows the NMS both to request all of the objects for any particular agent and to search a table without knowing its size beforehand.

2.3.1.2. Object Type Syntax

The syntax is the formal definition of an object type's structure using the ASN.1 notation. This syntax defines the abstract data structure corresponding to that particular object. Four standard attributes must be defined for each object in order to have properly declared objects for the MIB.

These four attributes are:

◆ syntax type

◆ access mode

◆ status

◆ name value

The syntax type is one of a set of predefined ASN.1 `ObjectSyntax` choices. Twelve choices are currently defined and these choices can be subdivided into three basic groups: `simple`, `application-wide`, and `simply-constructed`. The `simple` category consists of `INTEGER`, `OCTET STRING`, `OBJECT IDENTIFIER`, and `NULL`. The `Application-wide` group is comprised of `IpAddress`, `NetworkAddress`, `Counter`, `Gauge`, `TimeTicks`, and `Opaque`. The `simply-constructed` set contains `list` and `table`.

The access mode is a permissions level that the agent examines per request for each object. Four access values are currently defined: read-only, read-write, write-only, and not-accessible. Read-only objects can be read but not written, Read-write objects can be both read and written, write-only objects cannot be read but may be written, and not-accessible objects may be neither read nor written.

The status defines the managed node's responsibility for implementing this particular object. Three currently defined statuses are available: mandatory, optional, and obsolete. Mandatory objects must be implemented, optional objects may be implemented, and obsolete objects need no longer be implemented.

The name value is a short textual name, termed the object descriptor, that is equal to its corresponding object identifier.

2.3.1.3. *Object Type Encoding*

Once the instances of the object types have been defined and declared, their value may be transmitted to and from the agent and NMS by applying the specified encoding rules of ASN.1 to the syntax for the object type. The transfer syntax notation used in SNMP is the Basic Encoding Rules (BER).

2.3.2. MANAGEMENT INFORMATION BASE

The MIB defines the collection of objects that can be accessed through the network management protocol. The first group of RFCs defining the MIB was referred to as MIB-I. Subsequent additions led to the current superset of standard MIB objects. This new set, called MIB-II, is a Full Standard as defined in RFC 1213. An overview of the MIB developments appears in Figure 2-12.

The Management Information Base		
History	**Date**	**RFC Number**
MIB-I first defined	August 1988	1066
MIB-I modified	May 1990	1156
MIB-II introduced	May 1990	1158
MIB-II modified	March 1991	1213

Figure 2-12. MIB Summary

Whereas the SMI provides the general framework for the definition of the managed objects, the Management Information Base declares the particular instances for each object and then binds a value to each. The MIB is frequently referred to as a virtual database of managed objects.

MIB-I was originally designed for a minimal SNMP implementation. Most of these object definitions dealt with configuration or fault management, especially for routers and gateways. MIB-I contained 114 objects divided into eight groups.

The subsequent modification to MIB-I, named MIB-II, broadened SNMP's management scope by adding 57 new objects and two new groups. It is upwardly compatible and basically reflects new requirements for the complexity of the managed nodes, that is, multi-protocol devices, objects dealing with new media types, objects dealing with the SNMP itself, and so forth.

2.3.3. SNMP PROTOCOL

SNMP is the definition of the application protocol for the network management service. It was first defined in August 1988, and later reached Full Standard status with RFC 1157. Figure 2-13 lists the major milestones in the protocol's development.

The SNMP Protocol		
History	Date	RFC Number
SNMP first defined	August 1988	1067
SNMP modified	April 1989	1098
SNMP modified	May 1990	1157

Figure 2-13. SNMP Protocol Summary

SNMP is an asynchronous request and response protocol between an NMS and the agent. The NMS is capable of sending three different messages containing the Protocol Data Units (PDUs). These three PDUs are the GetRequest-PDU, the GetNextRequest-PDU, and the SetRequest-PDU. The agent is capable of sending two different messages: a response acknowledgment with the GetResponse-PDU to a proper request from an NMS, and also a message with a Trap-PDU, which is an unsolicited event sent when the agent has discovered a predefined extraordinary event.

With the SNMP protocol, monitoring a network device's state is accomplished primarily by polling for appropriate values of meaningful agent MIB variables. The agent can send a limited number of traps to guide the NMS's focus and timing of that polling. The scheme favored for SNMP implementations is called trap-directed polling.

The SNMP communicates its management information through the exchange of SNMP protocol messages. Each message is completely and independently represented within a single datagram as presented to the UDP transport service. Each of these messages contains a version identifier, the SNMP community name, and the PDU.

The version identifier is a constant used for version control that the NMS and agents must know. Under SNMP, no version arbitration is available. If the NMS or agent receives an SNMP message containing an invalid or unsupported version number, the message is discarded. Under Version 1, the version field always carries the value of 0; for SNMPv2, it must be a 1.

The SNMP community name is a string that identifies a particular group of NMSs and agents. Members of a community enforce authentication by using a crude password scheme. This simple use of a non-encrypted, plain-text community name by communicating NMSs and its agents is called the Trivial Authentication Scheme. For SNMP Version 1 it is the only SNMP security measure in place. The community name is represented as a string of octets. The community name "public" is often used as a default configuration setting.

As an additional reference, Appendix A presents the key dates and events in the development of SNMP.

2.4. THE SNMP REFERENCE MODEL

The SNMP Reference Model, as diagrammed in Figure 2-14, shows the generalized, overall structure of the SNMP network management framework. This includes the individual components of the system and the relationship among them.

The SNMP Reference Model consists of four major components:

◆ The internetwork

◆ The network protocols

◆ The Network Manager

◆ The Managed Network Entity

2.4.1. THE INTERNETWORK

In the SNMP Reference Model, an internetwork is a collection of one or more networks that use a common protocol and are connected by gateways. Any two end-points can communicate with each other if the proper global addressing

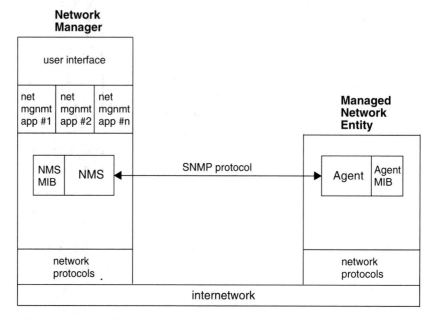

Figure 2-14. The SNMP Reference Model

scheme is implemented, if standardized protocols are used, and if a routing scheme is in place for the proper delivery of messages in a timely and reliable way.

When using SNMP, the Network Protocols of interest are primarily the TCP/IP protocol suite for use on the internetwork.

2.4.2. THE NETWORK PROTOCOLS

The Network Protocols are the rules that allow internetwork communication to be feasible. For internetwork communication using TCP/IP, various protocols operate at each of the well-defined four layers that comprise the TCP/IP protocol suite. A host, for example, will have implemented at least one protocol from each layer. The Network Protocols are often referred to as the "protocol stack."

2.4.2.1. *The Lower Layer*

The Lower Layer of the protocol stack is the layer "closest" to the hardware. In the TCP/IP protocol suite, this layer is called the Network Access Layer. Its chief function is to provide reliable host-to-network data exchange. A wide variety of network access protocols exist, each one corresponding to the many types of different networks that can be connected on the internetwork.

2.4.2.2. The Internet Layer

The Internetwork Layer is responsible for carrying data from a source host to a destination host. The Internet Layer's prime component is the Internet Protocol (IP). IP is a connectionless, datagram protocol that does not guarantee end-to-end delivery. IP's features include the ability to specify the type of service, internet layer addressing, fragmentation and reassembly, checksumming, and rudimentary security. Another important protocol included in the Internet Layer is the Internetwork Control Message Protocol (ICMP), which is used for error and congestion reporting.

2.4.2.2.1. The Internet Protocol

IP was specified and implemented approximately a decade ago to provide a connectionless network layer protocol for internetworking. The RFC for IP Version 4 is RFC 791. The responsibility for end-to-end reliable message transfers is the responsibility of the higher Transport Layer. Note that if the Transport facility above IP is unreliable (such as UDP), the responsibility for accurate data transfer is up to the Application Layer.

The messages that are transferred between the Transport Layer and the IP are called datagrams and are limited to 64 Kbytes. These datagrams are exchanged with the Interface Layer to be sent and received on the internet. If intermediate devices cannot handle large datagrams, these datagrams are broken up into fragments for reassembly at their final destination.

An IP datagram consists of two major parts: The IP Header and the IP Data Area. The Header consists of a 20-byte fixed portion and an optional header portion. Note that the length of the header is stored in the fixed portion. Figure 2-15 shows the layout of the IP datagram.

The header consists of 14 fields of various bit lengths. Figure 2-16 gives a brief description of each of these fields.

2.4.2.2.2. IP Addressing Formats

One requirement for the successful operation of IP is that every network device must have a unique IP address.

Version	length	type of service	total length
identification		fragment flags	fragment offset
time to live		protocol	checksum
source address			
destination address			
options (variable)			padding (variable)

Figure 2-15. The IP Header Format

Field	Size (in bits)	Meaning
Version	4	identifies IP version
IP Header Length (IHL)	4	header length in 32-bit words. Minimum value is *5*, i.e., 20 octets.
Type of Service (TOS)	8	used to specify reliability, precedence, delay, and throughput
Total Length	16	total length of datagram including the header in octets
Identification	16	datagram originator ID used with addresses and protocol number to uniquely identify each datagram
Fragment Flags	3	bit-flags used for fragmentation operation
Fragment Offset	13	indicates fragment's position in the datagram for reassembly; measured in 64-bit units.
Time to Live (TTL)	8	lifetime counter measured in one-second increments. When it reaches *0,* datagram is discarded.

Figure 2-16. The IP Header Fields

Field	Size (in bits)	Meaning
Protocol	8	transport protocol number
Header Checksum	16	checksum calculated when IP is sent and then recalculated when received with same algorithm; if the checksums are not equal, the datagram is discarded.
Source Address	32	sender's IP address
Destination Address	32	destination IP address
Options	(variable)	various IP options can be specified here. Option 0: if options do not stop at header Option 1: no operation Option 2: security and handling Option 3: loose source routing Option 4: internet timestamp Option 7: record route Option 8: stream identifier Option 9: strict source routing
Padding	(variable)	added to make IP header end on a 32-byte boundary. Zeros are used.

Figure 2-16. The IP Header Fields *(continued)*

A discussion of the IP Header format must include the five formats that the IP source and destination addresses can assume from this 32-bit field. Figure 2-17 shows the bit positions for the five possible formats of Internet Addresses.

Class A	0	netid (7 bits)			hostid (24 bits)	
Class B	1	0	netid (14 bits)		hostid (16 bits)	
Class C	1	1	0	netid (21 bits)	hostid (8 bits)	
Class D	1	1	1	0	multicast address (28 bits)	
Class E	1	1	1	1	0	reserved for future (27 bits)

Figure 2-17. The IP Address Formats

The five formats are comprised of three major portions. The leading significant bits determine the class of the address. One field contains the network identification, the netid, and also a field for the id of the host, the hostid. The IP address is usually written as four decimal numbers separated by decimal points. This is called dotted decimal notation. Each decimal number represents eight bits of the address.

The Class A format is used when you have a large number of host computers and a small number of networks. Class A addresses use seven bits for the netid and 24 bits for the hostid. This setup allows for 16,777,214 host network devices and only 128 networks. The dotted decimal notation range is from 00.nnn.nnn.nnn to 127.nnn.nnn.nnn.

The Class B format strikes a compromise between the number of hosts and the number of networks by allotting 14 bits for the netid and 16 bits for the hostid. This setup allows for 16,384 network addresses and 65,534 host device addresses. The dotted decimal notation range for Class B is from 128.000.nnn.nnn to 191.255.nnn.nnn.

When you have a need for a large number of networks with fewer network devices attached, the Class C addressing format is used. It uses 21 bits for the netid and 8 bits for the hostid. This setup allows for 2,097,152 networks, each with a maximum of 254 attached host devices. The dotted decimal notation range is from 192.000.000.nnn to 223.255.255.nnn.

Class D addresses are reserved for multicasting, a limited broadcasting facility where traffic can be sent to a group of hosts arranged in a multicast group. This setup allows hosts to operate on more than one physical network for sending certain types of traffic. The possible dotted decimal notation range is from 244.000.000.000 to 239.255.255.254, although the Internet does not allow 224.000.000.000 to be used and reserves 224.000.000.001 for the special "all hosts" designation.

Class E is a future format, and as such, is reserved for experimental purposes and should not be used for general internetwork IP communications. The possible dotted decimal notation range for this group is from 244.000.000.000 to 255.255.255.254.

2.4.2.2.3. *Subnet Addresses*

Another important concept is closely allied with the IP address formats: subnetting. Subnetting is a way of dividing networks into logical subnetworks by assigning a special subnet addressing scheme. A 32-bit address called the subnet mask can make the netid/hostid pair into a netid/siteid/hostid triple by stealing some of the bits. Which bits are used is a function of the IP class format used.

2.4.2.2.4. The Domain Name Service

The Domain Name Service (DNS) matches the numeric IP addressess to the more friendly format of human recognizable names. A hierarchy of name servers throughout an internetwork can maintain varying views of a database that correlate an IP address to an IP host name. The IP host names are also represented in a dotted fashion, reflecting their place in an internetwork hierarchy.

2.4.2.2.5. Internet Layer Address Resolution Protocols

Also, two important protocols from the TCP/IP protocol suite handle the name resolution between the physical network access address and the IP address: the Address Resolution Protocol (ARP) and the Reverse Address Resolution Protocol (RARP).

These two protocols are necessary for resolving the different addressing schemes and formats used in each of these two layers. The lowest-level address is typically assigned by the manufacturer, and the IP address is derived from one of the Internet IP Address Classes.

ARP allows a network device to find the network access address, also called the media access address (MAC), of another network device by only knowing the target device's IP address. This process occurs through a low-level broadcasting scheme. RARP allows a network device to find its IP address from a network server that maintains a table that correlates physical MAC and IP addresses. RARP is especially important for disk-less workstations that do not know their IP addresses at power-up.

2.4.2.2.6. The Internet Control Message Protocol

The Internet Control Message Protocol (ICMP) is a required protocol that must be implemented with IP. The RFC for ICMP is RFC 792. It uses the IP services to send various error and status messages. Figure 2-18 presents the key fields in an ICMP message.

Figure 2-19 lists the size and a brief description of each of the ICMP message fields.

type	code	checksum
parameters		
information		

Figure 2-18. The ICMP Message Format

Field	Size (in bits)	Meaning
Type	8	specifies the ICMP message type
Code	8	used when message parameters can be encoded in a few bits
Checksum	16	checksum of entire ICMP message
Parameters	32	used for longer parameter values
Information	(variable)	contains any additional information that goes with the message

Figure 2-19. The ICMP Header Fields

Thirteen ICMP messages exist, each with a unique type value. Figure 2-20 lists the various ICMP messages and their associated type values.

Message	Type Value
echo reply	0
destination unreachable	3
source quench	4
redirect	5
echo request	8
time exceeded	11
parameter unintelligible	12

Figure 2-20. ICMP Message Types

Message	Type Value
timestamp request	13
timestamp reply	14
information request	15
information reply	16
address mask request	17
address mask reply	18

Figure 2-20. ICMP Message Types *(continued)*

The ICMP protocol is most famous for its use in the PING program. PING, the Packet Internet Groper, sends an ICMP message of type echo request and waits for an echo reply to signify that an IP connection exists between the two end-points.

2.4.2.3. *The Transport Layer*

The Transport Layer provides for the end-to-end transfer of data between processes, either reliably by using TCP or unreliably by using UDP.

2.4.2.3.1. *The Transport Control Protocol*

Because the underlying IP is an unreliable service, the Transport level can provide the required reliability features for the network applications by using TCP. TCP offers this measure of reliability by providing various time-out, sequencing, and check-sum features. Its source RFC is RFC 793.

As with the IP, the maximum message in the TCP layer is 64 Kbytes. TCP messages are also called datagrams. TCP handles fragmentation and message sequencing so that in the event datagrams and/or fragments arrive out of order at the destination, TCP will reassemble the fragments and present the datagrams in the correct order to the application.

TCP sequences each data byte by providing private sequence numbers. The use of 32 bits for a sequence number makes the probability that sequence numbers are repeated because of wrapping nearly zero. Duplicate retransmissions are also handled with the use of a three-way handshake.

A TCP datagram also consists of two major parts: the TCP Header and the TCP Data Portion. Just as with IP, the minimum TCP Header consists of a 20 byte fixed portion and an optional header portion. The length of the header is stored in the fixed portion. Figure 2-21 shows the layout of the TCP header.

source port								destination port
sequence number								
acknowledgment number								
length	(res.)	u r g	a c k	p s h	r s t	s y n	f i n	window
checksum								urgent pointer
options (variable)								padding (variable)

Figure 2-21. The TCP Header Format

The header, shown in Figure 2-22, consists of 17 fields of various bit lengths.

Field	Size (in bits)	Meaning
Source Port	16	identifies sender's source port
Destination Port	16	identifies destination port
Sequence Number	32	assigned sequence number for each datagram used for reassembly of larger message
Acknowledgment #	32	acknowledgment number for received datagrams
TCP Header Length	4	header length in 32-bit words
(Reserved)	6	reserved for future use
URG	1	urgent pointer flag
ACK	1	acknowledgment flag
PSH	1	push function flag
RST	1	connection reset flag

Figure 2-22. The TCP Header Fields

Field	Size (in bits)	Meaning
SYN	1	sequence number synchronization flag
FIN	1	end of data flag
Window	16	flow control parameter. Octet number count that a sender is able to accept.
Checksum	16	checksum calculated when datagram is sent, and then recalculated when received with same algorithm; if the checksums are not equal, the datagram is discarded.
Urgent Pointer	16	points to data following urgent data, thereby indicating length of urgent data
Options	(variable)	options, such as maximum acceptable segment size
Padding	(variable)	added to make IP header end on a 32-byte boundary. Zeros are used.

Figure 2-22. The TCP Header Fields *(continued)*

TCP's service interface provides functions for setting up and shutting down connections, transmitting and receiving data, and inquiring on the status of the connection.

2.4.2.3.2. *The User Datagram Protocol*

The User Datagram Protocol (UDP) is a simple transport service that allows applications to use the IP network services. Its source RFC is RFC 768. It is a datagram-oriented protocol. The service that it provides is connectionless and is, therefore, unreliable in the sense that the higher-level application protocol is responsible for making sure that the messages are delivered properly. It does not provide transport-level acknowledgment or the capability of detecting and retransmitting lost datagrams. An application must use such mechanisms as timeouts to determine whether retransmissions are necessary. UDP is also incomplete in its lack of flow control, congestion control, or datagram sequencing.

UDP does add two transport services:

◆ the capability for distinguishing multiple destinations, called ports, from multiple sources

◆ the support for an additional and optional checksum facility

The UDP header has four components: the source port, the destination port, the length of the datagram's data, and the transport level checksum. Figure 2-23 depicts this layout. Each of these four components is two octets in length.

source port	destination port
datagram length	datagram checksum

Figure 2-23. The UDP Header Format

Figure 2-24 lists the size and meaning of each of the header fields.

Field	Size (in bits)	Meaning
Source Port	16	indicates the port number of sending process. Optional; if not used should be 0.
Destination Port	16	indicates the port number the receiving process is waiting on
Datagram Length	16	contains datagram length in octets. This length includes length of the header. Therefore, minimum value is 8.
Datagram checksum	16	16-bit one's complement of the pseudo-header from the IP header, the UDP header, and the data padded with 0 octets at the end if necessary to make a multiple of 2 octets.

Figure 2-24. The UDP Header Fields

2.4.2.4. *The Upper Layer*

The Upper Layer of the Network Protocols of the TCP/IP protocol stack is the Process or Application Layer. This layer provides services directly to an end-user or application. Common examples are Telnet, FTP, SMTP, and SNMP, of course!

2.4.3. THE NETWORK MANAGER

The SNMP Reference Model shows the Network Manager as a network device that uses the network protocols and the SNMP protocol to communicate over the internetwork with the Managed Network Entity. The Network Manager consists of four major components:

◆ The Network Management Station

◆ The NMS MIB and Database

◆ The Network Management Applications

◆ The Network Management User Interface

2.4.3.1. The Network Management Station (NMS)

The NMS is the processing entity that monitors and controls the agents that it is responsible for on the internetwork. The NMS and its agents make up a community. The NMS can read and write certain MIB objects in each agent to manage that network device. It can also store pertinent management information on each of the agents in its own database.

2.4.3.2. The NMS MIB

The Management Information Base of the NMS contains a master list for the MIBs from all of the agents in its community. If an NMS is to control each agent's MIB variables, it must know or be able to discover the variable's presence. Often the NMS maintains its MIB and additional management information in its database.

2.4.3.3. The Network Management Applications

The Network Management Applications are the programs that turn the SNMP data into usable information for the Network Manager user. They are a vast array of programs that poll the agents, format get and set requests, and handle the reception of trap messages. These network management applications are responsible for an increasingly growing number of useful network management functions. [Long-time Internet insider, Dave Crocker] "believes SNMP's genius lies in forcing people to think about the important part of managing a network: the application and what to do with management information."[16]

2.4.3.4. *The Network Manager User Interface*

The end-user's view of the Network Manager device is through the User Interface. Most Network Managers offer a graphical user interface (GUI) to present performance statistics, accounting summaries, fault reports, configuration inventories, forms for creating queries, topology maps, and so forth. Popular GUIs available today are Microsoft Windows, Windows 95, Windows NT, IBM Presentation Manager under OS/2, and the various interfaces available with the X Windows System, such as Motif and Open Look.

2.4.4. THE MANAGED NETWORK ENTITY

The SNMP Reference Model shows the Managed Network Entity as the network device that contains the agent. It also uses the network protocols and the SNMP protocol to communicate over the internetwork with the Network Manager's NMS. The Managed Network Entity consists of two key components:

◆   The Agent
◆   The Agent MIB

2.4.4.1. *The Agent*

The Agent is the processing entity that receives requests from NMSs in its community, processes them if they are valid, and sends the appropriate response. Agents can also be configured to send trap messages to report asynchronous, predefined events. The agent uses instrumentation routines that manipulate the local data structures to retrieve and set the various MIB objects it controls.

2.4.4.2. *The Agent MIB*

The Management Information Base of the agent is its collection of variables of interest. The MIB groups that comprise a particular agent's MIB are dependent on the functionality of the device and which resources it manages.

REFERENCES FOR CHAPTER 2

[1] Bartlett, John. *Bartlett's Familiar Quotations* (15th Edition). Boston: Little, Brown, and Company. 1980.

[2] Esar, Evan. *20,000 Quips and Quotes*. Garden City, NY: Doubleday and Company, Inc. 1968.

[3] Comer, Douglas E., and David L. Stevens. *Design, Implementation, and Internals. Volume II of Internetworking with TCP/IP*. Englewood Cliffs, NJ: Prentice Hall. 1991.

[4] Case, Jeffrey. "Ask Dr. SNMP." *The Simple Times*. May/June 1992: 9.

[5] Schneier, Bruce. *Applied Cryptography* (Second Edition). New York: John Wiley and Sons, 1996.

[6] Jander, Mary. "Coming Soon to a Network Near You." *Data Communications*. November 1992: 68.

[7] McCloghrie, Keith. "The SNMP Framework." *The Simple Times*. Vol. 4, No. 3. July 1996: 15-16.

[8] McCloghrie, Keith. "The SNMP Framework." *The Simple Times*. Vol. 4, No. 2. April 1996: 17-18.

[9] McCloghrie, Keith. "The SNMP Framework." *The Simple Times*. Vol. 4, No. 1. January 1996: 9-10.

[10] Waters, Glenn. "The User-based Security Model for SNMPv2." *Connexions*. May 1996: 12-21.

[11] Partain, David. "An Introduction to SNMPv2*." *Connexions*. May 1996: 22-33.

[12] Rose, Marshall. "Standards." *The Simple Times*. July 1996: 19-23.

[13] Nocastro, Linda. "Request For Comments, RFCs: Request and You Shall Receive." *UNIX Networking: A Supplement to Network Computing*. 1992: 12.

[14] Perkins, David T. "Standards." *The Simple Times*. May/June 1992: 12.

[15] Rose, Marshall. "Standards." *The Simple Times*. July 1996: 19-22.

[16] Borsook, Paulina. "Network Innovators: Jeff Case." *Network World*. December 7, 1992: 79.

CHAPTER 3

The Structure of Management Information for SNMP Version 1

I had an aunt in Yucatan
Who bought a Python from a man
And kept it as a pet.
She died, because she never knew
These simple little rules and few; —
The Snake is living yet.

"The Snake"
—Hilaire Belloc[1]

Perfect simplicity is unconsciously audacious.

—George Meredith[2]

The Structure of Management Information (SMI) is the first of the three key components of the SNMP network management framework. The SMI is the guideline for SNMP. It defines the arrangement, makeup, and identification of the information used for the SNMP framework. It provides the groundwork for describing the objects that are included in the MIB and also for describing the rules on how the protocol exchanges the messages.

The SMI used for SNMP version 1 is derived from the earlier development of a similar concept for the OSI network management scheme. As I discuss in Chapter 2, this SNMP SMI was originally defined in RFC 1065, *Structure and Identification of Management for TCP/IP-based Internet*, and then reissued with an updated status in RFC 1155. The updated MIB format defined in RFC 1212 is also considered part of the SMI standard. The SMI is a Full IAB standards protocol with recommended status per the IAB Official Protocol Standards.

This chapter discusses the SMI for version 1 (SMIv1). Chapter 4 introduces the new developments and modifications proposed for version 2 (SMIv2). For the most part, the SMI for version 2 is a superset of version 1.

One of the primary uses of the SMI is to define the managed objects used by SNMP. The managed objects in SNMP defined by the SMI each possess three attributes: a name, a syntax, and an encoding. Figure 3-1 provides summaries of the attributes.

Managed Object	
NAME	Every managed object has a unique *object identifier* as a name.
SYNTAX	The abstract data structure for each managed object is defined using Abstract Syntax Notation One (ASN.1).
ENCODING	An instance of a managed object is also encoded in ASN.1, and protocol messages sent and received containing the managed object values will be defined with Basic Encoding Rules (BER).

Figure 3-1. Managed Object Attributes

The SMI provides the templates for the managed objects that are defined in the MIB and used with the protocol. It defines the ASN.1 subset that is used, as well as how the BER are employed in transmitting and receiving SNMP messages.

Before delving deeper into the topic of the ASN.1 syntax, you need to fully understand the naming convention of the managed object's name—its Object Identifier. This abstraction is crucial in understanding how objects are named and how they derive their place in the global naming hierarchy.

Every object that is to be managed has a name. Its Object Identifier models a hierarchy where every object can be placed. Room is also allotted for all future objects that need to be added to an almost infinite level of depth. The way the name space is administered, once a name is used another object cannot reuse it. Objects can be created but never destroyed.

This hierarchy is represented as a global tree that begins with an unnamed root node and has nodes appended to it to represent the various objects that are named. Note that an object in these terms can be more than an SNMP managed MIB object name. This global naming scheme also accommodates nodes for organizations, specifications, and other objects of interest. Only when the tree is traversed to a specific sub-tree do you encounter the MIB variable names of SNMP.

The Object Identifier is represented as a string of decimal integers separated by periods. Each successive decimal group represents a deeper nesting level in the global naming hierarchy.

To be more specific, the root node has three child nodes appended to it that represent the organization in charge of administering that particular branch:

- The International Telegraph and Telephone Consultative Committee (CCITT) node
  (Note: the CCITT has now become the International Telecommunications Union-Telecommunications branch (ITU-T))

- The International Standards Organization (ISO) node

- A joint ISO-CCITT Administration node

Each node is assigned a numerical value that usually begins with a zero and has subsequent peer-level objects assigned in incremental values.

Figure 3-2 shows the highest level of the naming tree.

The branch of interest for the SNMP world starts at the iso sub-tree. This sub-tree is, in turn, subdivided into four branches with nodes:

- Standard node

- Registration-Authority node

- Member-Body node

- Identified-Organization node

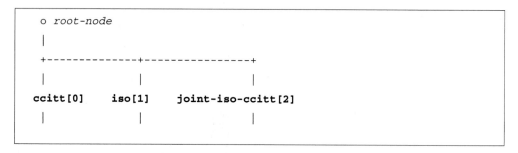

Figure 3-2. Standard Naming Hierarchy

Figure 3-3 shows the sub-branch nodes for the International Standards Organization.

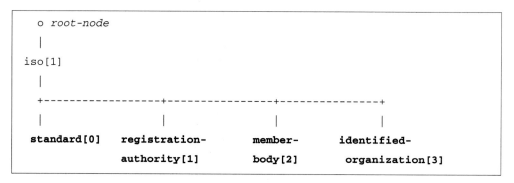

Figure 3-3. ISO Naming Branch

The branch of interest for SNMP from the `iso` sub-tree continues to the `identified-organization` branch. From there, branch 6 (`dod`), belonging to the Department of Defense, has assigned its first node to the Internet Architecture Board for use by the IAB. For those keeping score, the Object Identifier for the IAB node can be represented as:

iso.identified-organization.dod.IAB or { 1 3 6 1 } or 1.3.6.1

The IAB node is further subdivided into four branches with their corresponding nodes:

◆ Directory node

◆ Management node

◆ Experimental node

◆ Private node

Figure 3-4 displays the four branches administered by the IAB.

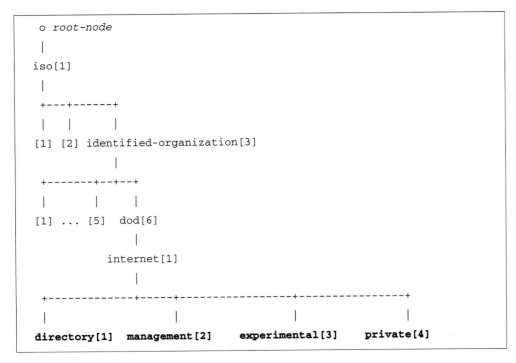

Figure 3-4. IAB Naming Branch

The `directory` branch is currently not used and is reserved for future OSI Directory services to be implemented on the Internet.

The `management` branch contains objects that are defined in the IAB documents, such as the RFCs. Under this branch, the SNMP standard MIB is placed as branch 1. Thus, all standard MIB objects begin with the same Object Identifier prefix: 1.3.6.1.2.1. The Internet Assigned Numbers Authority (IANA) administers the `management` branch and all of its sub-branches.

Objects used on an `experimental` basis for testing and research can be placed in the experimental branch. The IANA also administers the numbering of the Object Identifiers in this branch.

The `private` branch is the repository for objects defined unilaterally, that is, named by one group or organization. The primary use of the private branch is the addition of vendor MIB objects through the `enterprises` sub-branch. Each interested company can request a node number from the IANA where it can append its own objects. These objects are primarily the variables of interest that will be managed by SNMP for their specific products. Each company administers its object from this point in the naming tree. A current list of the `private` branch appears in Chapter 7.

A complete discussion of the SMI must include treatments of its definitional language, its transfer syntax, and a format for defining the managed objects found in the MIB. You can also read the formal SMI definition in this chapter.

3.1. ABSTRACT SYNTAX NOTATION ONE (ASN.1)

Abstract Syntax Notation One (ASN.1) provides a standard way of representing data traveling across the internetwork. This standardization is necessary because the data can be represented in incompatible ways within different network computing devices. ASN.1 is a high-level data-type definition language that describes the format of how SNMP messages can be sent between the agents and the network managers. You will also see how ASN.1 is used in SNMP to define the managed objects themselves.

The complete ASN.1 definition by the International Standards Organization is described in ISO Standard 8824, *Specification of Abstract Syntax Notation One (ASN.1)*.[3] The companion document that describes how the syntax is encoded is ISO Standard 8825, *Specification of Basic Encoding Rules for Abstract Syntax Notation One (ASN.1)*.[4] The ITU-T has also mirrored the ASN.1 and BER specifications in their series X.200 specifications on the OSI model and notation.[5, 6]

Douglas Steedman's reference, *Abstract Syntax Notation One (ASN.1): The Tutorial and Reference*,[7] is a complete discussion of the topic. A thorough presentation of how ASN.1 is used in the OSI environment is presented in Marshall Rose's *The Open Book: A Practical Perspective on OSI*.[8] In terms of the OSI Reference Model, ASN.1 fits into layer six, the Presentation Layer, as it provides for the basic data transformations needed for applications to communicate correctly. Remember, SNMP uses only a necessary subset of ASN.1 so that the implementations would remain "simple."

The ASN.1 concept of a module is used throughout SNMP to organize ASN.1 objects. A module in ASN.1 is a collection of related descriptions. These descriptions can refer to the SMI, the protocol, or to the many groups of MIB objects. Figure 3-5 (from [9]) shows the outline of what constitutes a module:

```
<<module>>   DEFINITIONS   ::=   BEGIN


<<linkage>>


<<declarations>>


END
```

Figure 3-5. ASN.1 Module Syntax

The module name (<<module>>) in SNMP often contains the specific RFC where these descriptions are contained. For example, the SMI version 1 module name is RFC1155-SMI. The linkage statement (<<linkage>>) allows for the importing and exporting of definitions between modules. Because the SMI module defines the guidelines used in SNMP, its linkage statement includes EVERYTHING—and then contains the list of objects that it exports. The declaration statement (<<declarations>>) contains the list of ASN.1 definitions comprising the module.

ASN.1 is both a formal grammar and an abstract notation, meaning that ASN.1 can be used as a notation for defining objects without regard to any specific machine-oriented incompatibilities.

◆ It helps solve such problems as the many basic incompatibilities that may exist between the diverse computing systems that may be connected to the internetwork.

◆ It helps resolve incompatible character data types, such as ASCII versus EBCDIC.

◆ It handles how the bytes are stored in computer memory, such as "big endian," where the most significant byte is stored in the lower address, versus "little endian," where the most significant byte is stored in the higher address.

◆ It deals with which bits are the high order bits and, conversely, which are the low order bits.

◆ It resolves how many octets represent an integer on a particular machine.

◆ It determines how big the integers are that are used to exchange the "integer" value, as well as other common data types.

◆ It standardizes whether structures are aligned on word- or byte-boundaries.

◆ It resolves other incompatibilities that could hinder interoperability.

Three major ASN.1 components are of interest for SNMP:

◆ Type notation for defining the data types of managed objects

◆ Value notation for defining data type values or instances

◆ Transfer syntax for transmitting and receiving the ASN.1 encoded messages

The type notation and value notation deal with ASN.1 syntax definitions and their values. The transfer syntax is a special topic that is defined by the Basic Encoding Rules. BER is an application of the ASN.1 rules.

The type notation used in SNMP is defined by the `ObjectSyntax` data type, which has been defined by ASN.1 as a Choice. A Choice is a union-like data structure definition that can take on one of a number of different data types. For SNMP the `ObjectSyntax` data structure can be one of three data types:

◆ simple

◆ simply-constructed

◆ application-wide

3.1.1. SIMPLE DATA TYPE

The Simple data types are the basic primitive data types that are common and necessary for all implementations. They are often referred to as non-aggregate types. Four simple data types are used in the SNMP subset. Figure 3-6 describes these primitives:

Simple	
Data Type	**Use**
INTEGER	a cardinal number, which is often enumerated for a data type to allow for bounds checking. The SMI RFC notes that if an INTEGER value is enumerated, the value of 0 should not be used.
OCTET STRING	zero or more octets. The value of each octet is between 0 and 255.
OBJECT IDENTIFIER	an object's name, represented as "dotted" decimal numbers, reflecting its place in the internetwork global naming tree.
NULL	a placeholder value. This is currently not used in SNMP.

Figure 3-6. SNMP Simple Data Types

3.1.2. SIMPLY-CONSTRUCTED DATA TYPE

The Simply-Constructed data type represents lists and tables. Lists and tables are two very important constructs used in SNMP. The Simply-Constructed data type is often referred to as an aggregate type. Two Simply-constructed data types are used in the SNMP subset: SEQUENCE and SEQUENCE OF. Figure 3-7 describes these two data types.

Simply-Constructed	
Data Type	**Use**
SEQUENCE	used for lists. This data type is analogous to the "structure," common in most programming languages. A SEQUENCE contains zero or more elements, each of which is another ASN.1 type.
SEQUENCE OF type	used for tables. This type is analogous to the "array," also common in most programming languages. A table can contain zero or more elements of the same ASN.1 type.

Figure 3-7. SNMP Simply-Constructed Data Types

3.1.3. APPLICATION-WIDE DATA TYPE

The Application-Wide data types are defined specially for SNMP. They are implicitly defined because they are derived from one of the simple data types discussed earlier in this chapter in Section 3.1.1. The SMI defines six Application-wide data types used in SNMP. Figure 3-8 lists these six data types.

Application-Wide	
Data Type	**Use**

IpAddress	represents an IP address in network order. Because it is a 32-bit value, it is defined as four octets:
	IpAddress ::=
	    [APPLICATION 0]
	        IMPLICIT OCTET STRING (SIZE (4))

Network Address	can represent different network address types. Because only the internet value is defined, this data type is equivalent to the IpAddress:
	Network Address :: = CHOICE {
	                    internet
	                    Ip Address }

Counter	a counting value that is incremented from zero to 4,294,967,295. When its maximum value is reached it wraps to zero.
	Counter ::=
	    [APPLICATION 1]
	        IMPLICIT INTEGER (0..4294967295)

Gauge	a counting value that can range from zero to 4,294,967,295 (increasing or decreasing). When it reaches the maximum value it *latches,* and remains there until reset.
	Gauge ::=
	    [APPLICATION 2]
	        IMPLICIT INTEGER (0..4294967295)

TimeTicks	a counting value that records time values in hundredths of a second intervals up to 4,294,967,295 units.
	TimeTicks ::=
	    [APPLICATION 3]
	        IMPLICIT INTEGER (0..4294967295)

Opaque	a special data type that can contain an arbitrary ASN.1 syntax encoding by *wrapping* it into an OCTET STRING.
	Opaque ::=
	    [APPLICATION 4]
	        IMPLICIT OCTET STRING

Figure 3-8. SNMP Application-Wide Data Types

3.2. BASIC ENCODING RULES (BER)

ISO Standard 8825, *Specification of Basic Encoding Rules for Abstract Syntax Notation One (ASN.1),*[4] specifies how the syntax is encoded into octets and transferred over the internetwork. The Basic Encoding Rules are an algorithm that takes the ASN.1 values and encodes the bits into the appropriate octet format for transmission over the internetwork. The BER specifies that the most significant bit is BIT 8 and the least significant bit is BIT 1. BIT 8 is the first bit presented to the network. This format is shown in Figure 3-9.

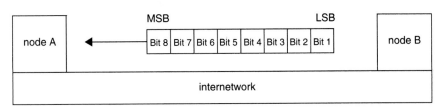

Figure 3-9. Using BER

Also noteworthy is the fact that integers that can be negative or positive are represented using the two's complement notation. For non-negative integer numbers, an unsigned representation can also be used to represent arbitrarily large, positive numbers.

An important part of BER and ASN.1, as they are used in SNMP, is how these various data types are used as a component of a larger data item abstraction. This data item is a triplet comprised of three variable-length parts: the tag, including the data type, the length, and the value. It is commonly referred to as the TLV triplet. (Note that the formal OSI documentation refers to this triplet as the Identifier/Length/Contents octets construct.) The SNMP messages that pass back and forth between the NMS and the agent are a complex nesting of ASN.1 encoded tag-length-value data items. Figure 3-10 shows the three parts that comprise the basic unit used in SNMP messages.

Figure 3-10. ASN.1 Data Item

In the BER standard an optional fourth part may be used when the data items are encoded, called the end-of-contents (EOC) delimiter sequence. The EOC may be used for encoding an indefinite length message. It consists of a single length octet of 10000000, followed by two octets of zeroes after the contents. These are considered the end-of-contents octets. Note: This form of encoding is not allowed in SNMP and should never be used.

3.2.1. THE TAG (TYPE IDENTIFIER)

Figure 3-11 shows the three parts of the Tag:

- The Class Bits (bits 8 and 7)
- The "F" (format) Bit (bit 6)
- The Tag Number Bits (bits 5, 4, 3, 2, and 1)

Class Bits	The "F" Bit	Tag Number Bits

Figure 3-11. The Tag Fields

The Class Bits determine the class type. Both the Simple and Simply-constructed data types belong to the Universal class type. The Application-wide data types belong to the class type with the same name, the Application-wide class type.

The Context-specific class type uniquely identifies a particular constructor type. These tags have no meaning outside the ASN.1 type for which they were specifically defined. This is the class that defines the SNMP PDUs used with the protocol.

The Private class is used for types defined by convention for a special purpose. It can be used with bilateral agreement for the private communication between vendors or enterprises.

Figure 3-12 shows the various possible bit settings for these different classes.

Bit 6 determines the format of the data type—whether it is simple or constructed. Figure 3-13 shows the meaning of this bit.

The meaning and value of the third field, the Tag Number, is dependent on the Class Type. For the Universal Class, five tag numbers are of interest. Four

Class Types		
bits 8 - 7		**Type**
0	0	Universal
0	1	Application-wide
1	0	Context-specific
1	1	Private

Figure 3-12. Class Types

Simple/Constructed Format	
bit 6	**Format Type**
0	Simple
1	Constructed

Figure 3-13. Format Types

are of the simple format, and one is constructed (actually, two, because the SEQUENCE and SEQUENCE OF data types share the same Universal Class Tag value of 16).

Figure 3-14 lists the tag value for each of the Universal class data types. The S/C column indicates the format type, whether the Universal type is simple (s) or constructed (c).

Universal Class Tags							
Type	**bits 5-4-3-2-1**					**decimal**	**S/C**
INTEGER	0	0	0	1	0	2	s
OCTET STRING	0	0	1	0	0	4	s
NULL	0	0	1	0	1	5	s
OBJECT IDENTIFIER	0	0	1	1	0	6	s
SEQUENCE, SEQUENCE OF	1	0	0	0	0	16	c

Figure 3-14. Universal Class Tag Types

For the Application-Wide Class, five tag numbers are also of interest. All five are of the simple format.

Figure 3-15 shows the tag value for each of the Application-Wide class data types. The S/C column indicates whether the Application-Wide type is of simple (s) or constructed (c) format type.

Application-Wide Class Tags							
Type	bits 5-4-3-2-1					decimal	S/C
IpAddress	0	0	0	0	0	0	s
Counter	0	0	0	0	1	1	s
Gauge	0	0	0	1	0	2	s
TimeTicks	0	0	0	1	1	3	s
Opaque	0	0	1	0	0	4	s

Figure 3-15. Application-Wide Class Tag Types

The Context-Specific class defines the SNMP PDUs used in the protocol exchanges. Their meaning is discussed in detail in Chapter 5, but it serves as an introduction to show what their tag number values are and how the bits are encoded for the various messages.

Five tag numbers are of interest for the Context-Specific class, corresponding to the number of PDUs defined in SNMP version 1. All five are of the constructed format.

Figure 3-16 lists the tag value for each of the Context-Specific class data types. The S/C column indicates whether the Context-Specific type format is simple (s) or constructed (c).

Context-Specific Class Tags							
Type	bits 5-4-3-2-1					decimal	S/C
Get-Request PDU	0	0	0	0	0	0	c
Get-Next-Request PDU	0	0	0	0	1	1	c
Get-Response PDU	0	0	0	1	0	2	c
Set-Request PDU	0	0	0	1	1	3	c
Trap PDU	0	0	1	0	0	4	c

Figure 3-16. Context-Specific Class Tag Types

Figure 3-17 summarizes the bit encodings for the Class, Format, and Tag value fields for the data types and the SNMP PDUs that SNMP implementations will encounter.

SNMP Type Identifiers Summary									
Type	bits								hex
	8	7	6	5	4	3	2	1	
INTEGER	0	0	0	0	0	0	1	0	02h
OCTET STRING	0	0	0	0	0	1	0	0	04h
NULL	0	0	0	0	0	1	0	1	05h
OBJECT IDENTIFIER	0	0	0	0	0	1	1	0	06h
SEQUENCE, SEQ. OF	0	0	1	1	0	0	0	0	30h
IpAddress	0	1	0	0	0	0	0	0	40h
Counter	0	1	0	0	0	0	0	1	41h
Gauge	0	1	0	0	0	0	1	0	42h
TimeTicks	0	1	0	0	0	0	1	1	43h
Opaque	0	1	0	0	0	1	0	0	44h
Get-Request PDU	1	0	1	0	0	0	0	0	A0h
Get-Next-Request PDU	1	0	1	0	0	0	0	1	A1h
Get-Response PDU	1	0	1	0	0	0	1	0	A2h
Set-Request PDU	1	0	1	0	0	0	1	1	A3h
Trap PDU	1	0	1	0	0	1	0	0	A4h

Figure 3-17. Common SNMP Type Identifiers Summary

ASN.1 provides a mechanism for specifying Tag Numbers larger than 30 (that is, having the least five bits, the Tag Number field, being set to all 1s) by using the convention of setting all of the bits to 1. If the tag field is all 1s, one or more of the subsequent octets will represent the tag number. Each subsequent octet—except the last one—has the most significant bit (MSB) set to 1. The last octet would have its MSB set to 0. The tag number is then formed by taking the seven least significant bits of each subsequent octet and concatenating them to form a binary number.

3.2.2. THE LENGTH IDENTIFIER

The Length Identifier also uses a similar convention to accommodate an arbitrarily large length value. It uses the Short/Long Form indicator bit to calculate whether the length is encoded in a single octet. This bit is the MSB of the Length Identifier octet as shown in Figure 3-18.

8	7	6	5	4	3	2	1
F-bit							

Figure 3-18. The Length Identifier Octet

If the indicator F-bit is a *0*, the short definite format, the least significant seven bits contain the length of the contents. The length can be between 0 and 127 octets, inclusive. If the F-bit is a *1*, the long definite format, the value of the least significant seven bits hold the number of subsequent length octets. These subsequent octets are then concatenated to give the number of contents octets. This would represent the length of the contents.

Examples as shown in Figure 3-19 can help support this explanation.

Contents Length	Length Octet(s) Binary Encoding	Format
0	00000000	short definite
1	00000001	short definite
128	10000001—10000000	long definite
256	10000010—10000000—00000000	long definite
2	10000001—00000010	long definite

Figure 3-19. Length Encoding Examples

Note that the fifth example indicates the use of the long definite format for a length value less than 128. This implementation wastes an extra octet, but is acceptable under the specification. "For the definite form, the length octets shall consist of one or more octets, and shall represent the number of octets in the contents octets using either the short form or the long form as the sender's option."[10]

3.2.3. THE VALUE (CONTENTS)

The value is the contents of each of the various SNMP types. The specific contents vary with each type. The length specifies how long the contents are.

3.3. MIB OBJECT DEFINITION FORMATS

In addition to specifying the formal syntax and encoding rules to be used in the network management framework, the SMI also specifies the format of the objects that the MIB will manage. Although I defer the specifics about the managed objects to Chapter 5, introducing the general template used in defining all of these objects is appropriate. As I mentioned earlier in this chapter, every managed object has a unique, administratively assigned name, an ASN.1 syntax for the abstract data structure that represents the object, and a corresponding BER encoding for its representation and communication using the protocol. Figure 3-20 shows the highest common level at which the objects are represented by the SMI.

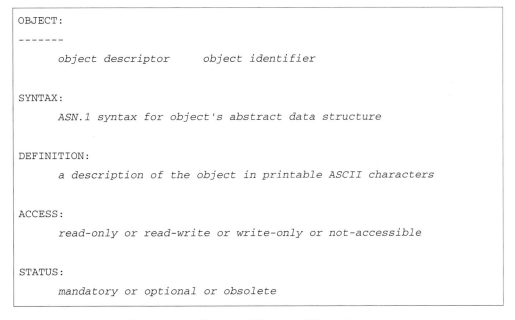

```
OBJECT:

-------

        object descriptor      object identifier


SYNTAX:
      ASN.1 syntax for object's abstract data structure


DEFINITION:
      a description of the object in printable ASCII characters


ACCESS:
      read-only or read-write or write-only or not-accessible


STATUS:
      mandatory or optional or obsolete
```

Figure 3-20. Top-Level Managed Object Template

The *object descriptor* is an abbreviated string that represents the object type. The *object identifier* is its ID, the series of decimal numbers separated by decimal points, that represents its place in the global naming hierarchy.

The *syntax* is its ASN.1 definition. The *definition* is a meaningful description of the object. The *access value* determines whether the object can be read or written, and the *status* determines its current implementation state.

In order to make the object definitions more easily processed, the SMI has defined a macro facility. The first macro introduced is called the OBJECT-TYPE. It presents a formal template for defining the objects that will constitute the Managed Information Base (MIB). Notice the macro's format; it includes several key words, block style BEGIN and END delimiters, and the enumerated values for an object's access and status.

Figure 3-21 shows the OBJECT-TYPE macro that defines the elements in the MIB.

```
OBJECT-TYPE MACRO ::=
BEGIN
    TYPE NOTATION ::= "SYNTAX" type (TYPE ObjectSyntax)
                      "ACCESS" Access
                      "STATUS" Status
    VALUE NOTATION ::= value (VALUE ObjectName)


    Access ::= "read-only"
               | "read-write"
               | "write-only"
               | "not-accessible"
    Status ::= "mandatory"
               | "optional"
               | "obsolete"
END
```

Figure 3-21. OBJECT-TYPE Macro

The SMI presents a straightforward formalism that is both simple and extensible in the way objects are to be represented and manipulated. Chapter 5 goes into the specifics as to how and which objects are selected and defined.

3.4. SMI DEFINITION

This discussion of the SMI would not be complete without including the formal definition from RFC 1155, *Structure and Identification of Management Information for TCP/IP-based Internets*. Figure 3-22 contains the SMI.

```
        RFC1155-SMI DEFINITIONS ::= BEGIN


        EXPORTS -- EVERYTHING
                internet, directory, mgmt,
                experimental, private, enterprises,
                OBJECT-TYPE, ObjectName, ObjectSyntax, SimpleSyntax,
                ApplicationSyntax, NetworkAddress, IpAddress,
                Counter, Gauge, TimeTicks, Opaque;


        -- the path to the root


        internet      OBJECT IDENTIFIER ::= { iso org(3) dod(6) 1 }


        directory     OBJECT IDENTIFIER ::= { internet 1 }


        mgmt          OBJECT IDENTIFIER ::= { internet 2 }


        experimental  OBJECT IDENTIFIER ::= { internet 3 }


        private       OBJECT IDENTIFIER ::= { internet 4 }
        enterprises   OBJECT IDENTIFIER ::= { private 1 }
```

Figure 3-22. SMI Formal Definition

```
        -- definition of object types


    OBJECT-TYPE MACRO ::=
    BEGIN
        TYPE NOTATION ::= "SYNTAX" type (TYPE ObjectSyntax)
                          "ACCESS" Access
                          "STATUS" Status
        VALUE NOTATION ::= value (VALUE ObjectName)


        Access ::= "read-only"
                        | "read-write"
                        | "write-only"
                        | "not-accessible"
        Status ::= "mandatory"
                        | "optional"
                        | "obsolete"
    END



-- names of objects in the MIB


    ObjectName ::=
        OBJECT IDENTIFIER


    -- syntax of objects in the MIB


    ObjectSyntax ::=
        CHOICE {
            simple
                SimpleSyntax,


    -- note that simple SEQUENCEs are not directly
    -- mentioned here to keep things simple (i.e.,
```

Figure 3-22. SMI Formal Definition *(continued)*

```
-- prevent mis-use).  However, application-wide
-- types which are IMPLICITly encoded simple
-- SEQUENCEs may appear in the following CHOICE

        application-wide
            ApplicationSyntax
  }

  SimpleSyntax ::=
      CHOICE {
          number
              INTEGER,

          string
              OCTET STRING,

          object
              OBJECT IDENTIFIER,

          empty
              NULL
      }

  ApplicationSyntax ::=
      CHOICE {
          address
              NetworkAddress,

          counter
              Counter,

          gauge
              Gauge,
```

Figure 3-22. SMI Formal Definition *(continued)*

```
                    ticks
                        TimeTicks,


                    arbitrary
                        Opaque


-- other application-wide types, as they are
-- defined, will be added here
    }



-- application-wide types

NetworkAddress ::=
    CHOICE {
        internet
            IpAddress
    }


IpAddress ::=
    [APPLICATION 0]          -- in network-byte order
        IMPLICIT OCTET STRING (SIZE (4))


Counter ::=
    [APPLICATION 1]
        IMPLICIT INTEGER (0..4294967295)


Gauge ::=
    [APPLICATION 2]
        IMPLICIT INTEGER (0..4294967295)


TimeTicks ::=
```

Figure 3-22. SMI Formal Definition *(continued)*

```
                        [APPLICATION 3]
                            IMPLICIT INTEGER (0..4294967295)


                Opaque ::=
                    [APPLICATION 4]              -- arbitrary ASN.1 value,
                        IMPLICIT OCTET STRING    --   "double-wrapped"


                END
```

Figure 3-22. SMI Formal Definition *(continued)*

REFERENCES FOR CHAPTER 3

[1] *The Oxford Dictionary of Quotations, Third Edition.* Oxford, UK: Oxford University Press, 1979.

[2] Tripp, Rhonda Thomas (compiler). *The International Thesaurus of Quotations.* New York: Thomas Y. Crowell Company. 1970.

[3] Information Processing Systems-Open Systems Interconnection. "Specification of Abstract Syntax Notation One (ASN.1)." International Organization for Standardization. International Standard 8824. 1987.

[4] Information Processing Systems-Open Systems Interconnection. "Specification of Basic Encoding Rules for Abstract Notation One (ASN.1)." International Organization for Standardization. International Standard 8825. 1987.

[5] International Telecommunication Union–Telecommunication Standardization Sector. "Specification of Abstract Syntax Notation One (ASN.1)." ITU-T Recommendation X.208. 1988.

[6] International Telecommunication Union-Telecommunication Standardization Sector. "Specification of Basic Encoding Rules for Abstract Syntax Notation One (ASN.1)." ITU-T Recommendation X.209. 1988.

[7] Steedman, Douglas. *Abstract Syntax Notation One (ASN.1): The Tutorial and Reference.* London: Technology Appraisals, Ltd. 1990.

[8] Rose, Marshall T. *The Open Book: A Practical Perspective on OSI*. Englewood Cliffs, NJ: Prentice Hall, Inc. 1990.

[9] Rose, Marshall T. *The Simple Book: An Introduction to Management of TCP/IP-based Internets*. Englewood Cliffs, NJ: Prentice Hall. 1991.

[10] International Telecommunication Union–Telecommunication Standardization Sector. "Specification of Basic Encoding Rules for Abstract Syntax Notation One (ASN.1)." ITU-T Recommendation X.209. 1988.

The Structure of Management Information for SNMP Version 2

A few strong instincts, and a few plain rules.

—*William Wordsworth*[1]

The art of art, the glory of expression and the sunshine of the light of letters, is simplicity.

— *Walt Whitman*[2]

Like the SMI for version 1, the Structure of Management Information (SMI) for SNMP version 2 defines how the management information for v2 can be represented using a subset of the ASN.1.[3] SMIv2 has the important second role of assigning key administrative values that are used in this framework. For this chapter, you need to understand how MIB objects are defined, ASN.1, and BER from Chapter 3 on SMIv1, because these concepts are carried forward into version 2. For convenience, I refer to this newer version of the SMI as SMIv2.

SMIv2 is a proper superset of the SMI used by SNMPv1. It was first defined as a proposed standard in RFC 1442 and included many of the modifications proposed from the secure SNMP and SMP efforts. The current draft standard of SMI that is used to implement community-based SNMPv2 is specified in RFC 1902, *Structure of Management Information for Version 2 of the Simple Network Management Protocol (SNMPv2)*.

The major improvements in the SMIv2 include the addition of several new data types; many new, expanded, and more clearly defined ASN.1 macros; and the addition of MIB compliance requirements and vendor capabilities statements.

This version makes the management definitions more "expressive" than the first version. It is the standard for writing new MIBs. All of the new IETF standard MIBs and many of the latest vendor information modules are written using SMIv2. Surprisingly, only the Counter64 data type is not supported by the version 1 protocol, making the coexistence and transitioning between the two versions relatively painless.

In addition to the formal SMI discussion, I also include the expanded set of standardized textual conventions presented in RFC 1903, *Textual Conventions for Version 2 of the Simple Network Management Protocol (SNMPv2)*, and the conformance statements discussed in RFC 1904, *Conformance Statements for Version 2 of the Simple Network Management Protocol (SNMPv2)*. The conformance statements define an implementation's acceptable lower bounds (compliance) and also the actual level that is achieved by that implementation (capability).

Since SMIv2 requires the definition of new objects, a new branch for SNMPv2 MIB objects has been added. It appears on the ISO/CCITT naming registration tree in Figure 4-1 as the snmpv2 branch. Its OID is 1.3.6.1.6. This branch currently has three sub-branches. The snmpDomains sub-tree contains transport domains, the snmpProxys sub-tree contains the transport proxies, and the snmpModules has the list of object identifiers for various modules. Note that since SMIv1 was defined in 1991, the security and mail branches have also been added.

4.1. SMI MODIFICATIONS FOR VERSION 2

After several years of implementation experience and discussion on how to improve the SNMP SMI, the SNMP working group members proposed several new additions.

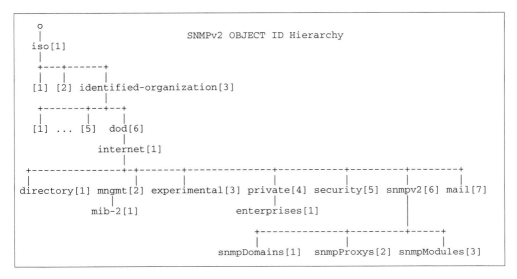

```
 o
 |                    SNMPv2 OBJECT ID Hierarchy
 |
iso[1]
 |
 |
 +---+------+
 |   |      |
[1] [2] identified-organization[3]
 |                    |
 +-------+--+--+
 |       |     |
[1] ... [5]  dod[6]
                |
             internet[1]
                |
 +--------------+-+-------+--------------+-----------+---------+--------+
 |                |       |              |           |         |        |
directory[1] mngmt[2] experimental[3] private[4] security[5] snmpv2[6] mail[7]
              |                           |                    |
           mib-2[1]                  enterprises[1]            |
                                          +--------------+---------+-----+
                                          |              |         |
                                    snmpDomains[1]  snmpProxys[2] snmpModules[3]
```

Figure 4-1. The Expanded SNMPv2 Object Identifier Hierarchy

New data types were introduced to allow for more precise definitions. Counters and gauges are now defined by their bit width: Counter32, Counter64, and Gauge32. Unsigned 32-bit integers are now of type Unsigned32. Bits can now be represented by the BITS construct that allows for the enumeration by bit. The NsapAddress for OSI network addresses that was defined for RFC 1442 was not kept for the draft version because its use proved to be unnecessary. Note that all of the other data types from Version 1 are still valid, although the Opaque type should not be used. It is present for backward-compatibility only. Please refer to the SMIv2 formal definition (Figure 4-20) for the full definitions for all of the data types.

At the highest level, the SMI is used to create an *information module*. This is a package of information that contains the relevant data used in the SNMP network management. The SMI defines three major types of information modules:

◆ MIB Modules

◆ Compliance Statements

◆ Capability Statements

The real importance of the SMI is its use in creating MIB modules; these, of course, are the collection of related managed objects that the management protocol manipulates.

111

Version 2 MIB modules contain the maximum requirement levels for managing this collection of objects. The Compliance Statements set a lower bound by stating the minimum level that should be provided. The Capability Statements finish the picture by allowing a particular vendor to describe its implementation details that represent that level of compliance.

The SMIv2 defines five constructs that are allowed in an SNMPv2 information module:

◆ the IMPORTS clause

◆ value definitions for OBJECT IDENTIFIERS

◆ type definitions for SEQUENCEs

◆ SNMPv2 restricted ASN.1 type assignments

◆ SNMPv2 ASN.1 macros

Before I go over the macros in detail, note that in practice the information modules create two different flavors: the standard modules and the modules made by each vendor or enterprise.

In addition to object definitions, the standard Information Module, usually referred to simply as *the MIB*, contains the module identity, the IMPORTS clause, and a compliance section. The module identity section is defined by the MODULE-IDENTITY macro. The compliance section is defined by the MODULE-COMPLIANCE macro.

A vendor Information Module or *enterprise MIB* also contains the module identity and the IMPORTS clause, but in place of the compliance section it contains its own capability macro. The capability macro is defined by using the AGENT-CAPABILITIES macro. It also contains the appropriate object definitions for what resources are to be managed.

The macros introduced with the SMIv2 have enriched the documentation and enhanced the maintainability of the management information. A firm grasp of the macros used in SMIv2 greatly aids the implementer in defining and understanding the MIB information modules and other notations that you encounter when working with SNMPv2.

Figure 4-2 lists the allowable macros that can be used in an SNMPv2 information module. The figure includes a brief description, and the RFC column cites the RFC that contains the full macro definition.

Now I look more closely into the specifics of each macro and its syntax.

Macro Name	Macro Description	RFC
MODULE-IDENTITY	describes the semantics of the whole information module	1902
OBJECT-IDENTITY	associates additional text to an OBJECT IDENTIFIER	1902
OBJECT-TYPE	the syntax and semantics of a managed object	1902
NOTIFICATION-TYPE	SNMPv2 notification syntax	1902
TEXTUAL-CONVENTION	refines syntax for standard data types	1903
OBJECT-GROUP	defines a collection of related managed objects	1904
NOTIFICATION-GROUP	defines a collection of notifications	1904
MODULE-COMPLIANCE	lists the MIB modules that are mandatory or optional	1904
AGENT-CAPABILITIES	details the specifics of a particular implementation	1904

Figure 4-2. SNMP Version 2 SMI Macros

4.1.1. MODULE-IDENTITY MACRO

The MODULE-IDENTITY macro adds a common identification section that gives a top-level textual description to the information module. It greatly adds to the documentation and control over managing the MIB modules. This macro includes organizational information, the OBJECT IDENTIFIER, and the revision level for this module.

Figure 4-3 shows the MODULE-IDENTITY macro definition.

The TYPE NOTATION clause shows that this macro contains four clauses for information on when this module was last updated, the organization responsible, whom to contact, a brief description, and revision information. The LAST-UPDATED field uses the ASN.1 standard notation for time and date called UTCTime. The format is *yymmddhhmm*. ORGANIZATION, CONTACT-INFO, and DESCRIPTION are text fields. The RevisionPart can contain zero or more Revisions that contain an Update field of the same UTCTime used above and an accompanying textual description. This entry is required for the initial revision.

The easiest way to see how such a macro template would be filled in is to cite an example. Figure 4-4 is the MODULE-IDENTITY macro declaration from the standard SNMPv2 MIB definition that would be implemented for every SNMPv2 entity.

```
MODULE-IDENTITY MACRO ::=
BEGIN
    TYPE NOTATION ::=
                    "LAST-UPDATED" value(Update UTCTime)
                    "ORGANIZATION" Text
                    "CONTACT-INFO" Text
                    "DESCRIPTION" Text
                    RevisionPart

    VALUE NOTATION ::=
                    value(VALUE OBJECT IDENTIFIER)

    RevisionPart ::=
                    Revisions
                  | empty
    Revisions ::=
                    Revision
                  | Revisions Revision
    Revision ::=
                    "REVISION" value(Update UTCTime)
                    "DESCRIPTION" Text

    -- uses the NVT ASCII character set
    Text ::= """" string """"
END
```

Figure 4-3. MODULE-IDENTITY Macro

```
snmpMIB MODULE-IDENTITY
    LAST-UPDATED "9511090000Z"
    ORGANIZATION "IETF SNMPv2 Working Group"
    CONTACT-INFO
            "           Marshall T. Rose

            Postal: Dover Beach Consulting, Inc.
                    420 Whisman Court
                    Mountain View, CA  94043-2186
                    US

               Tel: +1 415 968 1052

            E-mail: mrose@dbc.mtview.ca.us"
    DESCRIPTION
            "The MIB module for SNMPv2 entities."
    REVISION      "9304010000Z"
    DESCRIPTION
            "The initial revision of this MIB module was published as
            RFC 1450."
    ::= { snmpModules 1 }
```

Figure 4-4. Example of the MODULE-IDENTITY Macro Usage

The snmpMIB declaration of the MODULE-IDENTITY macro has a value of { snmpModules 1 } (which is shorthand for its *1.3.6.1.6.3.1* OID). It was last updated on November 11, 1995, at midnight by the IETF SNMPv2 working group. The contact person, Marshall T. Rose, and his address follow. The description states that this is the MIB module for managed SNMPv2 entities. The `RevisionPart` also states that the original version of this MIB was written on April 1, 1993, at midnight and presented in RFC 1450, *Management Information Base for Version 2 of the Simple Network Management Protocol (SNMPv2)*.

I examine the remaining macros in a similar way, but without a specific instantiation example. The syntax is very straightforward and many of the clauses are repeated.

4.1.2. OBJECT-IDENTITY MACRO

The OBJECT-IDENTITY macro is a general macro that allows for additional information to be applied to describe any OBJECT IDENTIFIER. This information includes status, a textual description, and an optional pointer to any associated reference. Figure 4-5 shows this macro.

```
OBJECT-IDENTITY MACRO ::=
BEGIN
    TYPE NOTATION ::=
                    "STATUS" Status
                    "DESCRIPTION" Text
                    ReferPart
    VALUE NOTATION ::=
                    value(VALUE OBJECT IDENTIFIER)

    Status ::=
                    "current"
                  | "deprecated"
                  | "obsolete"

    ReferPart ::=
                    "REFERENCE" Text
                  | empty

    Text ::= """" string """"
END
```

Figure 4-5. OBJECT-IDENTITY Macro

The Status field for an object can contain one of three values, as shown in Figure 4-6.

The DESCRIPTION is a text field and `ReferPart` is an optional textual reference. The reference clause can be a cross-reference to an object assignment described in another module. Note that in ASN.1, when a value includes the choice of *empty*, that clause is optional.

115

Status	Description
current	this definition is in use
deprecated	this definition is not endorsed and is in the process of being obsolete. It may still be supported to maintain backward compatibility.
obsolete	this definition is not in use and should not be implemented

Figure 4-6. Object Identity Status

4.1.3. OBJECT-TYPE MACRO

The OBJECT-TYPE macro is the key description of the version 2 managed object and carries all the information that SNMP needs to define this managed object. The macro appears in Figure 4-7.

```
OBJECT-TYPE MACRO ::=
BEGIN
    TYPE NOTATION ::=
                    "SYNTAX" Syntax
                    UnitsPart
                    "MAX-ACCESS" Access
                    "STATUS" Status
                    "DESCRIPTION" Text
                    ReferPart
                    IndexPart
                    DefValPart

    VALUE NOTATION ::=
                    value(VALUE ObjectName)

    Syntax ::=
                    type(ObjectSyntax)
                  | "BITS" "{" Kibbles "}"
    Kibbles ::=
                    Kibble
                  | Kibbles "," Kibble
    Kibble ::=
                    identifier "(" nonNegativeNumber ")"

    UnitsPart ::=
                    "UNITS" Text
                  | empty

    Access ::=
                    "not-accessible"
                  | "accessible-for-notify"
                  | "read-only"
                  | "read-write"
                  | "read-create"
```

Figure 4-7. OBJECT-TYPE Macro

```
        Status ::=
                        "current"
                      | "deprecated"
                      | "obsolete"

        ReferPart ::=
                        "REFERENCE" Text
                      | empty

        IndexPart ::=
                        "INDEX"     "{" IndexTypes "}"
                      | "AUGMENTS" "{" Entry       "}"
                      | empty
        IndexTypes ::=
                        IndexType
                      | IndexTypes "," IndexType
        IndexType ::=
                        "IMPLIED" Index
                      | Index
        Index ::=
                        -- use the SYNTAX value of the
                        -- correspondent OBJECT-TYPE invocation
                        value(Indexobject ObjectName)
        Entry ::=
                        -- use the INDEX value of the
                        -- correspondent OBJECT-TYPE invocation
                        value(Entryobject ObjectName)

        DefValPart ::=
                        "DEFVAL" "{" value(Defval Syntax) "}"
                      | empty

        -- uses the NVT ASCII character set
        Text ::= """" string """"
END
```

Figure 4-7. OBJECT-TYPE Macro *(continued)*

The OBJECT-TYPE macro can contain up to eight parts. Four are mandatory and four are optional.

1. SYNTAX

2. UnitsPart *(optional)*

3. MAX-ACCESS

4. STATUS

5. DESCRIPTION

6. ReferPart *(optional)*

7. IndexPart *(optional)*

8. DefValPart *(optional)*

The SYNTAX clause defines the object's data type from the ASN.1 definitions for ObjectSyntax. RFC 1902 defines the semantics for the thirteen data types that can be used. Figure 4-8 presents these data types. Note that all numerical values in this table are decimal.

Name	Description
Integer32	represents integer values from -2,147,483,648 to 2,147,483,647. Additionally, enumeration tags can be between 1 and 64 characters in length (although 32 or less is recommended) consisting of letters and digits (no hyphens). The first character must be a lowercase letter.
INTEGER	same as Integer32
OCTET STRING	arbitrary length string (although a maximum of 255 octets is recommended)
OBJECT IDENTIFIER	object identifier of up to 128 sub-identifiers. Each sub-identifier can have a maximum value of 4,294,967,295.
BITS	starting at zero, an enumeration of non-negative, contiguous valued, named bits. Labels should follow the same limitations as the enumeration tags used for the integer types above.
IpAddress	32-bit internet address (in network byte-order) specified as 4 octets
Counter32	a non-negative integer that goes from 0 to 4,294,967,295. When the maximum value is reached the counter value wraps to 0. Note that all counters in SNMP should not be defined with an initial value.
Gauge32	a non-negative integer that goes between 0 and 4,294,967,295. When the maximum value is reached the gauge latches, and can only be decreased.
TimeTicks	a non-negative integer that goes from 0 to 4,294,967,295. When the maximum value is reached the time value wraps to 0. A "tick" represents a centi-second (.01 of a second).
Opaque	used for passing an arbitrary syntax inside an OCTET STRING (i.e., the receiving application must understand the format of the opaque information). It is not used in SNMPv2 and is only presented for v1 compatibility. In fact a requirement for standard MIBs is to not use this construct.

Figure 4-8. Object Syntax Semantics

Name	Description
Counter64	twice as big as a Counter32; a non-negative integer that goes from 0 to 18,446,744,073,709,551,615. When the maximum value is reached the counter value wraps to 0.
Unsigned32	a non-negative integer that can be between 0 and 4,294,967,295
Conceptual Tables	syntax for tables and rows within the tables. A table is a sequence of rows, and each row is subsequently defined as an entry type. The rows are filled with the objects that can be accessed.

Figure 4-8. Object Syntax Semantics *(continued)*

ASN.1 sub-typing is allowed for several of these data types. The sub-typing more clearly defines the range, size, or enumeration values allowed for that object. For instance, if an object is an INTEGER and can only take on a small number of the over 4 billion possible values, it can be sub-classed to limit the range boundary for acceptable values (e.g., INTEGER (0..100). Appendix C in RFC 1902 gives detailed rules for sub-typing.

The UnitsPart of the OBJECT-TYPE macro is the text that describes the units used with the syntax, if appropriate. It is currently only present for documentation.

The MAX-ACCESS clause is the managed object's access level. The five access levels for SMIv2 are defined in Figure 4-9.

Access Level	Description
not-accessible	object instances cannot be read, written, or created
accessible-for-notify	object instances can be used for notifys
read-only	object instances can only be read
read-write	object instances can be read or written (but not created)
read-create	object instances can be read, written, or created

Figure 4-9. Object Access Levels

The STATUS clause for the object definition is the same as those defined for the object identity (see Figure 4-6 earlier in this chapter). It can be current, deprecated, or obsolete. The object can be described in the text DESCRIPTION clause. The reference, ReferPart, is an optional textual identification if this object is related to another object.

The IndexPart can contain the syntax for how table instances can be identified (INDEX) or how tabular extensions can be defined to add columns to an existing table (AUGMENTS).

The optional default value, DefValPart clause, can set initial default values when this object is instantiated on an agent. The syntax and values must be correct. Note that DEFVAL cannot be specified for Counter32 and Counter64 since they are defined as not having any initial value.

4.1.4. NOTIFICATION-TYPE MACRO

The NOTIFICATION-TYPE macro describes the format of the SNMPv2 notification and contains two mandatory fields and two optional clauses. It appears in Figure 4-10.

The ObjectsPart clause indicates which objects are included in this notification. It is optional.

The STATUS and DESCRIPTION clauses are mandatory and the same as the clauses found in the OBJECT-TYPE macro above. The ReferPart reference pointer is also similar to its counterpart in the OBJECT-TYPE macro. It is optional.

4.1.5. TEXTUAL-CONVENTION MACRO

The TEXTUAL-CONVENTION macro refines the syntax for the extensions to the standard data types. It appears in Figure 4-11. The full list of SMIv2 textual conventions presented in RFC 1903 is fully enumerated in Section 4.2, "SMI V2 Textual Conventions."

The Simple Book, rev. 2d ed.[4] notes that because this macro refines a data type instead of defining a new one, it should be invoked as follows:

```
NameOfType ::= TEXTUAL-CONVENTION
  <<clauses>>
  SYNTAX TYPE
```

The macro itself has five clauses: the display hint, the status, the description, the reference pointer, and the syntax.

```
NOTIFICATION-TYPE MACRO ::=
BEGIN
    TYPE NOTATION ::=
                    ObjectsPart
                    "STATUS" Status
                    "DESCRIPTION" Text
                    ReferPart

    VALUE NOTATION ::=
                    value(VALUE NotificationName)

    ObjectsPart ::=
                    "OBJECTS" "{" Objects "}"
                  | empty
    Objects ::=
                    Object
                  | Objects "," Object
    Object ::=
                    value(Name ObjectName)

    Status ::=
                    "current"
                  | "deprecated"
                  | "obsolete"

    ReferPart ::=
                    "REFERENCE" Text
                  | empty

    -- uses the NVT ASCII character set
    Text ::= """" string """"
END
```

Figure 4-10. NOTIFICATION-TYPE Macro

```
TEXTUAL-CONVENTION MACRO ::=
BEGIN
    TYPE NOTATION ::=
                    DisplayPart
                    "STATUS" Status
                    "DESCRIPTION" Text
                    ReferPart
                    "SYNTAX" Syntax

    VALUE NOTATION ::=
                    value(VALUE Syntax)

    DisplayPart ::=
                    "DISPLAY-HINT" Text
                  | empty

    Status ::=
                    "current"
                  | "deprecated"
                  | "obsolete"

    ReferPart ::=
```

Figure 4-11. TEXTUAL-CONVENTION Macro

```
                    "REFERENCE" Text
                  | empty

    -- uses the NVT ASCII character set
    Text ::= """" string """"

    Syntax ::=
                    type(ObjectSyntax)
                  | "BITS" "{" Kibbles "}"
    Kibbles ::=
                    Kibble
                  | Kibbles "," Kibble
    Kibble ::=
                    identifier "(" nonNegativeNumber ")"

END
```

Figure 4-11. TEXTUAL-CONVENTION Macro *(continued)*

The only clause not used in the previous macros is the DISPLAY-HINT. It is an optional field that indicates how a particular INTEGER or OCTET STRING value can be displayed.

For an INTEGER, a display hint consists of a character for the display format. If the display format is decimal, it may optionally have a precision indicator for pointing out where a decimal point can be placed. For example, d-2 for 10000 could be displayed as 100.00. Figure 4-12 shows the four acceptable display formats. Note that the ASCII representation is for OCTET STRINGs only.

Hint	Display Format
x	hexidecimal
d	decimal
o	octal
b	binary
a	ASCII

Figure 4-12. Display Hints Format Specifiers

For an OCTET STRING the hint comprises one or more octet-format specifications. Each octet-format specification can have up to five parts, which you see in Figure 4-13. A good example of the use of Display Hints is the Date-AndTime textual convention, which I discuss in Section 4.2.13.

Specification	Meaning
the repeat indicator	indicates that the current octet of value is used as the repeat count. It is an unsigned integer, greater than or equal to 0. It specifies how many times the remainder of this format specification will be successively applied. If it is not present the repeat count is 1. This field is optional.
the octet length	one or more decimal digits indicating the length of this field. It can be zero. Any high-order digits that cannot fit are truncated.
the display format	format; any of the specifiers from Figure 4-12 can be used except for b (binary).
the display separator character	any character except a digit or an asterisk that can separate octet specifications. This field is optional.
the repeat terminator character	any character except a digit or an asterisk that can be used to terminate an octet specification. This field is optional.

Figure 4-13. Octet-Format Specifications

4.1.6. OBJECT-GROUP MACRO

The OBJECT-GROUP macro defines a collection of related management objects and their associated conformance level. This macro provides a means for different implementations to describe how they conform by listing what groups they have implemented. It appears in Figure 4-14.

The macro has four parts: the OBJECTS clause, the STATUS clause, the DESCRIPTION clause, and the optional REFERENCE clause.

4.1.7. NOTIFICATION-GROUP MACRO

Similarly, the NOTIFICATION-GROUP macro defines a collection of notifications to indicate the level of conformance offered by this implementation. The macro listing appears in Figure 4-15.

The macro has four parts: the NOTIFICATIONS clause, the STATUS clause, the DESCRIPTION clause, and the optional REFERENCE clause.

```
OBJECT-GROUP MACRO ::=
BEGIN
    TYPE NOTATION ::=
                    ObjectsPart
                    "STATUS" Status
                    "DESCRIPTION" Text
                    ReferPart

    VALUE NOTATION ::=
                    value(VALUE OBJECT IDENTIFIER)

    ObjectsPart ::=
                    "OBJECTS" "{" Objects "}"
    Objects ::=
                    Object
                  | Objects "," Object
    Object ::=
                    value(Name ObjectName)

    Status ::=
                    "current"
                  | "deprecated"
                  | "obsolete"

    ReferPart ::=
                    "REFERENCE" Text
                  | empty

    -- uses the NVT ASCII character set
    Text ::= """" string """"
END
```

Figure 4-14. OBJECT-GROUP Macro

```
NOTIFICATION-GROUP MACRO ::=
BEGIN
    TYPE NOTATION ::=
                    NotificationsPart
                    "STATUS" Status
                    "DESCRIPTION" Text
                    ReferPart

    VALUE NOTATION ::=
                    value(VALUE OBJECT IDENTIFIER)

    NotificationsPart ::=
                    "NOTIFICATIONS" "{" Notifications "}"
    Notifications ::=
                    Notification
                  | Notifications "," Notification
    Notification ::=
                    value(Name NotificationName)

    Status ::=
                    "current"
                  | "deprecated"
                  | "obsolete"
```

Figure 4-15. NOTIFICATION-GROUP Macro

```
    ReferPart ::=
                "REFERENCE" Text
              | empty

    -- uses the NVT ASCII character set
    Text ::= """" string """"

END
```

Figure 4-15. NOTIFICATION-GROUP Macro *(continued)*

4.1.8. MODULE-COMPLIANCE MACRO

The MODULE-COMPLIANCE macro lists the modules that are mandatory or
optional. This listing shows the minimum implementation realized. It appears
in Figure 4-16.

```
MODULE-COMPLIANCE MACRO ::=
BEGIN
    TYPE NOTATION ::=
                "STATUS" Status
                "DESCRIPTION" Text
                ReferPart
                ModulePart

    VALUE NOTATION ::=
                value(VALUE OBJECT IDENTIFIER)

    Status ::=
                "current"
              | "deprecated"
              | "obsolete"

    ReferPart ::=
                "REFERENCE" Text
              | empty

    ModulePart ::=
                Modules
              | empty
    Modules ::=
                Module
              | Modules Module
    Module ::=
                -- name of module --
                "MODULE" ModuleName
                MandatoryPart
                CompliancePart

    ModuleName ::=
                modulereference ModuleIdentifier
                -- must not be empty unless contained
                -- in MIB Module
```

Figure 4-16. MODULE-COMPLIANCE Macro

```
                    | empty
       ModuleIdentifier ::=
                    value(ModuleID OBJECT IDENTIFIER)
                    | empty

    MandatoryPart ::=
                    "MANDATORY-GROUPS" "{" Groups "}"
                    | empty

    Groups ::=
                    Group
                    | Groups "," Group
    Group ::=
                    value(Group OBJECT IDENTIFIER)

    CompliancePart ::=
                    Compliances
                    | empty

    Compliances ::=
                    Compliance
                    | Compliances Compliance
    Compliance ::=
                    ComplianceGroup
                    | Object

    ComplianceGroup ::=
                    "GROUP" value(Name OBJECT IDENTIFIER)
                    "DESCRIPTION" Text

    Object ::=
                    "OBJECT" value(Name ObjectName)
                    SyntaxPart
                    WriteSyntaxPart
                    AccessPart
                    "DESCRIPTION" Text

    -- must be a refinement for object's SYNTAX clause
    SyntaxPart ::=
                    "SYNTAX" type(SYNTAX)
                    | empty

    -- must be a refinement for object's SYNTAX clause
    WriteSyntaxPart ::=
                    "WRITE-SYNTAX" type(WriteSYNTAX)
                    | empty

    AccessPart ::=
                    "MIN-ACCESS" Access
                    | empty
    Access ::=
                    "not-accessible"
                    | "accessible-for-notify"
                    | "read-only"
                    | "read-write"
                    | "read-create"

    -- uses the NVT ASCII character set
    Text ::= """" string """"
END
```

Figure 4-16. MODULE-COMPLIANCE Macro *(continued)*

The macro has four parts: the STATUS clause, the DESCRIPTION clause, the optional REFERENCE clause, and the MODULE clause. The MODULE clause indicates which groups are mandatory or optional for this implementation.

4.1.9. AGENT-CAPABILITIES MACRO

The AGENT-CAPABILITIES macro details the specifics of an agent's particular implementation. It is a concise summary of the details of how an agent supports the MIB modules that it claims it has implemented. This macro is written by the agent implementer and read by the manage side. The listing of the macro appears in Figure 4-17.

```
AGENT-CAPABILITIES MACRO ::=
BEGIN
    TYPE NOTATION ::=
                    "PRODUCT-RELEASE" Text
                    "STATUS" Status
                    "DESCRIPTION" Text
                    ReferPart
                    ModulePart

    VALUE NOTATION ::=
                    value(VALUE OBJECT IDENTIFIER)

    Status ::=
                    "current"
                  | "obsolete"

    ReferPart ::=
                    "REFERENCE" Text
                  | empty

    ModulePart ::=
                    Modules
                  | empty
    Modules ::=
                    Module
                  | Modules Module
    Module ::=
                    -- name of module --
                    "SUPPORTS" ModuleName
                    "INCLUDES" "{" Groups "}"
                    VariationPart

    ModuleName ::=
                    identifier ModuleIdentifier
    ModuleIdentifier ::=
                    value(ModuleID OBJECT IDENTIFIER)
                  | empty

    Groups ::=
                    Group
```

Figure 4-17. AGENT-CAPABILITIES Macro

```
                     | Groups "," Group
        Group ::=
                     value(Name OBJECT IDENTIFIER)

        VariationPart ::=
                     Variations
                   | empty
        Variations ::=
                     Variation
                   | Variations Variation

        Variation ::=
                     ObjectVariation
                   | NotificationVariation

        NotificationVariation ::=
                     "VARIATION" value(Name NotificationName)
                     AccessPart
                     "DESCRIPTION" Text

        ObjectVariation ::=
                     "VARIATION" value(Name ObjectName)
                     SyntaxPart
                     WriteSyntaxPart
                     AccessPart
                     CreationPart
                     DefValPart
                     "DESCRIPTION" Text

        -- must be a refinement for object's SYNTAX clause
        SyntaxPart ::=
                     "SYNTAX" type(SYNTAX)
                   | empty

        -- must be a refinement for object's SYNTAX clause
        WriteSyntaxPart ::=
                     "WRITE-SYNTAX" type(WriteSYNTAX)
                   | empty

        AccessPart ::=
                     "ACCESS" Access
                   | empty

        Access ::=
                     "not-implemented"
                   -- only "not-implemented" for notifications
                   | "accessible-for-notify"
                   | "read-only"
                   | "read-write"
                   | "read-create"
                   -- following is for backward-compatibility only
                   | "write-only"

        CreationPart ::=
                     "CREATION-REQUIRES" "{" Cells "}"
                   | empty

        Cells ::=
                     Cell
                   | Cells "," Cell
```

Figure 4-17. AGENT-CAPABILITIES Macro *(continued)*

```
    Cell ::=
                value(Cell ObjectName)

    DefValPart ::=
                "DEFVAL" "{" value(Defval ObjectSyntax) "}"
              | empty

    -- uses the NVT ASCII character set
    Text ::= """" string """"
END
```

Figure 4-17. AGENT-CAPABILITIES Macro *(continued)*

The macro has five parts: the PRODUCTS-RELEASE clause, the STATUS clause, the DESCRIPTION clause, the optional REFERENCE clause, and the MODULE clause.

4.2. SMI V2 TEXTUAL CONVENTIONS

Textual conventions (TC) are a refinement to the basic data types in order to provide more accurate specific data type notation. RFC 1903 states that a textual convention is a new type with a different name, a similar syntax, and more precise semantics. Ultimately, TCs are created for humans to make the MIBs easier to read and more self-documenting.

Figure 4-18 summarizes the textual conventions added for SNMPv2. Note that all of these Textual Conventions have a status of *current* except `InstancePointer`. The `InstancePointer` is now *obsolete* and should no longer be implemented. It has been refined and replaced by the two new TCs: `VariablePointer` and `RowPointer`. I discuss the format of the DISPLAY-HINT in section 4.1.1.5, "TEXTUAL-CONVENTION Macro."

Name	Syntax	Brief Description
DisplayString	OCTET STRING (SIZE (0..255))	ASCII text from NVT character set
PhysAddress	OCTET STRING	media or physical level address
MacAddress	OCTET STRING (SIZE (6))	802 media access layer address

Figure 4-18. SNMP Version 2 Textual Conventions

Name	Syntax	Brief Description
TruthValue	INTEGER { true(1), false(2) }	boolean value for true and false
TestAndIncr	INTEGER (0 .. 2147483647)	used for atomic set operations
AutonomousType	OBJECT IDENTIFIER	OID of a sub-tree containing additional information
InstancePointer	OBJECT IDENTIFIER	pointer to an OID instance. Note: this TC is now obsolete and is replaced by VariablePointer and RowPointer
VariablePointer	OBJECT IDENTIFIER	pointer to a specific OID instance (for non-tabular variables)
RowPointer	OBJECT IDENTIFIER	pointer to a conceptual row for tables
RowStatus	INTEGER { active (1), notInService(2), notReady(3), createAndGo(4), createAndWait(5), destroy(6) }	status used to control the creation and deletion of rows
TimeStamp	TimeTicks	value of $sysUpTime$ at the time of the event
TimeInterval	INTEGER (0 .. 2147483647)	period of time measured in .01 seconds
DateAndTime	OCTET STRING (SIZE 8 | 11))	date and time
StorageType	INTEGER { other (1), volatile(2), nonVolatile(3), permanent(4), readOnly(5) }	describes the type of memory used to store a conceptual row
TDomain	OBJECT IDENTIFIER	describes a transport service
TAddress	OCTET STRING (SIZE (1..255))	transport service address

Figure 4-18. SNMP Version 2 Textual Conventions *(continued)*

4.2.1. DISPLAYSTRING

The DisplayString TC defines a string data type of up to 255 ASCII characters. The NVT (Network Virtual Terminal) US-ASCII character set presented in RFC 854, *Telnet Protocol Specification*, is the character set of choice.

4.2.2. PHYSADDRESS

The PhysAddress TC defines the OSI Level 1 physical address data type. It can contain a media-level or physical-level address represented in an OCTET STRING that contains a set of hexadecimal numbers separated by colons.

4.2.3. MACADDRESS

The MacAddress TC defines the media access address type for IEEE 802 in *canonical order*. This means that the address should be represented least significant bit first, even though the protocol requires the address to be sent most significant bit first onto the wire. This address is represented in six octets.

4.2.4. TRUTHVALUE

The TruthValue TC defines the boolean value for true and false.

4.2.5. TESTANDINCR

The test and increment textual convention is a first-level check to verify that set operations have been done successfully. The TestAndIncr TC defines the test and increment integer data type in the range from *0* to *2,147,483,647*. Its purpose is to synchronize successful set operations between an NMS and an agent. When a set is requested by an NMS, the TestAndIncr value must be the same as the stored value. After a successful set, this value is bumped by 1 (and wraps back to 0 if necessary). If an agent is restarted, this value should be set to some random value.

4.2.6. AUTONOMOUSTYPE

The Autonomous Type TC is an OID that can identify a sub-tree with additional related MIB definitions. Alternatively, it can specify a particular type of hardware or software (chip set, protocol, etc.).

4.2.7. INSTANCEPOINTER

The InstancePointer TC is an obsolete data type that defined a generic OBJECT IDENTIFIER pointer data type. It has been replaced by the VariablePointer and RowPointer TCs.

4.2.8. VARIABLEPOINTER

The VariablePointer TC is an OBJECT IDENTIFIER that points to a specific object instance. It can retrieve non-tabular instances.

4.2.9. ROWPOINTER

The RowPointer TC is an OBJECT IDENTIFIER that can be used to retrieve instances from a table. It points at the first accessible columnar object in a conceptual row of the specified table.

4.2.10. ROWSTATUS

The RowStatus TC defines the row status data type. It is an enumerated value that can have the value of *active, notInService, notReady, createAndGo, createAndWait,* or *destroy.* This textual convention is used for creating, deleting, and modifying the rows in a table in a controlled fashion so that the integrity of the contents of a row can be maintained.

4.2.11. TIMESTAMP

The TimeStamp TC defines the value of `sysUpTime` at the time the event occurs—that is, the number of hundredths of a second (TimeTicks) since the agent was last reinitialized.

4.2.12. TIMEINTERVAL

The TimeInterval TC defines the time in hundredths of a second between two discrete events. The time interval is often referred to as an *epoch*.

4.2.13. DATEANDTIME

The DateAndTime TC defines the date and time data type. Figure 4-19 shows the fields, size, contents, and range of the fields.

Field	Octet	Contents	Range
1	1 – 2	year	0..65536
2	3	month	1..12
3	4	day	1..31
4	5	hour	0..23
5	6	minutes	0..59
6	7	seconds (use 60 for leap-second)	0..60
7	8	deci-seconds	0..9
8	9	direction from UTC	'+' | '-'
9	10	hours from UTC	0..11
10	11	minutes from UTC	0..59

Figure 4-19. Date and Time Textual Convention Format

The length is either 8 octets or 11 octets. The long form is used if information on time zones is included; the short form is used for local time. The acronym UTC is from the ASN.1 specification, and it stands for Universal Time (Coordinated). It has the same meaning as Greenwich Mean Time and is used for calculating time zones.

4.2.14. STORAGETYPE

The StorageType TC defines the type of memory storage used by the agent. It is an enumerated value that can have the value of *other, volatile, nonVolatile, permanent,* or *readOnly.* The storage type indicates the "lifetime" and the modifiability characteristics of the management information at the agent. For instance, if the management information is stored in non-volatile, permanent, or read only memory, it will persist after the node has been rebooted.

4.2.15. TDOMAIN

The TDomain TC defines the transport domain data type by specifying the OID for the relevant transport service. Choices include UDP, OSI connection-less network service (CLNS), OSI connection-oriented network service (CONS), Apple DDP, and Novell IPX.

4.2.16. TADDRESS

The TAddress TC defines transport address data type. Since many different formats exist for transport level addresses, this data type is expressed with a string that can contain 1 to 255 octets.

4.3. SMIV2 CONFORMANCE STATEMENTS

The SMIv2 Conformance Statements define the acceptable lower bounds and the actual level of implementation. The notation for these statements are detailed in RFC 1904, *Conformance Statements for Version 2 of the Simple Network Management Protocol (SNMPv2)*. The notation relies on the four macros defined in the RFC and discussed earlier in this chapter:

◆ The OBJECT-GROUP macro

◆ The NOTIFICATION-GROUP macro

◆ The MODULE-COMPLIANCE macro

◆ The AGENT-CAPABILITIES macro

The conformance statements introduced with SMIv2 have greatly aided in the documentation and maintenance of MIB modules and in manager and agent implementations.

4.4. SMI VERSION 2 DEFINITION

Figure 4-20 contains the formal definition for the draft standard version 2 of SMI as presented in RFC 1902, *Structure of Management Information for Version 2 of the Simple Network Management Protocol (SNMPv2)*. Notice that this listing contains the definitions of the MODULE-IDENTITY, OBJECT-IDENTITY, OBJECT-TYPE, and NOTIFICATION-TYPE macros discussed earlier in this chapter.

```
SNMPv2-SMI DEFINITIONS ::= BEGIN

-- the path to the root

org             OBJECT IDENTIFIER ::= { iso 3 }
dod             OBJECT IDENTIFIER ::= { org 6 }
internet        OBJECT IDENTIFIER ::= { dod 1 }

directory       OBJECT IDENTIFIER ::= { internet 1 }

mgmt            OBJECT IDENTIFIER ::= { internet 2 }
mib-2           OBJECT IDENTIFIER ::= { mgmt 1 }
transmission    OBJECT IDENTIFIER ::= { mib-2 10 }

experimental    OBJECT IDENTIFIER ::= { internet 3 }

private         OBJECT IDENTIFIER ::= { internet 4 }
enterprises     OBJECT IDENTIFIER ::= { private 1 }

security        OBJECT IDENTIFIER ::= { internet 5 }

snmpV2          OBJECT IDENTIFIER ::= { internet 6 }

-- transport domains
snmpDomains     OBJECT IDENTIFIER ::= { snmpV2 1 }

-- transport proxies
snmpProxys      OBJECT IDENTIFIER ::= { snmpV2 2 }

-- module identities
snmpModules     OBJECT IDENTIFIER ::= { snmpV2 3 }


-- definitions for information modules

MODULE-IDENTITY MACRO ::=
BEGIN
    TYPE NOTATION ::=
                "LAST-UPDATED" value(Update UTCTime)
                "ORGANIZATION" Text
                "CONTACT-INFO" Text
                "DESCRIPTION" Text
                RevisionPart

    VALUE NOTATION ::=
                value(VALUE OBJECT IDENTIFIER)
```

Figure 4-20. SMI Version 2 Formal Definition

```
     RevisionPart ::=
                    Revisions
                  | empty
     Revisions ::=
                    Revision
                  | Revisions Revision
     Revision ::=
                    "REVISION" value(Update UTCTime)
                    "DESCRIPTION" Text

     -- uses the NVT ASCII character set
     Text ::= """" string """"
END


OBJECT-IDENTITY MACRO ::=
BEGIN
     TYPE NOTATION ::=
                    "STATUS" Status
                    "DESCRIPTION" Text
                    ReferPart
     VALUE NOTATION ::=
                    value(VALUE OBJECT IDENTIFIER)

     Status ::=
                    "current"
                  | "deprecated"
                  | "obsolete"

     ReferPart ::=
                    "REFERENCE" Text
                  | empty

     Text ::= """" string """"
END


-- names of objects

ObjectName ::=
     OBJECT IDENTIFIER

NotificationName ::=
     OBJECT IDENTIFIER

-- syntax of objects

ObjectSyntax ::=
     CHOICE {
         simple
             SimpleSyntax,

          -- note that SEQUENCEs for conceptual tables and
          -- rows are not mentioned here...

         application-wide
             ApplicationSyntax
     }


-- built-in ASN.1 types
```

Figure 4-20. SMI Version 2 Formal Definition *(continued)*

```
SimpleSyntax ::=
    CHOICE {
        -- INTEGERs with a more restrictive range
        -- may also be used
        integer-value             -- includes Integer32
            INTEGER (-2147483648..2147483647),
-- OCTET STRINGs with a more restrictive size
        -- may also be used
        string-value
            OCTET STRING (SIZE (0..65535)),

        objectID-value
            OBJECT IDENTIFIER
    }


-- indistinguishable from INTEGER, but never needs more than
-- 32-bits for a two's complement representation
Integer32 ::=
    [UNIVERSAL 2]
        IMPLICIT INTEGER (-2147483648..2147483647)


-- application-wide types

ApplicationSyntax ::=
    CHOICE {
        ipAddress-value
            IpAddress,

        counter-value
            Counter32,

        timeticks-value
            TimeTicks,

        arbitrary-value
            Opaque,

        big-counter-value
            Counter64,

        unsigned-integer-value  -- includes Gauge32
            Unsigned32
    }

-- in network-byte order
-- (this is a tagged type for historical reasons)
IpAddress ::=
    [APPLICATION 0]
        IMPLICIT OCTET STRING (SIZE (4))

-- this wraps
Counter32 ::=
[APPLICATION 1]
        IMPLICIT INTEGER (0..4294967295)

-- this doesn't wrap
Gauge32 ::=
    [APPLICATION 2]
        IMPLICIT INTEGER (0..4294967295)
```

Figure 4-20. SMI Version 2 Formal Definition *(continued)*

137

```
-- an unsigned 32-bit quantity
-- indistinguishable from Gauge32
Unsigned32 ::=
    [APPLICATION 2]
        IMPLICIT INTEGER (0..4294967295)

-- hundredths of seconds since an epoch
TimeTicks ::=
    [APPLICATION 3]
        IMPLICIT INTEGER (0..4294967295)

-- for backward-compatibility only
Opaque ::=
    [APPLICATION 4]
        IMPLICIT OCTET STRING

-- for counters that wrap in less than one hour with only 32 bits
Counter64 ::=
    [APPLICATION 6]
        IMPLICIT INTEGER (0..18446744073709551615)


-- definition for objects

OBJECT-TYPE MACRO ::=
BEGIN
    TYPE NOTATION ::=
                    "SYNTAX" Syntax
                    UnitsPart
                    "MAX-ACCESS" Access
                    "STATUS" Status
                    "DESCRIPTION" Text
                    ReferPart
                    IndexPart
                    DefValPart

    VALUE NOTATION ::=
                    value(VALUE ObjectName)

    Syntax ::=
                    type(ObjectSyntax)
                  | "BITS" "{" Kibbles "}"
    Kibbles ::=
                    Kibble
                  | Kibbles "," Kibble
    Kibble ::=
                    identifier "(" nonNegativeNumber ")"

    UnitsPart ::=
                    "UNITS" Text
                  | empty

    Access ::=
                    "not-accessible"
                  | "accessible-for-notify"
                  | "read-only"
                  | "read-write"
                  | "read-create"

    Status ::=
                    "current"
```

Figure 4-20. SMI Version 2 Formal Definition *(continued)*

```
                         | "deprecated"
                         | "obsolete"

     ReferPart ::=
                         "REFERENCE" Text
                       | empty

     IndexPart ::=
                         "INDEX"      "{" IndexTypes "}"
                       | "AUGMENTS" "{" Entry       "}"
                       | empty
     IndexTypes ::=
                         IndexType
                       | IndexTypes "," IndexType
     IndexType ::=
                         "IMPLIED" Index
                       | Index
     Index ::=
                            -- use the SYNTAX value of the
                            -- correspondent OBJECT-TYPE invocation
                         value(Indexobject ObjectName)
     Entry ::=
                            -- use the INDEX value of the
                            -- correspondent OBJECT-TYPE invocation
                         value(Entryobject ObjectName)

     DefValPart ::=
"DEFVAL" "{" value(Defval Syntax) "}"
                       | empty

     -- uses the NVT ASCII character set
     Text ::= """" string """"
END

-- definitions for notifications

NOTIFICATION-TYPE MACRO ::=
BEGIN
     TYPE NOTATION ::=
                         ObjectsPart
                         "STATUS" Status
                         "DESCRIPTION" Text
                         ReferPart

     VALUE NOTATION ::=
                         value(VALUE NotificationName)

     ObjectsPart ::=
                         "OBJECTS" "{" Objects "}"
                       | empty
     Objects ::=
                         Object
                       | Objects "," Object
     Object ::=
                         value(Name ObjectName)

     Status ::=
                         "current"
                       | "deprecated"
                       | "obsolete"
```

Figure 4-20. SMI Version 2 Formal Definition *(continued)*

```
    ReferPart ::=
                "REFERENCE" Text
              | empty

    -- uses the NVT ASCII character set
    Text ::= """" string """"
END

-- definitions of administrative identifiers

zeroDotZero    OBJECT-IDENTITY
    STATUS     current
    DESCRIPTION
            "A value used for null identifiers."
    ::= { 0 0 }

END
```

Figure 4-20. SMI Version 2 Formal Definition *(continued)*

REFERENCES FOR CHAPTER 4

[1] Bartlett, John. *Familiar Quotations.* 15th ed. Boston: Little, Brown, and Co. 1980.

[2] Andrews, Robert. *The Columbia Dictionary of Quotations.* New York: Columbia University Press. 1993.

[3] Information Processing Systems-Open Systems Interconnection. "Specification of Abstract Syntax Notation One (ASN.1)." International Organization for Standardization, International Standard 8824. 1987.

[4] Rose, Marshall. *The Simple Book: An Introduction to Networking Management.* Upper Saddle River, NJ: Prentice Hall. 1996.

CHAPTER

5

The SNMP Version 1 Protocol

Cultivate simplicity, Coleridge. (letter to Coleridge, Nov. 8, 1796)

—Charles Lamb[1]

Beauty of style and harmony and grace and good rhythm depend on simplicity.

—Plato[2]

The SNMP network management protocol is the second key SNMP component. It is the application level protocol for allowing the Network Management Station to read-retrieve, get, or fetch—and write-alter, set, or store—the managed objects in each agent's MIB. It also defines the trap mechanism that allows an agent to transmit unsolicited alarm messages for certain predefined conditions. The protocol defines the message formats for commands and responses and also delineates authentication and authorization schemes used by the administrative framework.

This chapter introduces the protocol for SNMP version 1. The SNMP Extensions Working Group who wrote RFC 1157, *Simple Network Management Pro-*

tocol (*SNMP*), identified three major goals for the protocol architecture that they specified in the RFC:

1. minimize the number and complexity of management functions (lower agent development cost, lower internetwork resource requirements, fewer restrictions on management tools format and development).
2. design should be extensible to handle future needs of the network's operation and management.
3. architecture should be independent of other network devices (such as gateways and hosts) and vendor-specific issues, and implementation details as much as possible.

All communications using the protocol use the ASN.1 subset as defined by the SMI. The protocol uses a subset of the Basic Encoding Rules by specifying that only the definite-length form be used. Also, the non-constructor format is preferable over the constructor encoding whenever possible.

The network management stations and the agents use the protocol to communicate by exchanging SNMP Messages. In keeping with the SNMP goal of simplicity, UDP is specified as the transport protocol of choice. Due to SNMP's other goal of extensibility, other transport services can, and are being used, although UDP remains the recommended transport service and should be used if available. Every SNMP message must fit into a single UDP datagram. The standard specifies that any implementation is not required to receive messages greater than 484 octets (3872 bits), although a design should accommodate the largest UDP datagram possible.

The NMS and the agents receive all the SNMP Messages except the `Trap-PDU` at well-defined UDP port 161 of the socket interface. The `Trap-PDU` SNMP Messages are received by the NMS at well-defined UDP port 162.

5.1. AUTHENTICATION AND AUTHORIZATION

The SNMP administrative concerns involve the valid authentication and proper authorization of communicating NMSs and agents. Authentication is the process of checking and verifying the message sender's identity. Authorization is the check of the access-level for a particular authenticated message received by the agent.

SNMP uses a trivial authentication mechanism. This technique is simple and easy to implement but offers the barest of protection against malicious or erroneous SNMP messages. The key component of a trivial authentication scheme is the use of a community name. A community name is a string that represents the set of NMSs and agents that belong to a common and known group. While the community name can be a string of octets with any value, it is usually represented as a string of printable ASCII characters. The default community name often included in agent implementations is the string *public*. By including a default sting such as this, unknown managers can "browse" the agent's MIB.

An agent receives a command. When it checks the community field, it does a string compare operation of the community name field in the received message against the community name string stored in its configuration. If they match, the message is considered authentic by the protocol and is passed on for further processing. If the two strings are not successfully compared, the received message is discarded. Note that the string compare operation is case-sensitive and that the NMS's and agent's community names must match exactly for successful authentication.

A great deal of research and proposals are making an effort to implement less trivial, more secure authentication schemes based on keys, encryption, keyed-authentication, and several other security schemes. These efforts have not reached the SNMP standard as of this writing. As you see in Chapter 6, the current draft version of SNMPv2 still relies on this trivial authentication scheme defined in RFC 1157 (which is, ahem, over six years old!).

Once the SNMP message has been authenticated, the level of access then needs to be determined. Every member of the community knows which objects in the MIB can be accessed by other members. This group of objects is referred to as the view. Two access modes for the objects are in the view: read-only and read-write. By creating a matrix of these access modes and the access modes of the objects defined in the MIB-read-only, read-write, write-only, and not-accessible-the allowable SNMP operations can be listed. This table is called the community profile. Figure 5-1 lays out this matrix.

The SNMP operations get, get-next, set, and trap are embedded in the SNMP Message.

	MIB Object read-only	MIB Object read-write	MIB Object write-only	MIB Object not-accessible
community access mode read-only	get get-next trap	get get-next trap	no operations allowed	no operations allowed
community access mode read-write	get get-next trap	get, get-next set trap	get, get-next set trap	no operations allowed

Figure 5-1. Community Profiles

5.2. THE SNMP MESSAGE

The protocol specifies the command and response messages that can be used for the various dialogues between an NMS and its agents. Every command and response is an independent SNMPv1 message. Figure 5-2 shows the message and its fields.

The message field contains three required sub-fields:

◆ The Version Field

◆ The SNMP Community Name Field

◆ The Protocol Data Unit (PDU)

The Version Field is used for SNMP compatibility. The version number for version 1, according to RFC 1157, is *version-1*. When implemented, the version field is an integer type with value 0. SNMP version checking is a simple

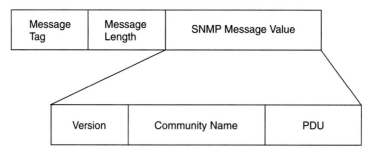

Figure 5-2. The SNMPv1 Message

144

mechanism that does not allow for any negotiation. If the version field of a received message is incorrect, the message is discarded.

The Community Name Field is the octet string that contains the community name used in the authentication process. An agent contains a list of valid community strings and checks the received SNMP message's community string against its list. If a match occurs, the message is processed. If no match occurs, the message is discarded. Each agent can be configured to send out the `authenticationFailure` trap to its correspondent NMSs if the community string is invalid.

SNMPv1 specifies that the Protocol Data Unit must be one of five supported types:

◆ GetRequest-PDU

◆ GetNextRequest-PDU

◆ GetResponse-PDU

◆ SetRequest-PDU

◆ Trap-PDU

The SNMPv1 Message is defined in the ASN.1 format as shown by Figure 5-3.

Note that SNMP version 1 supports only five PDUs. The choice to limit the command/response set is for reasons of simplicity and implementation ease. The bulk of the complexity and resource requirements are in the manager. The agent requires only a minimal implementation, fostering widespread implementations for a variety of devices.

In SNMP the imperative commands (get, get-next, and set) and the response command (get-response) contain a common structure. In SNMPv1, the `Trap-PDU` has a slightly different structure due to the information that it must contain.

Figure 5-4 shows the common structure for these four PDUs and the four fields that each contains:

◆ The Request ID Field

◆ The Error Status Field

◆ The Error Index Field

◆ The Variable Bindings List

Figure 5-5 shows the ASN.1 definition for these common constructs.

```
    -- top-level message

        Message ::=
            SEQUENCE {
                version         -- version-1 for RFC 1157
                    INTEGER {
                        version-1(0)
                    },

                community       -- community name
                    OCTET STRING,
                data            -- e.g., PDUs if trivial
                    ANY         -- authentication is being used
            }

    -- protocol data units

        PDUs :: =
            CHOICE {
                get-request
                    GetRequest-PDU,

                get-next-request
                    GetNextRequest-PDU,

                get-response
                    GetResponse-PDU,

                set-request
                    SetRequest-PDU,

                trap
                    Trap-PDU

            }
```

Figure 5-3. SNMPv1 Message ASN.1 Syntax

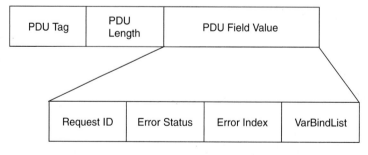

Figure 5-4. Common PDU Format

```
-- request/response information

RequestID ::=
        INTEGER

ErrorStatus ::=
        INTEGER {
            noError(0),
            tooBig(1),
            noSuchName(2),
            badValue(3),
            readOnly(4),
            genErr(5)
        }

ErrorIndex ::=
        INTEGER

-- variable bindings

VarBind :: =
        SEQUENCE  {
            name
                ObjectName,

            value
                ObjectSyntax
        }

VarBindList :: =
        SEQUENCE OF
            VarBind
```

Figure 5-5. Common PDU Format ASN.1 Syntax

The RequestID Field is an integer that numbers the requests sent from the NMS to the agent. This field is necessary for matching a subsequently received GetResponse-PDU from the agent. The onus of reliable SNMP message sequencing is solely on the management side. The RequestID field can handle the error condition of duplicate responses where two recently received responses have the same RequestID value, and the NMS can use a timer facility to gauge non-responses. An unknown RequestID would cause the NMS to discard the message.

The ErrorStatus Field is only used by the agent in sending a Get-Response-PDU. It indicates the status of the previous command. If it is non-zero, an error condition has occurred. In all other PDUs this field should have the value of *zero*.

Figure 5-6 shows the six values for the ErrorStatus field.

Like the ErrorStatus Field, the ErrorIndex Field is used in the Get-Response-PDU to provide more information on error conditions detected by

Status Name	Status Value
noError	0
tooBig	1
noSuchName	2
badValue	3
readOnly	4
genError	5

Figure 5-6. Error Status Field

the agent. The `ErrorIndex` points to the first variable in the Variable Bindings List that caused the error condition. Its value is the position of the variable within the list, starting at one.

The Variable Bindings List, often abbreviated as *VarBindList*, is the list of instances of the managed objects that are operated on by the message's command. SNMP allows the list to be a variable number of managed objects. The value field for each variable contains the Object Identifier Field and its corresponding value. Figure 5-7 shows the fields and the positions of the elements within the Variable Bindings List.

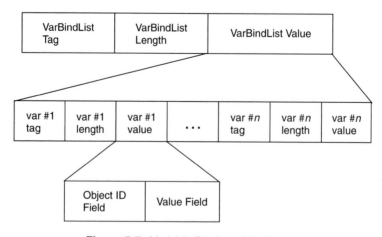

Figure 5-7. Variable Bindings List Format

The `Trap-PDU` has a different structure from the former four PDU types. The `Trap-PDU` has six mandatory fields for its format:

♦ The Enterprise Field

♦ The Agent Address Field

♦ The Generic Trap Field

♦ The Specific Trap Field

♦ The Time Stamp Field

♦ The Variable Bindings List

Figure 5-8 shows the six fields of the Trap-PDU used in SNMPv1.

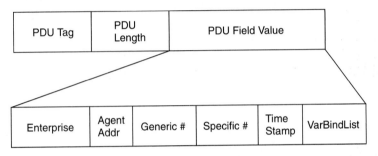

Figure 5-8. Trap-PDU Format

The Enterprise Field contains the Object Identifier for the network device generating the trap. This field is actually the `sysObjectID` in the System Group of its MIB (1.3.6.1.2.1.1.2); this name is akin to its SNMP name (more on this topic in Chapter 7).

The Agent Address Field is the agent's IP address. This further identifies the trap sender to the NMS that must receive and process the trap.

The Generic Trap Field contains an integer value that represents one of the standard predefined traps for SNMP. RFC 1157 defines seven generic traps:

1. coldStart

2. warmStart

3. linkDown

4. linkUp

5. authenticationFailure

6. egpNeighborLoss

7. enterpriseSpecific

The `enterpriseSpecific` trap indicates that the Specific Trap Field has an enterprise-specific trap and is further defined relative to the type of device it is. It is the protocol convention for providing a "hook" to allow vendors to define their own additional traps.

The Specific Trap Field contains that trap value defined for a particular enterprise. Note that this field is always present, even if the trap message is of the generic type. The values in the Specific Trap field are implementation-dependent and are defined in the vendor's MIB that is implemented for that device.

The Time Stamp Field contains the "time" the trap was generated. This value is the number of time ticks that have elapsed since the agent was initialized. This value is in units of hundredths of a second.

The Variable Bindings List contains supplemental implementation information when included in the Trap-PDU. Note that all five PDUs have in common the variable bindings list that contains the Object Identifiers for the managed objects with which a particular PDU deals. The variable bindings field contains "interesting information" associated with each generic or specific trap. This field contains zero or more variable binding pairs, which each contain an object name and the object value. The significance of the variable bindings list is implementation-specific, and its contents would be unique to each generic and specific trap. For example, for the standard `linkDown Trap-PDU`, the first element of its variable bindings is the name and value of the `ifIndex` instance. This informs the receiving manager the number of the interface whose link went down.

Now that I have explained the components of the SNMP message, I go on to examine each of the five PDU types in more detail.

5.2.1. THE GETREQUEST-PDU

The NMS uses the `GetRequest-PDU` to retrieve the specific values of the instances of known managed objects from the target agent's MIB. The valid response to this command is the `GetResponse-PDU` from the agent with the current values for those filled instances of the successful retrieval.

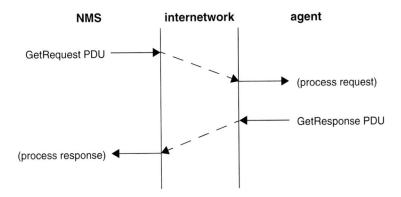

Figure 5-9. GetRequest Message

Figure 5-9 shows the NMS sending the `GetRequest-PDU`, having the agent process it, and then having the agent send the `GetResponse-PDU` for the NMS to process to complete the query.

The ASN.1 format of the `GetRequest-PDU` appears in Figure 5-10.

```
GetRequest-PDU ::=
    [0]
        IMPLICIT SEQUENCE {
            request-id
                RequestID,
            error-status        -- always 0
                ErrorStatus,
            error-index         -- always 0
                ErrorIndex,
            variable-bindings
                VarBindList
        }
```

Figure 5-10. GetRequest-PDU ASN.1 Format

The logic used by the agent in responding to the GetRequest command is very straightforward.

First, the agent verifies that each object specified in the variable bindings list of the command exists. Each object's access mode must be compatible: it must be either read-only or read-write. Attempting to read a non-accessible object, such as the aggregate types of a table name or entry (row definition), is incorrect. Another cause for an incorrect fetch is if the instrumentation code that retrieves the value detects an internal failure.

The first object that the agent encounters that is viewed as being incorrect, causes the agent to construct the `GetResponse-PDU` with the appropriate `errorStatus` and `errorIndex` fields set. If the agent cannot find an object, the `errorStatus` is set to *noSuchName*. If the object was an aggregate type, the `errorStatus` is also set to *noSuchName*. And if the instrumentation code detects a failure, *genErr* is the `errorStatus` used. The `errorIndex` field is set to the offset of the first object that caused the error.

The agent also can detect the failure condition for the case when the construction of an otherwise successful `GetResponse-PDU` results in a PDU of greater than maximum allowable SNMP message size. In this case the `GetResponse-PDU` is identical to the received `GetRequest-PDU`, except that the `errorStatus` is set to *tooBig* and the `errorIndex` field is assigned a value of *zero*.

If all of the managed object values are successfully found and retrieved, and the resulting `GetResponse-PDU` is of acceptable size, the `errorStatus` field is assigned the value of *noError* and the `errorIndex` field is set to *zero*.

In every case that the `GetResponse-PDU` is sent, the `requestID` field is set to the value retrieved from the corresponding previously received `GetRequest-PDU`. The message is then sent back to the NMS that originated the command.

Note that in SNMP version 1, if any error is indicated in the returned `GetResponse-PDU` to a get or a set operation, the entire contents in the Variable Bindings List are considered invalid and should not be referenced.

5.2.2. THE GETNEXTREQUEST-PDU

The format of the `GetNextRequest-PDU` is exactly the same as the `GetRequest-PDU`, except that the command number, called the *PDU type indication*, has a value of *one*. The ASN.1 format of the `GetNextRequest-PDU` appears in Figure 5-11.

Figure 5-12 shows the NMS sending the `GetNextRequest-PDU` across the internetwork and having the agent process it. The agent then sends the `GetResponse-PDU` that the NMS receives and processes to complete the query.

The `GetNextRequest` command is similar to `GetRequest`, except that the agent attempts to retrieve the lexicographically next larger value than the managed object instance requested. The use of this command is primarily for tree traversal and determining the elements of a table not known beforehand.

```
GetNextRequest-PDU ::=
    [1]
        IMPLICIT SEQUENCE {
            request-id
                RequestID,
            error-status        -- always 0
                ErrorStatus,
            error-index         -- always 0
                ErrorIndex,
            variable-bindings
                VarBindList
        }
```

Figure 5-11. GetNextRequest-PDU ASN.1 Format

It is the operation behind *MIB walking* or dynamically discovering an agent's MIB list that is seen when a MIB browser is invoked.

The agent verifies that an object lexicographically larger than the next object specified exists in the variable bindings list. The next managed object must have the proper access mode—read-only or read-write. If the instrumentation code that retrieves the value detects a failure, the agent records the error condition.

The first object the agent encounters that is viewed as being incorrect causes the agent to construct the `GetResponse-PDU` with the appropriate `error-Status` and `errorIndex` fields set. If the agent cannot find the next valid object, the `errorStatus` is set to *noSuchName*. If the instrumentation code detects a failure, the *genErr* `errorStatus` is used. The `errorIndex` field is set to the offset of the first object that caused the error.

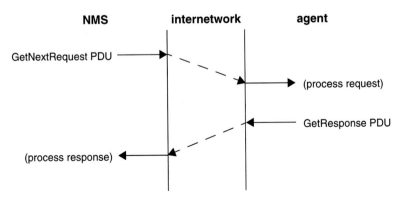

Figure 5-12. GetNextRequest Message

The agent can also detect the failure condition for the case when the construction of an otherwise successful GetResponse-PDU results in a PDU of greater than the maximum allowable SNMP message size. In this case the Get-Response-PDU is identical to the received GetNextRequest-PDU, except that the errorStatus is *tooBig* and the errorIndex field is assigned a zero value.

If all the managed object successor values are successfully found and retrieved, and the resulting GetResponse-PDU is of acceptable size, the errorStatus field is assigned the value of *noError* and the errorIndex field is set to zero. The variable bindings list of the GetResponse-PDU contains the variable name and value of the object representing the successor to each of the variable names requested. Each successor name and value represents the next object in the lexicographical ordering that has the proper access value for the particular MIB view.

In every case that the GetResponse-PDU is sent, the requestID field is set to the value found from the matching GetNextRequest-PDU received from the NMS. The message is then sent back to the NMS that originated the command.

The most often cited example for the use of the GetNextRequest operator is the traversal of the many tables of information stored within the agent's MIB.

The example scenario (taken from RFC 1157) shows how the GetNext-Request command can be used to retrieve the information in an agent's routing table. Three important variables in the table are: the destination, the next hop value, and the metric number. A sample routing table appears in Figure 5-13 with the MIB object name and their instantiated values for this example.

Destination (ipRouteDest)	Next Hop (ipRouteNextHop)	Metric (ipRouteMetric1)
10.0.0.99	89.1.1.42	5
9.1.2.3	99.0.0.3	3
10.0.0.51	89.1.1.42	5

Figure 5-13. Sample Routing Table

The exchange between the NMS and the agent appears in Figure 5-14. To start a table traversal, the NMS typically requests the objects with no instance

```
    NMS                                                      Agent

GetNextRequest(ipRouteDest, ipRouteNextHop, ipRouteMetric1)----->

              <----- GetResponse (( ipRouteDest.9.1.2.3 = "9.1.2.3" ),
                                  ( ipRouteNextHop.9.1.2.3 = "99.0.0.3" ),
                                  ( ipRouteMetric1.9.1.2.3 = 3 ))

GetNextRequest (ipRouteDest.9.1.2.3,
                ipRouteNextHop.9.1.2.3,
                ipRouteMetric1.9.1.2.3 )------>

              <-----GetResponse (( ipRouteDest.10.0.0.51 = "10.0.0.51" ),
                                 ( ipRouteNextHop.10.0.0.51 = "89.1.1.42" ),
                                 ( ipRouteMetric1.10.0.0.51 = 5 ))

GetNextRequest (ipRouteDest.10.0.0.51,
                ipRouteNextHop.10.0.0.51,
                ipRouteMetric1.10.0.0.51 )----->

              <-----GetResponse (( ipRouteDest.10.0.0.99 = "10.0.0.99" ),
                                 ( ipRouteNextHop.10.0.0.99 = "89.1.1.42" ),
                                 ( ipRouteMetric1.10.0.0.99 = 5 ))

GetNextRequest (ipRouteDest.10.0.0.99,
                ipRouteNextHop.10.0.0.99,
                ipRouteMetric1.10.0.0.99 )----->
```

Figure 5-14. GetNextRequest Example

value to be sure that the NMS will get returned the first value in the table. Also notice that the agent returns the table in order.

Because the routing table has been successfully traversed, the agent returns the successor names and values to the GetNextRequest variables. After the NMS examines the results of its fourth GetNextRequest, it is responsible for recognizing that the routing table has been entirely read by noticing that different object instances have been returned.

5.2.3. THE SETREQUEST-PDU

The format of the GetNextRequest-PDU is also exactly the same as the Get-Request-PDU, except that the command number has the value of *three*. The ASN.1 format of the SetRequest-PDU appears in Figure 5-15.

Figure 5-16 shows the NMS sending the SetRequest-PDU and having the agent process it. The agent then sends the GetResponse-PDU to the NMS who processes the returned information.

```
SetRequest-PDU ::=
    [3]
        IMPLICIT SEQUENCE {
            request-id
                RequestID,
            error-status            -- always 0
                ErrorStatus,
            error-index             -- always 0
                ErrorIndex,
            variable-bindings
                VarBindList
        }
```

Figure 5-15. SetRequest-PDU ASN.1 Format

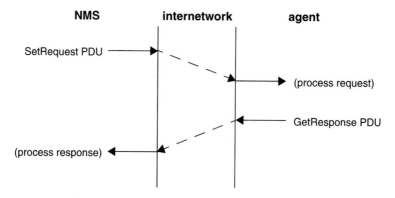

Figure 5-16. SetRequest Message

The `SetRequest-PDU` command is similar to the `GetRequest-PDU`, except that the agent attempts to set the value of the managed object instances specified instead of just reading it.

The agent verifies that each managed object exists and that it possesses a proper access mode of write-only or read-write. The ASN.1 format for the type, length, and value of the object must also be correct. If the instrumentation code that sets the value detects a failure, the agent records the error condition.

The first object the agent encounters that is viewed as being incorrect, causes the agent to construct the `GetResponse-PDU` with the appropriate `errorStatus` and `errorIndex` fields set. If the agent cannot find the object, the `errorStatus` is set to *noSuchName*. If the ASN.1 syntax was in error, the `errorStatus` of *badValue* is set in the response. If the instrumentation code detects a failure, the *genErr* errorStatus is used. The errorIndex field is set to the offset of the first object in the VarBindList that caused the error.

The agent can also detect the failure condition for the case when the construction of an otherwise successful GetResponse-PDU causes a PDU of greater than maximum allowable SNMP message size. In this case, the Get-Response-PDU is identical to the received SetRequest-PDU, except that the errorStatus is set to *tooBig* and the errorIndex field is assigned a value of zero.

If all the managed object values are successfully found and set, and the resulting GetResponse-PDU is of acceptable size, the errorStatus field is assigned the value of *noError* and the errorIndex field is set to zero. The variable bindings list of the GetResponse-PDU contains the variable name(s) and the new values for those objects.

Whether the resulting GetResponse-PDU indicates an error or not, the requestID field is set to the value saved from the SetRequest-PDU that initiated the request, and the message is then sent across the internetwork to the originating NMS.

5.2.4. THE GETRESPONSE-PDU

The format of the GetResponse-PDU is exactly the same as the Get-Request-PDU except that the command number has the value of *two*. The ASN.1 format of the GetResponse-PDU appears in Figure 5-17.

```
GetResponse-PDU ::=
    [2]
        IMPLICIT SEQUENCE {
            request-id
                RequestID,
            error-status
                ErrorStatus,
            error-index
                ErrorIndex,
            variable-bindings
                VarBindList
        }
```

Figure 5-17. GetResponse-PDU ASN.1 Format

The agent sends the GetResponse-PDU whenever it has processed a Get-Request-PDU, a GetNextRequest-PDU, or a SetRequest-PDU. The

NMS receiving the `GetResponse-PDU` needs to check the values of the fields in the message and then process the pertinent data.

The first field examined is the `requestID` field. It correlates the response to a previously sent command. Next, the `errorField` is checked to see if the command has been successful. If the error status in this field is *noError*, the variable bindings list is processed. If the error status is non-zero, the error is noted and logged. How the NMS handles `GetResponse` messages that report an error is an implementation detail.

Requests can be reattempted by omitting the incorrect variable in a multi-variable-request. Remember, the `errorIndex` field points to the first offending managed object that caused the error. This process can be reiterated until the NMS receives a valid response. If a request PDU contains one variable in the `VarBindList` and the response indicates a problem, the NMS must recognize that something is wrong with that particular request. If the error code was *tooBig*, a smaller request must be sent. The action an NMS must take can be determined by correctly interpreting the error status value in its context.

Figure 5-18 summarizes the various values for the different commands received.

GetResponse-PDU Error Fields				
command	error status	error index	meaning	action
GetRequest	noError	0	command successfully processed	[none]
GetRequest	noSuchName	offset of first variable in error	object does not exist; is aggregate type; wrong access code	verify object name and type; verify object is readable;
GetRequest	tooBig	0	response PDU too large	shorten VarBindList
GetRequest	genErr	offset of first variable in error	agent instrumentation routine failed	eliminate variable from VarBindList
GetNextRequest	noError	0	command successfully processed	[none]
GetNextRequest	noSuchName	offset of first variable in error	next object does not exist; wrong access code	verify object name; verify object is readable

Figure 5-18. GetResponse-PDU Error Fields

command	error status	error index	meaning	action
GetNextRequest	tooBig	0	response PDU too large	shorten VarBindList
GetNextRequest	genErr	offset of first variable in error	agent instrumentation routine failed	eliminate variable from VarBindList
SetRequest	noError	0	command successfully processed	[none]
SetRequest	noSuchName	offset of first variable in error	object does not exist; is aggregate type; wrong access code	verify object name and type; verify object is writeable
SetRequest	badValue	offset of first variable in error	incorrect ASN.1 type, length or value	correct ASN.1 encoding of variable
SetRequest	tooBig	0	response PDU too large	shorten VarBindList
SetRequest	genErr	offset of first variable in error	agent instrumentation routine failed	eliminate variable from VarBindList

Figure 5-18. GetResponse-PDU Error Fields *(continued)*

5.2.5. THE TRAP-PDU

Traps are asynchronous notifications an agent can send to the Network Management Station to inform the NMS of an extraordinary event. These extraordinary events are predefined in the MIB and must be known to both the agent and the NMS within the enterprise. Figure 5-19 shows the agent sending the `Trap-PDU` across the internetwork to the NMS for processing.

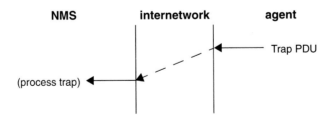

Figure 5-19. Trap Message

159

The SNMP standard has defined a core of seven generic trap messages. The way the trap design has been extended, however, is to have the seventh generic trap message, `enterpriseSpecific`, signal the examination of another field containing any number of defined specific traps that are designed and implemented expressly within the context of a particular enterprise. These enterprise-specific traps are defined in their respective MIB extensions.

The ASN.1 format of the Trap-PDU appears in Figure 5-20.

```
Trap-PDU ::=
    [4]
        IMPLICIT SEQUENCE {
            enterprise              -- type of object generating
                                    -- trap
                OBJECT IDENTIFIER,

            agent-addr              -- address of object generating
                NetworkAddress,     -- trap

            generic-trap            -- generic trap type
                INTEGER {
                    coldStart(0),
                    warmStart(1),
                    linkDown(2),
                    linkUp(3),
                    authenticationFailure(4),
                    egpNeighborLoss(5),
                    enterpriseSpecific(6)
                },

            specific-trap           -- specific code, present even
                INTEGER,            -- if generic-trap is not
                                    -- enterpriseSpecific

            time-stamp              -- time elapsed between the last
                TimeTicks,          -- (re)initialization of the network
                                    -- entity and the generation of the
                                    -- trap

            variable-bindings       -- "interesting" information
                VarBindList
        }
```

Figure 5-20. Trap PDU ASN.1 Foirmat

A Network Management Station can take two approaches to keeping abreast of the extraordinary, noteworthy events within the network:

◆ Interrupt-driven Reporting

◆ Polling

Interrupt-driven reporting is the sending of alarm messages in real-time as they occur at the agent station. The advantage of this approach is that notification is immediate, although it also has several disadvantages. Resources are needed at the agent for the generation of these trap messages, strict thresholds need to be implemented to prohibit excess network traffic, threshold checking can impede the agent's performance, and the agent is limited to its own view of the device.

Polling is the scheme whereby the NMS periodically asks each agent in its community whether it has any extraordinary events to report. The advantage of this approach is that the NMS knows the big picture of the enterprise network for its community. The polling is timely and intelligent. The disadvantage is that this polling takes time and resources and uses the network bandwidth.

The Internet-standard Network Management Framework model espouses the *trap-directed polling* paradigm. This approach is a hybrid of interrupt-driven reporting and polling.

When an extraordinary event occurs at the agent, the managed node usually sends a single, simple trap to the NMS. The NMS is then responsible for initiating further interactions with the agent on the managed node in order to determine the nature, time, and extent of the problem. This compromise is surprisingly effective. The impact on managed nodes remains small, the impact on the bandwidth is minimized, and problems can be dealt with in a timely fashion. Of course, because the traps are sent unreliably over UDP/IP, traps serve as an early warning. Low-frequency polling is often used by the NMS as a back-up scheme. Polling is also implemented at the NMS to keeps its topology map up-to-date.

5.2.5.1. Generic Traps

The generic trap field contains one of the traps predefined by SNMP. The seven traps defined for MIB-II are:

- **coldStart** (*0*): This trap signifies that the agent's device, called the *sending protocol entity*, is reinitializing itself such that the agent's configuration or the protocol entity implementation may be altered.

- **warmStart** (*1*): This trap signifies that the agent's device is reinitializing itself such that neither the agent's configuration nor the protocol entity implementation is altered.

- **linkDown** (*2*): This trap message signals that the agent's device recognizes a failure in one of the communication links represented in its configuration.

The `Trap-PDU` contains as the first element of its variable bindings, the name and value of the `ifIndex` instance for the affected interface.

◆ **linkUp** (3): This trap message signals that the agent's device recognizes that one of the communication links represented in the agent's configuration has come up. The `Trap-PDU` contains as the first element of its variable bindings, the name and value of the `ifIndex` instance for the affected interface.

◆ **authenticationFailure** (4): This trap signifies that the agent is the addressee of a protocol message that is not properly authenticated. Although implementations of the SNMP must be capable of generating this trap, they must also be capable of suppressing the emission of such traps through an implementation-specific mechanism such as a configuration parameter.

◆ **egpNeighborLoss** (5): This trap signifies that an Exterior Gateway Protocol (EGP) neighbor for whom the agent's device was an EGP peer has been marked down and the peer relationship no longer pertains. The first element in the variable bindings is the name and value of the `egpNeighAddr` instance for the affected neighbor.

◆ **enterpriseSpecific** (6): This trap signals that an agent has recognized that some predefined, enterprise-specific event has occurred. The specific-trap field identifies the particular trap that occurred.

5.2.5.2. *Specific Traps*

The specific trap field contains the predefined event known to both the agent and NMS implementations within the enterprise network. Many vendor MIBs contain specific traps implemented especially for their devices.

As an example, Figure 5-21 shows a specific trap defined for the Frame Relay MIB Group. This is taken from RFC 1315, *Management Information Base for Frame Relay DTEs*. It uses the Trap Macro template (TRAP-TYPE) for defining the fields and values of specific traps. Note that three variables are expected to be in the variable bindings list: the frame relay circuit interface index, the circuit DLCI, and the circuit state. Its specific trap value is 1.

5.2.5.3. *The Trap Macro*

In March 1991, Marshall Rose edited RFC 1215, *A Convention for Defining Traps for Use with the SNMP*. This RFC presents a concise and uniform format for de-

```
frDLCIStatusChange TRAP-TYPE
    ENTERPRISE frame-relay
    VARIABLES  { frCircuitIfIndex, frCircuitDlci, frCircuitState }
    DESCRIPTION
        "This trap indicates that the indicated Virtual Circuit has
        changed state. It has either been created or invalidated, or
        has toggled  between the active and inactive states."
    ::= 1
```

Figure 5-21. Example of a Specific Trap

fining traps. It is an Informational Standard but generally accepted as the proper way to define traps and to include the trap definitions into the MIB.

Figure 5-22 shows the template for this macro.

```
TRAP-TYPE MACRO ::=
BEGIN
  TYPE NOTATION ::= "ENTERPRISE" value
                   (enterprise OBJECT IDENTIFIER)
                   VarPart
                   DescrPart
                   ReferPart
  VALUE NOTATION ::= value (VALUE INTEGER)

  VarPart ::=
           "VARIABLES" "{" VarTypes "}"
             | empty
  VarTypes ::=
           VarType | VarTypes "," VarType
  VarType ::=
           value (vartype ObjectName)

  DescrPart ::=
           "DESCRIPTION" value (description DisplayString)
             | empty

  ReferPart ::=
           "REFERENCE" value (reference DisplayString)
             | empty

END
```

Figure 5-22. Trap Macro

5.3. HOW THE PROTOCOL WORKS

In preparation for the discussion on the implementation aspects of the protocol, an appropriate introduction is to present a quick overview of how the NMS and agent operate with regards to how the protocol is used.

From the point of view of the NMS, a command initiates the construction of an SNMP request. This operation may be a set, a get, or a get-next type of request. The NMS software creates an SNMP message by filling in the appropriate header values needed for transmitting the message over the internetwork to the destination agent. It assigns the community name, version number, and request ID. The PDU type is chosen and the members of the variable binding list are inserted into the message. The SNMP message is delivered to the UDP transport layer for transmission. The message is sent. The NMS must remember the request ID it has inserted in the request, in order to pair a response it should subsequently receive. Timers are also started to handle time-out conditions. At any time, the NMS must be prepared to receive and process traps sent by agents in its community.

After initializing, agents are waiting to receive the SNMP messages at the destination network device's UDP transport port 161. After the agent successfully receives a message, it calls its parse routine to decode the ASN.1 format into a more usable internal format.

If the message is in improper ASN.1 format, it is discarded and the agent simply returns to its wait loop. The next step is verifying the version number. If it is incorrect, this message is also discarded and the agent returns to wait for the next message.

After the message has successfully passed these first two checks, the authentication function is then called to verify the message. If it fails here and the agent has the ability to send the `authenticationFailure` trap message, the trap is sent and the message is discarded. If the message is authentic, the transport information is saved for the response message and the agent is now ready to continue decoding the SNMP message.

While the agent is decoding the ASN.1 format of the message, it can now start building a `GetResponse-PDU` for the reply. At this point any error condition does not cause the incoming message to be discarded, but rather the `GetResponse-PDU` indicates the cause of the failure. The error information is inserted into the `ErrorStatus` and `ErrorIndex` fields.

The decoding functions examine all the fields in the message and check for proper ordering and the tag, length, and value of the fields. If the format is valid, the command is executed by having its operation applied to the variables in the variable bindings list. The instrumentation routines of the agent determine whether the variable instance exists, whether the NMS is authorized for the requested access level, and how to access the variable for the requested operation.

After the agent completes filling in the `GetResponse-PDU`, it encodes the message into ASN.1, presents it to the UDP transport service for transmission to the requesting NMS, and returns to its wait loop. All of the proper variables the agent uses to record its operation, such as the objects about SNMP itself, have been properly incremented for later inspection by the NMS.

5.4. TABLE HANDLING

Although I defer the specifics of how the variables are represented in the MIB to Chapter 7, I do want to introduce the topic of table handling. A table is a very important construct for storing variables in SNMP.

A table is defined as having zero or more rows. Each row comprises variables of interest called *columnar objects*. Key variables must be present in each row to define a unique index so that the row may be properly accessed. This index can comprise one or more variables. Also present in each row must be a variable that contains the row's state or *status*. This is the mediating value in determining whether the contents of the row are valid or not.

The row index and status are used for table handling. The following quotation from RFC 1212, *Concise MIB Definitions*, comments that for SNMPv1, you need to understand the structure of the table to effectively retrieve information from it.

"However, it must be emphasized that, at the protocol level, relationships among columnar objects in the same row is a matter of convention, not of protocol.

Note that there are good reasons why the tabular structure is not a matter of protocol. Consider the operation of the SNMP Get-Next-PDU acting on the last columnar object of an instance of a conceptual row; it returns the next column of the first conceptual row or the first object instance occurring after the table. In contrast, if the rows were a matter of protocol, then it would instead return an error. By not returning an error, a single PDU exchange informs the manager that not only has the end of the conceptual row/table been reached, but also provides information on the next object instance, thereby increasing the information density of the PDU exchange."

Two basic operations can be done on a table. A row can be created or it can be deleted. The operation of reading an entire table as one logical operation, called *bulk table retrieval*, is also an important concept for effective network management.

5.4.1. ROW CREATION

Since the definition of a row for any particular table is defined in the MIB, the NMS can create a new row by sending a `SetRequest-PDU` with the `VarBindList`, filled in with the appropriate columnar objects and their values. The agent implementation, however, could react in any of three ways, each acceptable within the confines of the protocol:

1. The simple agent can refuse the `SetRequest-PDU` because the row specified does not exist. It then sends a `GetResponse-PDU` with the `ErrorStatus` field set to *noSuchName* and the `ErrorIndex` set appropriately.

2. The more complex agent implementation can process the set command by recognizing that the request is for the creation of a new row. Each specified variable from the bindings list is then instantiated with the assigned value found in the command. Here again, if the agent determines that the value to be assigned is incorrect, the `GetResponse-PDU` contains an `ErrorStatus` of *badValue* and the `ErrorIndex` points at the improperly assigned variable.

3. The most complex agent implementation allows rows to be created with a minimal number of variables needed in the `SetRequest-PDU`. Column objects not present in the variable bindings list are instantiated automatically and then assigned default values.

The issue of validating initial row variable values also involves deciding when to check and when to notify the NMS of an error. Two opportunities exist to do validity checking—when the management station sets each parameter object, or when the management station sets the entry status object to valid. The former choice is preferred because the `ErrorStatus` returned directly indicates the first row object initialized in error.

The problem of multiple NMSs creating and deleting rows of the same table must also be considered. A status entry is needed whereby an attempt to create the same row more than once returns an error.

5.4.2. ROW DELETION

The column state variable conceptually deletes a row from a table. This variable typically is an enumerated value that can be either *valid* or *invalid*. This variable should always be the first field examined by the NMS when it retrieves a row. If this variable has the value *invalid*, the values of the other objects in a particular row should not be considered. Whether an agent actually deletes a row by resetting it contents when the status object for the row has been set to *invalid* is an implementation issue.

5.4.3. BULK TABLE RETRIEVAL

Bulk table retrieval is the process of requesting the contents of an entire table. The brute force method for this operation is to determine the start of a table and then send `GetNextRequest-PDUs` until the entire table is retrieved. This approach is very inefficient, and several methods have been suggested for improving the performance and elegance of this operation. Two methods were put forth in RFC 1187, *Bulk Table Retrieval with the SNMP*. They are:

- pipelined algorithm
- parallel algorithm

The first method starts several `GetNext` requests concurrently, and then correlates the responses for efficient table reading. The second algorithm combines more than one `GetNextRequest` into an SNMP message.

A third proposal for a more efficient retrieval method is discussed in the first issue of *The Simple Times* in an article called "A New View on Bulk Retrieval with SNMP."[3] The method involves the use of experimental extensions. This proposal advocates the use of a new operator called the `GetColumn` primitive for use with SNMP over TCP.

SNMP version 2 has seen bulk table retrieval as an area that needed addressing in order to make the protocol more efficient. Its solution is the creation of a new protocol command for reading tables, the `GetBulkRequest-PDU` operator. I discuss the specifics of this operator and how it works Chapter 6 (Section 6.2.5 *The GetBulkRequest-PDU*).

5.5. THE PROTOCOL DEFINITION

The discussion of the protocol would not be complete without including a listing of the standard specification from RFC 1157, *Simple Network Management Protocol (SNMP)*. Due to the length of the specification, I have added the listing as Appendix B, Section B.1, *The SNMPv1 Protocol Specification*.

REFERENCES FOR CHAPTER 5

[1] The *Oxford Dictionary of Quotations (4th ed)*. Oxford, UK: Oxford University Press. 1992.

[2] Tripp, Rhonda Thomas (compiler). *The International Thesaurus of Quotations*. New York: Thomas Y. Crowell Company.

[3] Satz, Greg L. "A New View on Bulk Retrieval with SNMP." *The Simple Times*. Vol 1, No. 1. March/April 1992: 1-4.

CHAPTER

6

The SNMP Version 2 Protocol

Manifest plainness,
Embrace simplicity,
Reduce selfishness,
Have few desires.

—Lao-tzu[1]

When a thought is too weak to be expressed simply, it should be rejected.
—Luc, Marquis de Vauvenargues[2]

The SNMP version 2 protocol builds upon the Version 1 protocol. Like Version 1, the SNMPv2 management protocol transfers the management information as SNMP messages between the v2 management station and its agents. In addition to the SNMPv2 message format modifications, a new message has been added to introduce the capability of transferring information between managers. The SNMPv2 message contains a message wrapper that is comprised of a header portion and a data portion. The data portion is called the protocol data unit (PDU). The set of rules defined for this version of the protocol is specified in RFC 1905, *Protocol Operations for Version 2 of the Simple Network Management Protocol (SNMPv2)*.

In addition to protocol operation modification, the current draft version of SNMPv2 represents the use of the new v2 SMI and MIB improvements. The key point to understand is that this version of SNMPv2 based on RFCs 1902-1908 does not include a new administrative framework. It uses the same community-based administrative framework defined for SNMPv1 and is therefore often referred to as SNMPv2c: community-based SNMP version 2. The fact that the Version 1 administrative framework is retained means that the message wrapper format remains unchanged for this version 2, and the only quantitative difference is that the version value in the header is 1, instead of 0. The manager and the agents still receive all the SNMP messages (except the trap) at the well-defined UDP port 161. The SNMP Message with the SNMPv2-Trap-PDU is received at the well-defined UDP port 162.

The major impetus for SNMPv2c is to allow the SMI, MIB, and protocol improvements to be deployed while the debate over the issues of security, a new administrative framework, remote configuration, and other additions continues.

6.1. AUTHENTICATION AND AUTHORIZATION IN VERSION 2

The SNMPv2 uses the same authentication and authorization scheme used in Version 1. The trivial authentication mechanism uses the community name to verify that the request is from a known source. Once the SNMPv2 message has been authenticated, the level of access can be determined, if views have been configured that could limit a specific community's ability to read or write certain MIB variables.

6.2. THE SNMPV2 MESSAGE

Since SNMPv2 currently uses the SNMPv1 framework, its message format is also the same as Version 1. Figure 6-1 shows the SNMPv2 message and its fields.

The SNMPv2 message is defined in the ASN.1 format as shown by Figure 6-2. This definition is presented in RFC 1901, *Introduction to Community-based SNMPv2*. Note that this RFC is an experimental protocol because work is continuing for the specification of an updated SNMPv2 administration model that will contain a new ASN.1 definition of the top-level SNMP message wrapper. A new message wrapper will be required to support the new security features.

The message contains three required fields:

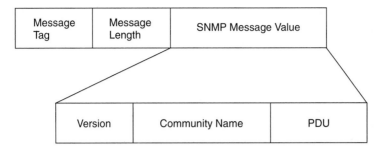

Figure 6-1. The SNMPv2 Message

```
-- top-level message

        Message ::=
                SEQUENCE {
                    version
                       INTEGER {
                         version(1)   -- modified from RFC 1157
                       },

                    community       -- community name
                       OCTET STRING,
                    data            -- e.g., SNMPv2PDUs
                         ANY
                }
```

Figure 6-2. The SNMPv2 Message ASN.1 Definition

◆ The Version Field

◆ The SNMP Community Name Field

◆ The Protocol Data Unit (PDU)

The Version Field for SNMPv2 messages must be set to a value of *1*.

The Community Name Field is the octet string that contains the community name used for the trivial authentication process. An agent may be configured with a list of valid community strings that can be used to check the received SNMP message's community string. If a match occurs, message processing continues. If no match occurs, the message is discarded. A trap may be sent out denoting that the community string was invalid. Each agent can be configured to send out the `authenticationFailure` trap to the managers on its list, in order to announce that this situation has occurred.

The PDUs are the data portion of the SNMP message that contains the command and the necessary associated data. A major improvement for this version

of SNMPv2 is that a consistent PDU format is introduced for all of the PDUs
(remember that in Version 1 the Trap PDU has a different layout). The consistent PDU format simplifies the processing of sending and receiving SNMP messages. For Version 2 eight PDU types now exist (seven, really, the `report-PDU`
and its use are still to be defined):

◆ `GetRequest-PDU`

◆ `GetNextRequest-PDU`

◆ `Response-PDU`

◆ `SetRequest-PDU`

◆ `GetBulkRequest-PDU`

◆ `InformRequest-PDU`

◆ `SNMPv2-Trap-PDU`

◆ `Report-PDU`

The SNMPv2 PDUs are defined in RFC 1905, *Protocol Operations for Version
2 of the Simple Network Management Protocol (SNMPv2)*, by using the ASN.1
CHOICE data structure. They appear in Figure 6-3.

```
-- protocol data units

PDUs ::=
    CHOICE {
        get-request
            GetRequest-PDU,

        get-next-request
            GetNextRequest-PDU,

        get-bulk-request
            GetBulkRequest-PDU,

        response
            Response-PDU,

        set-request
            SetRequest-PDU,

        inform-request
            InformRequest-PDU,

        snmpV2-trap
            SNMPv2-Trap-PDU,

        report
            Report-PDU,
    }
```

Figure 6-3. The SNMPv2 Protocol Data Units

Figure 6-4 shows the specific PDU values. The value of 4 (previously used to define the version 1 `Trap-PDU`) is now obsolete. The `Report-PDU` is defined but is currently not used in standard implementations.

```
-- PDUs

GetRequest-PDU ::=
    [0]
        IMPLICIT PDU

GetNextRequest-PDU ::=
    [1]
        IMPLICIT PDU

Response-PDU ::=
    [2]
        IMPLICIT PDU

SetRequest-PDU ::=
    [3]
        IMPLICIT PDU

-- [4] is obsolete

GetBulkRequest-PDU ::=
    [5]
        IMPLICIT BulkPDU

InformRequest-PDU ::=
    [6]
        IMPLICIT PDU

SNMPv2-Trap-PDU ::=
    [7]
        IMPLICIT PDU

--    Usage and precise semantics of Report-PDU are not presently
--    defined.  Any SNMP administrative framework making use of
--    this PDU must define its usage and semantics.
Report-PDU ::=
    [8]
        IMPLICIT PDU
```

Figure 6-4. The SNMPv2 Protocol Data Units

Figure 6-5 shows the specific ASN.1 syntax of the v2 PDU. Note the value of `max-bindings` is defined in the RFC 1905 as an INTEGER with a maximum value of *2,147,483,647*.

All seven SNMPv2 PDUs follow a common PDU format (the meanings of PDU field values, however, are different for the `GetBulkRequest-PDU`). Figure 6-6 shows the common structure for these six v2 PDUs and the four fields that they contain.

```
PDU ::=
    SEQUENCE {
        request-id
            Integer32,

        error-status                -- sometimes ignored
            INTEGER {
                noError(0),
                tooBig(1),
                noSuchName(2),      -- for proxy compatibility
                badValue(3),        -- for proxy compatibility
                readOnly(4),        -- for proxy compatibility
                genErr(5),
                noAccess(6),
                wrongType(7),
                wrongLength(8),
                wrongEncoding(9),
                wrongValue(10),
                noCreation(11),
                inconsistentValue(12),
                resourceUnavailable(13),
                commitFailed(14),
                undoFailed(15),
                authorizationError(16),
                notWritable(17),
                inconsistentName(18)
            },

        error-index               -- sometimes ignored
            INTEGER (0..max-bindings),

        variable-bindings    -- values are sometimes ignored
            VarBindList
    }


BulkPDU ::=                      -- MUST be identical in
    SEQUENCE {                   -- structure to PDU
        request-id
            Integer32,

        non-repeaters
            INTEGER (0..max-bindings),

        max-repetitions
            INTEGER (0..max-bindings),

        variable-bindings        -- values are ignored
            VarBindList
    }


-- variable binding

VarBind ::=
    SEQUENCE {
        name
            ObjectName,

        CHOICE {
```

Figure 6-5. The SNMPv2 PDU ASN.1 Syntax

174

```
            value
                ObjectSyntax,

            unSpecified            -- in retrieval requests
                    NULL,

                                   -- exceptions in responses
            noSuchObject[0]
                    IMPLICIT NULL,

            noSuchInstance[1]
                    IMPLICIT NULL,

            endOfMibView[2]
                    IMPLICIT NULL
        }
    }

-- variable-binding list

VarBindList ::=
    SEQUENCE (SIZE (0..max-bindings)) OF
        VarBind
```

Figure 6-5. The SNMPv2 PDU ASN.1 Syntax *(continued)*

- The Request ID Field
- The Error Status Field
- The Error Index Field
- The Variable Bindings List

The Request ID Field is an integer that numbers the requests sent from the NMS to the agent. This field is necessary for matching a subsequently received `Response-PDU` from the agent. The NMS can use a timer facility to gauge non-responses. The Request ID field is also used to handle the error condition of duplicate responses where two recently received responses have the same Request ID value.

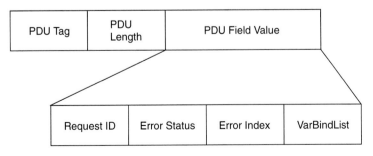

Figure 6-6. Common SNMPv2 PDU Format

The Error Status Field is set only when sending a `Response-PDU`. It indicates the status of the previous command. If it is non-zero, an error condition has occurred. In all other PDUs, this field should have the value of zero. The number of error conditions reported has been increased to provide better error reporting over Version 1, especially with regards to sets and the manipulation of rows in tables. The agent uses error codes 6-15 and 17-18 exclusively to report errors in a set operation. The Version 1 error codes were included for compatibility. Figure 6-7 shows the 19 values used for the Version 2 `ErrorStatus` field.

Name	Value	Description
noError	0	command successfully processed
tooBig	1	response PDU would be too large
noSuchName	2	not used; included for SNMPv1 compatibility
badValue	3	not used; included for SNMPv1 compatibility
readOnly	4	not used; included for SNMPv1 compatibility
genErr	5	internal agent error (instrumentation routine failed)
noAccess	6	variable not in community's view (access level)
wrongType	7	variable's ASN.1 data type does not match
wrongLength	8	variable's ASN.1 data length is incorrect
wrongEncoding	9	inconsistent ASN.1 encoding
wrongValue	10	variable's ASN.1 data value is not correct
noCreation	11	variable cannot be created
inconsistentValue	12	variable cannot be assigned a value
resourceUnavailable	13	allocation of resource needed to fulfill request not available
commitFailed	14	row commit operation failed for this variable
undoFailed	15	row undo operation failed for this variable
authorizationError	16	unrecognized community name
notWritable	17	variable cannot be created or modified
inconsistentName	18	variable cannot be created

Figure 6-7. Error Status Field

Like the Error Status Field, the Error Index Field is used in the Response-PDU to provide more information on detected error conditions. The Error Index points to the first variable in the Variable Bindings List that caused the error condition. Its value is the position of the variable within the list, starting at 1.

The Variable Bindings List, often abbreviated as "VarBindList," is the list of instances of the managed objects that are operated on by the message's command. SNMP allows the list to be a variable number of managed objects. The value field for each variable contains the Object Identifier Field and its corresponding value. Figure 6-8 shows the fields and the positions of the elements within the Variable Bindings List.

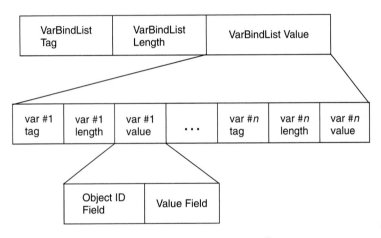

Figure 6-8. Variable Bindings List Format

The Value Field has been enhanced to allow the manager to check the validity of each individual returned value in the VarBindList. Remember, in Version 1, that a response was "atomic"; if any error was reported, the entire response had to be viewed as invalid, even if many entries were in the VarBindList and only one error.

The Version 2 protocol can now report either the requested value or an exception. The Value Fields and their descriptions appear in Figure 6-9.

As noted above, the GetBulkRequest-PDU has a similar format as the other PDUs, but the Error Status and Error Index fields have been replaced by the Non-Repeaters and Max-Repetitions fields. This replacement is required to specify the parameters needed for bulk retrieval. Figure 6-10 shows the PDU structure for the GetBulkRequest-PDU.

Value Field	Description
value	the request value (no error)
unspecified	a NULL value (used as placeholder value in a read operation)
noSuchObject	object is not implemented by the agent
noSuchInstance	instance not present at the agent
endOfMibView	no more instances (at the end of the MIB view)

Figure 6-9. Variable Bindings List Value Field

♦ The Request ID Field

♦ The Non-Repeaters Field

♦ The Max-Repetitions Field

♦ The Variable Bindings List

The Non-Repeaters field holds the number of variables that should be retrieved once, and the Max-Repetitions field contains the number of times that the remaining variables in the GetBulkRequest's VarBindList should be returned. The specifics of how the agent interprets these fields is discussed in the following section on this command. Notice that all of the other fields for this command have the same meaning as the SNMPv2 PDUs.

Now that I have explained the components of the SNMP message, examine each of the PDU types in more detail.

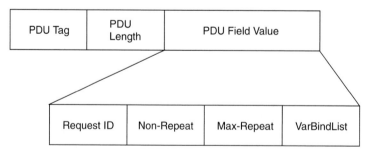

Figure 6-10. SNMPv2 PDU Format for GetBulkRequest-PDU

6.2.1. THE GETREQUEST-PDU

The NMS uses the `GetRequest-PDU` to retrieve the values of the specific instances of known managed objects from the target agent's MIB. This PDU is similar to Version 1. The response to this command is the `Response-PDU` from the agent with the current values for those instances filled in, if the retrievals were successful or value fields indicated otherwise.

The agent processes the `GetRequest-PDU` and then sends a `Response-PDU` back to the manager. The `GetRequest` requires that the variable instances requested in the `VarBindList` match exactly. The agent checks the object name and instance suffix for the match. If a match occurs, the agent places the value in the Value Field. If no match occurs for the object name prefix, the value field error is set to *noSuchObject*. If the object name matches, but the particular instance has not been found, the *noSuchInstance* value field error provides a finer error reporting.

If no errors occur, the Error Status field is set to *noError*. If an instance could not be found, the appropriate error status value is set and the Error Index points to the one-relative position of the error in the `VarBindList`. If the get request fails for any other error, the *genError* error status should be reported.

The only other possible error condition in creating the `Response-PDU` would be if the response generated a PDU that was too large to be sent. The *tooBig* error status indicates this problem. For this special exception, the Error Index is set to *0* and the response's `VarBindList` is empty. The RFC notes that in the strange case in which even this response is too large, the message is not sent but discarded. The `snmpSilentDrops` error counter is set. The NMS needs an error recovery procedure to handle the resulting time-out and see that this error counter has been incremented.

Figure 6-11 shows the NMS sending the GetRequest-PDU and the agent's actions.

6.2.2. THE GETNEXTREQUEST-PDU

The `GetNextRequest-PDU` is very similar to the command found in Version 1. The format of the `GetNextRequest-PDU` is exactly the same as the `GetRequest-PDU`, except that the command number, called the *PDU type indication*, has the value of *1*.

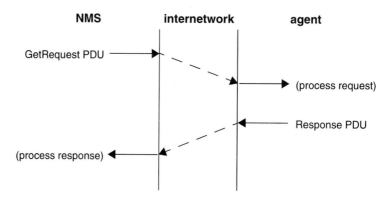

Figure 6-11. GetRequest Message

Figure 6-12 shows the NMS sending the GetNextRequest-PDU across the internetwork and having the agent process it. The agent then sends the Response-PDU and the NMS receives it and processes the Response-PDU.

The GetNextRequest command is a read-type command similar to the GetRequest, except that the agent attempts to retrieve the lexicographically next larger value than the managed object instance requests. The use of this command is primarily for tree traversal and determining the elements of a table not known beforehand. It is the operation behind MIB "browsing" or walking. This operator allows for the dynamic discovery of an agent's MIB list.

The agent verifies that an object exists that is lexicographically larger than the next object specified in the variable bindings list. The next managed object must have the proper access mode—read-only or read-write. Version 2 has the

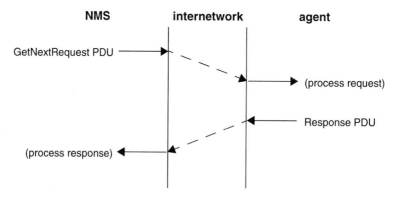

Figure 6-12. GetNextRequest Message

additional ability to set the Value Field to *endOfMibView*, in order to indicate that condition. Additionally, if the instrumentation code that retrieves the values detects a failure, the agent records the error condition.

The first object that the agent encounters that is viewed as being incorrect causes the agent to construct the `Response-PDU` with the appropriate `errorStatus` and `errorIndex` fields set. If the instrumentation code detects a failure, the *genErr* `errorStatus` is used. The `errorIndex` field is set to the offset of the first object that causes the error.

The agent can also detect the failure condition for the case when the construction of an otherwise successful `Response-PDU` results in a PDU larger than the maximum allowable SNMP message size. In this case, the `errorStatus` is set to *tooBig*, the `errorIndex` field is assigned a zero value, and the `VarBindList` is empty. Like the `GetRequest-PDU`, the RFC notes that if even this response is too large, the message is not sent but discarded and the `snmpSilentDrops` error counter is set.

If all the managed object successor values are successfully found and retrieved and the resulting `Response-PDU` is of acceptable size, the `errorStatus` field is assigned the value of *noError* and the `errorIndex` field is set to zero. The variable bindings list of the `Response-PDU` contains the variable name and value of the object representing the successor to each of the variable names requested. Each successor name and value represents the next object in the lexicographical ordering that has the proper access value for the particular MIB view.

In every case the `Response-PDU` is sent, the `requestID` field is set to the value found from the matching `GetNextRequest-PDU` received from the NMS. The message is then sent back to the NMS that originated the command.

6.2.3. THE RESPONSE-PDU

The `Response-PDU` is the acknowledgment for queries. Its format is derived from the successful completion of the instrumentation routines' abilities to retrieve the correct values or from the discovery of the various possible error conditions. After the NMS receives its `Response-PDU`, it must check to be sure that the `errorStatus` does not indicate an error (i.e., it has any value other than *noError*). If an error is indicated, the `errorIndex` field can retrieve the `VarBindList` entry that was incorrect. (Remember the VarBindList is numbered starting with *one*.)

6.2.4. THE SETREQUEST-PDU

The management applications use the `SetRequest` command to prompt the agent to modify the value of the managed object instances specified. The Version 2 `SetRequest-PDU` has augmented error-reporting abilities. Among other benefits, these provide improved table control. This control will greatly foster the use of SNMPv2 for the configuration of SNMP-manageable devices. The command number for the set has the value of 3.

Figure 6-13 shows the NMS sending the `SetRequest-PDU` and having the agent process it. The agent then sends a `Response-PDU` for the NMS to process.

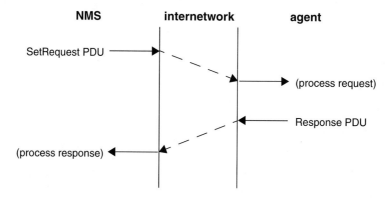

Figure 6-13. SetRequest Message

The first check the agent does is to be sure that the resulting `Response-PDU` response will not be too large to send back to the NMS. If it is, the *tooBig* error status is set. On exception, the Error Index is set to *0* and the response's `VarBindList` is empty. If this response was too large, the message is not sent but discarded. The `snmpSilentDrops` error counter is set, and the NMS is responsible for discovering the error. The NMS needs an error recovery procedure to handle the resulting time-out and to poll the agent to discover this particular error.

The set operation involves a two-pass procedure: a test of each value and then a modification for each value. All the variables in the `VarBindList` must be successfully written, or the set operation is considered a failure.

The first object that the agent encounters, during the test phase, that is viewed as being incorrect causes the agent to construct the `Response-PDU` with the appropriate `errorStatus` and `errorIndex` fields set. The error checking order is as follows:

1. Check if the object is accessible to the MIB view for this community. If it is not, the `errorStatus` is set to *noAccess*.

2. Check the Object Identifier prefix and be sure that the access level for the object is *read-write* or *read-create*. If it is not, the `errorStatus` is set to *notWritable*.

3. Verify the ASN.1 data type. If it doesn't match, the `errorStatus` is set to *wrongType*.

4. Verify the ASN.1 data length. If it is not valid, set the `errorStatus` to *wrongLength*.

5. Be sure that the ASN.1 encoding is correct. If it isn't, the `errorStatus` is set to *wrongEncoding*.

6. Check the value. If it is not assignable or is invalid for another reason, set the `errorStatus` to *wrongValue*.

7. If the variable doesn't exist and cannot be created under any circumstance, the `errorStatus` reported is *noCreation*.

8. If the variable doesn't exist but it can be created under certain circumstances, the *inconsistentName* `errorStatus` should be set.

9. If the variable exists but can't be written because it doesn't have the proper access definition, the `errorStatus` should be *notWritable*.

10. If the variable exists but it cannot be created under the current circumstances, the *inconsistentName* `errorStatus` should be set.

11. If the resources are not available at the agent to carry out the modification operation, the `errorStatus` reported should be *resourceUnavailable*.

12. If the operation fails for any other reason, such as an error in the internal agent instrumentation, the catch-all error of *genErr* is assigned to `errorStatus`.

If all of the managed object values are successfully found, tested, and altered, and the resulting `Response-PDU` is of acceptable size, the `errorStatus` field is assigned the value of *noError* and the `errorIndex` field is set to zero. The variable bindings list of the `Response-PDU` contains the variable name(s) and the new values for those objects.

Whether the resulting `Response-PDU` indicates an error or not, the `requestID` field is set to the value saved from the `SetRequest-PDU` that initiated the request, and the message is then sent across the internetwork to the originating NMS.

6.2.5. THE GETBULKREQUEST-PDU

The `GetBulkRequest-PDU` is new for Version 2 and introduces a mechanism for efficient bulk retrieval. This PDU appears in Figure 6-14. The NMS sends it at the request of the management application. The PDU is processed by the agent, which, in turn, generates the `Response-PDU` and sends the response back to the NMS for processing.

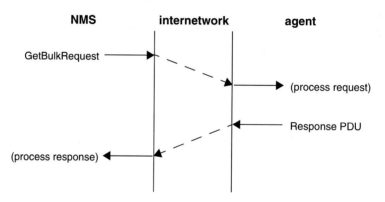

Figure 6-14. The GetBulkRequest Message

The `GetBulkRequest-PDU` uses the `non-repeaters` and `maximum-repetitions` fields of its PDU to specify how much information is returned. These two fields contain values that are used in an algorithm at the agent to determine how to populate the `VarBindList` of the `Response-PDU`. This algorithm generates the largest possible single response for this request.

The agent starts with the `non-repeaters` field. Starting at the beginning of the `VarBindList`, it contains the number of variables that should be retrieved once (typically non-tabular variables). After this requirement has been satisfied, and if room is still available, the `max-repetitions` field indicates the maximum number of times that the remaining variables can be retrieved

184

(as in columnar objects in a table). The exact algorithm specified in the protocol RFC is:

$$\text{Total Number of Requested Variable Bindings} = N + (M * R)$$

where N = minimum of non-repeaters field value, or number of variables
in VarBindList
M = max-repetitions field value
R = maximum number of variables in VarBindList minus N, or *zero*

(If either the non-repeaters or the max-repetitions fields contain a
negative value, that value is replaced with a *zero* in calculating the algorithm.)

Note that the agent does a "get next" retrieval of the OID specified in the list
so that an exact match is not required. The agent constantly keeps track of the
size of the generated response so that it can create the largest one specified in
the request. Because the agent is aware of the space requirements, it never
sends a response with the *tooBig* error status. The only possible error condition
in creating the Response-PDU for this request is *genErr*. The *endOfMib* field
value can be used if this condition is detected.

The RFC states that if the processing of the response takes "a significantly
greater amount of processing time than a normal request, then an agent may
terminate the request with less than the full number of repetitions, providing
at least one repetition is completed."

Marshall Rose notes that "In fact, after a little bit of thought, one could see
how to emulate the get-next operator using the get-bulk operator:

♦ simply make non-repeaters greater than or equal to the number of
variables in the request; or,

♦ simply set non-repeaters to *zero* and max-repetitions to *one*."[3]

The GetBulkRequest-PDU is a strong advance in making the protocol operation for retrieving large amounts of management data more efficient.

6.2.6. THE INFORMREQUEST-PDU

The InformRequest-PDU is also new for Version 2. It is important because
it is the first command that has been implemented for manager-to-manager

communication. This command can be used by one manager to send a pre-configured notification to another manager, indicating that a significant event has occurred. This type of communication is a first step in creating a hierarchy of managers where mid-level or *element* managers communicate to a centralized master management station. Typically, this master manager is the type of management station found in a Network Operations Center (NOC). It is an effective way of centralizing the management of a distributed enterprise-by dividing the enterprise into a number of smaller management domains. The steps involved in the sending and processing of an `InformRequest-PDU` appear in Figure 6-15.

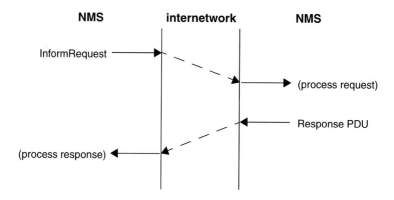

Figure 6-15. The InformRequest Message

The `InformRequest-PDU` is similar to the trap message in that both are defined with the NOTIFICATION-TYPE macro (defined in RFC 1902) and both are sent asynchronously when a predefined condition has been detected. Unlike the trap, however, this request requires a response to confirm that it has been received.

After a management application on a manager has determined that it wishes to send an `InformRequest-PDU`, it places its `sysUpTime` and `snmpTrap-OID` instances into the `VarBindList`. These instances tell the receiving manager who is sending this inform message and when. The `VarBindList` is then filled with the specific variables that are of interest and pertain specifically to this request.

When the receiving manager processes this request, it creates a `Response-PDU`. If no errors occur, the `errorStatus` field is set to *noError* and the contents are echoed back to the sending manager.

A possible error condition in creating the `Response-PDU` response is if the response generates a PDU that is too large to be sent. This situation is indicated by the *tooBig* error status. For this special exception, the `errorIndex` is set to *0* and the response's `VarBindList` is empty. Like the other request PDUs, if this response is too large, the message is not sent but discarded. The `snmp-SilentDrops` error counter is set.

6.2.7. THE SNMPV2-TRAP-PDU

The agent uses the `SNMPv2-Trap-PDU` to send an asynchronous notification of a predetermined event from the agent to the manager. For Version 2, the `SNMPv2-Trap-PDU` is defined with the NOTIFICATION-TYPE macro (defined in RFC 1902). The protocol does not require the manager to send a response to the agent.

After the agent has determined that it wishes to send an `SNMPv2-Trap-PDU`, it places its `sysUpTime` and `snmpTrapOID` instances into the `VarBindList`. These tell the receiving manager who is sending this trap and when. The `VarBindList` is then filled with the specific variables that are of interest and pertain specifically to this trap.

Figure 6-16 shows the agent sending the trap message across the internetwork to the manager. The agent must configure a list of managers that would receive each trap after it is generated.

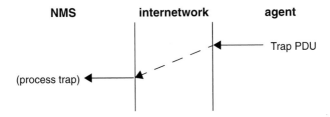

Figure 6-16. The SNMPv2 Trap Message

6.2.8. THE REPORT-PDU

The `Report-PDU` was added to the draft version of SNMPv2 in order to report errors dealing with the party-based SNMP message wrapper. Since the current community-based version of SNMPv2 still uses the v1 message wrapper, the Report-PDU is not needed. Its definition remains in the protocol specification, however, awaiting the arrival of any new administrative framework that may require an augmented message wrapper.

6.3. HOW THE VERSION 2 PROTOCOL WORKS

The Version 2 protocol builds on Version 1 by offering two new PDU types, improved error reporting, and other slight modifications to the protocol operation and message formats. The following section offers an introduction to present a quick overview on how the managers and agents operate with this new version of the protocol.

The NMS is the active participant in the management dialogue in the sense that network management applications initiate the construction of SNMP requests. This operation may be a setRequest, a getRequest, a getNext-Request, or getBulkRequest type of request. Additionally, in Version 2, a manager can send another manager an informRequest.

The NMS software creates an SNMP message by filling in the appropriate header values needed for transmitting the message over the internetwork to the destination management entity. The management application assigns the community name, version number, and request ID. The PDU type is chosen, and the members of the variable binding list are inserted into the message. The SNMP message is delivered to the UDP transport layer for transmission. The message is sent. The NMS must remember the requestID it has inserted in the request, in order to pair a response it expects to subsequently receive. Timers are also started to handle time-out conditions. At any time, the NMS must be prepared to receive and process both traps sent by agents and informs sent by other managers in its management domain.

After initializing, agents are waiting to receive the SNMP messages at its network device's UDP transport port 161. After the agent successfully receives a message, it calls its parse routine to decode the ASN.1 format into a more usable internal format. If the message is in improper ASN.1 format, it is discarded, and the agent simply returns to its wait loop. The next step is verifying the version number. If it is not a 1 (for version 2), this message is also discarded, and the agent returns to wait for the next message.

After the message has successfully passed these first two checks, the authentication function is then called to verify the message. If it fails here, and the agent has the ability to send the `authenticationFailure` trap message, the trap is sent and the message is discarded. If the message is authentic, the transport information is saved for the response message, and the agent is now ready to continue decoding the SNMP message.

While the agent is decoding the ASN.1 format of the message, it can start building a `Response-PDU` for the reply. At this point, any error condition does not cause the incoming message to be discarded, but rather the `Response-PDU` indicates the cause of the failure. The Value Field indicates a status for each variable in the `VarBindList`. Error information is inserted into the `ErrorStatus` and `ErrorIndex` fields.

The decoding functions examine all the fields in the message and check for proper ordering of the tag, length, and value of the fields. If the format is valid, the command is executed by having its operation applied to the variables in the variable bindings list. The instrumentation routines of the agent determine if the variable instance exists, whether the NMS is authorized for the requested access level, and how to access the variable for the requested operation.

After the agent completes filling in the `Response-PDU`, it encodes the message into ASN.1 using the BER, presents it to the UDP transport service for transmission to the requesting management entity, and returns to its wait loop. All of the proper variables the agent uses to record its operation, such as the objects about SNMP itself, are properly incremented for later inspection by the NMS.

6.4. VERSION 2 TABLE HANDLING

Table handling has been standardized for Version 2. Row creation, deletion, and modification are now done with standardized objects that are defined with textual conventions macros to describe the status of each row. The `RowStatus` TC has enumerated values to manipulate the current state of a particular row. Its values are: *active, notInService, notReady, createAndGo, createAndWait,* and *destroy.* Additionally, the `RowPointer` TC points to specific rows.

6.5. THE VERSION 2 PROTOCOL DEFINITION

A complete listing of the protocol from RFC 1905 is posted in Appendix B, Section B.2, *The SNMPv2 Protocol Specification.*

6.6. VERSION 2 TRANSPORT MAPPINGS

SNMPv2 can be extended to operate over non-UDP transport domains-although UDP is always the transport protocol of choice. These transport mappings are introduced in a standard way for the version 2 protocol. A full discussion of this mapping is included in RFC 1906, *Transport Mappings for Version 2 of the Simple Network Management Protocol (SNMPv2)*.

This RFC lists five transport domain mappings supported for the version 2 protocol:

◆ SNMPv2 over UDP

◆ SNMPv2 over OSI

◆ SNMPv2 over DDP

◆ SNMPv2 over IPX

◆ SNMPv2 Proxy For SNMPv1

For each transport domain, additional TEXTUAL-CONVENTION macros have been defined to facilitate implementation.

6.6.1. SNMPV2 OVER UDP

The preferred transport domain of the User Datagram Protocol (version 4) is specified with a TC for a UDP address. This appears in Figure 6-17.

```
-- SNMPv2 over UDP over IPv4

snmpUDPDomain  OBJECT-IDENTITY
    STATUS       current
    DESCRIPTION
          "The SNMPv2 over UDP transport domain.  The corresponding
           transport address is of type SnmpUDPAddress."
    ::= { snmpDomains 1 }

SnmpUDPAddress ::= TEXTUAL-CONVENTION
    DISPLAY-HINT "1d.1d.1d.1d/2d"
    STATUS       current
    DESCRIPTION
          "Represents a UDP address:

             octets    contents          encoding
              1-4      IP-address        network-byte order
              5-6      UDP-port          network-byte order
               "
    SYNTAX       OCTET STRING (SIZE (6))
```

Figure 6-17. SNMPv2 Over UDP

6.6.2. SNMPV2 OVER OSI

For SNMPv2 to run on the OSI connectionless (CLNS) and connection-oriented (CONS) transport stacks, the OSI address has been defined as the `Snmp-OSIAddress` TC. This definition is shown in Figure 6-18.

```
-- SNMPv2 over OSI

snmpCLNSDomain OBJECT-IDENTITY
    STATUS      current
    DESCRIPTION
            "The SNMPv2 over CLNS transport domain.  The corresponding
            transport address is of type SnmpOSIAddress."
    ::= { snmpDomains 2 }

snmpCONSDomain OBJECT-IDENTITY
    STATUS      current
    DESCRIPTION
            "The SNMPv2 over CONS transport domain.  The corresponding
            transport address is of type SnmpOSIAddress."
    ::= { snmpDomains 3 }

SnmpOSIAddress ::= TEXTUAL-CONVENTION
    DISPLAY-HINT "*1x:/1x:"
    STATUS      current
    DESCRIPTION
            "Represents an OSI transport-address:

            octets    contents            encoding
               1      length of NSAP      'n' as an unsigned-integer
                                            (either 0 or from 3 to 20)
            2..(n+1)  NSAP                concrete binary representation
            (n+2)..m TSEL                 string of (up to 64) octets
                    "
    SYNTAX      OCTET STRING (SIZE (1 | 4..85))
```

Figure 6-18. SNMPv2 Over OSI

6.6.3. SNMPV2 OVER DDP

The transport mapping and address TC for SNMPv2 over the AppleTalk Datagram Delivery Protocol (DDP) appears in Figure 6-19.

```
-- SNMPv2 over DDP

snmpDDPDomain  OBJECT-IDENTITY
    STATUS      current
    DESCRIPTION
            "The SNMPv2 over DDP transport domain.  The corresponding
            transport address is of type SnmpNBPAddress."
```

Figure 6-19. SNMPv2 Over DDP

```
    ::= { snmpDomains 4 }

SnmpNBPAddress ::= TEXTUAL-CONVENTION
    STATUS         current
    DESCRIPTION
          "Represents an NBP name:


                octets            contents            encoding
                  1               length of object    'n' as an unsigned integer
                2..(n+1)          object              string of (up to 32) octets
                  n+2             length of type      'p' as an unsigned integer
            (n+3)..(n+2+p)        type                string of (up to 32) octets
                n+3+p             length of zone      'q' as an unsigned integer
          (n+4+p)..(n+3+p+q)      zone                string of (up to 32) octets

          For comparison purposes, strings are case-insensitive All
          strings may contain any octet other than 255 (hex ff)."
    SYNTAX         OCTET STRING (SIZE (3..99))
```

Figure 6-19. SNMPv2 Over DDP *(continued)*

6.6.4. SNMPV2 OVER IPX

To run the SNMPv2 over the Novell Internetwork Packet Exchange (IPX) stack, the RFC introduces a TC for the SNMP IPX address. This definition appears in Figure 6-20.

```
-- SNMPv2 over IPX

snmpIPXDomain  OBJECT-IDENTITY
    STATUS       current
    DESCRIPTION
          "The SNMPv2 over IPX transport domain.  The corresponding
          transport address is of type SnmpIPXAddress."
    ::= { snmpDomains 5 }

SnmpIPXAddress ::= TEXTUAL-CONVENTION
    DISPLAY-HINT "4x.1x:1x:1x:1x:1x:1x.2d"
    STATUS       current
    DESCRIPTION
          "Represents an IPX address:

                octets    contents            encoding
                  1-4     network-number      network-byte order
                  5-10    physical-address    network-byte order
                 11-12    socket-number       network-byte order
                "
    SYNTAX        OCTET STRING (SIZE (12))
```

Figure 6-20. SNMPv2 Over IPX

6.6.5. SNMPV2 PROXY FOR SNMPV1

In order to proxy SNMPv1 with the SNMPv2 protocol, a transport domain is introduced. This definition appears in Figure 6-21. The behavior of this type of proxy agent is specified in RFC 1908, *Coexistence Between Version 1 and Version 2 of the Internet-standard Network Management Framework*.

```
-- for proxy to SNMPv1 (RFC 1157)

rfc1157Proxy    OBJECT IDENTIFIER ::= { snmpProxys 1 }

rfc1157Domain   OBJECT-IDENTITY
    STATUS      current
    DESCRIPTION
            "The transport domain for SNMPv1 over UDP.  The
            corresponding transport address is of type SnmpUDPAddress."
    ::= { rfc1157Proxy 1 }

--  ::= { rfc1157Proxy 2 }              this OID is obsolete
```

Figure 6-21. SNMPv2 Proxy for SNMPv1

6.7. VERSION 2 AND VERSION 1 COEXISTENCE

As SNMPv2 begins deployment, a period of time will occur when both versions must coexist. How long this period will be is anyone's guess right now, but proposed strategies exist for SNMPv1 to SNMPv2 migration. A discussion of this coexistence is the topic of RFC 1908, *Coexistence Between Version 1 and Version 2 of the Internet-standard Network Management Framework*.

The direct migration of version 1 to version 2 is straightforward when one understands the issues of the two versions of the SMI, the MIB updates, and the new capabilities of the protocol.

A coexistence strategy can be accomplished with either or both of these two methods:

◆ bi-lingual managers and or agents

◆ the use of proxies

A bilingual manager and agent can converse in both versions of SNMP. Keying on the Version Field in the header, both management entities can process the respective SNMP message, depending on the value. A proxy that converts Version 1 to Version 2, and vice versa, must understand what changes must be made to the message in order for the management information to be correctly processed. For more information on bi-lingual agents see RFC 2089, *V2 To V1 Mapping SNMPv2 onto SNMPv1 within a Bi-lingual SNMP Agent.*

REFERENCES FOR CHAPTER 6

[1] Bartlett, John. *Bartlett's Familiar Quotations.* 16th ed. Boston: Little, Brown, and Company. 1992.

[2] Andrews, Robert. *The Columbia Dictionary of Quotations.* New York: Columbia University Press. 1993.

[3] Rose, Marshall. *The Simple Book: An Introduction to Networking Management.* Upper Saddle River, NJ: Prentice Hall. 1996.

The Management Information Base for SNMP Version 1

The whole is simpler than the sum of the parts.

—William Gibbs[1]

The Management Information Base (MIB) is the third key component of the SNMP network management framework. The SNMPv1 MIB is defined by the Version 1 SMI. The MIB is the collection of all of the objects that can be managed by SNMP. This set includes the standard objects defined by the various IETF working groups, objects created for experimentation by universities and research facilities, and private objects defined by various vendors and other interested parties. The three current major branches for SNMP MIB objects appear on the ISO/CCITT naming registration tree in Figure 7-1.

In accordance with the naming convention and Internet administration, subsequent MIB objects are appended to the registration tree in their proper place. Every MIB object has its unique position, and therefore, a unique name and object identifier.

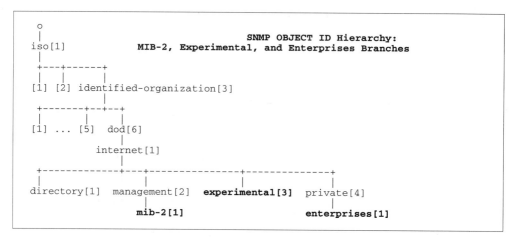

Figure 7-1. The SNMP Object Identifier Hierarchy

This unique, pre-assigned object identifier places the object in a known position in the SNMP Object ID Hierarchy. This method lends itself to conceptually viewing the MIB as a hierarchical tree structure with cascading sets of branches and nodes continuing down to an arbitrary level of depth as new objects are added. The last nodes of any branch are called the *leaf* nodes. Only these leaf nodes can contain objects that possess values accessible to the NMS. The object identifiers are never reissued, even if an object is no longer used— for example, when an object has its status changed to deprecated or obsolete.

The MIB can be viewed as the set of all groups of managed objects for SNMP—the MIB universe. Figure 7-2 depicts the abstract relationship among all of the possible MIB objects, the subset of objects that can be known by a particular NMS, and the subset of objects that can be known by any individual agent. A group is a part of the MIB that represents the managed objects for a particular component in the network device to be managed. An MIB group exists for TCP, for IP, for ICMP, and so forth. The MIB universe can also be viewed as the total sum of all of the MIB groups defined.

Because network devices are comprised of various components befitting their purpose as a network or host device, each device contains a certain subset of all possible MIB objects. It contains various MIB groups. Each agent's MIB subset is also referred to as its *individual MIB*. Its MIB is the virtual data storage for containing the set of objects maintained by that agent, and as such, these objects are the variables of interest for the Network Management Stations that know it and manage it.

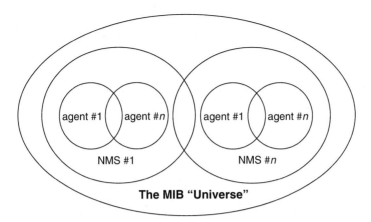

Figure 7-2. The MIB "Universe" of Objects

Although an agent's current MIB includes the core objects from the standard MIB-II definitions, it may be extended via any of these mechanisms:

♦ additions from new versions to the standard MIB from the management branch

♦ inclusion of experimental objects from the experimental branch

♦ inclusion of private objects defined in the enterprises branch

The SMIv1 has defined the format of the objects in the MIB using the SNMP ASN.1 subset, as shown in Figure 7-3.

As shown in Figure 7-3, an agent's MIB contains *n* objects, with each object having its three primary attributes of name, syntax, and encoding. Also remember that MIB objects are always arranged in groups.

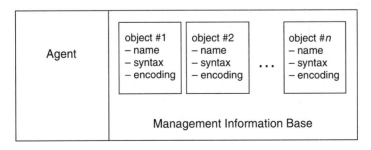

Figure 7-3. The Agent's Management Information Base

The object's name is its unique, pre-assigned object identifier that places it on the SNMP OBJECT ID Hierarchy. For example, the first object identifier that gets included in every agent's MIB is the System Description object. This MIB object is in the System Group and contains a string that describes the managed network entity. Its Object Identifier is

iso.identified-organization.dod.internet.management.mib-2.system.sysDescr

or

1.3.6.1.2.1.1.1

or

{ system 1 }

Note that the object identifier 1.3.6.1.2.1.1.1 can also be referred to as the object type `sysDescr`. The SMI allows the creation of macros in order to make the names more readable for humans. The suffix .1 that represents the `sysDescr` object type can also be represented as { system 1 }.

Three basic types of objects are defined for SNMP: a table, a row in that table, also called an *entry*, and the non-aggregate type, more commonly called a *leaf*. A leaf is a simple variable that is not in a table. A logical depiction of these three types appears in Figure 7-4.

As Figure 7-4 shows, a table comprises 1 to *n* rows. Each row must have the identical number of aggregate objects in it. One or more of these aggregate ob-

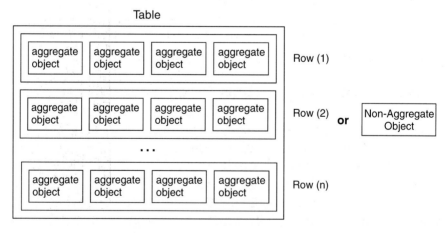

Figure 7-4. Three Types of Objects

jects are defined as an index for accessing that entry. The non-aggregate object is a simple variable that is not part of a table.

Now is an appropriate time to introduce the topic of *instantiation*, or the declaration of a unique instance of the object type used in the implementation. In order for an NMS to access an agent's MIB objects, the NMS must know the object type as well as the object instance of the particular management object it wishes to access. Think of the object type as the definition and the object instance as the declaration. The object instance is also called the *MIB variable*.

The declaration of non-aggregate variable names is straightforward. The variable names follow the format x.y, where x is the object type and y is the object identifier fragment. By convention, the y portion is the special value *0*. This implies that an agent can manage only one instance of a non-aggregate variable. For example, a specific instance of the System Description variable is 1.3.6.1.2.1.1.1.0. This notation greatly simplifies navigation through the MIB name space with the GetNext traversal operator.

Because SNMP is basically constructed to operate expressly on non-aggregate scalar values, the access to tabular objects is a bit more involved. Tables, aggregate object types, cannot be manipulated directly, and therefore require more complex instantiation rules to retrieve the column variable values. This retrieval is done with the use of the INDEX clause.

The INDEX clause defines the instance identification of tabular objects. The INDEX value for a particular table can be found by referring to the table's ENTRY definition that always follows each table definition in a MIB. The ENTRY definition defines a row in a table by listing its columns. The INDEX clause of the ENTRY definition serves as the key for manipulating the rows in that table for such operations as access, addition, and deletion. Note that as an SNMP convention, any object instance defined as a column entry does not have a suffix of .0.

By way of example, Figure 7-5 shows the table instantiation notation for the tables defined in MIB-I.

In addition to its name, an object has its syntax. This is the abstract data structure that represents the object. It is the object's definition as one of the predefined ASN.1 data types of the subset used by SNMP.

The encoding of the object is the representation of this syntax and how it is transmitted on the internetwork. The SMI has specified that the transmission of the SNMP message with any MIB objects encapsulated in it be the OSI Basic Encoding Rules for ASN.1.

Object Type Name	Special Instantiation Notation
ifTable	ifIndex value
atTable	atIfIndex value.atNetAddress value
ipAddrTable	ipAdEntAddr value
ipRoutingTable	ipRouteDest value
ipNetToMediaTable	ipNetToMediaIfIndex value.ipNetToMediaNetAddress value
tcpConnTable	tcpConnLocalAddress value.tcpConnLocalPort value. tcpConnRemAddress value.tcpConnRemPort value
udpTable	udpLocalAddress value.udpLocalPort value
egpNeighTable	egpNeighAddr value

Figure 7-5. MIB-I Table Instantiation

The format of the MIB Version 1 definitions has been specified by the Version 1 SMI. The OBJECT-TYPE macro compactly represents the key attributes of the object: name, syntax, access, status, and a textual description.

As an example, the MIB variable representing how long the agent has been up, `sysUpTime`, is presented with the OBJECT-TYPE macro, as shown in Figure 7-6.

```
sysUpTime OBJECT-TYPE
      SYNTAX      TimeTicks
      ACCESS      read-only
      STATUS      mandatory
      DESCRIPTION
          "The time (in hundredths of a second) since the
          network management portion of the system was last
          re-initialized."
      ::= { system 3 }
```

Figure 7-6. sysUpTime OBJECT-TYPE Definition

A more concise format for MIB definitions was introduced in RFC 1212, *Concise MIB Definitions*, and was recommended for all new MIB Version 1 definitions. Figure 7-7 shows this improved format.

This format expands on the OBJECT-TYPE macro definition by adding several new clauses. It also eliminates redundancy by making a more concise def-

```
OBJECT-TYPE MACRO ::=
BEGIN
  TYPE NOTATION ::=
                    -- must conform to RFC1155's ObjectSyntax
                "SYNTAX" type(ObjectSyntax)
                "ACCESS" Access
                "STATUS" Status
                DescrPart
                ReferPart
                IndexPart
                DefValPart
  VALUE NOTATION ::= value (VALUE ObjectName)
  Access ::= "read-only"
              | "read-write"
              | "write-only"
              | "not-accessible"
  Status ::= "mandatory"
              | "optional"
              | "obsolete"
              | "deprecated"
  DescrPart ::=
            "DESCRIPTION" value (description DisplayString)
            | empty
  ReferPart ::=
            "REFERENCE" value (reference DisplayString)
            | empty
  IndexPart ::=
            "INDEX" "{" IndexTypes "}"
            | empty
  IndexTypes ::=
            IndexType | IndexTypes "," IndexType
  IndexType ::=
                    -- if indexobject, use the SYNTAX
                    -- value of the correspondent
                    -- OBJECT-TYPE invocation
            value (indexobject ObjectName)
                    -- otherwise use named SMI type
                    -- must conform to IndexSyntax below
              | type (indextype)
  DefValPart ::=
            "DEFVAL" "{" value (defvalue ObjectSyntax) "}"
            | empty
END
```

Figure 7-7. Concise MIB Definition

inition for each MIB object. This definition is accomplished by merging the textual descriptions into the previous template for the OBJECT-TYPE macro. This specification is an IAB Full Standard for SNMPv1.

The SYNTAX clause is the ASN.1 abstract data structure representing the object. When the MIB objects are enumerated, they each have a syntax value in the ASN.1 SYNTAX column.

The ACCESS clause defines the read/write level for each object. The specification states that this is the minimum level of support that any particular object must provide. The implication is that an implementation may allow additional capability on a per-object basis. That is, a "read-only" data object may be updated to be "read-write" in certain cases. The following table, Figure 7-8, contains the various key values for the access modes.

Key	Value	Meaning
RO	"read-only"	object can be read but not written
RW	"read-write"	object can be both read or written
WO	"write-only"	object can be written but not read
NA	"not-accessible"	object cannot be read or written

Figure 7-8. Figure 7-8. Access Values and Meanings

The STATUS clause contains the value that describes the implementation state of the object. The following table, Figure 7-9, lists the keys for the various status attributes that an object may possess.

Key	Value	Meaning
M	"mandatory"	must be implemented
O	"optional"	may be implemented
B	"obsolete"	no longer needs to be implemented
D	"deprecated"	information presented by object is now better presented by other objects; however, still mandatory*

*objects with this status have a special "deprecated" value, in that the information that they provide has been supplanted by objects that contain a more meaningful definition. An example is the Address Translation Group objects that now have a deprecated status. The information that they contain is better provided by the corresponding objects in the Interfaces Group. Note that deprecated objects must still be implemented.

Figure 7-9. Status Values and Meanings

The Description clause is optional text (note that the "or" "empty" union value in the format makes this clause optional) that contains additional information about the object. The specification requires that this string be enclosed in quotation marks if present.

The optional Reference clause can contain a citation to other objects defined in another MIB module. This clause can serve as a useful cross-referencing tool for pertinent standards documents and other specifications dealing with this object.

The INDEX clause is added to provide information about how tables can be instantiated for access. For this reason, every table definition needs at least one index. Figure 7-10 shows that this index can have any one of the following ASN.1 values as its syntax.

```
IndexSyntax ::=
    CHOICE {
        number
    INTEGER (0..MAX),
        string
    OCTET STRING,
        object
    OBJECT IDENTIFIER,
        address
    NetworkAddress,
        ipAddress
    IpAddress
}
```

Figure 7-10. Index Values

DEFVAL is the optional default value an object can be assigned. The intent is to preassign values for table rows created via the `SetRequest-PDU` operation. When a `SetRequest` command creates a row in a table, all of the corresponding column entries can be created. The default values must be consistent with the object's syntax.

The total number of managed objects in the MIB is growing rapidly. As working groups specify and develop new MIB objects and groups by adding them to the `mib-2`, `experimental`, and `private` branches, a consistent format is necessary in order to understand all of the many details. This consistent format aids in a sound understanding of just what is to be managed and provides for a more quality implementation.

In the subsequent sections, I introduce each MIB individual group. You can discover its place in the SNMP OBJECT ID Hierarchy and find general information about the group. I list the appropriate RFC so that the complete set of objects can be retrieved.

The Standard MIB, originally referred to as MIB-I and since updated to MIB-II, has its object identifier values assigned from the `mib-2` branch. Therefore, all standard MIB objects begin with the identifier 1.3.6.1.2.1.

7.1. THE MIB-II SUB-TREE

The current Full Standard for the MIB for Version 1 is defined in RFC 1213, *Management Information Base for Network Management of TCP/IP-based Internets: MIB-II.* This version is called MIB-II. The current MIB-II standard tree evolved and is taken directly from MIB-I. For a historical perspective, examine MIB-I and see how it was amended to create MIB-II.

The list of objects included in MIB-I are the objects deemed essential for the original SNMP release by the working groups defining the MIB. This first release of standard MIB objects included those primarily needed for configuration control and fault monitoring. The list presented in RFC 1156 consists of objects arranged in eight groups. The total number of objects was 114.

Figure 7-11 shows where the MIB-I groups reside in the four-layer TCP/IP protocol suite model.

The eight groups in the MIB-I definition are:

1. System Group
2. Interfaces Group
3. Address Translation Group

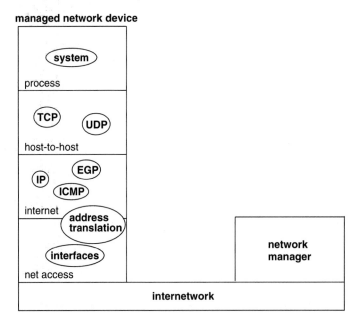

Figure 7-11. MIB-I Groups

4. Internet Protocol Group

5. Internet Control Message Protocol Group

6. Transmission Control Protocol Group

7. User Datagram Protocol Group

8. Exterior Gateway Protocol Group

The System Group has three objects, which contain descriptive information about the managed network device itself.

The 22 objects of the Interfaces Group deal with the device's lowest levels of connection to the network.

The Address Translation Group's three objects were a first cut at managing the IP address translation issue.

The largest group, 33 objects, needed to be defined for the Internet Protocol Group that was needed for IP layer management. In association with IP control, the Internet Control Message Protocol Group's 26 objects reported statistics on ICMP.

Twenty-one objects are available for the management of the transport layer. The monitoring and control of TCP was maintained by the 17 objects in the Transmission Control Protocol Group, and the User Datagram Protocol Group had four objects.

For the control of gateways and the EGP, the Exterior Gateway Protocol Group had defined six objects.

Note that the specifications clearly state that if a group is to be supported, every object in that group must be implemented. This requirement was not considered a burden, since the 114 MIB objects chosen were all deemed essential for offering management for any particular group. The designer has to decide which groups should be implemented for a particular device. For example, a typical host system that has no gateway capabilities would have implemented all of the objects in all of the groups in MIB-I, except for Group 8, the EGP Group.

In accordance with the SNMP philosophy of extensibility, experimentation and feedback from working implementations rapidly showed that MIB-I had to be augmented with the addition of new objects. RFC 1158, *Management Base for Network Management of TCP/IP-based Internets: MIB-II*, was released to include these modifications. MIB-II included two new groups and 57 new objects to reflect these changes. RFC 1158 was then made obsolete by RFC 1213, which was issued in March 1991. This RFC is a Full Standard (STD 17) and represents the latest version of the MIB II definition. It serves as the basis for the MIB discussion presented here.

To reiterate, MIB-II contains only the objects deemed essential for the core of SNMP management. The criteria for deciding which objects to include in MIB-II are spelled out in RFC 1213 and appear in Figure 7-12.

```
(1)An object needed to be essential for either fault or configuration
   management.

(2)Only weak control objects were permitted (weak meaning that tampering with
   them can do only limited damage). This criterion reflects the fact that the
   current management protocols are not sufficiently secure to do more
   powerful control operations.

(3)Evidence of current use and utility are required.

(4)In MIB-I, an attempt was made to limit the number of objects to about 100,
   in order to allow vendors to easily fully instrument their software. In MIB-
   II, this limit was raised, given the wide technological base now
   implementing MIB-I.

(5)To avoid redundant variables, no object could be included that can be
   derived from others in the MIB.

(6)Implementation specific objects (e.g., for BSD UNIX) were excluded.

(7)Heavily instrumented critical sections of code were avoided. The general
   guideline was one counter per critical section per layer.
```

Figure 7-12. MIB-II Object Selection Requirements

The two new groups added to the MIB are the Transmission Group and the SNMP Group. Their object identifiers are added to the standard MIB tree with node designators 10 and 11, respectively.

Figure 7-13 shows where the MIB-II groups reside in the four layer TCP/IP protocol suite model.

The ten groups in the current MIB-II definition are:

1. System Group
2. Interfaces Group
3. Address Translation Group (downgraded to "deprecated" status)
4. Internet Protocol Group
5. Internet Control Message Protocol Group

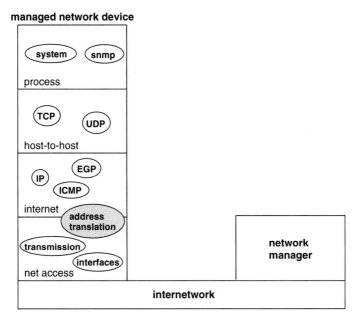

Figure 7-13. MIB-II Groups

6. Transmission Control Protocol Group

7. User Datagram Protocol Group

8. Exterior Gateway Protocol Group

9. Transmission Group

10. Simple Network Management Protocol Group

The Transmission Group as defined in RFC 1213 did not explicitly define MIB objects, but provided the place for objects dealing with various transmission media types to be located. Currently, at least 45 transmission groups have been defined. These include MIB groups for various LAN media such as Ethernet, Token Bus, Token Ring, and FDDI, as well as for other WAN and communications media. These include X.25 LABP and packet Level, DS1/E1, DS3/E3, SMDS, Frame-Relay, RS-232, Parallel, and IEEE 802.12 interfaces.

The SNMP Group included 30 new objects for the control and monitoring of the network management itself. The SNMP Group provides the essential capability of meta-management-managing the management! The remaining 27 new MIB objects were added to various places in the original eight standard groups.

Also note that two new data types were added in the latest MIB-II specification. These new types, defined in the textual conventions of the IMPORT section of the MIB modules are:

◆ DisplayString ::= OCTET STRING

◆ PhysAddress ::= OCTET STRING

The DisplayString is a special OCTET STRING that uses the NVT ASCII character set. DisplayString MIB objects can have a length from 0 to 255 octets.

The PhysAddress is also a special OCTET STRING. Its specific use is for modeling the various representations that can be used for media addresses of the network access layer. For many types of media, this will be a binary representation. For example, an Ethernet media address is represented as an OCTET STRING of 6 octets.

The remainder of this chapter discusses the individual MIB Groups. The appropriate RFC is cited for each group and should be consulted for all of the exact details. A great deal of additional information in each RFC is useful. This additional information includes the Working Group members that helped define the MIB Group, important references for many of the objects, specific details about an interface or protocol, and so forth. Two excellent sources for more information about the specifics on many of the technical aspects of using the MIB groups are *SNMP: A Guide to Network Management*[2] by Sidnie Feit and *How To Manage Your Network Using SNMP: The Network Management Practicum*[3] by Marshall Rose and Keith McCloghrie.

Since the MIBs have continued to evolve beyond the SNMPv1 standard, new MIB groups are continually being defined and MIBs are being updated. All the MIB groups are introduced in this chapter with reference to the latest RFC that contains its definition. Note that since the SMI for SNMPv2 was accepted as a draft standard, all new MIBs and all MIB updates since then are done in the new SMIv2. A full discussion of the SMIv2 MIBs occurs in Chapter 8.

7.1.1. THE SYSTEM GROUP

The System Group contains the objects that describe the top-level characteristics and general configuration information about the managed network device.

The System Group ASN.1 OBJECT IDENTIFIER is { mib-2 1 }. Figure 7-14 depicts the System Group's position in the SNMP OBJECT ID Hierarchy:

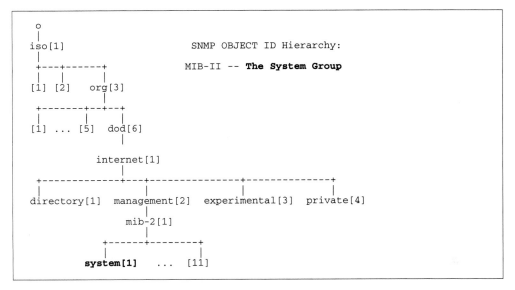

Figure 7-14. The System Group

The MIB-I definition of the System Group consisted of only three items:

◆ A string containing a full description of the node

◆ The node's ASN.1 OBJECT IDENTIFIER

◆ How long the device had been running

For MIB-II, four additional objects were defined to add more general information about the node:

◆ The name (and whereabouts) of the person responsible for the device

◆ A string with the node's name

◆ The location of the node

◆ A constant defining the system services supported by the node

Every object in this group is mandatory. If the agent is not configured for a value for any of these objects, the objects must have a default initialization value of *zero*.

7.1.2. THE INTERFACES GROUP

The Interfaces Group contains objects allowing for the management control of the lowest layer of the TCP/IP protocol suite, the interface layer. Since a network device can have more than one network interface, a count occurs of the number of interfaces present and also information relating to each one. This information includes 22 accessible items about a particular interface's state, various run-time statistics, packet lengths, queue lengths, and so forth. The Interfaces Group ASN.1 OBJECT IDENTIFIER is { mib-2 2 }. Figure 7-15 depicts the Interfaces Group's position in the SNMP OBJECT ID Hierarchy:

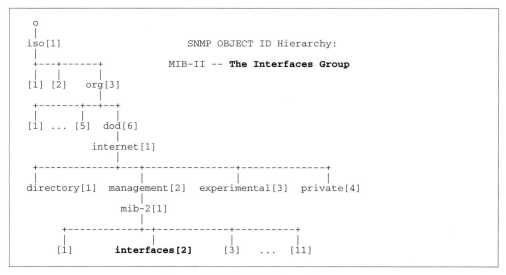

Figure 7-15. The Interfaces Group

The MIB-I definition of the Interfaces Group consisted of two major items for a total of 22 objects:

◆ An integer containing the number of interfaces supported

◆ An Interface Table of twenty-two columns with one row per interface

For MIB-II, the only addition to the original standard is an additional column in the Interface Table, the ifSpecific object. This object contains the OBJECT IDENTIFIER of the document that contains the information on that particular media. Additionally [in RFC1213], the way the ifNumber was defined was broadened to encompass non-IP supported interfaces. The access of the ifTable was corrected and several new ifType object values were added to accommodate new interface technologies (values 23 to 32).

Every object in this group is mandatory. If the agent is not configured for a value for any of these objects, the objects must have a default initialization value of *zero*. Again, the number of rows in the Interface Table corresponds to the number of interfaces supported by the device.

7.1.3. THE ADDRESS TRANSLATION GROUP

The Address Translation Group was implemented in MIB-I to provide a mapping of a network device's internetwork layer address (e.g., its IP address) and its interface layer address (also called *physical* or *subnetwork-specific address*).

Due to the unforeseen additional complexities of multiple address mappings, this definition was found to be too limiting, and address mapping information was included in other places in the MIB, such as in each network protocol group. The `ipNetToMediaTable` in the IP Group, for example, includes the exact information found in the `atTable`. Therefore, this group is given a deprecated status in MIB-II and must be included for compatibility with existing MIB-I implementations. The intent of the deprecated status is to indicate that the AT Group may be excluded from future specifications.

The Address Translation Group ASN.1 OBJECT IDENTIFIER is { mib-2 3 }. Figure 7-16 depicts the Address Translation Group's position in the SNMP OBJECT ID Hierarchy:

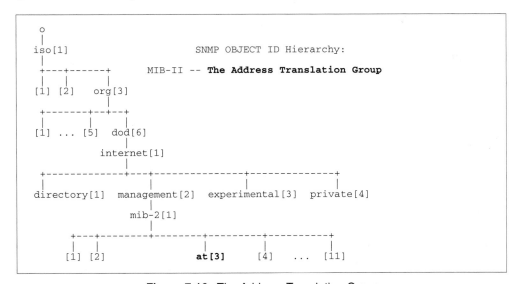

Figure 7-16. The Address Translation Group

The MIB-I definition of the Address Translation Group consists of the Address Translation Table with three columns. For MIB-II, the status for the table, and hence the whole group, is deprecated.

Every object in this group is deprecated.

7.1.4. THE INTERNET PROTOCOL GROUP

This group contains the managed objects for the Internet Protocol Group. The purpose of this group is to provide the information on IP operations such as IP routing tables and address conversion tables.

The IP Group ASN.1 OBJECT IDENTIFIER is { mib-2 4 }. Figure 7-17 depicts the Internet Protocol Group's position in the SNMP OBJECT ID Hierarchy:

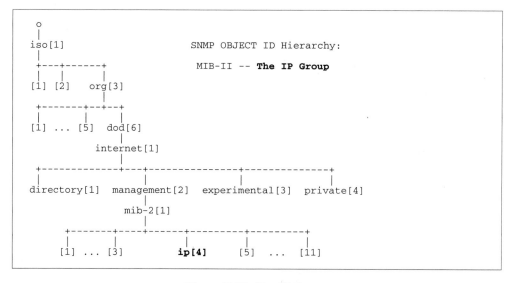

Figure 7-17. The IP Group

The MIB-I definition of the Internet Protocol Group consists of a group of 19 integers and counters used to keep various statistics on the IP and two tables:

◆ The IP Address Table

◆ The IP Route Table

MIB-I defined a total of 37 managed objects for this group.

For MIB-II, an additional column was added to the IP Address Table: ipAd-EntBcastAddr. Three additional columns were also added to the IP Route Table: ipRouteMask, ipRouteMetric5, and ipRouteInfo. The Network-To-Media Table was added for the handling of address translation between the IP and physical layers. It replaces the functionality of the Address Translation group. The object ipRoutingDiscards was also added to enhance error reporting. The MIB-II IP group now comprises 48 objects.

Every object in this group is mandatory. If the agent is not configured for a value for any of these objects, the objects must have a default initialization value of *zero*.

7.1.5. THE INTERNET CONTROL MESSAGE PROTOCOL GROUP

The ICMP group contains the Internet Control Message Protocol input and output statistics.

The ICMP Group ASN.1 OBJECT IDENTIFIER is { mib-2 5 }. Figure 7-18 depicts the ICMP Group's position in the SNMP OBJECT ID Hierarchy:

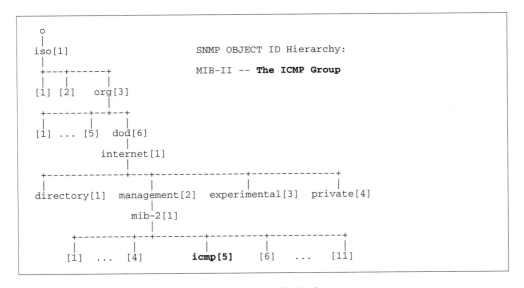

Figure 7-18. The ICMP Group

The MIB-I definition of the ICMP Group consists of 26 read-only counter objects for maintaining various statistics and error counts for the ICMP protocol. Two of these counters are for the number of ICMP messages sent and received, and two counters are for the number of ICMP error messages encountered. The other 22 counters are for 11 ICMP messages traveling in both the inbound and outbound directions. For quick reference these 11 ICMP messages are:

#	ICMP Message	#	ICMP Message
1	Destination Unreachable	7	Echo Reply
2	Time Exceeded	8	Timestamp Request
3	Parameter Problem	9	Timestamp Reply
4	Source Quench	10	Address Mask Request
5	Redirect	12	Address Mask Reply
6	Echo Request		

No changes were made to this group for MIB-II.

Every object in this group is mandatory. If the agent is not configured for a value for any of these objects, the objects must have a default initialization value of *zero*.

7.1.6. THE TRANSMISSION CONTROL PROTOCOL GROUP

The Transmission Control Protocol Group gathers statistics about the TCP connection. Note that instances of object types that represent information about a particular TCP connection are transient; they persist only as long as the connection in question.

The TCP Group ASN.1 OBJECT IDENTIFIER is { mib-2 6 }. Figure 7-19 depicts the TCP Group's position in the SNMP OBJECT ID Hierarchy.

The MIB-I definition of the TCP Group consists of 12 integers and counter objects for maintaining various statistics and error counts for TCP. It also includes the TCP Connection Table. MIB-I defines a total of 19 TCP management objects.

The tcpInErrs and tcpOutRsts objects were added for MIB-II.

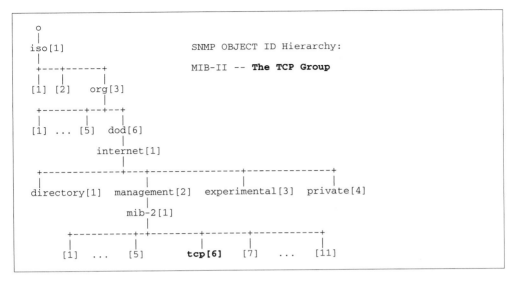

```
o
|
iso[1]                        SNMP OBJECT ID Hierarchy:
|
+---+------+                  MIB-II -- The TCP Group
|   |      |
[1] [2]  org[3]
|
+-------+--+--+
|       |     |
[1] ... [5]  dod[6]
|
internet[1]
|
+-------------+---+---------------+--------------+
|                 |               |              |
directory[1]  management[2]  experimental[3]  private[4]
|
mib-2[1]
|
+----------+-+--------+-------+-----------+
|          |          |       |           |
[1]  ...  [5]      tcp[6]    [7]   ...    [11]
```

Figure 7-19. The TCP Group

Every object in this group is mandatory. If the agent is not configured for a value for any of these objects, the objects must have a default initialization value of *zero*.

7.1.7. THE USER DATAGRAM PROTOCOL GROUP

This group contains the statistics and information about the User Datagram Protocol. UDP is the preferred transport service for SNMP.

The UDP Group ASN.1 OBJECT IDENTIFIER is { mib-2 7 }. Figure 7-20 depicts the UDP Group's position in the SNMP OBJECT ID Hierarchy.

The MIB-I definition of the UDP Group consists of four counter objects for maintaining various statistics and error counts for UDP.

A table was added for MIB-II to keep track of the IP address and port number of the local connections. This table brings the object total for the UDP group up to eight objects.

Every object in this group is mandatory. If the agent is not configured for a value for any of these objects, the objects must have a default initialization value of *zero*.

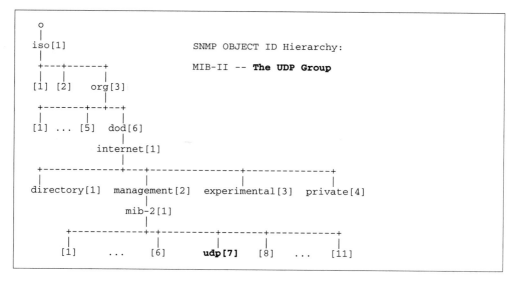

```
    o
    |
iso[1]                          SNMP OBJECT ID Hierarchy:
    |
    +---+------+                MIB-II -- The UDP Group
    |   |      |
   [1] [2]  org[3]
              |
    +-------+--+--+
    |       |     |
   [1] ... [5]  dod[6]
                  |
              internet[1]
                  |
   +-------------+---+---------------+--------------+
   |             |                   |              |
directory[1]  management[2]   experimental[3]  private[4]
                  |
              mib-2[1]
                  |
      +------------+-+---------+-------+-----------+
      |            |           |       |           |
     [1]    ...   [6]        udp[7]   [8]   ...    [11]
```

Figure 7-20. The UDP Group

7.1.8. THE EXTERIOR GATEWAY PROTOCOL GROUP

This group contains the managed objects needed for the Exterior Gateway Protocol.

The EGP Group ASN.1 OBJECT IDENTIFIER is { mib-2 8 }. Figure 7-21 depicts the EGP Group's position in the SNMP OBJECT ID Hierarchy.

The MIB-I definition for the EGP Group consists of four counters and the EGP Neighbor Table, for a total of eight objects.

For MIB-II, the EGP Neighbor Table was greatly expanded with the addition of 13 new columns. The egpAs object was also added.

Every object in this group is mandatory. If the agent is not configured for a value for any of these objects, the objects must have a default initialization value of *zero*.

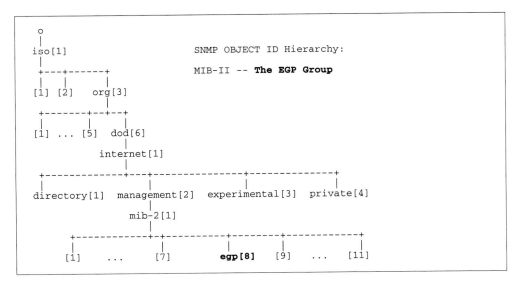

```
o
|
iso[1]                          SNMP OBJECT ID Hierarchy:
|
+---+------+                    MIB-II -- The EGP Group
|   |      |
[1] [2]   org[3]
|
+-------+--+--+
|       |     |
[1] ... [5]  dod[6]
              |
         internet[1]
              |
+------------+---+---------------+--------------+
|                |               |              |
directory[1]  management[2]  experimental[3]  private[4]
                 |
              mib-2[1]
                 |
    +------------+-+-----------+--------+-----------+
    |            |             |        |           |
   [1]    ...   [7]          egp[8]    [9]   ...   [11]
```

Figure 7-21. The EGP Group

7.1.9. THE TRANSMISSION GROUP

The Transmission Group contains the most prominent network access layer interface types that must be included if this media is to be managed on the network device. Originally, such definitions were first defined in the experimental MIB branch until they were used sufficiently to be included as part of the Internet standardization process. The general format of Transmission group types is:

type OBJECT IDENTIFIER   ::= { transmission number }

where type is the symbolic value used for the transmission media in the ifType column of the ifTable object (in the Interfaces Group). The transmission number is the corresponding integer value found in that table.

The Transmission Group ASN.1 OBJECT IDENTIFIER is { mib-2 10 }. Figure 7-22 depicts the Transmission Group's position in the SNMP OBJECT ID Hierarchy.

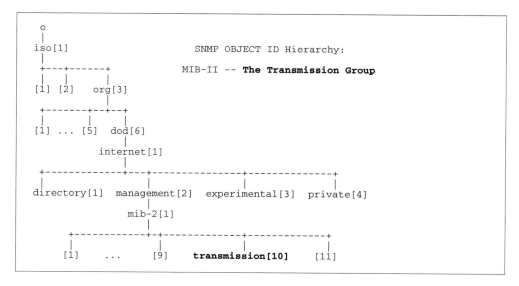

```
o
|
iso[1]                          SNMP OBJECT ID Hierarchy:
|
+---+------+                    MIB-II -- The Transmission Group
|   |      |
[1] [2]  org[3]
     |
+-------+--+--+
|   ...  |   |
[1] ... [5] dod[6]
             |
         internet[1]
             |
+------------+---+--------------+-------------+
|                |              |             |
directory[1]  management[2]  experimental[3]  private[4]
                 |
              mib-2[1]
                 |
     +------------+-+-------------+-------------+
     |            |               |             |
    [1]    ...   [9]      transmission[10]     [11]
```

Figure 7-22. The Transmission Group

Starting in January 1994, the MIBs began to be written to the new SMIv2 specification. Several of these transmission MIB Groups have already been updated using the new version 2 SMI, and their Version 1 MIBs have been obsoleted. Older technologies that are no longer implemented, such as 802.4 Token-Bus, have also been demoted to historical status. As of this writing, 16 defined MIB groups exist in the Transmission Group that have standard-track RFCs available for implementation. They are all presented in this chapter for convenience. I note in the appropriate section, where the MIB has been updated to the new SMIv2.

- X.25 Packet Layer Objects
- Ethernet-like Objects
- IEEE 802.5 Token Ring Objects
- FDDI Objects
- X.25 LAPB Link Layer Objects
- DS1/E1 Objects
- PPP Link Control Protocol Objects
- DS3/E3 Objects

- SMDS Interface Objects (SIP)

- Frame-Relay DTE Objects

- RS-232 Serial Device Objects

- Parallel Device Objects

- Multiprotocol over X.25 Objects

- Sonet/SDH Objects

- Frame Relay Service Objects

- IEEE 802.12 100 VG-AnyLAN Objects

Figure 7-23 shows the 16 currently defined Transmission MIB Groups with standard RFCs available. The table includes the MIB's OID, its latest RFC, and its current standard level. Several categories of MIB groups are for managing LAN and WAN technologies in a standardized fashion.

Three MIB groups deal with the X.25 packet technology. The X.25 Packet Layer Objects Group defines the objects for the MIB variables that represent the objects needed for managing the packet layer (level 3) of X.25. The X.25 Link Layer Objects Group defines the objects for the MIB variables that represent the objects needed for managing the link layer (level 2) of X.25. The Multi-protocol over X.25 Objects Group deals with implementing a variety of additional protocols to run over the packet network.

Three MIB groups exist for the common LAN technologies. The CSMA/CD-like Objects Group defines the objects for the ethernet-like specifications for carrier sense LANs. This "family" of network access protocols also includes the variants IEEE 802.3 standard for CSMA/CD, Ethernet, and StarLAN. The To-ken Ring-like Objects Group contains the objects needed to manage a Token Ring IEEE 802.5 LAN implementation. The 100 VG—AnyLAN Objects Group contains the objects needed to manage an IEEE 802.12 LAN interface.

The FDDI Objects Group defines the objects for the ANSI-specified FDDI LAN protocol. Since FDDI includes its own management scheme (Station Management, SMT), this MIB includes an interpretation of these key elements.

The DS1/E1 Carrier Objects Group and the DS3/E3 Interface Objects Group contain MIB objects for the physical interfaces based on the appropriate AT&T specifications.

The Transmission Groups			
Object Identifier	**MIB Transmission Group Name**	**RFC Number**	**Level**
1.3.6.1.2.1.10.5	X25 Packet Layer Objects	1382	proposed
1.3.6.1.2.1.10.7	CSMA/CD-like Objects	1643	full
1.3.6.1.2.1.10.9	Token Ring-like Objects	1748	draft
1.3.6.1.2.1.10.15	FDDI Objects	1512	proposed
1.3.6.1.2.1.10.16	X25 Link Layer Objects	1381	proposed
1.3.6.1.2.1.10.18	DS1/E1 Carrier Objects	1406	proposed
1.3.6.1.2.1.10.23	PPP Link Control Protocol Objects	1471	proposed
1.3.6.1.2.1.10.30	DS3/E3 Carrier Objects	1407	proposed
1.3.6.1.2.1.10.31	SMDS Interface Objects	1694	draft
1.3.6.1.2.1.10.32	Frame Relay DTE Objects	1315	proposed
1.3.6.1.2.1.10.33	RS-232 Objects	1659	draft
1.3.6.1.2.1.10.34	Parallel Printer Objects	1660	draft
1.3.6.1.2.1.10.38	Multiprotocol over X.25 Objects	1461	proposed
1.3.6.1.2.1.10.39	Sonet/SDH Objects	1595	proposed
1.3.6.1.2.1.10.44	Frame Relay Service Objects	1604	proposed
1.3.6.1.2.1.10.45	100VG- AnyLAN Objects	2020	proposed

Figure 7-23. The Transmission Groups

The Link Control Protocol for the PPP protocol Objects Group contains MIB objects for managing the Link Control Protocol and Link Quality Monitoring on subnetwork interfaces that use the Point-to-Point protocols.

The SMDS Interface Objects Group contains the MIB definitions for the use of IP over Switched Multi-megabit Data Service (SMDS). This includes management variables for the three layers defined for SMDS: SMDS over IP (SIP) Level 3, SIP Level 2, and the Physical Layer Convergence Protocol (PLCP) layer. An MIB Group also exists for Sonet and Synchronous Digital Hierarchy (SDH) protocols.

The Frame Relay DTE Objects Group contains objects for a Frame Relay interface to manage its data link connection, its circuits, and any errors that may occur. A Frame Relay Service Objects Group also exists.

MIB objects needed to manage synchronous or asynchronous serial, physical interfaces such as RS-232, RS-423, and V.35 are defined in the RS-232 Objects Group. The Parallel Printer Objects Group contains the MIB objects for defining the physical interface for parallel, printer-like interfaces.

I now present these 16 transmission MIB groups in more detail by listing the latest RFC that you should consult, its interface type value(s), its object identifier value, where it fits in the MIB-II Object Id hierarchy, and a brief overview of how the MIB objects are arranged for each group.

7.1.9.1. *The X.25 Packet Layer MIB Group*

The X.25 Packet Layer MIB Group contains the definitions for the MIB variables that represent the objects needed for managing the packet layer of X.25. The group is described in RFC 1382, *SNMP MIB Extension for the X.25 Packet Layer*. The `ifType` in the Interfaces Group distinguishes between the two types:

4	Dept. of Defense Version	(ddn-x25)
5	Internet Version	(rfc887-x25)

The X.25 Packet Layer MIB Group ASN.1 OBJECT IDENTIFIER is { transmission 5 }. Figure 7-24 depicts this group's position in the SNMP OBJECT ID Hierarchy.

The X.25 Packet Layer Group is composed of seven tables:

◆ X25AdmnTable

◆ X25OperTable

◆ X25StatTable

◆ X25ChannelTable

◆ X25CircuitTable

◆ X25Cleared CircuitTable

◆ X25CallParmTable

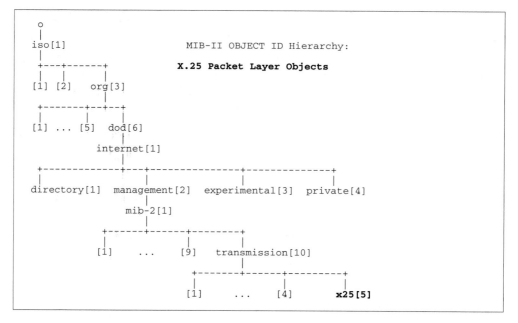

Figure 7-24. The X.25 Packet Layer Objects Group

7.1.9.2. Ethernet-Like MIB Group

The MIB extensions for the Ethernet-Like contention-based access protocol are defined in RFC 1643, *Definitions of Managed Objects for the Ethernet-Like Interface Types*. Three similar Interface Level protocols called "Ethernet-Like" use CSMA-CD. They vary in the media speed and header formats. The ifType in the Interfaces Group distinguishes among the three:

6	Standard Ethernet	(ethernet-csmacd)
7	IEEE 802.3	(iso88023-csmacd)
11	StarLAN Ethernet	(starLan)

This group is in the Object Identifier Hierarchy under the transmission branch with a value of seven or { transmission 7 }. Note that all objects in this group start with *dot3*, referring to the fact that this media is based on IEEE standard 802.3. This group must be implemented for network devices connected to the Internet via an Ethernet-Like medium. Figure 7-25 shows the MIB-II Object ID Hierarchy for Ethernet-Like objects:

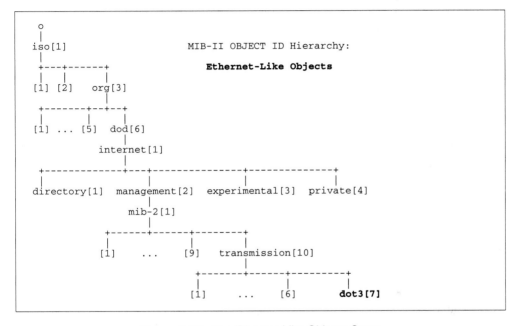

Figure 7-25. The Ethernet-Like Objects Group

This group is composed of three tables and several miscellaneous objects dealing with various tests and hardware chip sets. The five tables are:

◆ Status and Information Table

◆ Statistics Table

◆ Collisions Table

◆ Tests Table

◆ Error Table

7.1.9.3. IEEE 802.5 MIB Group

The MIB extensions for the Token Ring access protocol are defined in RFC 1748, *IEEE 802.5 Token Ring MIB using SNMPv2*. It is defined using the SNMPv2 SMI. The `ifType` in the Interfaces Group must be set to:

9	Token Ring	(iso88025-tokenRing)

This group is in the Object Identifier Hierarchy under the transmission branch with a value of nine or { transmission 9 }. Note that all objects in this group start with *dot5*, referring to the fact that this media is based on IEEE standard 802.5. The Figure 7-26 shows the MIB-II Object ID Hierarchy for Token-Ring objects:

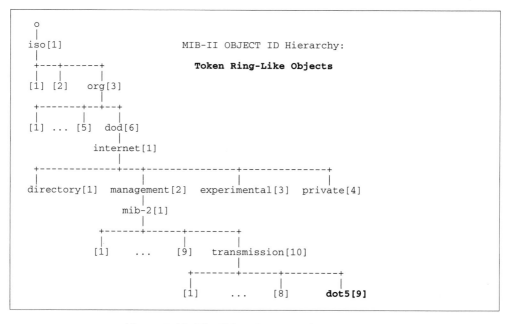

Figure 7-26. The Token Ring-Like Objects Group

This group is composed of four tables and several miscellaneous objects dealing with various tests and hardware chip sets. The four tables are:

♦ Interface Table

♦ Statistics Table

◆ Timer Table

◆ Interface Tests Table

This group must be implemented for network devices connected to the Internet using the Token Bus Controlled Protocol to access the medium.

7.1.9.4. FDDI MIB Group

The MIB extensions for the Fiber Distributed Data Interchange (FDDI) are defined in RFC 1512, *FDDI Management Information Base*. The ifType in the Interfaces Group must be set to:

15	FDDI	(fddi)

This group is in the Object Identifier Hierarchy under the transmission branch with a value of fifteen or { transmission 15 }.

Figure 7-27 shows the MIB-II Object ID Hierarchy for FDDI objects:

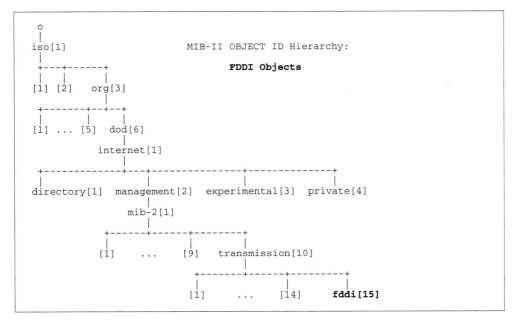

Figure 7-27. The FDDI Objects Group

225

This group is composed of six groups:

◆   The SMT Group

◆   The MAC Group

◆   The PATH Group

◆   The PORT Group

◆   The ATTACHMENT Group

◆   The Chip Sets Group

This group must be implemented for network devices connected to the Internet using the FDDI Protocol to access the medium.

7.1.9.5. X.25 LAPB MIB Group

The X.25 Link Layer (LAPB) MIB Group contains the definitions for the MIB variables that represent the objects needed for managing the link layer of X.25. The group is described in RFC 1381, *SNMP MIB Extension for the X.25 LAPB.* The ifType in the Interfaces Group is:

16	link access protocol (balanced)	(lapb)

The LAPB Group ASN.1 OBJECT IDENTIFIER is { transmission 16 }. Figure 7-28 depicts this group's position in the SNMP OBJECT ID Hierarchy.

The X.25 Link Layer Group is composed of four tables:

◆   lapbAdmnTable

◆   lapbOperTable

◆   lapbFlowTable

◆   lapbXidTable

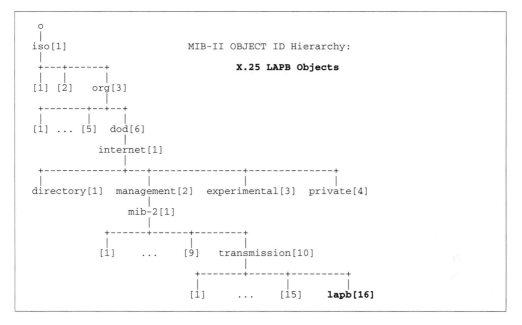

```
o
|
iso[1]                          MIB-II OBJECT ID Hierarchy:
|
+---+------+                        X.25 LAPB Objects
|   |      |
[1] [2]   org[3]
           |
+-------+--+--+
|       |     |
[1] ... [5]  dod[6]
              |
          internet[1]
              |
+-------------+---+---------------+--------------+
|                 |               |              |
directory[1]  management[2]  experimental[3]  private[4]
                  |
              mib-2[1]
                  |
          +------+------+--------+
          |             |        |
         [1]    ...    [9]   transmission[10]
                                  |
                      +-------+------+---------+
                      |              |         |
                     [1]    ...    [15]     lapb[16]
```

Figure 7-28. The X.25 LAPB Objects Group

7.1.9.6. *DS1 MIB Group*

The DS1 MIB Group contains the definitions for the MIB variables that represent the objects needed for managing DS1/E1 physical interfaces. The group is described in RFC 1406, *Definitions of Managed Objects for the DS1 and E1 Interface Types*. Two different DS1/E1 types are defined by the ifType in the Interfaces Group:

18	T-1 (1.544 Mbps)	(ds1)
19	European version of T-1	(e1)

The DS1 Group ASN.1 OBJECT IDENTIFIER is { transmission 18 }. Figure 7-29 depicts this group's position in the SNMP OBJECT ID Hierarchy.

The DS1 Group is composed of three sub-groups:

◆ DS1 Near End Group (mandatory)

◆ DS1 Far End Group (optional)

◆ Fractional Table (optional)

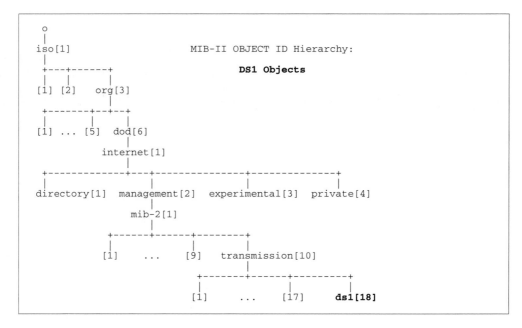

```
  o
  |
iso[1]                          MIB-II OBJECT ID Hierarchy:
  |
  +---+------+                      DS1 Objects
  |   |      |
 [1] [2]   org[3]
  |
  +-------+--+--+
  |       |     |
 [1] ... [5]  dod[6]
                 |
             internet[1]
                 |
  +------------+---+---------------+---------------+
  |            |                   |               |
directory[1] management[2]  experimental[3]  private[4]
                 |
             mib-2[1]
                 |
         +------+------+--------+
         |      |       |
        [1]    ...     [9]   transmission[10]
                                 |
                    +-------+------+--------+
                    |       |      |        |
                   [1]     ...    [17]    ds1[18]
```

Figure 7-29. The DS1 Objects Group

7.1.9.7. *PPP Link Control Protocol MIB Group*

This MIB Group contains the definitions for the MIB variables the Link Control Protocol and Link Quality Monitoring on subnetwork interfaces that use the Point-to-Point protocols require. The group is described in RFC 1471, *The Definitions of Managed Objects for the Link Control Protocol of the Point-to-Point Protocol*.

The PPP LCP Group ASN.1 OBJECT IDENTIFIER is { transmission 23 }. Figure 7-30 depicts this group's position in the SNMP OBJECT ID Hierarchy.

The PPP LCP MIB Group is comprised of six sub-groups:

- The PPP Link Group
- The PPP LQR Group
- The PPP LQR Extensions Group
- The PPP IP Group
- The PPP Bridge Group
- The PPP Security Group

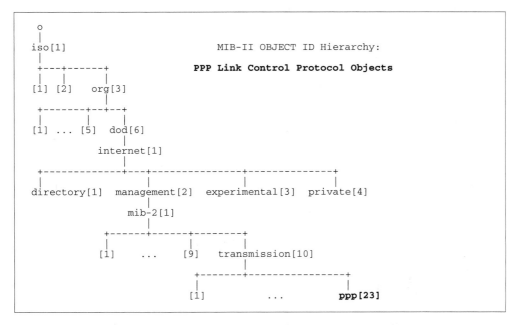

```
  o
  |
iso[1]                            MIB-II OBJECT ID Hierarchy:
  |
  +---+------+                    PPP Link Control Protocol Objects
  |   |      |
 [1] [2]  org[3]
            |
    +-------+--+--+
    |       |     |
   [1] ... [5]  dod[6]
                  |
             internet[1]
                  |
  +-------------+---+---------------+--------------+
  |             |                   |              |
directory[1]  management[2]    experimental[3]  private[4]
                  |
              mib-2[1]
                  |
        +------+------+--------+
        |      |       |
       [1]    ...     [9]   transmission[10]
                                  |
                       +-------+----------------+
                       |                        |
                      [1]           ...       ppp[23]
```

Figure 7-30. The PPP Link Control Protocol Objects Group

7.1.9.8. DS3 MIB Group

The DS3 MIB Group contains the definitions for the MIB variables that represent the objects needed for managing DS3 physical interfaces. The group is described in RFC 1407, *Definitions of Managed Objects for the DS3/E3 Interface Type*. The DS3 type defined by the `ifType` in the Interfaces Group is:

30	T-3	(ds3)

   The DS3 Group ASN.1 OBJECT IDENTIFIER is { transmission 30 }. Figure 7-31 depicts this group's position in the SNMP OBJECT ID Hierarchy.
   The DS3 Group is composed of three groups:

♦ D3/E3 Near End Group (mandatory)

♦ D3 Far End Group (optional)

♦ D3 Fractional Group (optional)

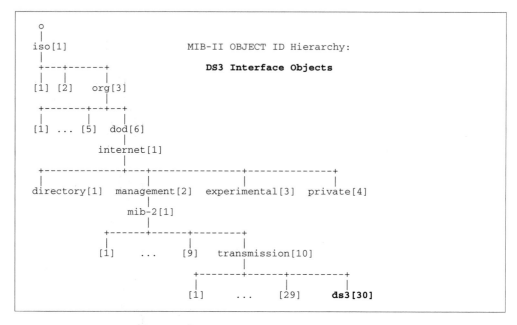

Figure 7-31. The DS3 Interface Objects Group

7.1.9.9. *SMDS Interface Objects (SIP) MIB Group*

The Switched Multi-megabit Data Service (SMDS) Interface Protocol (SIP) MIB Group contains the definitions for managing SIP objects. RFC 1694, *Definitions of Managed Objects for SMDS Interfaces using SNMPv2* presents the listing of these MIB objects. This MIB Group is defined using the SNMPv2 SMI and includes the newly defined access interfaces for running the SMDS service over Frame Relay and ATM.

The SIP MIB ASN.1 OBJECT IDENTIFIER is under the transmission branch with the Object Identifier of { transmission 31 }. Figure 7-32 depicts this Group's position in the SNMP OBJECT ID Hierarchy.

The SIP Group is comprised of six major groups:

◆ SIP Level 3 Table
◆ SIP Level 2 Table
◆ SIP Physical Layer Convergence Procedure (PLCP) Tables
◆ SMDS Applications
◆ SMDS Carrier Selection
◆ SIP Error Log

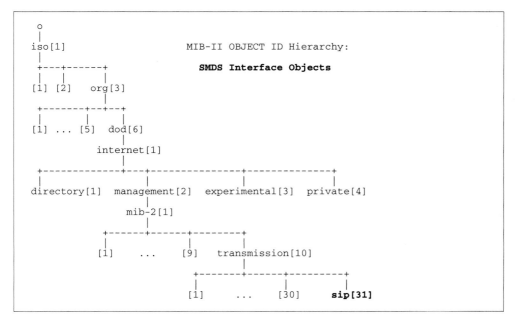

```
    o
    |
 iso[1]                      MIB-II OBJECT ID Hierarchy:
    |
    +---+------+              SMDS Interface Objects
    |   |      |
  [1] [2]   org[3]
             |
    +-------+--+--+
    |       |     |
  [1] ... [5]  dod[6]
                 |
            internet[1]
                 |
    +-------------+---+---------------+--------------+
    |                 |               |              |
 directory[1]  management[2]  experimental[3]  private[4]
                 |
              mib-2[1]
                 |
        +------+------+--------+
        |             |        |
      [1]     ...    [9]   transmission[10]
                              |
                 +-------+------+--------+
                 |              |        |
               [1]     ...    [30]    sip[31]
```

Figure 7-32. The SMDS Interface Objects Group

7.1.9.10. *Frame Relay DTE MIB Group*

The Frame Relay DTE MIB Group contains the definitions for the MIB variables that represent the objects needed for managing Frame Relay. The group is described in RFC 1315, *Management Information for Frame Relay DTEs*. The Frame Relay type defined by the `ifType` in the Interfaces Group is:

32	Frame-Relay protocol	(frame-relay)

The Frame Relay Group ASN.1 OBJECT IDENTIFIER is { transmission 32 }. Figure 7-33 depicts this group's position in the SNMP OBJECT ID Hierarchy.

This group is composed of two tables and several miscellaneous objects dealing with various global variables. The two tables are:

♦ Frame Relay Data Link Connection Management Interface (DLCMI) Table

♦ Frame Relay Circuit Table

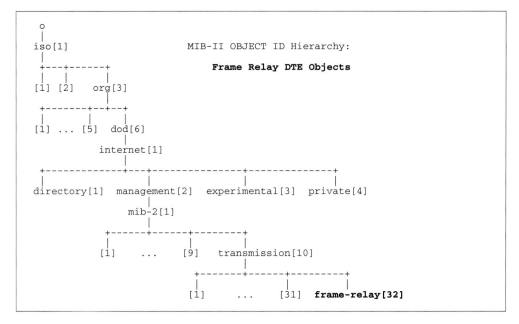

```
 o
 |
 iso[1]                        MIB-II OBJECT ID Hierarchy:
 |
 |                                Frame Relay DTE Objects
 +---+------+
 |   |      |
[1] [2]  org[3]
            |
 +-------+--+--+
 |       |     |
[1] ... [5]  dod[6]
              |
         internet[1]
              |
 +-------------+---+--------------+--------------+
 |             |                  |              |
directory[1]  management[2]  experimental[3]  private[4]
              |
          mib-2[1]
              |
     +------+------+--------+
     |      |      |        |
    [1]    ...    [9]  transmission[10]
                         |
          +-------+------+---------+
          |       |      |         |
         [1]     ...    [31]  frame-relay[32]
```

Figure 7-33. The Frame Relay DTE Objects Group

7.1.9.11. RS-232 MIB Group

The RS-232 MIB Group contains the definitions for the MIB variables that represent the objects needed for managing RS-232-like hardware devices at the physical layer. The group is described in RFC 1659, *Definitions Of Managed Objects For RS-232-Like Hardware Devices using SNMPv2*. It is defined using the SNMPv2 MIB.

The RS-232 Group ASN.1 OBJECT IDENTIFIER is { transmission 33 }. Figure 7-34 depicts this group's position in the SNMP OBJECT ID Hierarchy.

The RS232 Group is composed of a count and five tables:

◆ A Count of the Number of RS232 Ports

◆ RS232 Port Table

◆ Asynchronous Port Table

◆ Synchronous Port Table

◆ Input Signal Table

◆ Output Signal Table

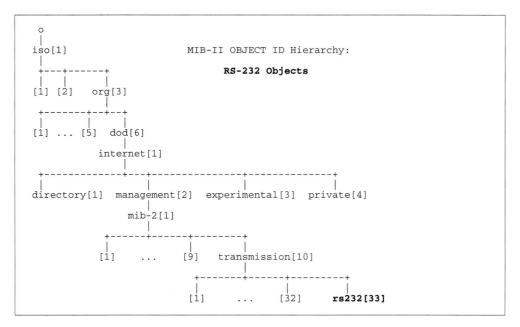

Figure 7-34. The RS-232 Objects Group

This group must be implemented for all network devices that have RS232-like hardware ports that are supported by higher-level software such as character streams or network interfaces.

7.1.9.12. Parallel-Printer-Like MIB Group

The Parallel-Printer-Like MIB Group contains the definitions for the MIB variables that represent the objects needed for managing parallel-printer-like hardware devices at the physical layer. The two common industry standards for parallel printer ports are the "Centronic" and "Data Products" type. RFC 1660, *Definitions Of Managed Objects For Parallel-Printer-Like Hardware Devices using SNMPv2*, describes the group. It is defined using the SNMPv2 SMI.

The Parallel-Printer-Like Group ASN.1 OBJECT IDENTIFIER is { transmission 34 }. Figure 7-35 depicts this group's position in the SNMP OBJECT ID Hierarchy.

The Parallel-Printer-Like Group is composed of a count and three tables:

♦ A Count of the Number of Parallel-Printer-like Ports

♦ Port Table

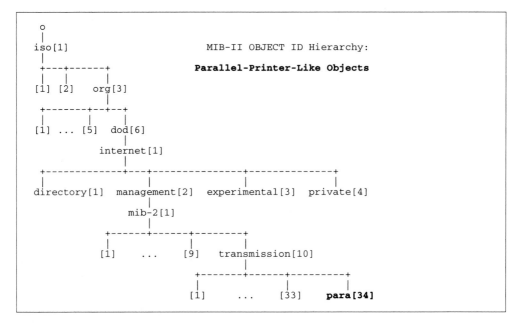

```
 o
 |
iso[1]                           MIB-II OBJECT ID Hierarchy:
 |
 +---+------+                    Parallel-Printer-Like Objects
 |   |      |
[1] [2]   org[3]
           |
 +-------+--+--+
 |       |     |
[1] ... [5]   dod[6]
               |
           internet[1]
               |
 +-------------+---+----------------+--------------+
 |                 |                |              |
directory[1]   management[2]   experimental[3]  private[4]
                   |
               mib-2[1]
                   |
           +------+------+--------+
           |      |      |        |
          [1]    ...    [9]   transmission[10]
                                   |
                       +-------+------+---------+
                       |       |      |         |
                      [1]     ...   [33]    para[34]
```

Figure 7-35. The Parallel-Printer-Like Objects Group

◆ Input Signal Table

◆ Output Signal Table

This group must be implemented for all network devices that have parallel-printer-like hardware ports that are supported by higher-level software such as character streams.

7.1.9.13. Multiprotocol Over X.25 MIB Group

The Multiprotocol Over X.25 MIB Group contains the definitions for the MIB variables that represent the objects needed for managing multiprotocol interconnect data traffic that runs over X.25. RFC 1461, *SNMP MIB Extensions for Multiprotocol Interconnect Over X.25*, describes the group.

The Multiprotocol Over X.25 Group ASN.1 OBJECT IDENTIFIER is { transmission 38 }. Figure 7-36 depicts this group's position in the SNMP OBJECT ID Hierarchy.

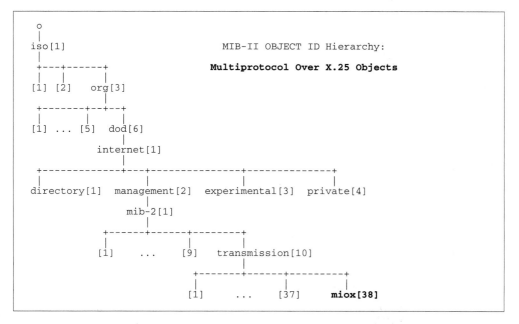

Figure 7-36. The Multiprotocol Over X.25 Objects Group

This group is composed of three tables. These three tables are:

◆ the mioxPleTable

◆ mioxPeerTable

◆ mioxPeerEncTable

7.1.9.14. *SONET/SDH MIB Group*

The SONET/SDH MIB Group contains the definitions for the MIB variables that represent the objects needed for managing SONET and Synchronous Digital Hierarchy (SDH). The group is described in RFC 1595, *Definitions of Managed Objects for the SONET/SDH Interface Types*. It is written using the version 2 SMI. The SONET/SDH type defined by the ifType in the Interfaces Group is:

39	Sonet	(sonet)

The SONET/SDH Group ASN.1 OBJECT IDENTIFIER is { transmission 39 }. Figure 7-37 depicts this group's position in the SNMP OBJECT ID Hierarchy:

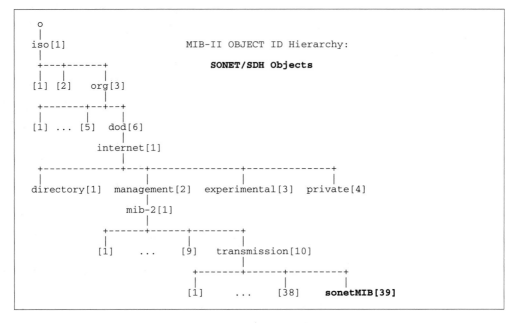

Figure 7-37. The SONET/SDH Group

This group is comprised of several subgroups required for managing SONET paths and connections.

7.1.9.15. Frame Relay Service MIB Group

The Frame Relay Service MIB Group contains the definitions for the MIB variables that represent the objects needed for managing Frame Relay Service. RFC 1604, *Definitions of Managed Objects for Frame Relay Service*, describes the group. It is defined using SMIv2. The Frame Relay type defined by the ifType in the Interfaces Group is:

44	Frame Relay Service	(frame relay service)

The Frame Relay Service Group ASN.1 OBJECT IDENTIFIER is { transmission 44 }. Figure 7-38 depicts this group's position in the SNMP OBJECT ID Hierarchy:

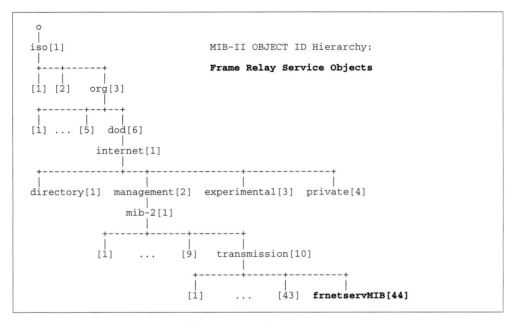

```
o
|
iso[1]                          MIB-II OBJECT ID Hierarchy:
|
+---+------+                    Frame Relay Service Objects
|   |      |
[1] [2]  org[3]
         |
   +-------+--+--+
   |       |     |
  [1] ... [5]  dod[6]
                |
          internet[1]
                |
 +-------------+---+--------------+--------------+
 |                 |              |              |
directory[1]  management[2]  experimental[3]  private[4]
                  |
              mib-2[1]
                  |
        +------+------+--------+
        |      |      |        |
       [1]    ...    [9]  transmission[10]
                              |
                    +-------+------+---------+
                    |       |      |         |
                   [1]     ...    [43]  frnetservMIB[44]
```

Figure 7-38. The Frame Relay Service Objects Group

This group is composed of five tables:

◆ Frame Relay Port Table

◆ Frame Relay Management VC Signaling Group

◆ The PVC End-Point Group

◆ The PVC Connection Group

◆ The Frame Relay Accounting Groups

7.1.9.16. 100 VG – AnyLAN MIB Group

The 100 VG – AnyLAN MIB Group contains the definitions for the MIB variables that represent the objects needed for managing IEEE 802.12 interfaces. The group is described in RFC 2020, *Definitions of Managed Objects for IEEE*

801.12 Interfaces. It is defined using SMIv2. The ifType in the Interfaces Group is:

55	IEEE 802.12	(ieee 80212)

The IEEE 802.12 Interface Group ASN.1 OBJECT IDENTIFIER is { transmission 45 }. Figure 7-39 depicts this group's position in the SNMP OBJECT ID Hierarchy.

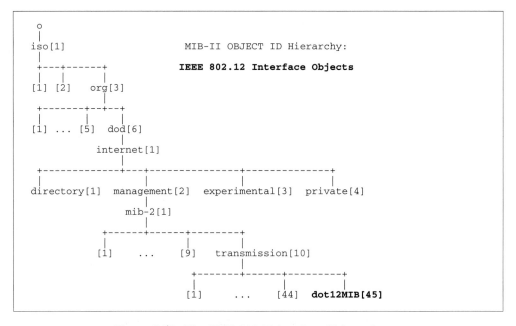

Figure 7-39. The IEEE 802.12 Interface Objects Group

This group is composed of two tables:

♦ 802.12 Interface Configuration Table

♦ 802.12 Status Table

The 100 VG – AnyLAN MIB Group is currently the "last" defined transmission group. The SNMP Group is the standard MIB-II group that follows the Transmission sub-tree.

7.1.10. THE SNMP GROUP

The Simple Network Management Protocol (SNMP) Group contains the objects that are about the SNMP itself. This group represents a collection of meaningful counters, status conditions, errors detected, and so forth.

The SNMP Group ASN.1 OBJECT IDENTIFIER is { mib-2 11 }. Figure 7-40 depicts the SNMP Group's position in the SNMP OBJECT ID Hierarchy.

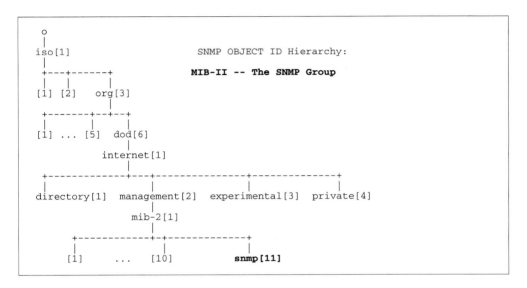

Figure 7-40. The SNMP Group

The MIB-I does not define the SNMP group.

MIB-II defined the SNMP group. In RFC 1213, two objects in the group were un-defined: `snmpInBadTypes` and `snmpOutReadOnlys`. Consistent with the ASN.1 naming hierarchy rules, these OBJECT IDENTIFIERS are reserved and cannot be reused. The object `snmpEnableAuthTraps` has its spelling changed to `snmpEnableAuthenTraps`. The SNMP group currently consists of 28 managed objects.

Every object in this group is mandatory. If the agent is not configured for a value for any of these objects, the objects must have a default initialization value of zero.

7.2. EXTENSIONS TO THE MIB-II SUB-TREE

The original design for MIB-II for SNMP included the standard sub-tree for the ten groups presented in the beginning of this chapter (remember that the CMOT group, 1.3.6.1.1.2.9. is not relevant for SNMP). Therefore, the highest numbered object identifier in this sub-tree was the SNMP Group (1.3.6.1.2.1.11.). Additional groups were to be assigned object identifiers in the `experimental` sub-tree (1.3.6.1.3.). These groups included various media-specific groups, additional protocols, and new types of network devices.

However, having to first define the groups in the `experimental` sub-tree introduced unnecessary complications. Once an `experimental` sub-tree branch was deemed satisfactory and suitable to be considered as a standard, it had to be pruned from the experimental sub-tree and then grafted into its new branch on the standard MIB-II branch. This structure also creates redundancy because once an object is named, it can never be removed. This fact is stated in RFC 1239, *Reassignment of Experimental MIBs to Standard MIBs*: "This practice required vendors to revise their implementations when a MIB went from Draft to Full Standard status, even though there was probably no substantive technical change in the definitions. This practice could also engender operational problems in the field at an undesirably late stage of the standardization process."

Not only would the implementations have to be retrofitted to accommodate the new object types, but many SNMP implementers might delay the release of their products until a particular MIB Group was granted the Full Standard appellation.

In order to anticipate the standardization of these new MIB groups, and also in keeping with the two key tenets of SNMP—simplicity and extensibility—the IAB wanted to assign the object identifiers for these new MIB Groups as early as possible. And because these identifiers are administratively assigned and unique, they would be retained throughout the standardization process.

Because the SNMP Group uses 1.3.6.1.2.1.11 as its object identifier, these new MIB Group extensions will be assigned the next contiguous values in the MIB-II namespace. With this in mind, 30 new groups are defined for the standards track at this writing:

◆ AppleTalk II Group

◆ Open Shortest Path First (Version 2) Group

- Border Gateway Protocol (Version 4) Group
- Remote Network Monitoring MIB Group
- Managed Objects for Bridges Group
- DECnet Phase IV MIB Extensions Group
- MIB for Character Stream Devices Group
- MIB For IEEE 802.3 Repeater Devices Group
- RIP Version 2 MIB Extensions
- Identification MIB Group
- Host Resources Group
- IEEE 802.3 Medium Attachment Unit Group
- Network Services Monitoring Group
- Mail Monitoring Group
- X.500 Directory Group
- Evolution of IF Group of MIB-II Objects Group
- DNS Server and Resolver Group
- Uninterruptible Power Supply Group
- SNA NAU Group
- Ether-like Interface Type (v2) Group
- SMDS Interface Protocol Group
- ATM Group
- Modem Group
- Relational Database Management System Group
- SNA DLC Group
- 802.5 Station Source Routing Objects Group
- Printer Group
- IP Mobility Support Objects Group
- Data Link Switching Objects Group
- Entity Group

I introduce and describe these groups in a similar manner to the MIB-II standard and transmission groups I already presented. This discussion involves giving a general introduction to the group and depicting its place in the SNMP Object ID hierarchy.

Figure 7-41 shows the 30 currently defined MIB groups that were added to the MIB-II branch. The groups for Generic Interface Extension Objects ({mib-2 12}) have been updated by RFC 1573, *Evolution of the Interfaces Group of MIB-II*, ({mib-2 31}). The two extensions for the proposed standard of SNMPv2 containing the MIBs for administration and security have also been relegated to historic status.

The Standard MIB Extension Groups			
Object Identifier	**MIB Extension Group Name**	**RFC Number**	**StandardLevel**
1.3.6.1.2.1.13	AppleTalk II Objects	1742	proposed
1.3.6.1.2.1.14	Open Shortest Path First (Version 2) Objects	1850	draft
1.3.6.1.2.1.15	Border Gateway Protocol (Version 4) Objects	1657	draft
1.3.6.1.2.1.16	Remote Network Monitoring Objects	1757	draft
1.3.6.1.2.1.17	Managed Objects for Bridges	1493	draft
1.3.6.1.2.1.18	DECnet Phase IV MIB Extensions Objects	1559	draft
1.3.6.1.2.1.19	MIB for Character Stream Devices Objects	1658	draft
1.3.6.1.2.1.22	MIB For IEEE 802.3 Repeater Devices Objects	1516	draft
1.3.6.1.2.1.23	RIP Version 2 MIB Extensions Objects	1724	draft
1.3.6.1.2.1.24	Identification Objects	1414	proposed
1.3.6.1.2.1.25	Host Resources Objects	1514	proposed
1.3.6.1.2.1.26	IEEE 802.3 Medium Attachment Unit Objects	1515	proposed
1.3.6.1.2.1.27	Network Services Monitoring Objects	1565	proposed
1.3.6.1.2.1.28	Mail Monitoring Objects	1566	proposed
1.3.6.1.2.1.29	X.500 Directory Objects	1567	proposed

Figure 7-41. The Standard MIB-II Extension Groups

Object Identifier	MIB Extension Group Name	RFC Number	StandardLevel
1.3.6.1.2.1.30	Evolution of IF Group of MIB-II Objects	1573	proposed
1.3.6.1.2.1.32	DNS Server and Resolver Objects	1611	proposed
1.3.6.1.2.1.33	Uninterruptible Power Supply Objects	1628	proposed
1.3.6.1.2.1.34	SNA NAU Objects	1666	proposed
1.3.6.1.2.1.35	Ether-like Interface Type (v2) Objects	1650	proposed
1.3.6.1.2.1.36	SMDS Interface Protocol Objects	1694	draft
1.3.6.1.2.1.37	ATM Objects	1695	proposed
1.3.6.1.2.1.38	Modem Objects	1696	proposed
1.3.6.1.2.1.39	Relational DB Management Objects	1697	proposed
1.3.6.1.2.1.41	SNA DLC Objects	1747	proposed
1.3.6.1.2.1.42	802.5 Station Source Routing Objects	1749	proposed
1.3.6.1.2.1.43	Printer Objects	1759	proposed
1.3.6.1.2.1.44	IP Mobility Support Objects	2006	proposed
1.3.6.1.2.1.46	Data Link Switching Objects	2024	proposed
1.3.6.1.2.1.47	Entity Objects	2037	proposed

Figure 7-41. The Standard MIB-II Extension Groups *(continued)*

The 30 currently defined Standard MIB-II Extension Groups allow for the management of a wide variety of Internet resources and protocols.

The AppleTalk Group has the definitions for objects needed to manage the protocols of the AppleTalk protocol suite.

Three MIB Group extensions are available for managing routers: the Open Shortest Path First (Version 2) Group contains the objects needed to manage a router that uses OSPF; the Border Gateway Protocol (Version 3) Group contains objects needed to manage a BGP-based router; and Routing Information Protocol (Version 2) Group contains objects for this interior gateway protocol.

The Remote Network Monitoring MIB Group defines the RMON objects. The first release of the RFC is solely for the monitoring of Ethernet-like segments, but work is progressing and is being added for Token Ring RMON management. Additionally, RMON2 will be released soon and will include the management of the higher level protocols.

The Managed Objects for Bridges Group contains the MIB objects for bridge management. It includes objects for both the IEEE 802.1d transparent bridging method and the IBM Token Ring source routing bridging method. The MIB For IEEE 802.3 Repeater Devices Group contains objects for the management of IEEE 802.3 10 Mbps baseband repeaters. These devices are also called *hubs*. An MIB group also exists for IEEE 802.3 Medium Attachment Unit Objects.

The DECnet Phase IV MIB Extensions Group contains the MIB definitions for the Digital Equipment Corporation's DECnet (Phase IV) protocol suite. It is specifically derived from the DECnet Architecture Network Management Functional Specification (4.0.0) from July 1983.

The MIB for Character Stream Devices Group contains objects for the management of virtual or physical character stream ports. The Printer Objects Group can manage the parallel streams primarily used by printers. Now, a standard MIB for modem management also exists. Uninterruptible Power Supply Objects can be implemented to manage UPS devices.

The Identification MIB Group contains the definitions for a set of objects that can identify the users associated with TCP connections. The Host Resources Objects Group contains objects for managing the hardware and software within a workstation or PC. The Host Resources MIB is used for systems management.

Network Services Monitoring Objects, Mail Monitoring Objects, and X.500 Directory Objects also have their own MIB groups for managing these important application level services. The Domain Name Server and Resolver Objects can be used for these network naming services. Relational DB Management Objects can be used to manage RDBMSs in a standard fashion.

SMDS Interface Protocol Objects and ATM Objects are present for managing these WAN protocols. The Ether-like Interface Type (v2) objects have been added on the LAN side.

Also, two MIBs exist for managing SNA on the Internet: the SNA DLC Objects Group and the SNA NAU Objects Group.

The latest three standard MIB-II MIBs deal with the new developments in networking and SNMP implementation. They include MIBs for managing IP Mobility Support, Data Link Switching, and the Entity MIB. The Entity MIB allows a single agent to support multiple instances of a MIB in a standard way.

It is useful for such cases as having multiple instances of repeaters or routers in a single network device that contains a single SNMP agent.

7.2.1. THE APPLETALK MIB GROUP

The AppleTalk Group contains the definitions for the MIB variables that represent the objects needed for managing an AppleTalk network. RFC 1742, *AppleTalk Management Information Base II* describes the group.

The AppleTalk Group ASN.1 OBJECT IDENTIFIER is { mib-2 13 }. Figure 7-42 depicts the AppleTalk Group's position in the SNMP OBJECT ID Hierarchy.

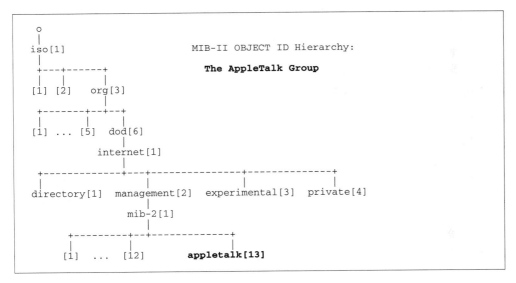

Figure 7-42. The AppleTalk Group

The AppleTalk Group is comprised of nine groups:

- LocalTalk Link Access Protocol (LLAP) Group
- AppleTalk Address Resolution Protocol (AARP) Group
- AppleTalk Port (ATPort) Group
- Datagram Delivery Protocol (DDP) Group
- Routing Table Maintenance Protocol (RTMP) Group
- Kinetics Internet Protocol (KIP) Group

- ◆ Zone Information Protocol (ZIP) Group
- ◆ Name Binding Protocol (NBP) Group
- ◆ AppleTalk Echo Protocol (ATEcho) Group

7.2.2. OPEN SHORTEST PATH FIRST MIB

The Open Shortest Path First (OSPF) MIB Group contains the definitions for the MIB variables that represent the objects needed for this interior routing protocol. They are described in RFC 1850, *OSPF Version 2 Management Information Base*.

The OSPF Group ASN.1 OBJECT IDENTIFIER is { mib-2 14 }. Figure 7-43 depicts this group's position in the SNMP OBJECT ID Hierarchy.

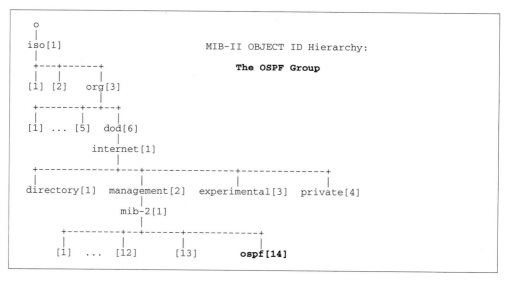

Figure 7-43. The OSPF Group

The OSPF Group is comprised of:

- ◆ General Variables
- ◆ Area Data Structure
- ◆ Area Stub Metric Table
- ◆ Link State Database

- Address Range Table

- Host Table

- Interface Table

- Interface Metric Table

- Virtual Interface Table

- Neighbor Table

- Virtual Neighbor Table

7.2.3. BORDER GATEWAY PROTOCOL MIB

The Border Gateway Protocol (BGP) MIB Group contains the definitions for the MIB variables that represent the objects needed for this interior routing protocol. They are described in RFC 1657, *Definitions of Managed Objects for the Fourth Version of the Border Gateway Protocol (BGP-4) using SMIv2*.

The BGP Group ASN.1 OBJECT IDENTIFIER is { mib-2 15 }. Figure 7-44 depicts this group's position in the SNMP OBJECT ID Hierarchy.

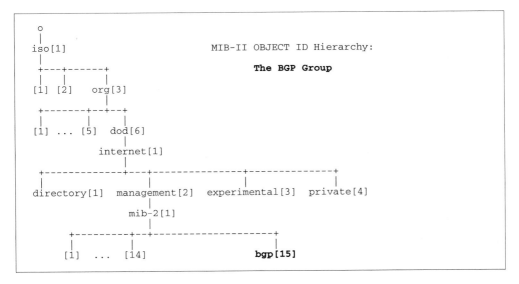

Figure 7-44. The BGP Group

The BGP Group is comprised of several important variables (such as the BGP version number, the local autonomous system number, and the local system identifier) and two tables:

◆ The Border Gateway Protocol Peer Table

◆ The Border Gateway Protocol Path Attribute Table

7.2.4. REMOTE NETWORK MONITORING MIB

The RMON group contains the definitions for the MIB variables that represent the objects needed for Remote Monitoring. It is described in RFC 1757, *Remote Network Monitoring Management Information Base.*

The RMON Group ASN.1 OBJECT IDENTIFIER is { mib-2 16 }. Figure 7-45 depicts the RMON Group's position in the SNMP OBJECT ID Hierarchy.

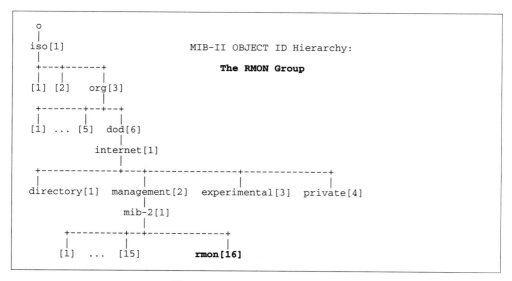

Figure 7-45. The RMON Group

The RMON Group is comprised of nine sub-groups:

◆ The Statistics Group

◆ The History Group

◆ The Alarm Group

◆ The Host Group

- ◆ The HostTopNGroup
- ◆ The Matrix Group
- ◆ The Filter Group
- ◆ The Packet Capture Group
- ◆ The Event Group

7.2.5. MANAGED OBJECTS FOR BRIDGES

The Managed Objects for Bridges MIB Group contains the definitions for the MIB variables that represent the objects needed for managing bridge devices. They are described in RFC 1493, *Definitions of Managed Objects for Bridges*.

The Bridge Group ASN.1 OBJECT IDENTIFIER is { mib-2 17 }. Figure 7-46 depicts this group's position in the SNMP OBJECT ID Hierarchy.

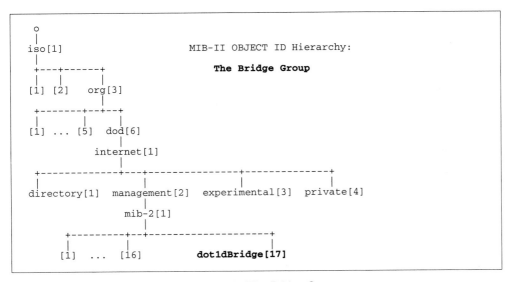

Figure 7-46. The Bridge Group

The Bridge MIB Group is comprised of five groups:

- ◆ The Common Base Group
- ◆ The Spanning Tree Protocol (STP) Group
- ◆ The Source Route Bridging Mode Group

◆ The Transparent Bridging Mode Group

◆ The Static (Destination-Address Filtering) Database Group

7.2.6. DECNET PHASE IV MIB EXTENSIONS

The DECnet Phase IV MIB Extensions Group contains the definitions for the MIB variables that represent the objects needed for managing the DECnet Phase IV set of protocols under the SNMP framework. This MIB extension group is described in RFC 1559, *DECnet Phase IV MIB Extensions*.

The DECnet Phase IV Group ASN.1 OBJECT IDENTIFIER is { mib-2 18 }. Figure 7-47 depicts this group's position in the MIB-II OBJECT ID Hierarchy.

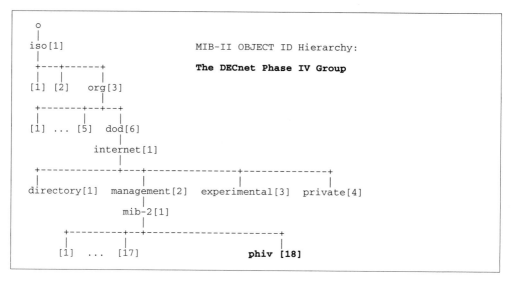

Figure 7-47. The DECnet Phase IV Group

The DECnet Phase IV Group is composed of 14 groups:

◆ System Group

◆ Network Management Group

◆ Session Group

◆ End Group

◆ Routing Group

- ◆ Circuit Group
- ◆ DDCMP Group
- ◆ DDCMP Multipoint Control Group
- ◆ Ethernet Group
- ◆ Counters Group
- ◆ Adjacency Group
- ◆ Line Group
- ◆ Non Broadcast Line Group
- ◆ Area Group

7.2.7. CHARACTER STREAM DEVICE MIB

The Character Stream Device group contains the definitions for the MIB variables that represent the objects needed for character stream devices. It is described in RFC 1658, *Definitions of Managed Objects For Character Stream Devices using SMIv2.*

The Character Stream Group ASN.1 OBJECT IDENTIFIER is { mib-2 19 }. Figure 7-48 depicts this group's position in the SNMP OBJECT ID Hierarchy.

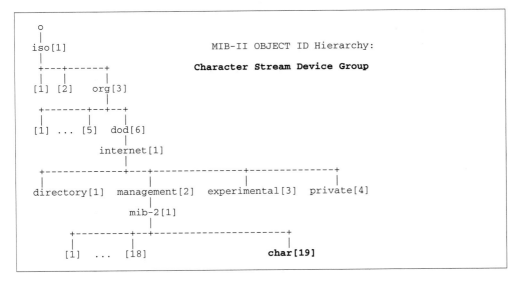

Figure 7-48. The Character Stream Device Group

251

The Character Stream Group is comprised of two tables:

♦ The Port Table
♦ The Session Table

This group must be implemented for all network devices that offer character ports.

7.2.8. MIB FOR IEEE 802.3 REPEATER DEVICES

The MIB for IEEE 802.3 Repeater Devices contains the definitions for the MIB variables that represent the objects needed for the management of these devices. IEEE 802.3 10 megabit/second baseband repeaters are often referred to as hubs. This MIB is described in RFC 1516, *Definitions of Managed Objects For IEEE 802.3 Repeater Devices.*

The Hub Group ASN.1 OBJECT IDENTIFIER is { mib-2 22 }. Figure 7-49 depicts this group's position in the SNMP OBJECT ID Hierarchy.

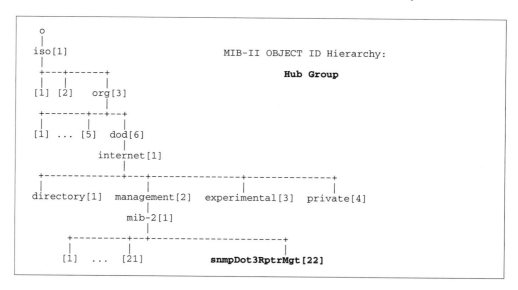

Figure 7-49. The Hub Group

The Hub MIB Group is comprised of three major groups:

♦ The Basic Group (a mandatory group containing information on the repeater, the port-group, and the ports)

◆ The Monitor Group (an optional group containing monitoring statistics for the repeater and its ports)

◆ The Address Tracking Group (DTE MAC address tracking information)

7.2.9. RIP VERSION 2 MIB EXTENSIONS

The MIB for the RIP (Version 2) Group contains the definitions for the MIB variables that represent the objects needed for the Routing Information Protocol. This is a routing protocol that uses a distance vector instead of a link state. The MIB is described in RFC 1724, *RIP Version 2 MIB Extension*.

The RIP 2 Group ASN.1 OBJECT IDENTIFIER is { mib-2 23 }. Figure 7-43 depicts this group's position in the SNMP OBJECT ID Hierarchy.

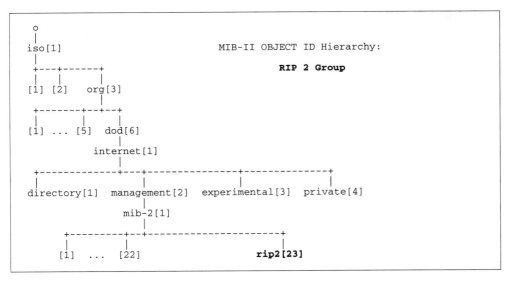

Figure 7-50. The RIP 2 Group

The RIP 2 Group is comprised of two global variables (for RIP route changes and global queries) and three tables:

◆ The RIP Interface Status Table

◆ The RIP Interface Configuration Table

◆ The RIP Peer Table

7.2.10. IDENTIFICATION MIB GROUP

The Identification MIB Group contains the definitions for a set of objects that can identify the users associated with TCP connections. The MIB is described in RFC 1414, *Identification MIB*.

The Identification Group ASN.1 OBJECT IDENTIFIER is { mib-2 24 }. Figure 7-43 depicts this group's position in the SNMP OBJECT ID Hierarchy.

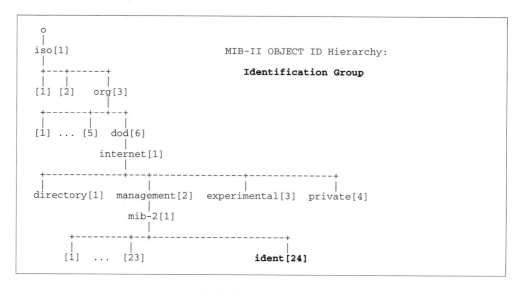

Figure 7-51. The Identification Group

The Identification Group is comprised of one table, the Identification Table.

7.2.11. HOST RESOURCES MIB GROUP

The Host Resources MIB Group contains the definitions for a set of objects that can manage the components in a typical host system. This MIB group is defined in RFC 1514, *Host Resources MIB*. It is a very important MIB group because it allows the SNMP framework to do what is traditionally known as Systems Management in a standardized manner.

The Host Resources Group ASN.1 OBJECT IDENTIFIER is { mib-2 25 }, and Figure 7-52 depicts this group's position in the SNMP OBJECT ID Hierarchy.

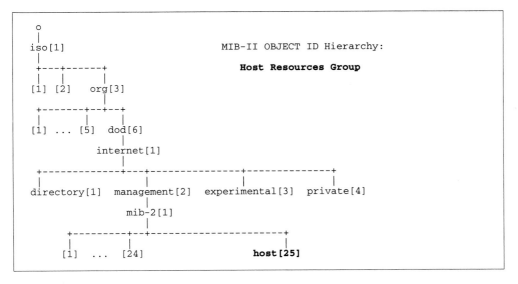

```
o
|
iso[1]                          MIB-II OBJECT ID Hierarchy:
|
+---+------+                      Host Resources Group
|   |      |
[1] [2]  org[3]
           |
    +-------+--+--+
    |       |     |
   [1] ... [5]  dod[6]
                  |
             internet[1]
                  |
  +-------------+---+---------------+--------------+
  |             |                   |              |
directory[1]  management[2]   experimental[3]  private[4]
                  |
              mib-2[1]
                  |
      +---------+--+----------------------+
      |         |                         |
     [1]  ...  [24]                    host[25]
```

Figure 7-52. The Host Resources Group

The Host Resources Group is comprised of six groups of variables:

- The Host Resources System Group

- The Host Resources Storage Group

- The Host Resources Device Group

- The Host Resources Running Software Group

- The Host Resources Running Software Performance Group

- The Host Resources Installed Software Group

7.2.12. IEEE 802.3 MAU MIB GROUP

The IEEE 802.3 MAU MIB Group defines the objects needed for managing IEEE 802.3 Medium Attachment Units (MAUs) that can be attached to repeaters or Ethernet interfaces. This MIB group is defined in RFC 1515, *Definitions of Managed Objects for IEEE 802.3 Medium Attachment Units (MAUs)*.

The IEEE 802.3 MAU MIB Group ASN.1 OBJECT IDENTIFIER is { mib-2 26 }, and Figure 7-53 depicts this group's position in the SNMP OBJECT ID Hierarchy.

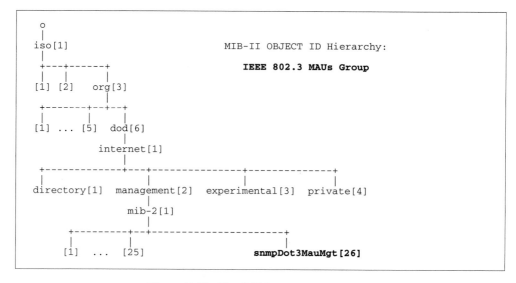

```
     o
     |
  iso[1]                             MIB-II OBJECT ID Hierarchy:
     |
  +---+------+                          IEEE 802.3 MAUs Group
  |   |      |
 [1] [2]  org[3]
            |
  +-------+--+--+
  |       |     |
 [1] ... [5]  dod[6]
               |
           internet[1]
               |
  +-------------+---+---------------+-------------+
  |             |                   |             |
directory[1]  management[2]   experimental[3]  private[4]
               |
            mib-2[1]
               |
  +---------+--+----------------------+
  |         |                         |
 [1]  ...  [25]                  snmpDot3MauMgt[26]
```

Figure 7-53. The IEEE 802.3 MAUs Group

This Group is comprised of three tables:

◆ The Basic Repeater MAU Table

◆ The Basic Interface MAU Table

◆ The Basic Broadband MAU Table

7.2.13. NETWORK SERVICES MONITORING MIB GROUP

The Network Services Monitoring MIB Group defines the objects needed for managing network service applications. This MIB group is defined in RFC 1565, *Network Services Monitoring MIB*.

The Network Services Monitoring MIB Group ASN.1 OBJECT IDENTIFIER is { mib-2 27 }, and Figure 7-54 depicts this group's position in the SNMP OBJECT ID Hierarchy.

The Network Services Monitoring Group is comprised of two tables:

◆ The Basic Application Table

◆ The Active Associations Table

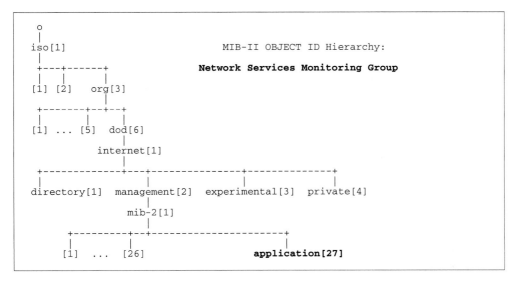

```
o
|
iso[1]                          MIB-II OBJECT ID Hierarchy:
|
+---+------+                  Network Services Monitoring Group
|   |      |
[1] [2]   org[3]
          |
+-------+--+--+
|       |     |
[1] ... [5]  dod[6]
             |
          internet[1]
             |
+-------------+---+---------------+--------------+
|             |                   |              |
directory[1]  management[2]  experimental[3]  private[4]
              |
           mib-2[1]
              |
     +---------+--+---------------------+
     |         |                        |
    [1]  ...  [26]                 application[27]
```

Figure 7-54. The Network Services Monitoring Group

7.2.14. MAIL MONITORING MIB GROUP

The Mail Monitoring MIB Group defines the objects needed for managing Message Transfer Agents (MTAs) and for monitoring the MTA components that can reside in a gateway used for mail. This MIB group is defined in RFC 1566, *Mail Monitoring MIB*.

The Mail Monitoring MIB Group ASN.1 OBJECT IDENTIFIER is { mib-2 28 }, and Figure 7-55 depicts this group's position in the SNMP OBJECT ID Hierarchy.

The Mail Monitoring Group is comprised of three tables:

◆ The Message Transfer Agent Table

◆ The Message Transfer Agent Group Table

◆ The Message Transfer Agent Group Name Table

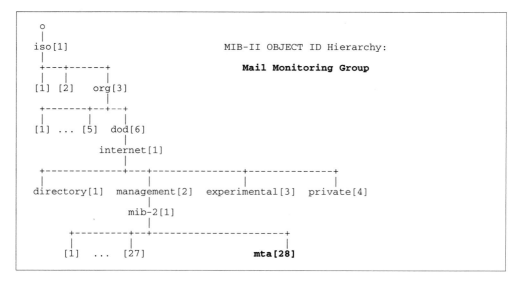

```
  o
  |
iso[1]                              MIB-II OBJECT ID Hierarchy:
  |
  +---+------+                         Mail Monitoring Group
  |   |      |
 [1] [2]   org[3]
            |
  +-------+--+--+
  |       |     |
 [1] ... [5]  dod[6]
                |
            internet[1]
                |
  +-------------+---+---------------+--------------+
  |                 |               |              |
 directory[1]  management[2]  experimental[3]  private[4]
                   mib-2[1]
                      |
     +---------+--+---------------------+
     |         |                        |
    [1]  ...  [27]                    mta[28]
```

Figure 7-55. The Mail Monitoring Group

7.2.15. X.500 DIRECTORY MIB GROUP

The X.500 Directory MIB Group defines the objects needed for monitoring the Directory System Agents (DSAs) used in the X.500 OSI directory service. This MIB group is defined in RFC 1567, *X.500 Directory Monitoring MIB*.

The X.500 Directory MIB Group ASN.1 OBJECT IDENTIFIER is { mib-2 29 }, and Figure 7-56 depicts this group's position in the SNMP OBJECT ID Hierarchy.

The X.500 Mail Monitoring Group is comprised of three tables:

◆ The DSA Operations Table

◆ The Entry Statistics and Cache Performance Table

◆ The Interaction History Table

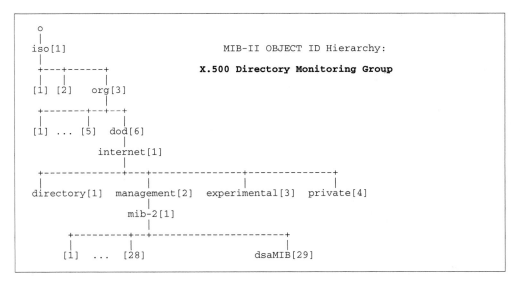

```
o
|
iso[1]                              MIB-II OBJECT ID Hierarchy:
|
+---+------+                    X.500 Directory Monitoring Group
|   |      |
[1] [2]  org[3]
            |
+-------+--+--+
|       |     |
[1] ... [5]  dod[6]
              |
          internet[1]
              |
+-------------+---+---------------+--------------+
|                 |               |              |
directory[1]  management[2]  experimental[3]  private[4]
                  |
               mib-2[1]
                  |
    +---------+--+---------------------+
    |         |                        |
   [1]  ...  [28]                  dsaMIB[29]
```

Figure 7-56. The X.500 Directory Monitoring Group

7.2.16. EVOLUTION OF IF GROUPS OF MIB-II MIB GROUP

The Evolution of Interface Groups of MIB-II MIB Group defines the objects needed for managing the various network interfaces that can be implemented on a device. This MIB group is defined in RFC 1573, *Evolution of the Interfaces Groups of MIB-II*.

The Evolution of Interface Groups of MIB-II MIB Group ASN.1 OBJECT IDENTIFIER is { mib-2 30 }, and Figure 7-57 depicts this group's position in the SNMP OBJECT ID Hierarchy.

The Interfaces Evolution Group is comprised of five tables:

◆ The Interfaces Table from MIB-II
◆ The Interfaces Evolution Table
◆ The Interfaces Stack Table
◆ The Interfaces Test Table
◆ The Interfaces Receive Address Table

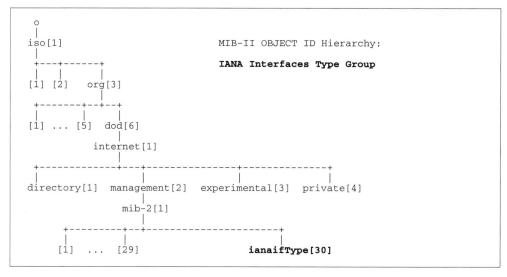

Figure 7-57. The IANA Interfaces Type Group

7.2.17. DNS SERVER AND RESOLVER MIB GROUP

The Domain Name Service Server and Resolver MIB Group define the objects needed to manage DNS name server and resolver software. This MIB group is defined in RFC 1611, *DNS Server MIB Extensions*, and RFC 1612, *DNS Resolver MIB Extensions*.

The Domain Name Service Server and Resolver MIB Group ASN.1 OBJECT IDENTIFIER is { mib-2 32 }, and Figure 7-58 depicts this group's position in the SNMP OBJECT ID Hierarchy.

.The Domain Name Service Server and Resolver MIB Group is comprised of ten sub-groups:

- The Server Configuration Group

- The Server Counter Group

- The Server Optional Counter Group

- The Server Zone Group

- The Resolver Configuration Group

- The Resolver Counter Group

- The Resolver Lame Delegation Group

- The Resolver Cache Group
- The Resolver Negative Cache Group
- The Resolver Optional Counter Group

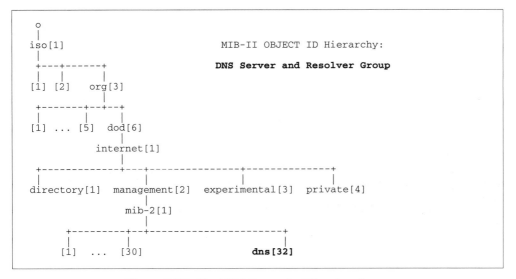

Figure 7-58. The DNS Server and Resolver Group

7.2.18. UNINTERRUPTIBLE POWER SUPPLY MIB GROUP

The Uninterruptible Power Supply MIB Group defines the objects needed for managing uninterruptible power supply systems. This MIB group is defined in RFC 1628, *UPS Management Information Base.*

The Uninterruptible Power Supply Group ASN.1 OBJECT IDENTIFIER is { mib-2 33 }, and Figure 7-59 depicts this group's position in the SNMP OB-JECT ID Hierarchy.

The Uninterruptible Power Supply Group is comprised of ten sub-groups:

- The Device Identification Group
- The Battery Group
- The Input Group
- The Output Group
- The Bypass Group

- The Alarm Group
- The Well Known Alarm Conditions Group
- The Test Group
- The Control Group
- The Configuration Group

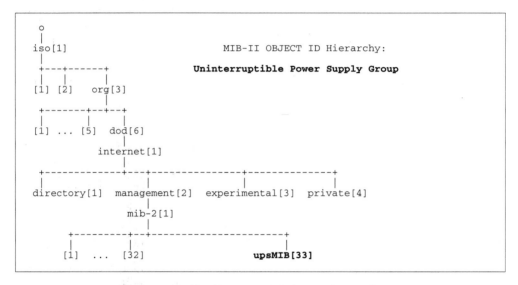

Figure 7-59. The Uninterruptible Power Supply Group

7.2.19. SNA NAU MIB GROUP

The SNA NAU MIB Group defines the objects for managing the configuration, monitoring, and control of Physical Units (PUs) and Logical Units (LUs) in an SNA environment. This MIB group is defined in RFC 1666, *Definitions of Managed Objects for SNA NAUs using SMIv2.*

The SNA NAU MIB Group ASN.1 OBJECT IDENTIFIER is { mib-2 34 }, and Figure 7-60 depicts this group's position in the SNMP OBJECT ID Hierarchy.

The SNA NAU Group is comprised of three sub-groups:

◆ The SNA NAU Group

◆ The SNA Logical Unit Group

◆ The SNA Management Tools Group

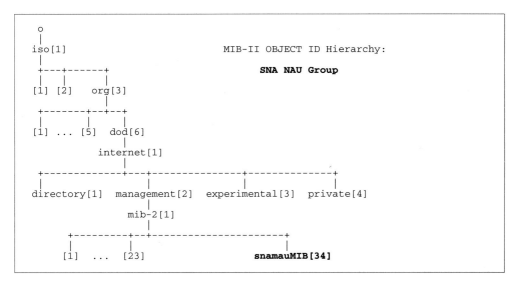

Figure 7-60. The SNA NAU Group

7.2.20. ETHERNET-LIKE INTERFACE TYPE MIB GROUP

The Ethernet-Like Interface Type MIB Group defines the objects needed for managing ethernet-like objects. This MIB group is defined in RFC 1650, *Definitions of Managed Objects for the Ethernet-Like Interface Types using SMIv2*.

The Ethernet-Like Interface Type MIB Group ASN.1 OBJECT IDENTIFIER is { mib-2 35 }, and Figure 7-61 depicts this group's position in the SNMP OBJECT ID Hierarchy.

The Ethernet-Like Interface Types Group is comprised of two tables:

◆ The Ethernet-like Statistics Table

◆ The Ethernet-like Collision Statistics Table

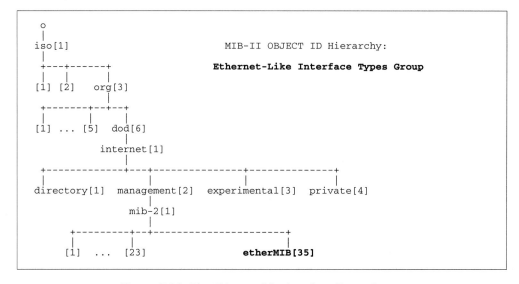

```
 o
 |
 iso[1]                          MIB-II OBJECT ID Hierarchy:
 |
 +---+------+                    Ethernet-Like Interface Types Group
 |   |      |
[1] [2]   org[3]
            |
 +-------+--+--+
 |       |     |
[1] ... [5]  dod[6]
              |
          internet[1]
              |
 +-------------+---+---------------+--------------+
 |             |                   |              |
directory[1]  management[2]  experimental[3]  private[4]
               |
            mib-2[1]
               |
    +---------+--+----------------------+
    |         |                         |
   [1]  ...  [23]                   etherMIB[35]
```

Figure 7-61. The Ethernet-Like Interface Types Group

7.2.21. SMDS INTERFACE MIB GROUP

The SMDS Interface MIB Group defines the objects needed for managing SMDS access interfaces. This MIB group is defined in RFC 1694, *Definitions of Managed Objects for SMDS Interfaces using SMIv2.*

The SMDS Interface MIB Group ASN.1 OBJECT IDENTIFIER is { mib-2 36 }, and Figure 7-62 depicts this group's position in the SNMP OBJECT ID Hierarchy.

The SMDS Interface Group is comprised of seven tables:

◆ The SIP Level 3 Table

◆ The SIP Level 2 Table

◆ The SIP DS1 PLCP Table

◆ The SIP DS3 PLCP Table

◆ The IP Over SMDS Table

◆ The SIP Level 3 PDU Error Table

◆ The DXI Table

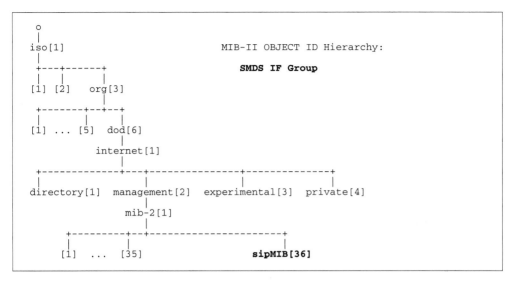

Figure 7-62. The SMDS Interface Group

7.2.22. ATM MIB GROUP

The Asynchronous Transfer Mode MIB Group defines the objects needed for managing ATM-based interfaces, devices, networks, and services. This MIB group is defined in RFC 1695, *Definitions of Managed Objects for ATM Management Version 8.0 using SMIv2.*

The ATM Group ASN.1 OBJECT IDENTIFIER is { mib-2 37 }, and Figure 7-63 depicts this group's position in the SNMP OBJECT ID Hierarchy.

The ATM Group is comprised of six basic sub-groups:

◆ The ATM Interface Configuration Group

◆ The ATM Interface DS3 PLCP Group

◆ The ATM Interface TC Sublayer Group

◆ The ATM Interface Virtual Link (VPL/VCL) Configuration Groups

◆ The ATM VP/VC Cross-Connect Groups

◆ The AAL5 Connection Performance Statistics Group

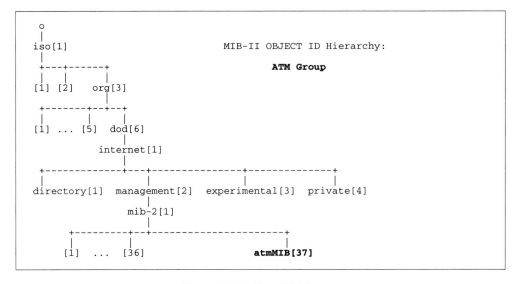

```
o
|
iso[1]                                MIB-II OBJECT ID Hierarchy:
|
+---+------+                              ATM Group
|   |      |
[1] [2]   org[3]
           |
+-------+--+--+
|       |     |
[1] ... [5]  dod[6]
              |
           internet[1]
              |
+-------------+---+---------------+--------------+
|                 |               |              |
directory[1]  management[2]  experimental[3]  private[4]
                  |
              mib-2[1]
                 |
      +---------+--+---------------------+
      |         |                        |
     [1]  ...  [36]                  atmMIB[37]
```

Figure 7-63. The ATM Group

7.2.23. MODEM MIB GROUP

The Modem MIB Group defines the objects needed for managing dial-up modems. This MIB group is defined in RFC 1696, *Modem Management Information Base (MIB) using SMIv2*.

The Modem MIB Group ASN.1 OBJECT IDENTIFIER is { mib-2 38 }, and Figure 7-64 depicts this group's position in the SNMP OBJECT ID Hierarchy.

The Modem MIB Group is comprised of six tables:

- The Modem ID Table
- The Modem Line Interface Table
- The DTE Interface Table
- The Call Control Table
- The Stored Dial String Table
- The Modem Statistics Table

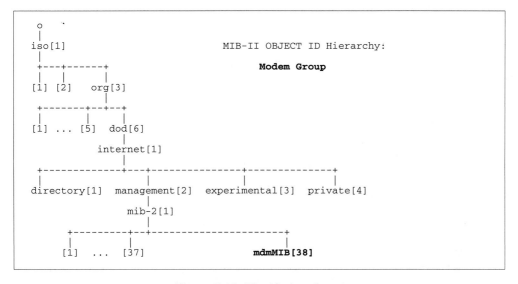

```
 o    ˙
 |
iso[1]                        MIB-II OBJECT ID Hierarchy:
 |
 +---+------+                      Modem Group
 |   |      |
[1] [2]  org[3]
          |
 +-------+--+--+
 |       |     |
[1] ... [5]  dod[6]
              |
          internet[1]
              |
 +------------+---+--------------+--------------+
 |                |              |              |
directory[1]  management[2]  experimental[3]  private[4]
                  |
              mib-2[1]
                  |
      +---------+--+----------------------+
      |         |                         |
     [1]  ...  [37]                   mdmMIB[38]
```

Figure 7-64. The Modem Group

7.2.24. RELATIONAL DATABASE SYSTEM MIB GROUP

The Relational Database Management System MIB Group defines the objects needed to manage relational database (RDBMS) implementations. This MIB group is defined in RFC 1697, *Relational Database Management System (RDBMS) Management Information Base (MIB) using SMIv2*.

The Relational Database Management System MIB Group ASN.1 OBJECT IDENTIFIER is { mib-2 39 }, and Figure 7-65 depicts this group's position in the SNMP OBJECT ID Hierarchy.

The Relational Database System Group is comprised of nine tables:

◆ The Installed Host/System Database Table

◆ The Actively Opened Database Table

◆ The Database Configuration Parameters Table

◆ The Limited Resources Database Table

◆ The Installed Server Database Table

◆ The Active Database Servers Table

◆ The Server Database Configuration Parameters Table

♦ The Server Limited Resources Table

♦ The Server and Database Relation on a Host Table

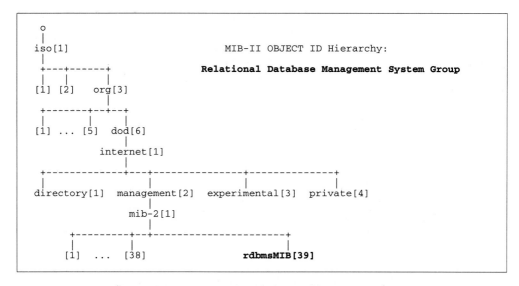

Figure 7-65. The Relational Database Management Group

7.2.25. SNA DLC MIB GROUP

The SNA DLC MIB Group defines the objects needed to manage devices running the SDLC protocol. This MIB group is defined in RFC 1747, *Definitions of Managed Objects for SNA Data Link Control (SDLC) using SMIv2*.

The SNA DLC MIB Group ASN.1 OBJECT IDENTIFIER is { mib-2 41 }, and Figure 7-66 depicts this group's position in the SNMP OBJECT ID Hierarchy.

The SNA DLC Group is comprised of six tables:

♦ The Port Administration Table

♦ The Port Operation Table

♦ The Port Statistics Table

♦ The Link Station Administration Table

♦ The Link Station Operation Table

♦ The Link Station Statistics Table

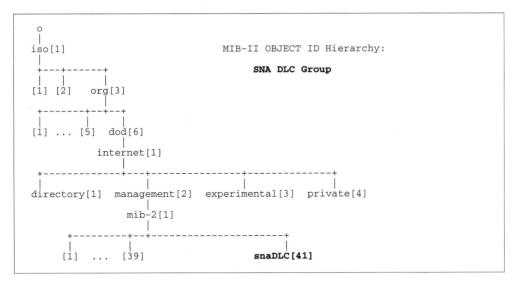

Figure 7-66. The SNA DLC Group

7.2.26. 802.5 STATION SOURCE ROUTING MIB GROUP

The 802.5 Station Source Routing MIB Group defines the objects for managing the source route end stations on an IEEE 802.5 Token Ring network. This MIB group is defined in RFC 1749, *IEEE 802.5 Station Source Routing MIB using SMIv2*.

The 802.5 Station Source Routing MIB Group ASN.1 OBJECT IDENTIFIER is { mib-2 42 }, and Figure 7-67 depicts this group's position in the SNMP OBJECT ID Hierarchy.

The 802.5 Source Routing Group is comprised of one table, the 802.5 Station Source Route Table.

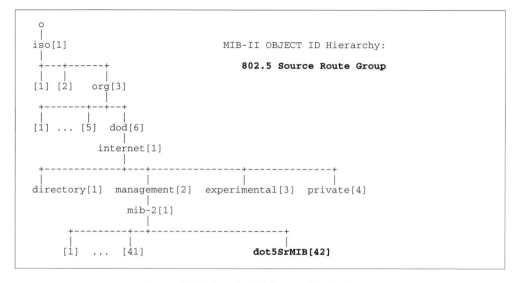

Figure 7-67. The 802.5 Source Route Group

7.2.27. PRINTER OBJECTS MIB GROUP

The Printer Objects MIB Group defines the objects needed for managing printers and their associated printing functions. This MIB group is defined in RFC 1759, *Printer MIB*.

The Printer Objects MIB Group ASN.1 OBJECT IDENTIFIER is { mib-2 43 }, and Figure 7-68 depicts this group's position in the SNMP OBJECT ID Hierarchy.

The Printer Group is comprised of 16 sub-groups:

◆ The General Printer Group

◆ The Input Group

◆ The Extended Input Group

◆ The Input Media Group

◆ The Output Group

◆ The Extended Output Group

◆ The Output Dimensions Group

◆ The Output Features Group

◆ The Marker Group

- The Marker Supplies Group

- The Marker Colorant Group

- The Media Path Group

- The Channel Group

- The Interpreter Group

- The Console Group

- The Alerts Group

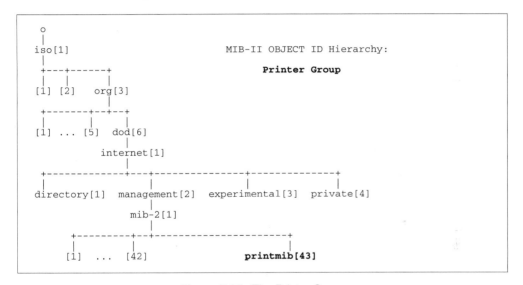

Figure 7-68. The Printer Group

7.2.28. IP MOBILITY SUPPORT OBJECTS MIB GROUP

The IP Mobility Support Objects MIB Group describes the managed objects needed for the management of the Mobile Node, Foreign Agent, and Home Agent for the Mobile IP Protocol. This MIB group is defined in RFC 2006, *The Definitions of Managed Objects for IP Mobility Support Using SMIv2.*

The IP Mobility Support Objects MIB Group ASN.1 OBJECT IDENTIFIER is { mib-2 44 }, and Figure 7-69 depicts this group's position in the SNMP OBJECT ID Hierarchy.

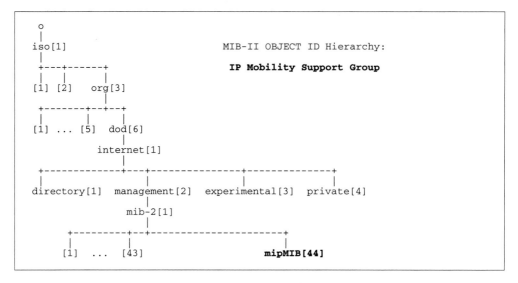

Figure 7-69. The IP Mobility Support Group

The IP Mobility Support Group is comprised of 12 groups:

◆ The Mobility IP Support System Group
◆ The Mobility IP Security Association Group
◆ The Mobility IP Security Violation Group
◆ The Mobility Node System Group
◆ The Mobility Node Discovery Group
◆ The Mobility Node Registration Group
◆ The Mobility Agent Advertisement Group
◆ The Foreign Agent System Group
◆ The Foreign Agent Advertisement Group
◆ The Foreign Agent Registration Group
◆ The Home Agent Registration Group
◆ The Home Agent Registration Node Counters Group

7.2.29. DATA LINK SWITCHING OBJECTS MIB GROUP

The Data Link Switching Objects MIB Group defines the objects needed for monitoring, controlling, and configuring a Data Link Switch (DLSw) device. This MIB group is defined in RFC 2024, *Definitions of Managed Objects for Data Link Switching Using SNMPv2*.

The Data Link Switching Group ASN.1 OBJECT IDENTIFIER is { mib-2 46 }, and Figure 7-70 depicts this group's position in the SNMP OBJECT ID Hierarchy.

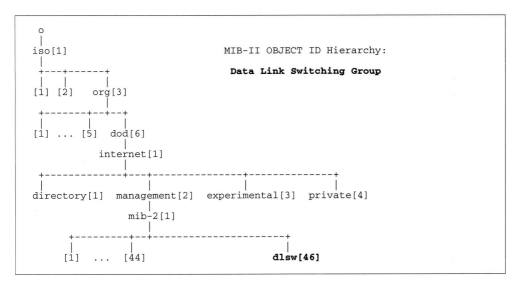

Figure 7-70. The Data Link Switching Group

The Data Link Switching Group is comprised of six groups:

◆ The Node Group

◆ The Adjacent DLSw Partners Group

◆ The Interface Group

◆ The Local and Remote Resources Directory Group

◆ The Established Circuits Group

◆ The SDLC Data Link Switched Devices Group

7.2.30. ENTITY OBJECTS MIB GROUP

The Entity Objects MIB Group describes the objects used for managing multiple logical and physical entities that a single SNMP agent can manage. This MIB presents a standard way that a single agent in a single device can control multiple instances of one MIB. This standard is useful for multiple instances of such things as repeaters and bridges that are now implemented in one network device.

This MIB group is defined in RFC 2037, *Entity MIB*, which states that the Entity Objects Group ASN.1 OBJECT IDENTIFIER is { mib-2 47 }. Figure 7-71 depicts this group's position within the SNMP OBJECT ID Hierarchy.

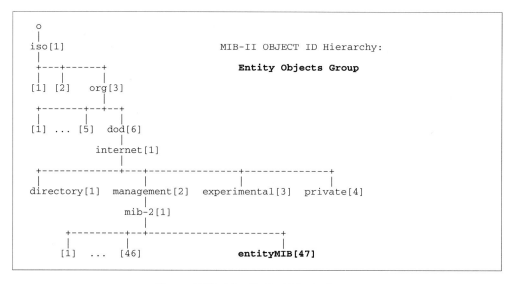

Figure 7-71. The Entity Objects Group

The Entity Objects Group is comprised of four groups:

◆ The Physical Entity Group
◆ The Logical Entity Group
◆ The Entity Mapping Group
◆ The General Entity Group

The Entity MIB Group represents the "last" defined standard MIB-II group for this chapter. The `experimental` sub-tree is the group that follows the MIB-II branch.

7.3. THE EXPERIMENTAL SUB-TREE

The `experimental` sub-tree contains MIB groups that are created for testing, research, and a variety of other experimental purposes. The IANA administers the numbering of the OBJECT IDENTIFIERS in this branch. All of these MIB groups and their objects begin with the OBJECT IDENTIFIER prefix 1.3.6.1.3, as shown in Figure 7-72.

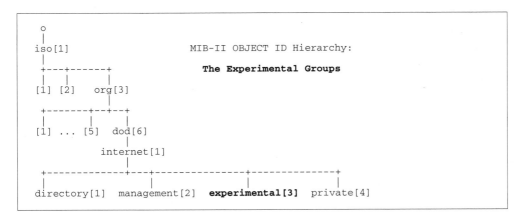

Figure 7-72. The Experimental Branch

Figure 7-73 shows the currently defined Experimental names and Object Identifiers that have been assigned by the IANA as specified in RFC 1700, *Assigned Numbers*.

7.3.1. THE CONNECTIONLESS NETWORK PROTOCOL MIB GROUP

The Connectionless Network Protocol (CLNS) MIB Group contains the experimental definitions for use with the Connectionless Network Protocol and End System to Intermediate Systems. It is an example of an experimental MIB

The Experimental MIB Groups		
Object Identifier	**Experimental Group Name**	**Description**
1.3.6.1.3.0	*Reserved*	*not applicable*
1.3.6.1.3.1	CLNS	ISO CLNS Objects
1.3.6.1.3.2	T1-Carrier	T1 Carrier Objects**
1.3.6.1.3.3	IEEE802.3	Ethernet-like Objects**
1.3.6.1.3.4	IEEE802.5	Token Ring-like Objects**
1.3.6.1.3.5	DECNet-PHIV	DECNet Phase IV**
1.3.6.1.3.6	Interface	Generic Interface Objects**
1.3.6.1.3.7	IEEE802.4	Token Bus-like Objects**
1.3.6.1.3.8	FDDI	FDDI Objects**
1.3.6.1.3.9	LANMGR-1	LAN Manager V1 Objects
1.3.6.1.3.10	LANMGR-TRAPS	LAN Manager Trap Objects
1.3.6.1.3.11	Views	SNMP View Objects
1.3.6.1.3.12	SNMP-AUTH	SNMP Authentication Objects
1.3.6.1.3.13	BGP	Border Gateway Protocol**
1.3.6.1.3.14	Bridge	Bridge MIB**
1.3.6.1.3.15	DS3	DS3 Interface Type**
1.3.6.1.3.16	SIP	SMDS Interface Protocol**
1.3.6.1.3.17	AppleTalk	AppleTalk Networking**
1.3.6.1.3.18	PPP	PPP Objects
1.3.6.1.3.19	Character MIB	Character MIB**
1.3.6.1.3.20	RS-232 MIB	RS-232 MIB**
1.3.6.1.3.21	Parallel MIB	Parallel MIB**
1.3.6.1.3.22	atsign-proxy	Proxy via Community

Figure 7-73. The Experimental MIB Groups

Object Identifier	Experimental Group Name	Description
1.3.6.1.3.23	OSPF	OSPF MIB**
1.3.6.1.3.24	Alert-Man	Alert-Man
1.3.6.1.3.25	FDDI-Synoptics	FDDI-Synoptics
1.3.6.1.3.26	Frame Relay	Frame Relay MIB**
1.3.6.1.3.27	rmon	Remote Network Monitor MIB**
1.3.6.1.3.28	IDPR	IDPR MIB
1.3.6.1.3.29	HUBMIB	IEEE 802.3 Hub MIB
1.3.6.1.3.30	IPFWDTBLMIB	IP Forwarding Table MIB
1.3.6.1.3.31	LATM MIB	LATM MIB
1.3.6.1.3.32	SONET MIB	Synchronous Optical Network MIB
1.3.6.1.3.33	IDENT	Identification MIB
1.3.6.1.3.34	MIME-MHS	Multipurpose Internet Mail Ext. MIB
1.3.6.1.3.35	MAUMIB	IEEE 802.3 MAU MIB
1.3.6.1.3.36	Host Resources	Host Resources MIB
1.3.6.1.3.37	ISIS-MIB	Integrated ISIS Protocol MIB
1.3.6.1.3.38	Chassis	Chassis MIB
1.3.6.1.3.39	ups	Uninterruptible Power Supply MIB
1.3.6.1.3.40	App-Mon	Application Monitoring MIB
1.3.6.1.3.41	ATM UNI	Asynchronous Transfer Mode MIB
1.3.6.1.3.42	FC	Fibre Channel
1.3.6.1.3.43	DNS	Domain Name Service**
1.3.6.1.3.44	X.25	X.25 MIB
1.3.6.1.3.45	Frame Relay Srvc.	Frame Relay Service MIB
1.3.6.1.3.46	Madman Apps	Mail and Directory Applications

Figure 7-73. The Experimental MIB Groups *(continued)*

Object Identifier	Experimental Group Name	Description
1.3.6.1.3.47	Madman-MTA	Madman Message Transfer Agents
1.3.6.1.3.48	Madman-DSA	Madman DSA
1.3.6.1.3.49	Modem	Modem MIB
1.3.6.1.3.50	SNA NAU	SNA NAU MIB
1.3.6.1.3.51	SDLC	SDLC MIB
1.3.6.1.3.52	DNS	Domain Name Service
1.3.6.1.3.53	net obj ip info	Network Objects IP Info X.500
1.3.6.1.3.54	printmib	Printer MIB
1.3.6.1.3.55	rdbmsmib	RDBMS MIB
1.3.6.1.3.56	sipMIB	SMDS over IP MIB
1.3.6.1.3.57	stllmib	ST-II Protocol MIB
1.3.6.1.3.58	802.5 SSR MIB	Station Source Routing MIB (802.5)

** These Experimental MIB Groups have been made obsolete by being relocated to their appropriate place as Standard MIB-II Extension Groups, or by being placed under the Transmission Group.

Figure 7-73. The Experimental MIB Groups *(continued)*

group and is described in RFC 1238, *CLNS MIB-for use with Connectionless Network Protocol (ISO 8473) and End System to Intermediate System (ISO 9542).*

The CLNS ASN.1 OBJECT IDENTIFIER is { experimental 1 }. Figure 7-74 depicts this group's position in the SNMP OBJECT ID Hierarchy.

The CLNS Group is composed of four groups:

◆ The CLNP Group

◆ The Error Group

◆ The Echo Group

◆ The ES-IS Group

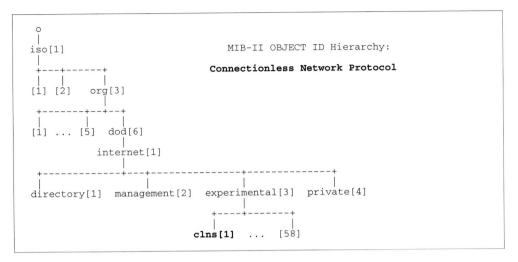

Figure 7-74. The Connectionless Network Protocol Group

7.4. THE PRIVATE SUB-TREE

The private sub-tree contains MIB groups that are created for unilaterally defined objects. Currently, its only sub-branch is the enterprises branch, which stores vendor-specific MIB objects. The IANA administers the numbering of the OBJECT IDENTIFIERS in this branch. All enterprise MIB groups and their objects begin with the same OBJECT IDENTIFIER prefix 1.3.6.1.4.1, as shown in Figure 7-75.

Figure 7-76 shows the current listing of the vendor controlled branches of the enterprises sub-tree; over 3,000 organizations have been granted enterprise numbers as of April 1997. As just another indication of SNMP's tremendous growth, the number of SNMP enterprises has increased six-fold from the 461 enterprises registered when the first edition was published just three years ago! The complete list is available over the World Wide Web:

```
ftp://ftp.isi.edu/in-notes/iana/assignments/enterprise-numbers
```

An enterprise number assignment can be obtained by sending the complete company name, address, fax number, and phone number, along with the con-

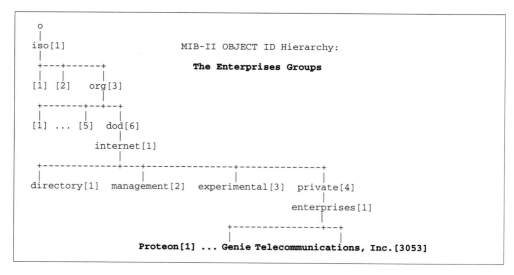

Figure 7-75. The Enterprises Branch

tact's person complete name, address, phone number, and e-mail address in an e-mail message to: `iana-mib@isi.edu`.

The Enterprises Groups	
Group Object Identifier	**Enterprise Name**
1.3.6.1.4.1.0	*reserved*
1.3.6.1.4.1.1	Proteon
1.3.6.1.4.1.2	IBM
1.3.6.1.4.1.3	CMU
1.3.6.1.4.1.4	Unix
1.3.6.1.4.1.5	ACC
1.3.6.1.4.1.6	TWG
1.3.6.1.4.1.7	CAYMAN
1.3.6.1.4.1.8	PSI
1.3.6.1.4.1.9	cisco
1.3.6.1.4.1.10	NSC
1.3.6.1.4.1.11	Hewlett Packard
1.3.6.1.4.1.12	Epilogue
1.3.6.1.4.1.13	University of Tennessee
1.3.6.1.4.1.14	BBN
1.3.6.1.4.1.15	Xylogics, Inc.
1.3.6.1.4.1.16	Timeplex
1.3.6.1.4.1.17	Canstar

Figure 7-76. The Enterprises Groups

The Enterprises Groups	
Group Object Identifier	**Enterprise Name**
1.3.6.1.4.1.18	Wellfleet
1.3.6.1.4.1.19	TRW
1.3.6.1.4.1.20	MIT
1.3.6.1.4.1.21	EON
1.3.6.1.4.1.22	Fibronics
1.3.6.1.4.1.23	Novell
1.3.6.1.4.1.24	Spider Systems
1.3.6.1.4.1.25	NSFNET
1.3.6.1.4.1.26	Hughes LAN Systems
1.3.6.1.4.1.27	Intergraph
1.3.6.1.4.1.28	Interlan
1.3.6.1.4.1.29	Vitalink Communications
1.3.6.1.4.1.30	Ulana
1.3.6.1.4.1.31	NSWC
1.3.6.1.4.1.32	Santa Cruz Operation
1.3.6.1.4.1.33	Xyplex
1.3.6.1.4.1.34	Cray
1.3.6.1.4.1.35	Bell Northern Research
1.3.6.1.4.1.36	DEC
1.3.6.1.4.1.37	Touch
1.3.6.1.4.1.38	Network Research Corporation
1.3.6.1.4.1.39	Baylor College of Medicine
1.3.6.1.4.1.40	NMFECC-LLNL
1.3.6.1.4.1.41	SRI
1.3.6.1.4.1.42	Sun Microsystems
1.3.6.1.4.1.43	3Com
1.3.6.1.4.1.44	CMC
1.3.6.1.4.1.45	SynOptics
1.3.6.1.4.1.46	Cheyenne Software
1.3.6.1.4.1.47	Prime Computer
1.3.6.1.4.1.48	MCNC/North Carolina Data Network
1.3.6.1.4.1.49	Chipcom
1.3.6.1.4.1.50	Optical Data Systems
1.3.6.1.4.1.51	gated
1.3.6.1.4.1.52	Cabletron Systems
1.3.6.1.4.1.53	Apollo Computers
1.3.6.1.4.1.54	DeskTalk Systems, Inc.
1.3.6.1.4.1.55	SSDS
1.3.6.1.4.1.56	Castle Rock Computing
1.3.6.1.4.1.57	MIPS Computer Systems
1.3.6.1.4.1.58	TGV, Inc.

Figure 7-76. The Enterprises Groups *(continued)*

The Enterprises Groups	
Group Object Identifier	**Enterprise Name**
1.3.6.1.4.1.59	Silicon Graphics, Inc.
1.3.6.1.4.1.60	University of British Columbia
1.3.6.1.4.1.61	Merit
1.3.6.1.4.1.62	NetEdge
1.3.6.1.4.1.63	Apple Computer, Inc.
1.3.6.1.4.1.64	Gandalf
1.3.6.1.4.1.65	Dartmouth
1.3.6.1.4.1.66	David Systems
1.3.6.1.4.1.67	Reuter
1.3.6.1.4.1.68	Cornell
1.3.6.1.4.1.69	LMS
1.3.6.1.4.1.70	Locus Computing Corporation
1.3.6.1.4.1.71	NASA
1.3.6.1.4.1.72	Retix
1.3.6.1.4.1.73	Boeing
1.3.6.1.4.1.74	AT&T
1.3.6.1.4.1.75	Ungermann-Bass
1.3.6.1.4.1.76	Digital Analysis Corporation
1.3.6.1.4.1.77	LAN Manager
1.3.6.1.4.1.78	Netlabs
1.3.6.1.4.1.79	ICL
1.3.6.1.4.1.80	Auspex Systems
1.3.6.1.4.1.81	Lannet Company
1.3.6.1.4.1.82	Network Computing Devices
1.3.6.1.4.1.83	Raycom Systems
1.3.6.1.4.1.84	Pirelli Focom, Ltd.
1.3.6.1.4.1.85	Datability Software Systems
1.3.6.1.4.1.86	Network Application Technology
1.3.6.1.4.1.87	LINK (Lokales Informatik-Netz Karlsruhe)
1.3.6.1.4.1.88	NYU
1.3.6.1.4.1.89	RND
1.3.6.1.4.1.90	InterCon Systems Corporation
1.3.6.1.4.1.91	Coral Network Corporation
1.3.6.1.4.1.92	Webster Computer Corporation
1.3.6.1.4.1.93	Frontier Technologies Corporation
1.3.6.1.4.1.94	Nokia Data Communications
1.3.6.1.4.1.95	Allen-Bradley Company
1.3.6.1.4.1.96	CERN
1.3.6.1.4.1.97	Sigma Network Systems, Inc.
1.3.6.1.4.1.98	Emerging Technologies, Inc.
1.3.6.1.4.1.99	SNMP Research

Figure 7-76. The Enterprises Groups *(continued)*

The Enterprises Groups	
Group Object Identifier	**Enterprise Name**
1.3.6.1.4.1.100	Ohio State University
1.3.6.1.4.1.101	Ultra Network Technologies
1.3.6.1.4.1.102	Microcom
1.3.6.1.4.1.103	Lockheed Martin
1.3.6.1.4.1.104	Micro Technology
1.3.6.1.4.1.105	Process Software Corporation
1.3.6.1.4.1.106	Data General Corporation
1.3.6.1.4.1.107	Bull Company
1.3.6.1.4.1.108	Emulex Corporation
1.3.6.1.4.1.109	Warwick University Computing Services
1.3.6.1.4.1.110	Network General Corporation
1.3.6.1.4.1.111	Oracle
1.3.6.1.4.1.112	Control Data Corporation
1.3.6.1.4.1.113	Hughes Aircraft Company
1.3.6.1.4.1.114	Synernetics, Inc.
1.3.6.1.4.1.115	Mitre
1.3.6.1.4.1.116	Hitachi, Ltd.
1.3.6.1.4.1.117	Telebit
1.3.6.1.4.1.118	Salomon Technology Services
1.3.6.1.4.1.119	NEC Corporation
1.3.6.1.4.1.120	Fibermux
1.3.6.1.4.1.121	FTP Software, Inc.
1.3.6.1.4.1.122	Sony
1.3.6.1.4.1.123	Newbridge Networks Corporation
1.3.6.1.4.1.124	Racal-Datacom
1.3.6.1.4.1.125	CR SYSTEMS
1.3.6.1.4.1.126	DSET Corporation
1.3.6.1.4.1.127	Computone
1.3.6.1.4.1.128	Tektronix, Inc.
1.3.6.1.4.1.129	Interactive Systems Corporation
1.3.6.1.4.1.130	Banyan Systems, Inc.
1.3.6.1.4.1.131	Sintrom Datanet, Ltd.
1.3.6.1.4.1.132	Bell Canada
1.3.6.1.4.1.133	Crosscomm Corporation
1.3.6.1.4.1.134	Rice University
1.3.6.1.4.1.135	OnStream Networks
1.3.6.1.4.1.136	Concurrent Computer Corporation
1.3.6.1.4.1.137	Basser
1.3.6.1.4.1.138	Luxcom
1.3.6.1.4.1.139	Artel
1.3.6.1.4.1.140	Independence Technologies, Inc. (ITI)

Figure 7-76. The Enterprises Groups *(continued)*

The Enterprises Groups	
Group Object Identifier	**Enterprise Name**
1.3.6.1.4.1.141	Frontier Software Development
1.3.6.1.4.1.142	Digital Computer, Ltd.
1.3.6.1.4.1.143	Eyring, Inc.
1.3.6.1.4.1.144	Case Communications
1.3.6.1.4.1.145	Penril DataComm, Inc.
1.3.6.1.4.1.146	American Airlines
1.3.6.1.4.1.147	Sequent Computer Systems
1.3.6.1.4.1.148	Bellcore
1.3.6.1.4.1.149	Konkord Communications
1.3.6.1.4.1.150	University of Washington
1.3.6.1.4.1.151	Develcon
1.3.6.1.4.1.152	Solarix Systems
1.3.6.1.4.1.153	Unifi Communications Corporation
1.3.6.1.4.1.154	Roadnet
1.3.6.1.4.1.155	Network Systems Corporation
1.3.6.1.4.1.156	ENE (European Network Engineering)
1.3.6.1.4.1.157	Dansk Data Elektronik A/S
1.3.6.1.4.1.158	Morning Star Technologies
1.3.6.1.4.1.159	Dupont EOP
1.3.6.1.4.1.160	Legato Systems, Inc.
1.3.6.1.4.1.161	Motorola
1.3.6.1.4.1.162	European Space Agency (ESA)
1.3.6.1.4.1.163	BIM
1.3.6.1.4.1.164	Rad Data Communications, Ltd.
1.3.6.1.4.1.165	Intellicom
1.3.6.1.4.1.166	Shiva Corporation
1.3.6.1.4.1.167	Fujikura America
1.3.6.1.4.1.168	Xlnt Designs INC (XDI)
1.3.6.1.4.1.169	Tandem Computers
1.3.6.1.4.1.170	BICC
1.3.6.1.4.1.171	D-Link Systems, Inc.
1.3.6.1.4.1.172	AMP, Inc.
1.3.6.1.4.1.173	Netlink
1.3.6.1.4.1.174	C. Itoh Electronics
1.3.6.1.4.1.175	Sumitomo Electric Industries (SEI)
1.3.6.1.4.1.176	DHL Systems, Inc.
1.3.6.1.4.1.177	Network Equipment Technologies
1.3.6.1.4.1.178	APTEC Computer Systems
1.3.6.1.4.1.179	Schneider & Koch & Co, Datensysteme GmbH
1.3.6.1.4.1.180	Hill Air Force Base
1.3.6.1.4.1.181	ADC Kentrox

Figure 7-76. The Enterprises Groups *(continued)*

The Enterprises Groups	
Group Object Identifier	**Enterprise Name**
1.3.6.1.4.1.182	Japan Radio Co.
1.3.6.1.4.1.183	Versitron
1.3.6.1.4.1.184	Telecommunication Systems
1.3.6.1.4.1.185	Interphase
1.3.6.1.4.1.186	Toshiba Corporation
1.3.6.1.4.1.187	Clearpoint Research Corporation
1.3.6.1.4.1.188	Ascom
1.3.6.1.4.1.189	Fujitsu America
1.3.6.1.4.1.190	NetCom Solutions, Inc.
1.3.6.1.4.1.191	NCR
1.3.6.1.4.1.192	Dr. Materna GmbH
1.3.6.1.4.1.193	Ericsson Business Communications
1.3.6.1.4.1.194	Metaphor Computer Systems
1.3.6.1.4.1.195	Patriot Partners
1.3.6.1.4.1.196	The Software Group Limited (TSG)
1.3.6.1.4.1.197	Kalpana, Inc.
1.3.6.1.4.1.198	University of Waterloo
1.3.6.1.4.1.199	CCL/ITRI
1.3.6.1.4.1.200	Coeur Postel
1.3.6.1.4.1.201	Mitsubish Cable Industries, Ltd.
1.3.6.1.4.1.202	SMC
1.3.6.1.4.1.203	Crescendo Communication, Inc.
1.3.6.1.4.1.204	Goodall Software Engineering
1.3.6.1.4.1.205	Intecom
1.3.6.1.4.1.206	Victoria University of Wellington
1.3.6.1.4.1.207	Allied Telesis, Inc.
1.3.6.1.4.1.208	Cray Communications A/S
1.3.6.1.4.1.209	Protools
1.3.6.1.4.1.210	Nippon Telegraph and Telephone Corporation
1.3.6.1.4.1.211	Fujitsu, Ltd.
1.3.6.1.4.1.212	Network Peripherals Inc.
1.3.6.1.4.1.213	Netronix, Inc.
1.3.6.1.4.1.214	University of Wisconsin - Madison
1.3.6.1.4.1.215	NetWorth, Inc.
1.3.6.1.4.1.216	Tandberg Data A/S
1.3.6.1.4.1.217	Technically Elite Concepts, Inc.
1.3.6.1.4.1.218	Labtam Australia Pty., Ltd.
1.3.6.1.4.1.219	Republic Telcom Systems, Inc.
1.3.6.1.4.1.220	ADI Systems, Inc.
1.3.6.1.4.1.221	Microwave Bypass Systems, Inc.
1.3.6.1.4.1.222	Pyramid Technology Corporation

Figure 7-76. The Enterprises Groups *(continued)*

The Enterprises Groups	
Group Object Identifier	**Enterprise Name**
1.3.6.1.4.1.223	Unisys_Corp
1.3.6.1.4.1.224	LANOPTICS, Ltd., Israel
1.3.6.1.4.1.225	NKK Corporation
1.3.6.1.4.1.226	MTrade UK, Ltd.
1.3.6.1.4.1.227	Acals
1.3.6.1.4.1.228	ASTEC, Inc.
1.3.6.1.4.1.229	Delmarva Power
1.3.6.1.4.1.230	Telematics International, Inc.
1.3.6.1.4.1.231	Siemens Nixdorf Informations Syteme AG
1.3.6.1.4.1.232	Compaq
1.3.6.1.4.1.233	NetManage, Inc.
1.3.6.1.4.1.234	NCSU Computing Center
1.3.6.1.4.1.235	Empirical Tools and Technologies
1.3.6.1.4.1.236	Samsung Group
1.3.6.1.4.1.237	Takaoka Electric Mfg. Co., Ltd.
1.3.6.1.4.1.238	Netrix Systems Corporation
1.3.6.1.4.1.239	WINDATA
1.3.6.1.4.1.240	RC International A/S
1.3.6.1.4.1.241	Netexp Research
1.3.6.1.4.1.242	Internode Systems Pty., Ltd.
1.3.6.1.4.1.243	netCS Informationstechnik GmbH
1.3.6.1.4.1.244	Lantronix
1.3.6.1.4.1.245	Avatar Consultants
1.3.6.1.4.1.246	Furukawa Electoric Co., Ltd.
1.3.6.1.4.1.247	Nortel Dasa Network Systems GmbH & Co.
1.3.6.1.4.1.248	Richard Hirschmann GmbH & Co.
1.3.6.1.4.1.249	G2R, Inc.
1.3.6.1.4.1.250	University of Michigan
1.3.6.1.4.1.251	Netcomm, Ltd.
1.3.6.1.4.1.252	Sable Technology Corporation
1.3.6.1.4.1.253	Xerox
1.3.6.1.4.1.254	Conware Computer Consulting GmbH
1.3.6.1.4.1.255	Compatible Systems Corporation
1.3.6.1.4.1.256	Scitec Communications Systems, Ltd.
1.3.6.1.4.1.257	Transarc Corporation
1.3.6.1.4.1.258	Matsushita Electric Industrial Co., Ltd.
1.3.6.1.4.1.259	ACCTON Technology
1.3.6.1.4.1.260	Star-Tek, Inc.
1.3.6.1.4.1.261	Codenoll Tech. Corporation
1.3.6.1.4.1.262	Formation, Inc.
1.3.6.1.4.1.263	Seiko Instruments, Inc. (SII)

Figure 7-76. The Enterprises Groups *(continued)*

The Enterprises Groups	
Group Object Identifier	**Enterprise Name**
1.3.6.1.4.1.264	RCE (Reseaux de Communication d'Entreprise S.A.)
1.3.6.1.4.1.265	Xenocom, Inc.
1.3.6.1.4.1.266	KABELRHEYDT
1.3.6.1.4.1.267	Systech Computer Corporation
1.3.6.1.4.1.268	Visual
1.3.6.1.4.1.269	SDD (Scandinavian Airlines Data Denmark A/S)
1.3.6.1.4.1.270	Zenith Electronics Corporation
1.3.6.1.4.1.271	TELECOM FINLAND
1.3.6.1.4.1.272	BinTec Computersystems
1.3.6.1.4.1.273	EUnet Germany
1.3.6.1.4.1.274	PictureTel Corporation
1.3.6.1.4.1.275	Michigan State University
1.3.6.1.4.1.276	GTE Government Systems - Network Management Organization
1.3.6.1.4.1.277	Cascade Communications Corporation
1.3.6.1.4.1.278	Hitachi Cable, Ltd.
1.3.6.1.4.1.279	Olivetti
1.3.6.1.4.1.280	Vitacom Corporation
1.3.6.1.4.1.281	INMOS
1.3.6.1.4.1.282	AIC Systems Laboratories, Ltd.
1.3.6.1.4.1.283	Cameo Communications, Inc.
1.3.6.1.4.1.284	Diab Data AB
1.3.6.1.4.1.285	Olicom A/S
1.3.6.1.4.1.286	Digital-Kienzle Computersystems
1.3.6.1.4.1.287	CSELT(Centro Studi E Laboratori Telecomunicazioni)
1.3.6.1.4.1.288	Electronic Data Systems
1.3.6.1.4.1.289	McData Corporation
1.3.6.1.4.1.290	Harris Corporation
1.3.6.1.4.1.291	Technology Dynamics, Inc.
1.3.6.1.4.1.292	DATAHOUSE Information Systems, Ltd.
1.3.6.1.4.1.293	Securicor 3net (NDL), Ltd.
1.3.6.1.4.1.294	Texas Instruments
1.3.6.1.4.1.295	PlainTree Systems, Inc.
1.3.6.1.4.1.296	Hedemann Software Development
1.3.6.1.4.1.297	Fuji Xerox Co., Ltd.
1.3.6.1.4.1.298	Asante Technology
1.3.6.1.4.1.299	Stanford University
1.3.6.1.4.1.300	Digital Link
1.3.6.1.4.1.301	Raylan Corporation
1.3.6.1.4.1.302	Datacraft
1.3.6.1.4.1.303	Hughes
1.3.6.1.4.1.304	Farallon Computing, Inc.

Figure 7-76. The Enterprises Groups *(continued)*

The Enterprises Groups	
Group Object Identifier	**Enterprise Name**
1.3.6.1.4.1.305	GE Information Services
1.3.6.1.4.1.306	Gambit Computer Communications
1.3.6.1.4.1.307	Livingston Enterprises, Inc.
1.3.6.1.4.1.308	Star Technologies
1.3.6.1.4.1.309	Micronics Computers, Inc.
1.3.6.1.4.1.310	Basis, Inc.
1.3.6.1.4.1.311	Microsoft
1.3.6.1.4.1.312	US West Advance Technologies
1.3.6.1.4.1.313	University College London
1.3.6.1.4.1.314	Eastman Kodak Company
1.3.6.1.4.1.315	Network Resources Corporation
1.3.6.1.4.1.316	Atlas Telecom
1.3.6.1.4.1.317	Bridgeway
1.3.6.1.4.1.318	American Power Conversion Corporation
1.3.6.1.4.1.319	DOE Atmospheric Radiation Measurement Project
1.3.6.1.4.1.320	VerSteeg CodeWorks
1.3.6.1.4.1.321	Verilink Corp
1.3.6.1.4.1.322	Sybus Corporation
1.3.6.1.4.1.323	Tekelec
1.3.6.1.4.1.324	NASA Ames Research Center
1.3.6.1.4.1.325	Simon Fraser University
1.3.6.1.4.1.326	Fore Systems, Inc.
1.3.6.1.4.1.327	Centrum Communications, Inc.
1.3.6.1.4.1.328	NeXT Computer, Inc.
1.3.6.1.4.1.329	Netcore, Inc.
1.3.6.1.4.1.330	Northwest Digital Systems
1.3.6.1.4.1.331	Andrew Corporation
1.3.6.1.4.1.332	DigiBoard
1.3.6.1.4.1.333	Computer Network Technology Corporation
1.3.6.1.4.1.334	Lotus Development Corporation
1.3.6.1.4.1.335	MICOM Communication Corporation
1.3.6.1.4.1.336	ASCII Corporation
1.3.6.1.4.1.337	PUREDATA Research
1.3.6.1.4.1.338	NTT DATA
1.3.6.1.4.1.339	Empros Systems International
1.3.6.1.4.1.340	Kendall Square Research (KSR)
1.3.6.1.4.1.341	ORNL
1.3.6.1.4.1.342	Network Innovations
1.3.6.1.4.1.343	Intel Corporation
1.3.6.1.4.1.344	Proxar
1.3.6.1.4.1.345	Epson Research Center

Figure 7-76. The Enterprises Groups *(continued)*

The Enterprises Groups	
Group Object Identifier	**Enterprise Name**
1.3.6.1.4.1.346	Fibernet
1.3.6.1.4.1.347	Box Hill Systems Corporation
1.3.6.1.4.1.348	American Express Travel Related Services
1.3.6.1.4.1.349	Compu-Shack
1.3.6.1.4.1.350	Parallan Computer, Inc.
1.3.6.1.4.1.351	Stratacom
1.3.6.1.4.1.352	Open Networks Engineering, Inc.
1.3.6.1.4.1.353	ATM Forum
1.3.6.1.4.1.354	SSD Management, Inc.
1.3.6.1.4.1.355	Automated Network Management, Inc.
1.3.6.1.4.1.356	Magnalink Communications Corporation
1.3.6.1.4.1.357	Kasten Chase Applied Research
1.3.6.1.4.1.358	Skyline Technology, Inc.
1.3.6.1.4.1.359	Nu-Mega Technologies, Inc.
1.3.6.1.4.1.360	Morgan Stanley & Co., Inc.
1.3.6.1.4.1.361	Integrated Business Network
1.3.6.1.4.1.362	L & N Technologies, Ltd.
1.3.6.1.4.1.363	Cincinnati Bell Information Systems, Inc.
1.3.6.1.4.1.364	OSCOM International
1.3.6.1.4.1.365	MICROGNOSIS
1.3.6.1.4.1.366	Datapoint Corporation
1.3.6.1.4.1.367	RICOH Co., Ltd.
1.3.6.1.4.1.368	Axis Communications AB
1.3.6.1.4.1.369	Pacer Software
1.3.6.1.4.1.370	3COM/Axon
1.3.6.1.4.1.371	Brixton Systems, Inc.
1.3.6.1.4.1.372	GSI
1.3.6.1.4.1.373	Tatung Co., Ltd.
1.3.6.1.4.1.374	DIS Research, Ltd.
1.3.6.1.4.1.375	Quotron Systems, Inc.
1.3.6.1.4.1.376	Dassault Electronique
1.3.6.1.4.1.377	Corollary, Inc.
1.3.6.1.4.1.378	SEEL, Ltd.
1.3.6.1.4.1.379	Lexcel
1.3.6.1.4.1.380	Sophisticated Technologies, Inc.
1.3.6.1.4.1.381	OST
1.3.6.1.4.1.382	Megadata Pty., Ltd.
1.3.6.1.4.1.383	LLNL Livermore Computer Center
1.3.6.1.4.1.384	Dynatech Communications
1.3.6.1.4.1.385	Symplex Communications Corporation
1.3.6.1.4.1.386	Tribe Computer Works

Figure 7-76. The Enterprises Groups *(continued)*

The Enterprises Groups	
Group Object Identifier	**Enterprise Name**
1.3.6.1.4.1.387	Taligent, Inc.
1.3.6.1.4.1.388	Symbol Technologies, Inc.
1.3.6.1.4.1.389	Lancert
1.3.6.1.4.1.390	Alantec
1.3.6.1.4.1.391	Ridgeback Solutions
1.3.6.1.4.1.392	Metrix, Inc.
1.3.6.1.4.1.393	Symantec Corporation
1.3.6.1.4.1.394	NRL Communication Systems Branch
1.3.6.1.4.1.395	I.D.E. Corporation
1.3.6.1.4.1.396	Matsushita Electric Works, Ltd.
1.3.6.1.4.1.397	MegaPAC
1.3.6.1.4.1.398	Pinacl Communication Systems, Ltd.
1.3.6.1.4.1.399	Hitachi Computer Products (America), Inc.
1.3.6.1.4.1.400	METEO FRANCE
1.3.6.1.4.1.401	PRC, Inc.
1.3.6.1.4.1.402	Wal*Mart Stores, Inc.
1.3.6.1.4.1.403	Nissin Electric Company, Ltd.
1.3.6.1.4.1.404	Distributed Support Information Standard
1.3.6.1.4.1.405	SMDS Interest Group (SIG)
1.3.6.1.4.1.406	SolCom Systems, Ltd.
1.3.6.1.4.1.407	Bell Atlantic
1.3.6.1.4.1.408	Advanced Multiuser Technologies Corporation
1.3.6.1.4.1.409	Mitsubishi Electric Corporation
1.3.6.1.4.1.410	C.O.L. Systems, Inc.
1.3.6.1.4.1.411	University of Auckland
1.3.6.1.4.1.412	Desktop Management Task Force (DMTF)
1.3.6.1.4.1.413	Klever Computers, Inc.
1.3.6.1.4.1.414	Amdahl Corporation
1.3.6.1.4.1.415	JTEC Pty, Ltd.
1.3.6.1.4.1.416	Matra Communcation
1.3.6.1.4.1.417	HAL Computer Systems
1.3.6.1.4.1.418	Lawrence Berkeley Laboratory
1.3.6.1.4.1.419	Dale Computer Corporation
1.3.6.1.4.1.420	IPTC, Universitaet of Tuebingen
1.3.6.1.4.1.421	Bytex Corporation
1.3.6.1.4.1.422	Cogwheel, Inc.
1.3.6.1.4.1.423	Lanwan Technologies
1.3.6.1.4.1.424	Thomas-Conrad Corporation
1.3.6.1.4.1.425	TxPort
1.3.6.1.4.1.426	Compex, Inc.
1.3.6.1.4.1.427	Evergreen Systems, Inc.

Figure 7-76. The Enterprises Groups *(continued)*

The Enterprises Groups	
Group Object Identifier	**Enterprise Name**
1.3.6.1.4.1.428	HNV, Inc.
1.3.6.1.4.1.429	U.S. Robotics, Inc.
1.3.6.1.4.1.430	Canada Post Corporation
1.3.6.1.4.1.431	Open Systems Solutions, Inc.
1.3.6.1.4.1.432	Toronto Stock Exchange
1.3.6.1.4.1.433	Mamakos\TransSys Consulting
1.3.6.1.4.1.434	EICON
1.3.6.1.4.1.435	Jupiter Systems
1.3.6.1.4.1.436	SSTI
1.3.6.1.4.1.437	Grand Junction Networks
1.3.6.1.4.1.438	Anasazi, Inc.
1.3.6.1.4.1.439	Edward D. Jones and Company
1.3.6.1.4.1.440	Amnet, Inc.
1.3.6.1.4.1.441	Chase Research
1.3.6.1.4.1.442	PEER Networks
1.3.6.1.4.1.443	Gateway Communications, Inc.
1.3.6.1.4.1.444	Peregrine Systems
1.3.6.1.4.1.445	Daewoo Telecom
1.3.6.1.4.1.446	Norwegian Telecom Research
1.3.6.1.4.1.447	WilTel
1.3.6.1.4.1.448	Ericsson-Camtec
1.3.6.1.4.1.449	Codex
1.3.6.1.4.1.450	Basis
1.3.6.1.4.1.451	AGE Logic
1.3.6.1.4.1.452	INDE Electronics
1.3.6.1.4.1.453	ISODE Consortium
1.3.6.1.4.1.454	J.I. Case
1.3.6.1.4.1.455	Trillium
1.3.6.1.4.1.456	Bacchus Inc.
1.3.6.1.4.1.457	MCC
1.3.6.1.4.1.458	Stratus Computer
1.3.6.1.4.1.459	Quotron
1.3.6.1.4.1.460	Beame & Whiteside
1.3.6.1.4.1.461	Cellular Technical Services
1.3.6.1.4.1.462	Shore Microsystems, Inc.
1.3.6.1.4.1.463	Telecommunications Techniques Corporation
1.3.6.1.4.1.464	DNPAP (Technical University Delft)
1.3.6.1.4.1.465	Plexcom, Inc.
1.3.6.1.4.1.466	Tylink
1.3.6.1.4.1.467	Brookhaven National Laboratory
1.3.6.1.4.1.468	Computer Communication Systems

Figure 7-76. The Enterprises Groups *(continued)*

The Enterprises Groups	
Group Object Identifier	**Enterprise Name**
1.3.6.1.4.1.469	Norand Corporation
1.3.6.1.4.1.470	MUX-LAP
1.3.6.1.4.1.471	Premisys Communications, Inc.
1.3.6.1.4.1.472	Bell South Telecommunications
1.3.6.1.4.1.473	J. Stainsbury PLC
1.3.6.1.4.1.474	Ki Research, Inc.
1.3.6.1.4.1.475	Wandel and Goltermann Technologies
1.3.6.1.4.1.476	Emerson Computer Power
1.3.6.1.4.1.477	Network Software Associates
1.3.6.1.4.1.478	Procter and Gamble
1.3.6.1.4.1.479	Meridian Technology Corporation
1.3.6.1.4.1.480	QMS, Inc.
1.3.6.1.4.1.481	Network Express
1.3.6.1.4.1.482	LANcity Corporation
1.3.6.1.4.1.483	Dayna Communications, Inc.
1.3.6.1.4.1.484	kn-X Ltd.
1.3.6.1.4.1.485	Sync Research, Inc.
1.3.6.1.4.1.486	PremNet
1.3.6.1.4.1.487	SIAC
1.3.6.1.4.1.488	New York Stock Exchange
1.3.6.1.4.1.489	American Stock Exchange
1.3.6.1.4.1.490	FCR Software, Inc.
1.3.6.1.4.1.491	National Medical Care, Inc.
1.3.6.1.4.1.492	Dialogue Communication Systemes, S.A.
1.3.6.1.4.1.493	NorTele
1.3.6.1.4.1.494	Madge Networks, Inc.
1.3.6.1.4.1.495	Memotec Communications
1.3.6.1.4.1.496	CTON
1.3.6.1.4.1.497	Leap Technology, Inc.
1.3.6.1.4.1.498	General DataComm, Inc.
1.3.6.1.4.1.499	ACE Communications, Ltd.
1.3.6.1.4.1.500	Automatic Data Processing (ADP)
1.3.6.1.4.1.501	Programa SPRITEL
1.3.6.1.4.1.502	Adacom
1.3.6.1.4.1.503	Metrodata, Ltd.
1.3.6.1.4.1.504	Ellemtel Telecommunication Systems Laboratories
1.3.6.1.4.1.505	Arizona Public Service
1.3.6.1.4.1.506	NETWIZ, Ltd.
1.3.6.1.4.1.507	Science and Engineering Research Council (SERC)
1.3.6.1.4.1.508	The First Boston Corporation
1.3.6.1.4.1.509	Hadax Electronics, Inc.

Figure 7-76. The Enterprises Groups *(continued)*

The Enterprises Groups	
Group Object Identifier	**Enterprise Name**
1.3.6.1.4.1.510	VTKK
1.3.6.1.4.1.511	North Hills Israel, Ltd.
1.3.6.1.4.1.512	TECSIEL
1.3.6.1.4.1.513	Bayerische Motoren Werke (BMW) AG
1.3.6.1.4.1.514	CNET Technologies
1.3.6.1.4.1.515	MCI
1.3.6.1.4.1.516	Human Engineering AG (HEAG)
1.3.6.1.4.1.517	FileNet Corporation
1.3.6.1.4.1.518	NFT-Ericsson
1.3.6.1.4.1.519	Dun & Bradstreet
1.3.6.1.4.1.520	Intercomputer Communications
1.3.6.1.4.1.521	Defense Intelligence Agency
1.3.6.1.4.1.522	Telesystems SLW, Inc.
1.3.6.1.4.1.523	APT Communications
1.3.6.1.4.1.524	Delta Airlines
1.3.6.1.4.1.525	California Microwave
1.3.6.1.4.1.526	Avid Technology, Inc.
1.3.6.1.4.1.527	Integro Advanced Computer Systems
1.3.6.1.4.1.528	RPTI
1.3.6.1.4.1.529	Ascend Communications, Inc.
1.3.6.1.4.1.530	Eden Computer Systems, Inc.
1.3.6.1.4.1.531	Kawasaki-Steel Corporation
1.3.6.1.4.1.532	Barclays
1.3.6.1.4.1.533	B.U.G., Inc.
1.3.6.1.4.1.534	Exide Electronics
1.3.6.1.4.1.535	Superconducting Supercollider Lab.
1.3.6.1.4.1.536	Triticom
1.3.6.1.4.1.537	Universal Instruments Corporation
1.3.6.1.4.1.538	Information Resources, Inc.
1.3.6.1.4.1.539	Applied Innovation, Inc.
1.3.6.1.4.1.540	Crypto AG
1.3.6.1.4.1.541	Infinite Networks, Ltd.
1.3.6.1.4.1.542	Rabbit Software
1.3.6.1.4.1.543	Apertus Technologies
1.3.6.1.4.1.544	Equinox Systems, Inc.
1.3.6.1.4.1.545	Hayes Microcomputer Products
1.3.6.1.4.1.546	Empire Technologies, Inc.
1.3.6.1.4.1.547	Glaxochem, Ltd.
1.3.6.1.4.1.548	Software Professionals, Inc.
1.3.6.1.4.1.549	Agent Technology, Inc.
1.3.6.1.4.1.550	Dornier GMBH

Figure 7-76. The Enterprises Groups *(continued)*

The Enterprises Groups	
Group Object Identifier	**Enterprise Name**
1.3.6.1.4.1.551	Telxon Corporation
1.3.6.1.4.1.552	Entergy Corporation
1.3.6.1.4.1.553	Garrett Communications, Inc.
1.3.6.1.4.1.554	Agile Networks, Inc.
1.3.6.1.4.1.555	Larscom
1.3.6.1.4.1.556	Stock Equipment
1.3.6.1.4.1.557	ITT Corporation
1.3.6.1.4.1.558	Universal Data Systems, Inc.
1.3.6.1.4.1.559	Sonix Communications, Ltd.
1.3.6.1.4.1.560	Paul Freeman Associates, Inc.
1.3.6.1.4.1.561	John S. Barnes, Corporation
1.3.6.1.4.1.562	Northern Telecom, Ltd.
1.3.6.1.4.1.563	CAP Debris
1.3.6.1.4.1.564	Telco Systems NAC
1.3.6.1.4.1.565	Tosco Refining Co.
1.3.6.1.4.1.566	Russell Info Sys.
1.3.6.1.4.1.567	University of Salford
1.3.6.1.4.1.568	NetQuest Corporation
1.3.6.1.4.1.569	Armon Networking, Ltd.
1.3.6.1.4.1.570	IA Corporation
1.3.6.1.4.1.571	AU-System Communication AB
1.3.6.1.4.1.572	GoldStar Information & Communications, Ltd.
1.3.6.1.4.1.573	SECTRA AB
1.3.6.1.4.1.574	ONEAC Corporation
1.3.6.1.4.1.575	Tree Technologies
1.3.6.1.4.1.576	GTE Government Systems
1.3.6.1.4.1.577	Denmac Systems, Inc.
1.3.6.1.4.1.578	Interlink Computer Sciences, Inc.
1.3.6.1.4.1.579	Bridge Information Systems, Inc.
1.3.6.1.4.1.580	Leeds and Northrup Australia (LNA)
1.3.6.1.4.1.581	BHA Computer
1.3.6.1.4.1.582	Newport Systems Solutions, Inc.
1.3.6.1.4.1.583	azel Corporation
1.3.6.1.4.1.584	ROBOTIKER
1.3.6.1.4.1.585	PeerLogic, Inc.
1.3.6.1.4.1.586	Digital Transmittion Systems
1.3.6.1.4.1.587	Far Point Communications
1.3.6.1.4.1.588	Xircom
1.3.6.1.4.1.589	Mead Data Central
1.3.6.1.4.1.590	Royal Bank of Canada
1.3.6.1.4.1.591	Advantis, Inc.

Figure 7-76. The Enterprises Groups *(continued)*

The Enterprises Groups	
Group Object Identifier	**Enterprise Name**
1.3.6.1.4.1.592	Chemical Banking Corporation
1.3.6.1.4.1.593	Eagle Technology
1.3.6.1.4.1.594	British Telecom
1.3.6.1.4.1.595	Radix BV
1.3.6.1.4.1.596	TAINET Communication System Corporation
1.3.6.1.4.1.597	Comtek Services, Inc.
1.3.6.1.4.1.598	Fair Issac
1.3.6.1.4.1.599	AST Research, Inc.
1.3.6.1.4.1.600	Soft*Star s.r.l. Ing.
1.3.6.1.4.1.601	Bancomm
1.3.6.1.4.1.602	Trusted Information Systems, Inc.
1.3.6.1.4.1.603	Harris & Jeffries, Inc.
1.3.6.1.4.1.604	Axel Technology Corporation
1.3.6.1.4.1.605	GN Navtel, Inc.
1.3.6.1.4.1.606	CAP debis
1.3.6.1.4.1.607	Lachman Technology, Inc.
1.3.6.1.4.1.608	Galcom Networking, Ltd.
1.3.6.1.4.1.609	BAZIS
1.3.6.1.4.1.610	SYNAPTEL
1.3.6.1.4.1.611	Investment Management Services, Inc.
1.3.6.1.4.1.612	Taiwan Telecommunication Lab
1.3.6.1.4.1.613	Anagram Corporation
1.3.6.1.4.1.614	Univel
1.3.6.1.4.1.615	University of California, San Diego
1.3.6.1.4.1.616	CompuServe
1.3.6.1.4.1.617	Telstra - OTC Australia
1.3.6.1.4.1.618	Westinghouse Electric Corporation
1.3.6.1.4.1.619	DGA, Ltd.
1.3.6.1.4.1.620	Elegant Communications, Inc.
1.3.6.1.4.1.621	Experdata
1.3.6.1.4.1.622	Unisource Business Networks Sweden AB
1.3.6.1.4.1.623	Molex, Inc.
1.3.6.1.4.1.624	Quay Financial Software
1.3.6.1.4.1.625	VMX, Inc.
1.3.6.1.4.1.626	Hypercom, Inc.
1.3.6.1.4.1.627	University of Guelph
1.3.6.1.4.1.628	DIaLOGIKa
1.3.6.1.4.1.629	NBASE Switch Communication
1.3.6.1.4.1.630	Anchor Datacomm bv
1.3.6.1.4.1.631	PACDATA
1.3.6.1.4.1.632	University of Colorado

Figure 7-76. The Enterprises Groups *(continued)*

The Enterprises Groups	
Group Object Identifier	**Enterprise Name**
1.3.6.1.4.1.633	Tricom Communications, Ltd.
1.3.6.1.4.1.634	Santix Software GmbH
1.3.6.1.4.1.635	FastComm Communications Corporation
1.3.6.1.4.1.636	The Georgia Institute of Technology
1.3.6.1.4.1.637	Alcatel Data Networks
1.3.6.1.4.1.638	GTECH
1.3.6.1.4.1.639	UNOCAL Corporation
1.3.6.1.4.1.640	First Pacific Network
1.3.6.1.4.1.641	Lexmark International
1.3.6.1.4.1.642	Qnix Computer
1.3.6.1.4.1.643	Jigsaw Software Concepts (Pty), Ltd.
1.3.6.1.4.1.644	VIR, Inc.
1.3.6.1.4.1.645	SFA Datacomm, Inc.
1.3.6.1.4.1.646	SEIKO Communication Systems, Inc.
1.3.6.1.4.1.647	Unified Management
1.3.6.1.4.1.648	RADLINX, Ltd.
1.3.6.1.4.1.649	Microplex Systems, Ltd.
1.3.6.1.4.1.650	Objecta Elektronik & Data AB
1.3.6.1.4.1.651	Phoenix Microsystems
1.3.6.1.4.1.652	Distributed Systems International, Inc.
1.3.6.1.4.1.653	Evolving Systems, Inc.
1.3.6.1.4.1.654	SAT GmbH
1.3.6.1.4.1.655	CeLAN Technology, Inc.
1.3.6.1.4.1.656	Landmark Systems Corporation
1.3.6.1.4.1.657	Netone Systems Co., Ltd.
1.3.6.1.4.1.658	Loral Data Systems
1.3.6.1.4.1.659	Cellware Broadband Technology
1.3.6.1.4.1.660	Mu-Systems
1.3.6.1.4.1.661	IMC Networks Corporation
1.3.6.1.4.1.662	Octel Communications Corporation
1.3.6.1.4.1.663	RIT Technologies, Ltd.
1.3.6.1.4.1.664	Adtran
1.3.6.1.4.1.665	PowerPlay Technologies, Inc.
1.3.6.1.4.1.666	Oki Electric Industry Co., Ltd.
1.3.6.1.4.1.667	Specialix International
1.3.6.1.4.1.668	INESC (Instituto de Engenharia de Sistemas e Computadores)
1.3.6.1.4.1.669	Globalnet Communications
1.3.6.1.4.1.670	Product Line Engineer SVEC Computer Corporation
1.3.6.1.4.1.671	Printer Systems Corporation
1.3.6.1.4.1.672	Contec Micro Electronics USA
1.3.6.1.4.1.673	Unix Integration Services

Figure 7-76. The Enterprises Groups *(continued)*

The Enterprises Groups	
Group Object Identifier	**Enterprise Name**
1.3.6.1.4.1.674	Dell Computer Corporation
1.3.6.1.4.1.675	Whittaker Electronic Systems
1.3.6.1.4.1.676	QPSX Communications
1.3.6.1.4.1.677	Loral WDI
1.3.6.1.4.1.678	Federal Express Corporation
1.3.6.1.4.1.679	E-COMMS, Inc.
1.3.6.1.4.1.680	Software Clearing House
1.3.6.1.4.1.681	Antlow Computers, Ltd.
1.3.6.1.4.1.682	Emcom Corporation
1.3.6.1.4.1.683	Extended Systems, Inc.
1.3.6.1.4.1.684	Sola Electric
1.3.6.1.4.1.685	Esix Systems, Inc.
1.3.6.1.4.1.686	3M/MMM
1.3.6.1.4.1.687	Cylink Corporation
1.3.6.1.4.1.688	Znyx Advanced Systems Division, Inc.
1.3.6.1.4.1.689	Texaco, Inc.
1.3.6.1.4.1.690	McCaw Cellular Communication Corporation
1.3.6.1.4.1.691	ASP Computer Product, Inc.
1.3.6.1.4.1.692	HiPerformance Systems
1.3.6.1.4.1.693	Regionales Rechenzentrum
1.3.6.1.4.1.694	SAP AG
1.3.6.1.4.1.695	ElectroSpace System, Inc.
1.3.6.1.4.1.696	unassigned
1.3.6.1.4.1.697	MultiPort Corporation
1.3.6.1.4.1.698	Combinet, Inc.
1.3.6.1.4.1.699	TSCC
1.3.6.1.4.1.700	Teleos Communications, Inc.
1.3.6.1.4.1.701	Alta Research
1.3.6.1.4.1.702	Independence Blue Cross
1.3.6.1.4.1.703	ADACOM Station Interconnectivity, Ltd.
1.3.6.1.4.1.704	MIROR Systems
1.3.6.1.4.1.705	Merlin Gerin
1.3.6.1.4.1.706	Owen-Corning Fiberglass
1.3.6.1.4.1.707	Talking Networks, Inc.
1.3.6.1.4.1.708	Cubix Corporation
1.3.6.1.4.1.709	Formation, Inc.
1.3.6.1.4.1.710	Lannair, Ltd.
1.3.6.1.4.1.711	LightStream Corporation
1.3.6.1.4.1.712	LANart Corporation
1.3.6.1.4.1.713	University of Stellenbosch
1.3.6.1.4.1.714	Wyse Technology

Figure 7-76. The Enterprises Groups *(continued)*

The Enterprises Groups	
Group Object Identifier	**Enterprise Name**
1.3.6.1.4.1.715	DSC Communications Corporation
1.3.6.1.4.1.716	NetEc
1.3.6.1.4.1.717	Breltenbach Software Engineering GmbH
1.3.6.1.4.1.718	Victor Company of Japan, Ltd.
1.3.6.1.4.1.719	Japan Direx Corporation
1.3.6.1.4.1.720	NECSY Network Control Systems S.p.A.
1.3.6.1.4.1.721	ISDN Systems Corporation
1.3.6.1.4.1.722	Zero-One Technologies, Ltd.
1.3.6.1.4.1.723	Radix Technologies, Inc.
1.3.6.1.4.1.724	National Institute of Standards and Technology
1.3.6.1.4.1.725	Digital Technology, Inc.
1.3.6.1.4.1.726	Castelle Corporation
1.3.6.1.4.1.727	Presticom, Inc.
1.3.6.1.4.1.728	Showa Electric Wire & Cable Co., Ltd.
1.3.6.1.4.1.729	SpectraGraphics
1.3.6.1.4.1.730	Connectware, Inc.
1.3.6.1.4.1.731	Wind River Systems
1.3.6.1.4.1.732	RADWAY International, Ltd.
1.3.6.1.4.1.733	System Management ARTS, Inc.
1.3.6.1.4.1.734	Persoft, Inc.
1.3.6.1.4.1.735	Xnet Technology, Inc.
1.3.6.1.4.1.736	Unison-Tymlabs
1.3.6.1.4.1.737	Micro-Matic Research
1.3.6.1.4.1.738	B.A.T.M. Advance Technologies
1.3.6.1.4.1.739	University of Copenhagen
1.3.6.1.4.1.740	Network Security Systems, Inc.
1.3.6.1.4.1.741	JNA Telecommunications
1.3.6.1.4.1.742	Encore Computer Corporation
1.3.6.1.4.1.743	Central Intelligent Agency
1.3.6.1.4.1.744	ISC (GB) Limited
1.3.6.1.4.1.745	Digital Communication Associates
1.3.6.1.4.1.746	CyberMedia, Inc.
1.3.6.1.4.1.747	Distributed Systems International, Inc.
1.3.6.1.4.1.748	Peter Radig EDP-Consulting
1.3.6.1.4.1.749	Vicorp Interactive Systems
1.3.6.1.4.1.750	Inet, Inc.
1.3.6.1.4.1.751	Argonne National Laboratory
1.3.6.1.4.1.752	Tek Logix
1.3.6.1.4.1.753	North Western University
1.3.6.1.4.1.754	Astarte Fiber Networks
1.3.6.1.4.1.755	Diederich & Associates, Inc.

Figure 7-76. The Enterprises Groups *(continued)*

The Enterprises Groups	
Group Object Identifier	**Enterprise Name**
1.3.6.1.4.1.756	Florida Power Corporation
1.3.6.1.4.1.757	ASK/INGRES
1.3.6.1.4.1.758	Open Network Enterprise
1.3.6.1.4.1.759	The Home Depot
1.3.6.1.4.1.760	Pan Dacom Telekommunikations
1.3.6.1.4.1.761	NetTek
1.3.6.1.4.1.762	Karlnet Corporation
1.3.6.1.4.1.763	Efficient Networks, Inc.
1.3.6.1.4.1.764	Fiberdata
1.3.6.1.4.1.765	Lanser
1.3.6.1.4.1.766	Telebit Communications A/S
1.3.6.1.4.1.767	HILAN GmbH
1.3.6.1.4.1.768	Network Computing, Inc.
1.3.6.1.4.1.769	Walgreens Company
1.3.6.1.4.1.770	Internet Initiative Japan, Inc.
1.3.6.1.4.1.771	GP van Niekerk Ondernemings
1.3.6.1.4.1.772	Queen's University Belfast
1.3.6.1.4.1.773	Securities Industry Automation Corporation
1.3.6.1.4.1.774	SYNaPTICS
1.3.6.1.4.1.775	Data Switch Corporation
1.3.6.1.4.1.776	Telindus Distribution
1.3.6.1.4.1.777	MAXM Systems Corporation
1.3.6.1.4.1.778	Fraunhofer Gesellschaft
1.3.6.1.4.1.779	EQS Business Services
1.3.6.1.4.1.780	CNet Technology, Inc.
1.3.6.1.4.1.781	Datentechnik GmbH
1.3.6.1.4.1.782	Network Solutions, Inc.
1.3.6.1.4.1.783	Viaman Software
1.3.6.1.4.1.784	Schweizerische Bankgesellschaft Zuerich
1.3.6.1.4.1.785	University of Twente - TIOS
1.3.6.1.4.1.786	Simplesoft, Inc.
1.3.6.1.4.1.787	Stony Brook, Inc.
1.3.6.1.4.1.788	Unified Systems Solutions, Inc.
1.3.6.1.4.1.789	Network Appliance Corporation
1.3.6.1.4.1.790	Ornet Data Communication Technologies, Ltd.
1.3.6.1.4.1.791	Computer Associates International
1.3.6.1.4.1.792	Multipoint Network, Inc.
1.3.6.1.4.1.793	NYNEX Science & Technology
1.3.6.1.4.1.794	Commercial Link Systems
1.3.6.1.4.1.795	Adaptec, Inc.
1.3.6.1.4.1.796	Softswitch

Figure 7-76. The Enterprises Groups *(continued)*

The Enterprises Groups	
Group Object Identifier	**Enterprise Name**
1.3.6.1.4.1.797	Link Technologies, Inc.
1.3.6.1.4.1.798	IIS
1.3.6.1.4.1.799	Mobile Solutions, Inc.
1.3.6.1.4.1.800	Xylan Corporation
1.3.6.1.4.1.801	Airtech Software Forge, Ltd.
1.3.6.1.4.1.802	National Semiconductor
1.3.6.1.4.1.803	Video Lottery Technologies
1.3.6.1.4.1.804	National Semiconductor Corporation
1.3.6.1.4.1.805	Applications Management Corporation
1.3.6.1.4.1.806	Travelers Insurance Company
1.3.6.1.4.1.807	Taiwan International Standard Electronics, Ltd.
1.3.6.1.4.1.808	US Patent and Trademark Office
1.3.6.1.4.1.809	Hynet, Ltd.
1.3.6.1.4.1.810	Aydin Corporation
1.3.6.1.4.1.811	ADDTRON Technology Co., Ltd.
1.3.6.1.4.1.812	Fannie Mae
1.3.6.1.4.1.813	MultiNET Services
1.3.6.1.4.1.814	GECKO mbH
1.3.6.1.4.1.815	Memorex Telex
1.3.6.1.4.1.816	Advanced Communications Networks (ACN) SA
1.3.6.1.4.1.817	Telekurs AG
1.3.6.1.4.1.818	Victron bv
1.3.6.1.4.1.819	CF6 Company
1.3.6.1.4.1.820	Walker Richer and Quinn, Inc.
1.3.6.1.4.1.821	Saturn Systems
1.3.6.1.4.1.822	Mitsui Marine and Fire Insurance Co., Ltd.
1.3.6.1.4.1.823	Loop Telecommunication International, Inc.
1.3.6.1.4.1.824	Telenex Corporation
1.3.6.1.4.1.825	Bus-Tech, Inc.
1.3.6.1.4.1.826	ATRIE
1.3.6.1.4.1.827	Gallagher & Robertson A/S
1.3.6.1.4.1.828	Networks Northwest, Inc.
1.3.6.1.4.1.829	Conner Peripherials
1.3.6.1.4.1.830	Elf Antar France
1.3.6.1.4.1.831	Lloyd Internetworking
1.3.6.1.4.1.832	Datatec Industries, Inc.
1.3.6.1.4.1.833	TAICOM
1.3.6.1.4.1.834	Brown's Operating System Services, Ltd.
1.3.6.1.4.1.835	MiLAN Technology Corporation
1.3.6.1.4.1.836	NetEdge Systems, Inc.
1.3.6.1.4.1.837	NetFrame Systems

Figure 7-76. The Enterprises Groups *(continued)*

The Enterprises Groups	
Group Object Identifier	**Enterprise Name**
1.3.6.1.4.1.838	Xedia Corporation
1.3.6.1.4.1.839	Pepsi
1.3.6.1.4.1.840	Tricord Systems, Inc.
1.3.6.1.4.1.841	Proxim Inc.
1.3.6.1.4.1.842	Applications Plus, Inc.
1.3.6.1.4.1.843	Pacific Bell
1.3.6.1.4.1.844	Scorpio Communications
1.3.6.1.4.1.845	TPS-Teleprocessing Systems
1.3.6.1.4.1.846	Technology Solutions Company
1.3.6.1.4.1.847	Computer Site Technologies
1.3.6.1.4.1.848	NetPort Software
1.3.6.1.4.1.849	Alon Systems
1.3.6.1.4.1.850	Tripp Lite
1.3.6.1.4.1.851	NetComm, Ltd.
1.3.6.1.4.1.852	Precision Systems, Inc. (PSI)
1.3.6.1.4.1.853	Objective Systems Integrators
1.3.6.1.4.1.854	Simpact, Inc.
1.3.6.1.4.1.855	Systems Enhancement Corporation
1.3.6.1.4.1.856	Information Integration, Inc.
1.3.6.1.4.1.857	CETREL S.C.
1.3.6.1.4.1.858	Platinum Technology, Inc.
1.3.6.1.4.1.859	Olivetti North America
1.3.6.1.4.1.860	WILMA
1.3.6.1.4.1.861	ILX Systems, Inc.
1.3.6.1.4.1.862	Total Peripherals, Inc.
1.3.6.1.4.1.863	SunNetworks Consultant
1.3.6.1.4.1.864	Arkhon Technologies, Inc.
1.3.6.1.4.1.865	Computer Sciences Corporation
1.3.6.1.4.1.866	Philips Communication d'Entreprise
1.3.6.1.4.1.867	Katron Technologies, Inc.
1.3.6.1.4.1.868	Transition Engineering, Inc.
1.3.6.1.4.1.869	Altos Engineering Applications, Inc.
1.3.6.1.4.1.870	Nicecom, Ltd.
1.3.6.1.4.1.871	Fiskars/Deltec
1.3.6.1.4.1.872	AVM GmbH
1.3.6.1.4.1.873	Comm Vision
1.3.6.1.4.1.874	Institute for Information Industry
1.3.6.1.4.1.875	Legent Corporation
1.3.6.1.4.1.876	Network Automation
1.3.6.1.4.1.877	NetTech
1.3.6.1.4.1.878	Coman Data Communications, Ltd.

Figure 7-76. The Enterprises Groups *(continued)*

The Enterprises Groups	
Group Object Identifier	**Enterprise Name**
1.3.6.1.4.1.879	Skattedirektoratet
1.3.6.1.4.1.880	Client-Server Technologies
1.3.6.1.4.1.881	Societe Internationale de Telecommunications Aeronautiques
1.3.6.1.4.1.882	Maximum Strategy, Inc.
1.3.6.1.4.1.883	Integrated Systems, Inc.
1.3.6.1.4.1.884	E-Systems
1.3.6.1.4.1.885	Reliance Comm/Tec
1.3.6.1.4.1.886	Summa Four, Inc.
1.3.6.1.4.1.887	J & L Information Systems
1.3.6.1.4.1.888	Forest Computer, Inc.
1.3.6.1.4.1.889	Palindrome Corporation
1.3.6.1.4.1.890	ZyXEL Communications Corporation
1.3.6.1.4.1.891	Network Managers (UK), Ltd.
1.3.6.1.4.1.892	Sensible Office Systems, Inc.
1.3.6.1.4.1.893	Informix Software
1.3.6.1.4.1.894	Dynatek Communications
1.3.6.1.4.1.895	Versalynx Corporation
1.3.6.1.4.1.896	Potomac Scheduling Communications Company
1.3.6.1.4.1.897	Sybase, Inc.
1.3.6.1.4.1.898	DiviCom, Inc.
1.3.6.1.4.1.899	Datus elektronische Informationssysteme GmbH
1.3.6.1.4.1.900	Matrox Electronic Systems, Ltd.
1.3.6.1.4.1.901	Digital Products, Inc.
1.3.6.1.4.1.902	Scitex Corporation, Ltd.
1.3.6.1.4.1.903	RAD Vision
1.3.6.1.4.1.904	Tran Network Systems
1.3.6.1.4.1.905	Scorpion Logic
1.3.6.1.4.1.906	Inotech, Inc.
1.3.6.1.4.1.907	Controlled Power Co.
1.3.6.1.4.1.908	Elsag Bailey, Inc.
1.3.6.1.4.1.909	J.P. Morgan
1.3.6.1.4.1.910	Clear Communications Corporation
1.3.6.1.4.1.911	General Technology, Inc.
1.3.6.1.4.1.912	Adax, Inc.
1.3.6.1.4.1.913	Mtel Technologies, Inc.
1.3.6.1.4.1.914	Underscore, Inc.
1.3.6.1.4.1.915	SerComm Corporation
1.3.6.1.4.1.916	Baxter Healthcare Corporation
1.3.6.1.4.1.917	Tellus Technology
1.3.6.1.4.1.918	Continuous Electron Beam Accelerator Facility
1.3.6.1.4.1.919	Canoga Perkins

Figure 7-76. The Enterprises Groups *(continued)*

The Enterprises Groups	
Group Object Identifier	**Enterprise Name**
1.3.6.1.4.1.920	R.I.S Technologies
1.3.6.1.4.1.921	INFONEX Corporation
1.3.6.1.4.1.922	WordPerfect Corporation
1.3.6.1.4.1.923	NRaD
1.3.6.1.4.1.924	Hong Kong Telecommunications, Ltd.
1.3.6.1.4.1.925	Signature Systems
1.3.6.1.4.1.926	Alpha Technologies, Ltd.
1.3.6.1.4.1.927	PairGain Technologies, Inc.
1.3.6.1.4.1.928	Sonic Systems
1.3.6.1.4.1.929	Steinbrecher Corporation
1.3.6.1.4.1.930	Centillion Networks, Inc.
1.3.6.1.4.1.931	Network Communication Corporation
1.3.6.1.4.1.932	Sysnet A.S.
1.3.6.1.4.1.933	Telecommunication Systems Lab
1.3.6.1.4.1.934	QMI
1.3.6.1.4.1.935	Phoenixtec Power Co., Ltd.
1.3.6.1.4.1.936	Hirakawa Hewtech Corporation
1.3.6.1.4.1.937	No Wires Needed bv
1.3.6.1.4.1.938	Primary Access
1.3.6.1.4.1.939	FD Software AS
1.3.6.1.4.1.940	Grabner & Kapfer GnbR
1.3.6.1.4.1.941	Nemesys Research, Ltd.
1.3.6.1.4.1.942	Pacific Communication Sciences, Inc. (PSCI)
1.3.6.1.4.1.943	Level One Communications, Inc.
1.3.6.1.4.1.944	Fast Track, Inc.
1.3.6.1.4.1.945	Andersen Consulting, OM/NI Practice
1.3.6.1.4.1.946	Bay Technologies Pty., Ltd.
1.3.6.1.4.1.947	Integrated Network Corporation
1.3.6.1.4.1.948	Epoch, Inc.
1.3.6.1.4.1.949	Wang Laboratories, Inc.
1.3.6.1.4.1.950	Polaroid Corporation
1.3.6.1.4.1.951	Sunrise Sierra
1.3.6.1.4.1.952	Silcon Group
1.3.6.1.4.1.953	Coastcom
1.3.6.1.4.1.954	4th DIMENSION SOFTWARE, Ltd.
1.3.6.1.4.1.955	SEIKO SYSTEMS, Inc.
1.3.6.1.4.1.956	PERFORM
1.3.6.1.4.1.957	TV/COM International
1.3.6.1.4.1.958	Network Integration, Inc.
1.3.6.1.4.1.959	Sola Electric, A Unit of General Signal
1.3.6.1.4.1.960	Gradient Technologies, Inc.

Figure 7-76. The Enterprises Groups *(continued)*

The Enterprises Groups	
Group Object Identifier	**Enterprise Name**
1.3.6.1.4.1.961	Tokyo Electric Co., Ltd.
1.3.6.1.4.1.962	Codonics, Inc.
1.3.6.1.4.1.963	Delft Technical University
1.3.6.1.4.1.964	Carrier Access Corporation
1.3.6.1.4.1.965	eoncorp
1.3.6.1.4.1.966	Naval Undersea Warfare Center
1.3.6.1.4.1.967	AWA, Ltd.
1.3.6.1.4.1.968	Distinct Corporation
1.3.6.1.4.1.969	National Technical University of Athens
1.3.6.1.4.1.970	BGS Systems, Inc.
1.3.6.1.4.1.971	McCaw Wireless Data Inc.
1.3.6.1.4.1.972	Bekaert
1.3.6.1.4.1.973	Epic Data, Inc.
1.3.6.1.4.1.974	Prodigy Services Co.
1.3.6.1.4.1.975	First Pacific Networks (FPN)
1.3.6.1.4.1.976	Xylink, Ltd.
1.3.6.1.4.1.977	Relia Technologies Corporation
1.3.6.1.4.1.978	Legacy Storage Systems, Inc.
1.3.6.1.4.1.979	Digicom, SPA
1.3.6.1.4.1.980	Ark Telecom
1.3.6.1.4.1.981	National Security Agency (NSA)
1.3.6.1.4.1.982	Southwestern Bell Corporation
1.3.6.1.4.1.983	Virtual Design Group, Inc.
1.3.6.1.4.1.984	Rhone Poulenc
1.3.6.1.4.1.985	Swiss Bank Corporation
1.3.6.1.4.1.986	ATEA N.V.
1.3.6.1.4.1.987	Computer Communications Specialists, Inc.
1.3.6.1.4.1.988	Object Quest, Inc.
1.3.6.1.4.1.989	DCL System International, Ltd.
1.3.6.1.4.1.990	SOLITON SYSTEMS K.K.
1.3.6.1.4.1.991	U S Software
1.3.6.1.4.1.992	Systems Research and Applications Corporation
1.3.6.1.4.1.993	University of Florida
1.3.6.1.4.1.994	Dantel, Inc.
1.3.6.1.4.1.995	Multi-Tech Systems, Inc.
1.3.6.1.4.1.996	Softlink, Ltd.
1.3.6.1.4.1.997	ProSum
1.3.6.1.4.1.998	March Systems Consultancy, Ltd.
1.3.6.1.4.1.999	Hong Technology, Inc.
1.3.6.1.4.1.1000	Internet Assigned Numbers Authority
1.3.6.1.4.1.1001	PECO Energy Co.

Figure 7-76. The Enterprises Groups *(continued)*

The Enterprises Groups	
Group Object Identifier	**Enterprise Name**
1.3.6.1.4.1.1002	United Parcel Service
1.3.6.1.4.1.1003	Storage Dimensions, Inc.
1.3.6.1.4.1.1004	ITV Technologies, Inc.
1.3.6.1.4.1.1005	TCPSI
1.3.6.1.4.1.1006	Promptus Communications, Inc.
1.3.6.1.4.1.1007	Norman Data Defense Systems
1.3.6.1.4.1.1008	Pilot Network Services, Inc.
1.3.6.1.4.1.1009	Integrated Systems Solutions Corporation
1.3.6.1.4.1.1010	SISRO
1.3.6.1.4.1.1011	NetVantage
1.3.6.1.4.1.1012	Marconi S.p.A.
1.3.6.1.4.1.1013	SURECOM
1.3.6.1.4.1.1014	Royal Hong Kong Jockey Club
1.3.6.1.4.1.1015	Gupta
1.3.6.1.4.1.1016	Tone Software Corporation
1.3.6.1.4.1.1017	Opus Telecom
1.3.6.1.4.1.1018	Cogsys, Ltd.
1.3.6.1.4.1.1019	Komatsu, Ltd.
1.3.6.1.4.1.1020	ROI Systems, Inc.
1.3.6.1.4.1.1021	Lightning Instrumentation SA
1.3.6.1.4.1.1022	TimeStep Corporation
1.3.6.1.4.1.1023	INTELSAT
1.3.6.1.4.1.1024	Network Research Corporation Japan, Ltd.
1.3.6.1.4.1.1025	Relational Development, Inc.
1.3.6.1.4.1.1026	Emerald Systems Corporation
1.3.6.1.4.1.1027	Mitel Corporation
1.3.6.1.4.1.1028	Software AG
1.3.6.1.4.1.1029	MillenNet, Inc.
1.3.6.1.4.1.1030	NK-EXA Corporation
1.3.6.1.4.1.1031	BMC Software
1.3.6.1.4.1.1032	StarFire Enterprises, Inc.
1.3.6.1.4.1.1033	Hybrid Networks, Inc.
1.3.6.1.4.1.1034	Quantum Software GmbH
1.3.6.1.4.1.1035	Openvision Technologies, Ltd.
1.3.6.1.4.1.1036	Healthcare Communications, Inc. (HCI)
1.3.6.1.4.1.1037	SAIT Systems
1.3.6.1.4.1.1038	SAT
1.3.6.1.4.1.1039	CompuSci, Inc.
1.3.6.1.4.1.1040	Aim Technology
1.3.6.1.4.1.1041	CIESIN
1.3.6.1.4.1.1042	Systems & Technologies International

Figure 7-76. The Enterprises Groups *(continued)*

The Enterprises Groups	
Group Object Identifier	**Enterprise Name**
1.3.6.1.4.1.1043	Israeli Electric Company (IEC)
1.3.6.1.4.1.1044	Phoenix Wireless Group, Inc.
1.3.6.1.4.1.1045	SWL
1.3.6.1.4.1.1046	nCUBE
1.3.6.1.4.1.1047	Cerner, Corporation
1.3.6.1.4.1.1048	Andersen Consulting
1.3.6.1.4.1.1049	Lincoln Telephone Company
1.3.6.1.4.1.1050	Acer
1.3.6.1.4.1.1051	Cedros
1.3.6.1.4.1.1052	AirAccess
1.3.6.1.4.1.1053	Expersoft Corporation
1.3.6.1.4.1.1054	Eskom
1.3.6.1.4.1.1055	SBE, Inc.
1.3.6.1.4.1.1056	EBS, Inc.
1.3.6.1.4.1.1057	American Computer and Electronics Corporation
1.3.6.1.4.1.1058	Syndesis, Ltd.
1.3.6.1.4.1.1059	Isis Distributed Systems, Inc.
1.3.6.1.4.1.1060	Priority Call Management
1.3.6.1.4.1.1061	Koelsch & Altmann GmbH
1.3.6.1.4.1.1062	WIPRO INFOTECH. Ltd.
1.3.6.1.4.1.1063	Controlware
1.3.6.1.4.1.1064	Mosaic Software
1.3.6.1.4.1.1065	Canon Information Systems
1.3.6.1.4.1.1066	America Online
1.3.6.1.4.1.1067	Whitetree Network Technologies, Inc.
1.3.6.1.4.1.1068	Xetron Corporation
1.3.6.1.4.1.1069	Target Concepts, Inc.
1.3.6.1.4.1.1070	DMH Software
1.3.6.1.4.1.1071	Innosoft International, Inc.
1.3.6.1.4.1.1072	Controlware GmbH
1.3.6.1.4.1.1073	Telecommunications Industry Association (TIA)
1.3.6.1.4.1.1074	Boole & Babbage
1.3.6.1.4.1.1075	System Engineering Support, Ltd.
1.3.6.1.4.1.1076	SURFnet
1.3.6.1.4.1.1077	OpenConnect Systems, Inc.
1.3.6.1.4.1.1078	PDTS (Process Data Technology and Systems)
1.3.6.1.4.1.1079	Cornet, Inc.
1.3.6.1.4.1.1080	NetStar, Inc.
1.3.6.1.4.1.1081	Semaphore Communications Corporation
1.3.6.1.4.1.1082	Casio Computer Co., Ltd.
1.3.6.1.4.1.1083	CSIR

Figure 7-76. The Enterprises Groups *(continued)*

The Enterprises Groups	
Group Object Identifier	**Enterprise Name**
1.3.6.1.4.1.1084	APOGEE Communications
1.3.6.1.4.1.1085	Information Management Company
1.3.6.1.4.1.1086	Wordlink, Inc.
1.3.6.1.4.1.1087	PEER
1.3.6.1.4.1.1088	Telstra Corporation
1.3.6.1.4.1.1089	Net X, Inc.
1.3.6.1.4.1.1090	PNC PLC
1.3.6.1.4.1.1091	DanaSoft, Inc.
1.3.6.1.4.1.1092	Yokogawa-Hewlett-Packard
1.3.6.1.4.1.1093	Universities of Austria/Europe
1.3.6.1.4.1.1094	Link Telecom, Ltd.
1.3.6.1.4.1.1095	Xirion bv
1.3.6.1.4.1.1096	Centigram Communications Corporation
1.3.6.1.4.1.1097	Gensym Corporation
1.3.6.1.4.1.1098	Apricot Computers, Ltd.
1.3.6.1.4.1.1099	CANAL+
1.3.6.1.4.1.1100	Cambridge Technology Partners
1.3.6.1.4.1.1101	MoNet Systems, Inc.
1.3.6.1.4.1.1102	Metricom, Inc.
1.3.6.1.4.1.1103	Xact, Inc
1.3.6.1.4.1.1104	First Virtual Holdings, Inc.
1.3.6.1.4.1.1105	NetCell Systems, Inc.
1.3.6.1.4.1.1106	Uni-Q
1.3.6.1.4.1.1107	DISA Space Systems Development Division
1.3.6.1.4.1.1108	INTERSOLV
1.3.6.1.4.1.1109	Vela Research, Inc.
1.3.6.1.4.1.1110	Tetherless Access, Inc.
1.3.6.1.4.1.1111	Magistrat Wien, AT
1.3.6.1.4.1.1112	Franklin Telecom, Inc.
1.3.6.1.4.1.1113	EDA Instruments, Inc.
1.3.6.1.4.1.1114	EFI Electronics Corporation
1.3.6.1.4.1.1115	GMD
1.3.6.1.4.1.1116	Voicetek Corporation
1.3.6.1.4.1.1117	Avanti Technology, Inc.
1.3.6.1.4.1.1118	ATLan, Ltd.
1.3.6.1.4.1.1119	Lehman Brothers
1.3.6.1.4.1.1120	LAN-hopper Systems, Inc.
1.3.6.1.4.1.1121	Web-Systems
1.3.6.1.4.1.1122	Piller GmbH
1.3.6.1.4.1.1123	Symbios Logic, Inc.
1.3.6.1.4.1.1124	NetSpan Corporation

Figure 7-76. The Enterprises Groups *(continued)*

307

The Enterprises Groups	
Group Object Identifier	**Enterprise Name**
1.3.6.1.4.1.1125	Nielsen Media Research
1.3.6.1.4.1.1126	Sterling Software
1.3.6.1.4.1.1127	Applied Network Technology, Inc.
1.3.6.1.4.1.1128	Union Pacific Railroad
1.3.6.1.4.1.1129	Tec Corporation
1.3.6.1.4.1.1130	Datametrics Systems Corporation
1.3.6.1.4.1.1131	Intersection Development Corporation
1.3.6.1.4.1.1132	BACS Limited, GB
1.3.6.1.4.1.1133	Engage Communication
1.3.6.1.4.1.1134	Fastware, S.A.
1.3.6.1.4.1.1135	LONGSHINE Electronics Corporation
1.3.6.1.4.1.1136	BOW Software, Inc.
1.3.6.1.4.1.1137	emotion, Inc.
1.3.6.1.4.1.1138	Rautaruukki steel factory, Information systems
1.3.6.1.4.1.1139	EMC Corp
1.3.6.1.4.1.1140	University of West England
1.3.6.1.4.1.1141	Com21
1.3.6.1.4.1.1142	Compression Technologies, Inc.
1.3.6.1.4.1.1143	Buslogic, Inc.
1.3.6.1.4.1.1144	Firefox Corporation
1.3.6.1.4.1.1145	Mercury Communications, Ltd.
1.3.6.1.4.1.1146	COMPUTER PROTOCOL MALAYSIA SDN. BHD.
1.3.6.1.4.1.1147	Institute for Information Industry
1.3.6.1.4.1.1148	Pacific Electric Wire & Cable Co., Ltd.
1.3.6.1.4.1.1149	MPR Teltech, Ltd.
1.3.6.1.4.1.1150	P-COM, Inc.
1.3.6.1.4.1.1151	Anritsu Corporation
1.3.6.1.4.1.1152	SPYRUS
1.3.6.1.4.1.1153	NeTpower, Inc.
1.3.6.1.4.1.1154	Diehl ISDN GmbH
1.3.6.1.4.1.1155	CARNet
1.3.6.1.4.1.1156	AS-TECH
1.3.6.1.4.1.1157	SG2 Innovation et Produits
1.3.6.1.4.1.1158	CellAccess Technology, Inc.
1.3.6.1.4.1.1159	Bureau of Meteorology
1.3.6.1.4.1.1160	Hi-TECH Connections, Inc.
1.3.6.1.4.1.1161	Thames Water Utilities, Ltd.
1.3.6.1.4.1.1162	Micropolis Corporation
1.3.6.1.4.1.1163	Integrated Systems Technology
1.3.6.1.4.1.1164	Brite Voice Systems, Inc.
1.3.6.1.4.1.1165	Associated Grocer

Figure 7-76. The Enterprises Groups *(continued)*

The Enterprises Groups	
Group Object Identifier	**Enterprise Name**
1.3.6.1.4.1.1166	General Instrument
1.3.6.1.4.1.1167	Stanford Telecom
1.3.6.1.4.1.1168	ICOM Informatique
1.3.6.1.4.1.1169	MPX Data Systems, Inc.
1.3.6.1.4.1.1170	Syntellect
1.3.6.1.4.1.1171	Perihelion Technology, Ltd.
1.3.6.1.4.1.1172	Shoppers Drug Mart
1.3.6.1.4.1.1173	Apollo Travel Services
1.3.6.1.4.1.1174	Time Warner Cable, Inc.
1.3.6.1.4.1.1175	American Technology Labs, Inc.
1.3.6.1.4.1.1176	Dow Jones & Company, Inc.
1.3.6.1.4.1.1177	FRA
1.3.6.1.4.1.1178	Equitable Life Assurance Society
1.3.6.1.4.1.1179	Smith Barney, Inc.
1.3.6.1.4.1.1180	Compact Data, Ltd.
1.3.6.1.4.1.1181	I.Net Communications
1.3.6.1.4.1.1182	YAMAHA Corporation
1.3.6.1.4.1.1183	Illinois State University
1.3.6.1.4.1.1184	RADGuard, Ltd.
1.3.6.1.4.1.1185	Calypso Software Systems, Inc.
1.3.6.1.4.1.1186	ACT Networks, Inc.
1.3.6.1.4.1.1187	Kingston Communications
1.3.6.1.4.1.1188	Incite
1.3.6.1.4.1.1189	VVNET, Inc.
1.3.6.1.4.1.1190	Ontario Hydro
1.3.6.1.4.1.1191	CS-Telecom
1.3.6.1.4.1.1192	ICTV, Inc.
1.3.6.1.4.1.1193	CORE International, Inc.
1.3.6.1.4.1.1194	Mibs4You
1.3.6.1.4.1.1195	ITK
1.3.6.1.4.1.1196	Network Integrity, Inc.
1.3.6.1.4.1.1197	BlueLine Software, Inc.
1.3.6.1.4.1.1198	Migrant Computing Services, Inc.
1.3.6.1.4.1.1199	Linklaters & Paines
1.3.6.1.4.1.1200	EJV Partners, L.P.
1.3.6.1.4.1.1201	Software and Systems Engineering, Ltd.
1.3.6.1.4.1.1202	VARCOM Corporation
1.3.6.1.4.1.1203	Equitel
1.3.6.1.4.1.1204	The Southern Company
1.3.6.1.4.1.1205	Dataproducts Corporation
1.3.6.1.4.1.1206	National Electrical Manufacturers Association

Figure 7-76. The Enterprises Groups *(continued)*

The Enterprises Groups	
Group Object Identifier	**Enterprise Name**
1.3.6.1.4.1.1207	RISCmanagement, Inc.
1.3.6.1.4.1.1208	GVC Corporation
1.3.6.1.4.1.1209	timonWare, inc.
1.3.6.1.4.1.1210	Capital Resources Computer Corporation
1.3.6.1.4.1.1211	Storage Technology Corporation
1.3.6.1.4.1.1212	Tadiran Telecomunications, Ltd.
1.3.6.1.4.1.1213	NCP
1.3.6.1.4.1.1214	Operations Control Systems (OCS)
1.3.6.1.4.1.1215	The NASDAQ Stock Market, Inc.
1.3.6.1.4.1.1216	Tiernan Communications, Inc.
1.3.6.1.4.1.1217	Goldman, Sachs Company
1.3.6.1.4.1.1218	Advanced Telecommunications Modules, Ltd.
1.3.6.1.4.1.1219	Phoenix Data Communications
1.3.6.1.4.1.1220	Quality Consulting Services
1.3.6.1.4.1.1221	MILAN
1.3.6.1.4.1.1222	Instrumental, Inc.
1.3.6.1.4.1.1223	Yellow Technology Services, Inc.
1.3.6.1.4.1.1224	Mier Communications, Inc.
1.3.6.1.4.1.1225	Cable Services Group, Inc.
1.3.6.1.4.1.1226	Forte Networks, Inc.
1.3.6.1.4.1.1227	American Management Systems, Inc.
1.3.6.1.4.1.1228	Choice Hotels International
1.3.6.1.4.1.1229	SEH Computertechnik Gm
1.3.6.1.4.1.1230	McAFee Associates, Inc.
1.3.6.1.4.1.1231	Network Intelligent, Inc.
1.3.6.1.4.1.1232	Luxcom Technologies, Inc.
1.3.6.1.4.1.1233	ITRON, Inc.
1.3.6.1.4.1.1234	Linkage Software, Inc.
1.3.6.1.4.1.1235	Spardat AG
1.3.6.1.4.1.1236	VeriFone, Inc.
1.3.6.1.4.1.1237	Revco D.S., Inc.
1.3.6.1.4.1.1238	HRB Systems, Inc.
1.3.6.1.4.1.1239	Litton Fibercom
1.3.6.1.4.1.1240	XCD, Inc.
1.3.6.1.4.1.1241	ProsjektLeveranser AS
1.3.6.1.4.1.1242	Halcyon, Inc.
1.3.6.1.4.1.1243	SBB
1.3.6.1.4.1.1244	LeuTek
1.3.6.1.4.1.1245	Zeitnet, Inc.
1.3.6.1.4.1.1246	Visual Networks, Inc.
1.3.6.1.4.1.1247	Coronet Systems

Figure 7-76. The Enterprises Groups *(continued)*

The Enterprises Groups	
Group Object Identifier	**Enterprise Name**
1.3.6.1.4.1.1248	SEIKO EPSON CORPORATION
1.3.6.1.4.1.1249	DnH Technologies
1.3.6.1.4.1.1250	Deluxe Data
1.3.6.1.4.1.1251	Michael A. Okulski, Inc.
1.3.6.1.4.1.1252	Saber Software Corporation
1.3.6.1.4.1.1253	Mission Systems, Inc.
1.3.6.1.4.1.1254	Siemens Plessey Electronics Systems
1.3.6.1.4.1.1255	Applied Communications, Inc.
1.3.6.1.4.1.1256	Transaction Technology, Inc.
1.3.6.1.4.1.1257	HST, Ltd.
1.3.6.1.4.1.1258	Michigan Technological University
1.3.6.1.4.1.1259	Next Level Communications
1.3.6.1.4.1.1260	Instinet Corporation
1.3.6.1.4.1.1261	Analog & Digital Systems, Ltd.
1.3.6.1.4.1.1262	Ansaldo Trasporti SpA
1.3.6.1.4.1.1263	ECCI
1.3.6.1.4.1.1264	Imatek Corporation
1.3.6.1.4.1.1265	PTT Telecom bv
1.3.6.1.4.1.1266	Data Race, Inc.
1.3.6.1.4.1.1267	Network Safety Corporation
1.3.6.1.4.1.1268	Application des Techniques Nouvelles en Electronique
1.3.6.1.4.1.1269	MFS Communications Company
1.3.6.1.4.1.1270	Information Services Division
1.3.6.1.4.1.1271	Ciena Corporation
1.3.6.1.4.1.1272	Ascom Nexion
1.3.6.1.4.1.1273	Standard Networks, Inc.
1.3.6.1.4.1.1274	Scientific Research Corporation
1.3.6.1.4.1.1275	micado SoftwareConsult GmbH
1.3.6.1.4.1.1276	Concert Management Services, Inc.
1.3.6.1.4.1.1277	University of Delaware
1.3.6.1.4.1.1278	Bias Consultancy, Ltd.
1.3.6.1.4.1.1279	Micromuse PLC.
1.3.6.1.4.1.1280	Translink Systems
1.3.6.1.4.1.1281	PI-NET
1.3.6.1.4.1.1282	Amber Wave Systems
1.3.6.1.4.1.1283	Superior Electronics Group, Inc.
1.3.6.1.4.1.1284	Network Telemetrics, Inc.
1.3.6.1.4.1.1285	BSW-Data
1.3.6.1.4.1.1286	ECI Telecom, Ltd.
1.3.6.1.4.1.1287	BroadVision
1.3.6.1.4.1.1288	ALFA, Inc.

Figure 7-76. The Enterprises Groups *(continued)*

The Enterprises Groups	
Group Object Identifier	**Enterprise Name**
1.3.6.1.4.1.1289	TELEFONICA SISTEMAS, S.A.
1.3.6.1.4.1.1290	Image Sciences, Inc.
1.3.6.1.4.1.1291	Mitsubishi Electric Information Network Corporation (MIND)
1.3.6.1.4.1.1292	Central Flow Management Unit
1.3.6.1.4.1.1293	Woods Hole Oceanographic Institution
1.3.6.1.4.1.1294	Raptor Systems, Inc.
1.3.6.1.4.1.1295	TeleLink Technologies, Inc.
1.3.6.1.4.1.1296	First Virtual Corporation
1.3.6.1.4.1.1297	Network Services Group
1.3.6.1.4.1.1298	SilCom Manufacturing Technology, Inc.
1.3.6.1.4.1.1299	NETSOFT Inc.
1.3.6.1.4.1.1300	Fidelity Investments
1.3.6.1.4.1.1301	Telrad Telecommunications
1.3.6.1.4.1.1302	Arcada Software, Inc.
1.3.6.1.4.1.1303	LeeMah DataCom Security Corporation
1.3.6.1.4.1.1304	SecureWare, Inc.
1.3.6.1.4.1.1305	USAir, Inc.
1.3.6.1.4.1.1306	Jet Propulsion Laboratory
1.3.6.1.4.1.1307	ABIT Co.
1.3.6.1.4.1.1308	Dataplex Pty., Ltd.
1.3.6.1.4.1.1309	Creative Interaction Technologies, Inc.
1.3.6.1.4.1.1310	Network Defenders, Inc.
1.3.6.1.4.1.1311	Optus Communications
1.3.6.1.4.1.1312	Klos Technologies, Inc.
1.3.6.1.4.1.1313	ACOTEC
1.3.6.1.4.1.1314	Datacomm Management Sciences, Inc.
1.3.6.1.4.1.1315	MG SOFT Co.
1.3.6.1.4.1.1316	Plessey Tellumat SA
1.3.6.1.4.1.1317	PaineWebber, Inc.
1.3.6.1.4.1.1318	DATASYS, Ltd.
1.3.6.1.4.1.1319	QVC, Inc.
1.3.6.1.4.1.1320	IPL Systems
1.3.6.1.4.1.1321	Pacific Micro Data, Inc.
1.3.6.1.4.1.1322	DeskNet Systems, Inc.
1.3.6.1.4.1.1323	TC Technologies
1.3.6.1.4.1.1324	Racotek, Inc.
1.3.6.1.4.1.1325	CelsiusTech AB
1.3.6.1.4.1.1326	Xing Technology Corporation
1.3.6.1.4.1.1327	dZine n.v.
1.3.6.1.4.1.1328	Electronic Merchant Services, Inc.
1.3.6.1.4.1.1329	Linmor Information Systems Management, Inc.

Figure 7-76. The Enterprises Groups *(continued)*

The Enterprises Groups	
Group Object Identifier	**Enterprise Name**
1.3.6.1.4.1.1330	ABL Canada, Inc.
1.3.6.1.4.1.1331	University of Coimbra
1.3.6.1.4.1.1332	Iskratel, Ltd., Telecommunications Systems
1.3.6.1.4.1.1333	ISA Co., Ltd.
1.3.6.1.4.1.1334	CONNECT, Inc.
1.3.6.1.4.1.1335	Digital Video
1.3.6.1.4.1.1336	InterVoice, Inc.
1.3.6.1.4.1.1337	Liveware Tecnologia a Servico a Ltda
1.3.6.1.4.1.1338	Precept Software, Inc.
1.3.6.1.4.1.1339	Heroix Corporation
1.3.6.1.4.1.1340	Holland House bv
1.3.6.1.4.1.1341	Dedalus Engenharia S/C Ltda
1.3.6.1.4.1.1342	GEC ALSTHOM I.T.
1.3.6.1.4.1.1343	Deutsches Elektronen-Synchrotron (DESY) Hamburg
1.3.6.1.4.1.1344	Switchview, Inc.
1.3.6.1.4.1.1345	Dacoll, Ltd.
1.3.6.1.4.1.1346	NetCorp, Inc.
1.3.6.1.4.1.1347	KYOCERA Corporation
1.3.6.1.4.1.1348	The Longaberger Company
1.3.6.1.4.1.1349	ILEX
1.3.6.1.4.1.1350	Conservation Through Innovation, Ltd.
1.3.6.1.4.1.1351	Software Technologies Corporation
1.3.6.1.4.1.1352	Multex Systems, Inc.
1.3.6.1.4.1.1353	Gambit Communications, Inc.
1.3.6.1.4.1.1354	Central Data Corporation
1.3.6.1.4.1.1355	CompuCom Systems, Inc.
1.3.6.1.4.1.1356	Generex Systems GMBH
1.3.6.1.4.1.1357	Periphonics Corporation
1.3.6.1.4.1.1358	Freddie Mac
1.3.6.1.4.1.1359	Digital Equipment bv
1.3.6.1.4.1.1360	PhoneLink plc
1.3.6.1.4.1.1361	Voice-Tel Enterprises, Inc.
1.3.6.1.4.1.1362	AUDILOG
1.3.6.1.4.1.1363	SanRex Corporation
1.3.6.1.4.1.1364	Chloride
1.3.6.1.4.1.1365	GA Systems, Ltd.
1.3.6.1.4.1.1366	Microdyne Corporation
1.3.6.1.4.1.1367	Boston College
1.3.6.1.4.1.1368	France Telecom
1.3.6.1.4.1.1369	Stonesoft Corp
1.3.6.1.4.1.1370	A. G. Edwards & Sons, Inc.

Figure 7-76. The Enterprises Groups *(continued)*

The Enterprises Groups	
Group Object Identifier	**Enterprise Name**
1.3.6.1.4.1.1371	Attachmate Corporation
1.3.6.1.4.1.1372	LSI Logic
1.3.6.1.4.1.1373	interWAVE Communications, Inc.
1.3.6.1.4.1.1374	mdl-Consult
1.3.6.1.4.1.1375	Bunyip Information Systems, Inc.
1.3.6.1.4.1.1376	Nashoba Networks, Inc.
1.3.6.1.4.1.1377	Comedia Information AB
1.3.6.1.4.1.1378	Harvey Mudd College
1.3.6.1.4.1.1379	First National Bank of Chicago
1.3.6.1.4.1.1380	Department of National Defence (Canada)
1.3.6.1.4.1.1381	CBM Technologies, Inc.
1.3.6.1.4.1.1382	InterProc, Inc.
1.3.6.1.4.1.1383	Glenayre R&D, Inc.
1.3.6.1.4.1.1384	Telenet GmbH Kommunikationssysteme
1.3.6.1.4.1.1385	Softlab GmbH
1.3.6.1.4.1.1386	Storage Computer Corporation
1.3.6.1.4.1.1387	Nine Tiles Computer Systems, Ltd.
1.3.6.1.4.1.1388	Network People International
1.3.6.1.4.1.1389	Simple Network Magic Corporation
1.3.6.1.4.1.1390	Stallion Technologies Pty., Ltd.
1.3.6.1.4.1.1391	Loan System
1.3.6.1.4.1.1392	DLR - Deutsche Forschungsanstalt fuer Luft- und Raumfahrt e.V.
1.3.6.1.4.1.1393	ICRA, Inc.
1.3.6.1.4.1.1394	Probita
1.3.6.1.4.1.1395	NEXOR, Ltd.
1.3.6.1.4.1.1396	American International Facsimile Products
1.3.6.1.4.1.1397	Tellabs
1.3.6.1.4.1.1398	DATAX
1.3.6.1.4.1.1399	IntelliSys Corporation
1.3.6.1.4.1.1400	Sandia National Laboratories
1.3.6.1.4.1.1401	Synerdyne Corporation
1.3.6.1.4.1.1402	UNICOM Electric, Inc.
1.3.6.1.4.1.1403	Central Design Systems, Inc.
1.3.6.1.4.1.1404	The Silk Road Group, Ltd.
1.3.6.1.4.1.1405	Positive Computing Concepts
1.3.6.1.4.1.1406	First Data Resources
1.3.6.1.4.1.1407	INETCO Systems, Ltd.
1.3.6.1.4.1.1408	NTT Mobile Communications Network, Inc.
1.3.6.1.4.1.1409	Target Stores
1.3.6.1.4.1.1410	Advanced Peripherals Technologies, Inc.
1.3.6.1.4.1.1411	Funk Software, Inc.

Figure 7-76. The Enterprises Groups *(continued)*

The Enterprises Groups	
Group Object Identifier	**Enterprise Name**
1.3.6.1.4.1.1412	DunsGate, a Dun & Bradstreet Company
1.3.6.1.4.1.1413	AFP
1.3.6.1.4.1.1414	Comsat RSI Precision Controls Division
1.3.6.1.4.1.1415	Williams Energy Services Company
1.3.6.1.4.1.1416	ASP Technologies, Inc.
1.3.6.1.4.1.1417	Philips Communication Systems
1.3.6.1.4.1.1418	Dataprobe, Inc.
1.3.6.1.4.1.1419	ASTROCOM CORPORATION
1.3.6.1.4.1.1420	CSTI(Communication Systems Technology, Inc.)
1.3.6.1.4.1.1421	Sprint Majdi Abuelbassal
1.3.6.1.4.1.1422	Syntax
1.3.6.1.4.1.1423	LIGHT-INFOCON Mr
1.3.6.1.4.1.1424	Performance Technology, Inc.
1.3.6.1.4.1.1425	CXR Telecom
1.3.6.1.4.1.1426	Amir Technology Labs
1.3.6.1.4.1.1427	ISOCOR
1.3.6.1.4.1.1428	Array Technology Corportion
1.3.6.1.4.1.1429	Scientific-Atlanta, Inc.
1.3.6.1.4.1.1430	GammaTech, Inc.
1.3.6.1.4.1.1431	Telkom SA
1.3.6.1.4.1.1432	CIREL SYSTEMES
1.3.6.1.4.1.1433	Redflex Limited Australia
1.3.6.1.4.1.1434	Hermes - Enterprise Messaging LTD
1.3.6.1.4.1.1435	Acacia Networks, Inc.
1.3.6.1.4.1.1436	NATIONAL AUSTRALIA BANK , Ltd.
1.3.6.1.4.1.1437	SineTec Technology Co., Ltd.
1.3.6.1.4.1.1438	Badger Technology, Inc.
1.3.6.1.4.1.1439	Arizona State University
1.3.6.1.4.1.1440	Xionics Document Technologies, Inc.
1.3.6.1.4.1.1441	Southern Information System, Inc.
1.3.6.1.4.1.1442	Nebula Consultants, Inc.
1.3.6.1.4.1.1443	SITRE, SA
1.3.6.1.4.1.1444	Paradigm Technology, Ltd.
1.3.6.1.4.1.1445	Telub AB
1.3.6.1.4.1.1446	Communications Network Services, Virginia Tech
1.3.6.1.4.1.1447	Martis Oy
1.3.6.1.4.1.1448	ISKRA TRANSMISSION
1.3.6.1.4.1.1449	QUALCOMM, Inc.
1.3.6.1.4.1.1450	Netscape Communications Corporation
1.3.6.1.4.1.1451	BellSouth Wireless, Inc.
1.3.6.1.4.1.1452	NUKO Information Systems, Inc.

Figure 7-76. The Enterprises Groups *(continued)*

The Enterprises Groups	
Group Object Identifier	**Enterprise Name**
1.3.6.1.4.1.1453	IPC Information Systems, Inc.
1.3.6.1.4.1.1454	Estudios y Proyectos de Telecomunicacion, S.A.
1.3.6.1.4.1.1455	Winstar Wireless
1.3.6.1.4.1.1456	Terayon Corporation
1.3.6.1.4.1.1457	CyberGuard Corporation
1.3.6.1.4.1.1458	Silicon Systems, Inc.
1.3.6.1.4.1.1459	Jupiter Technology, Inc.
1.3.6.1.4.1.1460	Delphi Internet Services
1.3.6.1.4.1.1461	Kesmai Corporation
1.3.6.1.4.1.1462	Compact Devices, Inc.
1.3.6.1.4.1.1463	OPTIQUEST
1.3.6.1.4.1.1464	Loral Defense Systems-Eagan
1.3.6.1.4.1.1465	OnRamp Technologies
1.3.6.1.4.1.1466	Mark Wahl
1.3.6.1.4.1.1467	Loran International Technologies, Inc.
1.3.6.1.4.1.1468	S & S International PLC
1.3.6.1.4.1.1469	Atlantech Technologies, Ltd.
1.3.6.1.4.1.1470	IN-SNEC
1.3.6.1.4.1.1471	Melita International Corporation
1.3.6.1.4.1.1472	Sharp Laboratories of America
1.3.6.1.4.1.1473	Groupe Decan
1.3.6.1.4.1.1474	Spectronics Micro Systems, Ltd.
1.3.6.1.4.1.1475	pc-plus COMPUTING GmbH
1.3.6.1.4.1.1476	Microframe, Inc.
1.3.6.1.4.1.1477	Telegate Global Access Technology, Ltd.
1.3.6.1.4.1.1478	Merrill Lynch & Co., Inc.
1.3.6.1.4.1.1479	JCPenney Co., Inc.
1.3.6.1.4.1.1480	The Torrington Company
1.3.6.1.4.1.1481	GS-ProActive
1.3.6.1.4.1.1482	BARCO Communication Systems
1.3.6.1.4.1.1483	vortex Computersysteme GmbH
1.3.6.1.4.1.1484	DataFusion Systems (Pty), Ltd.
1.3.6.1.4.1.1485	Allen & Overy
1.3.6.1.4.1.1486	Atlantic Systems Group
1.3.6.1.4.1.1487	Kongsberg Informasjonskontroll AS
1.3.6.1.4.1.1488	ELTECO a.s. Ing.
1.3.6.1.4.1.1489	Schlumberger, Ltd.
1.3.6.1.4.1.1490	CNI Communications Network International GmbH
1.3.6.1.4.1.1491	M&C Systems, Inc.
1.3.6.1.4.1.1492	OM Systems International (OMSI)
1.3.6.1.4.1.1493	DAVIC (Digital Audio-Visual Council)

Figure 7-76. The Enterprises Groups *(continued)*

The Enterprises Groups	
Group Object Identifier	**Enterprise Name**
1.3.6.1.4.1.1494	ISM GmbH
1.3.6.1.4.1.1495	E.F. Johnson Co.
1.3.6.1.4.1.1496	Baranof Software, Inc.
1.3.6.1.4.1.1497	University of Texas Houston
1.3.6.1.4.1.1498	Ukiah Software Solutions/EDS/HDS
1.3.6.1.4.1.1499	STERIA
1.3.6.1.4.1.1500	ATI Australia Pty., Ltd.
1.3.6.1.4.1.1501	The Aerospace Corporation
1.3.6.1.4.1.1502	Orckit Communications, Ltd.
1.3.6.1.4.1.1503	Tertio, Ltd.
1.3.6.1.4.1.1504	COMSOFT GmbH
1.3.6.1.4.1.1505	Innovative Software
1.3.6.1.4.1.1506	Technologic, Inc.
1.3.6.1.4.1.1507	Vertex Data Science, Ltd.
1.3.6.1.4.1.1508	ESIGETEL
1.3.6.1.4.1.1509	Illinois Business Training Center
1.3.6.1.4.1.1510	Arris Networks, Inc.
1.3.6.1.4.1.1511	TeamQuest Corporation
1.3.6.1.4.1.1512	Sentient Networks
1.3.6.1.4.1.1513	Skyrr
1.3.6.1.4.1.1514	Tecnologia y Gestion de la Innovacion
1.3.6.1.4.1.1515	Connector GmbH
1.3.6.1.4.1.1516	Kaspia Systems, Inc.
1.3.6.1.4.1.1517	SmithKline Beecham
1.3.6.1.4.1.1518	NetCentric Corporation
1.3.6.1.4.1.1519	ATecoM GmbH
1.3.6.1.4.1.1520	Citibank Canada
1.3.6.1.4.1.1521	MMS (Matra Marconi Space)
1.3.6.1.4.1.1522	Intermedia Communications of Florida, Inc.
1.3.6.1.4.1.1523	School of Computer Science, University Science of Malaysia
1.3.6.1.4.1.1524	University of Limerick
1.3.6.1.4.1.1525	ACTANE
1.3.6.1.4.1.1526	Collaborative Information Technology Research Institute(CITRI)
1.3.6.1.4.1.1527	Intermedium A/S
1.3.6.1.4.1.1528	ANS CO+RE Systems, Inc.
1.3.6.1.4.1.1529	UUNET Technologies, Inc.
1.3.6.1.4.1.1530	Securicor Telesciences
1.3.6.1.4.1.1531	QSC Audio Products
1.3.6.1.4.1.1532	Australian Department of Employment, Education and Training
1.3.6.1.4.1.1533	Network Media Communications, Ltd.
1.3.6.1.4.1.1534	Sodalia

Figure 7-76. The Enterprises Groups *(continued)*

The Enterprises Groups	
Group Object Identifier	**Enterprise Name**
1.3.6.1.4.1.1535	Innovative Concepts, Inc.
1.3.6.1.4.1.1536	Japan Computer Industry, Inc.
1.3.6.1.4.1.1537	Telogy Networks, Inc.
1.3.6.1.4.1.1538	Merck & Company, Inc.
1.3.6.1.4.1.1539	GeoTel Communications Corporation
1.3.6.1.4.1.1540	Sun Alliance (UK)
1.3.6.1.4.1.1541	AG Communication Systems
1.3.6.1.4.1.1542	Pivotal Networking, Inc.
1.3.6.1.4.1.1543	TSI TelSys, Inc.
1.3.6.1.4.1.1544	Harmonic Systems, Inc.
1.3.6.1.4.1.1545	ASTRONET Corporation
1.3.6.1.4.1.1546	Frontec
1.3.6.1.4.1.1547	NetVision
1.3.6.1.4.1.1548	FlowPoint Corporation
1.3.6.1.4.1.1549	TRON B.V. Datacommunication
1.3.6.1.4.1.1550	Nuera Communication, Inc.
1.3.6.1.4.1.1551	Radnet, Ltd.
1.3.6.1.4.1.1552	Oce Nederland bv
1.3.6.1.4.1.1553	Air France
1.3.6.1.4.1.1554	Communications & Power Engineering, Inc.
1.3.6.1.4.1.1555	Charter Systems
1.3.6.1.4.1.1556	Performance Technologies, Inc.
1.3.6.1.4.1.1557	Paragon Networks International
1.3.6.1.4.1.1558	Skog-Data AS
1.3.6.1.4.1.1559	mitec a/s
1.3.6.1.4.1.1560	THOMSON-CSF / Departement Reseaux d'Entreprise
1.3.6.1.4.1.1561	Ipsilon Networks, Inc.
1.3.6.1.4.1.1562	Kingston Technology Corporation
1.3.6.1.4.1.1563	Harmonic Lightwaves
1.3.6.1.4.1.1564	InterActive Digital Solutions
1.3.6.1.4.1.1565	Coactive Aesthetics, Inc.
1.3.6.1.4.1.1566	Tech Data Corporation
1.3.6.1.4.1.1567	Z-Com
1.3.6.1.4.1.1568	COTEP
1.3.6.1.4.1.1569	Raytheon Company
1.3.6.1.4.1.1570	Telesend, Inc.
1.3.6.1.4.1.1571	NCC
1.3.6.1.4.1.1572	Forte Software, Inc.
1.3.6.1.4.1.1573	Secure Computing Corporation
1.3.6.1.4.1.1574	BEZEQ
1.3.6.1.4.1.1575	Technical University of Braunschweig

Figure 7-76. The Enterprises Groups *(continued)*

The Enterprises Groups	
Group Object Identifier	**Enterprise Name**
1.3.6.1.4.1.1576	Stac, Inc.
1.3.6.1.4.1.1577	StarNet Communications
1.3.6.1.4.1.1578	Universidade do Minho
1.3.6.1.4.1.1579	Department of Computer Science, University of Liverpool
1.3.6.1.4.1.1580	Tekram Technology, Ltd.
1.3.6.1.4.1.1581	RATP
1.3.6.1.4.1.1582	Rainbow Diamond, Ltd.
1.3.6.1.4.1.1583	Magellan Communications, Inc.
1.3.6.1.4.1.1584	Bay Networks, Inc.
1.3.6.1.4.1.1585	Quantitative Data Systems (QDS)
1.3.6.1.4.1.1586	ESYS, Ltd.
1.3.6.1.4.1.1587	Switched Network Technologies (SNT)
1.3.6.1.4.1.1588	Brocade Communications Systems, Inc.
1.3.6.1.4.1.1589	Computer Resources International A/S (CRI)
1.3.6.1.4.1.1590	LuchtVerkeersBeveiliging
1.3.6.1.4.1.1591	PST
1.3.6.1.4.1.1592	XactLabs Corporation
1.3.6.1.4.1.1593	NetPro Computing, Inc.
1.3.6.1.4.1.1594	TELESYNC
1.3.6.1.4.1.1595	BOSCH Telecom
1.3.6.1.4.1.1596	INS GmbH
1.3.6.1.4.1.1597	Distributed Processing Technology
1.3.6.1.4.1.1598	Tivoli Systems, Inc.
1.3.6.1.4.1.1599	Network Management Technologies
1.3.6.1.4.1.1600	SIRTI
1.3.6.1.4.1.1601	TASKE Technology, Inc.
1.3.6.1.4.1.1602	CANON, Inc.
1.3.6.1.4.1.1603	Systems and Synchronous, Inc.
1.3.6.1.4.1.1604	XFER International
1.3.6.1.4.1.1605	Scandpower A/S
1.3.6.1.4.1.1606	Consultancy & Projects Group srl
1.3.6.1.4.1.1607	STS Technologies, Inc.
1.3.6.1.4.1.1608	Mylex Corporation
1.3.6.1.4.1.1609	CRYPTOCard Corporation
1.3.6.1.4.1.1610	LXE, Inc.
1.3.6.1.4.1.1611	BDM International, Inc.
1.3.6.1.4.1.1612	GE Spacenet Services, Inc.
1.3.6.1.4.1.1613	Datanet GmbH
1.3.6.1.4.1.1614	Opcom, Inc.
1.3.6.1.4.1.1615	Mlink Internet, Inc.
1.3.6.1.4.1.1616	Netro Corporation

Figure 7-76. The Enterprises Groups *(continued)*

The Enterprises Groups	
Group Object Identifier	**Enterprise Name**
1.3.6.1.4.1.1617	Net Partners, Inc.
1.3.6.1.4.1.1618	Peek Traffic - Transyt Corporation
1.3.6.1.4.1.1619	Comverse Information Systems
1.3.6.1.4.1.1620	Data Comm for Business, Inc.
1.3.6.1.4.1.1621	CYBEC Pty., Ltd.
1.3.6.1.4.1.1622	Mitsui Knowledge Industry Co., Ltd.
1.3.6.1.4.1.1623	NORDX/CDT, Inc.
1.3.6.1.4.1.1624	Blockade Systems Corporation
1.3.6.1.4.1.1625	Nixu Oy
1.3.6.1.4.1.1626	Australian Software Innovations (Services) Pty., Ltd.
1.3.6.1.4.1.1627	Omicron Telesystems, Inc.
1.3.6.1.4.1.1628	DEMON Internet, Ltd.
1.3.6.1.4.1.1629	PB Farradyne, Inc.
1.3.6.1.4.1.1630	Telos Corporation
1.3.6.1.4.1.1631	Manage Information Technologies
1.3.6.1.4.1.1632	Harlow Butler Broking Services, Ltd.
1.3.6.1.4.1.1633	Eurologic Systems, Ltd.
1.3.6.1.4.1.1634	Telco Research Corporation
1.3.6.1.4.1.1635	Mercedes-Benz AG
1.3.6.1.4.1.1636	HOB electronic GmbH
1.3.6.1.4.1.1637	NOAA
1.3.6.1.4.1.1638	Cornerstone Software
1.3.6.1.4.1.1639	Wink Communications
1.3.6.1.4.1.1640	Thomson Electronic Information Resources (TEIR)
1.3.6.1.4.1.1641	HITT Holland Institute of Traffic Technology bv
1.3.6.1.4.1.1642	KPMG
1.3.6.1.4.1.1643	Loral Federal Systems
1.3.6.1.4.1.1644	S.I.A.- Societa Interbancaria per l'Automazione
1.3.6.1.4.1.1645	United States Cellular Corporation
1.3.6.1.4.1.1646	AMPER DATOS S.A.
1.3.6.1.4.1.1647	Carelcomp
1.3.6.1.4.1.1648	Open Environment Australia
1.3.6.1.4.1.1649	Integrated Telecom Technology, Inc.
1.3.6.1.4.1.1650	Langner Gesellschaft fuer Datentechnik mbH
1.3.6.1.4.1.1651	Wayne State University
1.3.6.1.4.1.1652	SICC (SsangYong Information & Communications Corporation)
1.3.6.1.4.1.1653	THOMSON - CSF
1.3.6.1.4.1.1654	Teleconnect Dresden GmbH
1.3.6.1.4.1.1655	Panorama Software, Inc.
1.3.6.1.4.1.1656	CompuNet Systemhaus GmbH
1.3.6.1.4.1.1657	JAPAN TELECOM CO., Ltd.

Figure 7-76. The Enterprises Groups *(continued)*

The Enterprises Groups	
Group Object Identifier	**Enterprise Name**
1.3.6.1.4.1.1658	TechForce Corporation
1.3.6.1.4.1.1659	Granite Systems, Inc.
1.3.6.1.4.1.1660	Bit Incorporated
1.3.6.1.4.1.1661	Companhia de Informatica do Parana - Celepar
1.3.6.1.4.1.1662	Rockwell International Corporation
1.3.6.1.4.1.1663	Ancor Communications
1.3.6.1.4.1.1664	· Royal Institute of Technology, Sweden (KTH)
1.3.6.1.4.1.1665	SUNET, Swedish University Network
1.3.6.1.4.1.1666	Sage Instruments, Inc.
1.3.6.1.4.1.1667	Candle Corporation
1.3.6.1.4.1.1668	CSO GmbH
1.3.6.1.4.1.1669	M3i Systems, Inc.
1.3.6.1.4.1.1670	CREDINTRANS
1.3.6.1.4.1.1671	BIT Communications
1.3.6.1.4.1.1672	Pierce & Associates
1.3.6.1.4.1.1673	Real Time Strategies, Inc.
1.3.6.1.4.1.1674	R.I.C. Electronics
1.3.6.1.4.1.1675	Amoco Corporation
1.3.6.1.4.1.1676	Qualix Group, Inc.
1.3.6.1.4.1.1677	Sahara Networks, Inc.
1.3.6.1.4.1.1678	Hyundai Electronics Industries Co., Ltd.
1.3.6.1.4.1.1679	RICH, Inc.
1.3.6.1.4.1.1680	Amati Communications Corporation
1.3.6.1.4.1.1681	P.H.U. RysTECH
1.3.6.1.4.1.1682	Data Labs, Inc.
1.3.6.1.4.1.1683	Occidental Petroleum Services, Inc.
1.3.6.1.4.1.1684	Rijnhaave Internet Services
1.3.6.1.4.1.1685	Lynx Real-Time Systems, Inc.
1.3.6.1.4.1.1686	Pontis Consulting
1.3.6.1.4.1.1687	SofTouch Systems, Inc.
1.3.6.1.4.1.1688	Sonda S.A.
1.3.6.1.4.1.1689	McCormick Nunes Company
1.3.6.1.4.1.1690	Ume E5 Universitet
1.3.6.1.4.1.1691	NetIQ Corporation
1.3.6.1.4.1.1692	Starlight Networks
1.3.6.1.4.1.1693	Informacion Selectiva S.A. de C.V. (Infosel)
1.3.6.1.4.1.1694	HCL Technologies, Ltd.
1.3.6.1.4.1.1695	Maryville Data Systems, Inc.
1.3.6.1.4.1.1696	EtherCom Corporation
1.3.6.1.4.1.1697	MultiCom Software
1.3.6.1.4.1.1698	BEA Systems, Ltd.

Figure 7-76. The Enterprises Groups *(continued)*

The Enterprises Groups	
Group Object Identifier	**Enterprise Name**
1.3.6.1.4.1.1699	Advanced Technology, Ltd.
1.3.6.1.4.1.1700	Mobil Oil
1.3.6.1.4.1.1701	Technical Software
1.3.6.1.4.1.1702	Netsys International (Pty), Ltd.
1.3.6.1.4.1.1703	Titan Information Systems Corporation
1.3.6.1.4.1.1704	Cogent Data Technologies
1.3.6.1.4.1.1705	Reliasoft Corporation
1.3.6.1.4.1.1706	Midland Business Systems, Inc.
1.3.6.1.4.1.1707	Optimal Networks
1.3.6.1.4.1.1708	Gresham Computing plc
1.3.6.1.4.1.1709	Science Applications International Corporation (SAIC)
1.3.6.1.4.1.1710	Acclaim Communications
1.3.6.1.4.1.1711	BISS, Ltd.
1.3.6.1.4.1.1712	Caravelle, Inc.
1.3.6.1.4.1.1713	Diamond Lane Communications Corporation
1.3.6.1.4.1.1714	Infortrend Technology, Inc.
1.3.6.1.4.1.1715	Orda-B N.V.
1.3.6.1.4.1.1716	Ariel Corporation
1.3.6.1.4.1.1717	Datalex Communications, Ltd.
1.3.6.1.4.1.1718	Server Technology, Inc.
1.3.6.1.4.1.1719	Unimax Systems Corporation
1.3.6.1.4.1.1720	DeTeMobil GmbH
1.3.6.1.4.1.1721	INFONOVA GmbH
1.3.6.1.4.1.1722	Kudelski SA
1.3.6.1.4.1.1723	Pronet GmbH
1.3.6.1.4.1.1724	Westell, Inc.
1.3.6.1.4.1.1725	Nupon Computing, Inc.
1.3.6.1.4.1.1726	CIANET Ind e Com Ltda (CIANET Inc.)
1.3.6.1.4.1.1727	Aumtech of Virginia (amteva)
1.3.6.1.4.1.1728	CheongJo Data Communication, Inc.
1.3.6.1.4.1.1729	Genesys Telecommunications Laboratories Inc. (Genesys Labs.)
1.3.6.1.4.1.1730	Progress Software
1.3.6.1.4.1.1731	ERICSSON FIBER ACCESS
1.3.6.1.4.1.1732	Open Access Pty., Ltd.
1.3.6.1.4.1.1733	Sterling Commerce
1.3.6.1.4.1.1734	Predictive Systems, Inc.
1.3.6.1.4.1.1735	Architel Systems Corporation
1.3.6.1.4.1.1736	US West !nterAct
1.3.6.1.4.1.1737	Eclipse Technologies, Inc.
1.3.6.1.4.1.1738	Navy
1.3.6.1.4.1.1739	Bindi Technologies, Pty., Ltd.

Figure 7-76. The Enterprises Groups *(continued)*

The Enterprises Groups	
Group Object Identifier	**Enterprise Name**
1.3.6.1.4.1.1740	Hallmark Cards, Inc.
1.3.6.1.4.1.1741	Object Design, Inc.
1.3.6.1.4.1.1742	Vision Systems
1.3.6.1.4.1.1743	Zenith Data Systems (ZDS)
1.3.6.1.4.1.1744	Gobi Corporation
1.3.6.1.4.1.1745	Universitat de Barcelona
1.3.6.1.4.1.1746	Institute for Simulation and Training (IST)
1.3.6.1.4.1.1747	US Agency for International Development
1.3.6.1.4.1.1748	Tut Systems, Inc.
1.3.6.1.4.1.1749	AnswerZ Pty., Ltd. (Australia)
1.3.6.1.4.1.1750	H.Bollmann Manufacturers, Ltd. (HBM)
1.3.6.1.4.1.1751	Lucent Technologies
1.3.6.1.4.1.1752	phase2 networks, Inc.
1.3.6.1.4.1.1753	Unify Corporation
1.3.6.1.4.1.1754	Gadzoox Microsystems, Inc.
1.3.6.1.4.1.1755	Network One, Inc.
1.3.6.1.4.1.1756	MuLogic bv
1.3.6.1.4.1.1757	Optical Microwave Networks, Inc.
1.3.6.1.4.1.1758	SITEL, Ltd.
1.3.6.1.4.1.1759	Cerg Finance
1.3.6.1.4.1.1760	American Internet Corporation
1.3.6.1.4.1.1761	PLUSKOM GmbH
1.3.6.1.4.1.1762	Dept. of Communications, Graz University of Technology
1.3.6.1.4.1.1763	MindSpring Enterprises, Inc.
1.3.6.1.4.1.1764	Db-Tech, Inc.
1.3.6.1.4.1.1765	Apex Voice Communications, Inc.
1.3.6.1.4.1.1766	National DataComm Corporation
1.3.6.1.4.1.1767	Telenor Conax AS
1.3.6.1.4.1.1768	Patton Electronics Company
1.3.6.1.4.1.1769	The Fulgent Group, Ltd.
1.3.6.1.4.1.1770	BroadBand Technologies, Inc.
1.3.6.1.4.1.1771	Myricom, Inc.
1.3.6.1.4.1.1772	DecisionOne
1.3.6.1.4.1.1773	Tandberg Television
1.3.6.1.4.1.1774	AUDITEC SA
1.3.6.1.4.1.1775	PC Magic
1.3.6.1.4.1.1776	Philips Electronics NV
1.3.6.1.4.1.1777	ORIGIN
1.3.6.1.4.1.1778	CSG Systems
1.3.6.1.4.1.1779	Alphameric Technologies, Ltd.
1.3.6.1.4.1.1780	NCR Austria

Figure 7-76. The Enterprises Groups *(continued)*

The Enterprises Groups	
Group Object Identifier	**Enterprise Name**
1.3.6.1.4.1.1781	ChuckK, Inc.
1.3.6.1.4.1.1782	PowerTV, Inc.
1.3.6.1.4.1.1783	Active Software, Inc.
1.3.6.1.4.1.1784	Enron Capitol & Trade Resources
1.3.6.1.4.1.1785	ORBCOMM
1.3.6.1.4.1.1786	Jw direct shop
1.3.6.1.4.1.1787	B.E.T.A.
1.3.6.1.4.1.1788	Healtheon
1.3.6.1.4.1.1789	Integralis, Ltd.
1.3.6.1.4.1.1790	Folio Corporation
1.3.6.1.4.1.1791	ECTF
1.3.6.1.4.1.1792	WebPlanet
1.3.6.1.4.1.1793	nStor Corporation
1.3.6.1.4.1.1794	Deutsche Bahn AG
1.3.6.1.4.1.1795	Paradyne
1.3.6.1.4.1.1796	Nastel Technologies, Inc.
1.3.6.1.4.1.1797	Metaphase Technology, Inc.
1.3.6.1.4.1.1798	Zweigart & Sawitzki
1.3.6.1.4.1.1799	PIXEL
1.3.6.1.4.1.1800	WaveAccess, Inc.
1.3.6.1.4.1.1801	The SABRE Group
1.3.6.1.4.1.1802	Far Point Systems
1.3.6.1.4.1.1803	PBS
1.3.6.1.4.1.1804	Consensus Development Corporation
1.3.6.1.4.1.1805	SAGEM SA
1.3.6.1.4.1.1806	I-Cube, Inc.
1.3.6.1.4.1.1807	Intracom S.A (Hellenic Telecommunication and Electronics Industry)
1.3.6.1.4.1.1808	Aetna, Inc.
1.3.6.1.4.1.1809	Dow Jones Telerate Systems, Inc.
1.3.6.1.4.1.1810	Czech Railways s.o. CIT
1.3.6.1.4.1.1811	Scan-Matic A/S
1.3.6.1.4.1.1812	DECISION Europe
1.3.6.1.4.1.1813	VTEL Corporation
1.3.6.1.4.1.1814	Bloomberg, L.P.
1.3.6.1.4.1.1815	Eyretel, Ltd.
1.3.6.1.4.1.1816	Rose-Hulman Institute of Technology
1.3.6.1.4.1.1817	Aether Technologies
1.3.6.1.4.1.1818	Infonet Software Solutions
1.3.6.1.4.1.1819	CSTI (Compagnie des Signaux / Technologies Informatiques)
1.3.6.1.4.1.1820	LEROY MERLIN
1.3.6.1.4.1.1821	Total Entertainment Network

Figure 7-76. The Enterprises Groups *(continued)*

The Enterprises Groups	
Group Object Identifier	**Enterprise Name**
1.3.6.1.4.1.1822	Open Port Technology
1.3.6.1.4.1.1823	Mikroelektronik Anwendungszentrum Hamburg GmbH
1.3.6.1.4.1.1824	International Management Consulting, Inc.
1.3.6.1.4.1.1825	Scalable Networks, Inc.
1.3.6.1.4.1.1826	MTech Systems
1.3.6.1.4.1.1827	RxSoft, Ltd.
1.3.6.1.4.1.1828	Dept. Computer Studies, Loughborough University
1.3.6.1.4.1.1829	Beta80 S.p.A.
1.3.6.1.4.1.1830	Galiso, Inc.
1.3.6.1.4.1.1831	S2 Systems, Inc.
1.3.6.1.4.1.1832	Optivision, Inc.
1.3.6.1.4.1.1833	Countrywide Home Loans
1.3.6.1.4.1.1834	OA Laboratory Co., Ltd.
1.3.6.1.4.1.1835	SDX Business Systems, Ltd.
1.3.6.1.4.1.1836	West End Systems Corporation
1.3.6.1.4.1.1837	DK Digital Media
1.3.6.1.4.1.1838	Westel
1.3.6.1.4.1.1839	Fujitsu Telecommunications Europe, Ltd.
1.3.6.1.4.1.1840	Inmarsat
1.3.6.1.4.1.1841	TIMS Technology, Ltd.
1.3.6.1.4.1.1842	CallWare Technologies
1.3.6.1.4.1.1843	NextLink, L.L.C.
1.3.6.1.4.1.1844	TurnQuay Solutions, Ltd.
1.3.6.1.4.1.1845	Accusort Systems, Inc.
1.3.6.1.4.1.1846	DEUTSCHER BUNDESTAG
1.3.6.1.4.1.1847	Joint Research Centre
1.3.6.1.4.1.1848	FaxSav
1.3.6.1.4.1.1849	Chevy Chase Applications Design
1.3.6.1.4.1.1850	Bank Brussel Lambert (BBL)
1.3.6.1.4.1.1851	OutBack Resource Group, Inc.
1.3.6.1.4.1.1852	Screen Subtitling Systems, Ltd.
1.3.6.1.4.1.1853	Cambridge Parallel Processing, Ltd.
1.3.6.1.4.1.1854	Boston University
1.3.6.1.4.1.1855	News Datacom, Ltd.
1.3.6.1.4.1.1856	NuTek 2000, Inc.
1.3.6.1.4.1.1857	Overland Mobile Communication AB
1.3.6.1.4.1.1858	Axon IT AB
1.3.6.1.4.1.1859	Gradient Medical Systems
1.3.6.1.4.1.1860	WaveSpan Corporation
1.3.6.1.4.1.1861	Net Research, Inc.
1.3.6.1.4.1.1862	Crowncroft Community Church

Figure 7-76. The Enterprises Groups *(continued)*

The Enterprises Groups	
Group Object Identifier	**Enterprise Name**
1.3.6.1.4.1.1863	Net2Net Corporation
1.3.6.1.4.1.1864	US Internet
1.3.6.1.4.1.1865	Absolute Time
1.3.6.1.4.1.1866	VPNet
1.3.6.1.4.1.1867	NTech
1.3.6.1.4.1.1868	Nippon Unisoft Corporation
1.3.6.1.4.1.1869	Optical Transmission Labs, Inc.
1.3.6.1.4.1.1870	CyberCash, Inc.
1.3.6.1.4.1.1871	NetSpeed, Inc.
1.3.6.1.4.1.1872	Alteon Networks, Inc.
1.3.6.1.4.1.1873	Internet Middleware Corporation
1.3.6.1.4.1.1874	ISOnova GmbH
1.3.6.1.4.1.1875	Amiga IOPS Project
1.3.6.1.4.1.1876	Softbank Services Group
1.3.6.1.4.1.1877	Sourcecom Corporation
1.3.6.1.4.1.1878	Telia Promotor AB
1.3.6.1.4.1.1879	HeliOss Communications, Inc.
1.3.6.1.4.1.1880	Optical Access International, Inc.
1.3.6.1.4.1.1881	MMC Networks, Inc.
1.3.6.1.4.1.1882	Lanyon, Ltd.
1.3.6.1.4.1.1883	Rubico
1.3.6.1.4.1.1884	Quantum Telecom Solutions, Inc.
1.3.6.1.4.1.1885	Archinet
1.3.6.1.4.1.1886	i-cubed, Ltd.
1.3.6.1.4.1.1887	Siemens Switzerland, Ltd.
1.3.6.1.4.1.1888	GigaLabs, Inc.
1.3.6.1.4.1.1889	MET Matra-Ericsson
1.3.6.1.4.1.1890	JBM Electronics
1.3.6.1.4.1.1891	OPTIM Systems, Inc.
1.3.6.1.4.1.1892	Software Brewery
1.3.6.1.4.1.1893	WaveLinQ
1.3.6.1.4.1.1894	Siemens Stromberg-Carlson
1.3.6.1.4.1.1895	IEX Corporation
1.3.6.1.4.1.1896	TrueTime
1.3.6.1.4.1.1897	HT Communications, Inc.
1.3.6.1.4.1.1898	Avantcomp Oy
1.3.6.1.4.1.1899	InfoVista
1.3.6.1.4.1.1900	Unwired Planet
1.3.6.1.4.1.1901	Sea Wonders
1.3.6.1.4.1.1902	HeadStart Enterprise
1.3.6.1.4.1.1903	B-SMART, Inc.

Figure 7-76. The Enterprises Groups *(continued)*

The Enterprises Groups	
Group Object Identifier	**Enterprise Name**
1.3.6.1.4.1.1904	ISMA, Ltd.
1.3.6.1.4.1.1905	3DV Technology, Inc.
1.3.6.1.4.1.1906	StarCom Technologies, Inc.
1.3.6.1.4.1.1907	L.L.Bean
1.3.6.1.4.1.1908	NetIcs, Inc.
1.3.6.1.4.1.1909	Infratec plus GmbH
1.3.6.1.4.1.1910	The 3e Group
1.3.6.1.4.1.1911	GISE mbH
1.3.6.1.4.1.1912	lan & pc services
1.3.6.1.4.1.1913	RedPoint Software Corporation
1.3.6.1.4.1.1914	QUADRATEC
1.3.6.1.4.1.1915	I-95-CC
1.3.6.1.4.1.1916	Extreme Networks
1.3.6.1.4.1.1917	Village of Rockville Centre
1.3.6.1.4.1.1918	Swichtec Power Systems
1.3.6.1.4.1.1919	Deutscher Wetterdienst
1.3.6.1.4.1.1920	Bluebird Software
1.3.6.1.4.1.1921	Svaha Interactive Media, Inc.
1.3.6.1.4.1.1922	Sully Solutions
1.3.6.1.4.1.1923	Blue Line
1.3.6.1.4.1.1924	Castleton Network Systems Corporation
1.3.6.1.4.1.1925	Visual Edge Software, Ltd.
1.3.6.1.4.1.1926	NetGuard Technologies, Inc.
1.3.6.1.4.1.1927	SoftSell, Inc.
1.3.6.1.4.1.1928	MARNE SOFTWARE
1.3.6.1.4.1.1929	Cadia Networks, Inc.
1.3.6.1.4.1.1930	Milton
1.3.6.1.4.1.1931	Del Mar Solutions, Inc.
1.3.6.1.4.1.1932	KUMARAN SYSTEMS
1.3.6.1.4.1.1933	Equivalence
1.3.6.1.4.1.1934	Homewatch International, Inc.
1.3.6.1.4.1.1935	John Rivers
1.3.6.1.4.1.1936	Remark Services, Inc.
1.3.6.1.4.1.1937	Deloitte & Touche Consulting Group
1.3.6.1.4.1.1938	Flying Penguin Productions
1.3.6.1.4.1.1939	The Matrix
1.3.6.1.4.1.1940	Eastern Computers, Inc.
1.3.6.1.4.1.1941	Princeton BioMedica Inc.
1.3.6.1.4.1.1942	SanCom Technology, Inc.
1.3.6.1.4.1.1943	National Computing Centre, Ltd.
1.3.6.1.4.1.1944	Aval Communications

Figure 7-76. The Enterprises Groups *(continued)*

The Enterprises Groups	
Group Object Identifier	**Enterprise Name**
1.3.6.1.4.1.1945	WORTEC SearchNet CO.
1.3.6.1.4.1.1946	Dogwood Media
1.3.6.1.4.1.1947	Allied Domecq
1.3.6.1.4.1.1948	Telesoft Russia
1.3.6.1.4.1.1949	UTStarcom, Inc.
1.3.6.1.4.1.1950	comunit
1.3.6.1.4.1.1951	Traffic Software, Ltd.
1.3.6.1.4.1.1952	Qualop Systems Corporation
1.3.6.1.4.1.1953	Vinca Corporation
1.3.6.1.4.1.1954	AMTEC spa
1.3.6.1.4.1.1955	GRETACODER Data Systems AG
1.3.6.1.4.1.1956	KMSystems, Inc.
1.3.6.1.4.1.1957	GEVA
1.3.6.1.4.1.1958	Red Creek Communications, Inc.
1.3.6.1.4.1.1959	BORG Technology, Inc.
1.3.6.1.4.1.1960	Concord Electronics
1.3.6.1.4.1.1961	Richard Ricci DDS
1.3.6.1.4.1.1962	Link International Corporation
1.3.6.1.4.1.1963	Intermec Corp
1.3.6.1.4.1.1964	OPTIMUM Data AG
1.3.6.1.4.1.1965	Innova Corporation
1.3.6.1.4.1.1966	Perle Systems, Ltd.
1.3.6.1.4.1.1967	inktomi corporation
1.3.6.1.4.1.1968	TELE-TV Systems, L.P.
1.3.6.1.4.1.1969	Fritz-Haber-Institut
1.3.6.1.4.1.1970	mediaone.net
1.3.6.1.4.1.1971	SeaChange International
1.3.6.1.4.1.1972	CASTON Corporation
1.3.6.1.4.1.1973	Local Net
1.3.6.1.4.1.1974	JapanNet
1.3.6.1.4.1.1975	Nabisco
1.3.6.1.4.1.1976	micrologica GmbH
1.3.6.1.4.1.1977	NDG Software
1.3.6.1.4.1.1978	Northrop Grumman-Canada, Ltd.
1.3.6.1.4.1.1979	Global MAINTECH, Inc.
1.3.6.1.4.1.1980	Tele2 AB
1.3.6.1.4.1.1981	CLARiiON Advanced Storage Solutions
1.3.6.1.4.1.1982	ITS Corporation
1.3.6.1.4.1.1983	CleverSoft, Inc.
1.3.6.1.4.1.1984	The Perseus Group, Inc.
1.3.6.1.4.1.1985	Joe's WWW Pages

Figure 7-76. The Enterprises Groups *(continued)*

The Enterprises Groups	
Group Object Identifier	**Enterprise Name**
1.3.6.1.4.1.1986	Everything Internet Store
1.3.6.1.4.1.1987	LANology, Inc.
1.3.6.1.4.1.1988	Lycoming County PA
1.3.6.1.4.1.1989	Statens Institutions styrelse SiS
1.3.6.1.4.1.1990	INware Solutions, Inc.
1.3.6.1.4.1.1991	StarRidge Networks, Inc.
1.3.6.1.4.1.1992	Deutsche Bank
1.3.6.1.4.1.1993	Xyratex
1.3.6.1.4.1.1994	Bausch Datacom bv
1.3.6.1.4.1.1995	Advanced Radio Telecom (ART)
1.3.6.1.4.1.1996	Copper Mountain Communications, Inc.
1.3.6.1.4.1.1997	PlaNet Software
1.3.6.1.4.1.1998	Carltan Computer Corporation
1.3.6.1.4.1.1999	Littva Mitchell, Inc.
1.3.6.1.4.1.2000	TIBCO, Inc.
1.3.6.1.4.1.2001	Oki Data Corporation
1.3.6.1.4.1.2002	GoTel
1.3.6.1.4.1.2003	Adobe Systems, Inc.
1.3.6.1.4.1.2004	Sentricity
1.3.6.1.4.1.2005	Aeroports De Paris
1.3.6.1.4.1.2006	ECONZ, Ltd.
1.3.6.1.4.1.2007	TELDAT, S.A.
1.3.6.1.4.1.2008	Offset Info Service srl
1.3.6.1.4.1.2009	A. J. Boggs & Company
1.3.6.1.4.1.2010	Stale Odegaard AS
1.3.6.1.4.1.2011	HUAWEI Technology Co., Ltd.
1.3.6.1.4.1.2012	Schroff GmbH
1.3.6.1.4.1.2013	Rehabilitation Institute of Chicago
1.3.6.1.4.1.2014	ADC Telecommunications, Inc.
1.3.6.1.4.1.2015	SYSTOR AG
1.3.6.1.4.1.2016	GralyMage, Inc.
1.3.6.1.4.1.2017	Symicron Computer Communications, Ltd.
1.3.6.1.4.1.2018	Scandorama AB
1.3.6.1.4.1.2019	I-NET
1.3.6.1.4.1.2020	Xland, Ltd.
1.3.6.1.4.1.2021	U.C. Davis, ECE Dept..
1.3.6.1.4.1.2022	CANARY COMMUNICATIONS, Inc.
1.3.6.1.4.1.2023	NetGain
1.3.6.1.4.1.2024	West Information Publishing Group
1.3.6.1.4.1.2025	Deutsche Bundesbank
1.3.6.1.4.1.2026	Digicom System, Inc.

Figure 7-76. The Enterprises Groups *(continued)*

The Enterprises Groups	
Group Object Identifier	**Enterprise Name**
1.3.6.1.4.1.2027	GAUSS GmbH
1.3.6.1.4.1.2028	Aldiscon
1.3.6.1.4.1.2029	Vivid Image
1.3.6.1.4.1.2030	AfriQ*Access, Inc.
1.3.6.1.4.1.2031	Reliant Networks Corporation
1.3.6.1.4.1.2031	ENVOY Corporation
1.3.6.1.4.1.2032	SEMA Group Telecoms
1.3.6.1.4.1.2033	McKinney Lighting & Sound
1.3.6.1.4.1.2034	Whole Systems Design, Inc.
1.3.6.1.4.1.2035	O'Reilly & Associates
1.3.6.1.4.1.2036	ATL Products
1.3.6.1.4.1.2037	Ernst and Young LLP
1.3.6.1.4.1.2038	Teleware Oy
1.3.6.1.4.1.2039	Fiducia Informationszentrale AG
1.3.6.1.4.1.2040	Kinetics, Inc.
1.3.6.1.4.1.2041	EMCEE Broadcast Products
1.3.6.1.4.1.2042	Clariant Corporation
1.3.6.1.4.1.2043	IEEE 802.5
1.3.6.1.4.1.2044	Open Development Corporation
1.3.6.1.4.1.2045	RFG Systems
1.3.6.1.4.1.2046	Aspect Telecommunications
1.3.6.1.4.1.2047	Leo & Associates
1.3.6.1.4.1.2048	SoftLinx, Inc.
1.3.6.1.4.1.2049	Generale Bank
1.3.6.1.4.1.2050	Windward Technologies, Inc.
1.3.6.1.4.1.2051	NetSolve, Inc.
1.3.6.1.4.1.2052	Xantel
1.3.6.1.4.1.2053	arago, Institut fuer komplexes Datenmanagement GmbH
1.3.6.1.4.1.2054	Kokusai Denshin Denwa Co., Ltd.
1.3.6.1.4.1.2055	GILLAM-SATEL
1.3.6.1.4.1.2056	MOEBIUS SYSTEMS
1.3.6.1.4.1.2057	Financial Internet Technology
1.3.6.1.4.1.2058	MARC Systems
1.3.6.1.4.1.2059	Bova Gallery
1.3.6.1.4.1.2060	OSx Telecomunicacoes
1.3.6.1.4.1.2061	Telecom Solutions
1.3.6.1.4.1.2062	HolonTech Corporation
1.3.6.1.4.1.2063	Ardent Communications Corporation
1.3.6.1.4.1.2064	Aware, Inc.
1.3.6.1.4.1.2065	Racal Radio, Ltd.
1.3.6.1.4.1.2066	Control Resources Corporation

Figure 7-76. The Enterprises Groups *(continued)*

The Enterprises Groups	
Group Object Identifier	**Enterprise Name**
1.3.6.1.4.1.2067	Advanced Fibre Communications (AFC)
1.3.6.1.4.1.2068	Elproma Electronica B.V.
1.3.6.1.4.1.2069	MTA SZTAKI
1.3.6.1.4.1.2070	Consensys Computers, Inc.
1.3.6.1.4.1.2071	Jade Digital Research Co.
1.3.6.1.4.1.2072	Byte This Interactive Pty., Ltd.
1.3.6.1.4.1.2073	Financial Network Technologies, Inc.
1.3.6.1.4.1.2074	BROKAT Informationssysteme GmbH
1.3.6.1.4.1.2075	MediaWise Networks
1.3.6.1.4.1.2076	Future Software
1.3.6.1.4.1.2077	Commit Information Systems
1.3.6.1.4.1.2078	Virtual Access, Ltd.
1.3.6.1.4.1.2079	JDS FITEL, Inc.
1.3.6.1.4.1.2080	IPM DATACOM
1.3.6.1.4.1.2081	StarBurst Communications Corporation
1.3.6.1.4.1.2082	Tollgrade Communications, Inc.
1.3.6.1.4.1.2083	Wildfire Communications, Inc.
1.3.6.1.4.1.2084	Sanken Electric Co., Ltd.
1.3.6.1.4.1.2085	Isolation Systems, Ltd.
1.3.6.1.4.1.2086	AVIDIA Systems, Inc.
1.3.6.1.4.1.2087	WavePhore Networks, Inc.
1.3.6.1.4.1.2088	Radstone Technology Plc
1.3.6.1.4.1.2089	Philips Business Communications
1.3.6.1.4.1.2090	FMS Services
1.3.6.1.4.1.2091	Supernova Communications
1.3.6.1.4.1.2092	Murphy & Murphy Real Estate
1.3.6.1.4.1.2093	Multi-Platform Information Systems
1.3.6.1.4.1.2094	Allegro Consultants, Inc.
1.3.6.1.4.1.2095	AIAB
1.3.6.1.4.1.2096	Preview Multimedia Services
1.3.6.1.4.1.2097	Access Beyond
1.3.6.1.4.1.2098	SunBurst Technology, Inc.
1.3.6.1.4.1.2099	sotas
1.3.6.1.4.1.2100	CyberSouls Eternal Life Systems, Inc.
1.3.6.1.4.1.2101	HANWHA CORPORATION/TELECOM
1.3.6.1.4.1.2102	COMET TELECOMMUNICATIONS, Inc.
1.3.6.1.4.1.2103	CARY SYSTEMS, Inc.
1.3.6.1.4.1.2104	Peerless Systems Corporation
1.3.6.1.4.1.2105	Adicom Wireless, Inc.
1.3.6.1.4.1.2106	High Technology Software Corporation
1.3.6.1.4.1.2107	Lynk

Figure 7-76. The Enterprises Groups *(continued)*

The Enterprises Groups	
Group Object Identifier	**Enterprise Name**
1.3.6.1.4.1.2108	Robin's Limousine
1.3.6.1.4.1.2109	Secant Network Tech
1.3.6.1.4.1.2110	Orion Pictures Corporation
1.3.6.1.4.1.2111	Global Village Communication, Inc.
1.3.6.1.4.1.2112	ioWave, Inc.
1.3.6.1.4.1.2113	Signals and Semaphores
1.3.6.1.4.1.2114	Mayo Foundation
1.3.6.1.4.1.2115	KRONE AG
1.3.6.1.4.1.2116	Computer Networking Resources, Inc.
1.3.6.1.4.1.2117	Telenetworks
1.3.6.1.4.1.2118	Staffordshire University
1.3.6.1.4.1.2119	Broadband Networks, Inc.
1.3.6.1.4.1.2120	Federal Aviation Administration
1.3.6.1.4.1.2121	Technical Communications Corporation
1.3.6.1.4.1.2122	REZO+
1.3.6.1.4.1.2123	GrafxLab, Inc.
1.3.6.1.4.1.2124	Savant Corp
1.3.6.1.4.1.2125	COMTEC SYSTEMS CO., Ltd.
1.3.6.1.4.1.2126	Satcom Media
1.3.6.1.4.1.2127	UconX Corporation
1.3.6.1.4.1.2128	TPG Network
1.3.6.1.4.1.2129	CNJ, Inc.
1.3.6.1.4.1.2130	Greenbrier & Russel
1.3.6.1.4.1.2131	mainnet
1.3.6.1.4.1.2132	Comnet Datensysteme
1.3.6.1.4.1.2133	Novadigm, Inc.
1.3.6.1.4.1.2134	Alfatech, Inc.
1.3.6.1.4.1.2135	Financial Sciences Corporation
1.3.6.1.4.1.2136	Electronics For Imaging, Inc.
1.3.6.1.4.1.2137	Casabyte
1.3.6.1.4.1.2138	AssureNet Pathways, Inc.
1.3.6.1.4.1.2139	Alexander LAN, Inc.
1.3.6.1.4.1.2140	Gill-Simpson
1.3.6.1.4.1.2141	MCNS, L.P.
1.3.6.1.4.1.2142	Future Systems, Inc.
1.3.6.1.4.1.2143	IMGIS
1.3.6.1.4.1.2144	Skywire Corporation
1.3.6.1.4.1.2145	Irdeto Consultants B.V.
1.3.6.1.4.1.2146	Peasantworks
1.3.6.1.4.1.2147	Onion Peel Software
1.3.6.1.4.1.2148	PS Partnership

Figure 7-76. The Enterprises Groups *(continued)*

The Enterprises Groups	
Group Object Identifier	**Enterprise Name**
1.3.6.1.4.1.2149	IRdg, Inc.
1.3.6.1.4.1.2150	SDS, Ltd.
1.3.6.1.4.1.2151	Promus Hotel Corporation
1.3.6.1.4.1.2152	Cavid Lawrence Center
1.3.6.1.4.1.2153	Insider Technologies, Ltd.
1.3.6.1.4.1.2154	Berkeley Networks
1.3.6.1.4.1.2155	Infonautics Corporation
1.3.6.1.4.1.2156	Easy Software
1.3.6.1.4.1.2157	CESG
1.3.6.1.4.1.2158	SALIX Technologies, Inc.
1.3.6.1.4.1.2159	Essential Communications
1.3.6.1.4.1.2160	University of Hawaii
1.3.6.1.4.1.2161	Foxtel Management Pty.
1.3.6.1.4.1.2162	Advent Network Management
1.3.6.1.4.1.2163	Vayris, S.A.
1.3.6.1.4.1.2164	Telecom Multimedia Systems, Inc.
1.3.6.1.4.1.2165	Guardall, Ltd.
1.3.6.1.4.1.2166	WKK SYSTEMS, Inc.
1.3.6.1.4.1.2167	Prominet Corporation
1.3.6.1.4.1.2168	LMC Lan Management Consulting GmbH
1.3.6.1.4.1.2169	Lewis Enterprise
1.3.6.1.4.1.2170	Teles AG
1.3.6.1.4.1.2171	PCSI (Phoenix Control)
1.3.6.1.4.1.2172	Fourth Wave Designs, Inc.
1.3.6.1.4.1.2173	MediaGate, Inc.
1.3.6.1.4.1.2174	Interactive Online Services, Inc.
1.3.6.1.4.1.2175	Mutek Transcom, Ltd.
1.3.6.1.4.1.2176	University of Dortmund, IRB
1.3.6.1.4.1.2177	Network Diagnostic Clinic
1.3.6.1.4.1.2178	TSI - Telecom Systems, Ltd.
1.3.6.1.4.1.2179	Rheyn Techologies, Inc.
1.3.6.1.4.1.2180	Versanet Communications, Inc.
1.3.6.1.4.1.2181	EUnet Communications Services bv
1.3.6.1.4.1.2182	pow communications
1.3.6.1.4.1.2183	AM Communications, Inc.
1.3.6.1.4.1.2184	Open Architecture Systems Integration Solutions (OASIS), Inc.
1.3.6.1.4.1.2185	NetPartner s.r.o.
1.3.6.1.4.1.2186	Vina Technologies
1.3.6.1.4.1.2189	Deutsches Klimarechenzentrum GmbH
1.3.6.1.4.1.2190	ABSYSS
1.3.6.1.4.1.2191	Quadrophonics, Inc.

Figure 7-76. The Enterprises Groups *(continued)*

The Enterprises Groups	
Group Object Identifier	**Enterprise Name**
1.3.6.1.4.1.2192	Hypercore Technology, Inc.
1.3.6.1.4.1.2193	OBTK, Inc., dba Network Designs Corporation
1.3.6.1.4.1.2194	VOIS Corporation
1.3.6.1.4.1.2195	IXO S.A.
1.3.6.1.4.1.2196	Macro4 Open Systems, Ltd.
1.3.6.1.4.1.2197	Security Dynamics Technologies, Inc.
1.3.6.1.4.1.2198	NextWave Wireless, Inc.
1.3.6.1.4.1.2199	Pisces Consultancy
1.3.6.1.4.1.2200	TPS Call Sciences, Inc. (TPS)
1.3.6.1.4.1.2201	ICONSULT
1.3.6.1.4.1.2202	Third Point Systems Richard Parker
1.3.6.1.4.1.2203	MAS Technology, Ltd.
1.3.6.1.4.1.2204	Advanced Logic Research, Inc. (ALR)
1.3.6.1.4.1.2205	Documentum, Inc.
1.3.6.1.4.1.2206	Siemens Business Communication Systems, Inc.
1.3.6.1.4.1.2207	Telmax Communications Corporation
1.3.6.1.4.1.2208	Zypcom, Inc.
1.3.6.1.4.1.2209	Remote Sense
1.3.6.1.4.1.2210	OOTek Corporation
1.3.6.1.4.1.2211	eSoft, Inc.
1.3.6.1.4.1.2212	anydata, Ltd.
1.3.6.1.4.1.2213	Data Fellows, Ltd.
1.3.6.1.4.1.2214	Productions Medialog, Inc.
1.3.6.1.4.1.2215	Inovamerci, Lda
1.3.6.1.4.1.2216	OKITEC
1.3.6.1.4.1.2217	Vertex Networks, Inc.
1.3.6.1.4.1.2218	Pulse Communications
1.3.6.1.4.1.2219	CXA Communications, Ltd.
1.3.6.1.4.1.2220	IDD Information Service
1.3.6.1.4.1.2221	Atlas Computer Equipment, Inc.
1.3.6.1.4.1.2222	Syntegra
1.3.6.1.4.1.2223	CCC Information Services
1.3.6.1.4.1.2224	W. Quinn Associates
1.3.6.1.4.1.2225	Broadcom Eireann Research, Ltd.
1.3.6.1.4.1.2226	Risk Management Services llc
1.3.6.1.4.1.2227	Watkins-Johnson Company
1.3.6.1.4.1.2228	Eric E. Westbrook
1.3.6.1.4.1.2229	Martinho-Davis Systems, Inc.
1.3.6.1.4.1.2230	XYPOINT Corporation
1.3.6.1.4.1.2231	Innovat Communications, Inc.
1.3.6.1.4.1.2232	Charleswood & Co.

Figure 7-76. The Enterprises Groups *(continued)*

The Enterprises Groups	
Group Object Identifier	**Enterprise Name**
1.3.6.1.4.1.2233	ID Software AS
1.3.6.1.4.1.2234	Telia AB
1.3.6.1.4.1.2235	Exploration Enterprises, Inc.
1.3.6.1.4.1.2236	Daimler-Benz Aerospace AG
1.3.6.1.4.1.2237	Xara Networks, Ltd.
1.3.6.1.4.1.2238	The FreeBSD Project
1.3.6.1.4.1.2239	World Merchandise Exchange (WOMEX), Ltd.
1.3.6.1.4.1.2240	lysis
1.3.6.1.4.1.2241	CFL Research
1.3.6.1.4.1.2242	NET-TEL Computer Systems, Ltd.
1.3.6.1.4.1.2243	Sattel Communications
1.3.6.1.4.1.2244	Promatory Communications, Inc.
1.3.6.1.4.1.2245	Syncsort, Inc.
1.3.6.1.4.1.2246	LloydsTSB Group Plc
1.3.6.1.4.1.2247	IT Consultancy Engineering Management Group, Ltd.
1.3.6.1.4.1.2248	LITE-ON COMMUNICATIONS CORPORATION
1.3.6.1.4.1.2249	The New Millennium
1.3.6.1.4.1.2250	Quatraco Yugoslavia
1.3.6.1.4.1.2251	BR Business Systems
1.3.6.1.4.1.2252	WheelGroup Corporation
1.3.6.1.4.1.2253	Ultimate Technology, Inc.
1.3.6.1.4.1.2254	Delta Electronics, Inc.
1.3.6.1.4.1.2255	Waffle Productions
1.3.6.1.4.1.2256	Korea Internet
1.3.6.1.4.1.2257	BAeSEMA
1.3.6.1.4.1.2258	THOMSON BROADCAST SYSTEMS
1.3.6.1.4.1.2259	Workflow Automation Company, Ltd.
1.3.6.1.4.1.2260	Associated RT, Inc.
1.3.6.1.4.1.2261	Codem Systems, Inc.
1.3.6.1.4.1.2262	RIGHT TIME WATCH CENTER
1.3.6.1.4.1.2263	Advanced-Vision Technologies, Inc.
1.3.6.1.4.1.2264	Applied Intelligence Group
1.3.6.1.4.1.2265	Acorn Computers, Ltd.
1.3.6.1.4.1.2266	Tempest Consulting, Inc.
1.3.6.1.4.1.2267	Digital Sound Corporation
1.3.6.1.4.1.2268	Fastlan Solutions, Inc.
1.3.6.1.4.1.2269	Ordinox Network, Inc.
1.3.6.1.4.1.2270	Telinc Corporation
1.3.6.1.4.1.2271	DRS Consulting Group
1.3.6.1.4.1.2272	Rapid City Communication
1.3.6.1.4.1.2273	Invisible Fence Sales Company

Figure 7-76. The Enterprises Groups *(continued)*

The Enterprises Groups	
Group Object Identifier	**Enterprise Name**
1.3.6.1.4.1.2274	Troika Management Services
1.3.6.1.4.1.2275	Vxtreme, Inc.
1.3.6.1.4.1.2276	CryptSoft Pty., Ltd.
1.3.6.1.4.1.2277	Brooktrout Technology
1.3.6.1.4.1.2278	GRASS mbH
1.3.6.1.4.1.2279	EPiCon, Inc.
1.3.6.1.4.1.2280	SAD Trasporto Locale S.p.a
1.3.6.1.4.1.2281	Giganet, Ltd.
1.3.6.1.4.1.2282	INCAA Informatica Italia srl
1.3.6.1.4.1.2283	Vermont Firmware Corporation
1.3.6.1.4.1.2284	Automated Concepts
1.3.6.1.4.1.2285	Flash Networks, Ltd.
1.3.6.1.4.1.2286	Oracom, Inc.
1.3.6.1.4.1.2287	Shell Services Company
1.3.6.1.4.1.2288	Black Pigs of Death
1.3.6.1.4.1.2289	N3ERZ
1.3.6.1.4.1.2290	Technology Rendezvous, Inc.
1.3.6.1.4.1.2291	ZapNet!, Inc.
1.3.6.1.4.1.2292	Premier Technologies
1.3.6.1.4.1.2293	Tennyson Technologies
1.3.6.1.4.1.2294	Artecon
1.3.6.1.4.1.2295	DH Technology, Inc.
1.3.6.1.4.1.2296	DAGAZ Technologies, Inc.
1.3.6.1.4.1.2297	Ganymede Software, Inc.
1.3.6.1.4.1.2298	Tele-Communications, Inc.
1.3.6.1.4.1.2299	FreeGate Corportation
1.3.6.1.4.1.2300	MainControl, Inc.
1.3.6.1.4.1.2301	Luminate Software Corporation
1.3.6.1.4.1.2302	K2Net
1.3.6.1.4.1.2303	Aurora Communciations Pty., Ltd.
1.3.6.1.4.1.2304	LANscape, Ltd.
1.3.6.1.4.1.2305	Gateway Technologies, Inc.
1.3.6.1.4.1.2306	Zergo, Ltd.
1.3.6.1.4.1.2307	C4U Solutions
1.3.6.1.4.1.2308	Boll+Reich Engineering AG
1.3.6.1.4.1.2309	Internet Mail Consortium
1.3.6.1.4.1.2310**	College of Mathematics and Science - Univ. of Central Oklahoma
1.3.6.1.4.1.3000	IDB Systems, a Division of WorldCom, Inc.
1.3.6.1.4.1.3001	BAILO
1.3.6.1.4.1.3002	ADAXIS Group
1.3.6.1.4.1.3003	Packet Engines, Inc.

Figure 7-76. The Enterprises Groups *(continued)*

The Enterprises Groups	
Group Object Identifier	**Enterprise Name**
1.3.6.1.4.1.3004	Softwire Corporation
1.3.6.1.4.1.3005	TDS (Telecoms Data Systems)
1.3.6.1.4.1.3006	HCI Technologies
1.3.6.1.4.1.3007	TOPCALL International
1.3.6.1.4.1.3008	Open Service, Inc.
1.3.6.1.4.1.3009	Aichi Electronics Co., Ltd.
1.3.6.1.4.1.3010	university of aizu
1.3.6.1.4.1.3011	VideoServer, Inc.
1.3.6.1.4.1.3012	Space & Telecommunications Systems Pte., Ltd.
1.3.6.1.4.1.3013	Bicol Infonet System, Inc.
1.3.6.1.4.1.3014	MediaSoft Telecom
1.3.6.1.4.1.3015	Synaxis Corporation
1.3.6.1.4.1.3016	OzEmail, Ltd.
1.3.6.1.4.1.3017	Arcxel Technologies, Inc.
1.3.6.1.4.1.3018	EnterNet Corporation
1.3.6.1.4.1.3019	Jones Waldo Holbrook McDonough
1.3.6.1.4.1.3020	University Access
1.3.6.1.4.1.3021	Sendit AB
1.3.6.1.4.1.3022	Telecom Sciences Corporation, Ltd.
1.3.6.1.4.1.3023	Quality Quorm, Inc.
1.3.6.1.4.1.3024	Grapevine Systems, Inc.
1.3.6.1.4.1.3025	The Panda Project, Inc.
1.3.6.1.4.1.3026	Mission Control Development
1.3.6.1.4.1.3027	IONA Technologies, Ltd.
1.3.6.1.4.1.3028	Dialogic Corporation
1.3.6.1.4.1.3029	Digital Data Security
1.3.6.1.4.1.3030	ISCNI
1.3.6.1.4.1.3031	daoCon
1.3.6.1.4.1.3032	Beaufort Memorial Hospital
1.3.6.1.4.1.3033	Informationstechnik
1.3.6.1.4.1.3034	URMET SUD s.p.a.
1.3.6.1.4.1.3035	Avesta Technologies, Inc.
1.3.6.1.4.1.3036	Hyundai Electronics America
1.3.6.1.4.1.3037	DMV, Ltd.
1.3.6.1.4.1.3038	Fax International, Inc.
1.3.6.1.4.1.3039	MidAmerican Energy Company (MEC)
1.3.6.1.4.1.3040	Bellsouth.net
1.3.6.1.4.1.3041	Assured Access Technology, Inc.
1.3.6.1.4.1.3042	Logicon - Eagle Technology
1.3.6.1.4.1.3043	FREQUENTIS Nachrichtentechnik Ges.m.b.H
1.3.6.1.4.1.3044	ISIS 2000

Figure 7-76. The Enterprises Groups *(continued)*

The Enterprises Groups	
Group Object Identifier	**Enterprise Name**
1.3.6.1.4.1.3045	james e. gray, atty
1.3.6.1.4.1.3046	Jamaica Cable T.V. & Internet Services
1.3.6.1.4.1.3047	Information Technology Consultants Pty., Ltd.
1.3.6.1.4.1.3048	LinickGrp.com
1.3.6.1.4.1.3049	Yankee Know-How
1.3.6.1.4.1.3050	SeAH group
1.3.6.1.4.1.3051	Cinco Networks, Inc.
1.3.6.1.4.1.3052	Omnitronix, Inc.
1.3.6.1.4.1.3053	Genie Telecommunication, Inc.
** Note that there is a break in the sequence numbers and enterprise numbers 2311-2999 are not included.	

Figure 7-76. The Enterprises Groups *(continued)*

7.5. THE MIB DEFINITION

The discussion of the MIB would not be complete without including a listing of the standard specification from RFC 1213. Because of the length of the specification, the listing has been added as Appendix C.

REFERENCES FOR CHAPTER 7

[1] Esar, Evan. *20,000 Quips and Quotes.* Garden City, NY: Doubleday and Company, Inc. 1968.

[2] Feit, Sidnie. *SNMP: A Guide to Network Management.* New York: McGraw-Hill, Inc. 1995.

[3] Rose, Marshall, and Keith McCloghrie. *How To Manage Your Network Using SNMP: The Networking Management Practicum.* Englewood Cliffs, NJ: Prentice Hall. 1995.

The Management Information Base for SNMP Version 2

Thou canst not adorn simplicity. What is naked or defective is susceptible of decoration: what is decorated is simplicity no longer.

—*Walter Savage Landor*[1]

For SNMP Version 2, the MIBs are now defined with the Version 2 SMI and all of the additional macros that these information modules use. Since SMIv2 is a superset of SMIv1, the migration to its use is straightforward. Since 1994, all new standards-track MIBs have been written with SMIv2.

A standard MIB has also been defined for all network managers and agents that implement SNMPv2. RFC 1907, *Management Information Base for Version 2 of the Simple Network Management Protocol (SNMPv2)*, contains the managed objects of the System and SNMP Groups that describe how the SNMPv2 agent and managers behave. This MIB contains an updated subset of these two groups from the SNMPv1 MIB defined in RFC 1213.

8.1. UPDATES TO SNMPV2 MIBS

Since the SMIv2 is more expressive and has many benefits over the original, the recommendation is that all new MIBs be developed with this syntax. The migration from SNMPv1 MIBs to SNMPv2 is spelled out in RFC 1908, *Coexistence Between Version 1 and Version 2 of the Internet-standard Network Management Framework*. The RFC contains four important lists on how this process can be accomplished.

The first checklist contains the steps in updating a Version 1 MIB to Version 2.

1. The IMPORTS statement should be changed from RFC1155-SMI and RFC-1212 to SNMPv2-SMI.

2. The MODULE-IDENTITY macro has to be invoked right after any IMPORTs statement.

3. If any descriptor or label for a named-number enumeration or enumerated INTEGER has a hyphen character, the hyphen character should be removed from the name.

4. Any INTEGERs (without a range restriction) should have a syntax of Integer32.

5. Any `Counter` objects should be replaced with `Counter32`.

6. Any `Gauge` objects should be replaced with `Gauge32`.

7. Replace all the ACCESS clauses with MAX-ACCESS. The value is not changed unless another value makes "protocol sense" as the maximal level of access for the object. For example, all instances that can be set should be upgraded to have a MAX-ACCESS clause of "read-create." If the value of the ACCESS clause is "write-only," then the value of the MAX-ACCESS clause should be changed to "read-write." The DESCRIPTION clause explains that reading this object results in implementation-specific results.

8. Replace all occurrences of "mandatory" to "current" in the STATUS clause.

9. Replace all occurrences of "optional" to "obsolete" in the STATUS clause.

10. The DESCRIPTION clause must be defined for every object.

11. For all objects that represent a conceptual row, the row must have either an INDEX clause or the AUGMENTS clause defined for it.

12. For any object with an INDEX clause that references an object with a syntax of `NetworkAddress`, the value of the STATUS clause of both objects must be changed to "obsolete."

13. For any object containing a default value DEFVAL clause with an OBJECT IDENTIFIER value that is expressed as a collection of sub-identifiers, the value must be changed to reference a single ASN.1 identifier.

This next checklist contains optional changes that are "desirable, but not necessary."

1. If a Version 1 MIB contains conceptual tables that allow for row creation and deletion, the objects relating to those tables should be deprecated. They should be replaced with objects that use the new SMIv2 table manipulation textual conventions.

2. All OCTET STRINGs should be defined with lower- and upper-bounds for the size.

3. The TEXTUAL-CONVENTION should be used wherever possible as the formal macro definition.

4. If an object represents a measurement, the UNITS clause should be added to the definition of that object for documentation and possible future use.

5. If a conceptual row is an extension of another conceptual row, an AUGMENTS clause should be used in place of the INDEX clause, for the object corresponding to the conceptual row that is an extension to the first row.

The following list contains two common errors found in SNMPv1 MIBs that should be corrected for a proper implementation for SNMPv2. These deal with table handling.

1. If a non-columnar object is instanced as if it were immediately subordinate to a conceptual row, the value of the STATUS clause should be changed to "obsolete."

2. If a conceptual row object is not contained immediately subordinate to a conceptual table, the value of the STATUS clause of that object (and all subordinate objects) should be changed to "obsolete."

Finally, follow six considerations for upgrading Version 1 traps for use with Version 2.

1. Every occurrence of the TRAP-TYPE macro must be replaced with the NOTIFICATION-TYPE macro.

2. The IMPORTS statement must not reference RFC 1215. Remember, RFC 1215 was the informational RFC that contained the TRAP-TYPE macro that was used to define traps in Version 1.

3. Remove any occurrences of the ENTERPRISES clause.

4. Rename the VARIABLES clause to the OBJECTS clause.

5. The STATUS clause is now mandatory.

6. The invocation value of the NOTIFICATION-TYPE macro should be changed from INTEGER to OBJECT IDENTIFIER. If the value of the ENTERPRISE clause is not *snmp*, then the invocation value should become the value of the ENTERPRISE clause with two sub-identifiers: a *0* and the value of the invocation of the TRAP-TYPE.

As stated in the RFC 2037 (*Entity MIB*), "a semantically identical MIB conforming to the SNMPv1 SMI can be produced through the appropriate translation." A service is available at this writing that converts SMIv2 MIBs back to a corresponding SMIv1-based equivalent, if this is required for your implementation. You send the Version 2 MIB in the body of an e-mail message to:

```
mib-v2tov1@simple-times.org
```

Also available (from [2]) is an archive of standard MIB modules available in HTML format for your favorite Web browser at:

```
ftp://ftp.simple-times.org/pub/simple-times/html/
www://www.simple-times.org/pub/simple-times/html/
```

Since SMIv2 became available, the latest MIBs have all been created in the new format. Figure 8-1 lists the current standards-track MIBs that are in Version 2 format.

In order to better access the benefits of SMIv2 improved expressiveness, we will compare the UDP MIB Group from MIB-II with the new UDP MIB for SNMPv2.

RFC Title	RFC Number	Standard Level
Network Services Monitoring Objects	1565	proposed
Mail Monitoring Objects	1566	proposed
X.500 Directory Objects	1567	proposed
Evolution of IF Group of MIB-II Objects	1573	proposed
Sonet/SDH Objects	1595	proposed
Frame Relay Service Objects	1604	proposed
DNS Server and Resolver Objects	1611	proposed
Uninterruptible Power Supply Objects	1628	proposed
Ether-like Interface Type (v2) Objects	1650	proposed
Border Gateway Protocol (Version 4) Objects	1657	draft
MIB for Character Stream Devices Objects	1658	draft
RS-232 Objects	1659	draft
Parallel Printer Objects	1660	draft
SNA NAU Objects	1666	proposed
SMDS Interface Objects	1694	draft
ATM Objects	1695	proposed
Modem Objects	1696	proposed
Relational DB Management Objects	1697	proposed
RIP Version 2 MIB Extensions Objects	1724	draft
AppleTalk II Objects	1742	proposed
SNA DLC Objects	1747	proposed
Token Ring-like Objects	1748	draft
802.5 Station Source Routing Objects	1749	proposed
Remote Network Monitoring Objects	1757	draft
Printer Objects	1759	proposed
Open Shortest Path First (Version 2) Objects	1850	draft
IP Mobility Support Objects	2006	proposed
100VG- AnyLAN Objects	2020	proposed
Data Link Switching Objects	2024	proposed
Entity Objects	2037	proposed

Figure 8-1. Standards Track MIBs in SNMPv2 Format

8.2. COMPARING UDP MIB V1 VS. V2

Several of the important MIB Groups that were defined for MIB-II in RFC 1213 have been redefined with their own Version 2 MIB. The IP, TCP, and UDP MIB groups have been recently published as RFCs with their definitions expressed in the SMIv2 notation.

- RFC 2013, *SNMPv2 Management Information Base for the User Datagram Protocol using SMIv2*

- RFC 2012, *SNMPv2 Management Information Base for the Transmission Control Protocol*

- RFC 2011, *SNMPv2 Management Information Base for the Internet Protocol using SMIv2*

I first present the UDP MIB from RFC 1213 in Figure 8-2. It uses the SMIv2 macros for module identity, conformance, and compliance. It contains four counters and a UDP Listener Table for keeping information on the end-point connections.

```
UDP-MIB DEFINITIONS ::= BEGIN

IMPORTS
    MODULE-IDENTITY, OBJECT-TYPE, Counter32,
    IpAddress, mib-2                  FROM SNMPv2-SMI
    MODULE-COMPLIANCE, OBJECT-GROUP   FROM SNMPv2-CONF;


udpMIB MODULE-IDENTITY
    LAST-UPDATED "9411010000Z"
    ORGANIZATION "IETF SNMPv2 Working Group"
    CONTACT-INFO
           "          Keith McCloghrie

           Postal: Cisco Systems, Inc.
                   170 West Tasman Drive
                   San Jose, CA  95134-1706
                   US

           Phone:  +1 408 526 5260
           Email:  kzm@cisco.com"
    DESCRIPTION
           "The MIB module for managing UDP implementations."
    REVISION       "9103310000Z"
    DESCRIPTION
           "The initial revision of this MIB module was part of MIB-
           II."
    ::= { mib-2 50 }
```

Figure 8-2. The SNMPv2 UDP MIB

```
-- the UDP group

udp        OBJECT IDENTIFIER ::= { mib-2 7 }

udpInDatagrams OBJECT-TYPE
    SYNTAX      Counter32
    MAX-ACCESS  read-only
    STATUS      current
    DESCRIPTION
            "The total number of UDP datagrams delivered to UDP users."
    ::= { udp 1 }

udpNoPorts OBJECT-TYPE
    SYNTAX      Counter32
    MAX-ACCESS  read-only
    STATUS      current
    DESCRIPTION
            "The total number of received UDP datagrams for which there
            was no application at the destination port."
    ::= { udp 2 }

udpInErrors OBJECT-TYPE
    SYNTAX      Counter32
    MAX-ACCESS  read-only
    STATUS      current
    DESCRIPTION
            "The number of received UDP datagrams that could not be
            delivered for reasons other than the lack of an application
            at the destination port."
    ::= { udp 3 }

udpOutDatagrams OBJECT-TYPE
    SYNTAX      Counter32
    MAX-ACCESS  read-only
    STATUS      current
    DESCRIPTION
            "The total number of UDP datagrams sent from this entity."
    ::= { udp 4 }

-- the UDP Listener table

-- The UDP listener table contains information about this
-- entity's UDP end-points on which a local application is
-- currently accepting datagrams.

udpTable OBJECT-TYPE
    SYNTAX      SEQUENCE OF UdpEntry
    MAX-ACCESS  not-accessible
    STATUS      current
    DESCRIPTION
            "A table containing UDP listener information."
    ::= { udp 5 }

udpEntry OBJECT-TYPE
    SYNTAX      UdpEntry
    MAX-ACCESS  not-accessible
    STATUS      current
    DESCRIPTION
            "Information about a particular current UDP listener."
    INDEX   { udpLocalAddress, udpLocalPort }
    ::= { udpTable 1 }
```

Figure 8-2. The SNMPv2 UDP MIB *(continued)*

345

```
UdpEntry ::= SEQUENCE {
        udpLocalAddress  IpAddress,
        udpLocalPort     INTEGER
    }

udpLocalAddress OBJECT-TYPE
    SYNTAX      IpAddress
    MAX-ACCESS  read-only
    STATUS      current
    DESCRIPTION
            "The local IP address for this UDP listener.  In the case of
            a UDP listener which is willing to accept datagrams for any
            IP interface associated with the node, the value 0.0.0.0 is
            used."
    ::= { udpEntry 1 }

udpLocalPort OBJECT-TYPE
    SYNTAX      INTEGER (0..65535)
    MAX-ACCESS  read-only
    STATUS      current
    DESCRIPTION
            "The local port number for this UDP listener."
    ::= { udpEntry 2 }

-- conformance information

udpMIBConformance OBJECT IDENTIFIER ::= { udpMIB 2 }

udpMIBCompliances OBJECT IDENTIFIER ::= { udpMIBConformance 1 }
udpMIBGroups      OBJECT IDENTIFIER ::= { udpMIBConformance 2 }

-- compliance statements

udpMIBCompliance MODULE-COMPLIANCE
    STATUS  current
    DESCRIPTION
            "The compliance statement for SNMPv2 entities which
            implement UDP."
MODULE  -- this module
        MANDATORY-GROUPS { udpGroup
                    }
    ::= { udpMIBCompliances 1 }

-- units of conformance

udpGroup OBJECT-GROUP
    OBJECTS    { udpInDatagrams, udpNoPorts,
                udpInErrors, udpOutDatagrams,
                udpLocalAddress, udpLocalPort }
    STATUS     current
    DESCRIPTION
            "The udp group of objects providing for management of UDP
            entities."
    ::= { udpMIBGroups 1 }

END
```

Figure 8-2. The SNMPv2 UDP MIB *(continued)*

If you compare the new v2 UDP MIB with the "original" UDP MIB Group defined in RFC 1213, you see that they both contain the same managed objects but that the original definitions are defined using the SMIv1 OBJECT-TYPE macro. The Version 1 MIB-II also lacks the other SMIv2 macros that make the information modules semantically richer. The UDP MIB Group from RFC 1213 appears in Figure 8-3.

```
-- the UDP group

-- Implementation of the UDP group is mandatory for all
-- systems which implement the UDP.

udpInDatagrams OBJECT-TYPE
  SYNTAX   Counter
  ACCESS   read-only
  STATUS   mandatory
  DESCRIPTION
        "The total number of UDP datagrams delivered to
        UDP users."
  ::= { udp 1 }

udpNoPorts OBJECT-TYPE
  SYNTAX   Counter
  ACCESS   read-only
  STATUS   mandatory
  DESCRIPTION
        "The total number of received UDP datagrams for
        which there was no application at the destination
        port."
  ::= { udp 2 }

udpInErrors OBJECT-TYPE
  SYNTAX   Counter
  ACCESS   read-only
  STATUS   mandatory
  DESCRIPTION
        "The number of received UDP datagrams that could
        not be delivered for reasons other than the lack
        of an application at the destination port."
  ::= { udp 3 }

udpOutDatagrams OBJECT-TYPE
  SYNTAX   Counter
  ACCESS   read-only
  STATUS   mandatory
  DESCRIPTION
        "The total number of UDP datagrams sent from this
        entity."
  ::= { udp 4 }


-- the UDP Listener table

-- The UDP listener table contains information about this
-- entity's UDP end-points on which a local application is
-- currently accepting datagrams.

udpTable OBJECT-TYPE
  SYNTAX   SEQUENCE OF UdpEntry
```

Figure 8-3. The SNMPv1 UDP Managed Objects from MIB-II

```
        ACCESS   not-accessible
        STATUS   mandatory
        DESCRIPTION
            "A table containing UDP listener information."
        ::= { udp 5 }

    udpEntry OBJECT-TYPE
        SYNTAX   UdpEntry
        ACCESS   not-accessible
        STATUS   mandatory
        DESCRIPTION
            "Information about a particular current UDP
            listener."
        INDEX    { udpLocalAddress, udpLocalPort }
        ::= { udpTable 1 }

    UdpEntry ::=
        SEQUENCE {
            udpLocalAddress
              IpAddress,
            udpLocalPort
              INTEGER (0..65535)
        }

    udpLocalAddress OBJECT-TYPE
        SYNTAX   IpAddress
        ACCESS   read-only
        STATUS   mandatory
        DESCRIPTION
            "The local IP address for this UDP listener.  In
            the case of a UDP listener which is willing to
            accept datagrams for any IP interface associated
            with the node, the value 0.0.0.0 is used."
        ::= { udpEntry 1 }

    udpLocalPort OBJECT-TYPE
        SYNTAX   INTEGER (0..65535)
        ACCESS   read-only
        STATUS   mandatory
        DESCRIPTION
            "The local port number for this UDP listener."
        ::= { udpEntry 2 }
```

Figure 8-3. The SNMPv1 UDP Managed Objects from MIB-II *(continued)*

8.3. THE SNMPV2 MIB

The SNMPv2 MIB contains a list of management objects that an SNMPv2 management entity must instrument. It is an update of the System and SNMP groups found in MIB-II. This MIB includes standard objects that are used for defining trap messages. The SNMPv2 MIB also uses several of the new SMIv2 macros.

8.3.1. THE VERSION 2 SYSTEM GROUP

The System Group is the set of top-level descriptors that is common to all SNMP management entities. The seven original objects from MIB-II are included. These objects define a textual description, its Object ID, how long it's been running, a contact name, a node name, node location, and a value that indicates which communication protocols are implemented in this device. What is new for the Version 2 System Group is the addition of managed objects for an agent's dynamic object resources, for the support of additional MIBs. These objects include a "last change" time stamp and a table that contains entries describing each resource: its object ID, a textual description, and the sysUpTime value when this table entry was added.

8.3.2. THE VERSION 2 SNMP GROUP

The SNMP Group still contains the variables that are necessary to "manage the management," but the variables that are required have been reexamined and many of the original MIB-II SNMP Group variables were found to be ineffective and little used. V2 agents are now spared the responsibility for logging each and every possible processing condition and error. This reduction in the number of variables lessens the memory and processing requirements for the agent. Figure 8-4 shows the variables.

The SNMP Group			
OID	**Object Name**	**In V1?**	**In V2?**
1.3.6.1.4.1.11.1	snmpInPkts	X	X
1.3.6.1.4.1.11.2	snmpOutPkts	X	
1.3.6.1.4.1.11.3	snmpInBadVersions	X	X
1.3.6.1.4.1.11.4	snmpInBadCommunityNames	X	X
1.3.6.1.4.1.11.5	snmpInBadCommunityUses	X	X
1.3.6.1.4.1.11.6	snmpInASNParseErrs	X	X
1.3.6.1.4.1.11.7	*(not used)*		
1.3.6.1.4.1.11.8	snmpInTooBigs	X	

Figure 8-4. The SNMP Group for Version 1 and 2

OID	Object Name	In V1?	In V2?
1.3.6.1.4.1.11.9	snmpInNoSuchNames	X	
1.3.6.1.4.1.11.10	snmpInBadValues	X	
1.3.6.1.4.1.11.11	snmpInReadOnlys	X	
1.3.6.1.4.1.11.13	snmpInGenErrs	X	
1.3.6.1.4.1.11.14	snmpInTotalSetVars	X	
1.3.6.1.4.1.11.15	snmpInGetRequests	X	
1.3.6.1.4.1.11.16	snmpInGetNexts	X	
1.3.6.1.4.1.11.17	snmpInSetRequests	X	
1.3.6.1.4.1.11.18	snmpInGetResponses	X	
1.3.6.1.4.1.11.19	snmpInTraps	X	
1.3.6.1.4.1.11.20	snmpOutTooBigs	X	
1.3.6.1.4.1.11.21	snmpOutNoSuchNames	X	
1.3.6.1.4.1.11.22	snmpOutBadValues	X	
1.3.6.1.4.1.11.23	(not used)		
1.3.6.1.4.1.11.24	snmpOutGenErrors	X	
1.3.6.1.4.1.11.25	snmpOutGenRequests	X	
1.3.6.1.4.1.11.26	snmpOutGetNexts	X	
1.3.6.1.4.1.11.27	snmpOutSetRequests	X	
1.3.6.1.4.1.11.28	snmpOutGetResponses	X	
1.3.6.1.4.1.11.29	snmpOutTraps	X	
1.3.6.1.4.1.11.30	snmpEnableAuthenTraps	X	X
1.3.6.1.4.1.11.31	snmpSilentDrops		X
1.3.6.1.4.1.11.32	snmpProxyDrops		X

Figure 8-4. The SNMP Group for Version 1 and 2 *(continued)*

8.3.3. VERSION 2 STANDARDIZED TRAP OBJECTS

The third major group for the SNMPv2 MIB provides for standardized trap configuration for agents and also includes objects for improving set operation integrity for managers. The MIB now includes a Trap OID and enterprise tag that unambiguously define the origin of the trap. The Set Group currently has one variable–snmpSerialNo. This variable can be used as a locking scheme to coordinate sets to agents from various cooperating managers.

8.4. THE SNMPV2 MIB DEFINITION

Figure 8-5 contains the SNMPv2 MIB. This MIB is listed in RFC 1907, *Management Information Base for Version 2 of the Simple Network Management Protocol (SNMPv2)*.

```
SNMPv2-MIB DEFINITIONS ::= BEGIN

IMPORTS
    MODULE-IDENTITY, OBJECT-TYPE, NOTIFICATION-TYPE,
    TimeTicks, Counter32, snmpModules, mib-2
        FROM SNMPv2-SMI
    DisplayString, TestAndIncr, TimeStamp
        FROM SNMPv2-TC
    MODULE-COMPLIANCE, OBJECT-GROUP, NOTIFICATION-GROUP
        FROM SNMPv2-CONF;

snmpMIB MODULE-IDENTITY
    LAST-UPDATED "9511090000Z"
    ORGANIZATION "IETF SNMPv2 Working Group"
    CONTACT-INFO
            "           Marshall T. Rose

             Postal: Dover Beach Consulting, Inc.
                     420 Whisman Court
                     Mountain View, CA   94043-2186
                     US

                Tel: +1 415 968 1052

                E-mail: mrose@dbc.mtview.ca.us"
    DESCRIPTION
            "The MIB module for SNMPv2 entities."
    REVISION      "9304010000Z"
    DESCRIPTION
            "The initial revision of this MIB module was published as
            RFC 1450."
    ::= { snmpModules 1 }


snmpMIBObjects OBJECT IDENTIFIER ::= { snmpMIB 1 }

--  ::= { snmpMIBObjects 1 }      this OID is obsolete
--  ::= { snmpMIBObjects 2 }      this OID is obsolete
--  ::= { snmpMIBObjects 3 }      this OID is obsolete


-- the System group
```

Figure 8-5. The SNMPv2 Management Information Base

```
--
-- a collection of objects common to all managed systems.

system    OBJECT IDENTIFIER ::= { mib-2 1 }

sysDescr OBJECT-TYPE
    SYNTAX        DisplayString (SIZE (0..255))
    MAX-ACCESS    read-only
    STATUS        current
    DESCRIPTION
            "A textual description of the entity.  This value should
            include the full name and version identification of the
            system's hardware type, software operating-system, and
            networking software."
    ::= { system 1 }

sysObjectID OBJECT-TYPE
    SYNTAX        OBJECT IDENTIFIER
    MAX-ACCESS    read-only
    STATUS        current
    DESCRIPTION
            "The vendor's authoritative identification of the network
            management subsystem contained in the entity.  This value is
            allocated within the SMI enterprises subtree (1.3.6.1.4.1)
            and provides an easy and unambiguous means for determining
            `what kind of box' is being managed.  For example, if vendor
            `Flintstones, Inc.' was assigned the subtree
            1.3.6.1.4.1.4242, it could assign the identifier
            1.3.6.1.4.1.4242.1.1 to its `Fred Router'."
::= { system 2 }

sysUpTime OBJECT-TYPE
    SYNTAX        TimeTicks
    MAX-ACCESS    read-only
    STATUS        current
    DESCRIPTION
            "The time (in hundredths of a second) since the network
            management portion of the system was last re-initialized."
    ::= { system 3 }

sysContact OBJECT-TYPE
    SYNTAX        DisplayString (SIZE (0..255))
    MAX-ACCESS    read-write
    STATUS        current
    DESCRIPTION
            "The textual identification of the contact person for this
            managed node, together with information on how to contact
            this person.  If no contact information is known, the value
            is the zero-length string."
    ::= { system 4 }

sysName OBJECT-TYPE
    SYNTAX        DisplayString (SIZE (0..255))
    MAX-ACCESS    read-write
    STATUS        current
    DESCRIPTION
            "An administratively-assigned name for this managed node.
            By convention, this is the node's fully-qualified domain
            name.  If the name is unknown, the value is the zero-length
            string."
    ::= { system 5 }
```

Figure 8-5. The SNMPv2 Management Information Base *(continued)*

```
sysLocation OBJECT-TYPE
    SYNTAX       DisplayString (SIZE (0..255))
    MAX-ACCESS   read-write
    STATUS       current
    DESCRIPTION
            "The physical location of this node (e.g., `telephone
            closet, 3rd floor').  If the location is unknown, the value
            is the zero-length string."
    ::= { system 6 }

sysServices OBJECT-TYPE
    SYNTAX       INTEGER (0..127)
    MAX-ACCESS   read-only
    STATUS       current
    DESCRIPTION
            "A value which indicates the set of services that this
            entity may potentially offers.  The value is a sum.  This
            sum initially takes the value zero, Then, for each layer, L,
            in the range 1 through 7, that this node performs
            transactions for, 2 raised to (L - 1) is added to the sum.
            For example, a node which performs only routing functions
            would have a value of 4 (2^(3-1)).  In contrast, a node
            which is a host offering application services would have a
            value of 72 (2^(4-1) + 2^(7-1)).  Note that in the context
            of the Internet suite of protocols, values should be
            calculated accordingly:

                    layer       functionality
                      1         physical (e.g., repeaters)
                      2         datalink/subnetwork (e.g., bridges)
                      3         internet (e.g., supports the IP)
                      4         end-to-end  (e.g., supports the TCP)
                      7         applications (e.g., supports the SMTP)

            For systems including OSI protocols, layers 5 and 6 may also
            be counted."
    ::= { system 7 }


-- object resource information
--
-- a collection of objects which describe the SNMPv2 entity's
-- (statically and dynamically configurable) support of
-- various MIB modules.

sysORLastChange OBJECT-TYPE
    SYNTAX       TimeStamp
    MAX-ACCESS read-only
    STATUS       current
    DESCRIPTION
            "The value of sysUpTime at the time of the most recent
             change in state or value of any instance of sysORID."
    ::= { system 8 }


sysORTable OBJECT-TYPE
    SYNTAX       SEQUENCE OF SysOREntry
    MAX-ACCESS not-accessible
    STATUS       current
    DESCRIPTION
            "The (conceptual) table listing the capabilities of the
            local SNMPv2 entity acting in an agent role with respect to
```

Figure 8-5. The SNMPv2 Management Information Base *(continued)*

353

```
                    various MIB modules.  SNMPv2 entities having dynamically-
                    configurable support of MIB modules will have a
                    dynamically-varying number of conceptual rows."
    ::= { system 9 }

    sysOREntry OBJECT-TYPE
        SYNTAX       SysOREntry
        MAX-ACCESS not-accessible
        STATUS       current
        DESCRIPTION
                "An entry (conceptual row) in the sysORTable."
        INDEX       { sysORIndex }
        ::= { sysORTable 1 }

    SysOREntry ::= SEQUENCE {
        sysORIndex    INTEGER,
        sysORID       OBJECT IDENTIFIER,
        sysORDescr    DisplayString,
        sysORUpTime   TimeStamp
    }

    sysORIndex OBJECT-TYPE
        SYNTAX       INTEGER (1..2147483647)
        MAX-ACCESS not-accessible
        STATUS       current
        DESCRIPTION
                "The auxiliary variable used for identifying instances of
                the columnar objects in the sysORTable."
        ::= { sysOREntry 1 }

    sysORID OBJECT-TYPE
        SYNTAX       OBJECT IDENTIFIER
        MAX-ACCESS read-only
        STATUS       current
        DESCRIPTION
                "An authoritative identification of a capabilities statement
                with respect to various MIB modules supported by the local
                SNMPv2 entity acting in an agent role."
        ::= { sysOREntry 2 }

    sysORDescr OBJECT-TYPE
        SYNTAX       DisplayString
        MAX-ACCESS read-only
        STATUS       current
        DESCRIPTION
                "A textual description of the capabilities identified by the
                corresponding instance of sysORID."
        ::= { sysOREntry 3 }

    sysORUpTime OBJECT-TYPE
        SYNTAX       TimeStamp
        MAX-ACCESS read-only
        STATUS       current
        DESCRIPTION
                "The value of sysUpTime at the time this conceptual row was
                last instantiated."
        ::= { sysOREntry 4 }


    -- the SNMP group
    --
```

Figure 8-5. The SNMPv2 Management Information Base *(continued)*

```
-- a collection of objects providing basic instrumentation and
-- control of an SNMP entity.

snmp      OBJECT IDENTIFIER ::= { mib-2 11 }

snmpInPkts OBJECT-TYPE
    SYNTAX      Counter32
    MAX-ACCESS read-only
    STATUS      current
    DESCRIPTION
            "The total number of messages delivered to the SNMP entity
            from the transport service."
    ::= { snmp 1 }

snmpInBadVersions OBJECT-TYPE
    SYNTAX      Counter32
    MAX-ACCESS read-only
    STATUS      current
    DESCRIPTION
            "The total number of SNMP messages which were delivered to
            the SNMP entity and were for an unsupported SNMP version."
    ::= { snmp 3 }

snmpInBadCommunityNames OBJECT-TYPE
    SYNTAX      Counter32
    MAX-ACCESS read-only
    STATUS      current
    DESCRIPTION
            "The total number of SNMP messages delivered to the SNMP
            entity which used a SNMP community name not known to said
            entity."
    ::= { snmp 4 }

snmpInBadCommunityUses OBJECT-TYPE
    SYNTAX      Counter32
    MAX-ACCESS read-only
    STATUS      current
    DESCRIPTION
            "The total number of SNMP messages delivered to the SNMP
            entity which represented an SNMP operation which was not
            allowed by the SNMP community named in the message."
    ::= { snmp 5 }

snmpInASNParseErrs OBJECT-TYPE
    SYNTAX      Counter32
    MAX-ACCESS read-only
    STATUS      current
    DESCRIPTION
            "The total number of ASN.1 or BER errors encountered by the
            SNMP entity when decoding received SNMP messages."
    ::= { snmp 6 }

snmpEnableAuthenTraps OBJECT-TYPE
    SYNTAX      INTEGER { enabled(1), disabled(2) }
    MAX-ACCESS read-write
    STATUS      current
    DESCRIPTION
            "Indicates whether the SNMP entity is permitted to generate
            authenticationFailure traps.  The value of this object
            overrides any configuration information; as such, it
            provides a means whereby all authenticationFailure traps may
```

Figure 8-5. The SNMPv2 Management Information Base *(continued)*

```
                 be disabled.

                 Note that it is strongly recommended that this object be
                 stored in non-volatile memory so that it remains constant
                 across re-initializations of the network management system."
         ::= { snmp 30 }

snmpSilentDrops OBJECT-TYPE
     SYNTAX       Counter32
     MAX-ACCESS read-only
     STATUS       current
     DESCRIPTION
                 "The total number of GetRequest-PDUs, GetNextRequest-PDUs,
                 GetBulkRequest-PDUs, SetRequest-PDUs, and InformRequest-PDUs
                 delivered to the SNMP entity which were silently dropped
                 because the size of a reply containing an alternate
                 Response-PDU with an empty variable-bindings field was
                 greater than either a local constraint or the maximum
                 message size associated with the originator of the request."
         ::= { snmp 31 }

snmpProxyDrops OBJECT-TYPE
     SYNTAX       Counter32
     MAX-ACCESS read-only
     STATUS       current
     DESCRIPTION
                 "The total number of GetRequest-PDUs, GetNextRequest-PDUs,
                 GetBulkRequest-PDUs, SetRequest-PDUs, and InformRequest-PDUs
                 delivered to the SNMP entity which were silently dropped
                 because the transmission of the (possibly translated)
                 message to a proxy target failed in a manner (other than a
                 time-out) such that no Response-PDU could be returned."
         ::= { snmp 32 }


-- information for notifications
--
-- a collection of objects which allow the SNMPv2 entity, when
-- acting in an agent role, to be configured to generate
-- SNMPv2-Trap-PDUs.

snmpTrap        OBJECT IDENTIFIER ::= { snmpMIBObjects 4 }


snmpTrapOID OBJECT-TYPE
     SYNTAX       OBJECT IDENTIFIER
     MAX-ACCESS accessible-for-notify
     STATUS       current
     DESCRIPTION
                 "The authoritative identification of the notification
                 currently being sent.  This variable occurs as the second
                 varbind in every SNMPv2-Trap-PDU and InformRequest-PDU."
         ::= { snmpTrap 1 }

--  ::= { snmpTrap 2 }    this OID is obsolete

snmpTrapEnterprise OBJECT-TYPE
     SYNTAX       OBJECT IDENTIFIER
     MAX-ACCESS accessible-for-notify
     STATUS       current
     DESCRIPTION
```

Figure 8-5. The SNMPv2 Management Information Base *(continued)*

```
            "The authoritative identification of the enterprise
            associated with the trap currently being sent.  When a
            SNMPv2 proxy agent is mapping an RFC1157 Trap-PDU into a
            SNMPv2-Trap-PDU, this variable occurs as the last varbind."
    ::= { snmpTrap 3 }

--  ::= { snmpTrap 4 }    this OID is obsolete


-- well-known traps

snmpTraps       OBJECT IDENTIFIER ::= { snmpMIBObjects 5 }

coldStart NOTIFICATION-TYPE
    STATUS   current
    DESCRIPTION
            "A coldStart trap signifies that the SNMPv2 entity, acting
            in an agent role, is reinitializing itself and that its
            configuration may have been altered."
    ::= { snmpTraps 1 }

warmStart NOTIFICATION-TYPE
    STATUS   current
    DESCRIPTION
            "A warmStart trap signifies that the SNMPv2 entity, acting
            in an agent role, is reinitializing itself such that its
            configuration is unaltered."
    ::= { snmpTraps 2 }

-- Note the linkDown NOTIFICATION-TYPE ::= { snmpTraps 3 }
-- and the linkUp NOTIFICATION-TYPE ::= { snmpTraps 4 }
-- are defined in RFC 1573

authenticationFailure NOTIFICATION-TYPE
    STATUS   current
    DESCRIPTION
            "An authenticationFailure trap signifies that the SNMPv2
            entity, acting in an agent role, has received a protocol
            message that is not properly authenticated.  While all
            implementations of the SNMPv2 must be capable of generating
            this trap, the snmpEnableAuthenTraps object indicates
            whether this trap will be generated."
    ::= { snmpTraps 5 }

-- Note the egpNeighborLoss NOTIFICATION-TYPE ::= { snmpTraps 6 }
-- is defined in RFC 1213

-- the set group
--
-- a collection of objects which allow several cooperating
-- SNMPv2 entities, all acting in a manager role, to
-- coordinate their use of the SNMPv2 set operation.

snmpSet         OBJECT IDENTIFIER ::= { snmpMIBObjects 6 }


snmpSetSerialNo OBJECT-TYPE
    SYNTAX      TestAndIncr
    MAX-ACCESS read-write
    STATUS      current
    DESCRIPTION
```

Figure 8-5. The SNMPv2 Management Information Base *(continued)*

357

```
                "An advisory lock used to allow several cooperating SNMPv2
                entities, all acting in a manager role, to coordinate their
                use of the SNMPv2 set operation.

                This object is used for coarse-grain coordination.  To
                achieve fine-grain coordination, one or more similar objects
                might be defined within each MIB group, as appropriate."
        ::= { snmpSet 1 }


-- conformance information

snmpMIBConformance
                OBJECT IDENTIFIER ::= { snmpMIB 2 }

snmpMIBCompliances
                OBJECT IDENTIFIER ::= { snmpMIBConformance 1 }
snmpMIBGroups  OBJECT IDENTIFIER ::= { snmpMIBConformance 2 }


-- compliance statements

--    ::= { snmpMIBCompliances 1 }       this OID is obsolete

snmpBasicCompliance MODULE-COMPLIANCE
    STATUS   current
    DESCRIPTION
            "The compliance statement for SNMPv2 entities which
            implement the SNMPv2 MIB."
MODULE  -- this module
        MANDATORY-GROUPS { snmpGroup, snmpSetGroup, systemGroup,
                           snmpBasicNotificationsGroup }

        GROUP   snmpCommunityGroup
        DESCRIPTION
            "This group is mandatory for SNMPv2 entities which
            support community-based authentication."

    ::= { snmpMIBCompliances 2 }

-- units of conformance

--   ::= { snmpMIBGroups 1 }          this OID is obsolete
--   ::= { snmpMIBGroups 2 }          this OID is obsolete
--   ::= { snmpMIBGroups 3 }          this OID is obsolete
--   ::= { snmpMIBGroups 4 }          this OID is obsolete

snmpGroup OBJECT-GROUP
    OBJECTS { snmpInPkts,
              snmpInBadVersions,
              snmpInASNParseErrs,
              snmpSilentDrops,
              snmpProxyDrops,
              snmpEnableAuthenTraps }
    STATUS   current
    DESCRIPTION
            "A collection of objects providing basic instrumentation and
            control of an SNMPv2 entity."
    ::= { snmpMIBGroups 8 }

snmpCommunityGroup OBJECT-GROUP
```

Figure 8-5. The SNMPv2 Management Information Base *(continued)*

```
        OBJECTS { snmpInBadCommunityNames,
                  snmpInBadCommunityUses }
        STATUS  current
        DESCRIPTION
                "A collection of objects providing basic instrumentation of
                a SNMPv2 entity which supports community-based
                authentication."
        ::= { snmpMIBGroups 9 }

snmpSetGroup OBJECT-GROUP
        OBJECTS { snmpSetSerialNo }
        STATUS  current
        DESCRIPTION
                "A collection of objects which allow several cooperating
                SNMPv2 entities, all acting in a manager role, to coordinate
                their use of the SNMPv2 set operation."
        ::= { snmpMIBGroups 5 }

systemGroup OBJECT-GROUP
        OBJECTS { sysDescr, sysObjectID, sysUpTime,
                  sysContact, sysName, sysLocation,
                  sysServices,
                  sysORLastChange, sysORID,
                  sysORUpTime, sysORDescr }
        STATUS  current
        DESCRIPTION
                "The system group defines objects which are common to all
                managed systems."
        ::= { snmpMIBGroups 6 }

snmpBasicNotificationsGroup NOTIFICATION-GROUP
        NOTIFICATIONS { coldStart, authenticationFailure }
        STATUS        current
        DESCRIPTION
                "The two notifications which an SNMPv2 entity is required to
                implement."
        ::= { snmpMIBGroups 7 }


-- definitions in RFC 1213 made obsolete by the inclusion of a
-- subset of the snmp group in this MIB

snmpOutPkts OBJECT-TYPE
        SYNTAX      Counter32
        MAX-ACCESS  read-only
        STATUS      obsolete
        DESCRIPTION
                "The total number of SNMP Messages which were
                passed from the SNMP protocol entity to the
                transport service."
        ::= { snmp 2 }

-- { snmp 7 } is not used

snmpInTooBigs OBJECT-TYPE
        SYNTAX      Counter32
        MAX-ACCESS  read-only
        STATUS      obsolete
        DESCRIPTION
                "The total number of SNMP PDUs which were
                delivered to the SNMP protocol entity and for
```

Figure 8-5. The SNMPv2 Management Information Base *(continued)*

```
              which the value of the error-status field is
              `tooBig'."
      ::= { snmp 8 }

snmpInNoSuchNames OBJECT-TYPE
     SYNTAX        Counter32
     MAX-ACCESS    read-only
     STATUS        obsolete
     DESCRIPTION
              "The total number of SNMP PDUs which were
              delivered to the SNMP protocol entity and for
              which the value of the error-status field is
              `noSuchName'."
      ::= { snmp 9 }

snmpInBadValues OBJECT-TYPE
     SYNTAX        Counter32
     MAX-ACCESS    read-only
     STATUS        obsolete
     DESCRIPTION
              "The total number of SNMP PDUs which were
              delivered to the SNMP protocol entity and for
              which the value of the error-status field is
              `badValue'."
      ::= { snmp 10 }

snmpInReadOnlys OBJECT-TYPE
     SYNTAX        Counter32
     MAX-ACCESS    read-only
     STATUS        obsolete
     DESCRIPTION
              "The total number valid SNMP PDUs which were
              delivered to the SNMP protocol entity and for
              which the value of the error-status field is
              `readOnly'.  It should be noted that it is a
              protocol error to generate an SNMP PDU which
              contains the value `readOnly' in the error-status
              field, as such this object is provided as a means
              of detecting incorrect implementations of the
              SNMP."
      ::= { snmp 11 }

snmpInGenErrs OBJECT-TYPE
     SYNTAX        Counter32
     MAX-ACCESS    read-only
     STATUS        obsolete
     DESCRIPTION
              "The total number of SNMP PDUs which were
              delivered to the SNMP protocol entity and for
              which the value of the error-status field is
              `genErr'."
      ::= { snmp 12 }

snmpInTotalReqVars OBJECT-TYPE
     SYNTAX        Counter32
     MAX-ACCESS    read-only
     STATUS        obsolete
     DESCRIPTION
              "The total number of MIB objects which have been
              retrieved successfully by the SNMP protocol entity
              as the result of receiving valid SNMP Get-Request
```

Figure 8-5. The SNMPv2 Management Information Base *(continued)*

```
                    and Get-Next PDUs."
         ::= { snmp 13 }

snmpInTotalSetVars OBJECT-TYPE
     SYNTAX        Counter32
     MAX-ACCESS    read-only
     STATUS        obsolete
     DESCRIPTION
              "The total number of MIB objects which have been
              altered successfully by the SNMP protocol entity
              as the result of receiving valid SNMP Set-Request
              PDUs."
         ::= { snmp 14 }

snmpInGetRequests OBJECT-TYPE
     SYNTAX        Counter32
     MAX-ACCESS    read-only
     STATUS        obsolete
     DESCRIPTION
              "The total number of SNMP Get-Request PDUs which
              have been accepted and processed by the SNMP
              protocol entity."
         ::= { snmp 15 }

snmpInGetNexts OBJECT-TYPE
     SYNTAX        Counter32
     MAX-ACCESS    read-only
     STATUS        obsolete
     DESCRIPTION
              "The total number of SNMP Get-Next PDUs which have
              been accepted and processed by the SNMP protocol
              entity."
         ::= { snmp 16 }

snmpInSetRequests OBJECT-TYPE
     SYNTAX        Counter32
     MAX-ACCESS    read-only
     STATUS        obsolete
     DESCRIPTION
              "The total number of SNMP Set-Request PDUs which
              have been accepted and processed by the SNMP
              protocol entity."
         ::= { snmp 17 }

snmpInGetResponses OBJECT-TYPE
     SYNTAX        Counter32
     MAX-ACCESS    read-only
     STATUS        obsolete
     DESCRIPTION
              "The total number of SNMP Get-Response PDUs which
              have been accepted and processed by the SNMP
              protocol entity."
         ::= { snmp 18 }

snmpInTraps OBJECT-TYPE
     SYNTAX        Counter32
     MAX-ACCESS    read-only
     STATUS        obsolete
     DESCRIPTION
              "The total number of SNMP Trap PDUs which have
              been accepted and processed by the SNMP protocol
```

Figure 8-5. The SNMPv2 Management Information Base *(continued)*

```
            entity."
    ::= { snmp 19 }

snmpOutTooBigs OBJECT-TYPE
    SYNTAX        Counter32
    MAX-ACCESS  read-only
    STATUS        obsolete
    DESCRIPTION
            "The total number of SNMP PDUs which were
            generated by the SNMP protocol entity and for
            which the value of the error-status field is
            `tooBig.'"
    ::= { snmp 20 }

snmpOutNoSuchNames OBJECT-TYPE
    SYNTAX        Counter32
    MAX-ACCESS  read-only
    STATUS        obsolete
    DESCRIPTION
            "The total number of SNMP PDUs which were
            generated by the SNMP protocol entity and for
            which the value of the error-status is
            `noSuchName'."
    ::= { snmp 21 }

snmpOutBadValues OBJECT-TYPE
    SYNTAX        Counter32
    MAX-ACCESS  read-only
    STATUS        obsolete
    DESCRIPTION
            "The total number of SNMP PDUs which were
            generated by the SNMP protocol entity and for
            which the value of the error-status field is
            `badValue'."
    ::= { snmp 22 }


-- { snmp 23 } is not used

snmpOutGenErrs OBJECT-TYPE
    SYNTAX        Counter32
    MAX-ACCESS  read-only
    STATUS        obsolete
    DESCRIPTION
            "The total number of SNMP PDUs which were
            generated by the SNMP protocol entity and for
            which the value of the error-status field is
            `genErr'."
    ::= { snmp 24 }

snmpOutGetRequests OBJECT-TYPE
    SYNTAX        Counter32
    MAX-ACCESS  read-only
    STATUS        obsolete
    DESCRIPTION
            "The total number of SNMP Get-Request PDUs which
            have been generated by the SNMP protocol entity."
    ::= { snmp 25 }

snmpOutGetNexts OBJECT-TYPE
    SYNTAX        Counter32
```

Figure 8-5. The SNMPv2 Management Information Base *(continued)*

```
        MAX-ACCESS  read-only
        STATUS      obsolete
        DESCRIPTION
                "The total number of SNMP Get-Next PDUs which have
                been generated by the SNMP protocol entity."
        ::= { snmp 26 }

snmpOutSetRequests OBJECT-TYPE
        SYNTAX      Counter32
        MAX-ACCESS  read-only
        STATUS      obsolete
        DESCRIPTION
                "The total number of SNMP Set-Request PDUs which
                have been generated by the SNMP protocol entity."
        ::= { snmp 27 }

snmpOutGetResponses OBJECT-TYPE
        SYNTAX      Counter32
        MAX-ACCESS  read-only
        STATUS      obsolete
        DESCRIPTION
                "The total number of SNMP Get-Response PDUs which
                have been generated by the SNMP protocol entity."
        ::= { snmp 28 }

snmpOutTraps OBJECT-TYPE
        SYNTAX      Counter32
        MAX-ACCESS  read-only
        STATUS      obsolete
        DESCRIPTION
                "The total number of SNMP Trap PDUs which have
                been generated by the SNMP protocol entity."
        ::= { snmp 29 }

snmpObsoleteGroup OBJECT-GROUP
        OBJECTS { snmpOutPkts, snmpInTooBigs, snmpInNoSuchNames,
                snmpInBadValues, snmpInReadOnlys, snmpInGenErrs,
                snmpInTotalReqVars, snmpInTotalSetVars,
                snmpInGetRequests, snmpInGetNexts, snmpInSetRequests,
                snmpInGetResponses, snmpInTraps, snmpOutTooBigs,
                snmpOutNoSuchNames, snmpOutBadValues, snmpOutGenErrs,
                snmpOutGetRequests, snmpOutGetNexts, snmpOutSetRequests,
                snmpOutGetResponses, snmpOutTraps }
        STATUS  obsolete
        DESCRIPTION
                "A collection of objects from RFC 1213 made obsolete by this
                MIB."
        ::= { snmpMIBGroups 10 }

END
```

Figure 8-5. The SNMPv2 Management Information Base *(continued)*

REFERENCES FOR CHAPTER 8

[1] Tripp, Rhonda Thomas (compiler). *The International Thesaurus of Quotations.* New York: Thomas Y. Crowell Company. 1970.

[2] Rose, Marshall. *The Simple Book: An Introduction to Networking Management.* Upper Saddle River, NJ: Prentice-Hall. 1996.

The "Practice" of SNMP Version 1

Practice is nine-tenths.

—Ralph Waldo Emerson[1]

Practice is everything.

—Periander of Corinth[1]

The "practice" of SNMP is the design and implementation of the pieces that make up the management framework. This chapter contains the details and specifics for the design and implementation of the SNMP agent and the NMS.

9.1. THE SNMP REFERENCE MODEL REVISITED

Figure 2-14 in Chapter 2 shows the general structure of the SNMP network management framework. It shows the individual components of the system and the relationships between them.

Two distinct SNMP processing systems are of interest—the Network Management Station implementation and the agent implementation. For Version 2, the dual-role entity also includes both. Because SNMP is comprised of only a few different PDU types, any core implementation would include a generic SNMP Protocol Engine that executes the functions common for any implementation. The SNMP implementation must also include the interface to the transport system.

9.2. THE SNMP PROTOCOL ENGINE

The SNMP Protocol Engine contains the core protocol processes. In a well-thought-out design, both the NMS and the agent can be implemented around the protocol engine, simplifying the task of instrumenting network devices with an agent and of developing the NMS for the Network Manager.

In addition to the protocol engine, an SNMP implementation must have the proper software to interface to the transport layer, and to encode and decode the received SNMP messages in their ASN.1 format. It must contain the proper initialization and error handling code and any device-specific routines needed to specifically manage a particular device's hardware and software components.

To enhance portability and maintainability, the SNMP Protocol Engine and the necessary support functions are often bundled into one or more library modules. With this library, any SNMP implementation—be it an NMS or an agent—would only need to compile and link its platform-specific code with this SNMP library.

Note that I present the "practice" of SNMP in very general terms. The CASE diagrams contain components, data flows, and data stores that would be present in most implementations. The coding samples are a C/pseudo-code mixture, the intention of which is to demonstrate the procedural flow of an implementation. Any working code would need to provide all of the complementary software necessary to create an executable module representing a complete implementation for a specific device. This working code would include the header files, any additional support functions, debugging aids, MIB support tools, and so forth. Any of the freely available reference implementations available on the Internet contain all of the necessary components to make a working SNMP protocol engine.

The SNMP Library contains the necessary functions for any SNMP implementation. An SNMP Library includes some or all of these types of routines.

◆ Memory allocation and deallocation routines

◆ Buffer handling functions

◆ Print and display routines for debugging and local output

◆ ASN.1 decoding and encoding routines handling tags, lengths, and values

◆ PDU encoding and decoding routines, including Trap handling

◆ String manipulation routines

◆ Various error handling and processing procedures

◆ Transport service interface for sending and receiving SNMP Messages

◆ Authentication routines for version and community fields

◆ MIB handling and support functions

◆ "Hooks" for MIB variable instrumentation routines (dispatch tables, etc.)

◆ General routines: timers, memory copy functions, and so on

The discussion of the implementation uncovers the uses of these routines.

9.3. THE DESIGN OF THE AGENT

The agent software must be able to read and write the management variables, receive and transmit SNMP messages through the transport interface, and generate trap messages to configured managers in its community. Although the standard permits one or more transport interfaces, this design only considers UDP (the SNMP transport stack of choice).

9.3.1. SNMP AGENT DESIGN REFINEMENT

The agent design begins with a Context Diagram (CD) and is refined with the use of Data Flow Diagrams (DFD). The Context Diagram shows the system as one central process and represents the highest level of abstraction dealt with in the design. The Data Flow Diagrams depict the basic data objects needed for the system; they refine the Context Diagram. The design considers what actions are performed on these objects and also analyzes the necessary data flows and interactions with external processes.

9.3.1.1. *Agent Top Level Context Diagram*

The Context Diagram for the agent is the highest level diagram for the design. It shows the boundary between the agent process and its environment. The agent is represented by a single object type representing the processing it performs. The external entities represent the other components in the environment with which the agent must interact. The data flows represent real-world data used in the interactions.

In the CD are two major external entities, two data stores, and data flows connecting them all to the central agent process. Figure 9-1 depicts the Agent's Top Level Context Diagram.

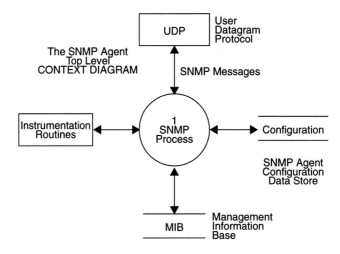

Figure 9-1. The SNMP Agent Top Level Context Diagram

9.3.1.1.1. *SNMP Process (1)*

The SNMP Process is the major process in the system, and it represents the agent. All of the processing to be done is represented as a single data process shown as the "large bubble."

9.3.1.1.2. *UDP External Process*

The User Datagram Protocol (UDP) is a connectionless-mode transport protocol that communicates between network entities on the internetwork. It, in turn, uses the Internet Protocol (IP), which interfaces to the Network Access hardware.

What is important to know for the agent design is that UDP receives and transmits application messages through well-defined ports of its socket interface. Each SNMP request, response, or trap message is transformed into a corresponding UDP datagram packet to be sent or received on the network.

The agent is designed as a server application. After being successfully initialized, it enters a "forever" loop waiting to receive SNMP requests from its client (i.e., the NMS). After it receives a request, it processes it, and, if appropriate, it sends a response. A provision has also been made so that the server can send asynchronous trap events to the client, informing the NMS of some predefined, extraordinary condition that has occurred.

9.3.1.1.3. *Host Instrumentation Code External Processes*

The Host Instrumentation Code External Processes are the agent instrumentation routines for MIB variables that reside on the agent's network device. These routines determine if the requested object is in the agent's MIB, verifies the access mode, knows where the object is located, and can retrieve or set its value.

9.3.1.1.4. *Configuration Data Store*

The Configuration Data Store stores the configuration information the agent needs. This information is typically read at initialization time, to retrieve the necessary parameters, addresses, and other information necessary to start up operations and to enter the loop to read and write SNMP messages.

Specific elements that can be contained in this data store are implementation-dependent, but several examples include such things as initial start-up parameters, default mode settings for options, initial NMSs' IP addresses for traps, the community string(s), transmission and internal buffer sizes, and so forth.

◆ The Community Name: defines the community name for the agent

◆ The View: defines the collection(s) of managed objects

◆ Trap NMS Destinations: define locations of NMSs where traps can be sent

◆ System Group variables: contain description, contact, name, and location

◆ Logging: configures local logging facility

9.3.1.1.5. *MIB Data Store*

The MIB Data Store is the virtual storage area for the managed objects in the MIB.

9.3.1.2. *Agent First Level Data Flow Diagram*

The Data Flow Diagrams (DFD) for the agent refine the CD and show its processing activities. Each DFD is comprised of processes, data stores, and data flow. The processes are diagrammed as circles, the data stores as parallel horizontal bars, and the flow of data in the system as arrows with the arrowheads indicating the direction of the data flow.

In this DFD are three processes, two major external entities (UDP and the Instrumentation Routines), two data stores (the MIB and the Configuration file), and data flows connecting them. Figure 9-2 depicts the Agent's First Level Data Flow Diagram.

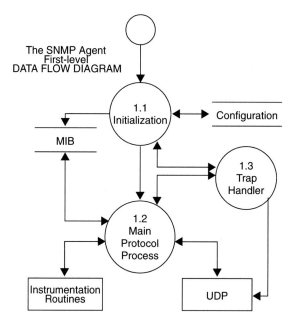

Figure 9-2. The SNMP Agent First Level Data Flow Diagram

9.3.1.2.1. Initialization Process (1.1)

The Initialization Process processes the Configuration data store, initializes the transport interface, and does any necessary MIB set-up and initial assignment.

9.3.1.2.2. Main Protocol Process (1.2)

The Main Protocol Process handles the receiving, decoding, parsing, translating, executing, encoding, and transmitting of SNMP Messages.

9.3.1.2.3. Trap Handler Process (1.3)

The Trap Handler Process handles the processing of Traps by realizing a trap needs to be sent. The Trap message is formatted and then sent to the appropriate NMS(s) in its list.

9.3.1.3. Agent Second Level Data Flow Diagram: Initialization

Figure 9-3 refines the top level DFD. Three processes are in this DFD: Process Configuration Data, Initialize the UDP Interface, and Initialize MIB. The UDP external process and the MIB and Configuration data stores also appear.

9.3.1.3.1. Process Configuration Data (1.1.1)

The Process Configuration Data process handles reading the Configuration file and using those values to set the appropriate values in the agent and MIB software.

9.3.1.3.2. Initialize UDP Interface (1.1.2)

The Initialize UDP Interface process sets up the application/transport interface. If a socket-type interface has been implemented, the agent must first do a socket call to get the socket descriptor handle and then "bind" to the socket ports. The agent is now ready to receive data from UDP.

9.3.1.3.3. Initialize MIB (1.1.3)

The Initialize MIB initializes the MIB by setting appropriate initial and default values.

9.3.1.4. Agent Second Level DFD: Main Protocol Process

Figure 9-4 also refines the top level DFD. The six processes that compose this DFD are the core of the SNMP agent code:

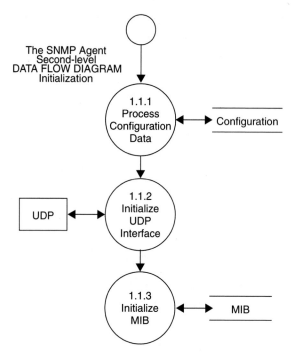

Figure 9-3. The SNMP Agent Second Level DFD:
Initialization

◆ Receive Incoming SNMP Request

◆ Parse and Translate into Internal Format

◆ Map MIB Variable into Local Equivalent

◆ Perform Requested Get/Set Operation

◆ Translate Reply to External Format

◆ Send Response to Requesting Client

The UDP send and receive external processes, the Instrumentation Routines, and the MIB data store also appear in Figure 9-4.

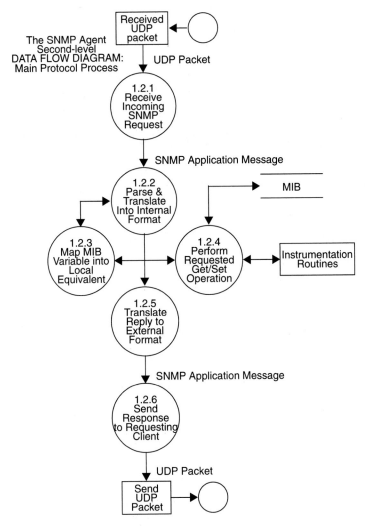

Figure 9-4. The SNMP Agent Second Level DFD: Main Protocol Process

9.3.1.4.1. *Receive Incoming SNMP Request (1.2.1)*

The Receive Incoming SNMP Request process reads an incoming request from the transport interface. If the socket interface is present, the `recvfrom()` call is made. It places it into an internal buffer and remembers the size of the packet.

9.3.1.4.2. Parse and Translate into Internal Format (1.2.2)

Because the ASN.1 format allows for variable length fields, the SNMP Message fields cannot be mapped directly into a fixed internal data structure in the agent's code. The Parse and Translate Into Internal Format process handles the parsing and converting of the input SNMP Message into a usable internal data structure from which the agent code can then operate.

9.3.1.4.3. Map MIB Variable into Local Equivalent (1.2.3)

The requested MIB variables are mapped into an internal, local format, in order to have the instrumentation routines begin their work. The first job of the code is to determine if the requested MIB object is present in this agent's MIB.

9.3.1.4.4. Perform Requested Get/Set Operation (1.2.4)

If the MIB object is present, the Perform Requested Get/Set Operation verifies the access mode and then performs the requested `GetRequest-PDU`, `Get-NextRequest-PDU`, or `SetRequest-PDU` operation on the objects in the SNMP Message's variable binding list. This process also must handle any error that occurs in this processing. For Version 2, the `GetBulkRequest-PDU` operation is also performed.

9.3.1.4.5. Translate Reply to External Format (1.2.5)

After the command has been carried out, the internal buffer needs to be transformed back into ASN.1 format for transmission to the NMS in the internetwork.

9.3.1.4.6. Send Response to Requesting Client (1.2.6)

The Send Response to Requesting Client process sends the SNMP packet to the UDP layer for transmission back to the NMS. If the agent is using the socket interface, the agent makes a `sendto()` call with the outgoing SNMP Message as the data is being sent.

9.3.1.5. Agent Second Level DFD: Trap Handler

Figure 9-5 represents the third refinement of the top level DFD. Three processes are in this DFD: Process Trap Request, Serialize into ASN.1 Format, and Send Response to Requesting Client. Figure 9-5 also shows the UDP external process.

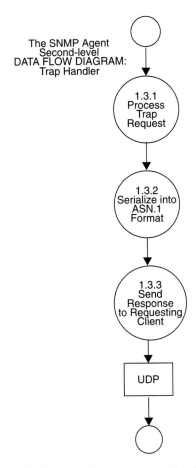

Figure 9-5. The SNMP Agent Second Level DFD: Trap Handler

9.3.1.5.1. *Process Trap Request (1.3.1)*

The Process Trap Request process is called by the agent code in the appropriate place when a trap needs to be sent. This determination of when and if a trap needs to be sent includes sending a `coldStart` or `warmStart` trap at initialization time, sending `linkUp` and `linkDown` traps if this condition is detected, sending any enterprise specific traps, and so forth. Note that the agent must be configured to send traps; otherwise, this function merely returns and doesn't send the `Trap-PDU` Message.

9.3.1.5.2. *Serialize into ASN.1 Format (1.3.2)*

This procedure takes the internal information and formats it into ASN.1 syntax, if a trap is to be sent. It places the appropriate values in the proper places of the SNMP Trap Message. Note that the formats for Version 1 and Version 2 are slightly different. The agent allocates and frees memory for this buffer, if necessary.

9.3.1.5.3. *Send Response to Requesting Client (1.3.3)*

The Send Response to Requesting Client process sends the SNMP Trap Message to the UDP layer for transmission back to the NMS. If the agent is using the socket interface, the agent will make a `sendto()` call with the outgoing SNMP Message as the data is being sent. The agent must know the internet address of the NMS(s) to which this trap will be sent. This address is typically a configuration item.

9.3.1.6. *Agent Third Level DFD: Receive Incoming Request*

Figure 9-6 refines the second level DFD process, Receive Incoming SNMP Request (1.2.1). Six processes are in this DFD:

◆ Check ASN.1 Type

◆ Check ASN.1 Value

◆ Check ASN.1 Length

◆ Validate SNMP Version

◆ Validate SNMP Community

◆ Allocate Buffer

A data flow to the Trap Handler Process (1.3) also appears in Figure 9-6, in case an invalid Community name is received and the agent is configured to send a trap for this condition.

9.3.1.6.1. *Check ASN.1 Type (1.2.1.1)*

This process checks the ASN.1 Type Field to be sure that it is valid.

9.3.1.6.2. *Check ASN.1 Value (1.2.1.2)*

This process checks and validates the ASN.1 Value Field.

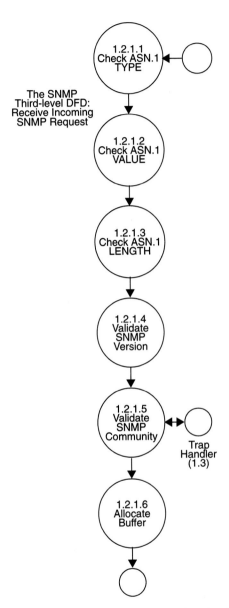

Figure 9-6. The SNMP Agent Third Level DFD: Receive SNMP Request

9.3.1.6.3. Check ASN.1 Length (1.2.1.3)

The ASN.1 Length Field is checked and validated by this process.

9.3.1.6.4. Validate SNMP Version (1.2.1.4)

The Validate SNMP Version process compares the received SNMP version number value with its configured SNMP version value, to be sure that they are the same. No negotiation mechanism is currently defined for the protocol, and a mismatch of the version numbers causes the received message to be discarded. Version 1 is a *0* and Version 2 is a *1*.

9.3.1.6.5. Validate SNMP Community (1.2.1.5)

The Validate SNMP Community process compares the received SNMP community name with the community name for which the agent is configured. If they do not match and the agent is configured to send a trap for this condition (snmpEnableAuthenTraps = *true*), the Trap handling function is called. The message is discarded.

9.3.1.6.6. Allocate Buffer (1.2.1.6)

This process allocates a buffer from the agent's memory space to handle the internal processing of the message. Typically the agent assumes the request will generate a response and begins to fill this buffer as the request is processed with information that is common to every response.

9.3.1.7. Agent Third Level DFD: Parse and Translate

Figure 9-7 refines the second level DFD process, Parse and Translate into Internal Format (1.2.2). Nine processes are in this DFD for Version 1. For Version 2, the additional GetBulkRequest-PDU function needs to be added.

♦ Process PDU Type

♦ Get Request PDU

♦ Get-Next Request PDU

♦ Set Request PDU

♦ Invalid Request PDU

♦ Get Request Common PDU Process

♦ Process Set Request PDU

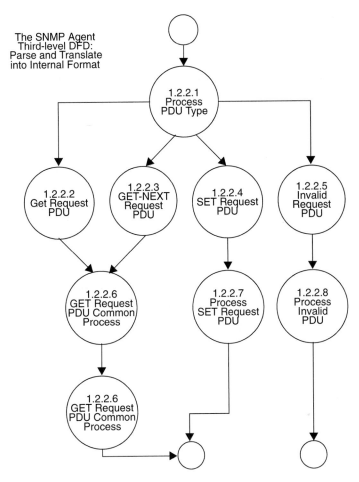

The SNMP Agent
Third-level DFD:
Parse and Translate
into Internal Format

Figure 9-7. The SNMP Agent 3rd Level DFD: Parse and Translate

- Process Invalid PDU
- Process Get Request Class

9.3.1.7.1. *Process PDU Type (1.2.2.1)*

This process determines the PDU type of the SNMP Message Request. It then calls the appropriate function to process that particular PDU type.

9.3.1.7.2. Get Request PDU (1.2.2.2)

This process handles the GetRequest-PDU type.

9.3.1.7.3. Get-Next PDU Request PDU (1.2.2.3)

This process handles the GetNextRequest-PDU type.

9.3.1.7.4. Set Request PDU (1.2.2.4)

This process handles the SetRequest-PDU type.

9.3.1.7.5. Invalid Request PDU (1.2.2.5)

If the PDU type is invalid (that is, not one of the three aforementioned types), the Invalid Request PDU function is called to handle this condition.

9.3.1.7.6. Get Request PDU Common Process (1.2.2.6)

Once the Get-Next target object has been identified, the "getting" operation of the Get and Get-Next are the same. The GetRequest-PDU Common Process handles this implementation commonality.

9.3.1.7.7. Process Set Request PDU (1.2.2.7)

This process does the subsequent actions of mapping the set request into internal format by setting up the necessary fields.

9.3.1.7.8. Process Invalid PDU (1.2.2.8)

This process handles the internal mapping of the invalid PDU condition and prepares the get response message with the error condition noted.

9.3.1.7.9. Process Get Request Class (1.2.2.9)

This process does the subsequent actions of mapping the get request into the internal format by setting up the requisite fields.

9.3.1.8. Agent Third Level DFD: Map MIB Variable

Figure 9-8 refines the second level DFD process, Map MIB Variable into Local Equivalent (1.2.3). One process is in this DFD: Create Variable Binding List.

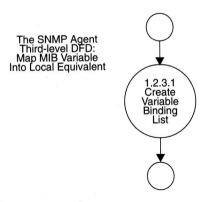

The SNMP Agent
Third-level DFD:
Map MIB Variable
Into Local Equivalent

1.2.3.1
Create
Variable
Binding
List

Figure 9-8. The SNMP Agent Third Level DFD:
Map MIB Into Local

9.3.1.8.1. *Create Variable Binding List (1.2.3.1)*

The Create Variable Binding List process prepares the internal representation for the object identifiers that are for the requested objects from the variable bindings list.

9.3.1.9. *Agent Third Level DFD: Perform Get/Set Operation*

Figure 9-9 refines the second level DFD process, Perform Requested Get/Set Operation (1.2.4). Two processes are in this DFD: Check for Existence and Call Object Instrumentation Routine. The Instrumentation Routine's external process also appears in Figure 9-9.

9.3.1.9.1. *Check for Existence (1.2.4.1)*

The purpose of this process is to determine whether the now-in-internal-format object identifiers for the objects requested, in fact, exist for this agent's MIB.

9.3.1.9.2. *Call Object Instrumentation Routine (1.2.4.2)*

If the object exists, its corresponding instrumentation routine is called to carry out the prescribed command request on the variable. This process knows how to find and access the internal representation of the MIB variable to effect the management request desired by the NMS.

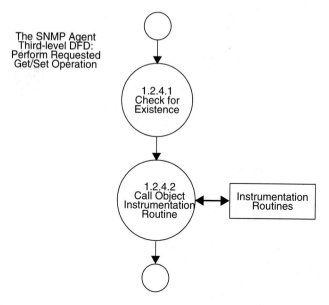

Figure 9-9. The SNMP Agent Third Level DFD: Perform Operation

9.3.1.10. *Agent Third Level DFD: Translate Reply*

Figure 9-10 refines the second level DFD process, Translate Reply to External Format (1.2.5). Five processes are in this DFD. Note that this is specifically for Version 1. For Version 2, the Response-PDU type is required instead of `Get-Response-PDU`, and the error handling needs to include the Version 2 exception processing for *noSuchObject*, *noSuchInstance*, and *endOfMibView*.

- ◆ Insert PDU Type
- ◆ Insert PDU Length
- ◆ Insert PDU Request ID
- ◆ Insert Error Status and Index
- ◆ Insert Updated Variable Binding List

9.3.1.10.1. *Insert PDU Type (1.2.5.1)*

This process inserts the PDU type for the `GetResponse-PDU` type.

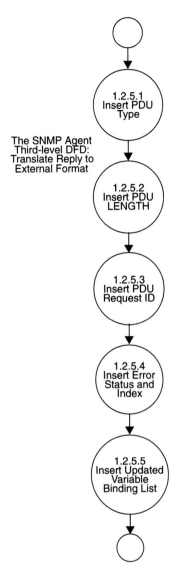

Figure 9-10. The SNMP Agent Third Level DFD: Translate Reply

9.3.1.10.2. *Insert PDU Length (1.2.5.2)*

This process inserts the PDU length for the GetResponse-PDU type.

9.3.1.10.3. Insert PDU Request ID (1.2.5.3)

This process inserts the PDU Request ID for the GetResponse-PDU type. This value was saved from a previously received Request ID from a request that caused this response to be generated.

9.3.1.10.4. Insert Error Status and Index (1.2.5.4)

This process inserts the Error Status and Error Index fields for the Get-Response-PDU type.

9.3.1.10.5. Insert Updated Variable Binding List (1.2.5.5)

This process inserts the now updated variable binding list into the response message buffer for the GetResponse-PDU type.

9.3.1.11. Agent Third Level DFD: Send Response

Figure 9-11 refines the second level DFD process, Send Response to Requesting Client (1.2.6). Five processes are in this DFD:

◆ Insert SNMP Community

◆ Insert SNMP Version

◆ Insert ASN.1 Type

◆ Insert ASN.1 Value

◆ Insert ASN.1 Length

These functions complete the necessary fields for the outgoing response that is sent to the NMS: GetResponse-PDU for Version 1 and Response-PDU for Version 2.

9.3.1.11.1. Insert SNMP Community (1.2.6.1)

This process inserts the agent's SNMP community name string.

9.3.1.11.2. Insert SNMP Version (1.2.6.2)

This process inserts the agent's SNMP version number field value: 0 for Version 1 and 1 for Version 2.

9.3.1.11.3. Insert ASN.1 Type (1.2.6.3)

This process inserts the SNMP Message's ASN.1 Type.

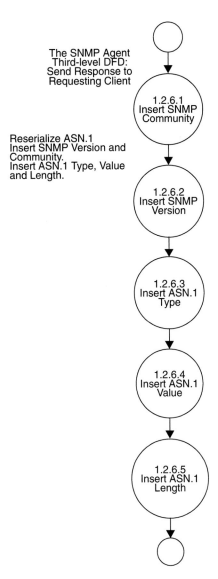

The SNMP Agent
Third-level DFD:
Send Response to
Requesting Client

Reserialize ASN.1
Insert SNMP Version and
Community.
Insert ASN.1 Type, Value
and Length.

Figure 9-11. The SNMP Agent Third Level DFD: Send Response

9.3.1.11.4. Insert ASN.1 Value (1.2.6.4)

This process inserts the SNMP Message's ASN.1 Value.

9.3.1.11.5. *Insert ASN.1 Length (1.2.6.5)*

This process inserts the SNMP Message's ASN.1 Length.

9.4. THE IMPLEMENTATION OF THE AGENT

Once the agent has successfully completed its initialization, it enters a "forever read loop." It waits to receive datagrams from the Transport Layer at its port, examines and decodes the SNMP message, executes the command it contains, calls the proper MIB instrumentation routines to set or get the variables, encodes and prepares the SNMP response Message, and finally transmits the message by encapsulating it as a UDP datagram and sending it on the SNMP port.

Figure 9-12 demonstrates that at the highest level, the agent process can be seen as six major functions. These functions are:

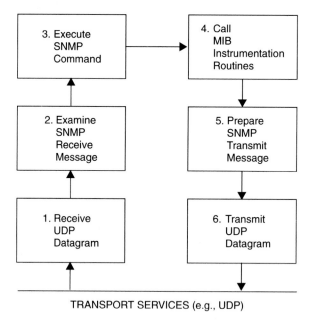

TRANSPORT SERVICES (e.g., UDP)

Figure 9-12. The SNMP Agent Top Level Flowchart

1. Receive the UDP Datagram
2. Examine the SNMP Receive Message
3. Execute the SNMP Command
4. Call the MIB Instrumentation Routines
5. Prepare the SNMP Transmit Message
6. Transmit the UDP Datagram

The intent of the following pseudocode sections is to give a top-level view of how the "main read loop" implementation can be done for a Version 1 SNMP agent. A complete implementation involves a great deal more code than I present here. "In practice, many small details complicate the code."[4] For a Version 2 implementation, additional functionality would include the GetBulk-PDU, the v2 exception processing, different use of the SNMP MIB-II counters, and other slight modifications and additions.

The following functions show a procedural flow in which the agent receives a message, decodes the ASN.1, converts it to an internal representation, executes the PDU command, creates a response, encodes the ASN.1, and then transmits the response PDU. That the initialization and agent configuration has been done successfully is assumed.

All of the coding examples are written in a C-like pseudocode with comments.

Only the six major functions are pseudocoded here. Many more minor details need to be included in the subsequent supporting functions and data structure definitions to provide for a complete implementation. All of the hardware and software device-specific issues have to be understood, designed, and coded. The necessary header files, make files, all sub-functions, error-handling routines, and any additional code also have to be written to create a complete executable agent implementation.

Also, the pseudocode is written to demonstrate functionality. All subsequent implementations can certainly be optimized and made more efficient. Singular ASN.1 tag decoding and encoding routines should be included. Routines for efficient memory management should be defined. How function parameters are defined and passed, how pointers are used, and how internal data structures are defined must be done correctly. Other activities include assuring proper modularity, writing robust error handling, reducing any redundancy in handling how the existence of the MIB variables is discovered, optimizing how the variables are read and written, and so forth. Any complete reference implementation that you view reveals these details and how things are implemented in slightly different fashions. The actual agent implementations are done in a variety of different programming languages for any number of environments.

The C and C++ programming languages have long been favorites for system- and application-level programming tasks such as SNMP implementations and network management applications. New programming languages are constantly evolving, offering new features that can be used for implementations such as SNMP agents and NMSs.

How to Manage Your Network Using SNMP: The Network Management Practicum[2] by Marshall Rose and Keith McCloghrie presents network management application code and other tools written in the scripting language TCL (Tool Command Language), with its accompanying GUI called Tk. Other implementations exist in PERL, various assembly languages, Java, Fortran, Basic, and many others.

9.4.1. RECEIVE THE UDP DATAGRAM

This function is called when an SNMP Message arrives for the agent. If the UDP Transport function (or the Socket Library interface, if used) returns successfully, the agent has an SNMP message in its buffer and its length. The code must have a buffer ready to accept the largest possible SNMP message.

```
/*(1)*******************************************************************/
/* FUNCTION NAME: Receive_The_UDP_Datagram()                         */
/* FUNCTION DESCRIPTION: This function returns with a received SNMP  */
/*     Message for the SNMP agent in a buffer.                       */
/* INPUTS: void                                                      */
/* OUTPUTS: BYTE -- result code from the received process:           */
/*       GOOD_RCV or BAD_RCV                                         */
/* OUTPUTS: BYTE -- result code from the received process            */
/* NOTE: For the purpose of example, the SNMP agent's receive buffer */
/*     and its length are made global for simplification.            */
/********************************************************************/
char MsgBuf[MAX_BUF_SIZE];      // constant equal to maximum receive pkt
unsigned int MsgLen;            // Message Length

BYTE Receive_The_UDP_Datagram(void)
   {
   BYTE ReceiveRC;              // result code of receive

   ReceiveRC = GOOD_RCV;        // initialize Result Code to success

   // Wait for Transport Layer Interface to return an SNMP Message
   // If the socket interface is used, code for handling SNMP socket
   //      must be added. The socket() and bind() calls should have
```

```
//      been successfully called, and the recvfrom() call waits for
//      the transport message.
// Transport Call should return GOOD or BAD

if ((MsgLen = Transport_Receive (MsgBuf)) <= 0)
   {
   ReceiveRC = BAD_RCV;           // less or = 0 indicates an error
                                  // should add error handling to return
                                  // and report exact error

   }
return (ReceiveRC);

} // endfunc: Receive_The_UDP_Datagram()
```

9.4.1.1. *Sample Input Data Path Data Flow Diagram*

Figure 9-13 shows an example of an input data flow for an Ethernet LAN network. Three processes and external entities exist for the network card and its device driver. The UDP port, the device driver output queue, and the Ethernet network also appear in Figure 9-13 as data stores. The SNMP Server process is the agent. The agent process reads from UDP port #161. The UDP Process implements the User Datagram Protocol and receives the UDP datagrams for the SNMP agent/server. The IP Process is the implementation of the Internet Protocol. It receives IP Packets for the UDP transport protocol above. It also interfaces to the network access layer below.

9.4.1.2. *The Socket Interface*

The socket interface is one of the most commonly used APIs for interfacing applications such as SNMP to the transport layer. Figure 9-14[3] shows the sequencing of function calls to the socket interface for a connectionless protocol such as UDP.

The socket() call takes the address "family" name, the type, and the protocol. The family name for the Internet protocols is the constant *AF_INET*. (Note: the actual constant values vary with implementations; these are common values, offered as examples. Please consult the documentation of your implementation for the specific syntax.) The type field is set for the datagram connection needed for UDP (e.g., *SOCK_DGRAM*). The protocol is, of course, UDP (e.g., *IPPROTO_UDP*). If this function is successful, the socket descriptor (*sd*) is returned. This *sd* is an important input parameter for the subsequent socket calls. If the call is not successful, various error codes are returned. These are typically negative values.

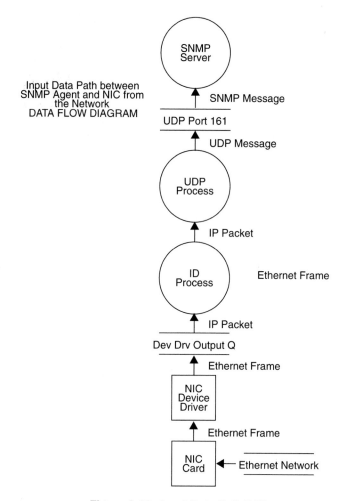

Input Data Path between
SNMP Agent and NIC from
the Network
DATA FLOW DIAGRAM

Figure 9-13. Input Data Path DFD

After the SNMP application gets a socket, it needs to bind to it in order to register the well-known SNMP port number with the interface. The bind() call is made with the socket descriptor, an address to the socket address data structure, and the length of that data structure. This function typically returns a 0 for success, and an error code, otherwise.

The recvfrom() call reads datagrams from the socket interface. The socket descriptor, a pointer to a receive buffer, and the maximum number of bytes that can be accepted are typically the formal input parameters. The maximum num-

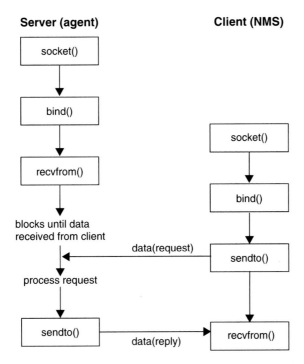

Figure 9-14. Socket Calls for Connectionless Protocol

ber of bytes that can be received equals the maximum size of the input buffer. If the read is successful, this function returns the number of bytes received. If an error occurred, a negative number representing the error is returned.

The `sendto()` call sends datagrams. The formal input parameters are generally the socket descriptor, a pointer to a transmit buffer, and the number of bytes to be sent. If the write is successful, this function returns the number of bytes transmitted. If an error occurs, a negative number representing that error is returned.

The WinSock API is an important standard socket interface API for Windows-based applications that implement the TCP/IP protocol suite. In addition to providing the socket interface, the WinSock specification includes standardized interfaces for database routines and Microsoft Windows-specific extensions.

Winsock was first released as Version 1.1 in 1993. Version 2.0 is currently available. It includes support for other transport services, such as Novell's IPX protocol. A primary source for WinSock code and information is `http://www.stardust.com`.

9.4.2. EXAMINE THE SNMP RECEIVE MESSAGE

This group of functions decodes the received SNMP message by verifying the ASN.1 fields and values and making sure that any encoded lengths are correct. These functions also check the required fields of the SNMP Message, and categorize the message as one of the five SNMP PDU types for Version 1. Remember, the agent is expecting only the `SetRequest-PDU`, the `GetRequest-PDU`, or the `GetNextRequest-PDU`. Any other PDU type received by an agent implementation is an error. The Version 2 agent must also process the `GetBulk-PDU`.

The software assumes that it has received a valid SNMP message, and as soon as the preliminary decoding succeeds, the construction of a working internal representation of the SNMP Message begins.

If a field is extracted and found to be incorrect, the corresponding SNMP counter tracking a particular error condition is incremented and the error handling is invoked. If the decoding fails in the early stages, error processing simply discards the message and a response PDU acknowledgment is not sent. The NMS can subsequently poll the SNMP MIB variables that contain the error counters, to get a more accurate portrait of what is happening at a particular agent.

```
/*(2)****************************************************************/
/* FUNCTION NAME: Examine_SNMP_Receive_Message()                   */
/* FUNCTION DESCRIPTION: This function begins the decoding of the SNMP*/
/*    message.                                                      */
/* INPUTS: void (for this example, the SNMP Message Buffer (MsgBuf) */
/*    and its length (MsgLen) are stored in "global" memory).       */
/* OUTPUTS: BYTE -- result code from the decoding process           */
/*    error codes need to be #'defined; DECODED for success;        */
/*****************************************************************/
BYTE Examine_SNMP_Receive_Message(void)
    {
    BYTE ReceiveDecodeResult;      // result code of decoding this message
    SNMP_MESSAGE *MsgPtr;          // SNMP message pointer

    MsgPtr = MsgBuf;                       // point at the received message
    ReceiveDecodeResult = DECODED_OK;      // initialize the Result Code

    // First, decode the "outer" message wrapper: TAG and LENGTH
    // +-------------------------------------------------+--------+-------+
    // | TAG: universal constructed sequence -- 0x30 | LENGTH | VALUE |
    // +-------------------------------------------------+--------+-------+
```

```
// The TAG or TYPE IDENTIFIER (see section 3.2.1.1. The Tag (Type
// Identifier) consists of 3 parts: Class, "F" bit, and Tag Number.
// The first TAG encountered should be: Universal, Constructed, and
// Sequence or: 00-1-1000 (0x30 in hex). Any ASN.1 Tag decoding and
// encoding routine must deal with the three parts of the TAG.
//
if the GetTag() function does not return UNIVERSAL_CONSTRUCTED_SEQUENCE
    {
    snmpInASNParseErrs++; // increment the snmpInASNParseErrs counter
    ReceiveDecodeResult = BAD_TAG_VALUE;
    return (ReceiveDecodeResult);
    }
if the GetASN1Len() function returns INVALID_ASN1_LENGTH_FORMAT
    {
    snmpInASNParseErrs++; // increment the snmpInASNParseErrs counter
    ReceiveDecodeResult = BAD_LENGTH_FORMAT;
    return (ReceiveDecodeResult);
    }

// The length calculated must be in valid format. The ASN.1 length
// decoding function must handle both the short and long forms (i.e.,
// whether the length is encoded in a single octet or not; see
// section 3.2.1.2. The Length Identifier for the specifics).
//
// Now, compare the decoded length with actual input parameter value
// given when the function was called (MsgLen). The decoded length in
// any part of the SNMP Packet indicates the size of the value field.
if (the lengths do not match)
    {
    ReceiveDecodeResult = BAD_LENGTH_VALUE;
    return (ReceiveDecodeResult);
    }

// Now that the message looks good, the agent should allocate an
// internal buffer of sufficient size and start processing the SNMP
// Message. The Allocate Memory function returns a pointer to the
// buffer if successful.
if (Allocate Memory() function fails)
    {
    snmpInGenErrs++;              // increment the snmpInGenErrs counter
    ReceiveDecodeResult = BAD_MEM_ALLOC;
    return (ReceiveDecodeResult);
    }

// The first field in the SNMP Message is the VERSION Field. Its ASN.1
// Tag, Length, and Value Field must be decoded and verified.
// VERSION FIELD:
// +---------------------+----------------+--------------------+
// | TAG: INTEGER -- 0x02 | LENGTH -- (0x01)| VALUE (usually 0x00)|
// +---------------------+----------------+--------------------+
//
if the GetVersion() function does not return INTEGER
    {
    snmpInASNParseErrs++; // increment the snmpInASNParseErrs counter
    ReceiveDecodeResult = BAD_VERSION_FORMAT;
    return (ReceiveDecodeResult);
    }
if the GetASN1Len() function returns INVALID_ASN1_LENGTH_FORMAT
    {
    snmpInASNParseErrs++; // increment the snmpInASNParseErrs counter
    ReceiveDecodeResult = BAD_LENGTH_FORMAT;
    return (ReceiveDecodeResult);
    }
```

```
// The agent now gets & validates the Version number (it's usually 0).
//
VersionNumber = GetVersionNumber();
if ValidateVersion(VersionNumber) function does not return MATCH
   {
   snmpInBadVersions++; // increment the snmpInBadVersions counter
   ReceiveDecodeResult = BAD_VERSION_VALUE;
   return (ReceiveDecodeResult);
   }


// The second field in the SNMP Message is the Community Name Field.
// Its ASN.1 Tag, Length, and Value Field must be decoded and verified.
// COMMUNITY NAME FIELD:
// +-------------------------+-------------------+---------------+
// | TAG: OCTET STRING -- 0x04 | LENGTH -- (varies)| VALUE (varies)|
// +-------------------------+-------------------+---------------+
//
if the GetCommunityName() function does not return OCTET STRING
   {
   snmpInASNParseErrs++; // increment the snmpInASNParseErrs counter
   ReceiveDecodeResult = BAD_COMMUNITY_NAME_FORMAT;
   return (ReceiveDecodeResult);
   }
if the GetASN1Len() function returns INVALID_ASN1_LENGTH_FORMAT
   {
   snmpInASNParseErrs++; // increment the snmpInASNParseErrs counter
   ReceiveDecodeResult = BAD_LENGTH_FORMAT;
   return (ReceiveDecodeResult);
   }

// The agent now gets & validates the Community Name. The string
// "public" is often used as a common default value.
//
CommunityName = GetCommunityNumber();    // Note this is a string
if ValidateCommunity(CommunityName) function does not return MATCH
   {
   snmpInBadCommunityNames++;  // increment snmpInBadCommunityNames
   ReceiveDecodeResult = BAD_COMMUNITY_NAME_VALUE;
   // At this point, if the agent is so configured it sends out an
   // Authentication Failure Trap to all of the NMSs in its community.
   Generate_Auth_Fail_Trap();

   // NOTE: this function checks the Authentication flag and then calls
   // the generic trap sending routine. The trap sending function should
   // know the IP Address of the NMS(s). Remember, the traps are not
   // acknowledged by the NMSs, so you don't get a response.
   //
   //      void Generate_Auth_Fail_Trap(void)
   //         {
   //         if (snmpEnableAuthTraps == TRUE)
   //            {
   //            Send_Trap(AUTHENTICATION_FAILURE);
   //            snmpOutPkts++;      // increment Output Packet counter
   //            snmpOutTraps++;     // increment Trap counter
   //            }
   //         return;
   //         } //endfunc: Generate_Auth_Fail_Trap()
   //
   return (ReceiveDecodeResult);
   }

// The third field in the SNMP Message is the PDU Field.
```

```
// Its ASN.1 Tag, Length, and Value Field must be decoded and verified.
// PDU FIELD:
// +------------------+------------------+--------------------+
// | TAG:  -- *0xA(n) | LENGTH -- (varies)| VALUE (PDU: varies)|
// +------------------+------------------+--------------------+
// *Note: the TAG field is CONTEXT-SPECIFIC CONSTRUCTED VALUE that has
// 0xAn where "n" is the value of the PDU. Therefore:
//
//       GetRequest PDU TAG Value     == 0xA0 -- rcv by agent
//       GetNextRequest PDU TAG Value == 0xA1 -- rcv by agent
//       GetResponse PDU TAG Value    == 0xA2 -- rcv by NMS
//       SetRequest PDU TAG Value     == 0xA3 -- rcv by agent
//       Trap PDU TAG Value           == 0xA4 -- rcv by NMS
//
if the PDUOpCode = GetPDUTag() does not return 0xA0, 0xA1, or 0xA3
    {
    snmpInASNParseErrs++; // increment the snmpInASNParseErrs counter
    ReceiveDecodeResult = BAD_PDU_FORMAT;
    return (ReceiveDecodeResult);
    }
if the GetASN1Len() function returns INVALID_ASN1_LENGTH_FORMAT
    {
    snmpInASNParseErrs++; // increment the snmpInASNParseErrs counter
    ReceiveDecodeResult = BAD_LENGTH_FORMAT;
    return (ReceiveDecodeResult);
    }

// The agent now has the PDU: GetRequest, GetNextRequest, or SetRequest.
// Because these three PDUs have a common format, we save the PDU type
// (in PDUOpCode) and then check the value of the PDU Field: Request ID
// Field, the Error Status Field, and the Error Index Field. We then
// start examining the Variable Bindings List where the list of
// variables that the PDU command operates on is located.
//
// The Value Field of the PDU is in turn composed of 4 fields:
//
//       o The Request ID Field
//       o The Error Status Field
//       o The Error Index Field
//       o The Variable Bindings List (VarBindList) Field
//

// The Request ID's ASN.1 Tag, Length, and Value Field must be decoded
// and verified. Its value depends on what the NMS has inserted.
// REQUEST ID FIELD:
// +---------------------+------------------+--------------------+
// | TAG: INTEGER -- 0x02 | LENGTH -- (varies)| VALUE (PDU: varies)|
// +---------------------+------------------+--------------------+
//
if the GetRequestIDField() function does not return INTEGER
    {
    snmpInASNParseErrs++; // increment the snmpInASNParseErrs counter
    ReceiveDecodeResult = BAD_REQUEST_ID_FORMAT;
    return (ReceiveDecodeResult);
    }
if the GetASN1Len() function returns INVALID_ASN1_LENGTH_FORMAT
    {
    snmpInASNParseErrs++; // increment the snmpInASNParseErrs counter
    ReceiveDecodeResult = BAD_LENGTH_FORMAT;
    return (ReceiveDecodeResult);
    }
RequestID = GetRequestIDValue();  // Now, fetch and save Request ID
```

395

```
// The Error Status Field's ASN.1 Tag, Length, and Value Field must be
// decoded and verified. When the agent receives the message this field
// should have a value of 0.
// ERROR STATUS FIELD:
// +--------------------+----------------+----------------+
// | TAG: INTEGER -- 0x02 | LENGTH -- (0x01)| VALUE -- (0x00)|
// +--------------------+----------------+----------------+
//
if the GetErrorStatusField() function does not return INTEGER
    {
    snmpInASNParseErrs++; // increment the snmpInASNParseErrs counter
    ReceiveDecodeResult = BAD_ERROR_STATUS_FORMAT;
    return (ReceiveDecodeResult);
    }
if the GetASN1Len() function returns INVALID_ASN1_LENGTH_FORMAT
    {
    snmpInASNParseErrs++; // increment the snmpInASNParseErrs counter
    ReceiveDecodeResult = BAD_LENGTH_FORMAT;
    return (ReceiveDecodeResult);
    }
if (ErrorStatus = GetErrorStatusValue() doesn't = 0)
    {
    ReceiveDecodeResult = INVALID_ERROR_STATUS_RCVD;
    return (ReceiveDecodeResult);
    }

// The Error Index Field's ASN.1 Tag, Length, and Value Field must be
// decoded and verified. After the agent receives a message, this field
// also has a value of 0.
// ERROR INDEX FIELD:
// +--------------------+----------------+----------------+
// | TAG: INTEGER -- 0x02 | LENGTH -- (0x01)| VALUE -- (0x00)|
// +--------------------+----------------+----------------+
//
if the GetErrorIndexField() function does not return INTEGER
    {
    snmpInASNParseErrs++; // increment the snmpInASNParseErrs counter
    ReceiveDecodeResult = BAD_ERROR_INDEX_FORMAT;
    return (ReceiveDecodeResult);
    }
if the GetASN1Len() function returns INVALID_ASN1_LENGTH_FORMAT
    {
    snmpInASNParseErrs++; // increment the snmpInASNParseErrs counter
    ReceiveDecodeResult = BAD_LENGTH_FORMAT;
    return (ReceiveDecodeResult);
    }
if (ErrorIndex = GetErrorIndexValue() doesn't = 0)
    {
    ReceiveDecodeResult = INVALID_ERROR_INDEX_RCVD;
    return (ReceiveDecodeResult);
    }

// Now the agent is ready to examine the Variables --
// The VarBindList Field ASN.1 Tag, Length, and Value Field must be
// decoded and verified. The Value Field contains one or more variables
// that are to be acted upon, depending on what the PDU command type is.
// VARIABLE BINDINGS LIST FIELD:
// +--------------+----------------+--------------------------+
// | TAG: *(0x30) | LENGTH -- (varies)| VALUE (VarBindList: varies)|
// +--------------+----------------+--------------------------+
// Note: Tag for the Variable Bindings List is the Universal Constructed
// Sequence. The hexadecimal value for this Tag is 0x30.
//
```

```
if (GetVarBindTag() function does not return 0x30)
    {
    snmpInASNParseErrs++; // increment the snmpInASNParseErrs counter
    ReceiveDecodeResult = BAD_VARBINDLIST_TAG_VALUE;
    return (ReceiveDecodeResult);
    }
if the GetASN1Len() function returns INVALID_ASN1_LENGTH_FORMAT
    {
    snmpInASNParseErrs++; // increment the snmpInASNParseErrs counter
    ReceiveDecodeResult = BAD_LENGTH_FORMAT;
    return (ReceiveDecodeResult);
    }
//
// The length is continually checked to determine how much is to follow.
// The VarBindList length can be used as the loop counter to determine
// when all the variables have been processed. For example, the list
// may be processed with the "while" construct. A global variable can
// also be used to keep an internal count of how many variables are in
// the VarBindList for this message. This count can be used to know
// how many times the MIB instrumentation routines should be called when
// the decoded message will be "executed."
//
//      varCount = 0;                      // initialize the variable counter
//      while(the VarBindListLength > 0)
//          {
//          process a "variable bind element"
//          decrement the VarBindListLength accordingly
//          varCount++;
//          }    // while loop ends when all data is processed

// The Value Field for the VarBindList consists of 1 to "n"
// variables. Each variable is also encoded as an ASN.1 TAG/LENGTH/VALUE
// triplet. These fields must be decoded and verified. The Value Field
// for each variable yields the final nesting of the OID Field/Value
// Field. Each of these two fields has their TAG/LENGTH/VALUE triplet.
// +-------------+------------------+-------------------------+
// | TAG: *(0x30) | LENGTH -- (varies)| VALUE (bind value: varies)|
// +-------------+------------------+-------------------------+
// Note: Tag for each Variable is the Universal Constructed
// Sequence. The hexadecimal value for this Tag is 0x30.
//
if (GetVarTag() function does not return 0x30)
    {
    snmpInASNParseErrs++; // increment the snmpInASNParseErrs counter
    ReceiveDecodeResult = BAD_VARIABLE_TAG_VALUE;
    return (ReceiveDecodeResult);
    }
if the GetASN1Len() function returns INVALID_ASN1_LENGTH_FORMAT
    {
    snmpInASNParseErrs++; // increment the snmpInASNParseErrs counter
    ReceiveDecodeResult = BAD_LENGTH_FORMAT;
    return (ReceiveDecodeResult);
    }
// The Value field of each variable includes its OID field that defines
// its unique OBJECT IDENTIFIER value, and the Value Field that
// holds the "value" for the object after the PDU command has been
// executed.
//
// The OID Field
// +---------------+------------------+----------------------------+
// | TAG: OID(0x06) | LENGTH -- (varies)| VALUE (OID encoding integers)|
// +---------------+------------------+----------------------------+
//
```

```
    if (GetOIDTag() function does not return 0x06)
        {
        snmpInASNParseErrs++; // increment the snmpInASNParseErrs counter
        ReceiveDecodeResult = BAD_OID_TAG_VALUE;
        return (ReceiveDecodeResult);
        }
    if the GetASN1Len() function returns INVALID_ASN1_LENGTH_FORMAT
        {
        snmpInASNParseErrs++; // increment the snmpInASNParseErrs counter
        ReceiveDecodeResult = BAD_LENGTH_FORMAT;
        return (ReceiveDecodeResult);
        }
    // With the length, the retrieve_OID() function reads and stores
    // the actual OID value. This value is stored in an internal
    // representation so that it can be subsequently checked by the
    // agent against its MIB list.
    retrieve_OID();

    // The Value Field
    // +--------------+-------------------+----------------------+
    // | TAG: (varies) | LENGTH -- (varies)| VALUE (value: varies)|
    // +--------------+-------------------+----------------------+
    //
    // The Value Field may be NULL in a received message and is usually
    // only needed for the GetResponse PDU. This is the field that will
    // contain the result of the operation on the variable: Get, GetNext,
    // or Set. After the operation is completed, the TAG, Length, and
    // Value are encoded in ASN.1 and placed in the response buffer
    // for transmission back to the NMS.
    //
    //
    // Done decoding the received SNMP Packet. Now I "execute"
    // the PDU command and operate on the variable list included.
    //
    return (ReceiveDecodeResult);     // we made it, return with Success
    } // endfunc: Examine_SNMP_Receive_Message()
```

9.4.3. EXECUTE THE SNMP COMMAND

This function carries out one of the possible valid commands that can be contained in the PDU field for the variables listed. Remember that in SNMP only one command exists per message. For each command, the MIB instrumentation routines are called with the command type, and a count occurs of the number of variables to be processed that were contained in the variable bindings list. At this point, the SNMP packet is now decoded into a usable internal format. The lengths are computed, all information for the response such as the community name and request ID, are stored, the PDU command is known, and the variables are ready for processing.

```
/*(3)*******************************************************************/
/* FUNCTION NAME: Execute_The_SNMP_Command()                           */
/* FUNCTION DESCRIPTION: This function carries out the requested        */
/*    operation on the variable list.                                  */
/* INPUTS: For purposes of this example, the SNMP packet has been       */
/*    decoded into an internal format. The lengths are computed, all    */
/*    information for the response (community name, request ID, etc.)   */
/*    is saved, the PDU command is known, and the variable OIDs are     */
/*    ready for processing.                                            */
/* OUTPUTS: BYTE -- result code from the execution phase               */
/**********************************************************************/
BYTE Execute_The_SNMP_Command(void)
    {
    BYTE ExecuteResult;              // result code of executing this message

    ExecuteResult = EXECUTED_OK;      // initialize the Result Code

    switch (PDUOpCode)
        {
        // Get Request PDU Command
        case GET_REQUEST_PDU:
          snmpInGetRequests++;        // increment the Get Request counter
          if (Call_MIB_Instrumentation_Routines(GET, varCount) == MIB_CALL_OK)
            snmpOutGetResponses++;     // increment Out Get counter
          else
            ExecuteResult = BAD_MIB_RTN;
          break;

        // Get Next Request PDU Command
        case GET_NEXT_REQUEST_PDU:
          snmpInGetNextRequests++; // increment Get Next Request counter
          if (Call_MIB_Instrumentation_Routines(GETN, varCount) == MIB_CALL_OK)
            snmpOutGetNextResponses++;    // increment Out Get Next counter
          else
            ExecuteResult = BAD_MIB_RTN;
          break;

        // Set Request PDU Command
        case SET_REQUEST_PDU:
          snmpInSetRequests++;       // increment the Set Request counter
          if (Call_MIB_Instrumentation_Routines(SET, varCount) == MIB_CALL_OK)
            snmpOutSetResponses++;     // increment Out Set counter
          else
            ExecuteResult = BAD_MIB_RTN;
          break;

        // Should never happen; already validated PDU Type
        default:
          snmpInBadTypes++;           // increment the snmpInBadTypes counter
          ExecuteResult = BAD_PDU_TYPE;
          return (ExecuteResult);
          break;
        } // endswitch

    snmpOutPkts++;                  // increment the Out Packets counter
    return(ExecuteResult);
    } // endfunc: Examine_The_SNMP_Command()
```

9.4.4. CALL THE MIB INSTRUMENTATION ROUTINES

This function calls the MIB instrumentation routines that are present for the MIB variables controlled by this agent. The functionality presented here is purposefully generalized because the MIB variables controlled by any particular agent implementation vary with the MIB groups the agent controls. Also, the tables compiled and generated for a specific agent implementation are a function of the particular MIB compiler employed. This function is called with the PDU type and the number of variables in the `VarBindList` that are to be acted upon.

For this discussion, assume that the input ASCII MIB file for this agent is compiled by a compliant MIB compiler into an object image that can be linked into the executable agent module. (A full discussion of MIB compilers occurs in Chapter 11.) The output format from the compiler is a table that contains an entry for each MIB variable. Each entry contains the following elements:

- the Object Identifier for this MIB variable in internal format

- its Syntax

- its Access Mode that must be compared to the MIB view

- a Function that determines if the variable "exists" for this command

- functions that determine how the associated value can be accessed for the Get, GetNext, and Set PDU commands. (This area is certainly one where implementations can optimize the design and implementation.)

After the Instrumentation Routines have been called, the SNMP Response Message is prepared. If these instrumentation routines are successful, the result variable values are transferred from the internal working area into the response buffer. Any error causes the Error Status and Error Index fields to be filled in with the appropriate values. The operations for an SNMP PDU are Pass/Fail—if even one error occurs in the processing of the variable list, the values in the `VarBindList` should be considered invalid for this SNMP request. The NMS must possess the intelligence to determine which variable(s) cause the error and then reformat and resend the request.

```
/*(4)*****************************************************************/
/* FUNCTION NAME: Call_MIB_Instrumentation_Routines()              */
/* FUNCTION DESCRIPTION: This function calls the instrumentation    */
/*   routines for the variables in the VarBindList. It checks for the*/
/*   object's existence, its syntax, its access mode, and then calls */
/*   the proper access routine depending on the PDU command code.   */
/* INPUTS: command -- the PDU type                                  */
/*         count -- number of variables associated with command     */
/* OUTPUTS: BYTE -- result code from calling the instrumentation rtns.*/
/*******************************************************************/
BYTE Call_MIB_Instrumentation_Routines(int command, int count)
    {
    BYTE MIBResult;           // result code of MIB instrumentation routine

    MIBResult = MIB_CALL_OK;              // initialize the Result Code

    while (count)
        {
        if (Does_Var_Exist(OID_num) == TRUE)
            {
            // How the MIB variables are arranged and then accessed is a
            // key design and implementation issue. Comer and Stevens discuss
            // the use of a "bucket hashing" technique for handling the
            // resolution of the ASN.1 OIDs and how the MIB variables are
            // stored internally by the agent in Internetworking with
            // TCP/IP [4].
            if (Access_Mode_in_MIB_View() == OK)
                {
                switch (command)
                    {
                    case GET:
                        Access_Get_Value();      // do the GET operation
                        break;
                    case GETN:
                        Access_GetNext_Value();  // do the GET NEXT operation
                        break;
                    case SET:                    // do the SET operation
                        Access_Set_Value();
                        break;
                    default:                     // shouldn't happen -- error
                        break;
                    } // endswitch
                }
            else   // improper access code for this MIB view
                {
                // the reason an access will fail is if a write is requested
                // for a read-only variable for this profile
                snmpInReadOnly++     // increment Read only counter
                break;               // break on error; remember error for response
                MIBResult = MIB_CALL_ERROR;    // return error
                }
            }
        else   // the name was not found -- error
            {
            snmpInNoSuchNames++    // increment the Name not found counter
            break;                 // break on error; remember error for response
            MIBResult = MIB_CALL_ERROR;    // return error
            }
        count--;                   // decrement the number of variables
        snmpInTotalReqVars++;      // increment In Total Variables counter
        } //endwhile

    return(MIBResult);
    } // endfunc: Call_MIB_Instrumentation_Routines()
```

9.4.5. PREPARE THE SNMP TRANSMIT MESSAGE

This function prepares the now decoded and executed SNMP message by creating a response message. If the instrumentation routines were all successful, the value fields in the VarBindList contain the results of the requested operation for each variable. If an error in the processing occurred, the Error Status Field and Error Index Field contain the cause and location of the first error.

After this function has executed successfully, a fully encoded SNMP Response Message is in a buffer ready for transmission. Its length is also known.

```
/*(5)***************************************************************/
/* FUNCTION NAME: Prepare_SNMP_Transmit_Message()                  */
/* FUNCTION DESCRIPTION: This function...                          */
/* INPUTS: SNMPMsg -- the received SNMP Message                    */
/*         MsgLen -- the length of the received message            */
/* OUTPUTS: BYTE -- result code from the preparation process       */
/*****************************************************************/
BYTE Prepare_SNMP_Transmit_Message(void)
    {
    BYTE PrepareRC;                    // result code of preparation for transmit

    PrepareRC = GOOD_Prepare;     // initialize Result Code

    // Now that the message has been decoded and executed, the internal
    // buffer can be "freed" or reused for the creation of the SNMP
    // Get Response Message. Again, the maximum buffer size is sufficient
    // because the response must fit into a single UDP datagram.
    //
    // The process of creating the response is the inverse process of how
    // the decoding and evaluating was done. The response message's fields
    // are calculated, encoded into ASN.1, and then put into the response
    // buffer so that it can be subsequently transmitted to the NMS.
    //

    Encode_VarBindList();            //Tag, Length, & Values (for var #1 -- #n)
    Encode_Error_Index_Field();      //Tag, Length, & Value fields
    Encode_Error_Status_Field();     //Tag, Length, & Value fields
    Encode_Request_ID_Field();       //Tag, Length, & Value fields
    Encode_PDU_Field();              //Tag, Length, & Value (i.e., the PDU)
    Encode_Community_Name_Field();   //Tag, Length, & Value fields
    Encode_Version_Field();          //Tag, Length, & Value fields
    Encode_Outer_Wrapper_For_Message(); //Tag, Length, Value fields
    // Note that the encoding process has been overly simplified here. Each
    // routine should do error checking and handling to insure that
    // each operation was done successfully. Lengths must be calculated
    // and encoded properly also.
    //
    snmpOutResponses++;       // increment the Out Get Response Counter

    return (PrepareRC);
    } // endfunc: Prepare_SNMP_Transmit_Message()
```

9.4.6. TRANSMIT THE UDP DATAGRAM

This function is called when the processed SNMP Response Message is ready to be sent to the NMS. This routine needs to know the location of the transmit buffer that contains the SNMP Message and its length. For simplicity, this code assumes that these two data items are stored globally and can be retrieved by this function.

```
/*(6)********************************************************************/
/* FUNCTION NAME: Transmit_The_UDP_Datagram()                          */
/* FUNCTION DESCRIPTION: This function presents the SNMP Response       */
/*    Message to the Transport Interface.                               */
/* INPUTS: void                                                         */
/* OUTPUTS: BYTE -- result code from the transmit process              */
/* NOTE: For the purpose of example, the SNMP agent's transmit buffer */
/*    and its length are available globally for simplification.        */
/**********************************************************************/
BYTE Transmit_The_UDP_Datagram(void)
   {
   BYTE TransmitRC;                    // result code of transmit

   TransmitRC = GOOD_XMT;              // initialize Result Code

   // If the socket interface is used, use the sendto() call
   //     with appropriate parameters (socket descriptor, length, etc.)
   // Transport Call should return GOOD or BAD
   if (Transport_Receive (XmtMsgBuf, &XmtMsgLen) == BAD)
      TransmitRC = BAD_XMT;          // should include error codes

   return (TransmitRC);
   } // endfunc: Transmit_The_UDP_Datagram()
```

Figure 9-15 shows an example of an output data flow for an Ethernet LAN network. The example includes three processes and external entities for the network card and its device driver. The UDP ports, the IP transmit queue, the device driver output queue, and the Ethernet network also appear in Figure 9-15 as data stores.

The SNMP Server process is the agent. It reads and writes all of its response PDUs to UDP port #161. The Trap-PDU SNMP Messages are sent to UDP port #162.

The UDP Process implements the User Datagram Protocol and sends the UDP datagrams for the SNMP agent/server.

The IP Process is the implementation of the Internet Protocol. It sends the IP Packets for the UDP transport protocol above. It also interfaces to the network access layer below.

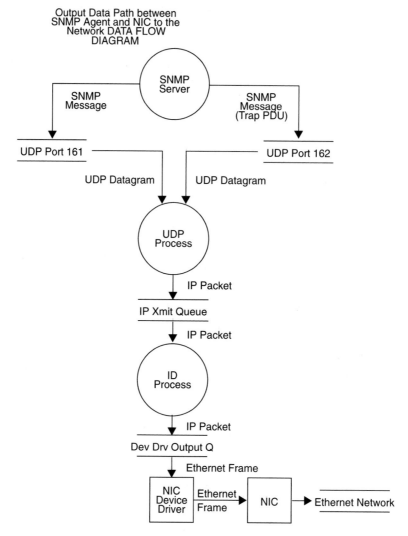

Figure 9-15. Output Data Path DFD

9.5. THE IMPLEMENTATION OF THE NMS

The NMS software uses the protocol to communicate with the agents in its community. This software must be able to format and send SNMP Message commands for retrieval and modification: `GetRequest-PDU`, `GetNext-`

PDU, and `SetRequest-PDU` for Version 1 and additionally, the `GetBulk-PDU` and `Inform-PDU` for Version 2. Both versions need to receive and process the SNMP response: `GetResponse-PDU` for Version 1 and `Response-PDU` for Version 2. A response here also includes the agent-generated `Trap-PDU` for its respective version's format. Figure 9-16 demonstrates the two basic functions of the NMS: sending and receiving SNMP Messages.

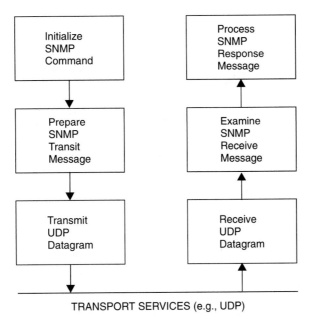

TRANSPORT SERVICES (e.g., UDP)

Figure 9-16. The NMS Top Level Flowchart

Network Management applications send requests to the NMS. The NMS software creates a request for a specified agent, encodes it into ASN.1 notation, and then uses the UDP Transport service to send the request over the internetwork. It then waits for the response message. The response is decoded and processed. The Request ID field filled in by the NMS is used as a check to match NMS requests and responses. The response is then passed back up to the awaiting network management application.

The NMS can also receive and process Trap messages. Trap messages do not need to be acknowledged in SNMP. Because SNMP implementations use a trap-directed polling strategy, the reception of a trap usually prompts the NMS to poll that agent for more information. This polling is a function of the information contained in the trap message.

Because the UDP datagram transport service is unreliable and not based on a connection, each NMS's responsibility is to handle the no response and duplicate response error conditions. A timer alerts the NMS that it has not received a response in a timely manner. The request ID ensures that the NMS does not receive two responses for the same command. Each response sent back by the agent has a different request ID.

The NMS processes a response by recording all of the pertinent data found in the message. These include any pre-determined activities programmed into the NMS, such as updating statistics and SNMP counters, filling in the database, updating poll timers, entering events in log files, noting changes for the topology map, and so forth.

Also, any user-initiated network management applications that are running need to be made current. The graphics for the User Interface screen should be updated, notifications may be sent to system administrators via e-mail or beepers, other support applications may be invoked, and so on. The area of developing FCAPS network management applications is a current key focus in NMS software design and implementation. Note that the specification for the SNMP network management applications and the design of the user interface are beyond the scope and therefore not included in the SNMP standards.

Before leaving the discussion of SNMP implementation, briefly review the two current design methods employed in this area.

9.6. PROCEDURAL DESIGN VERSUS OBJECT-ORIENTED DESIGN

Currently two major camps exist in the broader, more general topic of which software paradigm to choose when designing and implementing the agent and NMS software. These are procedural design and object oriented design (OOD). The character of the design and the method chosen can have a great deal of impact on such important issues as the maintainability and upgradeability of a particular managed installation.

The procedural method is the older of the two methodologies. It views the software effort as describing the problem to be solved as a series of steps that can be refined in a top-down or bottom-up fashion, until a manageable number of modules are created. Each group of these series of steps is called an "algorithm," and the algorithms use global and local data.

Procedural programming naturally lends itself to flowcharting and pseudocoding in describing the process flow of the system. The detailed design and implementation of the agent presented in this chapter is described in this fashion.

Object-oriented design deals with objects. These objects contain methods that operate on the data that is related to the object. OOD is becoming more and more the software design of choice but the learning curve involves a new way of thinking how problems are analyzed and how the software to solve that problem is designed. OOD comes with an entirely new set of terminology, also. Most new implementations are based on this method, and many current systems are being retrofitted to accommodate OOD. The programming approach and effort involved in these two software design methodologies can be very different.

9.6.1. PROCEDURAL PROGRAMMING

Procedural programming follows closely from the procedural design method. The software system to be designed is broken down into manageable units. Refinements to procedural programming include decomposing the system into the proper levels of abstraction by promoting a modular design. The end result is that the system can be viewed as a number of manageable sub-processes that can then be coded. The C programming language is often used for procedural programming.

9.6.2. OBJECT-ORIENTED PROGRAMMING

Object-Oriented Programming involves an iterative process where the software system to be defined is viewed in terms of objects and how they have to interact with each other in order for the system to work properly. The three major components of OOD—inheritance, encapsulation, and polymorphism—must be considered in the OOP effort.

Inheritance refers to the capability of one object to reuse the pertinent characteristics of an already defined object. *Encapsulation* is the ability to hide the internal workings of the system's objects for enforcing the abstraction of viewing the object in terms of the operations it performs, rather than merely in terms of its data structures or functions that pertain to it. Encapsulation allows each object to present its public interface. *Polymorphism* allows an object instance to be a member of various classes. It allows the object's member functions to be called without knowing the specifics of the parameter types. The C++ programming language and Java are prime examples of object-oriented programming languages.

REFERENCES FOR CHAPTER 9

[1] Bartlett, John. *Bartlett's Familiar Quotations*. 16th ed. Boston: Little, Brown, and Company. 1992.

[2] Rose, Marshall, and Keith McCloghrie. *How To Manage Your Network Using SNMP: The Network Management Practicum*. Englewood Cliffs, NJ: Prentice Hall. 1995.

[3] Stevens, W. Richard. *UNIX Network Programming*. Englewood Cliffs, NJ: Prentice Hall. 1990.

[4] Comer, Douglas E. *Principles, Protocols, and Architecture*. Vol. 1 of *Internetworking with TCP/IP*. Englewood Cliffs, NJ: Prentice Hall. 1991.

The "Practice" of SNMP Version 2

It seems that the idea of the simple is already to be found contained in that of the complex and in the idea of the analysis, and in such a way that we come to this idea quite apart from any examples of simple objects, or of the propositions which mention them, and we realize the existence of the simple object—a priori—as a logical necessity.

—Ludwig Wittgenstein (Notebooks)[1]

To beautify life is to give it an object.

—Jose Marti[2]

Since the "practice" of SNMP Version 1 began in the late 1980s, the velocity/development of the software engineering that is required to analyze, design, and implement network management solutions has been accelerating.

Object-oriented technology is employed in many areas of SNMP development. For the practice of SNMP Version 2 and beyond, object-oriented (OO) tools and models are being used. The area of network management application development is a prime example of how OO technology can enhance software development, reuse, maintainability, and quality.

10.1.SNMP IS "OBJECT-BASED"

The models of object-oriented paradigms can be viewed as three types. Each type of model has an increased support of objects.[3] The three are:

◆ Object-Based Models: Support objects
◆ Class-Based Models: Support objects and classes
◆ Object-Oriented Models: Support objects, classes, and inheritance

Strictly speaking, SNMP is considered object-based, primarily due to the requirements for minimal resources at the agent and a simplified framework as defined by the SMI. The SNMP agent does not have to implement inheritance and deal with object containment and associations. The management variables are simple and atomic.

10.2.USING THE OBJECT-ORIENTED APPROACH

The object-oriented approach is used for modeling complicated problems such as those dealt with by network management applications. A model can be a great help in abstracting a problem into manageable units. "Object-oriented modeling provides a framework within which large and complex systems may be organized both in terms of their structure and their behavior."[4]

Two excellent sources for learning about object-oriented modeling are the books by Grady Booch (*Object-Oriented Analysis and Design with Applications*, 2nd ed.[5]) and James Rumbaugh (*Object-Oriented Modeling and Design*[6]). Hand-in-hand with object-oriented analysis and design is the use of a tool to automate and validate the model. The OO CASE tool used in this chapter is Rational Rose from the Rational Software Corporation. (For more information see `http://www.rational.com/pst/products/rosefamily.html`.) A complete guide that presents a step-by-step example of how to use the Booch method with the Rational Rose tool for developing applications is Iseult White's handbook, *Using the Booch Method: A Rational Approach.*[7]

10.3.A NETWORK MANAGEMENT APPLICATION EXAMPLE

We have stated that object-oriented modeling and design is a powerful software technology that can be applied to many problem domains to create successful implementations.

Imagine creating a data communications company that develops networking equipment such as packet-switching and multi-protocol nodes that allow for the efficient and cost-effective use of communication facilities. Network management software is needed to monitor, control, and configure this equipment.

In order to manage these nodes a standardized network management platform is proposed titled *Open Network Management System* (OMS). This platform is based on a popular Network Management System. The most popular is the OpenView Windows (OVW) product from Hewlett-Packard. This tool provides a graphical user interface (GUI) and several application program interfaces (API) and libraries that allow companies to integrate network management applications into a standardized platform.

OVW supports SNMP that communicates with the devices in the network. SNMP is a network management framework that supports the manager/agent paradigm. OVW provides the "manager" portion, and the agents are implemented for each device in the enterprise that is to be managed.

A Fault Management System (FMS) is an important network management application that is to be part of OMS. In order to analyze, design, and implement this system, object-oriented technology will be used—specifically, the Booch method. The computer-aided software engineering (CASE) tool Rational Rose supports this methodology for analysis and design. This tool runs on all the popular workstation and PC platforms in use today.

For this undertaking, I introduce the FMS problem domain, describe the methodology, and state initial implementation considerations.

The FMS application is a "network discovery" process whose job is to learn about the nodes in a wide-area network (WAN). Discovered nodes are to be maintained in a database that tracks the hardware and software configuration and element status. An optional inventory can be kept for future accounting management applications.

The FMS resides on a workstation that is connected via Ethernet over a local area network (LAN) to an SNMP agent that proxies for all of the devices that are to be managed in the WAN. The Network Management Station (NMS) that contains OpenView talks over the UDP/IP protocol stack using the SNMP protocol. The SNMP agent then translates the SNMP request into a corresponding request that can be understood by the network devices. Your imaginary company has created one type of network switch that is to be managed by our OMS system.

SNMP NMS		SNMP Agent		Managed Device
net mgmt applications (e.g., FMS)		SNMP proxy agent		device application SW
SNMP		SNMP	proprietary remote handler software	proprietary remote handler software
UDP		UDP		
IP		IP		
ethernet		ethernet	X.25/ Frame Relay	X.25/ Frame Relay
	LAN		WAN	

Figure 10-1. FMS System Environment

Figure 10-1 shows the various hardware and software components that are of interest in our hypothetical enterprise.

What is of importance is that the FMS application can determine the managed devices that are present in a network, the hardware and software that comprise such nodes, and status where appropriate. Current proprietary network management schemes will be replaced by the SNMP standard protocol and the common management solution offered by OMS. Fault Management is an important piece of the functionality of network management.

By way of general introduction, I present Fault Management (FM) and review its functional requirements. See [8] for a full discussion of all the FCAPS applications.

Fault Management is the process of using network management to discover problems in the enterprise, understand their symptoms, and initiate corrective actions. FM reports can be logged for future reference and to speed problem recognition and correction. Note that Configuration Management works closely with Fault Management. Before the faults can be discovered and corrected, the network entities need to be identified (the "where" before the "what" and the "when").

Faults should be distinguished from errors. A fault is an abnormal condition that often requires the attention of a network administrator or management application to correct. Two key fault attributes are a failure to operate correctly or an excessive error count. Some types of errors may occur only occasionally and are not normally considered to be faults.

Implicit in the determination of whether a network device is operating properly is the knowledge of the "fault characteristics" of each device. Each device should have pre-defined fault thresholds. In conjunction with Configuration Management, these default thresholds should be changeable, either by having the NMS send set operations or by having these thresholds dynamically updated by the devices as they monitor the network operation.

Also, fault filtering should exist where faults can be prioritized to prevent the management station from being flooded by fault notifications. These priorities should also be configurable. This type of information is also used when dealing with fault propagation issues.

Routine preventive maintenance can also ensure properly functioning devices on the internetwork. Sophisticated Fault Management includes the proactive anticipation of failures. One way that this can be handled is by scheduling routine diagnostics to be run on the devices. Depending on the capabilities of the device, these tests can range from simple loopbacks to rigorous diagnostic test suites.

To summarize, the FMS application running on the NMS must:

1. Initially categorize fault categories and the specific faults within each category. Discover and record all of the network entities that are to be managed by the FMS system.

2. Monitor the network and receive specific faults it has been configured for.

3. Understand the nature of the faults and propagate status as configured.

4. Record the faults by keeping a log, updating the operational data store, etc. Maintenance on logs, traces, and data stores must be done as required.

5. Initiate corrective actions.

10.4. OBJECT-ORIENTED METHODOLOGY: THE BOOCH METHOD

The Booch Method is a popular methodology that uses a specific set of symbols and conventions to represent the various OO models that are created and refined for a particular problem. It espouses an iterative approach where analysis, design, and implementation are continually augmented and refined to create a solution that is generally more robust and easier to maintain than those created with ad hoc or more conventional Structured Design methodologies (the "waterfall" method). You do a little analysis, some design, part of the implementation, brief testing, and continue until the specifications have been met. The code that is created is part of the final system and not merely a "throw-away" demo.

OO methodology relates more closely to the real world in looking at a problem as a group of related objects. It provides a comprehensive analysis and allows the problem to be decomposed more easily. The iterative approach of an inward spiraling of refinements creates a series of incremental prototypical demos that merge and evolve into a well-thought-out design. OO-developed software provides the additional benefits of software reuse. Studies have shown that overall project maintenance is simplified.

The Booch Method consists of three major steps that are done in an iterative way. It is a feedback cycle where modifications and discoveries can be continually integrated into the various analysis, design, and implementation models that are being developed for the problem. The models are refined and optimized.

The three steps of the Booch method are:

- Analysis: Requirements and Domain Analysis
- Design: System Design
- Implementation: Coding (also can include Testing and Maintenance)

Analysis defines the basic system functions and lays out the system's main logical structure. It is the "what" of the problem. The Booch Method partitions analysis into Requirements Analysis and Domain Analysis.

Design is the "how." It takes the logical structure and maps it into a physical model. The architecture of the implementation is set up.

The implementation is the actual code that "solves" the problem. The Booch Method calls the software code "working executable releases."

10.4.1. REQUIREMENTS ANALYSIS

Requirements Analysis is the determination of what the system is to do, including the key functions and the scope of the problem domain.

Two major deliverables are in the Booch Method for this step:

- The System Charter
- The System Function Statement

10.4.1.1. The System Charter

The System Charter lists the key system responsibilities. It is brief and concise and is often the initial task of Requirements Analysis.

10.4.1.2. The System Function Statement

The System Function Statement contains an outline of the important "use cases" of the system. "Use cases" is a method of analysis developed by Ivar Jacobson (see [9]) where scenarios are drawn up for how the system is going to be used. A complete collection of these "use cases" would describe the total functionality of a system. These function statements are used throughout the analysis and design to indicate what classes and operations are needed. Use case analysis also provides a starting point for creating the test scenarios that are needed to make sure that the system meets its stated requirements. These test scenarios become the basis for the start of small "demos" or code prototypes that are developed further and mature as the final implementation. The System Function Statement initially introduces summaries of the use cases that are expanded throughout the OOA phase.

10.4.2. DOMAIN ANALYSIS

The Domain Analysis takes the requirements and defines a more directed model of the problem. Developers gain the detailed knowledge of the problem that is needed for the subsequent design and implementation. Classes, relationships, operations, attributes, and inheritance are defined.

Four major deliverables are in the Booch Method for this step:

◆ Class Diagrams

◆ Class Specifications

◆ Object-Scenario Diagrams

◆ Data Dictionary

10.4.2.1. Class Diagrams

Class Diagrams identify the major classes and relationships of the system. In the Booch Method classes are depicted as "dashed clouds," and they are joined by lines that illustrate the relationships between the classes. Full Class Diagrams include the key classes, the relationships, aggregations, inheritance, and cardinality. They can also show the attributes and operations for the classes.

10.4.2.2. Class Specifications

Class Specifications add to the class diagrams by listing the semantic definitions of the classes. The Booch Method provides a template that initially requires the class name, documentation source, and a class definition. Class Specifications are refined to include relationships, attributes, operations, constraints, and much other information that can pertain to a class.

10.4.2.3. Object-Scenario Diagrams

The Object-Scenario Diagrams show how the objects interact with each other. These diagrams show how the use cases can be traced by labeling and numbering the operations with parameters that can occur between objects. Typically an Object-Scenario Diagram is done for each major use case. These diagrams can be augmented by scripts that tell in simple language how the use case operates through time. They can help explain conditional statements and iteration that may be unclear solely from the diagram.

10.4.2.4. Data Dictionary

The Data Dictionary is the repository for information about the system's data. It includes a list of all of the domain "entities": classes, relationships, and attributes. It is continually updated throughout the analysis and design phases. The term "data dictionary" is a database term and in some systems so many entities exist that a database system is actually used to maintain the list.

10.4.2.5. Other Domain Analysis Techniques

Several other Domain Analysis techniques can be used that do not result in explicit deliverables from the Booch Method. These include Context Diagrams, Noun and Verb underlining, and CRC cards.

Context Diagrams show the problem to be analyzed as a large circle that communicates with other external processes. These external processes are shown as rectangles, and the data flows between any corresponding processes are labeled. Arrowheads show the direction of the message flow.

Noun and verb underlining is a simple technique that uses the problem statement as a starting point. Nouns and verbs are underlined, and they become class and relationship candidates, respectively. The candidates are "filtered" and a list of the key classes and relationships results. This type of analysis works best for more formal types of specifications.

A third type of informal analysis is the use of CRC cards. This is a simple and effective way to recognize key classes and analyze the system's scenarios. CRC is an acronym for Class/Responsibilities/Collaborators. This type of analysis is ideal for a "brainstorming" approach for small groups. Figure 10-2 is a sample of how a 3 by 5 inch card can be laid out.

Class Name	
Responsibilities	**Collaborations**
responsibility 1	collaboration 1
...	...
responsibility n	collaboration n

Figure 10-2. CRC Card

10.4.3. SYSTEM DESIGN

OO System Design turns the analysis models into design models where efficiency, cost-effectiveness, and many other factors are considered. The initial architecture is determined, the executable releases are planned and developed, and the design is iteratively refined and improved. Design focuses on the "how."

10.4.3.1. Architectural Descriptions

Architectural Descriptions contain major design decisions that become factors for the implementation. These include choice and number of processors, databases, operating systems, programming languages and tools, and so forth.

10.4.3.2. Executable Release Descriptions

The Executable Release Descriptions contain information about what successive releases will contain.

10.4.3.3. Class-Category Diagrams

The high-level classes and objects are partitioned into the Class-Category Diagrams. They help partition the logical model of the system. These diagrams are represented as named rectangles that represent highly related class clusters. These diagrams are very high level but help maintain the architectural elements of the design of the system.

10.4.3.4. Design Class Diagrams

Design Class Diagrams show the physical implementation abstractions, including detailed data types and structures. These help show how the logical elements of the model are mapped into the physical elements.

10.4.3.5. Design Object-Scenario Diagrams

Design Object-Scenario Diagrams show the details of the operational logic, including how the physical objects are used and how functions are carried out.

10.4.3.6. New Specifications

New Specifications can be created to support any of the new or modified diagrams. These are additional specifications.

10.4.3.7. Amended Class Specifications

Any operations that have complex algorithms, relationship implementations, and attribute typing are shown in the Amended Class Specifications. These are refinements that come to light through the iteration of the design.

10.4.3.8. Other Design Techniques

Other Design techniques can be used as needed.

10.4.4. IMPLEMENTATION CONSIDERATIONS

The Implementation deals with the software and its supporting hardware environment. Specific implementation issues include the code, memory usage, hardware considerations, compilers, object libraries, and any other tools that may be necessary. The considerations evolve throughout the implementation, and journals can be kept so that this information can be used in future OO projects. Implementation considerations can also affect testing and code maintenance.

10.5. APPLYING THE BOOCH METHOD FOR THE FMS APPLICATION

Now that we have detailed the major steps and deliverables of the Booch Method, we can apply this information to our network management FM application.

10.5.1. FMS APPLICATION ANALYSIS

The initial input for this project is a problem statement that comprises an introductory narrative for what the system should do. Since this problem statement is written in English, it is imprecise and very "top-level." The FMS application analysis appears in Figure 10-3. From this preliminary statement, the analysis continues by making the requirements and domain more clear.

```
    The application is a "network discovery" process whose job is to learn
about the nodes in a WAN. Discovered nodes are to be maintained in a database
that tracks hardware/software configuration and element status.

    Node hardware is composed of one or more cardfiles, a number of different
cards including processors, memory, and i/o cards that can have different
physical interfaces and different port counts. In addition, other hardware's
status may be managed, such as fan assemblies, disks, and power supplies.

    Node software is comprised of services such as X.25, frame relay, async,
and other protocols. Ports may be assigned to a software service.

    In addition to providing a hardware/software inventory function, the
application retrieves the status of the managed elements.

    Information is gathered from the network using SNMP through a standard HP
OpenView API. The information is stored in a database through another,
externally supplied API.

    The discovery process is initiated by user request or periodically run from
a script. When invoking discovery, the user can specify the starting point of
the discovery process, from the entire network, to all nodes in a given
domain, to a specific node, and ultimately to a specific managed element on a
node.

    The effect of "discovering" elements that are already known is to update
the status of the element in the FMS database.
```

Figure 10-3. Fault Management System Problem Statement

The OO Analysis for the FMS application uses the Booch Methodology by breaking this phase into two separate activities: the Requirements Analysis and the Domain Analysis. The Requirements Analysis creates the System Charter and the Function Statement. From these, the Domain Analysis diagrams and specifications are created and refined.

10.5.2. FMS REQUIREMENTS ANALYSIS

The FMS Requirements Analysis begins with a "first pass" as to "what" the FMS will do. Because the analysis is iterative, the creation of "use case" summaries listed in the System Function Statement starts off the OOA with the subsequent defining of the key classes and relationships of the system. The System Charter is taken as the most top-level list of the FMS system's major responsibilities.

As stated in the Introduction, two major deliverables contribute to the Requirements Analysis step according to the Booch methodology:

◆ The System Charter

◆ The System Function Statement

The FMS Requirements Analysis allows us to become familiar with the domain, understand the system's overall requirements, and formalize the major functions of the FMS.

10.5.2.1. FMS System Charter

The System Charter (Figure 10-4) shows the major responsibilities as a concise summary.

The Fault Management System, Release 1.0, will be able to:

◆ Initially populate the FMS database with network elements from either the configuration database or the actual network

◆ Add additional network elements to the FMS database as they are discovered in the configuration database or the actual network

◆ Delete existing network elements from the FMS database when they no longer exist in either the configuration database or the actual network

◆ Synchronize status of the FMS database network elements with status of actual network elements

---

Figure 10-4. FMS System Charter

10.5.2.2. FMS System Function Statement

Figure 10-5 shows the Function Statement. It is a summary of the important use cases that have been outlined for the Requirements Analysis:

> - add network elements to the FMS DB
> - delete network elements from the FMS DB
> - update network element status in FMS DB
> - compare network elements of the same type
> - determine if a given network element exists
> - get a network element

Figure 10-5. Fault Management System Function Statement

These function statements are often used as the basis for small prototype "demos" that are later incorporated into the final product and introduce the customer to the major functionality of the system. These demos are often called *proof of concept demonstrations*.

10.5.3. FMS DOMAIN ANALYSIS

The FMS Domain Analysis greatly refines the Requirements Analysis by adding knowledge of the domain to create a more detailed analysis model.

Four major deliverables exist for the Domain Analysis step:

- Class Diagrams

- Class Specifications

- Object-Scenario Diagrams

- Data Dictionary

The major objective of this portion of the analysis is to build a model that defines the key classes and relationships that are uncovered in the OOA. As you saw previously, other less "formal" techniques are used in domain analysis and add input to the deliverables. These techniques include the creation of a Context Diagram and Noun analysis from the problem statement.

10.5.3.1. Context Diagram

The creation of a Context Diagram is often a good starting point for Domain Analysis. This diagram is "borrowed" from earlier Structured Design methodologies and presents a way of defining the system as one process and laying out its boundaries and external process interfaces. If the proper context of the FMS is not set, time may be wasted analyzing objects that are outside the scope of the system or overlooking objects that should be included in the system.

The major purpose of the FMS application is to coordinate information across the various interfaces it serves and utilizes. Figure 10-6 depicts the Context Diagram for the FMS. This diagram models the system as the central process and shows the boundary between it and its environment. The central FMS "bubble" represents the "black box" processing that it performs. The external entities represent the other components in the environment with which the FMS must interact. Four external processes are defined: the User, the Network, the FMS Database, and other OMS applications. The data flows represent data used in these interactions that are sent and received over well-defined interfaces.

Four interfaces are defined for this system:

1. The User/FMS interface
2. The Network/FMS interface
3. The FMS Database/FMS interface
4. Other OMS applications/FMS interface

As stated in the Problem Statement, the User can initiate the discovery process by sending commands (requests) or by having the process be periodically started from a script. The FMS replies with the proper response.

The Network/FMS interface uses the HP OVW SNMP API to communicate with the network nodes. It uses SNMP gets to retrieve the appropriate managed variable values.

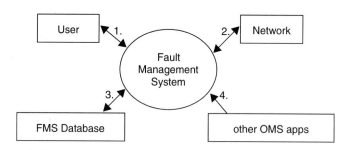

Figure 10-6. Fault Management System Context Diagram

The FMS DB/FMS interface populates the FMS database. This database is also called the *Operations Database*. It is a repository for such key information as the network status, operational state, and associated information for the network node's equipment and services along with their connections.

The FMS interface to other OMS applications could include Configuration Management System (CMS), Accounting Management System (AMS), Performance Management System (PMS), and Security Management System (SMS) network management applications. These applications could include inventory report generation, trouble-ticket production, and many others.

10.5.3.2. Noun Underlining

Noun Underlining is a simple, yet powerful technique for identifying key classes. The nouns and noun phrases are underlined from the Problem Statement, and each noun represents a candidate class or object. This technique is demonstrated for the FMS application in Figure 10-7. Note that refinements and clarifications to the original Problem Statement are italicized. Only the first instance of a noun needs to be underlined.

```
    The application is a "network discovery" process whose job is to learn
about the nodes in a wide-area network. Discovered nodes are to be maintained
in a database that tracks hardware/software configuration and element status.
    Node hardware is composed of one or more cardfiles, a number of different
cards including processors, memory, and i/o cards that can have different
physical interfaces and different port counts. In addition, other hardware's
status may be managed, such as fan assemblies, disks, and power supplies.
    Node software is comprised of services such as X.25, frame relay, async,
dsp, etc. Services are composed of one or more service categories. For
example, X.25 may have a link service category and an NUI service category.
Ports may be assigned to a software service.
    In addition to providing a hardware/software inventory function, the
application retrieves the status of the managed elements.
    Information is gathered from the network using SNMP through a standard HP
OpenView API. The information will be stored in a database through another,
externally supplied API.
    The discovery process is initiated by user request or periodically run from
a script. When invoking discovery, the user can specify the starting point of
the discovery process, from the entire network, to all nodes in a given
domain, to a specific node, and ultimately to a specific managed element on a
node.
    The effect of "discovering" elements that are already known is to update
the status of the element in the FMS database.
```

Figure 10-7. FMS Problem Statement (Refinement)

The resulting nouns and noun phrases are analyzed and "filtered" in Figure 10-8. The nouns that seem to be key classes are indicated in the third column. Figure 10-8 contains this table of analyzing key classes.

Noun	Analysis	Key Class?
Application	synonym for entire system; not one object	no
process	implementation concept; not a class	no
job	describes process; not a class	no
node	key abstraction; has attributes, operations, composed of hardware and software	yes
network	key abstraction; network composed of nodes	yes
database	FMS database is a key abstraction; repository for all operational data	yes
configuration	describes database; not a class	no
status	attribute of managed element	no
hardware	equipment is class name for nodal hardware	yes
cardfile	synonym for hardware; not a separate class	no
card	channel card; a node is composed of cards and "other hardware"	yes
processor	object; processor is an instance of channel card	no
memory	object; memory is an instance of channel card	no
i/o	object; i/o is an instance of channel card	no
interface	physical interface is an attribute of channel card	no
port	key abstraction; port is subclass of channel card	yes
other hardware	other component; node is composed of equipment or other components	yes
fan assembly	object; instance of other component	no
disk	object; instance of other component	no
power supply	object; instance of other component	no
software	synonym for preferred term of "service"	no
service	key abstraction; service is software class for node	yes
X.25	object; instance of service	no
frame relay	object; instance of service	no

Figure 10-8. FMS Noun Analysis Table

Noun	Analysis	Key Class?
async	object; instance of service	no
dsp	object; instance of service	no
service category	sub-class of service; service is composed of service categories	yes
link service category	object; instance of service category	no
NUI service category	object; instance of service category	no
inventory	vague term; not part of FMS application	no
managed element	key abstraction; many classes inherit the managed element class so that status can be updated	yes
information	vague term; synonym for status and collection of other node and network element attributes	no
SNMP	class that allows access to the network	yes
OpenView API	design and implementation detail	no
external API	design and implementation detail	no
user request	not a class, operation of user "actor"	no
script	not a class, operation of user "actor"	no
starting point	design detail; state of discovery process	no
domain	key abstraction; a network is composed of domains	yes

Figure 10-8. FMS Noun Analysis Table *(continued)*

Underlining verbs is a technique that can also be employed to detect candidate operations or relationships. Both noun and verb underlining techniques seem to work best when the problem statement is a formal set of requirements. These tend to be more complete and less ambiguous than their "English-language" counterparts.

10.5.3.3. FMS Class Diagrams

The first FMS Class Diagram that is created is the collection of "dashed clouds" that represent the key class abstractions initially discovered during the Domain Analysis. The FMS set of Class Diagrams appears in Figure 10-9.

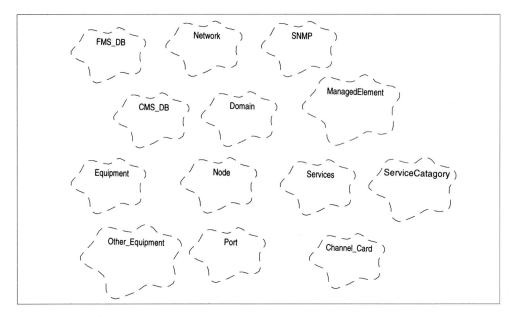

Figure 10-9. Key FMS Classes

This FMS Class Diagram is expanded and completed by adding and naming the associations between the classes. Cardinality and attributes are also added, as shown in Figure 10-10 and Figure 10-11.

10.5.3.4. FMS Class Specifications

The resulting key classes are listed as Class Specifications to more fully capture the semantics of the classes. The Booch Methodology has created a standard Class Specification template that is used here.

Class name:
>   Node

>   **Documentation:**
>   **Definition:**
>>   A Node is a component comprised of hardware and software that provides services for switching user traffic from one access point to another. The node may also act as a PAD (packet assembler/disassembler), providing services for protocol conversion to the packet protocol of the backbone.

>   **Export Control: Public**
>   **Cardinality: n**

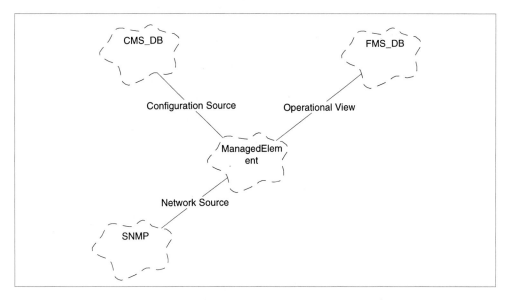

Figure 10-10. Class Diagram 1 (Managed Element)

Hierarchy:
    Superclasses: ManagedElement
Public Interface:
    Has-A Relationships:
        Equipment   Hardware
        Services   Software
    Attributes:
        String   nodeName
        Integer   nodeNumber

Class name:
Network

Documentation:
    Definition:
        The highest level managed element. A network is comprised of the collection of nodes that are managed by a single Proxy Agent running at a centralized location in the network.
    Constraints:
        The initial implementation will support only one network.

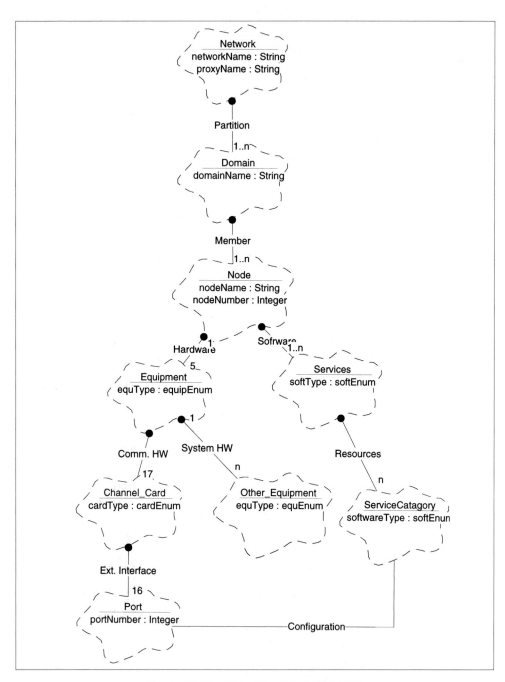

Figure 10-11. Class Diagram 2 (Network)

Export Control: Public
Cardinality: n
Hierarchy:
    Superclasses: ManagedElement
Public Interface:
    Has-A Relationships:
        Domain Partition
    Attributes:
        String   networkName
        String   proxyName

Class name:

FMS_DB

Documentation:
    Definition:
        The FMS DB is the local repository for operational images. This is an interface object that provides access to the actual relational database (RDB).
Export Control: Public
Cardinality: n
Hierarchy:
    Superclasses: none
Associations:
    ManagedElement Operational View

Class name:

Equipment

Documentation:
    Definition:
        Equipment refers to the primary hardware components that make up a node, including the backplane type that characterizes the optional hardware configuration.
Export Control: Public
Cardinality: n
Hierarchy:
    Superclasses: ManagedElement
Public Interface:
    Has-A Relationships:
        Other_EquipmentSystem HW
        Channel_CardComm. HW
    Attributes:
        equipEnum   equType

Class name:

CMS_DB

Documentation:
Definition:

The Configuration Database (CMS_DB) is the repository for the software config-uration of the network. The CMS_DB may be used as the alternate source for in-formation about managed elements that make up the FMS_DB.

Export Control: Public
Cardinality: n
Hierarchy:
  Superclasses: none
Associations:

ManagedElementConfiguration Source

Class name:

Channel_Card

Documentation:
Definition:

A channel card is a physical component of the node. Its function is to supply a number of ports. It resides in one of the fixed slots reserved for channel cards. Channel cards have 1, 2, 4, 8, or 16 ports supporting a single physical interface, but allowing multiple software services to be configured.

Export Control: Public
Cardinality: n
Hierarchy:
  Superclasses: ManagedElement
  Public Interface:
  Has-A Relationships:
    Port   Ext. Interface
Attributes:
    cardEnum   cardType

Class name:

Other_Equipment

Documentation:
Definition:

Other equipment is a class for any component that comprises the node but is not a channel card.

Export Control: Public
Cardinality: n
Hierarchy:
    Superclasses: ManagedElement
Public Interface:
    Has-A Relationships:
    Attributes:
        equEnum   equType

Class name:

    Service

Documentation:
    Definition:
        A service is a software application that runs on a node. Primary services include
        the WAN switching software (for X.25), and access PADs such as Async, DSP,
        SDLC, and others.
Export Control: Public
Cardinality: n
Hierarchy:
    Superclasses: ManagedElement
Public Interface:
    Has-A Relationships:
        ServiceCategoryResources
    Attributes:
        softEnum   softType

Class name:

    Port

Documentation:
    Definition:
        A port is a hardware interface that provides a connection point to some other
        piece of equipment. Ports are "owned" (i.e., controlled) by a service.
Export Control: Public
Cardinality: n
Hierarchy:
    Superclasses: ManagedElement
Public Interface:
    Has-A Relationships:
    Attributes:
        Integer   portNumber

Class name:

ManagedElement

Documentation:

Definition:

A parent class that is the basis of all "physical" components in the system. A managed element is any element in the network that can provide operational status to the management system. A managed element includes both hardware and software elements. Managed elements can be hardware such as power supplies or fan assemblies, or software such as X.25, or a combination such as an X.25 link assigned to a port.

Export Control: Public

Cardinality: n

Hierarchy:

   Superclasses: none

Public Interface:

   Has-A Relationships:

      contLevelEnum   containmentLevel

Class name:

SNMP

Documentation:

Definition:

SNMP is the interface to the actual Network. This is an interface object that provides the mapping of requests to the actual SNMP protocol operations (GET, GET-NEXT, etc.).

Constraints:

   SNMP reads the network's configuration from the Proxied node in the network. Therefore, the information on additional nodes is reliant on the configuration of the Proxy node.

Export Control: Public

Cardinality: n

Hierarchy:

   Superclasses: none

Associations:

   ManagedElementNetwork Source

Class name:

Domain

Documentation:

Definition:

The Domain is a logical grouping of nodes. Domains are created to subdivide the network into smaller, more manageable segments.

Export Control: Public
Cardinality: n
Hierarchy:
    Superclasses: ManagedElement
Public Interface:
    Has-A Relationships:
        Node   Member
    Attributes:
        String   domainName

Class name:

    ServiceCategory

Documentation:
    Definition:
        A service category is a collection of a specific type of managed elements under a service. Services may be one or more service categories. X.25, for example, may be composed of a link service category and an NUI service category.
Export Control: Public
Cardinality: n
Hierarchy:
    Superclasses: ManagedElement
Associations:
        Port   Configuration
Public Interface:
    Has-A Relationships:
        softEnum   softwareType

10.5.3.5. FMS Object-Scenario Diagrams

The following three FMS Object-Scenario Diagrams are key to understanding the FMS operation. Figure 10-12 shows the initial database population, Figure 10-13 shows how the database can be populated from the configuration database, and Figure 10-14 shows how the FMS database will be synchronized.

10.5.3.6. FMS Data Dictionary

The FMS Data Dictionary lists the domain entities as they are discovered. It is continually updated as the analysis and design are iterated. It establishes a vocabulary that is consistent throughout all of the phases of the project. A sample FMS Data Dictionary appears in Figure 10-15.

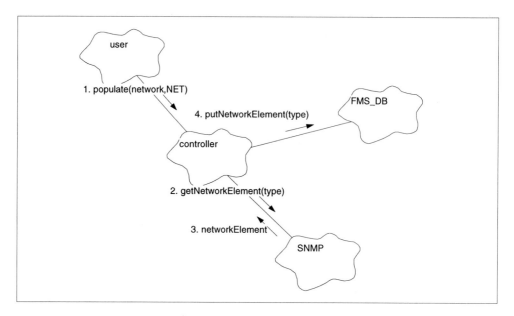

Figure 10-12. Initially Populate the FMS DB with Elements from Network

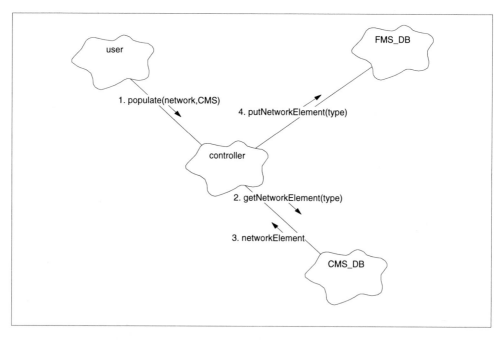

Figure 10-13. Initially Populate the FMS DB with Elements from CMS DB

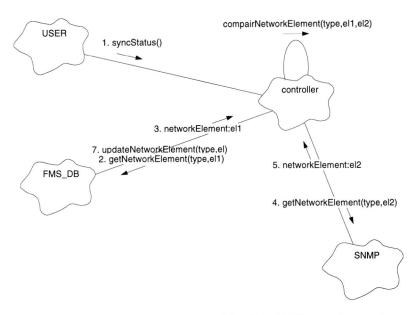

Figure 10-14. Synchronize Status of the FMS DB Network Elements
with the Status of the Actual Network Elements

Name	Type
Network	Class
Domain	Class
Node	Class
Equipment	Class
Channel Card	Class
Other Component	Class
Port	Class
Services	Class
ServiceCategory	Class

Figure 10-15. Fault Management System Data Dictionary

Name	Type
CMS Database	Class
FMS Database	Class
Managed Element	Class
SNMP	Class
Configuration Source	Relationship
Operational View	Relationship
Network Source	Relationship
Partition	Relationship
Member	Relationship
Hardware	Relationship
Software	Relationship
Communication Hardware	Relationship
Relationship	Relationship
External Interface	Relationship
Configuration	Relationship

Figure 10-15. Fault Management System Data Dictionary *(continued)*

10.5.4. FMS SYSTEM DESIGN

The FMS design centers around the creation of the physical model. The system designer creates the architecture for the implementation. The designer must also consider other issues such as common tactical policies and code reuse. The FMS analysis is expanded into a design and working implementation.

Seven possible deliverables are in the Booch Method for this step:

◆ Architectural Descriptions

◆ Executable Release Descriptions

◆ Class-Category Diagrams

- Design Class Diagrams
- Design Object-Scenario Diagrams
- New Specifications
- Amended Class Specifications

For the design, not all of the deliverables are required for every problem with the Booch Method. As with OOA, OOD is not done via a rigorous scientific formula. In general, the FMS design proceeds by iterating through three major steps:

1. Define the initial FMS architecture
2. Plan the Executable releases
3. Develop and refine the Executable releases

The Booch Design Deliverables are considered in each of these three phases.

One of the many benefits of the OO approach is that the design phase may cause a refinement to work already done in the analysis phase. This refinement leads to a sound implementation.

The key concept of the FMS Design is the creation of the architecture, which is the internal structure of the system. It lays out how the structure is organized.

The FMS is divided into partitions, each providing a specific service. This layering, or partitioning, method is common in system design for its many benefits such as abstraction and encapsulation. In the Booch Methodology, each partition is represented by a class category. Each of these categories provides a grouping of related services that have meaning for that particular level of abstraction. Each class category provides a well-defined interface that is to be implemented. The categories do not directly specify how the internal implementation is to be done, only the interfaces, so that each class category can be designed and implemented in an independent fashion. This use of class categories also greatly facilitates reuse.

The design shows how additional classes need to be added to the analysis model to carry out how the FMS application will work. These include application classes for a controller class and an event class that help support the key managed element class. Design also progressed through later iterations to reveal the need for additional internal classes that will be implemented. These will include classes to support the APIs for the database and the SNMP network communications.

The initial FMS architecture strategic decisions include interface consider-ations, object storage, communications, processes, and so forth. The system software that supports the application software needs to be considered here. For the FMS system this software includes:

◆ The Operating System

◆ The GUI

◆ Database Management Systems Interfaces

◆ Communications Interfaces

◆ Other System Software

The Architectural Services for the Fault Management System can be summa-rized as an Architectural Description in Figure 10-16.

The next important design step is to choose the Class Categories. They are based on the major functions of the FMS architecture. The FMS Class Catego-ries are:

◆ **FMS_System:** includes the domain classes defined in OOA and any additional ones that are needed to implement these classes (e.g., controller class, event class).

◆ **Persistent_Data:** provides database/storage functionality for persistent data items.

◆ **Data_Structures:** class library for all general data structures.

◆ **FMS_DB_Interface:** interface for the storing of information about the managed elements, including their status in the FMS Database.

◆ **SNMP_Net_Interface:** interface for the retrieval of information in the network via SNMP. A further iteration of the design will accommodate the retrieval of information from the configuration database. The analysis and design seems to indicate that the same interface may be used.

Figure 10-17 shows the FMS Class Categories and their relationship, as well as the "uses" association. The Data_Structures Class is global and is used by all classes. This class includes the necessary support libraries and internal classes that can be used by the other classes in the various class categories.

Another important design function is to recognize the dynamic aspects of the system. The dynamic aspects of FMS can be modeled via Design Class Di-

Architectural Services for the Fault Management System Platform
The FMS application runs as a process on a workstation (such as Sun SPARCstation). The platform must contain proper support hardware and drivers: 16MB RAM, Ethernet LAN card, 19" color monitor, 350MB hard drive, floppy disk, and mouse.

Operating System:
UNIX is used. The first release specifically uses Solaris 2.x from Sun Microsystems.

Platform User Interface:
Note: the FMS does not have a direct user interface but works with OpenView.
Motif is the GUI for the workstation platform.
Hewlett-Packard OpenView Windows is the Network Management GUI that provides an integration point for network management applications that run on the network management console workstation.

Database:
Ingres Relational Database Management System. SQL and a generic DB interface are implemented so that most common RDBMSs can be used. "Database portability" is a design consideration.

Communications Software:
The communications software is the protocol stack that talks to the devices on the network.
The protocol stack includes UDP, IP, and Ethernet. All devices that are to be managed must support this stack for communications and interoperability.

Network Management Software:
SNMP software from HP and another third party vendor implement the network management protocol.

Other System Software:
System software runs on the target (proxied) network devices.

Figure 10-16. FMS Architectural Services

agrams that show Control, Text-Scenario, and Object-Scenario diagrams of operational sequences that the application performs, and State Event Diagrams. These further reveal the operations that are necessary for the implementation.

The following diagram (Figure 10-18) is a Design Class Diagram with the addition of the Controller Class.

The creation of text for a scenario is another good method for modeling dynamic behavior. The following text is an example of a full status update. In this scenario the "user class" requests a full network, synchronized status update.

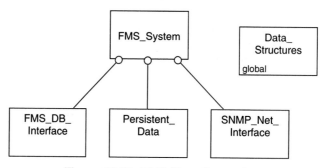

Figure 10-17. FMS Class Categories

The design indicates that the scenario is a start-up section and a set of three nested loops. This scenario appears in Figure 10-19.

The Event Trace Diagram also augments the text scenario by adding another level of detail. It traces the event flow between the classes involved in this scenario. It appears in Figure 10-20.

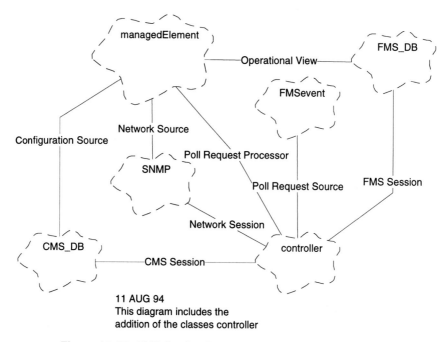

Figure 10-18. FMS Design Class Diagram (with Controller Class)

User requests full status update
Controller creates network object

TOP-LEVEL NETWORK LOOP
    Network object [at this containment level] gets source list [next level] from
    FMS DB
    For each domain in source list create [this level] object
    For each domain in new list create [this level] object from SNMP
    For each domain name create an object instance of a managed element
    Compare objects and generate FMS DB Update Events

MID-LEVEL DOMAIN LOOP
    For each domain in the new list, network object creates domain object
    Tell domain object to get source list of nodes from FMS DB
    Tell domain object to get new list of nodes from SNMP
    Compare lists and generate updates
    Build next level
    Exit to TOP-LEVEL NETWORK LOOP

LOW-LEVEL NODE LOOP
    For each node, create the node object
    Build the equipment list
    Build services list
    Exit to MID-LEVEL DOMAIN LOOP

Figure 10-19. Scenario: Request Full Network Status Synchronized Update

Another part of the FMS Design Model is the Design Object Scenario Diagram. Figure 10-21 depicts the user initiated full poll of the network. It shows key classes and numbered messages that flow between the objects.

Figure 10-22 is a State Event Diagram for the design of the Managed Element Class. This central class is very important for the discovering of network elements and their status. Figure 10-22 shows the key states, indicates the state operations, and describes the events where additional clarification is needed.

10.5.5. FMS EXECUTABLE RELEASE PLAN

The FMS Executable Release Plan indicates the "mini" releases that will be developed for the whole system. In the Booch method, the entire FMS application will be created from a series of "mini-systems," each with a pre-defined goal. These mini-systems are often called "slices" because they can be vertical views of how the design is implemented.

Total SNMP

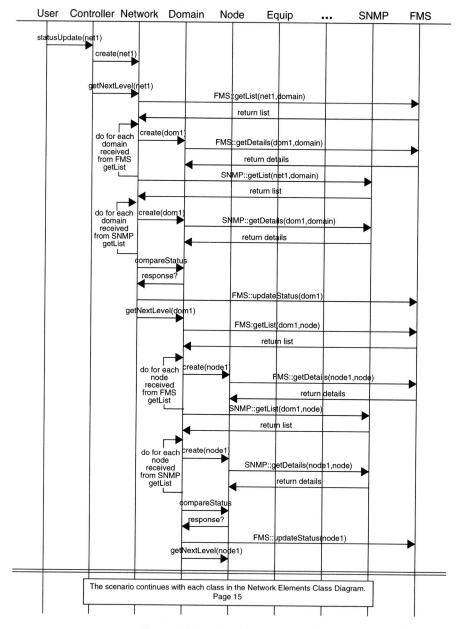

Figure 10-20. Event Trace Diagram

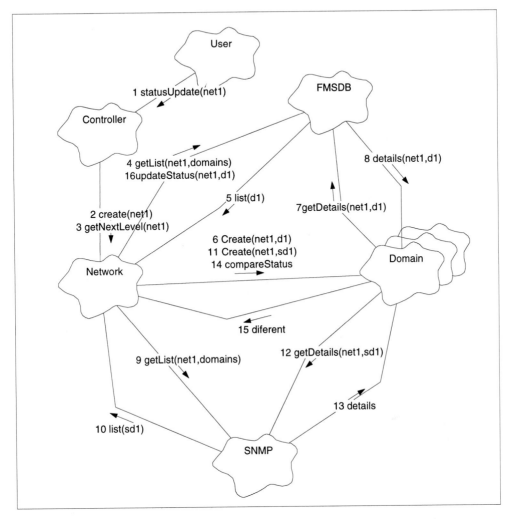

Figure 10-21. User Initiated Full Poll of Network Design Object Scenario Diagram

The FMS Executable Release Plan details:

◆ What new code will be added to the FMS application

◆ Which code modules have been completed, and what state they are currently in: debugged, tested, etc.

◆ Support code that is used to test working prototypes: test drivers, control scripts, etc.

443

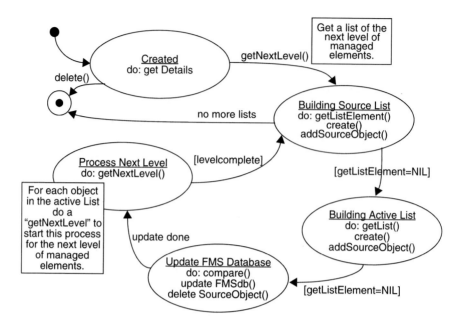

Figure 10-22. Managed Element State Diagram

- ◆ Simplified implementations of new and additional control and implementation classes that are needed, including library classes for global data, and so forth

10.5.6. FMS EXECUTABLE RELEASE DEVELOPMENT

A primary design task for implementation is the development of an Executable Release. The following template is recommended from the Booch methodology. It is a formalization, so that the implementation can be done by teams.

The following Executable Release (Figure 10-23) is an example for the FMS Controller Function.

Executable Release: FMS Controller

Goal:
Control interaction between the various FMS interfaces

Classes to be implemented:
Controller, Network, FMS_DB, Domain, SNMP

Previously implemented classes to use:
(None)

Use cases to be implemented:
Initiate the creation of the necessary network element

Inputs:
Receives input from "surrogate" user

Outputs:
Outputs the network name

Figure 10-23. FMS Executable Release Example

REFERENCES FOR CHAPTER 10

[1] Edwards, Paul (Editor-in-Chief). *The Encyclopedia of Philosophy*. Vol. 4. New York: Macmillan Publishing Co., Inc. 1967.

[2] Bartlett, John. *Familiar Quotations*. 15th ed. Boston: Little, Brown, and Co. 1980.

[3] Bapat, Subodh. *Object-Oriented Networks: Models for Architecture, Operations, and Management*. Englewood Cliffs, NJ: Prentice Hall. 1994.

[4] Bapat, Subodh. *Object-Oriented Networks: Models for Architecture, Operations, and Management*. Englewood Cliffs, NJ: Prentice Hall, 1994. p.19.

[5] Booch, Grady. *Object-Oriented Analysis and Design with Applications*. 2nd ed. Redwood City, CA: The Benjamin/Cummings Publishing Company, Inc. 1994.

[6] Rumbaugh, James, Michael Blaha, William Premerlani, Frederick Eddy, and William Lorensen. *Object-Oriented Modeling and Design*. Englewood Cliffs, NJ: Prentice Hall. 1991.

[7] White, Iseult. *Using the Booch Method: A Rational Approach*. Redwood City, CA: The Benjamin/Cummings Publishing Company, Inc. 1994.

[8] Leinwand, Allan, and Karen Fang Conroy. *Network Management: A Practical Perspective*. 2nd ed. Reading, MA: Addison-Wesley Publishing Company. 1996.

[9] Jacobson, Ivar, Magnus Christerson, Patrik Jonsson, and Gunnar Overgaard. *Object-Oriented Software Engineering, A Use Case Driven Approach*. Reading, MA: Addison-Wesley. 1995.

CHAPTER 11

SNMP Development and Support Tools

Every tool carries with it the spirit by which it has been created.

—Werner Karl Heisenberg[1]

For the implementation of SNMP NMSs and agents, you need a wide variety of development and support tools for the many different computing environments existing today. A vast array of tools and utilities are available from any number of SNMP vendors, internetworking hardware and software development houses, university research centers, and other involved parties. A quick "surf" with your favorite Web search engine reveals hundreds of hits at sites that contain information about SNMP tools.

11.1. SNMP DEVELOPMENT TOOLS

Because SNMP is primarily implemented in software, the mandatory development and testing environment must be present for any given implementation.

These include the programming language compilers, linkers, editors, and whatever other implementation-dependent tools that are required. The C and C++ programming languages are favorites for implementing network management software such as SNMP. Where code size and execution speed are a concern, assembly language is still used. Other high-level program languages used include ADA, Pascal, Modula-2, FORTRAN, and now Java. Scripting languages such as TCL and PERL are also gaining wide acceptance. The use of standard APIs such as WinSNMP and SNMP++ facilitate more efficient and bug-free SNMP implementations.

The operating systems of the target network devices are dependent on the nature of the device. High-end NMSs require a multi-tasking OS such as UNIX and its derivatives or Windows NT. Low-end NMSs often run under Windows 95 or 3.1. General-purpose host devices support all of the desktop operating systems: Windows, UNIX, OS/2, Apple OS, and others. Network devices such as routers and bridges contain proprietary and commercial, embedded real-time kernels for speed and efficiency. Less complex devices often contain a minimal implementation task scheduler to perform its services and support network management.

Marshall Rose draws the broad distinction between entities that have the network management software integrated into the device's general system software, such as routers and bridges, and devices where network management is a separate process, as in a general-purpose workstation. He labels these two types of implementations tightly-integrated and loosely-integrated, respectively (see [2]).

Development tools often include additional general support software such as source control software, testing tools, and other utilities such as loaders and cross-compilers, word processors, documentation aids, and so forth.

You need to understand the specific requirements for these development tools before attempting an SNMP implementation.

11.2. SNMP SUPPORT TOOLS

SNMP support tools are the additional software utility programs needed for such activities as creating and verifying various MIBs and their object instrumentation, testing the protocol commands and responses, checking the transport connection and internetwork traffic, and several other miscellaneous and implementation-specific tasks.

The class of SNMP support tools that deal with the MIB are called MIB tool kits and are available in a variety of forms from various vendors.[3] Two requisite utilities for creating and analyzing MIBs are MIB compilers and MIB editors, or "walk" programs.

The range of SNMP support tools varies greatly in their size, cost, and capabilities. Some allow for the automatic addition and validation of new MIB variables. Less complex versions require the user to "manually" enter new information. The tools also greatly vary on the amount of SNMP expertise a user must possess to fully utilize them. Different levels of expertise are needed in SNMP development and installation for device agents and for the NMS with its many, often complex, management applications. New systems include extensive help facilities. The general state of SNMP support tools seems to be evolving at least as quickly as SNMP itself.

11.2.1. MIB COMPILERS

The MIB compiler is one of the most essential SNMP support tools. It is an interpreter-type program that accepts a MIB input file in ASN.1 syntax, parses the definition file, and creates a MIB output file that can be used by the agent and NMS, provided no errors are discovered. David Perkins and Evan McGinnis point out in *Understanding SNMP MIBs* that MIB compilers can be "greatly misunderstood tools."[4] In addition to the compiler's duties of checking the syntax of the MIB, the compiler can "also apply to an entire class of tools that perform functions as diverse as drawing tree representations of a MIB, to automatically generating C code for a management application or agent."[5]

Figure 11-1 depicts the organization of a MIB compiler (from [6]).

The MIB Compiler model shown in Figure 11-1 decomposes the compiler into a front-end and one or more back-ends. The front-end accepts a MIB input file, processes it, and creates intermediate results. These intermediate results are then used as input to one or more back-end modules that process these formats and create the output of the compiler. The actual details are implementation-dependent, and the model can be realized as several separate programs, a stand-alone application, or even as an embedded module that resides inside an NMS or agent.

449

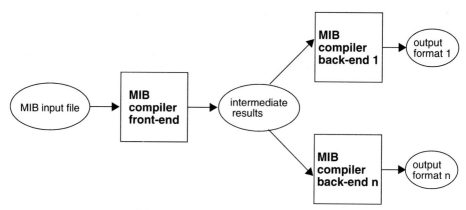

Figure 11-1. MIB Compiler Organization

The MIB input file is an ASCII text file that must be created in the proper format using ASN.1. Version 1 MIB compilers should support the Version 1 SMI (defined in RFCs 1155 and 1212), and the Version 2 MIB compilers should successfully parse RFC 1902 SMI defined information modules. As a review, Figure 11-2 shows the generalized format of what a MIB compiler is expecting as input object definitions for SNMPv1. The modified input object definition is required for SNMPv2.

```
object-name OBJECT-TYPE
        SYNTAX object-type
        ACCESS object-access
        STATUS object-status
        DESCRIPTION "description of the object." *
        REFERENCE reference*
        INDEX index**
        DEFVAL default-value*
::= { object-table object-id }
```
* optional
** only present in a Table Entry object

Figure 11-2. Generalized Concise MIB Object Definition (Version 1)

Although slight nuances exist for the different Version 1 MIB compiler implementations, the following general observations apply in nearly every case. One must look at a specific MIB compiler implementation and its documentation for all the details.

The object-name is the alphanumeric name for the MIB object. Each object-name should be unique throughout the MIB. Special characters should be avoided. The object-type is the variable's ASN.1 syntax type. It must be one of the valid ASN.1 types used by the SNMP subset. The object-access field must be one of the four allowable access values. The object-status field must also be one of the four valid status values. The Description, Reference, and Default Values clauses are optional but they are recommended, if possible, for documentation and clarity. The Index clause must be present in the Table Entry objects to define the table key. The Index also defines how the table instantiations are declared. The object-table object-id values specify the table or group that the object belongs to and its number in that table or group. Object IDs must be unique in their table.

The MIB module must also have the mandatory header section and the pertinent OBJECT IDENTIFIER tree structure to place this MIB in the SNMP name space. The MIB module header contains the MIB name (e.g., RFC1213-MIB), the DEFINITIONS ::= BEGIN clause, and the IMPORTS section needed for the proper linkage. Additional Textual Conventions can also be included.

A pair of dash characters typically signals the start of a comment. The comment continues until the end of the line:

```
-- This is a comment line in this MIB file.
```

The additional rules for the Version 2 SMI can be found in RFCs 1902, 1903, and 1904.

The front-end process has four main functions[7]:

♦ lexical analysis

♦ syntactic analysis

♦ semantic analysis

♦ error handling

The lexical analysis breaks the input file into small units called tokens. These tokens are then examined for the correct syntax. The tokens must conform to the rules of ASN.1. The *meaning* or semantics of the input are then verified within this context. If an error is discovered in any of the three analysis phases, the error handling routines are called and the appropriate action is taken.

The intermediary results of the front-end can be stored in memory or on disk files. This output becomes the input for the compiler back-end(s). The back-ends create the output of the compiler. Often, multiple options exist for the types of output the back-end processes can create.

One way the options can be invoked is through various command line arguments. The MIB compiler often supports a number of options that affect its operation in this way. A generalized command-line format for invoking a MIB compiler might be:

>mib_compiler_name   [-options list]   input_MIB_definitions_file

A sample of options for back-end output and overall compiler operation might include:

◆ configure and use a specified output file name
◆ invoke help on running the MIB compiler itself
◆ run the compiler in "verbose" mode
◆ create a corresponding Object Identifier list
◆ check for duplicate MIB entries
◆ create an output error file
◆ create a log file for auditing the compiler's activity
◆ create a schema file for the NMS
◆ create instrumentation code for the agent
◆ create a function prototypes file

The output file that contains code is important output from the MIB compiler. It is typically an ASCII file in the target programming language such as C or C++. This output source language file can then be compiled and linked with the SNMP implementation to form an executable file. Highly sophisticated MIB compilers may be capable of generating more than one source language format and may have additional tuning and configuration parameters.

This output file can contain the skeleton routines for the instrumentation code that is used in the agent implementation. Additional manual tweaking may be necessary to add any implementation-specific details.

The help option offers the user a list of the options that can be used with this MIB compiler. It may include additional information on some options.

Running the compiler in verbose mode gives the user feedback on how the compiler is processing the input file. Verbose output can be sent to the screen, to a file, or to a printer. This mode aids in debugging syntax or semantic errors in the input file. The compiler stops at the first fatal error and directs the user to the "offending" line. Verbose mode may also be configurable to print or not print banners, warnings, and so on.

The MIB compiler often has the ability to generate an Object Identifier list that can be informational and also aid in debugging. This list is a compilation of the objects included in a particular MIB arranged in lexicographical order to mirror the SNMP name space for MIB objects.

A partial sample from MIB-II may be similar to the listing shown in Figure 11-3.

```
// Listing of MIB Object Identifiers from mib2.txt
// compiled on Friday, 27jan97   09:26 AM
//
1                      iso
1.3                    org
1.3.6                  dod
1.3.6.1                internet
1.3.6.1.2              mgmt
1.3.6.1.2.1            mib-2
1.3.6.1.2.1.1          system
1.3.6.1.2.1.1.1        sysDescr
1.3.6.1.2.1.1.2        sysObjectID
1.3.6.1.2.1.1.3        sysUpTime
1.3.6.1.2.1.1.4        sysContact
1.3.6.1.2.1.1.5        sysName
1.3.6.1.2.1.1.6        sysLocation
1.3.6.1.2.1.1.7        sysServices
1.3.6.1.2.1.2          interfaces
1.3.6.1.2.1.2.1        ifNumber
1.3.6.1.2.1.2.2        ifTable
1.3.6.1.2.1.2.2.1      ifEntry
1.3.6.1.2.1.2.2.1.1    ifIndex
1.3.6.1.2.1.2.2.1.2    ifDescr
1.3.6.1.2.1.2.2.1.3    ifType
1.3.6.1.2.1.2.2.1.4    ifMtu
1.3.6.1.2.1.2.2.1.5    ifSpeed
1.3.6.1.2.1.2.2.1.6    ifPhysAddress
1.3.6.1.2.1.2.2.1.7    ifAdminStatus
1.3.6.1.2.1.2.2.1.8    ifOperStatus
1.3.6.1.2.1.2.2.1.9    ifLastChange
1.3.6.1.2.1.2.2.1.10   ifInOctets
1.3.6.1.2.1.2.2.1.11   ifInUcastPkts
1.3.6.1.2.1.2.2.1.12   ifInNUcastPkts
1.3.6.1.2.1.2.2.1.13   ifInDiscards
1.3.6.1.2.1.2.2.1.14   ifInErrors
1.3.6.1.2.1.2.2.1.15   ifInUnknownProtos
1.3.6.1.2.1.2.2.1.16   ifOutOctets
1.3.6.1.2.1.2.2.1.17   ifOutUcastPkts
1.3.6.1.2.1.2.2.1.18   ifOutNUcastPkts
1.3.6.1.2.1.2.2.1.19   ifOutDiscards
1.3.6.1.2.1.2.2.1.20   ifOutErrors
1.3.6.1.2.1.2.2.1.21   ifOutQLen
1.3.6.1.2.1.2.2.1.22   ifSpecific
```

Figure 11-3. MIB Compiler Object Identifier Output

A helpful option for most MIB compilers is the ability to detect duplicate MIB entries. Duplication in various forms can cause subtle errors that are difficult to detect.

The creation of an error file is very important in the initial stages of MIB development if any problems occur. The error file allows the problems to be examined and corrected.

The creation of a schema file is important for the NMS. The schema file is a special output format used by most NMSs to facilitate handling its MIB and all of the MIB variables it manages for the agents in its community. The schema file format is implementation-dependent to the database system implemented by the NMS. For rudimentary managers, a schema file may not be necessary.

The creation of a function prototypes file is also helpful for documentation and the debugging of SNMP implementations. These are the prototypes for the functions that would be used in a particular implementation. This file is especially helpful for the C++ language, because this language requires prototypes before a program can successfully compile.

In general, many different MIB compilers are currently available from a number of vendors. They should all successfully compile the standard MIB definitions and any extensions and vendor-specific objects that are needed for a particular SNMP implementation. They should provide several helpful optional capabilities.

11.2.2. OTHER MIB TOOLS

A MIB "walker" program is a special support tool that allows a user to view the MIB hierarchy tree structure. Some new versions of this program have an auto-discovery capability, where the tool interrogates a MIB and creates an ordered table of all of the objects in that MIB. A MIB walker is also called a MIB *browser* and less often a MIB *editor*.

This is a very handy tool that allows the user to traverse a particular tree in different ways to retrieve different "views" of the objects. It is very helpful in that its output is often graphical and depicts the abstraction of all of the MIB variables and where they reside on the tree.

Some MIB walkers are very sophisticated and allow a user to "click" on a particular object and view its description and all of its attributes.

MIB walkers are typically implemented as an application that does a series of GetNext commands. Since table indices cannot be 0, the application can "walk" a table by setting the suffix to the first `GetNext` request to ".0" and performing repeated `GetNexts`. The returned OID from the response is used as the input OID to the subsequent `GetNext` request. This process is repeated until the end of the table (or the MIB) is encountered, when the OID prefix changes. Note that the program doesn't know you have reached the end of the table until you retrieve the first value beyond it.

11.2.3. OTHER SNMP TOOLS

A wide variety of other SNMP tools also exist for many other purposes. Windowed and command line test programs simulate NMSs and agents. They allow for the creation of get and set SNMP Messages with variations on the PDU type, various field values, variable binding lists, and so forth. They allow for the entry of error values to test the correctness of the SNMP NMS, agent implementations, and the protocol processing. Traps can also be simulated and tested. Several intelligent data collection programs are also available.

11.3. AVAILABLE SNMP DEVELOPMENT AND SUPPORT TOOLS

SNMP development and support tools are available from a wide variety of commercial and public sources.

The two most popular are the SNMP Management Information Compiler (SMIC) and Managed Object Syntax-compiler (YACC-based) (MOSY). Both are freely available.

MOSY is included with the ISO Development Environment (ISODE) package. This package is written in C and runs under most UNIX operating system platforms. It contains many useful tools and utilities, including prototypes for agent and NMS implementations. You can find a copy of the ISODE distribution at:

```
ftp://ftp.uu.net/networking/osi/isode
```

SMIC is a very strict and comprehensive front-end compiler that runs under a variety of platforms. A new version is available called SMIC next generation (SMICng) that handles the new version SMI. Copies of the compilers are included on the CD that comes with *Understanding SNMP MIBs* (see *Annotated Bibliography*), or you can retrieve them via anonymous FTP at:

```
ftp.synoptics.com:/tmp/eng/mibcompiler/src/tar.z for SMIC, and
ftp.synoptics.com:/tmp/eng/mibcompiler2 for SMICng.
```

Another interesting SNMP tool called SNACC is an ASN.1 compiler that can create C code for BER encoding and decoding. The SNACC source is available at:

```
ftp://ftp.cs.ubc.ca/pub/local/src/snacc
```

All of the commercial NMSs and most of the agent vendors include their own MIB compilers and many useful tools that work with their product offerings. Please contact the various vendors to receive information on their SNMP development and support tools.

REFERENCES FOR CHAPTER 11

[1] Bartlett, John. *Bartlett's Familiar Quotations*. 16th ed. Boston: Little, Brown, and Company. 1992.

[2] Rose, Marshall T. *The Simple Book, An Introduction to Management of TCP/IP-based Internets*. Englewood Cliffs, NJ: Prentice Hall. 1991.

[3] Jander, Mary. "MIB Tools: Coping With the Not-So-Simple Side of SNMP," *Data Communications*. February 1992, 79-82.

[4] Perkins, David, and Evan McGinnis. *Understanding SNMP MIBs*. Upper Saddle River, NJ: Prentice Hall. 1996.

[5] Ibid. p. 325

[6] Roberts, Samuel M. "An Introduction to SNMP MIB Compilers." *The Simple Times*. January/February 1993, 1-5.

[7] Roberts, Samuel M. "An Introduction to SNMP MIB Compilers." *The Simple Times*. January/February 1993, 2.

CHAPTER

12

The Network Management Station

Management is known by the company it keeps.

—*(anonymous)*[1]

The Network Management Station (NMS) is the controlling entity that uses the SNMP protocol to manage its agents. The NMS is discussed in terms of the larger framework of the Network Manager. The Network Manager is the NMS bundled with its supporting components to create a usable management platform that can control and monitor the agents in its community. Often the terms NMS and Network Manager are used interchangeably, although for this chapter I assign a specific meaning to each. The Network Manager with the NMS appears in Figure 12-1.

Often a specific vendor's network manager product is called the Network Management Platform (NMP). Although the hardware and software involved in the implementation of the platform come in various flavors, depending on the extent of its functionality and other specific requirements, a general model can be described from similar components.

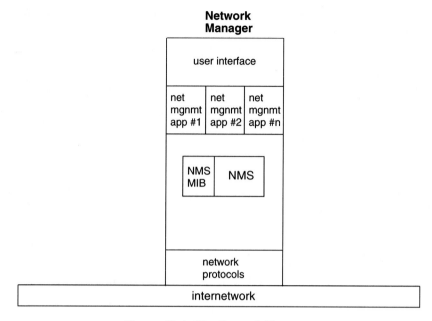

Figure 12-1. The Network Manager

12.1. COMPONENTS OF THE NETWORK MANAGER

The Network Manager is comprised of five key components:

♦ The Network Protocols

♦ The Network Management Station

♦ The NMS Management Information Base (MIB)

♦ The Network Management Applications

♦ The User Interface

12.1.1. THE NETWORK PROTOCOLS

As the overall SNMP Reference Model introduced in Section 2.4 shows, any device that is connected to the internetwork uses its network protocols to communicate to other devices. The Network Manager primarily uses the TCP/IP protocol suite for this, although SNMP can run over a variety of other transport domains. If the NMS is running the TCP protocol suite, it must have UDP implemented to send and receive SNMP Messages on UDP port 161 and also to receive traps on UDP port 162. It must also have the necessary IP protocols, a network access protocol for handling the connection to a specific media type, and whatever other networking protocols that are required for the specific implementation.

12.1.2. THE NETWORK MANAGEMENT STATION

The NMS is the software entity that processes the SNMP protocol. It encodes and decodes messages from ASN.1 to usable internal formats. For Version 1, it creates requests by making `GetRequest`, `SetRequest`, and `GetNextRequest-PDUs`. The NMS also processes `GetResponse-PDUs`, handles errors, and receives and takes action from Trap-PDUs. Version 2 handles the additional processing of the `GetBulk-PDU` and the modifications of the `Response-PDU`, the new trap format, and possibly the `InformRequest-PDU`. It also handles the other changes to the protocol discussed in Chapter 6.

The NMS interfaces to its MIB to recognize the proper set of managed objects that can be monitored and controlled. The NMS must interface to the UDP layer and the other network protocols to send and receive the SNMP Messages. It must also provide the necessary services for any requesting network management applications that may be present on the platform. Requests are made through the network management API. The management API may be a proprietary one implemented by an NMS vendor, or one of the new standard APIs being developed, such as WinSNMP for Windows-based managers.

12.1.3. THE NMS MIB

The NMS MIB contains the non-redundant superset of all of the MIBs from all of the agents in this manager's community. The NMS MIB must be translated into a local format that is more usable to the platform software. This format is often called the network manager's schema file.

The NMS MIB also usually encompasses a database and a database management system for additional management functionality that can be used by the applications. It may use a standard or proprietary storage API. The additional functionality includes such necessary activities as report generation, statistics gathering, accounting, usage metering, asset and configuration management, and so forth.

Often the managed physical network devices are stored as logical entries in the database. This abstraction makes the addition, deletion, and modification of the managed devices more straightforward. It can also represent various relationships between the devices in a network. The DBMS also offers the additional functionality of database queries, sort and search features, and different "views" of the managed objects.

12.1.4. THE NETWORK MANAGEMENT APPLICATIONS

The Network Management Applications are a hot area in SNMP network management today. The NMS gathers the necessary data, but the applications use the data to aid the network administrator to make intelligent decisions, provide proactive management, and extend the functionality of the platform in many directions. The first generation of network applications included report generation, trouble tickets, and audible alarms. The next generation of applications often include knowledge-based expert systems that can "beep" network personnel when serious problems occur, anticipate problems in various sections of the enterprise internetwork, use heuristics to aid in planning and operations, and provide valuable information that can be used to create informative displays on the user interface.

A key component of the network applications is the use of a standard management API. This allows multi-vendor applications to exist on a platform in order to offer the best mix of applications for a particular enterprise. The interface between the network management applications and the NMS should be well-defined–open and standards-based if possible.

12.1.5. THE USER INTERFACE

The Network User Interface is the primary interface between the end-user and the network manager. Most platforms offer a graphical user interface based on such standards as X-Windows Motif for UNIX, Microsoft Windows (3.1, 95, and NT), and perhaps OS/2 Presentation Manager. These GUIs offer multiple, movable, resizeable windows, many colors, multi-tasking, user-friendly controls, and ease of use. A consistent user interface to the network manager and its applications makes the network management personnel and any administrator's jobs more straightforward. Consistent and uniform user interfaces are easier to learn and easier to use. The User Interface also includes the use of a mouse or other pointing device to aid in the use of the GUI.

Note that the user interface is specifically not defined in the SNMP framework and is an implementation consideration.

12.2. NETWORK MANAGER FUNCTIONALITY

Due to the resource-intensive nature of the NMS processing, the network manager is usually a high-end workstation running a multi-tasking operating systems (such as UNIX, a UNIX derivative, or Windows NT). It often possesses a large amount of RAM, a fairly large hard disk, and other secondary storage and backup devices. Its resources should be scalable.

"The system must be easy to expand and customize. No single network management system can be built to accommodate every network by default. The system must facilitate the addition of applications and features required by a network engineer."[2]

Most NMSs possess a GUI with full-color, high resolution, bitmapped graphics displays. The screen that usually first greets the NMS user is the network management topology map.

This topology map shows all of the managed network devices present in the internetwork. This map can typically be sized and filtered depending on the location, number, and types of devices. Clicking with the mouse device often reveals several levels of definition in the map to show remote sites, floors in a building, and so forth. The intent is to get down to being able to identify and manage a specific network device.

Special icons represent types or class of devices. The icons often use "traffic lights" to indicate status: green is "go" (the device is up and running correctly), red (the device is down or a problem exists), and yellow (the device has a temporary problem, or some other type of inefficiency). Other colors are often used to convey any number of other indications. One possible convention for a color scheme to indicate device status appears in Figure 12-2 (from [2]).

The topology map also often allows a user to click on the device icon to uncover more information about the device. Configuration and other informa-

461

Color	Meaning
green	device is up with no errors
yellow	device may have an error
red	device is in error state
blue	device is up, but was previously in error state
orange	device is misconfigured
gray	no information is available about the device
purple	device is being polled

Figure 12-2. Color Conventions for NMS Icons

tional attributes can be interrogated and perhaps changed with the proper permission codes.

The NMS also includes an event logger or monitoring facility to display traps received from the agents in its community. It can also allow for the creation of a polling scheme to check on the network devices at specified intervals. The event logger is also configurable to filter and prioritize information that it captures and displays.

The ideal network manager and its applications implement and support the full suite of Network Management functions (remember FCAPS from Chapter 1?) for its managed devices.

◆ Fault Management

◆ Configuration Management

◆ Accounting Management

◆ Performance Management

◆ Security Management

Its NMS and network applications permit remote problem resolution by human or machine intervention. It functions in a multi-vendor, multi-protocol environment. It provides a means to anticipate potential bottlenecks. And it is also flexible and upgradeable. The use of standards and APIs makes this functionality possible.

Needless to say, dozens and dozens of vendors offer a myriad of network management products. Many offerings exist that range from complete platform solutions (hardware and software) to unique and interesting network applications that are specific to certain niches of the total SNMP network management scheme. Other companies specialize in APIs, network testing programs, various management tools, and so forth. Recent buyer's guides for Network Management Products offer a wide variety of the available products. Any current publication on networks is filled with present and future network manager product offerings.

REFERENCES FOR CHAPTER 12

[1] Esar, Evan. *20,000 Quips and Quotes*. Garden City, NY: Doubleday and Company, Inc. 1968.

[2] Leinwand, Allan, and Karen Fang, *Network Management: A Practical Perspective*. Reading, MA: Addison-Wesley Publishing Company. 1993.

The Agent

The Agent is the processing entity resident in each managed network entity. It receives requests and sends responses to and from the network manager in its community. Agents can also be configured to send trap messages. The agent uses its instrumentation routines to retrieve and set the various MIB objects it controls. The agent is usually discussed in terms of the larger framework of the Managed Network Entity. This is usually the network device that contains the agent software. The Managed Network Entity appears in Figure 13-1.

Although the hardware and software that compose the managed network entity are dependent on the functionality and services offered by the device, they can be modeled from similar components. The SNMP Agent must support its MIB, send and receive on the Transport interface, encode and decode the ASN.1 format of the SNMP Messages, and so forth.

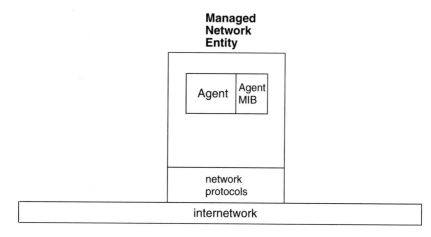

Figure 13-1. The Managed Network Entity

13.1.COMPONENTS OF THE MANAGED NETWORK ENTITY

The Managed Network Entity is comprised of three key components:

◆ The Network Protocols

◆ The Agent

◆ The Agent MIB

13.1.1. THE NETWORK PROTOCOLS

Any device that is connected to the internetwork uses its network protocols to communicate to other devices. The overall SNMP Reference Model in Figure 2-14 shows this setup. The Managed Network Entity can use the TCP/IP protocol suite for this purpose. It usually has UDP implemented to send and receive SNMP Messages on port 161. It must also be able to send traps on port 162. The agent must also have the necessary IP protocols, a network access protocol for connecting to its media, and whatever other networking protocols that are required for a specific implementation. As you saw earlier, SNMP can be implemented over alternative transport domains, although this option is less desirable.

13.1.2. THE AGENT

The Agent is the software entity that processes the SNMP protocol for its managed device. It encodes and decodes the SNMP set and get messages it receives from the NMS, from ASN.1 to usable internal formats. It then transmits responses, handles errors, and sends trap PDUs as required. It must implement SNMP Version 1, Version 2, or both.

The Agent interfaces to its MIB through its instrumentation routines to read and write the set of managed objects of interest requested by the NMS. It must interface to the UDP layer (or possibly, another transport service) and the other network protocols in the suite as needed, to send and receive the SNMP Messages.

A powerful extension to SNMP allows for a Proxy Agent to provide for the management of objects that are not under the direct control of the SNMP Agent or do not directly support the UDP/IP protocol stack.

13.1.3. THE AGENT MIB

The Agent MIB contains the set of all the variables of interest for the NMS. The Agent MIB contains all of the managed objects that can provide management information about this particular network device. If a group of MIB objects pertains to the services, protocols, and components supported by this device, they should be a part of the agent's MIB and implemented by this agent process.

13.2. THE AGENT FUNCTIONALITY

An important piece of the agent is its instrumentation routines. Once the agent process has determined that the object requested is in its MIB and is accessible, it calls an associated instrumentation function that determines how to actually retrieve or set the value of that particular MIB variable.

In SNMP, the instrumentation routines need to have knowledge of where and how to get at every MIB variable that the agent maintains. The instrumentation routines are very implementation-dependent and specific to each agent. (Contrast this to the very formalized instrumentation scheme for CMIS. Each protocol layer has its own Layer Management Entity (LME) that in turn interfaces to the System Management Application-Entity (SMAE). See [2].) Figure

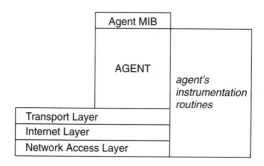

Figure 13-2. The Agent and Its Instrumentation Routines

13-2 shows a block diagram of how the agent interfaces to its protocol stack, its MIB, and its instrumentation routines. The instrumentation routines must be able to interrogate every layer that contains variables of interest to be read or written to by the agent.

13.3. TYPES OF SNMP AGENTS

SNMP agents are designed to be as simple as possible in order to minimize resource requirements and processing overhead. This design allows agents to be present in the widest number of network devices that are to be managed. It makes for the present manager-centric view of many agents and few network managers.

This generation of SNMP agents is not to be confused with all the recent talk about the intelligent agents circulating throughout the Internet. SNMP agents are passive—except for possibly sending out a trap or two. They do not roam about the network, they do not talk to other agents, and they do not leave their managed device in search of information (or adventure!). They live quietly in their community without thinking of forming a society. Perhaps the network management agent of the future will be hidden "manageBots" that work behind the scenes in our self-healing network, but for today they remain simple.

Five important types of agents are of concern for current SNMP Practice. They are:

◆ The SNMP Version 1 Agent

◆ The SNMP Version 2 Agent

- The Bilingual Agent

- The Proxy Agent

- The Extensible Agent

A representative list of agent vendors is included in Chapter 15.

13.3.1. THE SNMPV1 AGENT

The SNMPv1 agent implements the SNMP Version 1 protocol. It must receive and process the `GetRequest`, the `GetNextRequest`, and the `SetRequest`. It must be capable of responding with a `GetResponse` and also of sending out a trap.

13.3.2. THE SNMPV2 AGENT

The SNMPv2 agent implements the SNMP Version 2 protocol. It must receive and process the `GetRequest`, the `GetNextRequest`, `GetBulkRequest` and the `SetRequest`. It must be capable of responding with the `Response` and also of sending out a Version 2 trap message.

13.3.3. THE BILINGUAL AGENT

A bilingual agent must be able to speak both versions of SNMP by recognizing the version number and successfully processing the protocol operation. It knows which message to send to which network manager.

The implementation may actually be in SNMPv2 to reduce code redundancy if the agent maps SNMPv1 requests into SNMPv1 responses. This implementation is possible because the SMIv2 is a superset of SMIv1. The protocol operations are very similar, also. This translation entails mapping the error statuses, matching SNMPv2 exceptions to SNMPv1 errors, skipping `Counter64` and any other non-Version-1 syntax, and transforming Version 2 traps to Version 1 format. Figure 13-3 shows how the 19 Version 2 error statuses can be matched to their Version 1 counterparts.

Version 2 Error	Version 1 Error
noError	noError
tooBig	tooBig
noSuchName	noSuchName
badValue	badValue
readOnly	readOnly
genErr	genErr
wrongValue	badValue
wrongEncoding	badValue
wrongType	badValue
wrongLength	badValue
inconsistentValue	badValue
noAccess	noSuchName
notWritable	noSuchName
noCreation	noSuchName
inconsistentName	noSuchName
resourceUnavailable	genErr
commitFailed	genErr
undoFailed	genErr
authorizationError	noSuchName

Figure 13-3. Mapping Version 2 Errors to Version 1

13.3.4. THE PROXY AGENT

A proxy stands in between two parties to translate or substitute function for any activity that cannot be directly supported in a native manner. The proxy agent in the SNMP context is a powerful extension to management capabilities. "Simply put, a proxy is a software program that allows previously unmanageable network elements to be managed by a standard network management system."[3] In terms of SNMP, the proxy agent provides for the management of objects that are not under the direct control of the standard SNMP agent or do not directly support the UDP/IP protocol stack. Figure 13-4 shows a block diagram of how a proxy agent is positioned between the objects needing to be managed and the NMS.

Figure 13-4. The SNMP Proxy Agent

The solution to the first problem is to implement an application gateway proxy. This type of proxy needs to interpret the managed information and be able to "MIBify" it, to properly respond to the NMS. The second problem necessitates the use of a protocol gateway proxy to convert the native protocols into SNMP/UDP/IP traffic for communication to the NMS. The term *proxy agent* refers to both types of proxy translators.

Marshall Rose points out an interesting application of proxy agents. They can store answers to frequently asked inquiries to reduce the processing overhead at the managed device. "There is also a clever use of a proxy agent: caching of management information. In some environments, some management questions get asked frequently, so a proxy agent might be placed between the managed node and several management stations so as to minimize the processing burden on the managed node."[4] The application for these types of proxy agents may include administrative firewalls, caching firewalls, transport bridging, and protocol translation.[5]

13.3.5. THE EXTENSIBLE AGENT

The extensible agent ("Agent X") is an architecture that contains a master agent and sub-agents that communicate through a standard interface. The multiple sub-agents can be resident on the same device or on a connected proxied device. The master agent processes the SNMP protocol, and each sub-agent is responsible for a specific MIB view. The single sub-agent API implements a dynamic registering and de-registering of sub-agents while the main agent is running and communicating to the NMS.

The need for extensible agents arises from the fact that an SNMP agent is a statically compiled set of code that could not heretofore accommodate the run-time addition and deletion of MIB instances while the agent was running. The extensible agent also makes the set logic more robust by allowing the test, and then sets a two-step phase that assures the integrity of all of the individual sets done in one `SetRequest-PDU` (especially for operations on a table).

Figure 13-5 shows the extensible agent architecture.

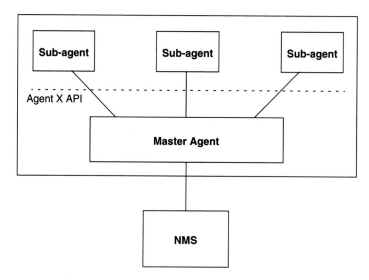

Figure 13-5. The Extensible Agent Architecture

Previously, sub-agents were implemented by experimental and proprietary techniques. An early effort, the SNMP Multiplexing Protocol (specified in RFC 1227, *SMUX MUX Protocol and MIB*), met with initial success, but was later found to be flawed. The RFC was then demoted to historical status and further SMUX implementations are now discouraged.

The Distributed Protocol API (DPAPI) (first released as RFC 1228, *SNMP-DPI: Simple Network Management Protocol Distributed Program Interface*, and then revised in RFC 1592, *Simple Network Management Protocol Distributed Protocol Interface Version 2.0*) is an experimental protocol that has been implemented successfully by several vendors. Other notable proprietary vendor efforts, such as SNMP Research's EMANATE product (Enhanced Management

Agent Through Extensions), have been widely deployed. All of these efforts have contributed technology that will be included in the AgentX effort and the final standard.

Work is continuing within the SNMP Agent Extensibility working group of the IETF to offer this technology in a standard way. The current Web site is:

```
http://www.scguild.com/agentx/
```

REFERENCES FOR CHAPTER 13

[1] Bartlett, John. *Bartlett's Familiar Quotations.* 16th ed. Boston: Little, Brown, and Company. 1992.

[2] Rose, Marshall T. *The Simple Book, An Introduction to Management of TCP/IP-based Internets.* Englewood Cliffs, NJ: Prentice Hall. 1991.

[3] Nichols, Elizabeth H., Ph.D. "Management by Proxy." *DG Review.* May 1992, 25.

[4] Rose, Marshall T. *The Simple Book, An Introduction to Management of TCP/IP-based Internets.* Englewood Cliffs, NJ: Prentice Hall. 1991.

[5] Rose, Marshall T. *The Simple Book, An Introduction to Network Management.* rev. 2nd ed. Upper Saddle River, NJ: Prentice Hall. 1996.

CHAPTER 14

Other Implementation Issues

Teach us delight in simple things,
And mirth that has no bitter springs;

—*Rudyard Kipling*[1]

Many other noteworthy implementation issues need to be examined for a full discussion of SNMP practice. SNMP is evolving to include the management of many interesting and diverse network objects and resources. The management charter has been expanded to include not only the network, but also the monitoring and control of the things connected to it. As a result, SNMP is now accelerating to include system management down to the desktop-including PCs and workstations and their applications. All users and their computers can now be monitored and accounted.

14.1. MANAGING EVERY NETWORK DEVICE

The ultimate goal of any network management framework is to automatically manage as many of its network devices as possible. The original SNMP has expanded beyond the monitor and control of gateways and routers and has grown to include many diverse and important hardware and software components. These include various communication protocol stacks, different network interfaces and transmission media types, and the SNMP itself. The RMON MIB Group allows control of the LAN "wire"; RMON-II proposes the control of the remaining higher layers. Thanks to its extensible framework, SNMP is constantly including many new experimental and private-enterprise MIB groups.

SNMP now manages nearly every type of LAN and WAN network devices such as bridges, routers, gateways, concentrators, channel and data service units, intelligent wiring hubs, modems, multiplexers, protocol analyzers, and terminal servers. It now also controls the host devices such as workstations, PCs, and servers.

SNMP is making inroads in the management of the many new network devices appearing. These include uninterruptible power supplies (UPS), network FAX servers, network printers, wireless devices, Web servers, and network imaging and storage devices.

Also, a great deal of activity is occurring in defining MIB groups for network software and new transmission technologies. New working groups are being formed to create MIBs for Asynchronous Transfer Mode (ATM), Synchronous Optical Network (SONET), SNA, 100 MBps Ethernet, and various mail and directory management services.

The implementation of SNMP may well go full circle. Whereas one of the first demonstrations of its use was in the tongue-in-cheek management of a toaster at the INTEROP show in 1988, it may well soon manage your toaster and all of the other electronic devices in your home!

14.2. MANAGING THE DESKTOP

One of the hottest areas of SNMP implementation is in managing the end-user's PC and its resources, the *desktop*. In a general sense, desktop network management is a collection of software products that reside in workstations, PCs, and servers that allow network administrators to monitor and control the PC workstations as managed network nodes. Several key developments include the Desktop Management Task Force (DMTF), the Host Resources MIB, and the use of SNMP in such products as Microsoft's System Management Server

(SMS). With the concomitant explosion of the agent/manager ratio, Network Manager environments need to be bolstered to handle this greatly increased number of agents. The way to truly bring network management to the enterprise includes well-thought-out designs for the managers and the implementation of sound network applications.

14.3. REVISITING FCAPS

Fault, Configuration, Accounting, Performance, and Security Management is the groundwork for what constitutes the functional requirements for any SNMP network management system. The data stored, retrieved, and manipulated in each agent's MIB becomes the information for management decision-making. It is time to revisit FCAPS, introduced in Chapter 1, to see more closely how these requirements are used under SNMP. I also give an example of how each functional area is implemented, to show how FCAPS specifically pertains to SNMP.

14.3.1. FAULT MANAGEMENT UNDER SNMP

Fault Management is often cited as one of the primary benefits of SNMP management. FM includes the detection, location, correction, and tracking of problems that can occur on the internetwork. SNMP is now managing an entire spectrum of faults ranging from the network printer running out of paper to a problem with the uninterruptible power supply (UPS) that backs up your most mission-critical server. SNMP can be used for all of the devices on the internetwork that contain an agent. The creation of a MIB for uninterruptible power supplies is a prime example of how FM is being implemented for SNMP and has become an essential part of network management.

An interesting implementation of fault management is the creation of a MIB for the standardized use of uninterruptible power supplies connected to the network. A working group for the UPS MIB was originally organized, and they held their first meeting in July 1992. The WG started with ten different UPS equipment vendors and other interested parties. Since the first edition of this book was published, the UPS MIB has become a proposed standard and has been revised and updated from implementation experience. The current UPS MIB RFC is RFC 1628, *UPS Management Information Base*.

477

The SNMP agent can be in the network UPS device directly, or it can proxy one or more UPSs to support this MIB. The UPSs can be monitored and controlled from the NMSs in their community. The traps defined in the UPS MIB can also be sent when power problems are detected.

Nine major MIB groups comprise the UPS MIB as shown in Figure 14-1:

Group	UPS Group Function
Device Identification	includes top-level information on the UPS, including manufacturer, model designation, software version, agent version, ID string, and a list of any attached devices.
Battery	provides information on the UPS battery, including status, how long it's been running on the battery, how much time is left on the battery, percentage of charge remaining, current voltage, battery's current, and the ambient temperature.
Input	contains input parameters such as out-of-tolerance condition counter, number of input lines, and an input table for each line (frequency, voltage, current, and true power rating).
Output	contains the output source, frequency, and output table for each line (voltage, current, power, and load).
Bypass	identifies bypass frequency, number of lines, and a bypass table for each line (voltage and current).
Alarm	contains the active number of alarm conditions and an alarm table for each alarm (ID, description, and time stamp). This group also includes 24 defined UPS alarm conditions.
Test	has information about UPS tests, including test IDs, a spin lock (for test synchronization from possible multiple NMSs), result summary, result detail, start time, elapsed time, and a set of five well-known UPS tests.
Control	has various control methods, including shutdown type, shutdown after delay, startup after delay, reboot with duration, and auto restart.
Configuration	includes input voltage and frequency, output voltage and frequency, nominal volt-amp rating, true output power rating, low battery time, audible status, low voltage transfer point, and high voltage transfer point.

Figure 14-1. The UPS MIB

The UPS MIB also includes four enterprise trap notifications. These report whether the UPS is running off its battery, whether a test has been completed, an entry has been added to the alarm table, and an entry has been deleted from the alarm table.

Where previously only expensive high-end UPSs were equipped with SNMP agents (or were capable of being proxied), now SNMP management is available from nearly every UPS vendor. A discussion of current UPS vendors and their products can be found in [2]. A more thorough explanation of UPS technology and how it works is in Gilbert Held's *LAN Management with SNMP and RMON.*[3]

14.3.2. CONFIGURATION MANAGEMENT UNDER SNMP

Configuration Management under SNMP deals with the *what*. Knowing and keeping track of what pieces comprise an enterprise and its internetwork is a primary concern of the network administrator. Because this task can be very time-intensive, it naturally invites automation. Many MIB objects can be used to create inventories of the various hardware and software components and their statuses. With the emphasis of including PCs and workstations under SNMP management, the creation of additional standard MIB groups such as the Host Resources MIB will greatly aid in CM under SNMP.

The Host Resources MIB goes beyond allowing for the management of the networking attributes of the device by also including a standardized list of MIB variables that pertain to the resources of the host itself. Since the first edition of this book, the Host Resources MIB has been updated to a proposed standard. RFC 1514, *Host Resources MIB*, by Grillo and Waldbusser is the latest revision.

Figure 14-2 shows the Host Resources MIB and its six groups.

Because the Host Resources MIB necessarily models a generic host, many SNMP agent vendors have created private MIB extensions tailored for the more popular desktop platforms (Microsoft Windows, Windows 95, NT, OS/2, Apple, UNIX and UNIX variants, and others). You can find a discussion of systems management and SNMP in [4].

14.3.3. ACCOUNTING MANAGEMENT UNDER SNMP

Accounting management under SNMP is primarily concerned with the usage of network resources by end-users. The particulars of cost, verification, usage

Group	Host Resources Group Function
System	contains general objects that describe the system, including how long it's been up, the local data and time, initial load device and parameters, the number of user sessions, and the maximum number of process contexts that can be supported by this host.
Storage	holds information about the storage types, capabilities, and other pertinent data about disks, memory, CDs, etc.
Device	describes the types and information about the hardware components resident and connected to the host, such as printers, modems, mouse, network adapter cards, other peripherals, etc.
Running SW	lists software currently running or loaded into main memory on the system, including the operating system, device drivers, and applications.
Running SW performance metrics	details performance statistics about the software found in the running software group, including CPU utilization, amount of memory used, and so on.
Installed SW	contains list of software installed on any local drives and pertinent information about each, including the type of software, its name, and the date it was installed. This table can be used for software auditing, checking for proper versions, etc.

Figure 14-2. The Host Resources MIB

time, and so forth are implementation-dependent attributes that can be handled in a variety of ways. Certain MIB objects can be used for AM implementations, but the primary thrust of SNMP-based AM is through the use of network management applications focusing in this area.

AM network management applications range in scope from simple monitoring to very rigorous control. For some networks, keeping track of the number of users accessing the system may be sufficient. For other networks, controls such as software distribution, licensing, and end-user usage need to be implemented in comprehensive network management AM applications. Some new AM packages perform duties ranging from distributing new software updates, to keeping the 51st user from using a network application installed with a 50-user license. AM network management application development is one current focus for many NMS applications developers.

More and more vendors are embracing SNMP to aid in expanding their existing proprietary products and allowing them to provide standardized interfaces. Microsoft has released a suite of products called the "Back Office," which includes the Systems Management Server that offers SNMP to provide accounting management.

Microsoft's System Management Server (SMS) is targeted at Windows-based PCs that now exist in the millions throughout the Internet. This product does a wide variety of accounting functions by discovering and inventorying the PC hardware and software in the network and storing the information in a database. This product can also distribute new software over the network. It includes diagnostic and remote control tools, security, and a network packet decoding facility.

Its SNMP interface support includes generating and forwarding traps that are created from Windows events. The SMS can both forward and receive traps from other SMS stations, as well as from HP OpenView, or from other SNMP devices that send traps.

The Web site for more information on SMS is `http://www.micro-soft.com/smsmgmt/`.

14.3.4. PERFORMANCE MANAGEMENT UNDER SNMP

Performance management under SNMP can help the network planner or administrator maintain a more efficiently running internetwork. The total performance of an internet is a composite of the various LAN/MAN/WAN network segments that comprise it. As the internet or intranet grows in both size and scope, PM can become a truly daunting task.

SNMP can help monitor the various networks and segments for bottlenecks and problem areas. It can control network operation by fine-tuning configurations and deciding where hardware (such as bridges and routers) and software need to be added in appropriate places. It can also do load balancing for various servers that exist on the network. It can even track the overhead required for network management.

Key SNMP variables can also provide data used by the NMS applications to perform capacity planning and network simulation for "what-if" scenarios. Proactive PM can also stand for "Preventive Maintenance" where important performance statistics can be used to set thresholds, collect operating data, and analyze the results looking for possible problems.

An innovative example of SNMP-based performance management is the use of the Remote Network Monitor (RMON) MIB.

A remote monitoring device listens to the traffic being carried on a network, starting at the physical media. It compiles and stores important information about the traffic activity that can be later used to adjust performance. It is designed to be configured and then left to run unattended. A specific class of stand-alone network devices have been dedicated solely for this purpose—called *probes*. These probes are placed in key locations throughout an internet, typically one per segment. Remote Monitoring devices and probes communicate performance statistics to special PM network management applications.

Remote monitoring has been standardized to work under the SNMP framework. It is called RMON. The IETF working group that developed an SNMP version for remote monitoring in the early 1990s included several interested vendor groups and researchers at Carnegie Mellon University. RFC 1271, *Remote Network Monitoring Management Information Base*, authored by Steven Waldbusser, included an introduction and a listing of the constituent MIB groups and their objects that would be required for monitoring lower layer protocols. The RMON Group is in the MIB-II naming tree and its ASN.1 OBJECT IDENTIFIER is { mib-2 16 }. Although remote monitoring can be implemented on any media type, this initial SNMP RMON release was specifically targeted for Ethernet LANs (layers 1 and 2).

RMON refers to the use of an SNMP agent that instruments the RMON MIB to listen to the broadcasts on a local network in order to collect statistics concerning traffic. Without RMON an NMS has difficulty constructing a profile of the network activity using standard tools on an individual network as a whole.

RFC 1271 has since been obsoleted by RFC 1757, *Remote Network Monitoring Management Information Base*. This RFC is currently a draft standard. A Token Ring version was made available in 1993 (RFC 1513, *Token Ring Extensions to the Remote Monitoring MIB*) to instrument the media-specific management objects for IEEE 802.5 Token Ring LANs. Other LAN protocols, such as FDDI, are being considered.

RFC 1757 states that five key goals can be realized from an RMON implementation:

♦ off-line operation: an RMON agent continues to collect statistics even if the connection between it and the NMS is temporarily disrupted.

♦ preemptive monitoring: If a failure occurs, the agent can preempt its normal monitoring duties and notify the NMS. The NMS can then request accumulated statistics for more insight into the problem or request that diagnostics be run.

♦ problem detection and reporting: The agent can be configured to log and report certain important error conditions.

♦ value-added data: Pertinent data can be collected and retrieved by the RMON agent for the NMS, exclusively for management purposes.

♦ multiple managers: The RMON agent must be able to support concurrent communications with more than one NMS.

The value-added data design goal is a key benefit for performance management. It significantly enhances the monitoring and control capabilities of the standard MIB-II and media-specific transmission groups. It also standardizes and augments proprietary network analyzers. Many new and exciting RMON network applications using the latest software technology, such as expert systems, increase internetwork performance by allowing the many network segments that comprise it to be monitored and tuned. Proactive failure notifications also ease maintenance duties. RMON is an important vehicle for monitoring subnetwork-wide behavior because it reduces the burden of the other SNMP agents and network management stations that are not directly concerned with performance management.

The RMON MIB from RFC 1271 has been divided into ten groups of managed variables. As is true for any SNMP implementation, if a group is implemented by an agent, every object in that group must be implemented.

Figure 14-3 lists the RMON MIB groups and their functions.

RMON adds to the monitor and control potential offered from MIB-II, by collecting statistics about the network itself, and not just the devices. It allows for thresholds to be set to catch minor problems before they escalate and bring down the network.

RMON also has the ability to save packets for use by the network management applications. These packets and other statistics can be used for creating graphs of network activity, performing historical analysis, anticipating possible problems, and optimizing the performance of the network and the internetwork. "Together, all of the statistics and other data that RMON makes available can be used to characterize the normal behavior of a network, thereby forming a 'baseline' characterization of the network. After the baseline is established, alarms can be set for conditions that exceed this baseline by a specified amount."[5]

Group	RMON Group Function
Ethernet Statistics	keeps track of important statistics collected by this RMON agent controlled device about the segment at the monitored interface. These statistics include various packet, byte, and error counts.
History Control	saves statistics over various time intervals for comparisons of the different periods.
Ethernet History	stores periodic statistics for each Ethernet interface on the device.
Alarm	allows for the setting of rising and falling thresholds for configurable alarm conditions. If a threshold is crossed, a notification is sent by the agent to the NMS. A hysteresis mechanism is used to govern when these alarms are sent.
Host	contains counters about a particular host device found on the network. The RFC states that the information found in this group can also be used to "discover" hosts on the network by keeping a list of the source and destination MAC Addresses seen in the good packets received from the network.
HostTopN	provides types of sorted lists of the various host statistics that can be used for report generation and comparison. The host list and the statistics sample interval are specified by the NMS.
Matrix	maintains statistics between two network addresses. As new "conversations" are created, additional entries are placed in the matrix table. It is very useful for comparing various connections.
Filter	allows packets to be matched from various settable filters. Matches can be saved or can cause notification events to the NMS.
Packet Capture	regulates which packets may be captured.
Event	allows for the logging of various statistics and the control of the generation of events to be sent to the NMS.

Figure 14-3. The RMON MIB

An exciting RMON development is RMON-II. The remote network monitor model has been extended by RMON-II to allow for the complete monitoring of OSI layers one through seven. Note that even though the OSI protocols themselves are not frequently implemented, the seven layer model is used for nearly every discussion of data communication protocols. RMON-II allows for the examination of network traffic such as IP, TCP, and other higher-level protocols. A probe that implements RMON-II can examine traffic at a higher perspective than RMON 1's limited view of the local subnetwork. Additionally, the probe can now monitor traffic to and from hosts for particular applications.

As of this writing, RMON-II is currently available only as an Internet Draft. It is expected to became a standards track RFC sometime in 1997. Also, work is being done involving the monitoring of wide area switching network protocols. This will allow for the monitoring of logical networks such as virtual and emulated LANs. This task is formidable since many current WAN switching strategies are proprietary.

A recommended text reference for RMON is William Stallings's book, *SNMP, SNMPv2, and RMON.*[6]

14.3.5. SECURITY MANAGEMENT UNDER SNMP

Security Management under SNMP must provide the ability to do management operations in a secure fashion and at the same time prohibit the misuse of the management protocol resulting from either accidental or malicious use. SM was seen as a major functional deficiency of Version 1 and the first area where proposed enhancements to the framework appeared. SM deals with the verification of the access and privileges for network users. It must handle the perils faced in the transmission of sensitive network management data across the Internet. These perils can include unauthorized users ("masquerading" as the system administrator), data modification, replayed messages, and general eavesdropping. As Internet use expands, security threats become even more insidious and difficult to detect and track.

As detailed in Chapter 2, the SNMP framework was enhanced in 1992 to incorporate security features. All of the efforts—Secure SNMP, SMP, and the proposed version of SNMPv2 (RFC 1441-1452)—failed to garner enough consensus to include it in the current SNMPv2 draft proposal. The party concept and its accompanying administrative overhead proved to have flaws and were not considered a sound design.

The current security proposal of SNMP "next generation" must succeed for SNMP to progress to full standard and for work to continue in the evolution of the framework. Security is viewed as a "must have" if SNMP is to be used for setting management variables for configuration and security management. Serious competition is also being felt from proprietary products that are available

485

now (such as Secure Socket Layer (SSL) developed by Netscape) and standards-based IETF efforts such as secure IP (IPsec).

The SNMPng Advisory team (formally, the Security and Administrative Framework Evolution for SNMP Advisory Team) was tasked with creating a new proposal for adding security to SNMP. They reported the results of their work at the 37th IETF meeting in December 1996 (see [7]). To a large extent, the results are a synthesis of the USEC and v2* proposals, with contributions from the working group and other interested individuals.

The issues the advisory team had to deal with included message timeliness, authentication, encryption, proxy handling, variable binding list processing, and other general administrative framework issues.

The new proposal defines a set of modules (further decomposed into submodules) and interfaces to the SNMP engine and other applications that perform functionality outside of the protocol processing. The three main modules are:

◆ Message Processing and Control

◆ Security Model

◆ Local Processing

Note that in addition to added administrative overhead, the SNMP message also needs to be modified to support the security features of authentication and/or encryption. This modification will include a possible global data area, a security model information area, and a naming context field in the header of the message. The PDU format will most likely come from the draft standard version defined in RFC 1905.

REFERENCES FOR CHAPTER 14

[1] *The Oxford Dictionary of Quotations*. 3rd ed. Oxford, UK: Oxford University Press. 1979.

[2] Newman, Jeff. "UPSes Keep Juices Flowing and Your Network Going." *Network Computing*. January 15, 1997, 128-137.

[3] Held, Gilbert. *LAN Management with SNMP and RMON*. New York: John Wiley and Sons, Inc. 1996.

[4] Krupczak, Bobby. "Systems Management and the Internet Management Framework." *ConneXions—The Interoperability Report*. August 1995, 2-9.

[5] Waldbusser, Steve, Mohan Nair, and Mark Hoerth. "SNMP Management Goes Down to the Wire." *Data Communications*. May 1992, 116.

[6] Stallings, William. *SNMP, SNMPv2, and RMON: Practical Network Management*. 2nd ed. Reading, MA: Addison-Wesley. 1996.

[7] Mundy, Russ. "SNMPng Advisory Team Status Report." *ConneXions – The Interoperability Report*. December 1996, 34-36.

CHAPTER

15

Current SNMP Implementation

Everything is simpler than you think, and more complex than you imagine.

—Goethe[1]

SNMP products and implementations are now a lion's share of the burgeoning Network Management market whose 1995 worldwide revenues were 1.369 billion dollars.[2] The U.S. market alone was over 650 million dollars.[2] The growth rate is estimated to be a very healthy 25 percent.[2]

SNMP implementations include the network manager products (including the hardware platforms and associated applications), management station aftermarket and add-on products, agent and sub-agent products, MIB compilers and tools, and many other supporting SNMP technology products. Many companies provide network management solutions with a wide variety of SNMP and related products.

15.1. CURRENT NETWORK MANAGER IMPLEMENTATIONS

Many network manager implementations are being developed, fielded, and refined as the need and use of SNMP grows. Although all of the Network Managers offer the core NMS functionality for processing the SNMP protocol, they can vary greatly in several important respects.

Three criteria for comparing Network Managers are:

◆ the environments in which they execute

◆ the scope of their abilities

◆ additional features

The NM environment is the hardware and software it comprises. Depending on where NM platforms are positioned, they are available across the entire spectrum of computing platforms. To render an overview, NMs can be divided into two major categories: high-end and low-end systems.

A high-end system is typically a powerful workstation. Most include, or are capable of supporting, more than one CPU. The workstation has a large, high resolution monitor. With the growing implementation of distributed computing and replicated databases, the network manager may actually be several computers working together in a client/server setup. In addition to SNMP, the network manager platform may support other network management protocols and proprietary vendor management systems. The platforms contain data stores such as a relational database management system (RDBMS). These systems are used in very large enterprises and are the basis for the Network Operations Center. They contain a wide variety of network management applications and tools. Most high-end systems run the UNIX and UNIX-variant operating systems, although the Windows NT OS is rapidly gaining popularity.

The low-end network management system consists of a less-powerful workstation or PC running Windows 95, Windows NT, UNIX or a UNIX derivative (like Linux). This system typically includes a large-screen graphics monitor for the GUI interface and may contain a database management system or large flat-file. This type of NM is a dedicated manager to a specific set of managed devices. If such an NM includes SNMPv2c, it is often a *dual-role entity*; it manages its local community and report important information via the Inform-PDU to a high-end manager located in a central site for the enterprise. The low-end network management system has a few specific network management applications and has much less scalability than the high-end type. Naturally, it is also less expensive.

The second differentiating factor between the two types of NMSs is the scope. The hallmark of a Network Manager's scope is the number and classes of agents it can monitor and control. This directly correlates to the different types of network devices and the varieties of network media and protocols that comprise an enterprise. Figure 15-1 shows the various network elements and protocols that can exist in the enterprise (from [3]).

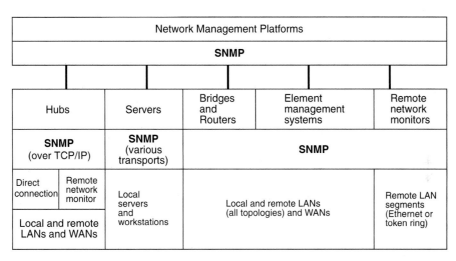

Figure 15-1. Network Management Elements and Protocols

The third, and in some ways the most important, criterion for comparison, is the additional features and functionality that can be provided. These additional features are the items that distinguish one vendor's NM from another—product differentiators. These features include the types of network management applications that can be supported, the platform's scalability, the inclusion of value-added tools such as MIB compilers, browsers, and import utilities, and its price/performance ratio. Other less tangible comparison points include how easy the NM is to install, configure, use, and customize; its performance and the overhead it introduces to the network; its report capabilities; the amount and quality of the vendor's technical support; licensing costs; and its documentation and overall packaging.

Many key areas of current development are in the NM arena. In addition to handling all of the latest protocol standards and private and standard MIB groups, NMs are now including one or more of the following current developments:

- integration of expert systems technology

- GUI enhancement (a good picture is worth how many words of management data?)

- the ability to accommodate the latest hardware and software upgrades (for scalability)

- movement towards object-oriented architecture and distributed objects

- providing APIs for innovative network applications

- migration path for full standard SNMPv2 security and administrative framework

- dynamic loading and unloading of MIB groups (sub-agents)

- distributed and replicated database management systems

- additional functionality that is currently beyond the realm of SNMP (such as network design and simulation, policy control, etc.)

Of particular interest to the people dealing with SNMP network management are the migration to the full standard SNMP Version 2 with security, and the evaluation and integration of the myriad network management applications that are being currently released.

The three elements of environment, scope, and additional features must be examined for each particular installation to determine which vendor's offering is a best fit.

The major NMs have evolved from several different directions. For some vendors, previously well-established pre-SNMP NMs were retrofitted with SNMP capabilities. These pre-SNMP NMs were often of a proprietary nature. Other vendors, traditionally considered network device hardware manufacturers, have generalized their management systems to include SNMP. These systems were originally designed to manage their specific devices or class of devices. Still other vendors have developed and made more comprehensive SNMP element management systems that typically managed a single type of network. Recently, several vendors have created network management products from scratch as the primary focus of their business.

Additionally, many software efforts are underway in the network management applications arena to augment an NM's capabilities and to more fully implement FCAPS management under SNMP. These efforts include the incorporation of RMON, RMON-II, and network design and simulation tools into network management applications.

The price range of the network management implementations also varies according to the base price, add-ons, specific network management applications, hardware and software platform resource requirements, number of devices to be managed, and several other factors. Consult the various vendors to get the latest quote on the price of the network management system that meets your enterprise's needs.

Since 1991, several prominent computer companies have strategically positioned their products as the NM market evolves. As the market matures, companies merge, new players are entering the scene and less successful ones leaving. A particular hot bed of interest for market differentiation is the development of innovative and useful network management applications that work with the network management APIs.

Contrast the high-end NM markets from 1991 to the present-the results are interesting. Figure 15-2 shows a snapshot of how the market was divided for the year 1991 (International Data Corporation, quoted in [4]).

Company (product)	1991 Market Share (%)
Hewlett-Packard (OpenView Network Node Manager)	24.5
SunConnect (SunNet Manager)	22.6
Others	20.5
Ungermann-Bass (NetDirector)	8.6
David Systems (ExpressView)	6.4
Cisco Systems	6.1
NetLabs (Manager 1000)	4.6
SynOptics	4.3
DEC (PolyCenter SNMP Manager 300)	2.4

Figure 15-2. Selected NM Market Share (1991 Shipments)

Figure 15-3 shows a snapshot of how the market was divided for the year 1995.[5] The high-end market currently is dominated by four major vendors who control over 88 percent of the business: Hewlett-Packard, Sun, Cabletron, and IBM. A recent article by Edwin Mier[6] gives a detailed comparison among these top four network management systems.

Company (product)	1995 Market Share (%)
Hewlett-Packard (OpenView Network Node Manager)	32.9
SunSoft (Solstice Domain Manager)	29.3
Cabletron (Spectrum)	17.6
IBM (NetView)	8.5
Others	6.9
Network Managers (NMC/3000)	4.8

Figure 15-3. Selected NM Market Share (1995 Shipments)

A quickly growing segment of the network manager market is the use of the Microsoft Windows NT platform. It is currently viewed as less expensive but not as scalable an alternative to the UNIX-based platform. Nearly every network manager vendor is porting or creating an NT-based management platform. Figure 15-4 shows the current market shares for Windows-based SNMP network management platforms (International Data Corporation, quoted in [9]). Currently, this market value is much smaller than the high-end market, but is growing larger every year.

Company (product)	1995 Market Share (%)
Hewlett-Packard (OpenView for Windows)	56.2
Novell (ManageWise/NMS)	32.8
Others	6.6
SunSoft (Site Manager)	2.3
Network Managers (NMC 1000)	2.1

Figure 15-4. Windows-Based NM Market Share (1995 Shipments)

Sections 15.1.1 through 15.1.5 present the five top current high-end NM offerings. These systems cover quite a range in their abilities, how they are architected, the platforms that they run on, and how they are positioned in the NM market.

The exact pricing for each product has been purposely omitted because of its variability. The address for each vendor is supplied so that you may request additional information regarding the latest version numbers, capabilities, and pricing structure. Remember, NM considered must be able to easily manage the devices of interest in your internetwork.

The list that follows is by no means all-inclusive. The products and prices are being continually upgraded and improved. Also, many other vendors are offering SNMP-related products and network management applications that work with and augment these network management systems.

15.1.1. HEWLETT-PACKARD: OPENVIEW NETWORK NODE MANAGER

Hewlett-Packard's OpenView Network Node Manager is the market leader and has maintained its position selling a comprehensive NM that includes a collection of integrated network applications and associated software for developing and supporting an SNMP network management environment. It is a very popular offering and serves as the basis for several of the NM systems sold by other vendors. The HP OpenView product family now includes network management solutions for any size network.

The OpenView Network Node Manager monitors and controls SNMP agents. This software runs on high-end workstations, such as Sun SPARCstations, IBM RISC/6000s, and HP 9000 series machines, supporting the X-Windows system. It now also runs on Windows NT. The OpenView NM includes applications for auto-discovery, topology map, application builder, and various types of data collection. It also includes a MIB browser and a MIB loader for third-party enterprise MIB group extensions. HP has also developed the OpenView Hub Manager, Bridge Manager, and Interconnect Manager applications for providing additional value-added management of specific network devices such as hubs, bridges, and routers. The Probe Manager can be used for LAN fault and performance management.

A key component of OpenView is that it provides a toolkit as a means for developing TCP/IP applications for network management. This API supports both the UNIX and Windows environments. Additionally, the Distributed

Management Platform includes support for OSI, proxy agents, and SQL to a relational database management system.

Third-party developers play an important role in OpenView's popularity. They have formed a group called the OpenView Forum that continually provides feedback to improve the product. Now, many hundreds of applications run under the OpenView platform.

OpenView
Hewlett-Packard Company
P. O. Box 7050
Colorado Springs, CO 80933-7050
Telephone: (719) 531-4414
http://www.hp.com/nsmd/ov/main.html/

15.1.2. SUNSOFT: SOLSTICE DOMAIN MANAGER

The original SunSoft network management product, SunNet Manager, has evolved into the Solstice family of network management systems. The high-end management system, Solstice Domain Manager, runs on Sun Microsystems SPARCsystems (with Solaris) with the OpenWindows GUI. It can also run on Pentium-based micro-computers. Its features include a comprehensive set of tools and management services. It includes a client/server design with sender and receiver "cooperative consoles" that allow for network management scaling. This product also supports scaling by defining one or more mid-level managers that can communicate with each other.

The management services include APIs for topology maps, and databases. Also, an API is available for building and integrating custom network management applications. This is an "open" NM whereby additional protocols and third-party applications can be easily integrated. These applications are used for configuration management, problem solving, capacity management, security, and resource accounting.

Because of its SunSoft division that created Java, Sun is sure to be one of the first and most prominent players in the Web-based management arena. Its new product, Solstice Enterprise manager, will include the Java Management API (JMAPI) that is seen by many as a new direction in network management and an alternative to SNMP.

> **Solstice Domain Manager**
> SunConnect, a Sun Microsystems Company
> 2550 Garcia Avenue
> Mountain View, CA 94043
> Telephone: (415) 960-1300
> `http://www.sun.com/solstice/index.html/`

15.1.3. CABLETRON: SPECTRUM

The network management system offered by Cabletron Systems, Inc., is called Spectrum. It runs under UNIX and Window NT. Spectrum is object-oriented and designed as a true client-server model. Two key components are the user interface client called SpectroGraph and the server, SpectroServer, which handles device polling, data collection and storing, and the other activities that are required to keep the state of the network.

A key strong point of this product is its various hierarchical views of the network. Three of these views are:

♦ The Location View

♦ The Topology View

♦ The Organization View

The Location View starts out with a global map and then allows users to zoom in for a more detailed look at their particular installation. A sample zoom may include country to state to city to building to floor to office. The Topology View shows the physical connections of the internetwork. The Organization View allows for the creation of groups based on the way a particular company is divided (by department, function, and so forth).

Cabletron has added other *specialty views* to aid in network troubleshooting. These additional views include: the Performance View for charting network statistics, the Alarms View for displaying current alarms, the Event Log View for listing events and alarms, the Lost and Found View for icons the system has trouble placing in a conventional view, and the Find View for quickly locating specific models or groups of models.

Spectrum also includes expert system technology in the form of an inductive modeling technique that "understands" how to use the models of the managed devices to make intelligent decisions about fault and configuration management. Other capabilities and tools that are included with Spectrum are automatic device discovery, a SQL database management system, a script scheduler, and several network management applications for such things as statistical analysis and trouble ticket generation.

Spectrum
Cabletron Systems, Inc.
35 Industrial Way
Rochester, NH 03867-0505
Telephone: (603) 332-9400
`http://www.ctron.com/spectrum`

15.1.4. IBM: TME 10/NETVIEW

IBM has merged its NetView platform with Tivoli's Management Environment (TME) system to create TME 10/Netview. It has been tailored to remove redundancies between the two offerings while retaining each platform's strong points. IBM's AIX NetView/6000 was IBM's SNMP NM product for managing TCP/IP network devices. On a larger scale it could interface with the legacy mainframe-based NetView. This was IBM's traditional network management system for SNA and other non-TCP/IP devices. AIX NetView/6000 was originally based on HP's OpenView product.

TME 10/NetView has many of the standard high-end manager features, including embedded event correlation, alarm filtering, and distributed event management. It also provides APIs for supporting a wide number of SNMP network management applications. It includes auto-discovery, MIB browser, and many of the other supporting tools and utilities.

TME 10/NetView
Tivoli
9442 Capital of Texas Highway North
Arboretum Plaza One, Suite 500
Austin, TX 78759
Telephone: (512) 794-9070
`http://www.tivoli.com/products/netview`

15.1.5. NETWORK MANAGERS: NMC 3000

Network Managers, Ltd., is an English firm that sells NMC/3000, a UNIX(Sun-OS)-based system that runs on SUN SPARCstations and compatibles. It works with additional modules such as IP Auto Discovery and the MIB Integrator. It also includes an integrated drawing package for creating icons, a utility for setting thresholds for key events, and a trouble ticket application that can be triggered from the reception of trap PDUs.

NMC 3000
Network Managers, Ltd.
73 Princeton St.
Suite 305
N. Chelmsford, MA 01863
Telephone: (508) 251-4111
`http://www.netmgrs.co.uk`

15.1.6. OTHER NETWORK MANAGER IMPLEMENTATIONS

All other network management companies hold the remaining 6.9 percent of the market. Two of these implementations are SNMPc from Castle Rock and the Integrated System Management NMS from Groupe Bull.

15.1.6.1. *Castle Rock: SNMPc*

The hallmark of Castle Rock's network manager, SNMPc, is its inexpensive price; this product is a full-featured network manager that offers a tremendous price/performance ratio. It was the first network manager that ran under MS Windows and currently can run as an application under HP OpenView.

> **SNMPc**
> Castle Rock Computing, Inc.
> 20863 Stevens Creek Blvd.
> Suite 530
> Cupertino, CA 95014
> Telephone: (408) 366-6540
> http://www.castlerock.com/

15.1.6.2. *Groupe Bull S.A.: Integrated System Management (ISM)*

The French company, Groupe Bull S.A., has been aggressively developing and marketing its network management system called Integrated System Management. It includes full support for SNMP-based devices. An additional key market differentiator is its emphasis on security features. "The vendor's success can be traced to its decision to add security to its management products. One year later [1995] no other platform vendor has yet matched Bull's enterprise-strength single sign-on security capabilities."[8]

> **Integrated System Management**
> Groupe Bull S.A.
> Bull Hn Information Systems, Inc.
> Technology Park
> Billerica, MA 01821
> Telephone: (508) 294-2354
> http://www-ism.bull.com/ism

15.2. CURRENT AGENT IMPLEMENTATIONS

Due to the nature of the business, many more companies are involved in the agent market. The list below is a sampling of several of the major agent vendors and their Web sites.

Company	Web Site
ACE*COMM	http://www.acec.com
BMC Software	http://www.bmc.com
Bridgeway	http://www.bridgeway.com
Empire Technologies	http://www.empiretech.com
Epilogue (ISI)	http://www.epilogue.com
Multiport	http://www.multiport.com
Paul Freeman Associates	http://world.std.com/~pfa
SNMP Research	http://www.snmp.com

Figure 15-5. Current Agent Implementation Companies

Contact these companies for product information. For agent implementation, custom consulting may also be needed. Other related activities for agent implementation can include design for sub-agents, agents for non-standard platforms and operating environments, special customization, support for private MIB extensions, proxy agents, and so forth. In general, agents tend to be much less plug-and-play than the managers.

In addition to commercial packages, a large number of freely available implementations exist. These require varying degrees of expertise—both in software engineering and SNMP—to get them up and running. They are available in many different types of programming and scripting languages. Two sites that contain popular SNMP implementations are:

```
ftp://ftp.ece.ucdavis.edu/pub/snmp (version of CMU code)
ftp://mercury.lcs.mit.edu/pub/snmp (version of MIT code)
```

15.3.OTHER SNMP COMPONENTS IMPLEMENTATIONS

Dozens of other related categories of SNMP-related products do not handily fit into the NMS or agent category. These include RMON probes and software, various development tools, debuggers, and reporting packages. Also available are help desk applications, trouble ticket generators, alarm and event correlation software tools, and many, many others. Review and search the World Wide Web and current relevant periodicals for these types of vendors and their products.

REFERENCES FOR CHAPTER 15

[1] Esar, Evan. *20,000 Quips and Quotes*. Garden City, NY: Doubleday and Company, Inc. 1968.

[2] *Data Communications Magazine*, "The 1995 Data Comm Market Forecast." December 1994, 75.

[3] *Data Communications Magazine*. "Network Management and Security." October 15, 1992, 136.

[4] Huntington-Lee, Jill. "Platforms to the Rescue: As Nets Get More Complex, Platforms Deliver Solutions." *Open Systems Today*. September 21, 1992, 26.

[5] Gillooly, Caryn. "HP and Cabletron Boost Management Systems." *Information Week*. March 4, 1996, 16.

[6] Mier, Edwin. "Battle Tactics: Arm Yourself Against Network Snafus with These Four Distributed Management Platforms." *Network World*. May 20, 1996, 54–59.

[7] _____. "Networking." *PC Week*. December 18, 1995, 57.

[8] Saunders, Steven. "The Brightest Ideas in Networking (Hot–Or Forgotten?)." *Data Communications*. January 1997, 36.

CHAPTER 16

Recent Directions and Developments

Knowledge leads us from the simple to the complex; wisdom leads us from the complex to the simple.

—*Oscar Wilde*[1]

I adore simple pleasures. They are the last refuge of the complex.

—*Oscar Wilde*[2]

The future direction for SNMP is still bright. Its two key attributes of simplicity and extensibility have made it the network management of choice far beyond the core Internet community. TCP/IP-based internets and intranets are ubiquitous. Its simplicity has continued to allow many new implementations to appear in a relatively short amount of time. Its extensibility has allowed its original charter to be expanded to include additional transport protocols and integration into other networking technologies such as SNA and telecommunications. Now, MIBs exist for just about everything! Even the perceived weaknesses of the SNMP Version 1 standard are being addressed by proposed changes and amendments in Version 2 and Version 3. A secure SNMP will (hopefully!) be a reality in 1997. Network Management working groups are being created and re-activated for all the latest technologies. Additionally, management by the Web is turning out to be a hot area for implementation and debate on how and how much SNMP will be part of this effort.

Many exciting areas are being investigated in the network management arena today. Key topics for the current development and direction of SNMP include:

- Web-Based Network Management
- Simple Network Management Protocol APIs
- Desktop Management Task Force (DMTF)
- The Role of Expert Systems in Network Management
- Network Management with Distributed Objects

16.1. NETWORK MANAGEMENT AND THE WEB

Web-Based management is the hottest thing to happen to network management since the SNMP-controlled toaster! Claims have become dramatically over-hyped to the point where some people believe they can throw away their current NMS platforms and manage their network for free with only their favorite Web browser. SNMP was "simple" but it was never "free." Beware, efforts are just underway in these areas, and further standardization and implementation experience is required before any true conclusions can be reached.

The term *Web-Based management* actually refers to two distinct management areas: management *by* the Web and management *of* the Web.

16.1.1. WEB-BASED NETWORK MANAGEMENT

Web management is the application of World Wide Web (WWW) tools and technology for the network management of devices connected over an internetwork. By utilizing the Hypertext Transfer Protocol (HTTP) over the TCP/IP protocol suite, a standard browser can monitor and control targeted devices that are supported by an associated HTTP server program. With supporting tools, programming languages and protocols such as Hypertext Markup Language (HTML), Common Gateway Interface (CGI), PERL, Java, C++, and

SNMP, management information can be created, delivered, and presented as static, dynamic, and form-based (interactive) screens.

Web-Based management is a new technology. The Web-Based server's mechanism and methods for accessing and presenting the management information for the devices it represents can be specified by several different models. Two reference models to consider are differentiated by the entities involved in the management communication.

16.1.1.1. Web Management with Browsing/Browsed Entities Model

The first model involves a scenario where the browser communicates directly with the HTTP server on the managed device. This scenario presents a deceptively simple reference model that masks many implementation details by essentially collapsing the managing and managed entities into a single *browsed* entity. The browsed entity contains an HTTP server and the necessary instrumentation support to set and get management variables. Figure 16-1 presents this reference model.

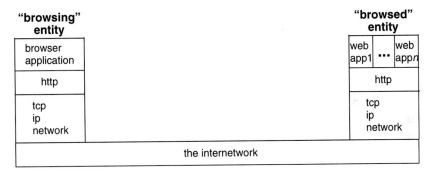

Figure 16-1. Web Management Reference Model Version 1

In this type of implementation, the target device must contain the necessary TCP/IP protocol stack and the collection of Web management applets (probably written in Java) that are downloaded to the browser client PC and executed. The target device can additionally contain HTML pages and all of the other capabilities of a Web server. The executing applets can be very sophisticated, capable of communicating back to the managed device, and contain links to other pages and applets. They include the GUI, the socket network interface, and many other possible features. In this model no need exists for the intermediary manager device such as an SNMP Network Manager Station.

Browser requests come to the HTTP server where management applets are stored. The applets are downloaded to the browser platform and executed.

16.1.1.2. Web Management with SNMP Managing/Managed Entities Model

The second model contains three major players and represents the merging and coexistence of Web-Based management with the current SNMP Network manager/agent paradigm. The manager can contain applets and HTML pages for many managed entities, differentiated by their location on the manager's disk. The NMS in this scenario is also the HTTP server.

Browser requests come to the CGI location where management applications are stored. Applications written in a script language such as PERL then call an interface (perhaps a Perl2SNMP translation library) that calls the appropriate methods in the SNMP library to make the SNMP operation to the specified agent in the target device. Figure 16-2 presents this reference model.

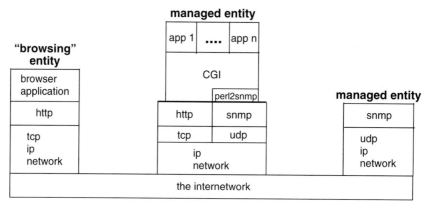

Figure 16-2. Web Management Reference Model Version 2

Two additional efforts are underway that may help to shape the direction of Web-Based management. One is a consortium of vendors working to propose a standard and the other is an entirely new API written for the Java programming language.

16.1.2. WEB-BASED ENTERPRISE MANAGEMENT (WBEM)

The Web-Based Enterprise Management (WBEM) consortium is a group of five companies that proposed an industry standard for network management using the Web in July 1996. The original five companies that started WBEM are:

- BMC Software (Houston, TX)
- Cisco Systems, Inc. (San Jose, CA)
- Compaq Computer Corporation (Houston, TX)
- Intel Corporation (Santa Clara, CA)
- Microsoft Corporation (Redmond, WA)

This effort includes the definition of three interfaces that provide a standardized network management approach. The WBEM effort is designed to work with SNMP along with other network management schemes. The three WBEM interfaces are:

- HyperMedia Management Schema (HMMS), which defines the data model
- HyperMedia Management Protocol (HMMP), which defines the communication protocol of running HMMS over HTTP
- HyperMedia Object Manager (HMOM), which is a development tool that enables WBEM applications to manipulate network elements as objects

For more information, the WBEM home page is: `http://wbem.free-range.com`.

16.1.3. JAVA MANAGEMENT API (JMAPI)

The Java Management API (JMAPI) is a new network management API from Sun that promises platform-independence. JMAPI is an object-oriented set of objects and methods written in the Java programming language that can be used to develop management applications. It includes user interface guidelines, management Java classes, and an SNMP interface. The Web site for JMAPI is `http://java.sun.com/products/JavaManagement`.

16.1.4. NETWORK MANAGEMENT OF WEB SERVERS

Network management of the Web pertains to the definition and understanding of the requirements for a standard way of managing Web servers. The informational RFC that currently applies to this is RFC 2039, *Applicability of Standards Track MIBs to Management of World Wide Web Servers*, by Carl Kalbfleisch.

16.2. SIMPLE NETWORK MANAGEMENT PROTOCOL APIS

An Application Programming Interface (API) is an important concept for providing standardized access to computing services for application programs. An

API allows for multi-platform independence and portability. APIs for SNMP are essential for extending its functionality, as well as providing a method for creating network management applications that run on the various NMs that are available.

Many new developments in SNMP provide APIs to make the information that they manage available to network management stations. These include the WinSNMP and SNMP++ efforts. Many network management vendors provide special APIs and software development kits for added functionality and custom application program development. In addition to management APIs, data storage APIs, user interface APIs, and others are under development.

16.2.1. WINSNMP

WinSNMP is a programming API for SNMP network management applications running under the Microsoft Windows operating system. It allows these applications to access an SNMP engine in a standardized fashion by making the API calls. It provides a single interface that all of the SNMP vendors that wish to use it can conform. The specification includes a complete technical description of the data structures, the program API, and other implementation information.

It offers three major benefits:

◆ It masks the lower level programming details of ASN.1 encoding and decoding and the SNMP protocol operation details.

◆ It offers implementation interoperability.

◆ It creates a uniform SNMP Version 1 and Version 2 implementation.

Additionally, the WinSNMP specification offers four levels of increasing implementation compliance:

Level	Meaning
Level 0	SNMP Message encoding and decoding only
Level 1	Level 0 plus interaction with Version 1 SNMP agents
Level 2	Level 1 plus interaction with Version 2 SNMP agents
Level 3	Level 2 plus interaction with other SNMPv2 managers

The 1.1 version of the specification in various formats is available at:

```
ftp://sunsite.unc.edu/pub/micro/pc-stuff/ms-windows/
winsnmp/winsnmp_app
```

WinSNMP has been added to many commercial products and work is continuing on its development.

16.2.2. SNMP++

SNMP++ is a set of C++ classes that define a network management API that facilitates the creation of NM applications in a standard way. It allows the network management applications that use it to work with both the Windows-based SNMP library (WinSNMP) and the UNIX SNMP library. These in turn run on top off their respective transport layer interfaces. Figure 16-3 shows a top-level view of how SNMP++ works in an SNMP manager implementation.

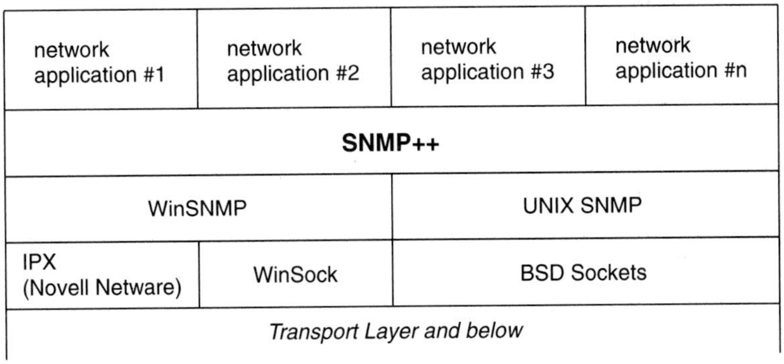

network application #1	network application #2	network application #3	network application #n
SNMP++			
WinSNMP		UNIX SNMP	
IPX (Novell Netware)	WinSock	BSD Sockets	
Transport Layer and below			

Figure 16-3. The SNMP++ Model

SNMP++ is a set of reusable class libraries that are platform-independent. The major three classes are the Oid class, the Vb class, and the SNMP class. The Oid class is the encapsulation of the object identifier; the Vb class is an encapsulation of the Variable Binding List; and the SNMP class is a top-level encapsulation of an SNMP session between the manager and the agent. Its methods include the various types of protocol commands that can be sent (sets and gets).

HP introduced an SNMP++ implementation in 1995 that is currently used in several commercial products. For more information, see the SNMP++ home page at: http://rosegarden.external.hp.com/snmp++. A detailed article on SNMP++ can be found in the March 1995, issue of *ConneXions*.[3]

16.3. DESKTOP MANAGEMENT TASK FORCE (DMTF)

The management of the desktop is an important thrust in SNMP deployment for total enterprise management integration. The Desktop Management Task Force (DTMF) is a consortium of industry vendors who have defined an API for managing host workstations (such as DOS-based and Windows-based PCs) and allowing the management of these workstations to be subsequently integrated into the SNMP management framework. Although the specification states that the interfaces are system-independent, network operating system-independent, and network management protocol-independent, one of the first ways in which managed information on the PC is accessed is through SNMP over the network.

The consortium was formed in May 1992, and was originally comprised of members from these companies:

◆ Intel Corporation (Santa Clara, CA)

◆ Novell, Inc. (San Jose, CA)

◆ SunConnect (Mountain View, CA)

◆ Microsoft Corporation (Redmond, WA)

◆ SynOptics Communications, Inc. (Santa Clara, CA)

Several more companies then joined in:

◆ International Business Machines Corporation (Armonk, NY)

◆ Digital Equipment Corporation (Maynard, MA)

◆ Hewlett-Packard (Palo Alto, CA)

This API defines how network management protocols (such as SNMP) and other applications can access information about the workstation. Although the initial focus is on SNMP, future management protocols and applications will include CMOL, local applications, special DMI test applications, and others to be determined.

The information about each workstation includes data on the workstation hardware, add-in boards, applications software, and systems software.

The workstation hardware includes configuration information about the various components present in the box. This inventory includes information about RAM/ROM memory, various drives (hard disk, diskette, CD-ROM, and so forth), the CPU, numerical co-processor, and so on.

Detailed information about the workstation's add-in boards is also present, including the board type, configuration information, diagnostics, and other attributes specific to a particular add-in board. Common examples of add-in boards are network interface cards, video cards, communications cards, and the new hardware to support multimedia.

The application software on the workstation is also audited for the various programs present, their versions, and licensing information. Information on the workstation's system software is also collected, particularly data on the operating system.

The DMTF's Desktop Management Interface (DMI) consists of the DMI Service Layer and its two constituent interfaces: the Management Interface (MI) above and the Component Interface (CI) below.

Figure 16-4 shows the DMTF API architecture.

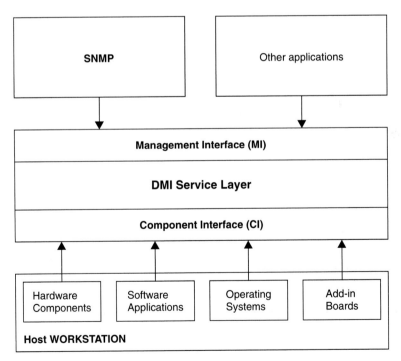

Figure 16-4. The DTMF API Architecture

The Management Interface provides standardized access for the various management and test applications that send requests to the DMI Service Layer and expect responses. The MI encourages sound NMS and test application development as it allows the focus to be placed on these applications instead of on the agent in the workstation.

The Component Interface is the common access for the various hardware and software components that can reside in the workstation. It allows for the management of the various vendors' products. The CI has been defined for the easy implementation of current and future hardware and software products.

The DMI Service Layer is where the various services are implemented that are needed for handling commands and responses for the MI and for setting and getting information on the workstation hardware and software information from the CI.

The home page for the DMTF is http://www.dmtf.org.

16.4. THE ROLE OF EXPERT SYSTEMS IN NETWORK MANAGEMENT

As the size and complexity of the enterprise internetwork grows, it becomes more important—perhaps even critical—that the human network managers, administrators, and their staff have help in managing their network.

The use of expert system technology from artificial intelligence research is becoming much more widespread. This complex software technology is aiding and even replacing many of the tasks that were previously done manually. Many of the currently released NMS management applications include expert system components and embedded expert system "engines" to aid in FCAPS management. They use inference to make decisions on the data the expert system garners from the agents and the NMS databases. Heuristics are utilized when procedural algorithms are not appropriate for a particular problem.

Fuzzy logic and neural networks are two additional areas from AI that are being investigated as technologies that can enhance network management implementation.

16.5. NETWORK MANAGEMENT WITH DISTRIBUTED OBJECTS

One of the leading-edge developments in network management today is the use of distributed objects to model network elements and their relationships.

One of the primary object models being deployed today is the Cooperative Object Requestor Broker Architecture (CORBA). Figure 16-5 compares the key features of SNMP Version 1, CMIP, and CORBA Objects (taken from [4]) in order to give a snapshot of the current state of these three frameworks.

Feature	SNMP(v1)	CMIP	CORBA Objects
Installed base	Huge	Small	Very small
Managed objects per managing station	Small	Large	Large
Management model	Manager and agents	Manager and agents	Communicating Objects
View of managed objects	Simple variables arranged in MIB trees	Objects with inheritance defined in MIBs	Objects with IDL defined interfaces, attributes, and multiple inheritance
Manager/agent interactions	Polling, infrequent traps	Event driven	Event driven
Explicit manager-to-agent command invocations	No	Yes	Yes
Security	No	Yes	Yes
Manager-to-manager exchanges	No	Yes	Yes
Bulk transfers	No	Yes	Yes
Create/delete managed objects	No	Yes	Yes
Communication model	Datagram	Session-based	ORB
Standards body	Internet	ISO	OMG
Approximate memory requirements	40-200 Kbytes	300-1000 KBytes	300-2000 Kbytes

Figure 16-5. SNMP, CMIP, and CORBA Objects: Features Comparison

16.6. SNMP NEXT GENERATION (SNMPNG)

SNMP Next Generation (SNMPng) is an important step in the SNMP evolution. After meeting with unbridled success, the security feature has proved to be quite a hurdle to overcome. SNMPv1 has been successfully deployed for many devices throughout the world. For the framework to evolve with a standard way to securely configure SNMP instrumented devices and to accommodate all of the security features in general, consensus must be reached on the security features and the administrative framework that is required to implement it.

As this book goes to print, a new SNMPv3 working group has started up to work on the SNMPng effort. It is the goal of the WG to create a set of documents (first as Internet drafts and then as RFCs) that specify the new direction of SNMP, including security. Five specifications are planned:

- SNMPv3 Modules and Interface Definitions
- SNMPv3 Message Processing and Control Module Specification
- SNMPv3 Security Model Module Specification
- SNMPv3 Local Processing Module Specification
- SNMPv3 Proxy Specification

Throughout 1997 work will be done on SNMPv3 and a proposed standard is tentatively scheduled for April, 1998. Interested parties can subscribe to the SNMPv3 mailing list at `snmpv3-request@tis.com`. Stay tuned.

16.7. FINAL OBSERVATIONS AND PREDICTIONS

The SNMP management framework has resoundingly demonstrated that simplicity can be a key to success.

The ability to simplify means to eliminate the unnecessary so that the necessary may speak.

—*Hans Hoffman*[5]

...simplicity should be a goal in its own right, not just because SNMP requires it, but because the end-result is better for being simpler. Even though adding complexity is often the easiest and quickest way to resolve issues, it leads to an inferior result in the long term.

—*Keith McCloghrie, Marshall Rose, and Craig Partridge*[6]

SNMP is certainly making inroads into an area that beckons for solutions. As the multi-vendor, heterogeneous networks that can comprise an enterprise steadily grow larger and more complex, and at the same time, the network management staff budget stands pat, the need for SNMP becomes evermore apparent.

SNMP also has shown itself to be a framework capable of change and improvement. This is a prerequisite for any type of enabling technology that is to be considered in such rapid-paced and ever-changing times as these. SNMP needs to accelerate as quickly as the technology it is designed to manage.

The future? Hopefully, implementation experience, reaction to changing technologies, and direction from the key architects and researchers will help guide SNMP through SNMP Version 3 and beyond. Perhaps someday SNMP will evolve into an autonomous network management system that will invisibly overlord a self-healing, global internetwork. It will have an intuitive three-dimensional user interface. We can call it the Ultimate Network Management Protocol. UNMP.

And to all the SNMPers, I leave you with a final maxim (if you can tolerate the anachronism; it is actually Lord Tennyson's eulogy for the Duke of Wellington! ☺):

Foremost Captain of his time,
Rich in saving common-sense,
And, as the greatest only are,
In his simplicity sublime.

—*Alfred, Lord Tennyson*[7]

REFERENCES FOR CHAPTER 16

[1] Esar, Evan. *20,000 Quips and Quotes.* Garden City, NY: Doubleday and Company, Inc. 1968.

[2] Andrews, Robert. *The Columbia Dictionary of Quotations.* New York: Columbia University Press. 1993.

[3] Banker, Kim, and Peter E. Mellquist. "SNMP++: A Portable Object Oriented Approach to Network Management Programming." *ConneXions—The Interoperability Report.* March 1995, 35–41.

[4] Orfali, Robert, Dan Harkey, and Jeri Edwards. *Essential Client/Server Survival Guide*. New York: Van Nostrand Reinhold. 1994.

[5] Tripp, Rhonda Thomas (compiler). *The International Thesaurus of Quotations*. New York: Thomas Y. Crowell Company. 1970.

[6] McCloghrie, Keith, Marshall Rose, and Craig Partridge. "Defining a Protocol-Independent Management Information Base." *Integrated Network Management, I: Proceedings of the IFIP TC 6/WG 6.6 Symposium on Integrated Network Management*. eds. Branislav Meandzija and Jil Westcott. New York: North-Holland. 1989, 193.

[7] *The Oxford Dictionary of Quotations*. 3rd ed. Oxford, UK: Oxford University Press. 1979.

An SNMP Chronology

The following SNMP Chronology is a listing of the key dates in the evolution of the Simple Networking Management Protocol.

1987

The now-famous dinner party at the Doubletree Inn in Monterey, California, attended by influential research and industry networking leaders to discuss key network management issues and desires occurs on March 18th. Among the notable attendants are Robert Braden from the National Science Foundation, Jeffrey Case from the University of Tennessee, Mark Fedor from the Cornell Supercomputer Theory Center, Marty Schoffstall from Rensselaer Polytechnic Institute, and several managers from Proteon. The discussion centers on the need for network management of the NSFNet running the TCP/IP protocol. "Almost as a dare, Proteon management agreed to come up with a network management agent. But in return, Proteon wanted the three complaining network users [Case, Fedor, and Schoffstall] to develop the management portion of the needed software."[1] Proteon is often considered the first commercial vendor of SNMP products. Professor Case and others work to release the Simple Gateway Network Protocol (SGMP), the direct predecessor of SNMP. Also from this meeting, the practice of using the INTEROP conference and trade show as a regular showplace for the newest innovations in SNMP and interoperability begins.

March was also notable for the publication of the first issue of *ConneXions— The Interoperability Report*, edited and published by Ole Jacobsen. This monthly publication contains several solid articles on the key technologies evolving with the Internet, including network management and SNMP. (A cumulative index from 1987 to present is available on-line at `ftp://ftp/ sbexpos.com/pub/cumulative_index.txt`).

In October, the specifications on HEMS by Craig Partridge and Glenn Trewitt are issued. The four related RFCs are: RFC 1021, *The High-Level Entity Management System*; RFC 1022, *The High-Level Entity Management Protocol*; RFC 1023, *The HEMS Monitoring and Control Language*; and RFC 1024, HEMS *Variable Definitions*.

The specification on SGMP, RFC 1028, *Simple Gateway Network Protocol*, by J. Davin, J. Case, M. Fedor, and M. L. Schoffstall is released in November. Although intended to manage router devices, it is used to monitor terminal servers and other host devices.

In the final month of 1987, 3 ISO documents describing CMIP are released:

♦ ISO/IEC JTC 1/21 N 2058, "2nd DP 9595-1 Information Processing Systems—Open Systems Interconnection—Management Information Service Definition—Part 1: Overview"

♦ ISO/IEC JTC 1/21 N 2059, "2nd DP 9595-2 Information Processing Systems—Open Systems Interconnection—Management Information Service Definition—Part 2: Common Management Information Service Definition"

♦ ISO/IEC JTC 1/21 N 2060, "2nd DP 9596-2 Information Processing Systems—Open Systems Interconnection—Management Information Protocol Specification—Part 2: Common Management Information Protocol"

1988

IAB Recommendations for the Development of Internet Network Management Standards (RFC 1052) by Vinton Cerf is issued in April. It discusses the IAB policy statement on network management from the meeting held on February 29th. The three major network management systems considered are SGMP, HEMS, and CMIP. SNMP (from SGMP) is chosen as a short-term solution, and CMIP becomes the long-term network management platform.

In August, the seminal RFCs that contain the three key elements of SNMP— the SMI, the MIB, and the protocol—are released. *Structure and Identification of Management Information for TCP/IP-based Internets* (RFC 1065) and *Management Information Base for Network Management of TCP/IP-based Internets* (RFC 1066) were written by Keith McCloghrie and Marshall Rose. RFC 1067 titled *A Simple Network Management Protocol* was written by Jeffrey Case, M. Fedor, M.L. Schoffstall, and J. Davin. These four people are often cited as the original SNMP authors, although certainly many other people have made significant contributions.

1989

In February, Schoffstall, Davin, Fedor, and Case write a brief RFC on how SNMP can be implemented on top of the Ethernet LAN protocol titled SNMP *Over Ethernet*, RFC 1089.

The March issue of *ConneXions—The Interoperability Report* is devoted to network management. The issue includes articles on SNMP and CMOT.

In April, Schoffstall, Davin, Fedor, and Case revise SNMP protocol and issue *Simple Network Management Protocol* (SNMP) as RFC 1098. In the Internet terminology, this RFC "obsoletes" the previous RFC 1067. Also, a Request for Comment on CMOT is released. RFC 1095, *Common Management Information Services and Protocol Over TCP/IP* (CMOT) is written by U.S. Warrier and L. Besaw.

RFC 1109, *Report of the Second Ad Hoc Network Management Review Group*, by Vinton Cerf, is issued in August. This RFC details the June 12th meeting where the SNMP/CMOT dual track was reaffirmed. Several vendors release SNMP implementations (Cicso, Proteon, the Wollongong Group). Free implementations from MIT and CMU are also made available. Still, no public CMOT implementations are available, and the dual track strategy appears tentative.

At the Fall INTEROP 1989 exhibition in October, demonstrations from over 20 vendors show a wide variety of SNMP implementations.

1990

The three SNMP RFCs on the SMI, MIB, and protocol are revised and reissued in May. They are: *Structure and Identification of Management Information for TCP/IP-based Internets*, RFC 1155; *Management Information Base for Network Management of TCP/IP-based Internets*, RFC 1156, by Rose and McCloghrie; and *Simple Network Management Protocol* (SNMP), RFC 1157, by Case, Fedor, Schoffstall, and Davin. Also, in the same month, the MIB-II specification is released. RFC 1158, *Management Information Base for Network Management of TCP/IP-based Internets: MIB II*, is edited by Marshall Rose.

In June, Marshall Rose writes a short RFC on how SNMP can be implemented on OSI stacks titled *SNMP Over OSI*, RFC 1161.

In August, *ConneXions—The Interoperability Report* devotes the entire issue to network management and security. The issue includes articles on SNMP and IP security.

The October INTEROP 1990 show has 128 vendors demonstrating SNMP operability. Rose, McCloghrie, and Davin issue an RFC on how tables can be retrieved more efficiently in SNMP, *Bulk Table Retrieval with SNMP*, RFC 1187. Also, an updated Request for Comment on CMOT is reissued. RFC 1189, *Common Management Information Services and Protocols for the Internet (CMOT and CMIP)*, by U.S. Warrier, L. Besaw, L. LaBarre, and B. D. Handspicker, obsoletes RFC 1095.

1991

In March, a revised format for MIB definitions is proposed by Rose and McCloghrie (editors) in RFC 1212, *Concise MIB Definitions*. Also, an update of MIB-II is released, *Management Information Base for Network Management of TCP/IP-based Internets: MIB-II*, RFC 1213, edited by Rose and McCloghrie. Rose also edits an informational RFC titled *Convention for Defining Traps for Use with SNMP*, RFC 1215, that is used to define traps for SNMPv1.

SNMP Version 1 has been firmly defined and now work begins to "mibify" the variables of interest. Hundreds of standard MIB variables are defined, and thousands of MIB variables are defined by hundreds of vendors interested in having their devices being managed in an open, standard way.

The OSI MIB RFC 1214 edited by L. LaBarre, *OSI Internet Management Base*, is issued in April.

In May, eight SNMP RFCs are issued:

◆ RFC 1224 by L. Steinberg, *Techniques for Managing Asynchronously Generated Alerts*, includes a discussion of the SNMP Trap functionality.

◆ RFC 1227 is titled *SNMP MUX Protocol and MIB* and authored by M. Rose.

◆ SNMP-DPI: *Simple Network Management Protocol Distributed Program Interface*, by G. Carpenter and B. Wijnen, deals with agent implementation and is RFC 1228.

◆ RFC 1229, *Extensions to the Generic-interface MIB*, is edited by K. McCloghrie.

◆ RFC 1230, titled *IEEE 802.4 Token Bus MIB*, is by K. McCloghrie and R. Fox.

◆ IEEE 802.5, *Token Ring MIB*, by McCloghrie, Fox, and Decker is issued as RFC 1231.

◆ RFC 1232, *Definitions for Managed Objects for the DS1 Interface Type*, is edited by F. Baker and C. P. Kolb.

◆ RFC 1233, *Definitions of Managed Objects for the DS3 Interface Type*, is edited by T.A. Cox and K. Tesink.

In June, RFC 1239 by J. K. Reynolds, *Reassignment of Experimental MIBs to Standard MIBs*, is issued.

MIB extensions for Apple networks is issued in the next month. RFC 1243, *AppleTalk Management Information Base* is edited by S. Waldbusser. RFC 1248, by F. Baker and R. Coltun, *OSPF Version 2: Management Information Base*, is also released.

In August, RFC 1248, *OSPF Version 2: Management Information Base* by Baker and Coltun, is obsoleted by RFC 1252 and then quickly by RFC 1253 in the same month.

In October, an RFC discussing the underlying protocols used with SNMP is issued by F. Kastenholz (editor) entitled *SNMP Communications Services*, RFC 1270. It points out that although using SNMP over a variety of transports is possible, UDP remains the transport protocol of choice for SNMP. The MIB extensions for the Border Gateway Protocol is also issued as RFC 1269, *Definitions of Managed Objects for the Border Gateway Protocol: Version 3*, by S. Willis and J. W. Burruss.

The Remote Network Monitoring (RMON) MIB Extension Specification is issued in November. RFC 1271, *Remote Network Monitoring Management Information Base*, is written by S. Waldbusser. Many view RMON as an exciting new application of SNMP principles.

Marshall Rose's RFC on how SNMP can be implemented on OSI stacks, *SNMP Over OSI, RFC 1283*, is reissued. This RFC obsoletes RFC 1161. Several more specifications on MIB extensions are also issued: RFC 1284, *Definitions of Managed Objects for the Ethernet-like Interface Types*, edited by J. Cook, RFC 1286, *Definitions of Managed Objects for Bridges*, by Decker, Langille, Rijsinghani, and McCloghrie, and RFC 1289, *DECnet Phase IV MIB Extensions*, by J. Saperia. Many transmission types and standard resources have MIBs defined for them.

1992

By 1992 the talk of SNMP Version 2 to improve the management framework is well underway. Work continues on developing standard and vendor MIBs. Implementation experience grows on many fronts.

The FDDI media MIB extensions RFC is issued in the first month of the year as RFC 1285, *FDDI Management Information Base*. It is written by J. Case.

In the second month of the year, integrating SNMP into Novell networks is discussed in RFC 1298, *SNMP Over IPX*, by R. B. Wormley and S. Bostock. RFC 1303, *Convention for Describing SNMP-based Agents*, by McCloghrie and Rose; and RFC 1304, *Definitions of Managed Objects for the SIP Interface Type*, edited by T. A. Cox and K. Tesink, are also issued.

In March, the first issue of *Simple Times* is distributed. It is published bimonthly until February 1994. This periodical is an excellent source of information on SNMP. It includes technical articles, industry comments, a letter column, review of standards activities, the status of working groups and the SNMP RFCs, and several book reviews. The major authors of SNMP all contribute. The current Web site is: `http://www.simple-times.org/pub/simple-times/issues/`. Another issue was released in August and three issues were written when publication was resumed in 1996.

In April 4 more specifications for MIB extensions are released:

◆ RFC 1315, *Management Information Base for Frame Relay DTEs*, by C. Brown, F. Baker, and C. Carvalho

◆ RFC 1316, *Definitions of Managed Objects for Character Stream Devices*, edited by B. Stewart

◆ RFC 1317, *Definitions of Managed Objects for RS-232-like Hardware Devices*, edited by B. Stewart

◆ RFC 1318, *Definitions of Managed Objects for Parallel-Printer-like Hardware Devices*, also edited by B. Stewart

The RFC that contains information about a key component to the newly suggested security features to be incorporated into SNMP, RFC 1321, *MD5 Message-Digest Algorithm*, by R. L. Rivest, is also released in this month. MD5 is still seen as the most popular algorithm for authentication in a network environment.

In July, the three RFCs that are considered the preliminary specification for Secure SNMP appear:

◆ RFC 1351, *SNMP Administrative Model*, is by J. Davin, K. McCloghrie, and J. Galvin.

◆ Proposed SNMP security features for data integrity, authentication, and confidentiality are discussed in RFC 1352, *SNMP Security Protocols*, by Galvin, McCloghrie, and Davin.

◆ The MIB objects for the enhancements to the Administration model are introduced in RFC 1353, *Definitions of Managed Objects for Administration of SNMP Parties*, also by McCloghrie, Davin, and Glavin.

An improvement of the MIB objects for the IP Forwarding Table in the Internet Group is proposed in RFC 1354, *IP Forwarding Table MIB* by F. Baker.

In October, the MIB Group for Hubs is issued as RFC 1368, *Definitions of Managed Objects for IEEE 802.3 Repeater Devices*, by D. McMaster and K. McCloghrie.

In November, the MIB Groups for X.25 are released. RFC 1381, *SNMP MIB Extension for X.25 LAPB*, by D. Throop and F. Baker, contains the link layer objects. The network layer objects are defined in RFC 1382, *SNMP MIB Extension for the X.25 Packet Layer*, edited by D. Throop.

1993

In January, the MIB Group for the RIP routing protocol is issued as RFC 1389, *RIP Version 2 MIB Extension*, by G. Malkin and F. Baker. RFC 1406, titled *Definitions of Managed Objects for the DS1 and E1 Interface Types*, edited by F. Baker and J. Watt, is also reissued to obsolete the previous MIB RFC for the management of T1 and E1, RFC 1232. The counterpart RFC for T3, RFC 1407, *Definitions of Managed Objects for the DS3/E3 Interface Type*, edited by T. Cox and K. Tesink, is also released, obsoleting its predecessor, RFC 1233.

In February, RFC 1414, *Identification MIB*, authored by M. St. Johns and M. Rose, comes out with the definitions for managing TCP user connections.

In March, three RFCs detail how SNMP can be used over non-UDP protocol stacks:

♦ RFC 1418: *SNMP Over OSI*, by M. Rose

♦ RFC 1419: *SNMP Over AppleTalk*, by G. Minshall and M. Ritter

♦ RFC 1420: *SNMP Over IPX*, by S. Bostock

The controversial proposed party-based RFCs of SNMPv2 are issued in April:

♦ RFC 1441: *Introduction to Version 2 of the Internet-standard Network Management Framework*, by Case, McCloghrie, Rose, and Waldbusser.

♦ RFC 1442: *Structure of Management Information for Version 2 of the Simple Network Management Protocol (SNMPv2)*, by Case, McCloghrie, Rose, and Waldbusser.

♦ RFC 1443: *Textual Conventions for Version 2 of the Simple Network Management Protocol (SNMPv2)*, by Case, McCloghrie, Rose, and Waldbusser.

♦ RFC 1444: *Conformance Statements for Version 2 of the Simple Network Management Protocol (SNMPv2)*, by Case, McCloghrie, Rose, and Waldbusser.

♦ RFC 1445: *Administrative Model for Version 2 of the Simple Network Management Protocol (SNMPv2)*, by Galvin and McCloghrie.

◆ RFC 1446: *Security Protocols for Version 2 of the Simple Network Management Protocol (SNMPv2)*, by Galvin and McCloghrie.

◆ RFC 1447: *Party MIB for Version 2 of the Simple Network Management Protocol (SNMPv2)*, by McCloghrie and Galvin.

◆ RFC 1448: *Protocol Operations for Version 2 of the Simple Network Management Protocol (SNMPv2)*, by Case, McCloghrie, Rose, and Waldbusser.

◆ RFC 1449: *Transport Mappings for Version 2 of the Simple Network Management Protocol (SNMPv2)*, by Case, McCloghrie, Rose, and Waldbusser.

◆ RFC 1450: *Management Information Base for Version 2 of the Simple Network Management Protocol (SNMPv2)*, by Case, McCloghrie, Rose, and Waldbusser.

◆ RFC 1451: *Manager-to-Manager Management Information Base*, by Case, McCloghrie, Rose, and Waldbusser.

◆ RFC 1452: *Coexistence between Version 1 and Version 2 of the Internet-standard Network Management Framework*, by Case, McCloghrie, Rose, and Waldbusser.

In May, RFC 1461, *SNMP MIB Extension for Multiprotocol Interconnect over X.25*, by D. Throop, details X.25 MIB object definitions. For the remainder of the year a fair number of standard MIBs and associated RFCs are released.

RFCs 1474, *The Definitions of Managed Objects for the Bridge Network Control Protocol of the Point-to-Point Protocol*, RFC 1473, *The Definitions of Managed Objects for the IP Network Control Protocol of the Point-to-Point Protocol*, RFC 1472, *The Definitions of Managed Objects for the Security Protocols of the Point-to-Point Protocol*, and RFC 1471, *The Definitions of Managed Objects for the Link Control Protocol of the Point-to-Point Protocol*, all by Frank Kastenholz, are printed in June.

RFC 1493, *Definitions of Managed Objects for Bridges*, by Decker, Langille, Rijsinghani, and McCloghrie, is released in July. The next month, an informational RFC about configuring SNMPv2 parties is available—RFC 1503, *Algorithms for Automating Administration in SNMPv2 Managers*. It is written by Keith McCloghrie and Marshall Rose.

Six RFCs are released in September:

- RFC 1512: *FDDI Management Information Base*, by Case and Rijsinghani
- RFC 1513: *Token Ring Extensions to the Remote Network Monitoring MIB*, by Waldbusser
- RFC 1514: *Host Resources MIB*, by Grillo and Waldbusser
- RFC 1515: *Definitions of Managed Objects for IEEE 802.3 Medium Attachment Units (MAUs)*, by McMaster, McCloghrie, and Roberts
- RFC 1516: *Definitions of Managed Objects for IEEE 802.3 Repeater Devices*, by McMaster and McCloghrie
- RFC 1525: *Definitions of Managed Objects for Source Routing Bridges*, by Decker, McCloghrie, Langille, and Rijsinghani

The year ends with the release of RFC 1559, *DECnet Phase IV MIB Extensions*, by J. Saperia, being released in December.

1994

Implementation of the draft SNMPv2 specifications are slow to appear from both manager and agent vendors. Many people are content to stay on the sidelines and wait for the problems of the party-based administrative framework to be worked out. Several brave vendors offer products, but these are not generally purchased.

The MIBs now appear using the SMIv2 syntax. Standard MIBs are updated to this new, improved format:

RFC #	Title	Author(s)	Month
1565	*Network Services Monitoring MIB*	Freed/Kille	January
1566	*Mail Monitoring MIB*	Freed/Kille	January
1567	*X.500 Directory Monitoring MIB*	Mansfield/Kille	January
1573	*Evolution of the Interfaces Group of MIB-II*	McCloghrie/ Kastenholz	January
1592	*Simple Network Management Protocol Distributed Protocol Interface Version 2.0*	Wijnen/Carpenter/ Curran/Sehgal/Waters	March
1593	*SNA APPN Node MIB*	McKenzie/Cheng	March
1595	*Definitions of Managed Objects for the SONET/SDH Interface Type*	Brown/Tesink	March

RFC #	Title	Author(s)	Month
1596	*Definitions of Managed Objects for Frame Relay Service*	Brown	March
1604	*Definitions of Managed Objects for Frame Relay Service*	Brown	March
1628	*UPS Management Information Base*	Case	May
1643	*Definitions of Managed Objects for the Ethernet-like Interface Types*	Kastenholz	July
1650	*Definitions of Managed Objects for the Ethernet-like Interface Types using SMIv2*	Kastenholz	August
1657	*Definitions of Managed Objects for the Fourth Version of the Border Gateway Protocol (BGP-4) using SMIv2*	Willis/Burruss/Chu	July
1658	*Definitions of Managed Objects for Character Stream Devices using SMIv2*	Stewart	July
1659	*Definitions of Managed Objects for RS-232-like Hardware Devices using SMIv2*	Stewart	July
1660	*Definitions of Managed Objects for Parallel-printer-like Hardware Devices using SMIv2*	Stewart	July
1665	*Definitions of Managed Objects for SNA NAUs using SMIv2*	Kielczewski/Kostick/ Shih	July
1666	*Definitions of Managed Objects for SNA NAUs using SMIv2*	Kielczewski/Kostick/ Shih	August
1694	*Definitions of Managed Objects for SMDS Interfaces using SMIv2*	Brown/Tesink	August
1695	*Definitions of Managed Objects for ATM Management Version 8.0 using SMIv2*	Ahmed/Tesink	August
1696	*Modem Management Information Base (MIB) using SMIv2*	Barnes/Brown/ Royston/Waldbusser	August
1697	*Relational Database Management System (RDBMS) Management Information Base (MIB) using SMIv2*	Brower/Purvy/Daniel/ Sinykin/Smith	August
1724	*RIP Version 2 MIB Extension*	Malkin/Baker	November
1743	*IEEE 802.5 MIB using SMIv2*	McCloghrie/Decker	December
1748	*IEEE 802.5 MIB using SMIv2*	McCloghrie/Decker	December
1749	*IEEE 802.5 Station Source Routing MIB using SMIv2*	McCloghrie/Baker/ Decker	December

---

1995

Fighting continues on what will constitute the draft version of SNMPv2; a serious consideration even exists for an SNMPv1.5 as an interim solution.

A few MIBs are re-released as updates:

RFC 1742, *AppleTalk Management Information Base II*, by S. Waldbusser and K. Frisa is issued in January to obsolete RFC 1243. Also in the first month, RFC 1747, *Definitions of Managed Objects for SNA Data Link Control: SDLC*, by J. Hilgeman, S. Nix, A. Bartky, and W. Clark, is released.

A major release of RMON is issued in February-RFC 1757, *Remote Network Monitoring Management Information Base*, by Steven Waldbusser. It obsoletes RFC 1271.

RFC 1759 *Printer MIB*, by R. Smith, F. Wright, T. Hastings, S. Zilles, and J. Gyllenskog, is available in March. *TCP/IPX Connection MIB Specification* (RFC 1792 by T. Sung) is issued in April. RFC 1850, *OSPF Version 2 Management Information Base*, by F. Baker and R. Coltun, is released in November to obsolete RFC 1253.

Work completes on SNMPv2c at the close of the year.

1996

The SNMPv2 community-based draft RFCs of SNMPv2 are issued in January. Note that RFC 1901 remains experimental and this version of SNMPv2 is implemented with the Version 1 message wrapper and community name authentication scheme.

◆ RFC 1901: *Introduction to Community-based SNMPv2*, by Case, McCloghrie, Rose, and Waldbusser.

◆ RFC 1902: *Structure of Management Information for Version 2 of the Simple Network Management Protocol (SNMPv2)*, by Case, McCloghrie, Rose, and Waldbusser.

◆ RFC 1903: *Textual Conventions for Version 2 of the Simple Network Management Protocol (SNMPv2)*, by Case, McCloghrie, Rose, and Waldbusser.

- RFC 1904: *Conformance Statements for Version 2 of the Simple Network Management Protocol (SNMPv2)*, by Case, McCloghrie, Rose, and Waldbusser.

- RFC 1905: *Protocol Operations for Version 2 of the Simple Network Management Protocol (SNMPv2)*, by Case, McCloghrie, Rose, and Waldbusser.

- RFC 1906: *Transport Mappings for Version 2 of the Simple Network Management Protocol (SNMPv2)*, by Case, McCloghrie, Rose, and Waldbusser.

- RFC 1907: *Management Information Base for Version 2 of the Simple Network Management Protocol (SNMPv2)*, by Case, McCloghrie, Rose, and Waldbusser.

- RFC 1908: *Coexistence Between Version 1 and Version 2 of the Internet-standard Network Management Framework*, by Case, McCloghrie, Rose, and Waldbusser.

RFCs 1909 (*An Administrative Infrastructure for SNMPv2*) and 1910 (*User-based Security Model for SNMPv2*) are issued in the next month dealing with the "usec" SNMPv2 proposal for an administrative framework that supports security. RFC 1909 is edited by Keith McCloghrie and RFC 1910 is edited by Glen Waters.

RFC 1988, *Conditional Grant of Rights to Specific Hewlett-Packard Patents in Conjunction with the Internet Engineering Task Force's Internet-Standard Network Management Framework*, by McAnally, Gilbert, and Flick, is released in August.

In October, five RFCs appear that introduce new standard MIBs:

- RFC 2006: *The Definitions of Managed Objects for IP Mobility Support using SMIv2*, by Cong, Hamlen, and Perkins

- RFC 2020: *Definitions of Managed Objects for IEEE 802.12 Interfaces*, by Flick

- RFC 2024: *Definitions of Managed Objects for Data Link Switching using SNMPv2*, by Chen, Gayek, and Nix

- RFC 2037: *Entity MIB*, by McCloghrie and Bierman

- RFC 2051: *Definitions of Managed Objects for APPC*, by Allen, Clouston, Kielczewski, Kwan, and Moore

Three RFCs appear in November that contain the SNMPv2 versions of the IP, TCP, and UDP MIBs done with the SMIv2. These are RFC 2011, *SNMPv2 Management Information Base for the Internet Protocol using SMIv2*, RFC 2012, *SNMPv2 Management Information Base for the Transmission Control Protocol*, and RFC 2013, *SNMPv2 Management Information Base for the User Datagram Protocol using SMIv2*. All three are written by Keith McCloghrie.

RFC 2039, *Applicability of Standards Track MIBs to Management of World Wide Web Servers*, by Carl Kalbfleisch, also appears in November. It deals with which MIBs are important for the management of Web Servers.

The December issue of *ConneXions—The Interoperability Report* contains the SNMPng advisory team status report by Russ Mundy as work continues on security for SNMP.

1997

The SNMPv2c implementations are now widely available from agent and manager vendors, although SNMPv1 is still the most pervasive form of network management.

A standard MIB for measuring traffic flow appears in January (RFC 2064: *Traffic Flow Measurement: Meter MIB*, by N. Brownlee). Also in the same month, an RFC on RMON MIB protocol identifiers is issued (RFC 2074, *Remote Network Monitoring MIB Protocol Identifiers*, by Bierman and Iddon), an RFC for Version 2 to Version 1 mapping within a bilingual agent (RFC 2089, *V2 To V1 Mapping SNMPv2 onto SNMPv1 Within a Bi-lingual SNMP Agent*, by Wijnen and Levi), and an updated RFC on the IP Forwarding Table (RFC 2096, *IP Forwarding Table MIB*, by Baker). In February RFC 2108, *Definitions of Managed Objects for IEEE 802.3 Repeater Devices Using SMIv2*, by DeGraaf, Romascanu, McMaster, and McCloghrie is published to update RFC 1516.

Two new MIBs written by G. Roeck are released in March: RFC 2128, *Dial Control Management Information Base Using SMIv2* and RFC 2127, *ISDN Management Information Base*.

The SNMPv3 Working Group is charted to begin work on the latest version of SNMP. Specifications in the form of Internet Drafts and then RFCs will be produced throughout 1997 with the tentative plan of releasing a proposed standard version of SNMPv3 with security in the first quarter of 1998.

REFERENCES APPENDIX A

[1] Borsook, Paulina. "Network Innovators: Jeff Case." *Network World*. December 7, 1992, 79.

SNMP Protocol Specifications

B.1. THE SNMPV1 PROTOCOL SPECIFICATION

The following definition is the SNMP Protocol Specification for version 1 from
RFC 1157, *Simple Network Management Protocol (SNMP)*.

```
RFC1157-SNMP DEFINITIONS ::= BEGIN

IMPORTS
    ObjectName, ObjectSyntax, NetworkAddress, IpAddress, TimeTicks
        FROM RFC1155-SMI;


    -- top-level message

    Message ::=
            SEQUENCE {
                version             -- version-1 for this RFC
                    INTEGER {
                        version-1(0)
                    },

                community           -- community name
                    OCTET STRING,
```

```
                data              -- e.g., PDUs if trivial
                    ANY           -- authentication is being used
            }


-- protocol data units

PDUs ::=
        CHOICE {
                    get-request
                        GetRequest-PDU,

                    get-next-request
                        GetNextRequest-PDU,

                    get-response
                        GetResponse-PDU,

                    set-request
                        SetRequest-PDU,

                    trap
                        Trap-PDU
                }

-- PDUs

GetRequest-PDU ::=
    [0]
        IMPLICIT PDU

GetNextRequest-PDU ::=
    [1]
        IMPLICIT PDU

GetResponse-PDU ::=
    [2]
        IMPLICIT PDU

SetRequest-PDU ::=
    [3]
        IMPLICIT PDU

PDU ::=
        SEQUENCE {
            request-id
                INTEGER,

            error-status      -- sometimes ignored
                INTEGER {
```

```
                    noError(0),
                    tooBig(1),
                    noSuchName(2),
                    badValue(3),
                    readOnly(4),
                    genErr(5)
                },

        error-index        -- sometimes ignored
            INTEGER,

        variable-bindings -- values are sometimes ignored
            VarBindList
    }

Trap-PDU ::=
    [4]
        IMPLICIT SEQUENCE {
            enterprise        -- type of object generating
                              -- trap, see sysObjectID in [5]


                OBJECT IDENTIFIER,

            agent-addr        -- address of object generating
                NetworkAddress, -- trap

            generic-trap      -- generic trap type
                INTEGER {
                    coldStart(0),
                    warmStart(1),
                    linkDown(2),
                    linkUp(3),
                    authenticationFailure(4),
                    egpNeighborLoss(5),
                    enterpriseSpecific(6)
                },

            specific-trap  -- specific code, present even
                INTEGER,   -- if generic-trap is not
                           -- enterpriseSpecific

            time-stamp     -- time elapsed between the last
                TimeTicks, -- (re)initialization of the network
                           -- entity and the generation of the trap

          variable-bindings -- "interesting" information
              VarBindList
    }
```

```
-- variable bindings

VarBind ::=
        SEQUENCE {
            name
                ObjectName,

            value
                ObjectSyntax
        }

VarBindList ::=
        SEQUENCE OF
            VarBind

END
```

B.2. THE SNMPV2 PROTOCOL SPECIFICATION

The following definition is the SNMP Protocol Specification for version 2 from
RFC 1905, *Protocol Operations for Version 2 of the Simple Network Management
Protocol (SNMPv2)*.

```
SNMPv2-PDU DEFINITIONS ::= BEGIN

IMPORTS
    ObjectName, ObjectSyntax, Integer32
        FROM SNMPv2-SMI;


-- protocol data units

PDUs ::=
    CHOICE {
        get-request
            GetRequest-PDU,

        get-next-request
            GetNextRequest-PDU,

        get-bulk-request
            GetBulkRequest-PDU,

        response
            Response-PDU,

        set-request
```

```
                SetRequest-PDU,

            inform-request
                InformRequest-PDU,

            snmpV2-trap
                SNMPv2-Trap-PDU,

            report
                Report-PDU,
        }


-- PDUs

GetRequest-PDU ::=
    [0]
        IMPLICIT PDU

GetNextRequest-PDU ::=
    [1]
        IMPLICIT PDU

Response-PDU ::=
    [2]
        IMPLICIT PDU

SetRequest-PDU ::=
    [3]
        IMPLICIT PDU

-- [4] is obsolete

GetBulkRequest-PDU ::=
    [5]
        IMPLICIT BulkPDU

InformRequest-PDU ::=
    [6]
        IMPLICIT PDU

SNMPv2-Trap-PDU ::=
    [7]
        IMPLICIT PDU

--    Usage and precise semantics of Report-PDU are not presently
--    defined.  Any SNMP administrative framework making use of
--    this PDU must define its usage and semantics.
Report-PDU ::=
    [8]
        IMPLICIT PDU
```

```
max-bindings
    INTEGER ::= 2147483647

PDU ::=
    SEQUENCE {
        request-id
            Integer32,

        error-status            -- sometimes ignored
            INTEGER {
                noError(0),
                tooBig(1),
                noSuchName(2),    -- for proxy compatibility
                badValue(3),      -- for proxy compatibility
                readOnly(4),      -- for proxy compatibility
                genErr(5),
                noAccess(6),
                wrongType(7),
                wrongLength(8),
                wrongEncoding(9),
                wrongValue(10),
                noCreation(11),
                inconsistentValue(12),
                resourceUnavailable(13),
                commitFailed(14),
                undoFailed(15),
                authorizationError(16),
                notWritable(17),
                inconsistentName(18)
            },

        error-index            -- sometimes ignored
            INTEGER (0..max-bindings),

        variable-bindings   -- values are sometimes ignored
            VarBindList
    }


BulkPDU ::=                    -- MUST be identical in
    SEQUENCE {                 -- structure to PDU
        request-id
            Integer32,

        non-repeaters
            INTEGER (0..max-bindings),

        max-repetitions
            INTEGER (0..max-bindings),
```

```
            variable-bindings        -- values are ignored
                VarBindList
        }


-- variable binding

VarBind ::=
    SEQUENCE {
        name
            ObjectName,

        CHOICE {
            value
                    ObjectSyntax,

            unSpecified        -- in retrieval requests
                    NULL,

                            -- exceptions in responses
            noSuchObject[0]
                    IMPLICIT NULL,

            noSuchInstance[1]
                    IMPLICIT NULL,

            endOfMibView[2]
                    IMPLICIT NULL
        }
    }


-- variable-binding list

VarBindList ::=
    SEQUENCE (SIZE (0..max-bindings)) OF
        VarBind
    END
```

MIB-II Specification

The following definition is the MIB-II Specification from RFC 1213, *Management Information Base for Network Management of TCP/IP-based Internets: MIB-II.*

```
RFC1213-MIB DEFINITIONS ::= BEGIN

IMPORTS
        mgmt, NetworkAddress, IpAddress, Counter, Gauge,
            TimeTicks
          FROM RFC1155-SMI
        OBJECT-TYPE
            FROM RFC-1212;

--   This MIB module uses the extended OBJECT-TYPE macro as
--   defined in [14];


--   MIB-II (same prefix as MIB-I)

mib-2 OBJECT IDENTIFIER ::= { mgmt 1 }

-- textual conventions

DisplayString ::=
   OCTET STRING
-- This data type is used to model textual information taken
```

```
-- from the NVT ASCII character set.  By convention, objects
-- with this syntax are declared as having
--
--       SIZE (0..255)

PhysAddress ::=
  OCTET STRING
-- This data type is used to model media addresses.  For many
-- types of media, this will be in a binary representation.
-- For example, an ethernet address would be represented as
-- a string of 6 octets.


-- groups in MIB-II

system OBJECT IDENTIFIER ::= { mib-2 1 }

interfaces  OBJECT IDENTIFIER ::= { mib-2 2 }

at      OBJECT IDENTIFIER ::= { mib-2 3 }

ip      OBJECT IDENTIFIER ::= { mib-2 4 }

icmp    OBJECT IDENTIFIER ::= { mib-2 5 }

tcp     OBJECT IDENTIFIER ::= { mib-2 6 }

udp     OBJECT IDENTIFIER ::= { mib-2 7 }

egp     OBJECT IDENTIFIER ::= { mib-2 8 }

-- historical (some say hysterical)
-- cmotOBJECT IDENTIFIER ::= { mib-2 9 }

transmission OBJECT IDENTIFIER ::= { mib-2 10 }

snmp    OBJECT IDENTIFIER ::= { mib-2 11 }


-- the System group

-- Implementation of the System group is mandatory for all
-- systems.  If an agent is not configured to have a value
-- for any of these variables, a string of length 0 is
-- returned.

sysDescr OBJECT-TYPE
  SYNTAX  DisplayString (SIZE (0..255))
  ACCESS  read-only
  STATUS  mandatory
  DESCRIPTION
```

```
            "A textual description of the entity.  This value
            should include the full name and version
            identification of the system's hardware type,
            software operating-system, and networking
            software.  It is mandatory that this only contain
            printable ASCII characters."
    ::= { system 1 }

sysObjectID OBJECT-TYPE
    SYNTAX  OBJECT IDENTIFIER
    ACCESS  read-only
    STATUS  mandatory
    DESCRIPTION
            "The vendor's authoritative identification of the
            network management subsystem contained in the
            entity.  This value is allocated within the SMI
            enterprises subtree (1.3.6.1.4.1) and provides an
            easy and unambiguous means for determining `what
            kind of box' is being managed.  For example, if
            vendor `Flintstones, Inc.' was assigned the
            subtree 1.3.6.1.4.1.4242, it could assign the
            identifier 1.3.6.1.4.1.4242.1.1 to its `Fred
            Router'."
    ::= { system 2 }

sysUpTime OBJECT-TYPE
    SYNTAX  TimeTicks
    ACCESS  read-only
    STATUS  mandatory
    DESCRIPTION
            "The time (in hundredths of a second) since the
            network management portion of the system was last
            re-initialized."
    ::= { system 3 }

sysContact OBJECT-TYPE
    SYNTAX  DisplayString (SIZE (0..255))
    ACCESS  read-write
    STATUS  mandatory
    DESCRIPTION
            "The textual identification of the contact person
            for this managed node, together with information
            on how to contact this person."
    ::= { system 4 }

sysName OBJECT-TYPE
    SYNTAX  DisplayString (SIZE (0..255))
    ACCESS  read-write
    STATUS  mandatory
    DESCRIPTION
            "An administratively-assigned name for this
```

```
              managed node.  By convention, this is the node's
              fully-qualified domain name."
        ::= { system 5 }

sysLocation OBJECT-TYPE
   SYNTAX  DisplayString (SIZE (0..255))
   ACCESS  read-write
   STATUS  mandatory
   DESCRIPTION
           "The physical location of this node (e.g.,
           `telephone closet, 3rd floor')."
        ::= { system 6 }

sysServices OBJECT-TYPE
   SYNTAX  INTEGER (0..127)
   ACCESS  read-only
   STATUS  mandatory
   DESCRIPTION
           "A value which indicates the set of services that
           this entity primarily offers.

           The value is a sum.  This sum initially takes the
           value zero.  Then, for each layer, L, in the range
           1 through 7, that this node performs transactions
           for, 2 raised to (L - 1) is added to the sum.  For
           example, a node which performs primarily routing
           functions would have a value of 4 (2^(3-1)).  In
           contrast, a node which is a host offering
           application services would have a value of 72
           (2^(4-1) + 2^(7-1)).Note that in the context of
           the Internet suite of protocols, values should be
           calculated accordingly:

                  layer   functionality
                    1   physical (e.g., repeaters)
                    2   datalink/subnetwork (e.g., bridges)
                    3   internet (e.g., IP gateways)
                    4   end-to-end  (e.g., IP hosts)
                    7   applications (e.g., mail relays)

           For systems including OSI protocols, layers 5 and
           6 may also be counted."
        ::= { system 7 }

-- the Interfaces group

-- Implementation of the Interfaces group is mandatory for
-- all systems.

ifNumber OBJECT-TYPE
   SYNTAX  INTEGER
```

544

```
    ACCESS  read-only
    STATUS  mandatory
    DESCRIPTION
          "The number of network interfaces (regardless of
          their current state) present on this system."
    ::= { interfaces 1 }


-- the Interfaces table

-- The Interfaces table contains information on the entity's
-- interfaces.  Each interface is thought of as being
-- attached to a `subnetwork'.  Note that this term should
-- not be confused with `subnet' which refers to an
-- addressing partitioning scheme used in the Internet suite
-- of protocols.

ifTable OBJECT-TYPE
    SYNTAX  SEQUENCE OF IfEntry
    ACCESS  not-accessible
    STATUS  mandatory
    DESCRIPTION
          "A list of interface entries.  The number of
          entries is given by the value of ifNumber."
    ::= { interfaces 2 }

ifEntry OBJECT-TYPE
    SYNTAX  IfEntry
    ACCESS  not-accessible
    STATUS  mandatory
    DESCRIPTION
          "An interface entry containing objects at the
          subnetwork layer and below for a particular
          interface."
    INDEX   { ifIndex }
    ::= { ifTable 1 }

IfEntry ::=
    SEQUENCE {
        ifIndex
          INTEGER,
        ifDescr
          DisplayString,
        ifType
          INTEGER,
        ifMtu
          INTEGER,
        ifSpeed
          Gauge,
        ifPhysAddress
          PhysAddress,
```

```
            ifAdminStatus
              INTEGER,
            ifOperStatus
              INTEGER,
            ifLastChange
              TimeTicks,
            ifInOctets
              Counter,
            ifInUcastPkts
              Counter,
            ifInNUcastPkts
              Counter,
            ifInDiscards
              Counter,
            ifInErrors
              Counter,
            ifInUnknownProtos
              Counter,
            ifOutOctets
              Counter,
            ifOutUcastPkts
              Counter,
            ifOutNUcastPkts
              Counter,
            ifOutDiscards
              Counter,
            ifOutErrors
              Counter,
            ifOutQLen
              Gauge,
            ifSpecific
              OBJECT IDENTIFIER
        }

ifIndex OBJECT-TYPE
    SYNTAX  INTEGER
    ACCESS  read-only
    STATUS  mandatory
    DESCRIPTION
            "A unique value for each interface.  Its value
            ranges between 1 and the value of ifNumber.  The
            value for each interface must remain constant at
            least from one re-initialization of the entity's
            network management system to the next re-
            initialization."
    ::= { ifEntry 1 }

ifDescr OBJECT-TYPE
    SYNTAX  DisplayString (SIZE (0..255))
    ACCESS  read-only
    STATUS  mandatory
```

```
      DESCRIPTION
            "A textual string containing information about the
            interface.  This string should include the name of
            the manufacturer, the product name, and the version
            of the hardware interface."
       ::= { ifEntry 2 }

  ifType OBJECT-TYPE
     SYNTAX  INTEGER {
                 other(1),      -- none of the following
                 regular1822(2),
                 hdh1822(3),
                 ddn-x25(4),
                 rfc877-x25(5),
                 ethernet-csmacd(6),
                 iso88023-csmacd(7),
                 iso88024-tokenBus(8),
                 iso88025-tokenRing(9),
                 iso88026-man(10),
                 starLan(11),
                 proteon-10Mbit(12),
                 proteon-80Mbit(13),
                 hyperchannel(14),
                 fddi(15),
                 lapb(16),
                 sdlc(17),
                 ds1(18),       -- T-1
                 e1(19),        -- european equiv. of T-1
                 basicISDN(20),
                 primaryISDN(21),-- proprietary serial
                 propPointToPointSerial(22),
                 ppp(23),
                 softwareLoopback(24),
                 eon(25),       -- CLNP over IP [11]
                 ethernet-3Mbit(26),
                 nsip(27),      -- XNS over IP
                 slip(28),      -- generic SLIP
                 ultra(29),     -- ULTRA technologies
                 ds3(30),       -- T-3
                 sip(31),       -- SMDS
                 frame-relay(32)
             }
     ACCESS  read-only
     STATUS  mandatory
     DESCRIPTION
            "The type of interface, distinguished according to
            the physical/link protocol(s) immediately `below'
            the network layer in the protocol stack."
       ::= { ifEntry 3 }

  ifMtu OBJECT-TYPE
```

547

```
        SYNTAX  INTEGER
        ACCESS  read-only
        STATUS  mandatory
        DESCRIPTION
            "The size of the largest datagram which can be
            sent/received on the interface, specified in
            octets.  For interfaces that are used for
            transmitting network datagrams, this is the size
            of the largest network datagram that can be sent
            on the interface."
        ::= { ifEntry 4 }

ifSpeed OBJECT-TYPE
        SYNTAX  Gauge
        ACCESS  read-only
        STATUS  mandatory
        DESCRIPTION
            "An estimate of the interface's current bandwidth
            in bits per second.  For interfaces which do not
            vary in bandwidth or for those where no accurate
            estimation can be made, this object should contain
            the nominal bandwidth."
        ::= { ifEntry 5 }

ifPhysAddress OBJECT-TYPE
        SYNTAX  PhysAddress
        ACCESS  read-only
        STATUS  mandatory
        DESCRIPTION
            "The interface's address at the protocol layer
            immediately `below' the network layer in the
            protocol stack.  For interfaces which do not have
            such an address (e.g., a serial line), this object
            should contain an octet string of zero length."
        ::= { ifEntry 6 }

ifAdminStatus OBJECT-TYPE
        SYNTAX  INTEGER {
                up(1),          -- ready to pass packets
                down(2),
                testing(3)    -- in some test mode
            }
        ACCESS  read-write
        STATUS  mandatory
        DESCRIPTION
            "The desired state of the interface.  The
            testing(3) state indicates that no operational
            packets can be passed."
        ::= { ifEntry 7 }

ifOperStatus OBJECT-TYPE
```

```
    SYNTAX  INTEGER {
            up(1),        -- ready to pass packets
            down(2),
            testing(3)    -- in some test mode
        }
    ACCESS  read-only
    STATUS  mandatory
    DESCRIPTION
        "The current operational state of the interface.
        The testing(3) state indicates that no operational
        packets can be passed."
    ::= { ifEntry 8 }

ifLastChange OBJECT-TYPE
    SYNTAX  TimeTicks
    ACCESS  read-only
    STATUS  mandatory
    DESCRIPTION
        "The value of sysUpTime at the time the interface
        entered its current operational state.  If the
        current state was entered prior to the last re-
        initialization of the local network management
        subsystem, then this object contains a zero
        value."
    ::= { ifEntry 9 }

ifInOctets OBJECT-TYPE
    SYNTAX  Counter
    ACCESS  read-only
    STATUS  mandatory
    DESCRIPTION
        "The total number of octets received on the
        interface, including framing characters."
    ::= { ifEntry 10 }

ifInUcastPkts OBJECT-TYPE
    SYNTAX  Counter
    ACCESS  read-only
    STATUS  mandatory
    DESCRIPTION
        "The number of subnetwork-unicast packets
        delivered to a higher-layer protocol."
    ::= { ifEntry 11 }

ifInNUcastPkts OBJECT-TYPE
    SYNTAX  Counter
    ACCESS  read-only
    STATUS  mandatory
    DESCRIPTION
        "The number of non-unicast (i.e., subnetwork-
        broadcast or subnetwork-multicast) packets
```

```
                    delivered to a higher-layer protocol."
           ::= { ifEntry 12 }

   ifInDiscards OBJECT-TYPE
     SYNTAX   Counter
     ACCESS   read-only
     STATUS   mandatory
     DESCRIPTION
           "The number of inbound packets which were chosen
           to be discarded even though no errors had been
           detected to prevent their being deliverable to a
           higher-layer protocol.  One possible reason for
           discarding such a packet could be to free up
           buffer space."
     ::= { ifEntry 13 }

   ifInErrors OBJECT-TYPE
     SYNTAX   Counter
     ACCESS   read-only
     STATUS   mandatory
     DESCRIPTION
           "The number of inbound packets that contained
           errors preventing them from being deliverable to a
           higher-layer protocol."
     ::= { ifEntry 14 }

   ifInUnknownProtos OBJECT-TYPE
     SYNTAX   Counter
     ACCESS   read-only
     STATUS   mandatory
     DESCRIPTION
           "The number of packets received via the interface
           which were discarded because of an unknown or
           unsupported protocol."
     ::= { ifEntry 15 }

   ifOutOctets OBJECT-TYPE
     SYNTAX   Counter
     ACCESS   read-only
     STATUS   mandatory
     DESCRIPTION
           "The total number of octets transmitted out of the
           interface, including framing characters."
     ::= { ifEntry 16 }

   ifOutUcastPkts OBJECT-TYPE
     SYNTAX   Counter
     ACCESS   read-only
     STATUS   mandatory
     DESCRIPTION
           "The total number of packets that higher-level
```

```
        protocols requested be transmitted to a
        subnetwork-unicast address, including those that
        were discarded or not sent."
  ::= { ifEntry 17 }

ifOutNUcastPkts OBJECT-TYPE
  SYNTAX  Counter
  ACCESS  read-only
  STATUS  mandatory
  DESCRIPTION
        "The total number of packets that higher-level
        protocols requested be transmitted to a non-
        unicast (i.e., a subnetwork-broadcast or
        subnetwork-multicast) address, including those
        that were discarded or not sent."
  ::= { ifEntry 18 }

ifOutDiscards OBJECT-TYPE
  SYNTAX  Counter
  ACCESS  read-only
  STATUS  mandatory
  DESCRIPTION
        "The number of outbound packets which were chosen
        to be discarded even though no errors had been
        detected to prevent their being transmitted. One
        possible reason for discarding such a packet could
        be to free up buffer space."
  ::= { ifEntry 19 }

ifOutErrors OBJECT-TYPE
  SYNTAX  Counter
  ACCESS  read-only
  STATUS  mandatory
  DESCRIPTION
        "The number of outbound packets that could not be
        transmitted because of errors."
  ::= { ifEntry 20 }

ifOutQLen OBJECT-TYPE
  SYNTAX  Gauge
  ACCESS  read-only
  STATUS  mandatory
  DESCRIPTION
        "The length of the output packet queue (in
        packets)."
  ::= { ifEntry 21 }

ifSpecific OBJECT-TYPE
  SYNTAX  OBJECT IDENTIFIER
  ACCESS  read-only
  STATUS  mandatory
```

```
DESCRIPTION
        "A reference to MIB definitions specific to the
        particular media being used to realize the
        interface.  For example, if the interface is
        realized by an Ethernet, then the value of this
        object refers to a document defining objects
        specific to Ethernet.  If this information is not
        present, its value should be set to the OBJECT
        IDENTIFIER { 0 0 }, which is a syntactically valid
        object identifier, and any conformant
        implementation of ASN.1 and BER must be able to
        generate and recognize this value."
::= { ifEntry 22 }


-- the Address Translation group

-- Implementation of the Address Translation group is
-- mandatory for all systems.  Note, however, that this group
-- is deprecated by MIB-II. That is, it is being included
-- solely for compatibility with MIB-I nodes, and will most
-- likely be excluded from MIB-III nodes.  From MIB-II and
-- onwards, each network protocol group contains its own
-- address translation tables.

-- The Address Translation group contains one table which is
-- the union across all interfaces of the translation tables
-- for converting a NetworkAddress (e.g., an IP address) into
-- a subnetwork-specific address.  For lack of a better term,
-- this document refers to such a subnetwork-specific address
-- as a `physical' address.

-- Examples of such translation tables are: for broadcast
-- media where ARP is in use, the translation table is
-- equivalent to the ARP cache; or, on an X.25 network where
-- non-algorithmic translation to X.121 addresses is
-- required, the translation table contains the
-- NetworkAddress to X.121 address equivalences.

atTable OBJECT-TYPE
   SYNTAX   SEQUENCE OF AtEntry
   ACCESS   not-accessible
   STATUS   deprecated
   DESCRIPTION
        "The Address Translation tables contain the
        NetworkAddress to `physical' address equivalences.
        Some interfaces do not use translation tables for
        determining address equivalences (e.g., DDN-X.25
        has an algorithmic method); if all interfaces are
        of this type, then the Address Translation table
        is empty, i.e., has zero entries."
```

```
    ::= { at 1 }

atEntry OBJECT-TYPE
   SYNTAX   AtEntry
   ACCESS   not-accessible
   STATUS   deprecated
   DESCRIPTION
        "Each entry contains one NetworkAddress to
        `physical' address equivalence."
   INDEX    { atIfIndex,
             atNetAddress }
   ::= { atTable 1 }

AtEntry ::=
   SEQUENCE {
       atIfIndex
          INTEGER,
       atPhysAddress
          PhysAddress,
       atNetAddress
          NetworkAddress
   }

atIfIndex OBJECT-TYPE
   SYNTAX   INTEGER
   ACCESS   read-write
   STATUS   deprecated
   DESCRIPTION
        "The interface on which this entry's equivalence
        is effective.  The interface identified by a
        particular value of this index is the same
        interface as identified by the same value of
        ifIndex."
   ::= { atEntry 1 }

atPhysAddress OBJECT-TYPE
   SYNTAX   PhysAddress
   ACCESS   read-write
   STATUS   deprecated
   DESCRIPTION
        "The media-dependent `physical' address.

        Setting this object to a null string (one of zero
        length) has the effect of invalidating the
        corresponding entry in the atTable object.  That
        is, it effectively dissasociates the interface
        identified with said entry from the mapping
        identified with said entry.  It is an
        implementation-specific matter as to whether the
        agent removes an invalidated entry from the table.
        Accordingly, management stations must be prepared
```

```
            to receive tabular information from agents that
            corresponds to entries not currently in use.
            Proper interpretation of such entries requires
            examination of the relevant atPhysAddress object."
    ::= { atEntry 2 }


atNetAddress OBJECT-TYPE
    SYNTAX  NetworkAddress
    ACCESS  read-write
    STATUS  deprecated
    DESCRIPTION
            "The NetworkAddress (e.g., the IP address)
            corresponding to the media-dependent `physical'
            address."
    ::= { atEntry 3 }



-- the IP group

-- Implementation of the IP group is mandatory for all
-- systems.

ipForwarding OBJECT-TYPE
    SYNTAX  INTEGER {
                forwarding(1),-- acting as a gateway
                not-forwarding(2) -- NOT acting as a gateway
            }
    ACCESS  read-write
    STATUS  mandatory
    DESCRIPTION
            "The indication of whether this entity is acting
            as an IP gateway in respect to the forwarding of
            datagrams received by, but not addressed to, this
            entity.  IP gateways forward datagrams.  IP hosts
            do not (except those source-routed via the host).

            Note that for some managed nodes, this object may
            take on only a subset of the values possible.
            Accordingly, it is appropriate for an agent to
            return a `badValue' response if a management
            station attempts to change this object to an
            inappropriate value."
    ::= { ip 1 }

ipDefaultTTL OBJECT-TYPE
    SYNTAX  INTEGER
    ACCESS  read-write
    STATUS  mandatory
    DESCRIPTION
            "The default value inserted into the Time-To-Live
            field of the IP header of datagrams originated at
```

```
        this entity, whenever a TTL value is not supplied
        by the transport layer protocol."
    ::= { ip 2 }

ipInReceives OBJECT-TYPE
    SYNTAX  Counter
    ACCESS  read-only
    STATUS  mandatory
    DESCRIPTION
        "The total number of input datagrams received from
        interfaces, including those received in error."
    ::= { ip 3 }

ipInHdrErrors OBJECT-TYPE
    SYNTAX  Counter
    ACCESS  read-only
    STATUS  mandatory
    DESCRIPTION
        "The number of input datagrams discarded due to
        errors in their IP headers, including bad
        checksums, version number mismatch, other format
        errors, time-to-live exceeded, errors discovered
        in processing their IP options, etc."
    ::= { ip 4 }

ipInAddrErrors OBJECT-TYPE
    SYNTAX  Counter
    ACCESS  read-only
    STATUS  mandatory
    DESCRIPTION
        "The number of input datagrams discarded because
        the IP address in their IP header's destination
        field was not a valid address to be received at
        this entity.This count includes invalid
        addresses (e.g., 0.0.0.0) and addresses of
        unsupported Classes (e.g., Class E). For entities
        which are not IP Gateways and therefore do not
        forward datagrams, this counter includes datagrams
        discarded because the destination address was not
        a local address."
    ::= { ip 5 }

ipForwDatagrams OBJECT-TYPE
    SYNTAX  Counter
    ACCESS  read-only
    STATUS  mandatory
    DESCRIPTION
        "The number of input datagrams for which this
        entity was not their final IP destination, as a
        result of which an attempt was made to find a
        route to forward them to that final destination.
```

In entities which do not act as IP Gateways, this
counter·will include only those packets which were
Source-Routed via this entity, and the Source-
Route option processing was successful."
::= { ip 6 }

ipInUnknownProtos OBJECT-TYPE
    SYNTAX   Counter
    ACCESS   read-only
    STATUS   mandatory
    DESCRIPTION
        "The number of locally-addressed datagrams
        received successfully but discarded because of an
        unknown or unsupported protocol."
    ::= { ip 7 }

ipInDiscards OBJECT-TYPE
    SYNTAX   Counter
    ACCESS   read-only
    STATUS   mandatory
    DESCRIPTION
        "The number of input IP datagrams for which no
        problems were encountered to prevent their
        continued processing, but which were discarded
        (e.g., for lack of buffer space). Note that this
        counter does not include any datagrams discarded
        while awaiting re-assembly."
    ::= { ip 8 }

ipInDelivers OBJECT-TYPE
    SYNTAX   Counter
    ACCESS   read-only
    STATUS   mandatory
    DESCRIPTION
        "The total number of input datagrams successfully
        delivered to IP user-protocols (including ICMP)."
    ::= { ip 9 }

ipOutRequests OBJECT-TYPE
    SYNTAX   Counter
    ACCESS   read-only
    STATUS   mandatory
    DESCRIPTION
        "The total number of IP datagrams which local IP
        user-protocols (including ICMP) supplied to IP in
        requests for transmission. Note that this counter
        does not include any datagrams counted in
        ipForwDatagrams."
    ::= { ip 10 }

ipOutDiscards OBJECT-TYPE

```
    SYNTAX  Counter
    ACCESS  read-only
    STATUS  mandatory
    DESCRIPTION
        "The number of output IP datagrams for which no
        problem was encountered to prevent their
        transmission to their destination, but which were
        discarded (e.g., for lack of buffer space).  Note
        that this counter would include datagrams counted
        in ipForwDatagrams if any such packets met this
        (discretionary) discard criterion."
    ::= { ip 11 }

ipOutNoRoutes OBJECT-TYPE
    SYNTAX  Counter
    ACCESS  read-only
    STATUS  mandatory
    DESCRIPTION
        "The number of IP datagrams discarded because no
        route could be found to transmit them to their
        destination.Note that this counter includes any
        packets counted in ipForwDatagrams which meet this
        `no-route' criterion.  Note that this includes any
        datagrams which a host cannot route because all of
        its default gateways are down."
    ::= { ip 12 }

ipReasmTimeout OBJECT-TYPE
    SYNTAX  INTEGER
    ACCESS  read-only
    STATUS  mandatory
    DESCRIPTION
        "The maximum number of seconds which received
        fragments are held while they are awaiting
        reassembly at this entity."
    ::= { ip 13 }

ipReasmReqds OBJECT-TYPE
    SYNTAX  Counter
    ACCESS  read-only
    STATUS  mandatory
    DESCRIPTION
        "The number of IP fragments received which needed
        to be reassembled at this entity."
    ::= { ip 14 }

ipReasmOKs OBJECT-TYPE
    SYNTAX  Counter
    ACCESS  read-only
    STATUS  mandatory
    DESCRIPTION
```

```
            "The number of IP datagrams successfully re-
            assembled."
     ::= { ip 15 }

ipReasmFails OBJECT-TYPE
   SYNTAX  Counter
   ACCESS  read-only
   STATUS  mandatory
   DESCRIPTION
            "The number of failures detected by the IP re-
            assembly algorithm (for whatever reason: timed
            out, errors, etc.).  Note that this is not
            necessarily a count of discarded IP fragments
            since some algorithms (notably the algorithm in
            RFC 815) can lose track of the number of fragments
            by combining them as they are received."
     ::= { ip 16 }

ipFragOKs OBJECT-TYPE
   SYNTAX  Counter
   ACCESS  read-only
   STATUS  mandatory
   DESCRIPTION
            "The number of IP datagrams that have been
            successfully fragmented at this entity."
     ::= { ip 17 }

ipFragFails OBJECT-TYPE
   SYNTAX  Counter
   ACCESS  read-only
   STATUS  mandatory
   DESCRIPTION
            "The number of IP datagrams that have been
            discarded because they needed to be fragmented at
            this entity but could not be, e.g., because their
            Don't Fragment flag was set."
     ::= { ip 18 }

ipFragCreates OBJECT-TYPE
   SYNTAX  Counter
   ACCESS  read-only
   STATUS  mandatory
   DESCRIPTION
            "The number of IP datagram fragments that have
            been generated as a result of fragmentation at
            this entity."
     ::= { ip 19 }

-- the IP address table

-- The IP address table contains this entity's IP addressing
```

```
-- information.

ipAddrTable OBJECT-TYPE
   SYNTAX  SEQUENCE OF IpAddrEntry
   ACCESS  not-accessible
   STATUS  mandatory
   DESCRIPTION
         "The table of addressing information relevant to
         this entity's IP addresses."
   ::= { ip 20 }

ipAddrEntry OBJECT-TYPE
   SYNTAX  IpAddrEntry
   ACCESS  not-accessible
   STATUS  mandatory
   DESCRIPTION
         "The addressing information for one of this
         entity's IP addresses."
   INDEX   { ipAdEntAddr }
   ::= { ipAddrTable 1 }

IpAddrEntry ::=
   SEQUENCE {
       ipAdEntAddr
         IpAddress,
       ipAdEntIfIndex
         INTEGER,
       ipAdEntNetMask
         IpAddress,
       ipAdEntBcastAddr
         INTEGER,
       ipAdEntReasmMaxSize
         INTEGER (0..65535)
   }

ipAdEntAddr OBJECT-TYPE
   SYNTAX  IpAddress
   ACCESS  read-only
   STATUS  mandatory
   DESCRIPTION
         "The IP address to which this entry's addressing
         information pertains."
   ::= { ipAddrEntry 1 }

ipAdEntIfIndex OBJECT-TYPE
   SYNTAX  INTEGER
   ACCESS  read-only
   STATUS  mandatory
   DESCRIPTION
         "The index value which uniquely identifies the
         interface to which this entry is applicable. The
```

```
                   interface identified by a particular value of this
                   index is the same interface as identified by the
                   same value of ifIndex."
            ::= { ipAddrEntry 2 }


        ipAdEntNetMask OBJECT-TYPE
           SYNTAX   IpAddress
           ACCESS   read-only
           STATUS   mandatory
           DESCRIPTION
                   "The subnet mask associated with the IP address of
                   this entry.  The value of the mask is an IP
                   address with all the network bits set to 1 and all
                   the hosts bits set to 0."
            ::= { ipAddrEntry 3 }


        ipAdEntBcastAddr OBJECT-TYPE
           SYNTAX   INTEGER
           ACCESS   read-only
           STATUS   mandatory
           DESCRIPTION
                   "The value of the least-significant bit in the IP
                   broadcast address used for sending datagrams on
                   the (logical) interface associated with the IP
                   address of this entry.  For example, when the
                   Internet standard all-ones broadcast address is
                   used, the value will be 1.  This value applies to
                   both the subnet and network broadcasts addresses
                   used by the entity on this (logical) interface."
            ::= { ipAddrEntry 4 }


        ipAdEntReasmMaxSize OBJECT-TYPE
           SYNTAX   INTEGER (0..65535)
           ACCESS   read-only
           STATUS   mandatory
           DESCRIPTION
                   "The size of the largest IP datagram which this
                   entity can re-assemble from incoming IP fragmented
                   datagrams received on this interface."
            ::= { ipAddrEntry 5 }


    -- the IP routing table

    -- The IP routing table contains an entry for each route
    -- presently known to this entity.

    ipRouteTable OBJECT-TYPE
       SYNTAX   SEQUENCE OF IpRouteEntry
       ACCESS   not-accessible
       STATUS   mandatory
       DESCRIPTION
```

```
              "This entity's IP Routing table."
    ::= { ip 21 }

ipRouteEntry OBJECT-TYPE
   SYNTAX  IpRouteEntry
   ACCESS  not-accessible
   STATUS  mandatory
   DESCRIPTION
          "A route to a particular destination."
   INDEX   { ipRouteDest }
   ::= { ipRouteTable 1 }

IpRouteEntry ::=
   SEQUENCE {
       ipRouteDest
          IpAddress,
       ipRouteIfIndex
          INTEGER,
       ipRouteMetric1
          INTEGER,
       ipRouteMetric2
          INTEGER,
       ipRouteMetric3
          INTEGER,
       ipRouteMetric4
          INTEGER,
       ipRouteNextHop
          IpAddress,
       ipRouteType
          INTEGER,
       ipRouteProto
          INTEGER,
       ipRouteAge
          INTEGER,
       ipRouteMask
          IpAddress,
       ipRouteMetric5
          INTEGER,
       ipRouteInfo
          OBJECT IDENTIFIER
   }

ipRouteDest OBJECT-TYPE
   SYNTAX  IpAddress
   ACCESS  read-write
   STATUS  mandatory
   DESCRIPTION
          "The destination IP address of this route.  An
          entry with a value of 0.0.0.0 is considered a
          default route.  Multiple routes to a single
          destination can appear in the table, but access to
```

```
                    such multiple entries is dependent on the table-
                    access mechanisms defined by the network
                    management protocol in use."
            ::= { ipRouteEntry 1 }


    ipRouteIfIndex OBJECT-TYPE
        SYNTAX  INTEGER
        ACCESS  read-write
        STATUS  mandatory
        DESCRIPTION
                "The index value which uniquely identifies the
                local interface through which the next hop of this
                route should be reached.  The interface identified
                by a particular value of this index is the same
                interface as identified by the same value of
                ifIndex."
            ::= { ipRouteEntry 2 }


    ipRouteMetric1 OBJECT-TYPE
        SYNTAX  INTEGER
        ACCESS  read-write
        STATUS  mandatory
        DESCRIPTION
                "The primary routing metric for this route.  The
                semantics of this metric are determined by the
                routing-protocol specified in the route's
                ipRouteProto value.  If this metric is not used,
                its value should be set to -1."
            ::= { ipRouteEntry 3 }


    ipRouteMetric2 OBJECT-TYPE
        SYNTAX  INTEGER
        ACCESS  read-write
        STATUS  mandatory
        DESCRIPTION
                "An alternate routing metric for this route.  The
                semantics of this metric are determined by the
                routing-protocol specified in the route's
                ipRouteProto value.  If this metric is not used,
                its value should be set to -1."
            ::= { ipRouteEntry 4 }


    ipRouteMetric3 OBJECT-TYPE
        SYNTAX  INTEGER
        ACCESS  read-write
        STATUS  mandatory
        DESCRIPTION
                "An alternate routing metric for this route.  The
                semantics of this metric are determined by the
                routing-protocol specified in the route's
                ipRouteProto value.  If this metric is not used,
```

```
              its value should be set to -1."
        ::= { ipRouteEntry 5 }


ipRouteMetric4 OBJECT-TYPE
    SYNTAX  INTEGER
    ACCESS  read-write
    STATUS  mandatory
    DESCRIPTION
            "An alternate routing metric for this route.  The
            semantics of this metric are determined by the
            routing-protocol specified in the route's
            ipRouteProto value.  If this metric is not used,
            its value should be set to -1."
        ::= { ipRouteEntry 6 }


ipRouteNextHop OBJECT-TYPE
    SYNTAX  IpAddress
    ACCESS  read-write
    STATUS  mandatory
    DESCRIPTION
            "The IP address of the next hop of this route.
            (In the case of a route bound to an interface
            which is realized via a broadcast media, the value
            of this field is the agent's IP address on that
            interface.)"
        ::= { ipRouteEntry 7 }


ipRouteType OBJECT-TYPE
    SYNTAX  INTEGER {
                other(1),     -- none of the following

                invalid(2),   -- an invalidated route

                              -- route to directly
                direct(3),    -- connected (sub-)network

                              -- route to a non-local
                indirect(4)   -- host/network/sub-network
            }
    ACCESS  read-write
    STATUS  mandatory
    DESCRIPTION
            "The type of route.  Note that the values
            direct(3) and indirect(4) refer to the notion of
            direct and indirect routing in the IP
            architecture.

            Setting this object to the value invalid(2) has
            the effect of invalidating the corresponding entry
            in the ipRouteTable object.  That is, it
            effectively dissasociates the destination
```

```
                identified with said entry from the route
                identified with said entry.  It is an
                implementation-specific matter as to whether the
                agent removes an invalidated entry from the table.
                Accordingly, management stations must be prepared
                to receive tabular information from agents that
                corresponds to entries not currently in use.
                Proper interpretation of such entries requires
                examination of the relevant ipRouteType object."
          ::= { ipRouteEntry 8 }

      ipRouteProto OBJECT-TYPE
          SYNTAX  INTEGER {
                    other(1),     -- none of the following

                                  -- non-protocol information,
                                  -- e.g., manually configured
                    local(2),     -- entries

                                  -- set via a network
                    netmgmt(3),   -- management protocol

                                  -- obtained via ICMP,
                    icmp(4),      -- e.g., Redirect

                                  -- the remaining values are
                                  -- all gateway routing
                                  -- protocols
                    egp(5),
                    ggp(6),
                    hello(7),
                    rip(8),
                    is-is(9),
                    es-is(10),
                    ciscoIgrp(11),
                    bbnSpfIgp(12),
                    ospf(13),
                    bgp(14)
                }
          ACCESS  read-only
          STATUS  mandatory
          DESCRIPTION
                "The routing mechanism via which this route was
                learned.  Inclusion of values for gateway routing
                protocols is not intended to imply that hosts
                should support those protocols."
          ::= { ipRouteEntry 9 }

      ipRouteAge OBJECT-TYPE
          SYNTAX  INTEGER
          ACCESS  read-write
```

```
   STATUS  mandatory
   DESCRIPTION
        "The number of seconds since this route was last
        updated or otherwise determined to be correct.
        Note that no semantics of `too old' can be implied
        except through knowledge of the routing protocol
        by which the route was learned."
   ::= { ipRouteEntry 10 }

ipRouteMask OBJECT-TYPE
   SYNTAX  IpAddress
   ACCESS  read-write
   STATUS  mandatory
   DESCRIPTION
        "Indicate the mask to be logical-ANDed with the
        destination address before being compared to the
        value in the ipRouteDest field.  For those systems
        that do not support arbitrary subnet masks, an
        agent constructs the value of the ipRouteMask by
        determining whether the value of the correspondent
        ipRouteDest field belongs to a class-A, B, or C
        network, and then using one of:

                mask          network
                255.0.0.0       class-A
                255.255.0.0     class-B
                255.255.255.0  class-C

        If the value of the ipRouteDest is 0.0.0.0 (a
        default route), then the mask value is also
        0.0.0.0.  It should be noted that all IP routing
        subsystems implicitly use this mechanism."
   ::= { ipRouteEntry 11 }

ipRouteMetric5 OBJECT-TYPE
   SYNTAX  INTEGER
   ACCESS  read-write
   STATUS  mandatory
   DESCRIPTION
        "An alternate routing metric for this route.  The
        semantics of this metric are determined by the
        routing-protocol specified in the route's
        ipRouteProto value.  If this metric is not used,
        its value should be set to -1."
   ::= { ipRouteEntry 12 }

ipRouteInfo OBJECT-TYPE
   SYNTAX  OBJECT IDENTIFIER
   ACCESS  read-only
   STATUS  mandatory
   DESCRIPTION
```

```
                    "A reference to MIB definitions specific to the
                    particular routing protocol which is responsible
                    for this route, as determined by the value
                    specified in the route's ipRouteProto value.  If
                    this information is not present, its value should
                    be set to the OBJECT IDENTIFIER { 0 0 }, which is
                    a syntactically valid object identifier, and any
                    conformant implementation of ASN.1 and BER must be
                    able to generate and recognize this value."
           ::= { ipRouteEntry 13 }


       -- the IP Address Translation table

       -- The IP address translation table contains the IpAddress to
       -- `physical' address equivalences.  Some interfaces do not
       -- use translation tables for determining address
       -- equivalences (e.g., DDN-X.25 has an algorithmic method);
       -- if all interfaces are of this type, then the Address
       -- Translation table is empty, i.e., has zero entries.

       ipNetToMediaTable OBJECT-TYPE
          SYNTAX  SEQUENCE OF IpNetToMediaEntry
          ACCESS  not-accessible
          STATUS  mandatory
          DESCRIPTION
                  "The IP Address Translation table used for mapping
                  from IP addresses to physical addresses."
          ::= { ip 22 }

       ipNetToMediaEntry OBJECT-TYPE
          SYNTAX  IpNetToMediaEntry
          ACCESS  not-accessible
          STATUS  mandatory
          DESCRIPTION
                  "Each entry contains one IpAddress to `physical'
                  address equivalence."
          INDEX   { ipNetToMediaIfIndex,
                    ipNetToMediaNetAddress }
          ::= { ipNetToMediaTable 1 }

       IpNetToMediaEntry ::=
          SEQUENCE {
              ipNetToMediaIfIndex
                 INTEGER,
              ipNetToMediaPhysAddress
                 PhysAddress,
              ipNetToMediaNetAddress
                 IpAddress,
              ipNetToMediaType
                 INTEGER
```

```
     }

ipNetToMediaIfIndex OBJECT-TYPE
   SYNTAX   INTEGER
   ACCESS   read-write
   STATUS   mandatory
   DESCRIPTION
         "The interface on which this entry's equivalence
         is effective.  The interface identified by a
         particular value of this index is the same
         interface as identified by the same value of
         ifIndex."
   ::= { ipNetToMediaEntry 1 }

ipNetToMediaPhysAddress OBJECT-TYPE
   SYNTAX   PhysAddress
   ACCESS   read-write
   STATUS   mandatory
   DESCRIPTION
         "The media-dependent `physical' address."
   ::= { ipNetToMediaEntry 2 }

ipNetToMediaNetAddress OBJECT-TYPE
   SYNTAX   IpAddress
   ACCESS   read-write
   STATUS   mandatory
   DESCRIPTION
         "The IpAddress corresponding to the media-
         dependent `physical' address."
   ::= { ipNetToMediaEntry 3 }

ipNetToMediaType OBJECT-TYPE
   SYNTAX   INTEGER {
               other(1),       -- none of the following
               invalid(2),     -- an invalidated mapping
               dynamic(3),
               static(4)
          }
   ACCESS   read-write
   STATUS   mandatory
   DESCRIPTION
         "The type of mapping.

         Setting this object to the value invalid(2) has
         the effect of invalidating the corresponding entry
         in the ipNetToMediaTable.  That is, it effectively
         dissasociates the interface identified with said
         entry from the mapping identified with said entry.
         It is an implementation-specific matter as to
         whether the agent removes an invalidated entry
         from the table.  Accordingly, management stations
```

```
                must be prepared to receive tabular information
                from agents that corresponds to entries not
                currently in use.  Proper interpretation of such
                entries requires examination of the relevant
                ipNetToMediaType object."
        ::= { ipNetToMediaEntry 4 }


    -- additional IP objects

    ipRoutingDiscards OBJECT-TYPE
        SYNTAX  Counter
        ACCESS  read-only
        STATUS  mandatory
        DESCRIPTION
                "The number of routing entries which were chosen
                to be discarded even though they are valid.  One
                possible reason for discarding such an entry could
                be to free-up buffer space for other routing
                entries."
        ::= { ip 23 }


    -- the ICMP group

    -- Implementation of the ICMP group is mandatory for all
    -- systems.

    icmpInMsgs OBJECT-TYPE
        SYNTAX  Counter
        ACCESS  read-only
        STATUS  mandatory
        DESCRIPTION
                "The total number of ICMP messages which the
                entity received.  Note that this counter includes
                all those counted by icmpInErrors."
        ::= { icmp 1 }

    icmpInErrors OBJECT-TYPE
        SYNTAX  Counter
        ACCESS  read-only
        STATUS  mandatory
        DESCRIPTION
                "The number of ICMP messages which the entity
                received but determined as having ICMP-specific
                errors (bad ICMP checksums, bad length, etc.)."
        ::= { icmp 2 }

    icmpInDestUnreachs OBJECT-TYPE
        SYNTAX  Counter
        ACCESS  read-only
```

```
     STATUS   mandatory
     DESCRIPTION
            "The number of ICMP Destination Unreachable
            messages received."
     ::= { icmp 3 }

icmpInTimeExcds OBJECT-TYPE
   SYNTAX   Counter
   ACCESS   read-only
   STATUS   mandatory
   DESCRIPTION
            "The number of ICMP Time Exceeded messages
            received."
     ::= { icmp 4 }

icmpInParmProbs OBJECT-TYPE
   SYNTAX   Counter
   ACCESS   read-only
   STATUS   mandatory
   DESCRIPTION
            "The number of ICMP Parameter Problem messages
            received."
     ::= { icmp 5 }

icmpInSrcQuenchs OBJECT-TYPE
   SYNTAX   Counter
   ACCESS   read-only
   STATUS   mandatory
   DESCRIPTION
            "The number of ICMP Source Quench messages
            received."
     ::= { icmp 6 }

icmpInRedirects OBJECT-TYPE
   SYNTAX   Counter
   ACCESS   read-only
   STATUS   mandatory
   DESCRIPTION
            "The number of ICMP Redirect messages received."
     ::= { icmp 7 }

icmpInEchos OBJECT-TYPE
   SYNTAX   Counter
   ACCESS   read-only
   STATUS   mandatory
   DESCRIPTION
            "The number of ICMP Echo (request) messages
            received."
     ::= { icmp 8 }

icmpInEchoReps OBJECT-TYPE
```

```
     SYNTAX  Counter
     ACCESS  read-only
     STATUS  mandatory
     DESCRIPTION
           "The number of ICMP Echo Reply messages received."
     ::= { icmp 9 }

icmpInTimestamps OBJECT-TYPE
     SYNTAX  Counter
     ACCESS  read-only
     STATUS  mandatory
     DESCRIPTION
           "The number of ICMP Timestamp (request) messages
           received."
     ::= { icmp 10 }

icmpInTimestampReps OBJECT-TYPE
     SYNTAX  Counter
     ACCESS  read-only
     STATUS  mandatory
     DESCRIPTION
           "The number of ICMP Timestamp Reply messages
           received."
     ::= { icmp 11 }

icmpInAddrMasks OBJECT-TYPE
     SYNTAX  Counter
     ACCESS  read-only
     STATUS  mandatory
     DESCRIPTION
           "The number of ICMP Address Mask Request messages
           received."
     ::= { icmp 12 }

icmpInAddrMaskReps OBJECT-TYPE
     SYNTAX  Counter
     ACCESS  read-only
     STATUS  mandatory
     DESCRIPTION
           "The number of ICMP Address Mask Reply messages
           received."
     ::= { icmp 13 }

icmpOutMsgs OBJECT-TYPE
     SYNTAX  Counter
     ACCESS  read-only
     STATUS  mandatory
     DESCRIPTION
           "The total number of ICMP messages which this
           entity attempted to send.  Note that this counter
           includes all those counted by icmpOutErrors."
```

```
    ::= { icmp 14 }

icmpOutErrors OBJECT-TYPE
   SYNTAX  Counter
   ACCESS  read-only
   STATUS  mandatory
   DESCRIPTION
         "The number of ICMP messages which this entity did
         not send due to problems discovered within ICMP
         such as a lack of buffers.  This value should not
         include errors discovered outside the ICMP layer
         such as the inability of IP to route the resultant
         datagram.  In some implementations there may be no
         types of error which contribute to this counter's
         value."
    ::= { icmp 15 }

icmpOutDestUnreachs OBJECT-TYPE
   SYNTAX  Counter
   ACCESS  read-only
   STATUS  mandatory
   DESCRIPTION
         "The number of ICMP Destination Unreachable
         messages sent."
    ::= { icmp 16 }

icmpOutTimeExcds OBJECT-TYPE
   SYNTAX  Counter
   ACCESS  read-only
   STATUS  mandatory
   DESCRIPTION
         "The number of ICMP Time Exceeded messages sent."
    ::= { icmp 17 }

icmpOutParmProbs OBJECT-TYPE
   SYNTAX  Counter
   ACCESS  read-only
   STATUS  mandatory
   DESCRIPTION
         "The number of ICMP Parameter Problem messages
         sent."
    ::= { icmp 18 }

icmpOutSrcQuenchs OBJECT-TYPE
   SYNTAX  Counter
   ACCESS  read-only
   STATUS  mandatory
   DESCRIPTION
         "The number of ICMP Source Quench messages sent."
    ::= { icmp 19 }
```

```
icmpOutRedirects OBJECT-TYPE
  SYNTAX  Counter
  ACCESS  read-only
  STATUS  mandatory
  DESCRIPTION
        "The number of ICMP Redirect messages sent.  For a
        host, this object will always be zero, since hosts
        do not send redirects."
  ::= { icmp 20 }

icmpOutEchos OBJECT-TYPE
  SYNTAX  Counter
  ACCESS  read-only
  STATUS  mandatory
  DESCRIPTION
        "The number of ICMP Echo (request) messages sent."
  ::= { icmp 21 }

icmpOutEchoReps OBJECT-TYPE
  SYNTAX  Counter
  ACCESS  read-only
  STATUS  mandatory
  DESCRIPTION
        "The number of ICMP Echo Reply messages sent."
  ::= { icmp 22 }

icmpOutTimestamps OBJECT-TYPE
  SYNTAX  Counter
  ACCESS  read-only
  STATUS  mandatory
  DESCRIPTION
        "The number of ICMP Timestamp (request) messages
        sent."
  ::= { icmp 23 }

icmpOutTimestampReps OBJECT-TYPE
  SYNTAX  Counter
  ACCESS  read-only
  STATUS  mandatory
  DESCRIPTION
        "The number of ICMP Timestamp Reply messages
        sent."
  ::= { icmp 24 }

icmpOutAddrMasks OBJECT-TYPE
  SYNTAX  Counter
  ACCESS  read-only
  STATUS  mandatory
  DESCRIPTION
        "The number of ICMP Address Mask Request messages
        sent."
```

```
     ::= { icmp 25 }

icmpOutAddrMaskReps OBJECT-TYPE
    SYNTAX  Counter
    ACCESS  read-only
    STATUS  mandatory
    DESCRIPTION
            "The number of ICMP Address Mask Reply messages
            sent."
    ::= { icmp 26 }


-- the TCP group

-- Implementation of the TCP group is mandatory for all
-- systems that implement the TCP.

-- Note that instances of object types that represent
-- information about a particular TCP connection are
-- transient; they persist only as long as the connection
-- in question.

tcpRtoAlgorithm OBJECT-TYPE
    SYNTAX  INTEGER {
                other(1),    -- none of the following

                constant(2),-- a constant rto
                rsre(3),     -- MIL-STD-1778, Appendix B
                vanj(4)        -- Van Jacobson's algorithm [10]
            }
    ACCESS  read-only
    STATUS  mandatory
    DESCRIPTION
            "The algorithm used to determine the timeout value
            used for retransmitting unacknowledged octets."
    ::= { tcp 1 }

tcpRtoMin OBJECT-TYPE
    SYNTAX  INTEGER
    ACCESS  read-only
    STATUS  mandatory
    DESCRIPTION
            "The minimum value permitted by a TCP
            implementation for the retransmission timeout,
            measured in milliseconds.  More refined semantics
            for objects of this type depend upon the algorithm
            used to determine the retransmission timeout.  In
            particular, when the timeout algorithm is rsre(3),
            an object of this type has the semantics of the
            LBOUND quantity described in RFC 793."
    ::= { tcp 2 }
```

```
tcpRtoMax OBJECT-TYPE
  SYNTAX  INTEGER
  ACCESS  read-only
  STATUS  mandatory
  DESCRIPTION
        "The maximum value permitted by a TCP
        implementation for the retransmission timeout,
        measured in milliseconds.  More refined semantics
        for objects of this type depend upon the algorithm
        used to determine the retransmission timeout.  In
        particular, when the timeout algorithm is rsre(3),
        an object of this type has the semantics of the
        UBOUND quantity described in RFC 793."
  ::= { tcp 3 }

tcpMaxConn OBJECT-TYPE
  SYNTAX  INTEGER
  ACCESS  read-only
  STATUS  mandatory
  DESCRIPTION
        "The limit on the total number of TCP connections
        the entity can support.  In entities where the
        maximum number of connections is dynamic, this
        object should contain the value -1."
  ::= { tcp 4 }

tcpActiveOpens OBJECT-TYPE
  SYNTAX  Counter
  ACCESS  read-only
  STATUS  mandatory
  DESCRIPTION
        "The number of times TCP connections have made a
        direct transition to the SYN-SENT state from the
        CLOSED state."
  ::= { tcp 5 }

tcpPassiveOpens OBJECT-TYPE
  SYNTAX  Counter
  ACCESS  read-only
  STATUS  mandatory
  DESCRIPTION
        "The number of times TCP connections have made a
        direct transition to the SYN-RCVD state from the
        LISTEN state."
  ::= { tcp 6 }

tcpAttemptFails OBJECT-TYPE
  SYNTAX  Counter
  ACCESS  read-only
```

```
   STATUS   mandatory
   DESCRIPTION
         "The number of times TCP connections have made a
         direct transition to the CLOSED state from either
         the SYN-SENT state or the SYN-RCVD state, plus the
         number of times TCP connections have made a direct
         transition to the LISTEN state from the SYN-RCVD
         state."
   ::= { tcp 7 }

tcpEstabResets OBJECT-TYPE
   SYNTAX   Counter
   ACCESS   read-only
   STATUS   mandatory
   DESCRIPTION
         "The number of times TCP connections have made a
         direct transition to the CLOSED state from either
         the ESTABLISHED state or the CLOSE-WAIT state."
   ::= { tcp 8 }

tcpCurrEstab OBJECT-TYPE
   SYNTAX   Gauge
   ACCESS   read-only
   STATUS   mandatory
   DESCRIPTION
         "The number of TCP connections for which the
         current state is either ESTABLISHED or CLOSE-
         WAIT."
   ::= { tcp 9 }

tcpInSegs OBJECT-TYPE
   SYNTAX   Counter
   ACCESS   read-only
   STATUS   mandatory
   DESCRIPTION
         "The total number of segments received, including
         those received in error.  This count includes
         segments received on currently established
         connections."
   ::= { tcp 10 }

tcpOutSegs OBJECT-TYPE
   SYNTAX   Counter
   ACCESS   read-only
   STATUS   mandatory
   DESCRIPTION
         "The total number of segments sent, including
         those on current connections but excluding those
         containing only retransmitted octets."
   ::= { tcp 11 }
```

```
tcpRetransSegs OBJECT-TYPE
   SYNTAX  Counter
   ACCESS  read-only
   STATUS  mandatory
   DESCRIPTION
        "The total number of segments retransmitted - that
        is, the number of TCP segments transmitted
        containing one or more previously transmitted
        octets."
   ::= { tcp 12 }


-- the TCP Connection table

-- The TCP connection table contains information about this
-- entity's existing TCP connections.

tcpConnTable OBJECT-TYPE
   SYNTAX  SEQUENCE OF TcpConnEntry
   ACCESS  not-accessible
   STATUS  mandatory
   DESCRIPTION
        "A table containing TCP connection-specific
        information."
   ::= { tcp 13 }

tcpConnEntry OBJECT-TYPE
   SYNTAX  TcpConnEntry
   ACCESS  not-accessible
   STATUS  mandatory
   DESCRIPTION
        "Information about a particular current TCP
        connection.  An object of this type is transient,
        in that it ceases to exist when (or soon after)
        the connection makes the transition to the CLOSED
        state."
   INDEX   { tcpConnLocalAddress,
             tcpConnLocalPort,
             tcpConnRemAddress,
             tcpConnRemPort }
   ::= { tcpConnTable 1 }

TcpConnEntry ::=
   SEQUENCE {
       tcpConnState
         INTEGER,
       tcpConnLocalAddress
         IpAddress,
       tcpConnLocalPort
         INTEGER (0..65535),
       tcpConnRemAddress
```

```
            IpAddress,
        tcpConnRemPort
            INTEGER (0..65535)
    }


tcpConnState OBJECT-TYPE
    SYNTAX  INTEGER {
                closed(1),
                listen(2),
                synSent(3),
                synReceived(4),
                established(5),
                finWait1(6),
                finWait2(7),
                closeWait(8),
                lastAck(9),
                closing(10),
                timeWait(11),
                deleteTCB(12)
            }
    ACCESS  read-write
    STATUS  mandatory
    DESCRIPTION
            "The state of this TCP connection.

            The only value which may be set by a management
            station is deleteTCB(12).  Accordingly, it is
            appropriate for an agent to return a `badValue'
            response if a management station attempts to set
            this object to any other value.

            If a management station sets this object to the
            value deleteTCB(12), then this has the effect of
            deleting the TCB (as defined in RFC 793) of the
            corresponding connection on the managed node,
            resulting in immediate termination of the
            connection.

            As an implementation-specific option, a RST
            segment may be sent from the managed node to the
            other TCP endpoint (note however that RST segments
            are not sent reliably)."
    ::= { tcpConnEntry 1 }

tcpConnLocalAddress OBJECT-TYPE
    SYNTAX  IpAddress
    ACCESS  read-only
    STATUS  mandatory
    DESCRIPTION
            "The local IP address for this TCP connection.  In
            the case of a connection in the listen state which
```

```
                  is willing to accept connections for any IP
                  interface associated with the node, the value
                  0.0.0.0 is used."
            ::= { tcpConnEntry 2 }

      tcpConnLocalPort OBJECT-TYPE
         SYNTAX  INTEGER (0..65535)
         ACCESS  read-only
         STATUS  mandatory
         DESCRIPTION
                  "The local port number for this TCP connection."
            ::= { tcpConnEntry 3 }

      tcpConnRemAddress OBJECT-TYPE
         SYNTAX  IpAddress
         ACCESS  read-only
         STATUS  mandatory
         DESCRIPTION
                  "The remote IP address for this TCP connection."
            ::= { tcpConnEntry 4 }

      tcpConnRemPort OBJECT-TYPE
         SYNTAX  INTEGER (0..65535)
         ACCESS  read-only
         STATUS  mandatory
         DESCRIPTION
                  "The remote port number for this TCP connection."
            ::= { tcpConnEntry 5 }


      -- additional TCP objects

      tcpInErrs OBJECT-TYPE
         SYNTAX  Counter
         ACCESS  read-only
         STATUS  mandatory
         DESCRIPTION
                  "The total number of segments received in error
                  (e.g., bad TCP checksums)."
            ::= { tcp 14 }

      tcpOutRsts OBJECT-TYPE
         SYNTAX  Counter
         ACCESS  read-only
         STATUS  mandatory
         DESCRIPTION
                  "The number of TCP segments sent containing the
                  RST flag."
            ::= { tcp 15 }
```

```
-- the UDP group

-- Implementation of the UDP group is mandatory for all
-- systems which implement the UDP.

udpInDatagrams OBJECT-TYPE
    SYNTAX   Counter
    ACCESS   read-only
    STATUS   mandatory
    DESCRIPTION
            "The total number of UDP datagrams delivered to
            UDP users."
    ::= { udp 1 }

udpNoPorts OBJECT-TYPE
    SYNTAX   Counter
    ACCESS   read-only
    STATUS   mandatory
    DESCRIPTION
            "The total number of received UDP datagrams for
            which there was no application at the destination
            port."
    ::= { udp 2 }

udpInErrors OBJECT-TYPE
    SYNTAX   Counter
    ACCESS   read-only
    STATUS   mandatory
    DESCRIPTION
            "The number of received UDP datagrams that could
            not be delivered for reasons other than the lack
            of an application at the destination port."
    ::= { udp 3 }

udpOutDatagrams OBJECT-TYPE
    SYNTAX   Counter
    ACCESS   read-only
    STATUS   mandatory
    DESCRIPTION
            "The total number of UDP datagrams sent from this
            entity."
    ::= { udp 4 }


-- the UDP Listener table

-- The UDP listener table contains information about this
-- entity's UDP end-points on which a local application is
-- currently accepting datagrams.

udpTable OBJECT-TYPE
```

```
      SYNTAX   SEQUENCE OF UdpEntry
      ACCESS   not-accessible
      STATUS   mandatory
      DESCRIPTION
            "A table containing UDP listener information."
      ::= { udp 5 }

udpEntry OBJECT-TYPE
   SYNTAX   UdpEntry
   ACCESS   not-accessible
   STATUS   mandatory
   DESCRIPTION
         "Information about a particular current UDP
         listener."
   INDEX   { udpLocalAddress, udpLocalPort }
   ::= { udpTable 1 }

UdpEntry ::=
   SEQUENCE {
       udpLocalAddress
          IpAddress,
       udpLocalPort
          INTEGER (0..65535)
   }

udpLocalAddress OBJECT-TYPE
   SYNTAX   IpAddress
   ACCESS   read-only
   STATUS   mandatory
   DESCRIPTION
         "The local IP address for this UDP listener.  In
         the case of a UDP listener which is willing to
         accept datagrams for any IP interface associated
         with the node, the value 0.0.0.0 is used."
   ::= { udpEntry 1 }

udpLocalPort OBJECT-TYPE
   SYNTAX   INTEGER (0..65535)
   ACCESS   read-only
   STATUS   mandatory
   DESCRIPTION
         "The local port number for this UDP listener."
   ::= { udpEntry 2 }


-- the EGP group

-- Implementation of the EGP group is mandatory for all
-- systems which implement the EGP.

egpInMsgs OBJECT-TYPE
```

```
      SYNTAX   Counter
      ACCESS   read-only
      STATUS   mandatory
      DESCRIPTION
            "The number of EGP messages received without
            error."
      ::= { egp 1 }

egpInErrors OBJECT-TYPE
      SYNTAX   Counter
      ACCESS   read-only
      STATUS   mandatory
      DESCRIPTION
            "The number of EGP messages received that proved
            to be in error."
      ::= { egp 2 }

egpOutMsgs OBJECT-TYPE
      SYNTAX   Counter
      ACCESS   read-only
      STATUS   mandatory
      DESCRIPTION
            "The total number of locally generated EGP
            messages."
      ::= { egp 3 }

egpOutErrors OBJECT-TYPE
      SYNTAX   Counter
      ACCESS   read-only
      STATUS   mandatory
      DESCRIPTION
            "The number of locally generated EGP messages not
            sent due to resource limitations within an EGP
            entity."
      ::= { egp 4 }


-- the EGP Neighbor table

-- The EGP neighbor table contains information about this
-- entity's EGP neighbors.

egpNeighTable OBJECT-TYPE
      SYNTAX   SEQUENCE OF EgpNeighEntry
      ACCESS   not-accessible
      STATUS   mandatory
      DESCRIPTION
            "The EGP neighbor table."
      ::= { egp 5 }

egpNeighEntry OBJECT-TYPE
```

```
            SYNTAX   EgpNeighEntry
            ACCESS   not-accessible
            STATUS   mandatory
            DESCRIPTION
                 "Information about this entity's relationship with
                 a particular EGP neighbor."
            INDEX   { egpNeighAddr }
            ::= { egpNeighTable 1 }

     EgpNeighEntry ::=
        SEQUENCE {
             egpNeighState
               INTEGER,
             egpNeighAddr
               IpAddress,
             egpNeighAs
               INTEGER,
             egpNeighInMsgs
               Counter,
             egpNeighInErrs
               Counter,
             egpNeighOutMsgs
               Counter,
             egpNeighOutErrs
               Counter,
             egpNeighInErrMsgs
               Counter,
             egpNeighOutErrMsgs
               Counter,
             egpNeighStateUps
               Counter,
             egpNeighStateDowns
               Counter,
             egpNeighIntervalHello
               INTEGER,
             egpNeighIntervalPoll
               INTEGER,
             egpNeighMode
               INTEGER,
             egpNeighEventTrigger
               INTEGER
        }

     egpNeighState OBJECT-TYPE
        SYNTAX   INTEGER {
                  idle(1),
                  acquisition(2),
                  down(3),
                  up(4),
                  cease(5)
             }
```

```
  ACCESS  read-only
  STATUS  mandatory
  DESCRIPTION
        "The EGP state of the local system with respect to
        this entry's EGP neighbor.  Each EGP state is
        represented by a value that is one greater than
        the numerical value associated with said state in
        RFC 904."
  ::= { egpNeighEntry 1 }

egpNeighAddr OBJECT-TYPE
  SYNTAX  IpAddress
  ACCESS  read-only
  STATUS  mandatory
  DESCRIPTION
        "The IP address of this entry's EGP neighbor."
  ::= { egpNeighEntry 2 }

egpNeighAs OBJECT-TYPE
  SYNTAX  INTEGER
  ACCESS  read-only
  STATUS  mandatory
  DESCRIPTION
        "The autonomous system of this EGP peer.  Zero
        should be specified if the autonomous system
        number of the neighbor is not yet known."
  ::= { egpNeighEntry 3 }

egpNeighInMsgs OBJECT-TYPE
  SYNTAX  Counter
  ACCESS  read-only
  STATUS  mandatory
  DESCRIPTION
        "The number of EGP messages received without error
        from this EGP peer."
  ::= { egpNeighEntry 4 }

egpNeighInErrs OBJECT-TYPE
  SYNTAX  Counter
  ACCESS  read-only
  STATUS  mandatory
  DESCRIPTION
        "The number of EGP messages received from this EGP
        peer that proved to be in error (e.g., bad EGP
        checksum)."
  ::= { egpNeighEntry 5 }

egpNeighOutMsgs OBJECT-TYPE
  SYNTAX  Counter
  ACCESS  read-only
  STATUS  mandatory
```

583

```
DESCRIPTION
     "The number of locally generated EGP messages to
     this EGP peer."
::= { egpNeighEntry 6 }

egpNeighOutErrs OBJECT-TYPE
  SYNTAX   Counter
  ACCESS   read-only
  STATUS   mandatory
  DESCRIPTION
     "The number of locally generated EGP messages not
     sent to this EGP peer due to resource limitations
     within an EGP entity."
::= { egpNeighEntry 7 }

egpNeighInErrMsgs OBJECT-TYPE
  SYNTAX   Counter
  ACCESS   read-only
  STATUS   mandatory
  DESCRIPTION
     "The number of EGP-defined error messages received
     from this EGP peer."
::= { egpNeighEntry 8 }

egpNeighOutErrMsgs OBJECT-TYPE
  SYNTAX   Counter
  ACCESS   read-only
  STATUS   mandatory
  DESCRIPTION
     "The number of EGP-defined error messages sent to
     this EGP peer."
::= { egpNeighEntry 9 }

egpNeighStateUps OBJECT-TYPE
  SYNTAX   Counter
  ACCESS   read-only
  STATUS   mandatory
  DESCRIPTION
     "The number of EGP state transitions to the UP
     state with this EGP peer."
::= { egpNeighEntry 10 }

egpNeighStateDowns OBJECT-TYPE
  SYNTAX   Counter
  ACCESS   read-only
  STATUS   mandatory
  DESCRIPTION
     "The number of EGP state transitions from the UP
     state to any other state with this EGP peer."
::= { egpNeighEntry 11 }
```

```
egpNeighIntervalHello OBJECT-TYPE
   SYNTAX  INTEGER
   ACCESS  read-only
   STATUS  mandatory
   DESCRIPTION
          "The interval between EGP Hello command
          retransmissions (in hundredths of a second). This
          represents the t1 timer as defined in RFC 904."
   ::= { egpNeighEntry 12 }

egpNeighIntervalPoll OBJECT-TYPE
   SYNTAX  INTEGER
   ACCESS  read-only
   STATUS  mandatory
   DESCRIPTION
          "The interval between EGP poll command
          retransmissions (in hundredths of a second). This
          represents the t3 timer as defined in RFC 904."
   ::= { egpNeighEntry 13 }

egpNeighMode OBJECT-TYPE
   SYNTAX  INTEGER { active(1), passive(2) }
   ACCESS  read-only
   STATUS  mandatory
   DESCRIPTION
          "The polling mode of this EGP entity, either
          passive or active."
   ::= { egpNeighEntry 14 }

egpNeighEventTrigger OBJECT-TYPE
   SYNTAX  INTEGER { start(1), stop(2) }
   ACCESS  read-write
   STATUS  mandatory
   DESCRIPTION
          "A control variable used to trigger operator-
          initiated Start and Stop events.  When read, this
          variable always returns the most recent value that
          egpNeighEventTrigger was set to.  If it has not
          been set since the last initialization of the
          network management subsystem on the node, it
          returns a value of `stop'.

          When set, this variable causes a Start or Stop
          event on the specified neighbor, as specified on
          pages 8-10 of RFC 904.  Briefly, a Start event
          causes an Idle peer to begin neighbor acquisition
          and a non-Idle peer to reinitiate neighbor
          acquisition.A stop event causes a non-Idle peer
          to return to the Idle state until a Start event
          occurs, either via egpNeighEventTrigger or
          otherwise."
```

```
        ::= { egpNeighEntry 15 }


-- additional EGP objects

egpAs OBJECT-TYPE
   SYNTAX   INTEGER
   ACCESS   read-only
   STATUS   mandatory
   DESCRIPTION
         "The autonomous system number of this EGP entity."
   ::= { egp 6 }

-- the Transmission group

-- Based on the transmission media underlying each interface
-- on a system, the corresponding portion of the Transmission
-- group is mandatory for that system.

-- When Internet-standard definitions for managing
-- transmission media are defined, the transmission group is
-- used to provide a prefix for the names of those objects.

-- Typically, such definitions reside in the experimental
-- portion of the MIB until they are "proven", then as a
-- part of the Internet standardization process, the
-- definitions are accordingly elevated and a new object
-- identifier, under the transmission group is defined. By
-- convention, the name assigned is:
--
--     type OBJECT IDENTIFIER    ::= { transmission number }
--
-- where "type" is the symbolic value used for the media in
-- the ifType column of the ifTable object, and "number" is
-- the actual integer value corresponding to the symbol.


-- the SNMP group

-- Implementation of the SNMP group is mandatory for all
-- systems which support an SNMP protocol entity.  Some of
-- the objects defined below will be zero-valued in those
-- SNMP implementations that are optimized to support only
-- those functions specific to either a management agent or
-- a management station. In particular, it should be
-- observed that the objects below refer to an SNMP entity,
-- and there may be several SNMP entities residing on a
-- managed node (e.g., if the node is hosting acting as
-- a management station).

snmpInPkts OBJECT-TYPE
```

```
   SYNTAX   Counter
   ACCESS   read-only
   STATUS   mandatory
   DESCRIPTION
        "The total number of Messages delivered to the
        SNMP entity from the transport service."
   ::= { snmp 1 }

snmpOutPkts OBJECT-TYPE
   SYNTAX   Counter
   ACCESS   read-only
   STATUS   mandatory
   DESCRIPTION
        "The total number of SNMP Messages which were
        passed from the SNMP protocol entity to the
        transport service."
   ::= { snmp 2 }

snmpInBadVersions OBJECT-TYPE
   SYNTAX   Counter
   ACCESS   read-only
   STATUS   mandatory
   DESCRIPTION
        "The total number of SNMP Messages which were
        delivered to the SNMP protocol entity and were for
        an unsupported SNMP version."
   ::= { snmp 3 }

snmpInBadCommunityNames OBJECT-TYPE
   SYNTAX   Counter
   ACCESS   read-only
   STATUS   mandatory
   DESCRIPTION
        "The total number of SNMP Messages delivered to
        the SNMP protocol entity which used a SNMP
        community name not known to said entity."
   ::= { snmp 4 }

snmpInBadCommunityUses OBJECT-TYPE
   SYNTAX   Counter
   ACCESS   read-only
   STATUS   mandatory
   DESCRIPTION
        "The total number of SNMP Messages delivered to
        the SNMP protocol entity which represented an SNMP
        operation which was not allowed by the SNMP
        community named in the Message."
   ::= { snmp 5 }

snmpInASNParseErrs OBJECT-TYPE
   SYNTAX   Counter
```

```
   ACCESS  read-only
   STATUS  mandatory
   DESCRIPTION
        "The total number of ASN.1 or BER errors
        encountered by the SNMP protocol entity when
        decoding received SNMP Messages."
   ::= { snmp 6 }

-- { snmp 7 } is not used

snmpInTooBigs OBJECT-TYPE
   SYNTAX  Counter
   ACCESS  read-only
   STATUS  mandatory
   DESCRIPTION
        "The total number of SNMP PDUs which were
        delivered to the SNMP protocol entity and for
        which the value of the error-status field is
        `tooBig'."
   ::= { snmp 8 }

snmpInNoSuchNames OBJECT-TYPE
   SYNTAX  Counter
   ACCESS  read-only
   STATUS  mandatory
   DESCRIPTION
        "The total number of SNMP PDUs which were
        delivered to the SNMP protocol entity and for
        which the value of the error-status field is
        `noSuchName'."
   ::= { snmp 9 }

snmpInBadValues OBJECT-TYPE
   SYNTAX  Counter
   ACCESS  read-only
   STATUS  mandatory
   DESCRIPTION
        "The total number of SNMP PDUs which were
        delivered to the SNMP protocol entity and for
        which the value of the error-status field is
        `badValue'."
   ::= { snmp 10 }

snmpInReadOnlys OBJECT-TYPE
   SYNTAX  Counter
   ACCESS  read-only
   STATUS  mandatory
   DESCRIPTION
        "The total number valid SNMP PDUs which were
        delivered to the SNMP protocol entity and for
        which the value of the error-status field is
```

```
            `readOnly'.  It should be noted that it is a
            protocol error to generate an SNMP PDU which
            contains the value `readOnly' in the error-status
            field, as such this object is provided as a means
            of detecting incorrect implementations of the
            SNMP."
      ::= { snmp 11 }

snmpInGenErrs OBJECT-TYPE
   SYNTAX  Counter
   ACCESS  read-only
   STATUS  mandatory
   DESCRIPTION
            "The total number of SNMP PDUs which were
            delivered to the SNMP protocol entity and for
            which the value of the error-status field is
            `genErr'."
      ::= { snmp 12 }

snmpInTotalReqVars OBJECT-TYPE
   SYNTAX  Counter
   ACCESS  read-only
   STATUS  mandatory
   DESCRIPTION
            "The total number of MIB objects which have been
            retrieved successfully by the SNMP protocol entity
            as the result of receiving valid SNMP Get-Request
            and Get-Next PDUs."
      ::= { snmp 13 }

snmpInTotalSetVars OBJECT-TYPE
   SYNTAX  Counter
   ACCESS  read-only
   STATUS  mandatory
   DESCRIPTION
            "The total number of MIB objects which have been
            altered successfully by the SNMP protocol entity
            as the result of receiving valid SNMP Set-Request
            PDUs."
      ::= { snmp 14 }

snmpInGetRequests OBJECT-TYPE
   SYNTAX  Counter
   ACCESS  read-only
   STATUS  mandatory
   DESCRIPTION
            "The total number of SNMP Get-Request PDUs which
            have been accepted and processed by the SNMP
            protocol entity."
      ::= { snmp 15 }
```

```
snmpInGetNexts OBJECT-TYPE
  SYNTAX  Counter
  ACCESS  read-only
  STATUS  mandatory
  DESCRIPTION
        "The total number of SNMP Get-Next PDUs which have
        been accepted and processed by the SNMP protocol
        entity."
  ::= { snmp 16 }

snmpInSetRequests OBJECT-TYPE
  SYNTAX  Counter
  ACCESS  read-only
  STATUS  mandatory
  DESCRIPTION
        "The total number of SNMP Set-Request PDUs which
        have been accepted and processed by the SNMP
        protocol entity."
  ::= { snmp 17 }

snmpInGetResponses OBJECT-TYPE
  SYNTAX  Counter
  ACCESS  read-only
  STATUS  mandatory
  DESCRIPTION
        "The total number of SNMP Get-Response PDUs which
        have been accepted and processed by the SNMP
        protocol entity."
  ::= { snmp 18 }

snmpInTraps OBJECT-TYPE
  SYNTAX  Counter
  ACCESS  read-only
  STATUS  mandatory
  DESCRIPTION
        "The total number of SNMP Trap PDUs which have
        been accepted and processed by the SNMP protocol
        entity."
  ::= { snmp 19 }

snmpOutTooBigs OBJECT-TYPE
  SYNTAX  Counter
  ACCESS  read-only
  STATUS  mandatory
  DESCRIPTION
        "The total number of SNMP PDUs which were
        generated by the SNMP protocol entity and for
        which the value of the error-status field is
        `tooBig.'"
  ::= { snmp 20 }
```

```
snmpOutNoSuchNames OBJECT-TYPE
   SYNTAX   Counter
   ACCESS   read-only
   STATUS   mandatory
   DESCRIPTION
          "The total number of SNMP PDUs which were
          generated by the SNMP protocol entity and for
          which the value of the error-status is
          `noSuchName'."
   ::= { snmp 21 }

snmpOutBadValues OBJECT-TYPE
   SYNTAX   Counter
   ACCESS   read-only
   STATUS   mandatory
   DESCRIPTION
          "The total number of SNMP PDUs which were
          generated by the SNMP protocol entity and for
          which the value of the error-status field is
          `badValue'."
   ::= { snmp 22 }

-- { snmp 23 } is not used

snmpOutGenErrs OBJECT-TYPE
   SYNTAX   Counter
   ACCESS   read-only
   STATUS   mandatory
   DESCRIPTION
          "The total number of SNMP PDUs which were
          generated by the SNMP protocol entity and for
          which the value of the error-status field is
          `genErr'."
   ::= { snmp 24 }

snmpOutGetRequests OBJECT-TYPE
   SYNTAX   Counter
   ACCESS   read-only
   STATUS   mandatory
   DESCRIPTION
          "The total number of SNMP Get-Request PDUs which
          have been generated by the SNMP protocol entity."
   ::= { snmp 25 }

snmpOutGetNexts OBJECT-TYPE
   SYNTAX   Counter
   ACCESS   read-only
   STATUS   mandatory
   DESCRIPTION
          "The total number of SNMP Get-Next PDUs which have
          been generated by the SNMP protocol entity."
```

```
      ::= { snmp 26 }

snmpOutSetRequests OBJECT-TYPE
  SYNTAX  Counter
  ACCESS  read-only
  STATUS  mandatory
  DESCRIPTION
        "The total number of SNMP Set-Request PDUs which
        have been generated by the SNMP protocol entity."
  ::= { snmp 27 }

snmpOutGetResponses OBJECT-TYPE
  SYNTAX  Counter
  ACCESS  read-only
  STATUS  mandatory
  DESCRIPTION
        "The total number of SNMP Get-Response PDUs which
        have been generated by the SNMP protocol entity."
  ::= { snmp 28 }

snmpOutTraps OBJECT-TYPE
  SYNTAX  Counter
  ACCESS  read-only
  STATUS  mandatory
  DESCRIPTION
        "The total number of SNMP Trap PDUs which have
        been generated by the SNMP protocol entity."
  ::= { snmp 29 }

snmpEnableAuthenTraps OBJECT-TYPE
  SYNTAX  INTEGER { enabled(1), disabled(2) }
  ACCESS  read-write
  STATUS  mandatory
  DESCRIPTION
        "Indicates whether the SNMP agent process is
        permitted to generate authentication-failure
        traps.  The value of this object overrides any
        configuration information; as such, it provides a
        means whereby all authentication-failure traps may
        be disabled.

        Note that it is strongly recommended that this
        object be stored in non-volatile memory so that it
        remains constant between re-initializations of the
        network management system."
  ::= { snmp 30 }

END
```

Selected RFC Index

The following is a list of RFCs presented in descending numerical order that pertain to SNMP, the TCP/IP protocol suite, and miscellaneous related issues that may be of interest. The list includes the RFC number, the title, the author(s) or editor(s), the date it was issued, and information on other RFCs that directly pertain to it. RFCs are now easily available over the Internet via anonymous FTP or in HTML format at several sites. A good starting point is to view the RFC index (e.g., `http://ds.internic.net/rfc/rfc-index.txt`).

2128 *Dial Control Management Information Base Using SMIv2*. Roeck, G. March 1997.

2127 *ISDN Management Information Base*. Roeck, G. March 1997.

2108 *Definitions of Managed Objects for IEEE 802.3 Repeater Devices Using SMIv2*. DeGraaf, K.; Romascanu, D.; McMaster, D.; McCloghrie, K. February 1997. (Updates RFC 1516) (Obsoletes RFC 1516)

2096 *IP Forwarding Table MIB*. Baker, F. January 1997. (Obsoletes RFC 1354)

2089 *V2 To V1 Mapping SNMPv2 onto SNMPv1 Within a Bi-lingual SNMP Agent*. Wijnen, B.; Levi, D. January 1997.

2074 *Remote Network Monitoring MIB Protocol Identifiers.* Bierman, A.; Iddon, R. January 1997.

2064 *Traffic Flow Measurement: Meter MIB.* Brownlee, N. January 1997.

2051 *Definitions of Managed Objects for APPC.* Allen, K.; Clouston, B.; Kielczewski, Z.; Kwan, W.; Moore, R. October 1996.

2039 *Applicability of Standards Track MIBs to Management of World Wide Web Servers.* Kalbfleisch, C. November 1996.

2037 *Entity MIB.* McCloghrie, K.; Bierman, A. October 1996.

2024 *Definitions of Managed Objects for Data Link Switching using SNMPv2.* Chen, D.; Gayek, P.; Nix, S. October 1996.

2020 *Definitions of Managed Objects for IEEE 802.12 Interfaces.* Flick, J. October 1996.

2013 *SNMPv2 Management Information Base for the User Datagram Protocol using SMIv2.* McCloghrie, K. November 1996.

2012 *SNMPv2 Management Information Base for the Transmission Control Protocol.* McCloghrie, K. November 1996.

2011 *SNMPv2 Management Information Base for the Internet Protocol using SMIv2.* McCloghrie, K. November 1996.

2006 *The Definitions of Managed Objects for IP Mobility Support using SMIv2.* Cong, D.; Hamlen, C., Perkins, C. October 1996.

1988 *Conditional Grant of Rights to Specific Hewlett-Packard Patents In Conjunction With the Internet Engineering Task Force's Internet-Standard Network Management Framework.* McAnally, G.; Gilbert, D.; Flick, J. August 1996.

1910 *User-based Security Model for SNMPv2.* Waters, G., ed. February 1996.

1909 *An Administrative Infrastructure for SNMPv2.* McCloghrie, K., ed. February 1996.

1908 *Coexistence Between Version 1 and Version 2 of the Internet-standard Network Management Framework.* Case, J.; McCloghrie, K.; Rose, M.; Waldbusser, S. January 1996.

1747 *Definitions of Managed Objects for SNA Data Link Control: SDLC.* J. Hilgeman, S. Nix, A. Bartky, W. Clark. January 1995.

1743 *IEEE 802.5 MIB using SMIv2.* K. McCloghrie, E. Decker. December 1994. (Obsoletes RFC 1231)

1742 *AppleTalk Management Information Base II.* S. Waldbusser, K. Frisa. January 1995. (Obsoletes RFC 1243)

1724 *RIP Version 2 MIB Extension.* G. Malkin, F. Baker. November 1994. (Obsoletes RFC 1389)

1697 *Relational Database Management System (RDBMS) Management Information Base (MIB) using SMIv2.* D. Brower, R. Purvy, A. Daniel, M. Sinykin, J. Smith. August 1994.

1696 *Modem Management Information Base (MIB) using SMIv2.* J. Barnes, L. Brown, R. Royston, S. Waldbusser. August 1994.

1695 *Definitions of Managed Objects for ATM Management Version 8.0 using SMIv2.* M. Ahmed, K. Tesink. August 1994.

1694 *Definitions of Managed Objects for SMDS Interfaces using SMIv2.* T. Brown, K. Tesink. August 1994. (Obsoletes RFC1304)

1666 *Definitions of Managed Objects for SNA NAUs using SMIv2.* Z. Kielczewski, D. Kostick, K. Shih. August 1994.

1665 *Definitions of Managed Objects for SNA NAUs using SMIv2.* Kielczewski, Z.; Kostick, D.; Shih, K. July 1994.

1660 *Definitions of Managed Objects for Parallel-printer-like Hardware Devices using SMIv2.* B. Stewart, July 1994. (Obsoletes RFC 1318)

1659 *Definitions of Managed Objects for RS-232-like Hardware Devices using SMIv2.* B. Stewart. July 1994. (Obsoletes RFC1317)

1658 *Definitions of Managed Objects for Character Stream Devices using SMIv2.* B. Stewart. July 1994. (Obsoletes RFC1316)

1657 *Definitions of Managed Objects for the Fourth Version of the Border Gateway Protocol (BGP-4) using SMIv2.* S. Willis, J. Burruss, J. Chu. July 1994.

1514 *Host Resources MIB.* Grillo, P.; Waldbusser, S. September 1993.

1513 *Token Ring Extensions to the Remote Network Monitoring MIB.* S. Waldbusser. September 1993. (Updates RFC1271)

1512 *FDDI Management Information Base.* J. Case, A. Rijsinghani. September 1993. (Updates RFC1285)

1503 *Algorithms for Automating Administration in SNMPv2 Managers.* K. McCloghrie, M. Rose. August 1993.

1495 *Mapping between X.400 and RFC-822 Message Bodies.* H. Alvestrand, S. Kille. R. Miles, M. Rose, S. Thompson. August 1993. (Updates RFC1327)

1493 *Definitions of Managed Objects for Bridges.* E. Decker, P. Langille, A. Rijsinghani, K. McCloghrie. July 1993. (Obsoletes RFC1286)

1474 *The Definitions of Managed Objects for the Bridge Network Control Protocol of the Point-to-Point Protocol.* F. Kastenholz. June 1993.

1473 *The Definitions of Managed Objects for the IP Network Control Protocol of the Point-to-Point Protocol.* F. Kastenholz. June 1993.

1472 *The Definitions of Managed Objects for the Security Protocols of the Point-to-Point Protocol.* F. Kastenholz. June 1993.

1471 *The Definitions of Managed Objects for the Link Control Protocol of the Point-to-Point Protocol.* F. Kastenholz. June 1993.

1470 *FYI on a Network Management Tool Catalog: Tools for Monitoring and Debugging TCP/IP Internets and Interconnected Devices.* R. Enger, J. Reynolds. June 1993. (FYI 2) (Obsoletes RFC1147)

1461 *SNMP MIB extension for MultiProtocol Interconnect over X.25.* D. Throop. May 1993.

1452 *Coexistence between version 1 and version 2 of the Internet-standard Network Management Framework.* Case, J.D.; McCloghrie, K.; Rose, M.T.; Waldbusser, S. April 1993.

1451 *Manager-to-Manager Management Information Base.* Case, J.D.; McCloghrie, K.; Rose, M.T.; Waldbusser, S. April 1993.

1414   *Identification MIB.* St. Johns, M.; Rose, M.T. February 1993.

1413   *Identification Protocol.* St. Johns, M. February 1993. (Obsoletes RFC 931)

1407   *Definitions of Managed Objects for the DS3/E3 Interface Type.* Cox, T.A.; Tesink, K., eds. January 1993. (Obsoletes RFC 1233)

1406   *Definitions of Managed Objects for the DS1 and E1 Interface Types.* Baker, F.; Watt, J., eds. January 1993. (Obsoletes RFC 1232)

1389   *RIP Version 2 MIB Extension.* Malkin, G.S.; Baker, F. January 1993.

1388   *RIP Version 2: Carrying Additional Information.* Malkin, G.S. January 1993. (Updates RFC 1058)

1387   *RIP Version 2 Protocol Analysis.* Malkin, G.S. January 1993.

1382   *SNMP MIB extensions for the X.25 packet layer.* Throop, D.D., ed. November 1992.

1381   *SNMP MIB extension for X.25 LAPB.* Throop, D.D.; Baker, F. November 1992.

1369   *Implementation notes and experience for the Internet Ethernet MIB.* Kastenholz, F.J. October 1992.

1368   *Definitions of managed objects for IEEE 802.3 repeater devices.* McMaster, D.; McCloghrie, K. October 1992.

1354   *IP forwarding table MIB.* Baker, F. July 1992.

1353   *Definitions of managed objects for administration of SNMP parties.* McCloghrie, K.; Davin, J.R.; Galvin, J.M. July 1992.

1352   *SNMP security protocols.* Galvin, J.M.; McCloghrie, K.; Davin, J.R. July 1992.

1351   *SNMP administrative model.* Davin, J.R.; Galvin, J.M.; McCloghrie, K. July 1992.

1321   *MD5 Message-Digest algorithm.* Rivest, R.L. April 1992.

1320   *MD4 Message-Digest algorithm.* Rivest, R.L. April 1992. (Obsoletes RFC 1186)

1267   *Border Gateway Protocol 3 (BGP-3).* Lougheed, K.; Rekhter, Y. October 1991. (Obsoletes RFC 1163)

1253   *OSPF version 2: Management Information Base.* Baker, F.; Coltun, R. August 1991. (Obsoletes RFC 1252)

1252   *OSPF version 2: Management Information Base.* Baker, F.; Coltun, R. August 1991. (Obsoletes RFC 1248; Obsoleted by RFC 1253)

1248   *OSPF version 2: Management Information Base.* Baker, F.; Coltun, R. July 1991. (Obsoleted by RFC 1252; Updated by RFC 1349)

1247   *OSPF version 2.* Moy, J. July 1991. (Obsoletes RFC 1131; Updated by RFC 1349)

1243   *AppleTalk Management Information Base.* Waldbusser, S., ed. July 1991.

1239   *Reassignment of experimental MIBs to standard MIBs.* Reynolds, J.K. June 1991. (Updates RFC 1229, RFC 1230, RFC 1231, RFC 1232, RFC 1233)

1238   *CLNS MIB for use with Connectionless Network Protocol (ISO 8473) and End System to Intermediate System (ISO 9542).* Satz, G. June 1991. (Obsoletes RFC 1162)

1233   *Definitions of managed objects for the DS3 Interface type.* Cox, T.A.; Tesink, K., eds. May 1991. (Obsoleted by RFC 1407; Updated by RFC 1239)

1232   *Definitions of managed objects for the DS1 Interface type.* Baker, F.; Kolb, C.P., eds. May 1991. (Obsoleted by RFC 1406; Updated by RFC 1239)

1231   *IEEE 802.5 Token Ring MIB.* McCloghrie, K.; Fox, R.; Decker, E. May 1991. (Updated by RFC 1239)

1230   *IEEE 802.4 Token Bus MIB.* McCloghrie, K.; Fox, R. May 1991. (Updated by RFC 1239)

1229   *Extensions to the generic-interface MIB.* McCloghrie, K., ed. May 1991. (Updated by RFC 1239)

1228   *SNMP-DPI: Simple Network Management Protocol Distributed Program Interface.* Carpenter, G.; Wijnen, B. May 1991.

1227 *SNMP MUX protocol and MIB.* Rose, M.T. May 1991.

1215 *Convention for defining traps for use with the SNMP.* Rose, M.T., ed. March 1991.

1214 *OSI internet management: Management Information Base.* LaBarre, L., ed. April 1991.

1213 *Management Information Base for network management of TCP/IP-based internets: MIB-II.* McCloghrie, K.; Rose, M.T., eds. March 1991. (Obsoletes RFC 1158)

1212 *Concise MIB definitions.* Rose, M.T.; McCloghrie, K., eds. March 1991.

1189 *Common Management Information Services and Protocols for the Internet (CMOT and CMIP).* Warrier, U.S.; Besaw, L.; LaBarre, L.; Handspicker, B.D. October 1990. (Obsoletes RFC 1095)

1187 *Bulk table retrieval with the SNMP.* Rose, M.T.; McCloghrie, K.; Davin, J.R. October 1990.

1186 *MD4 message digest algorithm.* Rivest, R.L. October 1990. (Obsoleted by RFC 1320)

1162 *Connectionless Network Protocol (ISO 8473) and End System to Intermediate System (ISO 9542) Management Information Base.* Satz, G. June 1990. (Obsoleted by RFC 1238)

1161 *SNMP over OSI.* Rose, M.T. June 1990. (Obsoleted by RFC 1283, RFC 1418)

1158 *Management Information Base for network management of TCP/IP-based internets: MIB-II.* Rose, M.T., ed. May 1990. (Obsoleted by RFC 1213)

1157 *Simple Network Management Protocol (SNMP).* Case, J.D.; Fedor, M.; Schoffstall, M.L.; Davin, C. May 1990. (Obsoletes RFC 1098)

1156 *Management Information Base for network management of TCP/IP-based internets.* McCloghrie, K.; Rose, M.T. May 1990. (Obsoletes RFC 1066)

1155 *Structure and identification of management information for TCP/IP-based internets.* Rose, M.T.; McCloghrie, K. May 1990. (Obsoletes RFC 1065)

1109   *Report of the second Ad Hoc Network Management Review Group.* Cerf, V.G. August 1989.

1098   *Simple Network Management Protocol (SNMP).* Case, J.D.; Fedor, M.; Schoffstall, M.L.; Davin, C. April 1989. (Obsoletes RFC 1067; Obsoleted by RFC 1157)

1095   *Common Management Information Services and Protocol over TCP/IP (CMOT).* Warrier, U.S.; Besaw, L. April 1989. (Obsoleted by RFC 1189)

1089   *SNMP over Ethernet.* Schoffstall, M.L.; Davin, C.; Fedor, M.; Case, J.D. February 1989.

1076   *HEMS monitoring and control language.* Trewitt, G.; Partridge, C. November 1988. (Obsoletes RFC 1023)

1067   *Simple Network Management Protocol.* Case, J.D.; Fedor, M.; Schoffstall, M.L.; Davin, J.R. August 1988. (Obsoleted by RFC 1098)

1066   *Management Information Base for network management of TCP/IP-based internets.* McCloghrie, K.; Rose, M.T. August 1988. (Obsoleted by RFC 1156)

1065   *Structure and identification of management information for TCP/IP-based internets.* McCloghrie, K.; Rose, M.T. August 1988. (Obsoleted by RFC 1155)

1052   *IAB recommendations for the development of Internet network management standards.* Cerf, V.G. April 1988.

1028   *Simple Gateway Monitoring Protocol.* Davin, J.R.; Case, J.D.; Fedor, M.; Schoffstall, M.L. November 1987.

1024   *HEMS variable definitions.* Partridge, C.; Trewitt, G. October 1987.

1023   *HEMS Monitoring and Control Language.* Trewitt, G.; Partridge, C. October 1987. (Obsoleted by RFC 1076)

1022   *High-level Entity Management Protocol (HEMP).* Partridge, C.; Trewitt, G. October 1987.

1021   *High-level Entity Management System (HEMS).* Partridge, C.; Trewitt, G. October 1987.

Annotated Bibliography

REFERENCES PRIMARILY ON SNMP:

Feit, Sidnie. *SNMP: A Guide to Network Management*. New York: McGraw-Hill. 1994.

Excellent reference on the use of SNMP to manage protocols and interfaces. Solid introduction to network management and SNMP. Includes up to SNMPv2 draft proposal (RFC 1441-1452). RFC index current to RFC 1573.

Harnedy, Sean. *TOTAL SNMP: Exploring the Simple Network Management Protocol*. Horsham, PA: CBM Books. 1994.

First edition of this book. Includes appendix with description of all standard MIB variables at the time. RFC index current to RFC 1452.

Hein, Mathais, and David Griffiths. *SNMP Versions 1 & 2 Simple Network Management Protocol Theory and Practice*. London: International Thomson Computer Press. 1995.

Sound reference on SNMP and OSI network management. Includes up to SNMPv2 draft proposal (RFC 1441-1452). RFC index current to RFC 1516.

Held, Gilbert. *LAN Management with SNMP and RMON*. New York: John Wiley and Sons, Inc. 1996.

Includes introduction to network management and SNMP. Deals primarily with the use of SNMPv1 for the management of Ethernet and token ring LANs, bridges, switching hubs, UPSs, and RMON. RFC index current to RFC 1792.

Miller, Mark A. *Managing Internetworks with SNMP: The Definitive Guide to the Simple Network Management Protocol (SNMP) and SNMP version 2*. New York: M&T Books. 1993.

Practical introduction to SNMP including a great deal of technical detail. Has case studies, analyzer dumps, and several useful appendices. Includes up to SNMPv2 draft proposal (RFC 1441-1452). RFC index current to RFC 1461.

Perkins, David, and Evan McGinnis. *Understanding SNMP MIBs*. Upper Saddle River, NJ: Prentice Hall. 1997.

Complete reference on MIBs and everything to do with them. General introduction on SNMP, MIB compilers, ASN.1 syntax, and much other useful information. Includes CD.

Rose, Marshall T. *The Simple Book: An Introduction to Management of TCP/IP-based Networks*. Upper Saddle River, NJ: Prentice Hall. 1990.

The Classic. First text on SNMP by one of SNMP's authors. Deals with SNMP version 1.

Rose, Marshall T. *The Simple Book: An Introduction to Internet Management*. 2nd ed. Upper Saddle River, NJ: Prentice Hall. 1994.

Second edition revised to cover SNMPv2 draft proposal (RFC 1441-1452).

Rose, Marshall T. *The Simple Book: An Introduction to Networking Management*. rev. 2nd ed. Upper Saddle River, NJ: Prentice Hall. 1996.

The "2.1" edition that covers SNMPv2 proposed version. Includes CD.

Rose, Marshall T., and McCloghrie, Keith Z. *How to Manage Your Network Using SNMP: The Network Management Practicum*. Upper Saddle River, NJ: Prentice Hall. 1995.

Book on network management applications with code done in TCL and Tk. Much information on technologies that can be managed with SNMP.

Stallings, William. *SNMP, SNMPv2, and CMIP: The Practical Guide to Network Management Standards*. Reading, MA: Addison-Wesley. 1993.

Excellent discussion of SNMP and CMIP. Much discussion of network management principles and analysis not found anywhere else. Covers draft version of SNMPv2.

Stallings, William. *SNMP, SNMPv2, and RMON: Practical Network Management 2nd ed*. Reading, MA: Addison-Wesley. 1996.

Updated for the proposed SNMPv2. RMON discussion has displaced CMIP and OSI discussion.

Townsend, Robert L. *SNMP Application Developer's Guide*. New York: Van Nostrand Reinhold. 1995.
Introduction to SNMP concepts. Includes 2 diskettes.

OTHER REFERENCES ON NETWORK MANAGEMENT (INCLUDING SNMP):

Aidarous, Salah, and Thomas Plevyak, eds. *Telecommunications Network Management into the 21st Century: Techniques, Standards, Technologies, and Applications*. New York: IEEE Press. 1994.
Discusses telecommunications and FCAPS. Includes much information on SNMP.

Ball, Larry L. *Cost-Efficient Network Management*. New York: McGraw-Hill, Inc. 1992.
Discusses cost factors in network management.

Black, Uyless. *Network Management Standards: The OSI, SNMP and CMOL Protocols*. New York: McGraw-Hill, Inc. 1992.
Discusses major network management frameworks in detail. Includes a section on OSI network manager implementations.

Black, Uyless. *Network Management Standards: SNMP, CMIP, TMN, MIBs, and Object Libraries*. 2nd ed. New York: McGraw-Hill, Inc. 1995.
Second edition includes high-level overview of OSI and IEEE 802 network management standards. Includes section on SNMP.

Comer, Douglas E., and David L. Stevens. *Design, Implementation, and Internals*. Vol. II of *Internetworking with TCP/IP*. Englewood Cliffs, NJ: Prentice Hall. 1991.
Very detailed look at TCP, including SNMP. contains very in-depth discussion and source code. Part of a three volume series that offers a very complete look at the Internet protocol suite.

Hegering, Heinz-Gerd, and Sebastian Abeck. *Integrated Network and System Management*. Reading, MA: Addison-Wesley. 1994.
Includes a discussion of "integrated" network management where different standard NM architectures and various other types of management tools are used together. Discussions of SNMP, OSI, and TMN are included.

Leinwand, Allan, and Karen Fang. *Network Management: A Practical Perspective*. Reading, MA: Addison-Wesley. 1993.
Provides an overview of FCAPS in network management areas. This book includes information on CMIP and SNMP.

Leinwand, Allan, and Karen Fang Conroy. *Network Management: A Practical Perspective.* 2nd ed. Reading, MA: Addison-Wesley. 1996.
Updated edition.

McConnell, John W. *Managing Client/Server Environments: Tools and Strategies for Building Solutions.* Upper Saddle River, NJ: Prentice Hall. 1996.
Overview of client/server management with discussion of practical application, including discussion of vendors and other tools.

Meandzija, Branislav, and Jil Westcott, eds. *Integrated Network Management, I: Proceedings of the IFIP TC 6/WG 6.6 Symposium on Integrated Network Management.* New York: North-Holland. 1989.
Contains various articles on leading-edge topics dealing with network management.

Piscitello, David, and A. L. Chapin. *Open Systems Networking: OSI and TCP/IP.* Reading, MA: Addison-Wesley. 1993.
Discussion of what open systems are, including use of SNMP and CMIP management. Includes the protocol processing of the 7 OSI layers and a discussion of other topics related to management (routing, electronic mail, etc.).

Terplan, Kornel, and Jill Huntington-Lee. *Applications for Distributed Systems and Network Management.* New York: Van Nostrand Reinhold. 1995.
Discussion of network management applications and vendor platforms.

ADDITIONAL REFERENCES OF INTEREST ON RELATED TOPICS:

Bapat, Subodh. *Object-Oriented Networks: Models for Architecture, Operations, and Management.* Englewood Cliffs, NJ: Prentice Hall. 1994.
Complete technical discussion of the use of object-oriented technology as it pertains to networking, including network management.

Booch, Grady. *Object-Oriented Analysis and Design with Applications.* 2nd ed. Redwood City, CA: The Benjamin/Cummings Publishing Company, Inc. 1994.
Grady Booch's explanation of object-oriented technology including his Booch method.

Jacobson, Ivar, Magnus Christerson, Patrik Jonsson, and Gunnar Overgaard. *Object-Oriented Software Engineering, A Use Case Driven Approach.* Reading, MA: Addison-Wesley. 1995.
Use Case Model is a requirements model that specifies all of the functionality of the system.

Orfali, Robert, Dan Harkey, and Jeri Edwards. *Essential Client/Server Survival Guide*. New York: Van Nostrand Reinhold. 1994.
Discussion of all of the many topics dealing with the client/server model; includes information on SNMP, DMTF, and CORBA.

Rose, Marshall T. *The Open Book: A Practical Perspective on OSI*. Englewood Cliffs, NJ: Prentice Hall. 1990.
Book on OSI; includes chapter on ASN.1.

Rumbaugh, James, Michael Blaha, William Premerlani, Frederick Eddy, and William Lorensen. *Object-Oriented Modeling and Design*. Englewood Cliffs, NJ: Prentice Hall. 1991.
Excellent object-oriented reference discussed with the use of the OMT tool.

Schneier, Bruce. *Applied Cryptography*. 2nd ed. New York: John Wiley and Sons, Inc. 1996.
Complete reference on cryptography. A must-read for anyone interested in security issues.

Steedman, Douglas. *Abstract Syntax Notation One (ASN.1): The Tutorial and Reference*. London: Technology Appraisals, Ltd. 1990.
Complete reference on ASN.1.

Stevens, W. Richard. *UNIX Network Programming*. Englewood Cliffs, NJ: Prentice Hall. 1990.
Guide to UNIX network programming, including protocols, sockets, etc..

Wayner, Peter. *Agents Unleashed*. Boston, MA: Academic Press. 1995.
Interesting discussion of intelligent (non-SNMP-like) agents and may be possible direction for network management in the future.

White, Iseult. *Using the Booch Method: A Rational Approach*. Redwood City, CA: The Benjamin/Cummings Publishing Company, Inc. 1994.
Guidebook for implementing an object-oriented application using the Rational Rose tool.

Acronyms

A

AARP	AppleTalk Address Resolution Protocol
ACK	Acknowledgment
ACSE	Association Control Service Element
AF	Address Family
AI	Artificial Intelligence
AM	Accounting Management
ANSI	American National Standards Institute
API	Application Program Interface
APPC	Advanced Peer-to-Peer Communication
APPN	Advanced Peer-to-Peer Network
ARP	Address Resolution Protocol
ARPA	Advanced Research Projects Agency
ARPANET	Advanced Research Projects Agency Network
AS	Autonomous System
ASCII	American Standard Code For Information Interchange
ASN.1	Abstract Syntax Notation "Dot" One
ATM	Asynchronous Transfer Mode

B

BER	Basic Encoding Rules
BGP	Border Gateway Protocol
BOF	Birds Of a Feather
BOOTP	Bootstrap Protocol
BPV	Bipolar Violation
BSD	Berkeley Software Distribution

C

C	C Programming Language
CASE	Computer Aided Software Engineering
CCITT	International Telegraph and Telephone Consultative Committee (*Comite Consultatif International de Telegraphique et Telephonique*)
CD	Compact Disk, *or* Context Diagram
CGI	Common Gateway Interface
CI	Component Interface
CLNP	Connectionless Network Protocol
CLNS	Connectionless-mode Network Service
CLTS	Connectionless-mode Transport Service
CM	Configuration Management
CMIP	Common Management Information Protocol
CMIS	Common Management Information Services
CMISE	Common Management Information Service Element
CMOL	CMIP over LLC
CMOT	CMIP over TCP/IP
CMU	Carnegie Mellon University
CONS	Connection-Oriented Network Service
CORBA	Common Object Request Broker Architecture
COTS	Connection Oriented Transport Service
CRC	Cyclic Redundancy Check, or Class/Responsibilities/Collaborators
CSMA/CD	Carrier Sense Multiple Access/Collision Detection
CSS	Controlled Slip Seconds
CSU	Channel Service Unit
CV	Code Violation

D

DARPA	Defense Advanced Research Projects Agency
DB	Database
DBMS	DB Management System

DCE	Distributed Computing Environment, *or* Data Circuit-terminating Equipment
DDCMP	Digital Data Communications Message Protocol
DDP	Datagram Delivery Protocol
DDN	Defense Data Network
DDS	Digital Data Service
DE	Discard Eligibility
DEC	Digital Equipment Corporation
DES	Data Encryption Standard
DFD	Data Flow Diagram
DIX	Digital Equipment Corporation/Intel/Xerox
DLC	Data Link Control
DLCI	Data Link Connection Identifier
DLCMI	Data Link Connection Management Interface
DLSw	Data Link Switch
DME	Distributed Management Environment
DMI	Desktop Management Interface
DMTF	Desktop Management Task Force
DNM	Desktop Network Management
DNS	Domain Name Service
DPI	Distributed Program Interface
DQDB	Distributed Queue Dual Bus
DSA	Directory System Agent
DSIS	Distributed Support Information Standards
DS1	Digital Signaling 1
DS3	Digital Signaling 3
DSU	Data (*or* Digital) Service Unit
DTE	Data Termination Equipment

E

EBCDIC	Extended Binary Coded Decimal Interchange Code
ECN	Explicit Congestion Control
ECO	Engineering Change Order
EGP	Exterior Gateway Protocol
EMANATE	Enhanced Management Agent Through Extensions
EOC	End of Contents
EOF	End of File
ERD	Entity Relationship Diagram
ES	Errored Seconds, *or* End System
ESF	Extended Superframe Format

F

FAQ	Frequently Asked Questions
FCAPS	Fault, Configuration, Accounting, Performance, Security
FCS	Frame Check Sequence
FDDI	Fiber Distributed Data Interchange
FIN	Final Segment
FM	Fault Management
FMS	Fault Management System
FR	Frame Relay
FTP	File Transfer Protocol
FYI	For Your Information

G

GGP	Gateway-to-Gateway Protocol
GOSIP	Government Open Systems Interconnection Profile
GUI	Graphical User Interface

H

HDLC	High-level Data Link Control
HEMS	High-level Entity Management System
HMMP	Hypermedia Management Protocol
HMMS	Hypermedia Management Schema
HMOM	Hypermedia Object Manager
HP	Hewlett-Packard Corporation
HTML	Hypertext Markup Language
HTTP	Hypertext Transfer Transport Protocol

I

IAB	Internet Architecture Board, *formerly* Internet Activities Board
IANA	Internet Assigned Numbers Authority
IBM	International Business Machines
ICMP	Internet Control Message Protocol
IDL	Interface Definition Language
IDPR	Inter-Domain Policy Routing
IEEE	Institute of Electrical and Electronics Engineers, Inc.
IESG	Internet Engineering Steering Group
IETF	Internet Engineering Task Force
IGP	Interior Gateway Protocol
IHL	Internet Header Length
IP	Internet Protocol

IPng	IP Next Generation (Version 6)
IPLPDN	Internet Protocol over Large Public Data Networks
IPsec	Secure IP
IPX	Internetwork Packet Exchange
IRSG	Internet Research Steering Group
IRTF	Internet Research Task Force
IS	Intermediate System
IS-IS	Intermediate System -- Intermediate System
ISDN	Integrated Services Digital Network
ISO	International Standards Organization
ISODE	International Standards Organization Development Environment
ITU-T	International Telecommunications Union – Telecommunications (area)

J

JMAPI	Java Management Application Program Interface

K

KIP	Kinetics Internet Protocol

L

LAN	Local Area Network
LAPB	Link Access Protocol Balanced
LAPD	Link Access Protocol for the D-Channel
LCP	Link Control Protocol
LLAP	LocalTalk Link Access Protocol
LLC	Logical Link Control
LME	Layer Management Entity
LOS	Loss Of Signal
LS	Link State
LSA	Link State Advertisement
LU	Logical Unit

M

MAC	Media Access Control
MAN	Metropolitan Area Network
MAP	Manufacturing Automation Protocol
MAU	Medium Attachment Unit
MD5	Message Digest 5
MI	Management Interface
MIB	Management Information Base

MIME	Multipurpose Internet Mail Extensions
MIT	Massachusetts Institute of Technology
MO	Managed Object
MOSY	Managed Object Syntax-compiler (YACC-based)
MTA	Message Transfer Agent
MTU	Maximum Transmission Unit

N

NAK	Negative Acknowledgment
NAU	Network Access Unit
NBP	Name Binding Protocol
NDIS	Network Driver Interface Specification
NETBIOS	Network Basic Input/Output System
NFS	Network File System
NIC	Network Interface Card, *or* Network Information Center
NIST	National Institute of Standards and Technology
NM	Network Management
NMC	Network Management Console
NMF	Network Management Forum
NMP	Network Management Platform
NMS	Network Management System (or Network Management Station)
NOC	Network Operations Center
NOS	Network Operating System
NREN	National Research and Education Network
NVT	Network Virtual Terminal

O

OAM&P	Operations, Administration, Maintenance & Provisioning
ODI	Open Data-Link Interface
OID	Object Identifier
OMG	Object Management Group
OO	Object-Oriented
OOA	OO Analysis
OOD	OO Design
OOF	Out Of Frame
OOP	Object-Oriented Programming
ORB	Object Request Broker
OSF	Open Systems Foundation
OSI	Open Systems Interconnection
OSPF	Open Shortest Path First
OVW	OpenView for Windows

P

PAD	Packet Assembler/Disassembler
PC	Personal Computer
PDU	Protocol Data Unit
PERL	Practical Extraction and Report Language
PHY	Physical Layer Protocol
PING	Packet Internet Groper
PLCP	Physical Layer Convergence Protocol
PLE	Packet Level Entity
PLS	Physical Layer Signaling
PM	Performance Management
PPP	Point-to-Point Protocol
PU	Physical Unit

R

RAM	Random Access Memory
RARP	Reverse Address Resolution Protocol
RDB	Relational Database
RDBMS	Relational Database Management System
RFC	Request For Comment
RIP	Routing Information Protocol
RMON	Remote Network Monitor
ROSE	Remote Operations Service Element
RPC	Remote Procedure Call
RTFM	Read The %$@!#* Manual
RTMP	Routing Table Maintenance Protocol

S

S.A.	
SD	Socket Descriptor
SDLC	Synchronous Data Link Protocol
SDH	Synchronous Digital Hierarchy
SEFS	Severely Errored Framing Second
SES	Severely Errored Seconds
SGMP	Simple Gateway Monitoring Protocol
SIP	SMDS Interface Protocol
SLIP	Serial Line Interface Protocol
SM	Security Management
SMAE	System Management Application-Entity
SMDS	Switched Multimegabit Data Service
SMI	Structure of Management Information

SMIC	SNMP Management Information Compiler
SMICng	SMIC Next Generation
SMP	Simple Management Protocol
SMS	System Management Server
SMT	Station Management
SMTP	Simple Mail Transfer Protocol
SMUX	SNMP Multiplexing Protocol
SNA	Systems Network Architecture
SNAP	Sub-Network Access Protocol
SNI	Subscriber Network Interface
SNMP	Simple Network Management Protocol
SNMPng	SNMP Next Generation
SNMPv1	SNMP Version 1
SNMPv2	SNMP Version 2
SNMPv3	SNMP Version 3
SONET	Synchronous Optical Network
SPF	Shortest Path First
SQL	Structured Query Language
SRI	Stanford Research Institute
SSL	Secure Socket Layer
STP	Spanning Tree Protocol

T

TC	Textual Convention
TCL	Tool Control Language
TCP	Transport Control Protocol
TDR	Time-Domain Reflectometry
TFTP	Trivial File Transfer Protocol
TME	Tivoli Management Environment
TMN	Telecommunications Management Network
TOP	Technical Office Protocol
TOS	Type of Service
TP4	Transport Service Class 4
TPFDB	Transparent Bridge Forwarding Database
TR	Token Ring
TTL	Time To Live

U

UA	Universal Agent
UDP	User Datagram Protocol
UPS	Uninterruptible Power Supply

US	Unavailable Seconds
USEC	User Security (SNMPv2 security model)
UTC	Universal Time (Coordinated)

W

WAN	Wide Area Network
WBEM	Web-Based Enterprise Management
WG	Working Group
WWW	World Wide Web

X

X	X Windows System
XNS	Xerox Network System

Y

YACC	Yet Another Compiler Compiler

Z

ZIP	Zone Information Protocol

Glossary

A

Abstract Syntax Notation one: OSI version of an abstract syntax notational language. Abstract syntax notation is used because it is implementation-dependent and can be used in a variety of internetwork environments to allow for interoperability. ASN.1 is defined in ISO documents 8824.2 and 8825.2.

accounting management: one of the five functional areas of network management. AM deals with network usage and utilization, billing, and other cost determinations.

address: unique identification of a network device that allows for unambiguous communications. Typically, a packet or frame contains both a source and destination address to facilitate communications.

Address Resolution Protocol: Internet protocol that correlates a device's four-octet IP address to its corresponding six-octet Ethernet addresses. ARP is defined in RFC 826.

administrative framework: set of policies defined for authentication, authorization, security, and other administrative concerns.

agent: a processing entity on the managed network device that has the proper routines to access the management variables (MIB variables) that it controls. It generally responds to requests from a network management system.

American National Standards Institute: major standards definition group in the United States. It represents the US at the international ISO meetings that charter worldwide standards.

American Standard Code for Information Interchange: seven-bit (with one bit for parity) representation used for representing characters. ASCII was established by the ANSI standards committee.

anonymous FTP: version of Internet protocol for file transfer that allows a well-known user ID of "anonymous" to retrieve publicly accessible files. Anonymous FTP can be used to retrieve RFCs.

AppleTalk: the Apple communications protocol suite that allows networking of Apple computers. It runs over Ethernet (EtherTalk), Token Ring (TokenTalk), and a 230Kbit serial line interface (LocalTalk). Other protocols and services include Datagram Delivery Protocol, AppleTalk Session Protocol, Name Binding Protocol, AppleShare, and AppleTalk Remote Access.

application layer: top layer of the OSI model that allows users to make use of the network services.

application program interface: set of programming functions and routines that provide access to the services of a particular layer (such as the network layer).

Arcnet: proprietary, token-passing, star topology LAN protocol developed by Datapoint Corporation. Its speed is 2.5Mbps and it is relatively inexpensive to implement.

asynchronous transfer mode: CCITT cell relay transmission standard using 53-octet fixed-length cells to carry data, voice, and video. It can be employed in both LAN and WAN environments.

authentication: the verification process of the claimed identity of a client's request. In SNMP Version 1, a trivial authentication scheme is used to compare the community names of the NMS and the agent.

authorization: level of access to the managed objects allowed by the managed entity to the requesting management station.

autonomous system: a singly-administered group of routers using an interior gateway protocol.

B

Basic Encoding Rules: OSI rules for defining the encoding of the data units and the network transfer syntax. BER is specified in ISO 8825.

big-endian: data representation format where the most significant bit is placed first.

Border Gateway Protocol: exterior gateway protocol defined in RFCs 1267 and 1268.

bridge: protocol-independent, media-dependent, internetworking device that connects network segments. It passes packets between these segments based on the packet's destination address. A bridge operates at level 2 of the OSI model (data link layer).

broadcast: a message sent to all network devices by using a reserved destination that is understood by all network devices.

brouter: hybrid internetworking device that combines bridge and router functions. It operates at level 2 of the OSI model and is protocol-independent like a bridge, but additionally media-independent like a router.

bus topology: network architecture where all of the devices are connected to a common media, called the *bus*.

C

carrier sense multiple access/collision detection: a protocol used on Ethernet and IEEE 802.3 LANs. When a station wishes to transmit, it listens to the media before attempting. If it is free, it transmits, or else it waits and sends later. If a collision occurs, the transmission is reattempted after a random back-off time.

channel service unit: customer premise equipment that interfaces to telephone lines by terminating T1 or DDS circuits. It also contains additional configuration and diagnostic capabilities.

client: application that requests the services provided by another application called the *server.*

Comite Consultatif International de Telegraphique et Telephonique: international organization that makes technical recommendations on telephony and data communication systems. The CCITT meets every four years.

Common Management Information Protocol: the protocol specification for the OSI network management framework. CMIP is defined in ISO standard 9595.

Common Management Information Service: the OSI network management service offered by the CMIP protocol.

Common Management Information Services and Protocol Over IEEE 802 Logical Link Control: the IEEE network management specification for running CMIS/CMIP over the logical link layer. CMOL was specified to run on LAN protocols.

Common Management Information Services Over Transport Control Protocol: the network management specification for using CMIS/CMIP over the Internet protocol suite. CMOT is specified in RFC 1189.

community: an administrative relationship defined by a community name between SNMP managers and agents who wish to communicate.

configuration management: one of the five functional areas of network management. CM deals with internetwork device setup and status.

connection-oriented service: service where a circuit is set up, used, and then taken down between the two communicating parties. This type of service has three phases: connection establishment, data transfer, and communication release.

connectionless service: service where each packet is independent and contains full source and destination addressing so that a circuit does not need to be established between the two communicating parties.

D

data communications equipment: equipment that establishes, maintains, and terminates a data transmission connection. An example of DCE is a modem.

Data Encryption Standard: standardized encryption scheme. DES was developed by the U.S. National Bureau of Standards and is part of SNMPv2 security.

datagram: independent packet containing both source and destination addresses. Typically used with connectionless service.

data link layer: layer two of the OSI seven-layer reference model that deals with the establishment and release of data link connections and the transmission of data units called frames on that connection.

data terminal equipment: equipment that transmits data to and from data communications equipment. An example of DTE is a computer.

DECnet: Digital Equipment Corporation's network architecture that runs primarily on point-to-point, X.25, and Ethernet networks. DECnet's link layer protocol is called DDC-MP, Digital Data Communications Message Protocol. The standard is released in "phases" and the current DECnet MIB is for Phase IV.

digital data service: digital data communications line service between 2400 and 56000Bps.

digital service unit: a customer premise device that interfaces to a digital circuit.

Distributed Computing Environment: architecture for distributed applications that can run on different computing environments. DCE is being developed by the Open Software Foundation.

Distributed Management Environment: architecture framework for integrating system and network management using an object-oriented approach. DME is being developed by the Open Software Foundation.

domain naming service: a hierarchical system for naming host computers on the Internet by grouping the subject hosts into categories. Typically, the names have meaningful extensions, such as .COM for hosts in commercial businesses, .EDU for computers in an educational setting, and so forth. DNS is defined in RFCs 1034 and 1035.

dotted decimal notation: also called "dotted quad" notation, this is the common notation for specifying IP addresses in the n.n.n.n format, where *n* represents one byte represented in decimal.

E

electronic mail: system where users and applications can exchange mail messages over the internetwork. It is often called *e-mail*.

encryption: algorithm where message data is modified so that only proper recipients can recover the true message.

Ethernet: LAN protocol that uses a carrier sense multiple access collision detection (CS-MA/CD) policy for transmissions. It is a 10Mbps standard that was originally developed by DEC, Intel, and Xerox. It is very similar to the IEEE 802.3 standard.

expert system: software system that uses heuristics and rules to make inferences when more straightforward procedural-based solutions are not adequate.

Extended Binary Coded Decimal Interchange Code: eight-bit encoding scheme. EBCDIC is primarily used in older IBM systems.

Exterior Gateway Protocol: gateway protocol that determines the reachability of another IP network. EGP is defined in RFC 904.

F

fault management: one of the five functional areas of network management. FM deals with network faults and their correction.

Fiber Distributed Data Interface: protocol for transmitting data over fiber optic cable. FDDI is an ANSI standard that specifies a rate up to 100Mbps.

File Transfer Protocol: protocol for exchanging files over the Internet. FTP is defined in RFC 959.

frame: data link level unit of transmission. It contains a header, data, and trailer information.

frame relay: packet switching WAN protocol with speeds from 56Kbps to 1.54Mbps (T1) that provides for greater throughput by having error detection and correction done by the higher-level protocols.

G

gateway: protocol-independent, media-independent, internetworking device that translates and routes various protocols. A gateway operates at level 7 of the OSI model (application layer).

get: the SNMP "read" operation for the requested instance.

get-next: the SNMP "read-next" operation where the lexicographically next variable instance is returned, if available.

graphical user interface: interface presented to the end-user. GUIs are represented as bit-map displays for workstation monitors.

H

High-Level Entity Management System: early network management framework proposal. HEMS is documented in RFC 1076.

host: in Internet parlance, a computer that can be used to communicate with other hosts on a network. Hosts are identified by addresses and also by host names.

host-to-host layer: the third layer of the TCP/IP network protocol that ensures reliable data transfer between TCP/IP hosts. It is similar to the transport layer of the OSI reference model.

hub: a network device that creates a "star" topology. A hub is also called a *concentrator.*

I

instance: the specific declaration of an object as realized by each agent implementation.

Institute of Electrical and Electronics Engineers: organization that helps define network standards. The IEEE ("eye-triple e") is active in creating and supporting many common communications specifications used today.

Integrated Services Digital Network: an international standard proposed by the CCITT. ISDN specifies the transmission of voice, data, and video over telephone lines.

International Standards Organization: international standards body that specifies standards for many network protocols. ISO is noted for the seven-layer OSI Reference Model.

Internet: The large and ever-expanding set of interconnected computers that use the Internet protocol suite. The Internet links many university, government, research, and commercial sites. In a general sense, an internet is a network of networks; the Internet is the largest internet in the world.

Internet Architecture Board: the group that oversees the general direction of the Internet groups, protocols, and other matters.

Internet Control Message Protocol: internet protocol that is part of IP that sends special error and status messages. ICMP messages are used by PING. This protocol is specified in RFC 792.

internet layer: the second layer of the TCP/IP protocol suite that provides services for allowing data to traverse hosts that can reside on multiple networks.

Internet Protocol: unreliable, connectionless, internet layer protocol that uses IP addresses to send and receive messages. RFC 791 specifies this protocol.

internet protocol suite: set of protocols that implement the four layers of the TCP/IP protocols used for internetworking.

internetwork: A network of networks. These networks are usually connected by such network devices as a router.

IP address: four-octet address specifying the network and host IDs. Both source and destination IP addresses exist.

J

Java Management API: an object-oriented management API introduced by SUN that uses java applets for network management.

L

local area network: a communications network that is characterized by being limited to a small geographic area, sharing a common media, and by using high-speed transmission. Two of the most common LAN topologies are Ethernet/802.3 and token ring/802.5.

logical link control: 802.2 logical link layer protocol used with LANs. LLC includes addressing and error detection information.

little-endian: data representation format where the least significant bit is placed first.

M

Management Information Base: virtual database of managed objects.

maximum transmission unit: largest datagram that can be sent for a particular network media type.

media access control: layer below LLC in LAN protocols. The MAC talks directly to the physical media.

N

network access layer: the lowest layer of the TCP/IP protocol suite that handles the connection between the host and the network.

network layer: layer three of the OSI seven-layer model that handles routing and circuits within a network.

network management station: processing entity that makes requests of agents that it manages.

node: a network device such as a bridge, router, or host.

O

Open Systems Interconnection model: seven-layer model developed by ISO that is the fundamental architecture used in explaining the interactions of protocols and networks. Each layer builds on the services provided by the layer beneath it.

P

packet: a unit of data that travels through the network.

performance management: one of the five functional areas of network management. PM deals with the efficiency and utilization of how the network is operating and how it is accessed.

personal computer: a host computer. Usually you have a one-to-one correspondence of PC to user.

physical layer: layer one of the OSI seven-layer reference model that deals with the connection of the device to the media for transmitting the bit stream.

PING: the Packet InterNet Groper application that uses ICMP echo messages to test for basic connectivity between two IP-addressed nodes.

poll: periodic request for status.

port: a communication connection point that may be realized in various ways in hardware or software.

presentation layer: sixth layer of the OSI reference model that deals with data formats.

process layer: highest level of the TCP/IP protocol suite that provides protocols needed to support application such as e-mail and file transfer.

protocol: a formal set of rules that define standards between communicating parties.

protocol data unit: a group of bytes in a known format that are delivered to and from peer applications. The SNMP PDU carries requests and responses between the NMSs and the agents.

proxy agent: agent that can provide management capabilities to network entities that cannot directly communicate with the NMS.

Q

query: a request for status and specific variable values.

R

repeater: media-dependent network device that regenerates physical signals to extend the range of the media. A repeater operates at level 1 of the OSI model (physical layer).

request for comments: documents that contain information about the Internet protocol suite. RFCs contain a variety of information about other topics dealing with the Internet.

Reverse Address Resolution Protocol: permits a host to discover its IP address. RARP is primarily used for diskless workstations.

route: a path through the internetwork used to send and receive messages between two communicating hosts.

router: protocol-dependent, media-independent, internetworking device that routes packets based on its destination address. A router operates at level 3 of the OSI model (network layer).

S

secure SNMP: name given to first proposals for enhancements to SNMP Version 1 to provide security features. Secure SNMP is defined in RFCs 1351- 1353.

security management: one of the five functional areas of network management. SM deals with access permissions, protection, and user authentication.

server: application that handles requests from clients and then carries out any requested actions.

session layer: fifth layer of the OSI reference model that deals with the reliable data exchange between users and the network.

set: an SNMP "write" operation on the requested instance.

Simple Gateway Monitoring Protocol: network management framework that evolved into SNMP. SGMP is defined in RFC 1028.

Simple Management Protocol: proposal in July 1992 to improve SNMP Version 1. SMP was used as the basis for SNMP Version 2.

Simple Network Management Protocol: the network management framework defined by the Internet community utilizing the TCP/IP protocol suite. SNMP is defined by RFCs 1155, 1157, and 1213.

Simple Network Management Protocol (Version 2): latest enhancement to SNMP framework. SNMPv2 draft version is described in RFCs 1902- 1908.

socket: a data structure that is used in a common interface for communicating with UDP, TCP, and IP.

Structure of Management Information: rules for defining objects within a network management framework.

subnetting: extension of IP addressing scheme where the network ID bytes can be further grouped into sub-networks.

switched multimegabit data service: packet-switching WAN communications technology that provides high-speed rates from T1 to T3. SMDS is available from the regional Bell operating companies and other carriers.

synchronous optical network: high-speed synchronous physical layer network technology that is designed to be carried over optical media. SONET provides up to 2.5Gbps.

T

T1: Digital transmission lines with speeds up to 1.54Mbps. The framing specification for T1 is called DS1.

T3: Digital transmission lines with speeds up to 44Mbps. The framing specification for T3 is called DS3.

Telnet: internet protocol that defines remote terminal connection service.

token ring: LAN topology where network devices wait for the reception of a small frame called the "token" before accessing the media. IEEE 802.5 is the specification for token ring.

transmission control protocol: internet transport protocol that uses connection-oriented, end-to-end, reliable transmission. It is specified in RFC 793.

transport layer: fourth layer of the OSI model that provides end-to-end data integrity.

trap: an SNMP alert that can be sent asynchronously by an agent to predetermined NMSs when a predefined condition has been detected.

Trivial File Transfer Protocol: simple version of FTP for transferring files. TFTP is defined in RFC 783.

U

UNIX: popular multi-tasking, multi-user operating system developed by AT&T used on many internetworking devices.

user datagram protocol: internet transport protocol that is connectionless, unreliable, and uses datagrams. It is defined in RFC 768.

V

view: the set of managed objects in an agent's MIB that are available to the NMSs in its community.

W

Web-Based Enterprise Management: a consortium of companies proposing a standard or network management using the World Wide Web.

Web-based management: the use of the World Wide Web technologies to manage devices on the Internet.

wide area network: a network that traverses large distances and often uses common carrier transmission services.

WinSNMP: a programming API for SNMP network managment applications running under Microsoft Windows.

workstation: a host computer or high-end personal computer.

X

X windows: network-based graphics windowing system that uses TCP/IP for transport. Originally developed at MIT, the system includes GUI managers such as Motif.

X.25: data communications interface that describes packet switched communications. It defines layers 1, 2, and 3.

Xerox network system: proprietary set of protocols defined by Xerox that defines the network and transport layer services.

Index

RFC 1381   61,220,226,525,602
RFC 1382   61,220,221,525,602
RFC 1387   602
RFC 1388   602
RFC 1389   63,526,602
RFC 1398   63
RFC 1406   61,220,227,526,602
RFC 1407   61,220,229,526,602
RFC 1413   602
RFC 1414   61,242,255,526,602
RFC 1418   526,601
RFC 1419   526,601
RFC 1420   526,601
RFC 1441   28,42,49,51, 63,487,526,601
RFC 1442   49, 51, 63,111,526,601
RFC 1443   49, 51, 63,526,601
RFC 1444   49, 51, 63,526,601
RFC 1445   49, 51, 63,526,601
RFC 1446   49, 51, 63,527,601
RFC 1447   49, 52, 63,527,601
RFC 1448   49, 52, 63,527,601
RFC 1449   49, 52, 63,527,601
RFC 1450   49, 52, 63,527,601
RFC 1451   28,47,49, 63,52,527,600
RFC 1452   42,49, 52, 63,487,527,600
RFC 1461   61,220,235,527,600
RFC 1470   62,600
RFC 1471   61,220,228,527,600
RFC 1472   61,527,600
RFC 1473   61,527,600
RFC 1474   61,527,600
RFC 1493   61,242,250,527,600
RFC 1495   600
RFC 1503   62,527,600
RFC 1512   61,220,225,528,600
RFC 1513   61,484,528,600
RFC 1514   61,243,255,481,528,600
RFC 1515   61,243,256,528,599
RFC 1516   61,242,253,528,532,599
RFC 1525   61,528,599
RFC 1559   61,242,251,528,599
RFC 1565   61,243,257,528,599
RFC 1566   62,243,258,528,599
RFC 1567   62,243,259,528,599
RFC 1573   242-243,260,528,599
RFC 1592   62,528,599

RFC 1593   528,599
RFC 1595   62,220,236,528,599
RFC 1596   63,529,599
RFC 1604   62,220,237,529,599
RFC 1611   62,243,261
RFC 1612   62
RFC 1623   63
RFC 1628   62,243,263,479,529,599
RFC 1643   61,220,222,529,599
RFC 1650   62,243,265,529,599
RFC 1657   61,242,247,529,598
RFC 1658   61,242,252,529,598
RFC 1659   61,220,232,529,598
RFC 1660   61,220,234,529,598
RFC 1665   63,529,598
RFC 1666   62,243,264,529,598
RFC 1694   61,220,230,243,265,529,598
RFC 1695   62,243,267,529,598
RFC 1696   62,243,267,529,598
RFC 1697   62,243,268,529,598
RFC 1700   276
RFC 1724   61,242,254,529,598
RFC 1742   61,242,245,530,598
RFC 1743   529,598
RFC 1747   62,243,270,529,530,598
RFC 1748   61,220,224,529,597
RFC 1749   62,243,271,529,597
RFC 1757   61,242,248,484,530,597
RFC 1759   62,243,271,530,597
RFC 1792   62,530,597
RFC 1850   61,242,246,530,597
RFC 1901   51,53,530,597
RFC 1902   25,28,42,
           51,55,113,135,186,452,453,530,597
RFC 1903   51,113,129,453,530,597
RFC 1904   51,113,453,531,597
RFC 1905   52,169,172-
           173,189,488,531,538,597
RFC 1906   52,531,597
RFC 1907   52,341,531,597
RFC 1908   25,28,42,
           52,55,193,342,531,596
RFC 1909   53,531,596
RFC 1910   53,531,596
RFC 1988   531,596
RFC 2006   243,273,531,596